THE QUESTION OF
SEX DIFFERENCES

Psychological, Cultural,
and Biological Issues

THE QUESTION OF SEX

DIFFERENCES

Psychological, Cultural, and Biological Issues

KATHARINE BLICK HOYENGA
KERMIT T. HOYENGA
Western Illinois University

LITTLE, BROWN and COMPANY
Boston   Toronto

Library of Congress Catalog Card No. 78–70852

First Printing

Published simultaneously in Canada
by Little, Brown & Company (Canada) Limited

Printed in the United States of America

Katharine Blick Hoyenga

To the people who believed in me long before I believed in myself; my family, Dr. Moncrieff Smith, Dr. Eugene Galanter, and Dr. Herbert Wells.

Kermit T. Hoyenga

To my parents, and to those whose only belief is in the search for a better answer.

Preface

This book is concerned with the question of why there are sex differences in behavior. To explain this question, we examine sex differences from a wide variety of perspectives, including genetics, hormones and behavior, cross-cultural comparisons, socialization, and social-psychology. Each of these perspectives answers differently the question of *why* there are sex differences.

This book can be easily adapted for use in courses on various levels. It can be read as background to questions, issues, and possible answers in the area of sex differences or as prelude and guide to the primary source material. Thus, it can be used as a text for upper level undergraduate or graduate courses in sex differences or to supplement courses concerned with sex roles, hormones and behavior, life-span developmental psychology, sex education, counseling, and community mental health. Little specific background is required other than an understanding of the basic psychological concepts and terminology presented in introductory level psychology courses. We explain the biological concepts without assuming any specific knowledge on the part of the reader.

Part 1 introduces our approach and points out possible problems of interpretation. The next two parts of the book describe the differences between the sexes that may lead to differences in behavior. Part 2 deals with sex differences in the internal environments of the two genders—that is, differences in chromosomes, hormones, and physiology-biology, biological biases that may contribute to differences in behavior.

For example, the sex difference in chromosomes ultimately determines whether a male or a female organism is born. Why and how? How might this difference in chromosomes contribute to sex differences in behavior? Why are there two sexes anyway—how is it advantageous to the survival of the species to have sexes that differ in both appearance and behavior? We analyze the differences that seem most advantageous by looking at those that occur in widely different species. Such comparisons tell us from an evolutionary point of view why there might be biologically biased sex differences. Males and females of all species also differ in the hormones in their bloodstreams, both before and after birth. Does this difference affect their brains and behavior? Are there other physical differences between the sexes that might lead to differences in behavior? If so, why? Finally, cross-cultural similarities in sex differences often have been interpreted as evidence that the difference is due to biology. Is this true?

Part 3 considers sex differences in the external environment, that is, differences in the ways society treats males and females. What are the major differences in development and socialization that could lead to differences in behavior? What *are* the differences in the environments of the two genders—how are men treated differently from women, and what expectations do we have for women and men in this society? What are some cross-cultural similarities in socialization that could lead to environmental biases for certain types of differences between males and females?

In Part 4 of this book we analyze the ways in which sex differences in the internal and external environments interact to produce sex differences in human behavior. Each behavior associated with sex differences is analyzed, whether the association can be experimentally verified or is based on commonly held beliefs, either stereotypic or prejudiced. Are women more nurturant than men? If so, *why?* Are men more aggressive than women? In what situations and why might this difference exist? We also inquire into differences in sexuality. Are men and women aroused by different kinds of erotic stimuli? And are males more easily aroused?

At the end of the book, we speculate about the implications of these sex differences for society as a whole and for individuals within the society—and about the implications of the fact that there are different ways of answering the question *why.* The text ends with a glossary of biological and psychological terms and a list of references.

An instructor's manual accompanies the text. As a teaching aid, it includes sample questions, suggestions for classroom demonstrations and discussion topics, and some suggested background readings that should prove useful to the instructor.

This book focuses on active areas of research rather than on an experiential approach to sex differences. Thus, consciousness raising is not deliberately built into it, but you as reader should find that your concept of yourself as a male or a female, behaving in more or less masculine or feminine ways, is changed by this book. You will find ideas about your body may be affecting your experiences, and how your experiences may in turn be affecting your body. You will also become more aware of the social pressures that may be subtly affecting your behavior, and of your unconscious masculine or feminine behavior. So this book, although it focuses on research rather than on the psychology of women or the psychology of change, should produce change and lead you to a better understanding of the different experiences of women and men in this society. It follows that the reasons why the "psychology of women" may not be the same as the "psychology of men" are implicit throughout the book.

We would like to express our appreciation to the people who have worked on this book; in particular, we would like to thank our editor, Marian R. Ferguson, and our book editor, Cynthia Chapin. Several reviewers also contributed their time and expertise to a painstaking reading of the manuscript in various stages. These include Lynne A. Bond-Dunn, Lorraine B. Dennis, Joan DiGiovanni, Justin Joffe, Alexandra Kaplan, John R. Moreland, and Joan Rabin. Lastly, the book could never have been finished without the intelligent and careful typing of our secretaries: Karen Nelson, Mary Webber, and Ruth Sizek.

Brief Contents

Contents

PART 1 _____

Introduction

CHAPTER 1

An Overview of Sex Differences

> Girls play with dolls and folderols,
>   And boys do not.
> Boys play with trains and hoisting cranes,
>   And girls do not.
> Why do we differ, I and you,
> In what we want and what we do?
> Something inside us tells us to,
>   I wonder what?
> Girls learn to bake pie crust and cake,
>   And boys won't try.
> Boys learn to box and take hard knocks,
>   And girls won't try.
> It's curious, yet it seems to be
> That what suits you will not suit me
> Because you're she and I am he,
>   I wonder why?
>
>   —J. M. Shaw, "Girls and Boys"*

In this chapter, the plan of the book will be discussed. The reasons for including various topics will be described, along with a statement of the authors' biases. We will introduce the terminology and the logic of research concerned with sex differences and with the effects of both biology and environment on those sex differences. Most importantly, this chapter discusses the possible areas of misinterpretation and bias and how they affect sex differences. After reading this chapter, you should have a better idea of the different answers to the question "Why are the sexes different?" Answering this question entails answering three others. What are the differences between the sexes, and why do they exist? What caused them? And what function might they have?

*Reprinted from J. M. Shaw, *The Things I Want: Poems to Two Children*, 1967, by permission of the Friends of the Florida State University Library.

GENDER IDENTITY AND GENDER ROLE

Who Are We?

> *Gender identity:* The sameness, unity and persistence of one's individuality as male or female (or ambivalent) in greater or lesser degree, especially as it is experienced in self-awareness and behavior.
>
> *Gender role:* Everything that a person says and does, to indicate to others or to the self the degree to which one is male or female or ambivalent. . . . Gender role is the public expression of gender identity, and gender identity is the private experience of gender role.*

Name _____ Date _____ Age _____ Sex _____
         Last   First   Middle   M or F

Nearly everyone would recognize the top portion of an IBM answer sheet for a multiple-choice test. And most of us would have no trouble filling out that part of the test, including the part "Sex _____." As a matter of fact, that might be the eas-
                                                         M or F
iest question on the whole test. But what if it were not the easiest question—can you imagine what it would be like not to be sure of the answer to that question?

Confusion over the answer to that question was what led, in part, to a statement made in *Psychology Today.* In an article called "The Danger of Knowing Too Much," the author discussed some of the pitfalls associated with genetic counseling. One in particular involved people with **testicular feminization, or androgen insensitivity.** These people have the chromosomes, internal gonads, and hormones of a male, but the external appearance of a female. Because of their appearance, they are generally reared as and regard themselves as females. However, since they are, of course, infertile, they often come to clinics for diagnosis and treatment of their infertility. The geneticist is in a quandary as to how to respond to their problem: "To all outward appearances they are perfectly normal women. And therein lies the problem. They're not women at all, but men. . . . The diagnosis of testicular feminization can be counted upon to set off an emotional powder keg. What is at stake is no less than the patient's sexual identity. In a sense, she is not a *she* at all but a *he*" (Restak, 1975, p. 88). The geneticist could imagine no more damaging discovery. However, there is more than one definition of gender, and when different definitions don't agree, one cannot assume that one definition is any more basic than another. A person's genetic gender is certainly not more basic or important than that person's gender of appearance or gender of identity.

Definitions of Gender

The eight different ways of defining gender that we will use in this book are all listed in Table 1.1. The first five are biological and the last three are psychological. **Chromosomal gender** refers to the sex of the genes or chromosomes, a

*Reprinted from J. Money and A. A. Ehrhardt, *Man and Woman, Boy and Girl.* Copyright © 1973, The Johns Hopkins University Press. Reprinted by permission.

TABLE 1.1

EIGHT DEFINITIONS OF GENDER

Type of Definition	Males	Females
Chromosomal Gender	XY	XX
Gonadal Gender	Testes	Ovaries
Hormonal Gender	Mostly androgens	Mostly estrogens and progestins
Gender of the Internal Sexual Accessory Organs	Prostate glands, ejaculatory ducts, vas deferens, and seminal vesicles	Uterus and Fallopian tubes
Gender of External Genitals	Penis and scrotal sacs	Clitoris, labia, and vagina
Gender of Rearing	"It's a boy!"	"It's a girl!"
Gender Identity	_X_ Male ____ Female	____ Male _X_ Female
Gender Role	Masculine behavior	Feminine behavior

person's sexual heredity. **Gonadal gender** refers to the type of internal sex glands, or gonads, present. **Hormonal gender** refers to the type of sex hormones (substances secreted by the gonads) present in the bloodstream. This definition usually, but not always, corresponds to gonadal gender. Hormonal gender before birth is generally the same as hormonal gender after birth, but there are exceptions here too; these exceptions occur either naturally or because of experimental manipulations. We will explore some of the consequences of having a prenatal male hormonal gender followed by a postnatal female hormonal gender.

Hormonal gender directly or indirectly determines the other definitions of gender in normal organisms. During fetal development, the presence or absence of hormones from the testes determines whether the **internal** and **external sex organs** will develop in the male or female direction. In turn, the **gender of rearing,** or that placed on the birth certificate and by which the parents rear the child, is determined by the external sex organs. Finally, there are **gender identity** and **gender role,** both of which were defined at the beginning of this chapter. Briefly, gender identity is the gender you believe yourself to be, the way you answer that question on the IBM sheet. Gender role refers to the behaviors a culture defines as appropriate for a given gender. Gender role includes, but is not limited to, the choice of a sexual object.

These definitions are congruent in normal people, but discrepancies do occur. One example would be a masculine acting individual with XX chromosomes. This person may well identify herself as female, based on gender of rearing and external appearance, but act out some of the achievement and dominance behaviors specified by our society as more appropriate for the male gender role. And how should the XX individual with a penis be classified? Or an XY individual with a vagina? There are also people who have male biological gender and who are reared as males but who nevertheless identity themselves as females; these are the male to female transsexuals. And to add to the confusion, not all of these transsexuals adopt aspects of the feminine gender role prior to the sex-change surgery.

Sex Differences—Why?

This book is essentially concerned with the question of why there are two sexes throughout most of the animal kingdom, and why these two sexes look and act differently. This question can take many different forms. What during development leads to the birth of a female rather than a male? What is good about having two sexes that differ in both appearance and behavior? How are the hormones and physiology of men and women different, and do these differences lead to differences in appearance and behavior? And in what ways, for what kinds of behavior, do social pressures exerted today cause the sexes to act differently? What happens when all these sources and types of sex differences are not congruent, as when an individual defies the socially defined sex roles and adopts both masculine and feminine types of behavior and becomes **androgynous**?

Our bias is that as many behavioral options as possible ought to be left open to people of both genders. Even if differences based on the biological definitions of gender result in different frequencies of behavioral preferences and choices, the choices should not be restricted by social sanctions. At the very least—and this is probably the most that can be expected—society ought to work to ensure that behaviors are not differently evaluated because of the gender of the person involved. Assertiveness and emotional expressiveness, for example, should be evaluated independently of the gender of the assertive or expressive person. That is not to say that everyone ought to be alike, only that judgments of behavior should not take gender into account. These are ideals—in all likelihood, ideals impossible to achieve—but we believe even the attempts to achieve them to be worthwhile, and that belief colors this book.

THE INTERACTION OF BIOLOGY AND ENVIRONMENT

Overview and Terminology

Sex differences in humans begin at conception when the female embryo receives one X chromosome from each parent and the male receives an X from his mother and a Y from his father. This genetic difference, if all goes normally, results in the physical sex differences in the embryos; these physical differences interact with the surrounding environment from the moment of conception through the person's life. All behavior, including sex-role behavior, is a continuing product of the interaction between inherited physical characteristics and environment.

The chromosomes directly influence the fetal gonads, causing the female fetus's primitive, undifferentiated gonads to develop into ovaries and the male's to develop into testes. These differentiated gonads then secrete their sex hormones, under the control of areas of the brain called the **hypothalamus** and the **pituitary gland.** Before birth, these hormones exert a so-called **inductive effect** on the brain and other parts of the body, determining the development and connections among various parts of the brain and therefore the later behavior of the organism. After birth, the sex hormones circulating in the bloodstream have an **activational effect** on various parts of the brain and other organs, either increasing or inhibiting their actions. The inductive effect is usually permanent or irreversible, but the activational effect depends on the level of hormones circulating through the body and can therefore vary from moment to moment.

These biological sex differences then interact with environmental sex differences. Four very influential theories try to explain the effects of environment on the development of sex differences in behavior. **Freud's psychoanalytic theory** has dominated thinking until recently; he believed that the child's **identification** with the like-sexed parent, which occurs at the end of the **Oedipal period**, results in the child acquiring the beliefs, values, and behaviors of that adult. **Parson's sociological theory** added to Freudian theory an emphasis on the impact society has on sex-role socialization in the family.

Two other developmental theories attach a lesser importance to the physical differences between the sexes. Mischel and Bandura developed **social-learning theory**, which says sex differences appear because the child is reinforced only for performing gender-appropriate behaviors and either is not reinforced or is punished for engaging in gender-inappropriate behaviors. Children also tend to **model** their behavior after those around them, and the behavior of like-sexed models is more often copied. Thus, according to social learning theory, the sexual stereotypes held by parents and teachers and presented in books and on television are largely responsible for sex differences in behavior. Kohlberg's **cognitive-developmental theory** emphasizes cognitive factors in sex-role development. Kohlberg hypothesized that stages of emotional and social development parallel Piaget's stages of cognitive development. Sex differences arise once children become aware of their gender identity and also realize, after observing parents and others, that different behaviors are appropriate for boys and girls.

This book will explain sex differences in terms of an interaction between biology and environment. The different questions about sex differences will be taken up by discussing the various influences that seem to promote or decrease the differences between the sexes. The biological influences will be reviewed first, followed by social pressures; then sex differences in behavior in a variety of areas will be reviewed in the context of the social-biological interaction.

Biology, Environment, and Preparedness

The question of the relative roles of biology and environment in determining sex differences is a controversial issue and difficult to answer. Most people today agree that biology and environment interact, and that an individual's behavior is a complex function of their current interaction and the outcome of their interaction in that person's past. Nevertheless, some people still attempt to evaluate the relative weight of environment (or biology) in determining a given type of behavior; in other words, their interaction is assumed, but it is also assumed that one factor is inherently more important than the other in influencing a given behavior. For example, many people now doing sex role research assume that environment has more influence than biology on human behavior; humans are said to be liberated from their hormones and from their genes.

These attempts to evaluate the relative importance of biology or environment are, however, somewhat short-sighted. For example, if heredity could be held constant, if a group of people could have all the same chromosomes (as do identical twins), then any differences in behavior would have to be entirely the result of environmental differences before and after birth. However, this does not mean that there was no genetic influence on their body structures or their behavior, but only that the influence was the same for all of them. In this case, genes would still exert their influence, but all differences in behavior between individuals would have been due to differences in environment. Alternatively, if environment could be kept constant, if a group of people could be raised exactly the same way, then all differences in body or behavior would have to be the result of differences in heredity. Environment would still have an important effect on all of them, but it would have the same effect on each of them. In fact, however, it is impossible to have either genetically or environmentally identical pairs of boys and girls (fraternal twins, consisting of one girl and one boy, are not identical). Because of this, sex differences come from the differences in chromosomes and hormones, the differences in the social environment, and the ways in which biology and environment interact. Instead of trying to evaluate the relative importance of biology and environment, we should ask under what conditions and with what results biology or social pressure can affect a given behavior.

One of the most useful concepts in understanding the implications of the interaction of biology and environment in terms of sex differences is Seligman's concept of **preparedness.** According to Seligman (1970), species differ in their ability to associate a stimulus to a response or to relate two stimuli, and this ability can be described as falling on a biological continuum of preparedness, from prepared through unprepared to contra-prepared. Prepared associations can be formed or acquired or related to each other within the first few times they occur together, in close temporal proximity; prepared associations can be formed without reward or reinforcement, and some special associations can even be formed when the two stimuli are separated by several hours. Contra-prepared associations cannot be acquired; the stimulus and response will not be related no matter how many times they are paired. For example, you can condition a rat to avoid a food with a novel taste by making the animal sick after it eats the food; however, you cannot make a rat avoid water that is accompanied by flashing lights and bells by making that rat sick afterwards. Thus, rats (and people) are prepared to associate illness with a novel taste, but they are contra-prepared to associate illness with bright, noisy water. Unprepared associations can be formed but will require more training than do prepared associations.

Some of preparedness can be understood from an evolutionary point of view. For example, it was adaptive for animals to learn to avoid a poisonous substance with a novel taste that made them ill, but how many times have our ancestors encountered bright, noisy, poisonous water? But it must be emphasized that preparedness is related to the ease of making the association, not to the ease of making the response or to the organism's sensitivity to the stimulus. The rat could get sick, and could taste, hear, and see, but the ability to make associations among those stimuli varied widely, probably because of evolutionary history.

Biological biases may make one gender or the other more prepared to be affected in a certain way by a certain kind of experience. For example, male rats remember the association between a novel taste and illness longer than do female rats (K. C. Chambers, 1976, K. C. Chambers and Sengstake, 1976). If sex differences occur only in the ease of associating certain behaviors with certain situations, then with sufficient experience even the less prepared gender can reach the same level of performance as the more prepared gender—the process will just take longer. If everyone is trained repeatedly to be aggressive, then there should be no sex differences in aggression. Even if males are biologically biased towards learning to be aggressive, if only females receive aggressive training, then females will be more aggressive than males since the bias of males wouldn't appear without training. In other words, if there is a sex difference in the preparedness to learn to be aggressive, then a sex difference in aggressiveness is not inevitable; it would simply be the case that one sex could associate aggressive responses with pleasant consequences more rapidly and readily than the other sex.

A second point relevant to preparedness can also be made. If biological factors bias organisms to respond in certain ways to certain stimuli, there should be no sex differences when those stimuli are absent. Therefore, these biases should be situation specific. As a result, a small change in the situation could eliminate the effect of the bias. Both because of the situation specificity and because preparedness refers only to the time required to learn an association, even biologically biased sex differences will be neither universal nor inevitable.

All the data presented in the first part of the book will help us to decide whether or not there are biological biases in any **sexually dimorphic trait** (any trait that occurs in different frequencies in females and in males). But the reader should always keep in mind that in every case differences in environment are also having their impact on sex differences in behavior, either magnifying or minimizing the effect of the biological bias. Another caution to keep in mind is that the data on biological biases are always subject to various experimental biases and possible distortions. This means that biological biases ought to be inferred only if their presence is supported by most of the data in the various kinds of research, from studies of inductive and activational hormonal effects, to studies using many different animals, including humans. Therefore, what should be looked for are commonalities that appear across studies using different methodologies and different species.

The kinds of effects that environment can have will be assessed by examining the types and range of consistent social influences on sex differences in humans. This will include everything from differences in parental treatment of newborn infants, based on the infants' gender, to the sources and effects of an internalized sexual stereotype on behavior. Then each of the major areas of human sexual dimorphism will be evaluated in terms of the interaction between biology and environment. Both possible biological and possible social biases will be examined in order to evaluate the way that experience interacts with biology in producing sex differences.

In all sections, we will attempt to focus not on how many and what types of sex differences there are, but on the causes and functions of sex differences. The circumstances that determine whether or not differences are apparent will be emphasized whenever relevant data exist. It seems important not just to list sex differences but to understand the details of each difference—when and why it appears, and how it can be manipulated—because only by knowing that can we understand the social impact of sex differences, and because by knowing that we can better understand our own behavior. And maybe at the end of it all, we will have a better idea of where to look for the answers to the question of why there are sex differences, and a better idea of what types of answers there might be.

DIFFERENT TYPES OF SEX DIFFERENCES

Before the interaction of biological biases and environment can be evaluated, some common sources of misinterpretation and bias must be considered. These problems make it difficult to determine the extent to which the genders actually differ from each other. In fact, in some respects, the data in the area of sex differences are more vulnerable to misinterpretation and bias than that of many other areas of psychology. For one thing, this area tends to arouse emotions, both because our gender identity is so central to our whole sense of self and because sex differences have been used to justify sexual discrimination. Questioning the validity of sex-role stereotypes as adequate predictors (or explainers) of behavior can threaten a person's sense of self.

There are other problems of interpretation in the study of sex differences. First, differences between sexes, even when they are reliable and consistent, tend to be small when compared to the differences found among people of the same gender. Also, since experimenters cannot randomly assign people to one gender or the other (the people would undoubtedly object), correlational data, with all of their associated problems of interpretation, are common in this area. Also, some additional factors operate to consistently bias the literature, making it very difficult to estimate the true nature and extent of sex differences. Finally, cultural stereotypes not only can determine what behaviors are selected to be studied in what kinds of people, but these same stereotypes can inadvertently determine the results of experiments.

The rest of this chapter will give some general background for the different types of sex differences, discussing some possible sources of erroneous conclusions and experimental bias and emphasizing the types of problems mentioned above. There are four ways in which the genders can differ, each of which can be expressed in terms of statistics. The genders can differ because one has more of something than the other, such as weight or height (differences in the statistical mean). The genders can also differ in the degree to which a person is similar to other people of the same gender (differences in variability). For example, females are found in fewer occupations than males, so it is easier to predict at birth what female will be likely to do as an adult than to predict what a male will do as an adult. Gender can also be a factor in the way that one variable influences another (differences in interaction): an impoverished early environment may have more effect on the intellectual development of males than females. Finally, the genders may differ in the way in which or the degree to which two variables are related to each other (differences in correlation). For example, IQ is more strongly related to occupational success in males than in females.

Differences in Means of Distributions

Suppose you were given the job of finding out whether or not men and women reliably or significantly differ in weight. To carry out this task, you would probably try to find a group of men and a group of women of the same age (or making the groups matched for ages) and measure the weight of each person, perhaps plotting a frequency distribution for each gender (see Appendix A). Suppose that you also found that the **median, modal,** and **mean** weight of men exceeded those of women; therefore, the typical weight of a typical man is higher than that of a typical woman. Then what?

Statistical Significance and Confidence Levels. Before evaluating any difference between mean scores of the genders along any measurable dimension, we will need to perform some sort of statistical test to tell us how much confidence we should place in our belief that there is in fact a real difference between the genders. Suppose, for example, that there were two jars containing marbles. Suppose also that both jars had seventy red marbles and thirty yellow marbles and that we had someone draw out ten marbles from each jar. If the person were blindfolded, and if the marbles were all the same size, weight, and texture and were well mixed, then **chance** alone would determine what marbles were taken out. But suppose that the person drew a sample of ten red marbles from one jar and a sample of ten yellow marbles from the other jar—an unlikely but not impossible occurrence (people do win lotteries). We obviously would be in error if we concluded on the basis of those two samples that the one jar had only red marbles and the other jar only yellow ones; in fact, we would have committed what is called a Type 1 error (see Appendix A).

Similarly, any difference found between groups divided on the basis of gender must be carefully evaluated to determine the likelihood that chance factors alone could have accounted for that difference. In the example of the jars, we would determine this chance factor by first drawing several samples from each jar and looking at the mean number of red marbles drawn in those samples. Then we would compare the differences in the average number of red marbles drawn from each jar to the variability observed in the number of red marbles across samples for each jar. This comparison would probably bring us close to the correct conclusion: each jar had exactly the same number of red marbles in it. In the case of sex differences, the size of the difference between the means of the two sexes is compared to the variability of scores within each sex to allow us to estimate the probability that the observed difference was due to chance factors alone, thus determining the degree of confidence with which we can conclude that there is a real difference between the sexes.

Psychology journals generally require that experimentally produced or measured differences between groups reach a certain arbitrarily chosen confidence level, or **significance level,** before the difference is to be regarded as real and worth communicating to other people. This significance level is generally set such that the observed difference between the groups would have occurred by chance factors alone in only five out of a hundred times the experiment was done. This is generally stated as $p < .05$, which means a chance probability of less than .05, or five times out of a hundred samples. If a difference has a confidence or significance level of $p <.001$, then only in one time out of a thousand would a difference have appeared by chance factors alone, and you could then place great confidence in the conclusion that the difference was real.

Common Problems and Misinterpretations. With a large enough sample size and a sufficiently stable measuring instrument, extremely small differences between groups can be reliably and confidently detected. But significance does not mean importance. For example, on the Graduate Record Examination, required for entrance into many graduate schools, the males' score on a scale of verbal abilities significantly differed from those of females at the .001 level. However, the standard deviation of both female and male scores was 124.5, while the difference between the mean scores of males and females was only ten (493 as opposed to 503). Thus, it is possible to find differences that are significant, but not very important in terms of predicting the behavior of a person only from a knowledge of that person's gender. In the above example, the difference between the sexes was less than 8 percent of one measure of the difference within each sex. So concluding that there is a real sex difference between the mean scores on a test does not necessarily mean that this is a relevant way to differentiate between groups; in order to predict task or job performance, it would be more accurate to divide groups into high and low scorers, regardless of sex.

One point to keep in mind in interpreting differences is that the test may be measuring different things for each sex. For example, females consistently receive higher mean scores on tests of need to affiliate. This does not necessarily mean that women are more affiliative. Instead, these scores seem to mean different things—they predict different behaviors—in men and in women. Men with a high need to affiliate, or a strong desire to be around people and to be liked, are perceived as unpopular and may be exhibitionists. This is not true for women who have a high need to affiliate. So even if there are differences in mean scores on a given test, the test may not be measuring the same trait in men as in women.

Also, the more tests of significance you make on the same subjects, the more likely you are to find a significant sex difference, due to chance factors alone. To correct for this, **alpha levels** should be adjusted (see Appendix A), but this is seldom done. Thus, the interpretation of a significant sex difference in the mean or average test score or behavioral measure will depend on the behavioral correlates of what is being measured and the number of other tests that were also performed on the same data.

Sex Differences in Variability

Researchers have found a second type of sex difference. There are sometimes significant differences in the **variability** of a trait in the two genders. Variability refers to individual differences, to how many people deviate from the typical, and by how much. The more variability there is, the more people differ from one another on what is being measured, the less accurately the typical or mean score describes the group or predicts individual behavior. For example, if there were no variability in a given trait, then everyone would be typical, or the mean score would be true for everyone. If, however, people tend to be very different from one another, if they vary greatly along a particular dimension, then the mean score will provide relatively little ability to predict what any one of them might be like.

To look for sex differences in variability, you again would measure something, say, weight, in a large group of men and an equally large group of women, all matched for age. You could again plot a frequency distribution for each group. This time, you would be likely to find not only that women tend to weigh less on the average, but also that they are more variable. That is, not only are there more thin women than thin men, there are also more fat women than fat men—more women well above and below the mean for women than there are men well above and below the mean for men. Thus, women tend to be more variable in weight, to be more different from one another along the dimension of weight.

Examples of Sex Differences in Variability.   Several phenomena have been explained by hypothesizing sex differences in variability. The relative lack of geniuses among women has been attributed by many people to a greater variability in intelligence in males; since men are more variable, more of them would be geniuses and idiots than would be the case with women. As another example, Vandenberg, McKusick, and McKusick (1962) found more variability among pairs of identical female twins than among pairs of identical male twins; that is, female twins tended to differ from each other more than did male twins. The researchers attributed this difference to the fact that the normal human female is a **genetic mosaic,** an organism whose body cells contain different chromosomes, but the normal male is not. These hypotheses will be discussed in greater detail in later chapters, but it is clear that the possibility of sex differences in variability should not be overlooked.

Range Location and Sex Differences.   Another closely related type of sex difference is the **location** of the range of scores, regardless of whether there are sex differences in variability. For example, Maccoby (1966) proposed that the sexes differ in the range location of scores on dimensions such as activation and aggression. Most females fall in the range from passive to moderately aggressive, while most males lie in the area from moderately to greatly aggressive. This would lead not only to differences in the mean scores for aggression for each sex, but it could also lead to sex differences in correlations, as discussed later in this chapter.

Implications of Variability.   The major point to be kept in mind with regard to sex differences and variability is that the variability within either gender is always larger than the mean difference between the genders. That is, knowledge of a person's gender does not allow for accurate predictions of that person's behavior. Also, differences in variability imply either that the more variable gender has the more variable biological or social environment, or that the interaction of biology and environment differs according to gender. For example, both genders have monthly changes in hormones, but the change in females from one day to another is greater than that in males. This could mean that any hormone-sensitive behavior would be more variable in women than in men. On the other hand, men are socialized so as to be able to take on more occupations than are women, so achievement behaviors might be more variable in men than in women. Finally, differences in the range location can affect the interpretation of other types of differences, such as sex differences in correlations.

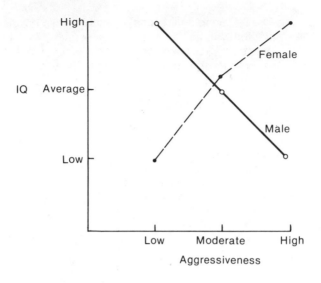

FIGURE 1.1

HYPOTHETICAL INTERACTION BETWEEN TWO VARIABLES

In an interaction, the effect one variable has on behavior depends on the level of another variable. In this example, the relationship of aggressiveness and IQ scores depends on the gender of the subject; aggressive women tend to have higher IQ scores; aggressive men tend to have lower IQ scores.

Gender Interacting with Other Variables

Suppose we were measuring both aggressiveness and IQ in a group of men and in a group of women to see how aggressiveness might be related to IQ. That is, suppose we measured how many times each person was willing to give a painful shock to another person who had insulted him or her, and we also had the IQ scores of all our subjects. What we would be looking for is the relationship between aggression and IQ according to sex, a third type of sex difference.

If we did such an experiment, what we might find is an **interaction,** which would mean that the effect of aggressiveness on IQ (or the effect of IQ on aggressiveness) would depend upon the gender of the person being tested. One form this interaction might take is illustrated in Figure 1.1. Another interaction would be if intelligent women were more aggressive, as illustrated in Figure 1.1, but aggression was not related to IQ in men. An interaction occurs whenever the relationship of one variable or behavior (such as aggression) to another variable or behavior (such as IQ score) is determined by or affected by the level or value of a third variable (such as gender).

Obviously, to look for interactions demands complex experiments, but to ignore the possibility of an interaction can lead to completely invalid conclusions. Thus, the possibility of an interactive explanation for any sex difference observed between means of distributions should never be overlooked.

Sex Differences in Correlations

Correlations among variables can be affected by gender and these form a fourth type of sex difference. For example, it has been suggested that the correlation between socioeconomic class and incidence of obesity is significant and negative; that is, the higher the socioeconomic class, the lower the incidence of obesity. However, the correlation between class and weight for women was more negative than that for men; that is, there were both more obese lower-class women and thin upper-class women than there were men in each case.

Nevertheless, before you can demonstrate a sex difference, you will have to ask whether or not the correlation between class and obesity for women is significantly greater (more negative) than the comparable correlation was for men. You will also need to know what degree of confidence should be placed in the conclusion that the two correlations were in fact different.

Thus, comparing correlations for women to the equivalent correlations for men and testing to see whether or not the two correlations are significantly different is another way of demonstrating sex differences in behavior. But before a correlation can be interpreted, several questions must be answered.

Correlation Is Not Causation. One reason that a correlation can be difficult to interpret comes from the common, but erroneous, assumption that it means that one of the variables in some way caused the other variable to happen. This is probably the case for the negative correlation between miles traveled and the number of gallons remaining in the gas tank, but is not necessarily the case in the following example. A positive and significant correlation might be demonstrated across cities between the number of cats in the city and the number of burglaries occurring per year. Since cat burglars are not really cats, there is obviously no causal relationship. It would also be possible to demonstrate a positive correlation between ice cream consumed and the number of drownings per day. But ice cream does not make people drown, and dead and drowned people do not eat more ice cream than live people, so there is obviously no causal relationship here either.

So, if two variables are correlated, several different possible causal relationships could be involved. The correlation could have arisen because one variable in some way led to changes in the other, as driving the car leads to the disappearance of gas from its tank. A significant correlation could also be produced because both variables were caused by a third, unexplored, and uncontrolled variable. For example, large cities have both more cats and more cat burglars, and on hot days more people eat ice cream and more people also go swimming (and drown). The same types of analyses could be made for the hypothetical correlation of aggression and IQ. Does intelligence increase aggression in women? Or does aggression increase intelligence? Or do male hormones or rejecting mothers increase both IQ and aggression in women? Therefore, with regard to correlational data, one question should always be asked: is there any reason to assume any particular causal relationship from this data?

Other Areas of Misinterpretation. Other errors in interpreting correlations are particularly likely to occur in the area of sex differences. For example, Kagan and Moss (1962) reported that parental attempts to accelerate (engaging in

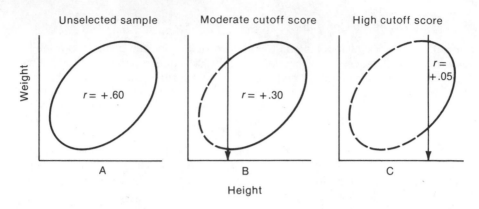

FIGURE 1.2

DIFFERENCE IN CORRELATIONS CAUSED BY RESTRICTING SCORE DISTRIBUTION

This figure shows the effect that truncating or restricting the distribution of scores on one measure has upon the correlation of that measure with another. Part A illustrates a correlation (r) of .60 between height and weight. Using higher and higher cutoff scores, as shown in parts B and C, progressively decreases the size of the correlation.

frequent sessions of having their child practice such activities as walking, talking, spelling, and counting) their three- to six-year-old children were significantly and positively correlated with that child's attempts to dominate other people, but only for girls, not for boys. What can we conclude on the basis of that information? Not much. We could conclude only that the correlation for girls would have occurred by chance alone less than five times out of a hundred, while the boys' correlation would have occurred by chance alone more than five times out of a hundred. We could not definitely state that the correlation for girls was significantly different from the correlation for boys, although that is one possibility. Other possibilities must first be ruled out by asking several other questions of the data.

A less than significant correlation for boys could have come about for several reasons. One possibility is that the range of either variable could have been less for boys than for girls, due to differences in rearing practices. If, for example, all parents tried to accelerate their sons but only some parents tried to accelerate their daughters because these particular parents felt that it was more important for boys to succeed, then this would result in a lower correlation between acceleration and dominance for boys than for girls. Figure 1.2 illustrates the possible effects of different range sizes (or cutoffs) on the correlations.

The difference in correlations might also be due to **sample size** (the number of subjects studied). Perhaps fewer boys than girls were studied. If so, the likelihood that any given value of a correlation could have occurred by chance alone would be greater for boys, making it less likely to reach the .05 confidence or significance level.

But perhaps both sexes had the same range and sample size. It could still be that more variables affect dominance in boys than in girls, or that variables other than parental acceleration have more effect on dominance in boys than girls. Thus, there might be more **scatter** around the relationship between dominance and acceleration for boys than for girls. In other words, acceleration may account for more of the variability in dominance scores in females than in males so that the degree to which the two variables were related depended on gender, with the relationship being stronger for females than for males.

These then are three possible explanations for the statement that the relationship was significant for girls but not for boys. In only one of these (the last) did gender actually affect the degree of relationship between the correlated variables. Here, the sex difference in the correlation, given the same range and sample sizes, means that more of the variability in one of the behaviors can be accounted for by its correlate for one sex than for the other—other variables may be more important relatively for that sex. Different range or sample sizes could also lead to different correlations, without there being any underlying sex difference in the actual degree of relationship between the two correlated variables. So in these latter cases, we cannot conclude that there was a significant effect of gender on the degree of the relationship of the variables.

Which is the true explanation for the Kagan and Moss data? In fact, as Kagan and Moss (1962) indicated, the significant correlation for girls was +.36, and the nonsignificant correlation for boys was +.37. Thus, we must conclude that the sample sizes differed. However, since authors of texts and research papers don't always report the values of nonsignificant correlations, or even test to see whether or not the male correlation is significantly different from the female correlation with regard to the tested pairs of variables, these possibilities must always be kept in mind.

The questions described in this section are those experimenters are least likely to ask of their data, so correlations in the area of sex differences can frequently lead to erroneous conclusions—if the reader is not wary. Only if there is a significant difference between the correlations for the scores of the two sexes can you say that there is a true sex difference—that the degree to which the two variables are related does in fact depend upon gender.

Conclusions. As we now see, correlation data in the area of sex differences can frequently lead to misinterpretations. You cannot assume that correlation means causation. You also cannot assume that there is a sex difference in the type or degree of relationship between two variables unless you can establish: (a) that there is a significant sex difference in the values of the correlations; and (b) that the genders have equivalent variability for the scores on the two variables. Finally, if more than a few correlations are calculated, the alpha level should be adjusted.

SOURCES OF BIAS

There are four possible types of differences between the genders. The data for each difference—whether they involve means, variability, interactions, or correlations—present unique problems of interpretation and difficulties to anyone trying to infer the existence of sex differences. However, these are not the only sources of problems that affect attempts to evaluate the extent of differences. Other problems come from the biasing effects of publication policies and from the beliefs, values, and expectations of the experimenters.

Publication Bias

One source of bias that affects our ability to estimate the true nature and extent of sex differences is the arbitrarily set significance level for all four types of sex differences. If one hundred different experimenters examined groups of males and groups of females, given the .05 level of significance, then five out of those hundred experimenters would find significant differences between the two groups at least at the .05 level, even if the differences were only the result of chance variations in sampling. The five experimenters who got positive results are much more likely to try to publish their results, and journals are much more likely to accept them than the negative results of the other ninety-five experimenters. Thus, any survey of the literature on sex differences could easily overemphasize positive results—those published and communicated—thereby exaggerating the number of sex differences.

Subject and Experimenter Selection

Another bias works in the opposite direction of the previous one. Several authors have noted that over 70 percent of the published papers using human subjects in which sex of subject was specified have tested only male college students (Holmes and Jorgensen, 1971; Schultz, 1969). Other studies did not specify the sex of the subject, and some studies, even though both sexes were used, did not analyze for any possible effects of sex on their results. Various reasons have been given for this bias. First, since most researchers are male, they are most interested in learning about themselves by studying other men. Also, since men have a relatively more prestigious role in our society, it might seem more important to study men than to study women. Finally, women might be viewed as having to be protected from some of the experimental manipulations that are often used.

But using only male subjects not only limits our ability to generalize from the research results, but also leads in the long run to an underestimation of the true extent of sex differences. In order to discover a sex difference, researchers have to study two sexes. So subject selection combines with publication biases to make it very difficult to estimate accurately the extent to which the sexes actually differ.

Not all research shows a bias toward male subjects. For example, sex-role research usually used mostly female subjects (Hochschild, 1973). So we have a lot of data about the role of the woman inside and outside the family, but relatively little data on men—and even less data on sex differences. The experimental design employed may also affect the gender of the subject chosen (McKenna and Kessler, 1977). For example, males are used more often than females in aggression research, and even when women are used, their aggression is more likely to be measured only indirectly, as by a paper and pencil test (the likelihood is 43 percent for women, and only 11 percent for men). Aggression in males was more often measured by looking at their overt behaviors (66 percent of males were measured that way, and only 35 percent of females). So perhaps these biases reflect the beliefs of experimenters that males are more active and females more passive.

A related source of bias was discussed by S. Harris (1971). The sex of the experimenter is often not specified in papers, and it is not always correct to assume that the author of the paper was the experimenter. In one case, it was found that male researchers engaged in more "intense and prolonged" contact with female than with male subjects, while female experimenters were equally remote from both genders (Wax, 1975). Thus, the experimenter's gender could inadvertently produce a spurious sex difference; in this example, male experimenters would be more likely to find a sex difference in their data. The true extent of sex differences cannot be estimated if gender is not varied, not specified, or its effects not analyzed for.

The Rosenthal Effect

Another source of bias was pointed out by Weisstein (1971). To the extent that researchers themselves have internalized the cultural sex-role stereotypes, they will have expectations as to the likely outcome of research concerned with sex differences. They could well look for results that confirm their expectations.

Rosenthal and his coworkers (Rosenthal, 1963, 1966) have shown that the hypothesis of the experimenter has significant effects on the outcome of the experiment, even if the subject is a rat (Rosenthal and Fode, 1960; Rosenthal and Lawson, 1961). These results were extended to a classroom situation. Students were tested and their teachers were told that some particular students showed great promise (actually, these students had been randomly selected). Later, the students were retested and those for whom the teachers had great expectations showed dramatic increases in IQ relative to the other students (Rosenthal and Jacobson, 1968). Thus, without proper controls and cautions, it would be possible for the cultural sex-role stereotype to be duplicated in and perpetuated by experimental results simply because of the experimenters' culturally-conditioned hypotheses. This is probably true even of biological data in studies of genes and hormones (M. Rosenberg, 1973).

SUMMARY AND CONCLUSIONS

This book will evaluate the possible influences that biological biases can have on sex differences, and the ways in which culture and society can create, increase, or decrease sex differences. The reasons for sex differences, both in terms of biological and social utility, will also be explored. Finally, ways in which the environmental and biological biases interact to influence behavior will be examined in several areas in which sex differences have often been assumed to exist or have actually been observed to exist.

To interpret these data, you should keep in mind the meaning of statistical statements about the different types of sex differences—both what the statistics do and do not say—and the types of bias that exist in this area of research. The major point to keep in mind is that this is an area in which people tend to have very strong beliefs, beliefs that are very important to their own self-identity, beliefs that when questioned often cause them to respond with anger or fear. Once, when we were at a friend's house, we picked up a book belonging to one of his children. The book contained a story of a girl and her brother. The brother attempted to ride a bicycle and succeeded; the girl also made the attempt, failed, and ended up an enthusiastic observer of her brother's success. We asked our friend—a professional psychologist—if that was what he wanted his little girl to grow up believing. He responded that it was better for her to believe that than to grow up not knowing she was a girl.

Beliefs about sex differences in behavior not only determine childrearing practices but also easily color the interpretation of data, the selection of subjects, and even the direction of experimental results. These beliefs can be self-fulfilling; if they are held strongly the data will be likely to support them, making them even stronger. So no great confidence should be placed in data that has not been replicated by experimenters with different points of view and that has not been supported by a variety of data across several different experimental areas. Otherwise, the answer to the question of why there are differences between the sexes might simply be, "because of experimenter bias."

KEY TERMS AND CONCEPTS

Gender identity
Gender role
Androgen insensitivity
Testicular feminization
Chromosomal gender
Gonadal gender
Hormonal gender
Gender of internal sex organs
Gender of external sex organs
Gender of rearing
Androgynous
Hypothalamus
Pituitary gland
Inductive effect of hormones
Activational effect of hormones
Freud's psychoanalytic theory
Identification
Oedipal period
Parson's sociological theory
Social-learning theory

Model
Kohlberg's cognitive-developmental theory
Preparedness
Biological biases
Sexual dimorphism
Median
Mode
Mean
Statistical significance
Chance
Genetic mosaic
Variability
Alpha level
Range location
Interaction
Correlations
Acceleration of children
Sample size
Scatter
Rosenthal effect

QUESTIONS ON KEY ISSUES

1. What is the nature of the interaction between environment and biology, and what is its relevance for sex differences?

2. What forms can the question of why there are sex differences take?

3. What are the four major types of sex differences (in terms of statistics)?

4. What are some common problems of interpretation that occur for each type of difference?

5. What are the major sources of bias in the data of sex differences? What can be done about them?

PART 2 _____

Biology and
Sex Differences

CHAPTER 2

On Being Born Male or Female

Why are we born either male or female? The answer to that question starts at conception, with the chromosomal gender. The presence of a Y chromosome leads to the development of testes; androgens from the testes produces a male baby and later a masculine looking adolescent. The absence of the Y, and the absence of the androgens produced by the testes, leads to the birth of a girl and later, under the influence of estrogen and progesterone from the ovaries, to a feminine looking adolescent who menstruates.

This chapter deals with the question of why there are two sexes by investigating how the sex chromosomes and sex hormones lead to the development of male and female people, and examining the implications of genetic sex differences. The possible effects of the chromosomal differences between the sexes will be analyzed in two different ways. First, the effects of chromosomal abnormalities will be examined to see what they imply about the effects of sex chromosomes on sex differences in genetically normal people. Second, the behavioral and physical traits that might be affected by the genes on the sex chromosomes are reviewed, because these traits ought then to appear with different frequencies in females and males. The effect of the sex hormones upon the brain before birth (the inductive effect of hormones) and after puberty (the activational effect of hormones) is considered in more detail in chapters 4 and 5.

INTRODUCTION TO SEXUAL HEREDITY

One answer to the question of why there are two sexes starts by looking at the moment of conception. At that time, the sex of the fetus is determined by its chromosomes; afterward, every cell in the body contains the label of the genetic sex of that individual, whether that person is normal or abnormal. What implications for sex differences does this genetic label have?

Genes: The Unit of Heredity

The Structure and Function of Genes. Fetal development and the functioning of every cell of every living organism is under the control of the genetic information contained in each cell's **chromosomes.** Each chromosome contains a large number of **genes**—approximately 3,000, although the number varies according to the size of the chromosone. Each gene is composed of a large molecule of a substance called **deoxyribonucleic acid,** or **DNA.** Genes serve as a template or code for the manufacture of proteins. These proteins may then determine the structure and function of the body cells, or else they act to either activate (induce) or inhibit (repress) the action of other genes in that cell or other cells.

The major point to remember is that genes have no direct effect on cellular activity, cellular structure, or development and behavior; genes exert their influence only by way of the proteins for which they are the code. And some genes act to control—induce or repress—other genes.

Genotype and Phenotype.   The total contribution of genes to an organism's inherited physical appearance and behavior is called the **genotype.** When the genes are expressed, in interaction with the environment and other genes, the result is called a **phenotype.** Since the environment may affect the way a gene is expressed, the phenotype often differs from the genotype.

Chromosomes in Humans

Humans have twenty-three pairs of chromosomes, making a total of forty-six chromosomes in all. In each person, one chromosome of each pair comes from the father and one from the mother. The twenty-three paternal chromosomes, one of each of the father's chromosome pairs plus an X or a Y, are selected randomly when the sperm is formed. The maternal contribution of twenty-three chromosomes, including one of her Xs, is contained in the ovum, or egg. When the sperm and ovum combine, the fertilized egg, or fetus, then has its full complement of twenty-three pairs. The chromosomes are divided into those that determine the sex of the organism, the **sex chromosomes**—and the other twenty-two pairs of chromosomes called **autosomes.**

Sex Chromosomes and the Karyotype.   In the male, the sex chromosomes are an X and a Y; a genetically normal male has a total of forty-six chromosomes and is designated as 46, XY. The genetically normal human female has a pair of X chromosomes and is designated as 46, XX. In the male, the Y chromosome came from his father; in the female, one X came from the mother and one from the father.

Figure 2.1 contains a diagram of a **karyotype,** the total number of genes and chromosomes of an individual, here rank ordered from largest to smallest. The X is one of the largest chromosomes and the Y one of the smallest. The Y thus has fewer genes on it than the X.

The Barr Body, X-Inactivation, and Mosaicism.   In 1949, Barr and Bertram discovered that individual nuclei of cells from female cats contained a body of darkly staining chromosome material (chromatin). Figure 2.1 also presents a picture of this material, which came to be called the **Barr body,** or the **Barr sex chromatin body.** Later it was found that this body occurs in many of the body cells (15 to 65 percent) of a great majority of female mammals, including humans. In 1959, Ohno and his colleagues (Ohno, 1967) established that this darkly staining body was one of the two X chromosomes of the female. In 1961, Lyon hypothesized that early during embryonic development, the genes on one of the X chromo-

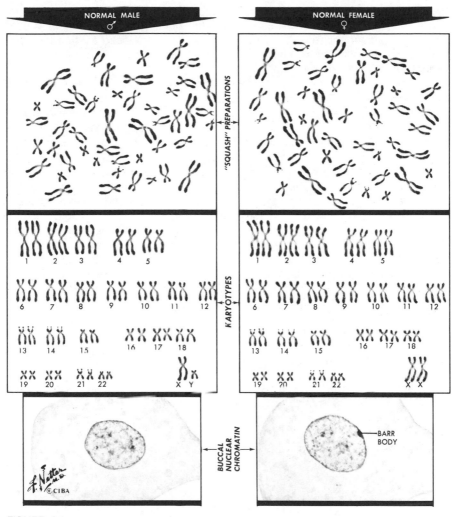

FIGURE 2.1

THE GENOTYPE OF A PERSON

At the top, cellular multiplication was arrested by a chemical agent, and a "squash" preparation made by spreading out cells under a cover slip. The total number of chromosomes and the type of sex chromosomes present comprise the karyotype, here arranged in order from largest to smallest. The Barr body (the second, inactivated X in females) is often identified by staining cells scraped from the mouth, the buccal mucosa.

somes are inactivated—which sometimes causes it to stain darkly—though which one is inactivated in each fetal cell is randomly determined. But once an X chromosome has been inactivated in a cell, all the cells produced by that fetal cell, both before and after birth, will have the same X inactivated. This makes the genetically normal female a natural mosaic.

Since Lyon formulated her hypothesis, others have found evidence to support the idea that the normal female is a genetic mosaic, with different Xs active in different body cells (Beutter, Yeh, and Fairbanks, 1962; R. G. Davidson, Nitowsky, and Childs, 1963). However, there seems to be some disagreement as to whether the inactivation is complete or whether some genes on the X chromosome might remain somewhat active (Lyon, 1972; Ohno, 1967). The implications of complete versus partial inactivation are not as yet clear, but some genes on the inactivated X may be necessary for normal ovaries.

One visible consequence of this inactivation of different X chromosomes in different cells is the calico coat of some cats. Most calicos are females, since the splotches of different colors depend on which X chromosome has been inactivated in a particular area of the skin. The only male calico cats are those who have at least two Xs in addition to a Y chromosome, and they are usually infertile. So the next time you see a calico cat, remember that you are seeing the effects of mosaicism in a genetically normal female (or in a genetically abnormal male).

SEX CHROMOSOME ABNORMALITIES AND BEHAVIOR

Much of our information about how sex chromosomes influence development and behavior has come from the study of individuals who have some abnormality in their sex chromosomes. Before you read the following discussion, however, caution must be advised. The studies discussed here often compared the incidence of a given genetic abnormality at birth to its incidence among individuals institutionalized because of mental disorders, retardation, or criminal behavior. The adequacy of the karyotyping procedure among newborns and the effect of different selection criteria for institutionalization have been questioned (see A. Robinson, 1975). This means that these studies must be interpreted carefully.

Also, environmental factors are just as important for individuals with chromosome abnormalities as for people with normal chromosomes. People with identical chromosome abnormalities will be affected both by their genes and by their environments in exactly the same way that genetically normal people are. But, if the environment had similar effects on genetically abnormal and genetically normal people, comparing them is one way to assess the effects of the extra or missing sex chromosomes upon behavior. Still, if the environment of people with chromosome abnormalities differs systematically from that of normal people, then the cause of any behavioral difference will remain obscure. For example, XXY males and XYY males are taller than normal males. If society treats tall and short men differently, then any differences between XXY or XYY men and XY men may be due to genes or environment. Such possible systematic biases must always be kept in mind.

Rosenthal effects and other biases may also contaminate data on genetic abnormalities. That is, their expectations may lead experimenters to subtly (and unknowingly) bias their data. Also, since the physical appearance of these people differs from that of normal people, parental attitudes and expectations may have been subtly communicated to the child. Later, the person's own awareness of his or her differences may change his or her behavior in ways that have nothing directly to do with genes. For example, men with Klinefelter's syndrome often exhibit low levels of sexual behavior. But these men often have feminized appearance, with small male genitals and some breast growth. Perhaps self-consciousness or lack of self-esteem causes them to be hesitant about initiating sexual behavior.

Data on genetic abnormalities support two conclusions. One is that, in humans, *it is the Y chromosome that determines gender.* Both people with only one X and those with more than two Xs are female in appearance. And no matter how many Xs are present, if a Y chromosome is also present, the individual will be born with a male appearance. The other conclusion suggested by the data is that *extra Xs may make males, but not females, somewhat more feminine; and extra Ys may make males more masculine than normal.*

47, XXX and 48, XXXX

In individuals with 47, XXX and 48, XXXX, there are one or two extra chromosomes, and the extra ones are Xs. This syndrome occurs in from .07 to .09 percent of all female births (Hamerton et al., 1975). There is usually one fewer Barr body than there are X chromosomes, indicating that all of the superfluous Xs have been inactivated. However, these women dramatically demonstrate that the inactivated, extra Xs do have an effect. Although they are usually of normal female appearance, they have diminished fertility (Court-Brown et al., 1964). Only about half to three quarters menstruate normally, and early menopause is common. Because the mothers of these women are often older than is usual, this disorder might be partially due to aging of egg cells.

These women are prone to a variety of psychological and intellectual abnormalities. Trisomy X (47, XXX) may predispose the individual toward a schizophrenialike illness (Maclean et al., 1968) or to a manic-depressive disorder (Kusumi, 1976). M. T. Tsuang (1974, 1975) has reported that among Chinese females with extra X chromosomes, there seems to be a high incidence of both schizophrenia and retardation. However, everyone with trisomy-X need not show all these disorders; for example, it is possible for such a person to test as bright normal (though this is not possible for a person with more than three X chromosomes).

One study (Tennes, et al., 1975) compared the development of eleven girls with a 47, XXX karyotype to that of twenty-three normal siblings. The authors reported that one-third of the trisomy-X group showed a delay in motor and speech development, a slight intellectual deficit, and a difficulty in relating to others. Another third of the trisomy-X girls had suffered mild developmental problems but the last third were described as having given no cause for concern. However, as the authors pointed out, "no one child suffered all the effects nor was any completely free" (p. 79).

Thus, the above research suggests that women with extra X chromosomes may have normal physical appearance, but they may be more likely than genetically normal women to be infertile, retarded, slow in development, and schizophrenic. The extra X did not feminize them, but it did affect their development and behavior, even though it usually was inactivated.

45, X, or Turner's Syndrome

In the case of Turner's syndrome, the fetus has only one X chromosome present and hence has no Barr body and yet is clearly female in external appearance (see Figure 2.2). The frequency of Turner's women is not related to the mother's age, but 74 percent of the time the one X did come from the mother (G. Fraser, 1963). This syndrome occurs in about .01 percent of all female births (Hamerton et al., 1975). Here again, we see that the inactivated X in the normal female is important, because without it, the woman with Turner's syndrome exhibits frequent behavioral, physical, and intellectual abnormalities (Lyon, 1972).

Physical Abnormalities.   Some of the typical physical abnormalities of the Turner's women include shortness (4 to 5 feet tall); the appearance of webbing around the neck; frequent cardiac difficulties; eyelid folds; shieldlike chest; small jaws; malformation of the nails, feet, and fingers; porous bones; swelling of lower limbs; and, almost always, infertility (Court-Brown et al., 1964; Money and Granoff, 1965). In addition, without estrogen therapy from adolescence onward, these women generally will not menstruate and they will have no breasts. In other words, they have to be given hormones to show the normal changes of puberty, because their own ovaries are merely nonfunctional streaks of tissue. They do not have normal amounts of any of the three major types of sex hormones.

Thus, the inactive X in genetically normal females seems indispensible for fertility and the normal functioning of the ovaries (Polani, 1974). Although the ovaries of Turner's fetuses seem to be normal up to about the third month of fetal life, by birth there are few if any egg-producing cells left. And by puberty, the majority of 45, X girls will have completely nonfunctional ovaries (Polani, 1972). So the inactivated X in genetically normal females seems to become important around the third month of fetal life.

Social and Emotional Behavior.   In one study of Turner's females, Money and Ehrhardt (1972) compared fifteen Turner's girls, aged eight to sixteen and a half, to a set of control girls matched for age, IQ, socioeconomic background, and race. They found that Turner's girls were less athletic and fought less in childhood, but had a greater interest in jewelry, perfume, and hair styling. Theilgaard (1972) also found that Turner's women dressed so as to exaggerate their gender identity.

FIGURE 2.2 —————————————————————————————————

A TURNER'S GIRL WITH KARYOTYPE OF 45, X

The high output of gonadotropins (pituitary hormones which control the gonads) will be discussed later in this chapter in the context of negative feedback effects.

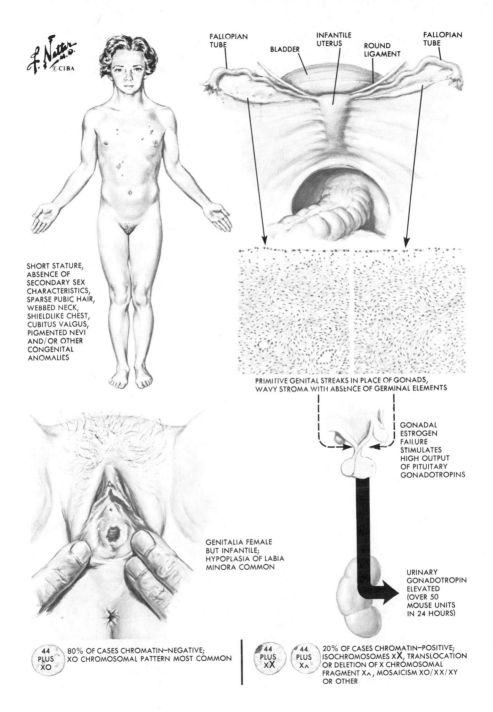

SHORT STATURE, ABSENCE OF SECONDARY SEX CHARACTERISTICS, SPARSE PUBIC HAIR, WEBBED NECK, SHIELDLIKE CHEST, CUBITUS VALGUS, PIGMENTED NEVI AND/OR OTHER CONGENITAL ANOMALIES

FALLOPIAN TUBE

BLADDER

INFANTILE UTERUS

ROUND LIGAMENT

FALLOPIAN TUBE

PRIMITIVE GENITAL STREAKS IN PLACE OF GONADS, WAVY STROMA WITH ABSENCE OF GERMINAL ELEMENTS

GONADAL ESTROGEN FAILURE STIMULATES HIGH OUTPUT OF PITUITARY GONADOTROPINS

GENITALIA FEMALE BUT INFANTILE; HYPOPLASIA OF LABIA MINORA COMMON

URINARY GONADOTROPIN ELEVATED (OVER 50 MOUSE UNITS IN 24 HOURS)

44 PLUS XO   80% OF CASES CHROMATIN–NEGATIVE; XO CHROMOSOMAL PATTERN MOST COMMON

44 PLUS XX   44 PLUS X^   20% OF CASES CHROMATIN–POSITIVE; ISOCHROMOSOMES XX, TRANSLOCATION OR DELETION OF X CHROMOSOMAL FRAGMENT X^, MOSAICISM XO/XX/XY OR OTHER

She stated that Turner's women often wore ruffles and bows, had a great deal of jewelry, and had feminine, curly hairstyles. In Money and Ehrhardt's group, all but one of the Turner's girls wanted to get married, and the one exception wanted to be a nun. All reported daydreaming about being pregnant, even though none of them could fulfill that fantasy. All but one played only with dolls, and the fifteenth girl preferred dolls to other toys.

Intellectual Ability.   Usually, Turner's women have at least a normal IQ, and some even have IQs above 130 (Money, 1964). Still, these women do show some interestingly specific deficits. On the Weschler Adult Intelligence Scale and the Weschler Intelligence Scale for Children, Turner's females show a mean **verbal IQ** slightly but not significantly above the normal mean ($\overline{X}$ =106, where 100 is the norm), but they were significantly below normal in **performance IQ** ($\overline{X}$ =88) (J. W. Shaffer, 1962). They also "had great difficulty understanding mathematics, especially algebra. One girl had an extremely poor sense of direction and frequently became lost. Another went through an elaborate ritual when putting away kitchen utensils since any departure from this procedure left her thoroughly confused" (J. W. Shaffer, 1962, p. 405).

So Turner's women apparently have specific deficiencies in perceptual organization, or **space-form intelligence,** the ability to accurately visualize and locate objects in three-dimensional space. This deficit would at least in part account for the low performance IQ scores, since that often involves performing spatial tasks as well as other tests requiring reasoning and applications of knowledge. Turner's women also have difficulty distinguishing left from right in map reading tests (Money, 1964), and do poorly on embedded figures tasks (Theilgaard, 1972), all of which may be related to their deficiency in spatial ability.

Summary and Interpretations.   Interpretation of the relationship between the 45, X karyotype and the physical abnormalities is made somewhat difficult by the fact that there is also a male Turner's syndrome. Turner's males also show the webbed neck, shield chest, small stature, and retarded sexual development typical of Turner's females (Flavell, 1943). But Turner's males are usually genetically normal, unlike the females.

Turner's women show that the second X in normal females is necessary. Without it, normal functioning of the fetal ovary cannot be maintained. And without it, the woman is neither genetically nor hormonally normal, and the rest of the physical stigmata and the intellectual deficits are the common result.

Turner's women also demonstrate that the second X is not necessary to being born female and even to being feminine. Turner's women have been referred to as showing "exaggeratedly 'female' characteristics" (Ounsted and Taylor, 1972, p. 252), because of their shortness, low performance IQ, difficulties with space-form (including embedded figures and map reading), difficulties with numbers, and interest in personal adornment and in having children. All these traits are more characteristic of the female's stereotypic gender role than of the male's. These differences are not likely to be secondary effects of physical differences, since these women look less feminine than normal in childhood, so it is hard to see how either their parents or peers could have expected them to act more feminine. Therefore, the presence of an extra X (as in 47, XXX) does not feminize females, but the absence of the second X may lead to some feminization.

47, XXY and 48, XXXY, or Klinefelter's Syndrome

People born with **Klinefelter's syndrome** are sometimes called genetic hermaphrodites since they have both the male (the XY) and the female (the XX) chromosome pattern. However, a true **hermaphrodite** is a person with both male and female gonads; other individuals with ambiguities of sex chromosomes or sex organs (like people with Klinefelter's) are usually referred to as **pseudohermaphrodites.**

Although Klinefelter's individuals are male in external appearance, they, like normal females, often have one or more Barr bodies, depending on how many extra Xs they have. Thus, Klinefelter's males will be genetic mosaics, like male calico cats. Whether or not a 47, XXY individual does or does not have the extra X inactivated does not seem to be related to their other abnormalities (Weaver et al., 1975). This disorder occurs in .1 to .2 percent of all male births, and is caused by some fault in the genetic control of cell division in their mother's egg cells (Court-Brown et al., 1964; Hamerton et al., 1975). Therefore, these boys tend to be born to older mothers (Cassiman et al., 1975; Simpson et al., 1974).

Physical Abnormalities. The males with a 47, XXY karyotype are tall and have disproportionately long arms and legs. Though male, many people with Klinefelter's are also somewhat female in appearance. They often show some breast enlargement and may have small penises (see Figure 2.3). The testes are also small and these individuals are often infertile (Court-Brown et al., 1964; Money and Ehrhardt, 1972). These men also show low levels of **testosterone,** the major androgen, or male sex hormone (Money and Ehrhardt, 1972; Smals, Kloppenborg, and Benroad, 1974). These low levels of testosterone probably account for the deficiency of body hair that frequently occurs in these men, and for the femalelike pattern of pubic hair (the female pattern is an inverted triangle; in males, hair grows up toward the belly button). This syndrome also seems to be frequently associated with cancer and with diseases of the immune system (S. H. Tsung and Heckman, 1974). These latter diseases are much more common in normal women than in normal men.

Electroencephalographs (recordings of the electrical activity of the brain, usually abbreviated **EEG**) of Klinefelter's men may show aberrations, indicative of some disorder of brain cell functioning. Nielsen and Tsuboi (1974) surveyed fifty-nine Klinefelter's males and found some EEG abnormalities in 37 percent of them, as compared with 12 to 15 percent in the general population. The frequency of these EEG aberratons was the same for Klinefelter's men found outside mental and prison institutions as for those found inside such institutions. Thus, the aberrations may be related to chromosomes rather than to institutionalization.

Emotional and Social Behavior. These men are more likely than the average genetically normal male to have social problems, many of which are related to gender identity. Money and Ehrhardt (1972) reported frequent occurrence of gender identity problems; that is, these men had some doubts as to what sex they actually were or as to how they ought to behave. Thielgaard (1972) also reported, on the basis of projective tests, that these men may have problems accepting the masculine role. These men may also show such sexual identity problems as transvestism, transsexualism, homosexuality, bisexuality, and lack of sex-

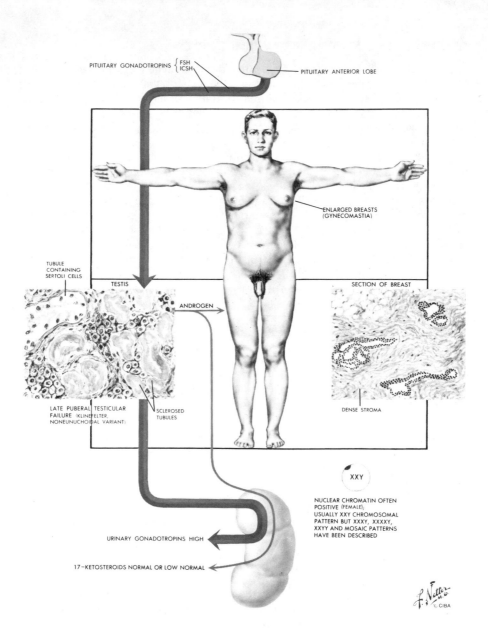

PITUITARY GONADOTROPINS { FSH / ICSH

PITUITARY ANTERIOR LOBE

ENLARGED BREASTS (GYNECOMASTIA)

TUBULE CONTAINING SERTOLI CELLS

TESTIS

ANDROGEN

SECTION OF BREAST

LATE PUBERAL TESTICULAR FAILURE (KLINEFELTER, NONEUNUCHOIDAL VARIANT)

SCLEROSED TUBULES

DENSE STROMA

XXY

NUCLEAR CHROMATIN OFTEN POSITIVE (FEMALE); USUALLY XXY CHROMOSOMAL PATTERN BUT XXXY, XXXXY, XXYY AND MOSAIC PATTERNS HAVE BEEN DESCRIBED

URINARY GONADOTROPINS HIGH

17–KETOSTEROIDS NORMAL OR LOW NORMAL

uality (Money and Ehrhardt, 1972). These problems might be caused by low hormone levels before birth or by the men's and others' reactions to their feminized appearance.

These men also may be more likely to be imprisoned than XY men. One survey of research studies reported that they showed up in maximum security hospitals or institutions for defective delinquents at a rate disproportionate to their numbers. One out of every 150 male inmates of these institutions had the XXY karyotype, which may be over six times the frequency of that karyotype at birth (Hook, 1973). The same high rate of appearance of XXY men has been found among males in psychiatric institutions (Nielsen, 1969) and in maximum security hospitals (Price et al., 1976).

Intellectual Ability. The XXY karyotype has also come to be associated with mental retardation (Witkin et al., 1976). Among mentally retarded males in institutions, the rate of the appearance of the XXY karyotype is about ten times the newborn rate (Nielsen, 1969). In Belgium, .58 percent of those in institutions for the retarded show this or 48, XXXY and 49, XXXXY sex chromosome abnormality, compared to .28 percent incidence at birth (Cassiman et al., 1975). The low IQ associated with the syndrome may be the reason that these men appear more often in prisons; it makes them more likely to get caught than the XY criminal with a normal IQ (Witkin et al., 1976).

However, in contrast to that in people with Turner's syndrome, the intellectual deficit in Klinefelter's men, when present, is general and covers a wide range of skills and abilities (Money, 1964). They do tend to have a performance IQ slightly greater than the verbal IQ: in a study of thirty-four men performance IQ led, 103.4 to 101.9 (Thielgaard, 1972). But genetically normal males of that IQ level often have performance IQs even higher than their verbal IQs. It should be emphasized that some XXY men show very high levels of IQ. But all the 48, XXXY and 49, XXXXY men found so far (fifty-seven cases) have been retarded and sterile (Kushnick and Colondrillo, 1975; Simpson et al., 1974).

Summary. Klinefelter's men are usually considered at risk for a variety of social, emotional, and intellectual problems. These men also seem somewhat feminized in some—but not all—aspects of behavior. They have a feminized appearance, with some breast development and a small penis. They also may have gender identity and gender role difficulties and perhaps a somewhat feminized IQ pattern, with verbal IQ being close or equal to performance IQ. They, like normal females, are more prone to diseases of the immune system. Finally, their fingerprint patterns are more similar to normal females than to normal males (Nanko, 1975). However, they are not feminized in all aspects. They tend to be taller, on the average, than 46, XY males. Also, the proportion of Klinefelter's males in prison is high, making them more masculine in that respect (more males than females are in prison).

FIGURE 2.3 ———————————————————————————————————————

A KLINEFELTER'S MALE

Note the long arms and legs, the breast enlargement, the small penis and testes of the Klinefelter's male. FSH and LH are hormones secreted by the pituitary which control the gonads.

But, as was pointed out earlier, it is not clear how many of the problems of these men are caused by their genes and the associated decrease in male sex hormones and IQ. Some (or all) of their problems might be caused by the abnormalities of the electrical activity of their brains or to some as yet undiscovered effect of the extra X. Some of their problems might also be caused by their physical appearance and how both they and others reacted to it.

47, XYY and 48, XYYY

Hamerton and his colleagues (Hamerton et al., 1975), in their review of six chromosome surveys of newborn infants, have estimated the frequency of occurrence of 47, XYY to be about .09 percent of all male births (27 out of 29,930 male infants surveyed). These men have been described as displaying "exaggeratedly 'male' characteristics" (Ounsted and Taylor, 1972, p. 252), both physically and emotionally. The XYY male has also been said to possess a criminal genotype. Is this true?

Physical Abnormalities.   These men tend to be even taller than Klinefelter's men, but otherwise they look normal. The only physical abnormalities found in these men are height, changes of fingerprint patterns, alterations in testes, some neurological changes, and some heart problems (Owen, 1972). Because of the changes in the testes, these men have reduced fertility, but some have fathered normal daughters and a few normal sons (Nielsen and Christensen, 1974; Polani, 1972). The testosterone levels in their blood and urine are usually within the normal range (Polani, 1972).

Nielsen and Tsuboi (1974) also reported that XYY males show an increased incidence of EEG abnormalities, as do XXY males. In their samples, 44 percent of the XYY males had some abnormality, which is quite similar to the 37 percent reported for the XXY males. As for the XXY male, this was the same whether or not the male had been institutionalized.

Emotional and Social Behaviors.   The XYY male, whether inside or outside institutions, has been characterized as impulsive and as having a low tolerance for frustration or anxiety (Nielsen and Christensen, 1974). They may lack persistence, and this may be the reason they leave school earlier than their genetically normal siblings. They also may have more difficulties in school and in keeping jobs. And they are not empathetic and may have difficulty in relating to other people.

One study concerned with the psychological characteristics of XYY males was particularly impressive (Noël et al., 1974). Seven XYY males found in a general screening of young male military draftees were each matched to two control subjects for age, socioeconomic status, and education; there was also very little difference in either mean height or IQ. In spite of the fact that neither the examiners nor the subjects were aware of the chromosomal diagnosis (it was a double-blind study), all subjects were correctly classified as either XYY or XY on the basis of interviews and psychological tests (Rorschach Test, Thematic Apperception Test, and two visual perception tests). The XYY males were said to be more excitable, impatient, and irritable. They showed either very poor impulse control, with ready outbursts of emotion, or else they were hypercontrolled and rigid. Both of the XYY groups seemed unable to cope with anxiety. They also seemed emotionally dependent, and many were quite boastful. They described themselves as "irritable, nervous, easily angered and distracted." Socially, they often felt ill at ease, and were rarely leaders or dominant in social situations. These men sometimes seemed aware of their aggressiveness and so tried to control it, becoming in fact hypercontrolled and rigid; nevertheless, they all seemed to enjoy violence on television and in movies, and their preferred leisure activities were hunting and judo. Thus, these men were often impulsively aggressive, especially when frustrated. These findings are impressive in view of the fact that only one of the men had any criminal record at all (he was on probation for a minor theft) and so these differences existed among XY and XYY men all living apparently normal lives in the general community.

The XYY Male as a Criminal.   The XYY genetic syndrome has caused the most public controversy of any genetic abnormality. In 1965, P. Jacobs and her colleagues published a survey called "Aggressive Behavior, Mental Subnormality and the XYY Male," which concluded that more XYY males were among dangerous criminals than could be accounted for by chance alone. Since then, the popular press has at times concluded that the extra Y chromosome in some way causes criminal behavior or homicidal mania. Richard Speck, convicted of murdering eight nurses, was falsely reported to be an XYY male. Here, due to the complexity of the issue and our lack of space, we will simply review some of the evidence to illustrate the controversy.

Some genetic surveys have found no evidence that the XYY is a criminal genotype. In 1971, Jacobs and her colleagues published a second survey. The entire institutionalized population of Scotland was examined, and the incidence of sex chromosome abnormalities was compared to the incidence found by the same researchers among newborn boys. The summary of the article stated that "there was no significant difference found between the incidence of males with an abnormality of the sex chromosomes in particular with an XYY complement in these establishments and the incidence of such males among the newborn." Two other reviews also concluded that there was no relationship between the XYY karyotype and criminality (Kessler and Moos, 1970; Owen, 1972).

Other surveys have come to opposite conclusions (see Price et al., 1976). For example, Nielsen and Christensen (1974) surveyed 1,247 males at a psychiatric hospital, 1,500 males in institutions for criminals, and 6,455 randomly selected males from the general population (3,840 randomly selected male draftees and 2,615 consecutive newborn boys—consecutive newborns were chosen to ensure no sample bias). The incidence rate of XYY males per thousand in each group was, in order, 3.21, 8.67, and 1.24. The authors concluded that "our finding of a significantly increased frequency of XYY males in certain prisons and institutions for criminals in Denmark, as well as the comparatively high frequency of criminality among males found outside institutions, indicates that the risk of criminality is higher than expected in XYY males" (p. 33). Finally, Hook (1973) surveyed and pooled thirty-five different studies of XYY males in mental and penal institutions and concluded that the average prevalence rate there was about 20 times the average newborn rate. Hook stated that "there is no question that the prevalence rate of XYYs is markedly increased over baseline" (p. 143).

However, even if the XYY male turns out to be a criminal more often than the XY male (and that is still not certain), he is not a homicidal or sexual maniac. In one study, Price and Whatmore (1967) compared nine XYY males to eighteen randomly selected normal males from the same penal institution. The XYY males had fewer instances of violence in their criminal histories than did the control males, although they had started their careers in crime earlier—at a mean age of 13.1 years. Both groups had severe personality disorders that were resistant to treatment. Other studies have also found that XYY males did not have more instances of violent crimes than their fellow inmates, but did have more instances of theft and, perhaps, minor sex offenses (Court-Brown, Price, and Jacobs, 1968; Griffiths et al., 1970; P. Jacobs et al., 1968; Witkin et al., 1976). Nielsen and Christensen (1974) also extensively studied thirty-five males with a 47, XYY karyotype. The fifteen found in institutions committed only the crime of arson more often than the XY criminal. So the XYY may more often be a criminal, but he is not more violent than his fellow inmate.

Intellectual Ability.   The XYY male is expected to be brighter than the XXY male, but is still apt to be slightly subnormal in intelligence (Court-Brown et al., 1968; Witkin et al., 1976). In terms of the pattern of intellectual abilities, these men showed a male pattern of IQ, with the verbal IQ lower than the performance IQ, with means of 94.4 and 97.1, respectively (Nielsen and Christensen, 1974). Also, although the lower IQ of XXY males can account for their more frequent appearances in prison, the lower IQ of XYY males can apparently account only for some and not for all of their more frequent prison appearances (Witkin et al., 1976).

Summary and Interpretations.   The XYY male is said to be a tall, impulsive loner who has difficulties staying either with school or with a job. Men with the XYY karyotype have been reported to be found in prisons more often than would be accounted for by chance alone. In some respects, the XYY man represents an exaggeration of the male stereotype. They are tall, impulsively aggressive, have a male pattern of IQ (performance higher than verbal scores), and may be less sensitive to and interested in other people. Did the extra Y masculinize them?

A point made by Nielsen and Christensen (1974) is very well taken: "it is evident that environmental factors play as great a role in the development of personality and behavior in XYY males as they do in males with karyotype 46, XY. The total phenotype—and particularly the personality and behavior phenotype—is the result of the total integration properties of the genome interacting with the environment" (p. 36). Thus, an XYY genotype does not ensure a criminal phenotype, although the impulsivity of the XYY male may lead him to get in more trouble than does the XY male.

Some General Effects of Extra Sex Chromosomes

If you look at all of the chromosome abnormalities as a group, some general conclusions about their effects are implied. The major conclusion is, of course, that the presence of a single Y chromosome, no matter how many Xs are also present, means that the individual is born with a male appearance. We can also conclude that more males than females are born with sex chromosome abnormalities. About one of every 400 male infants has a sex chromosome abnormality, while only one of every 700 females do (Hamerton et al., 1975; P. Jacobs, 1977).

TABLE 2.1

HEIGHT AS A FUNCTION OF ABNORMALITIES IN THE SEX CHROMOSOMES

Type	Number	Mean Height in Centimeters
45, X	128	141.80
46, XX	1	162.20
47, XXX	30	163.07
46, XY	1	174.70
47, XXY	118	175.69
48, XXYY	22	180.52
47, XYY	19	182.95

Source: From P. E. Polani, "Chromosome Phenotypes—Sex Chromosomes." In F. C. Fraser and V. A. McKusick (eds.), *Congenital Malformations*. Amsterdam: Excerpta Medica, 1970, p. 233–250.
[1] Based on normative data.

The total number of sex chromosomes may also be related to height, IQ, and fingerprint patterns. A survey done by Moor (cited by Gray and Drewett, in press) showed that the more extra Xs there were, the lower the IQ. An extra Y chromosome led to a further decline in IQ, although extra Xs seemed to have a more deleterious effect. Surveys have also found that the number of ridges in fingerprints are negatively correlated with the number of sex chromosomes (Penrose, 1968; Polani, 1969, Raqavi, 1969). Polani (1970) also claimed that height is related to the number of sex chromosomes; 45, X girls are abnormally short, and both XXY and XYY men tended to be tall. (Polani's data is presented in Table 2.1.)

Barlow (1973) attributed all these phenomena (except increased height) to the retarding effect extra chromosomes might have on fetal development. He cited the low birth weights of children with these abnormalities as evidence, along with a lower rate of cell divisions in cultures of cells taken from these individuals. So poor fetal development might cause the lower IQ seen in people with extra sex chromosomes.

Implications of Chromosome Abnormalities

One major implication for society of the research findings on chromosome abnormalities involves facing the decision about what to do with fetuses that have sex chromosome abnormalities. With the technique of **amniocentesis** (analyzing the amniotic fluid of the pregnant woman, which includes a karyotypic analysis of the fetal cells present in that fluid during the third month of pregnancy) the fetus can be karyotyped before birth. Do the fetuses with abnormalities of the sex chromosomes suffer enough behavioral and physical defects to warrant abortion? How much is enough? Or is abortion never warranted? How about those with four or five sex chromosomes, who are almost always profoundly retarded, with IQs ranging from 36 to 63 (Barlow, 1973)? What would you do if you were told that your three-month-old fetus had abnormal sex chromosomes?

Chromosome abnormalities can teach us about the development and behavior of people with normal chromosomes. The fact that there are often differences between genetically normal and abnormal people suggests that the chromosomes may have an impact on normal people. Among their other functions, sex chromosomes may affect the rate of fetal development. The differences between genetically normal and abnormal people in physical appearance, intellectual abilities, and sex-role stereotypic behavior suggest (but do not prove) that sex chromosomes may have some indirect effect on similar differences between normal males and females in appearance, ability, and behavior—as, for example, in aggression and maternal behavior. But women are not feminized by extra Xs, although the absence of the second X may lead to an exaggeration of the female stereotypic sex role—due to the lack of any kind of inductive hormones? Males may be feminized in some respects by extra Xs, although here too the effects might be more directly due to the decrease in inductive and activational male hormones. And extra Ys have been associated with an exaggeration of some aspects of the male sex role. Though biases do exist in the literature, it does seem significant that the aspects of behavior so often reported to be changed by chromosome abnormalities are sex-role stereotypic.

SEX-LINKAGE AND SEX-LIMITATION

Definitions

Sex chromosomes affect the inherited characteristics of individuals through **sex-linkage** and **sex-limitation**. Sex-linkage refers to a trait whose gene is located on one of the sex chromosomes, usually the X. Sex-limitation refers to a trait coded for by a gene on an autosome but expressed only or mostly in one sex or the other. A trait can be both X-linked and sex-limited. That is the case for androgen insensitivity, a syndrome in which a 46, XY individual is born with testes but with a female external appearance; females with this gene would be very little affected by it.

The likelihood of either a sex-linked or sex-limited trait being expressed in any given individual depends on whether that trait is dominant or recessive. A **dominant** trait will be expressed—will appear in the person's phenotype—regardless of what the analogous gene is on the other chromosome of the pair. A **recessive** trait will be expressed if and only if the opposite gene on the paired chromosome also carries the recessive trait. Cystic fibrosis is an example of an autosomal recessive disease. In this disease, people suffer from chronic lung obstruction and poor growth and usually die before the age of twenty. For a person to exhibit this disease, he/she must inherit the gene for it from both parents; since it is recessive, if a person got only one cystic fibrosis gene from one parent, and the dominant, nondisease gene from the other, the person would not show the disease, but would be a carrier. Thus, if a child has cystic fibrosis, both parents must have been carriers.

Sex-linked Traits

Y-Linked Traits.   The only trait that may be Y-linked is hairy ears, found among men in India. It is also interesting to note that the karyotype of 45, Y is always lethal; no one has ever been born with that chromosome pattern. Both facts may reflect the small size of the Y which therefore carries fewer genes than does the X. So the genes on the Y mainly code for "maleness" and very little else.

X-Linked Traits. If the trait coded for by a gene on an X chromosome is dominant, then the trait will be expressed in both men and women regardless of the paired gene on the other chromosome, the second X or Y. One such X-linked, dominant trait is a type of rickets that occurs in twice as many women as men (women have two Xs and so have twice as many chances of getting that particular gene as a man). However, males with that disease are more severely affected (C. O. Carter, 1972). This is probably because that particular X with the dominant rickets gene (assuming that the paired gene is not also coding for rickets) will be inactivated, forming a Barr body, in approximately half of a woman's body cells, whereas the gene will not be inactivated in any male cells.

If a trait is coded by by an X-linked recessive gene, it will always be expressed in the male who inherits an X with that gene because he has only the one X. The same trait will be expressed in a female only if she inherits a paired gene on the other X that is also coding for the same recessive trait. So she needs two Xs with that gene in order to have that trait. If the recessive gene appears in the population with a frequency of p, then that will also be the probability of it appearing in a man. Females, however, will have that trait expressed only with the frequency of p^2, since the daughter must receive the recessive trait from both parents before the trait will appear in her. This should also mean that the correlation between parents and offspring should follow a specific pattern for any X-linked, recessive trait; for example, the father-son correlation should be zero, since fathers cannot give their sons an X. However, in considering trait probabilities and parent-offspring correlations, you should also keep in mind the mosaic nature of normal females. The recessive trait will often be detectable in them although it may not be fully expressed.

Examples of X-linked, recessive traits include one form of muscular dystrophy, some types of metabolic disorders, one type of diabetes, and hemophilia. There are also three or four types of partially recessive mental retardation that may be X-linked (Yarbrough and Howard-Peebles, 1976). Some types of manic-depressive illnesses may also be X-linked (Loranger, 1975).

Two types of red-green color blindness are also X-linked and recessive. Since the gene for color blindness is recessive, the trait will be expressed only if the other X chromosome in genetically normal women also contains that same recessive X. Since men and Turner's women both have only one X, if that gene is present on their one X, they will be color-blind. Therefore, 8 percent of both genetically normal men and Turner's women are color-blind, but only .5 percent of normal women are. However, a very few women, despite having both the dominant and recessive genes, are almost completely color-blind; by chance, most of their retinal cells must have come from a fetal cell in which the dominant, non-color-blind gene was inactivated. Also, women may have very small patches of color-blind cells in their retina of which they are completely unaware. These patches correspond to areas in which the non-color-blind gene was inactivated, like the callico coat color in cats (Born, Grützner, and Hemminger, 1976).

Are Spatial and Mathematical Abilities X-Linked? Stafford (1961, 1963,

1972) has suggested that one of the genes responsible for good mathematical ability and one of the genes coding for good space-form ability are both X-linked and recessive. According to Stafford, this would then explain why men are better able to visualize objects in three-dimensional space and are good in math. Stafford and other investigators have found patterns of correlations of spatial ability that suggest some influences from an X-linked, recessive gene (Bock and Kolakowski, 1973; Corah, 1965; R. Guttman, 1974; Hartlage, 1970; W. Yen, 1975). In all of these studies, the father-son correlation in spatial abilities was essentially zero, and males consistently scored higher on tests of spatial ability than females did.

There are several difficulties with Stafford's hypothesis that spatial and mathematical abilities are affected by X-linked, recessive genes. One is that biologically advantageous traits like spatial and mathematical ability are seldom recessive. Another problem is that Turner's girls do even more poorly at spatial and mathematical tasks than does the average 46, XX female. Since Turner's girls, like normal males, have only one X, then according to Stafford's hypothesis, they ought to show an incidence of superior spatial ability equal to the incidence in men (Garron, 1970).

Another major problem with Stafford's hypothesis is that recent data do not fit its predictions, and might be better explained by another model. DeFries's recent data (DeFries, Vandenberg, and McClearn, 1976) on the spatial abilities of 5,077 people in 1,490 families did not fit an X-linked model at all. DeFries suggested that a **multifactorial, sex-modified threshold model** might better explain sex differences in this area. This model suggests that a variety of environmental, genetic, and hormonal factors could all additively combine to affect the likelihood of being able to express good spatial ability. Males would have a lower threshold, that is, they would have good spatial ability with fewer factors present than females. The sex-modified threshold model can thus include the influence of such factors as sex-role socialization, the influence of activational and inductive hormones, and the influence of genes (sex-linked, sex-limited, or simply autosomal). Only those individuals in whom these factors combine so that the likelihood crosses the threshold will have good spatial ability. This model assumes either that several genes are involved in spatial ability and/or that the genetic effect on spatial ability is relatively small compared to the effect of environment.

Thus, there are several problems with Stafford's hypothesis of an X-linked, recessive pattern of inheritance of spatial and mathematical abilities. The predictive abilities of the two models need to be compared, but in the meantime it appears that the sex-modified threshold model is the best working hypothesis. We will use it to explain sex differences in spatial ability; it has also been used to explain sex differences in alcoholism, retardation, and sociopathy (Cloninger, Reich, and Guze, 1975a, 1975b; Freire-Maia, Freire-Maia, and Morton, 1974; Reich, Winokur, and Mulhaney, 1975).

Sex-limited Traits

Sex-limited traits are coded for by genes on the autosomes, but these genes are either activated or inhibited by protein products of the sex chromosomes or by the hormones secreted by the gonads (Edelman, 1975). One sex-limited trait is male-pattern baldness, or the baldness of temples and crown that develops with age in men. This trait is an autosomal dominant one that is only expressed in the presence of sufficient testosterone (C. O. Carter, 1972). Thus, castration is the only effective treatment known for male-pattern baldness, although it is not a very practical one. In fact, any trait or behavior affected by either inductive or by activational hormones could also be said to be sex-limited, as chapters 4 and 5 of this text will demonstrate.

Summary

The sex chromosomes affect sex differences through sex-linked traits. A trait carried by a Y chromosome would of course be seen only in males. Any trait affected by an X-linked, dominant gene will be seen twice as often in females as in males. And any trait influenced by an X-linked, recessive gene will be exhibited by more males than females. Thus, the direction and degree of sex differences in the frequencies of many traits may be affected by whether or not the trait is Y-linked or X-linked, and if X-linked, whether it is dominant or recessive.

The multifactorial, sex-modified threshold model of heritability can also explain sex differences. If one sex has a lower threshold for a trait than the other, more people of that gender will show the trait. So genes, inductive hormones, activational hormones, and experience may all combine to affect a trait. But the trait may be seen in one gender more often than in the other, because that gender may need fewer predisposing factors to exhibit it.

The major indirect effect of sex chromosomes on sex differences is upon gonads during fetal development. Because of the sex chromosomes, either testes or ovaries will develop in the fetus, who will have either a male or a female pattern of hormones for the rest of his or her life. If some trait is affected by either inductive or activational sex hormones, then the trait would be sex-limited and would show sex differences in its frequency of appearance.

SEX DIFFERENCES IN FETAL DEVELOPMENT

The gender of the fetus is determined by the father's sperm. In turn, the sex chromosomes of the fetus determine whether testes or ovaries will develop. From that point on, the concentrations of the gonadal hormones will determine the way the internal sex organs, external sex organs, and brain will develop. Up to a point, the more male hormones a fetus has, the more masculine will be his or her internal and external organs and—perhaps—his or her brain.

The Effect of the Sex Chromosomes

Under normal conditions, the gender of the fetus is determined the moment the sperm of the father penetrates the ovum of the mother. The ovum always contains an X (the mother does not have a Y to give away), but the sperm will have either an X or a Y, thus determining the gender of the fetus.

Sex differences in the development of the fetus begin well after it has been

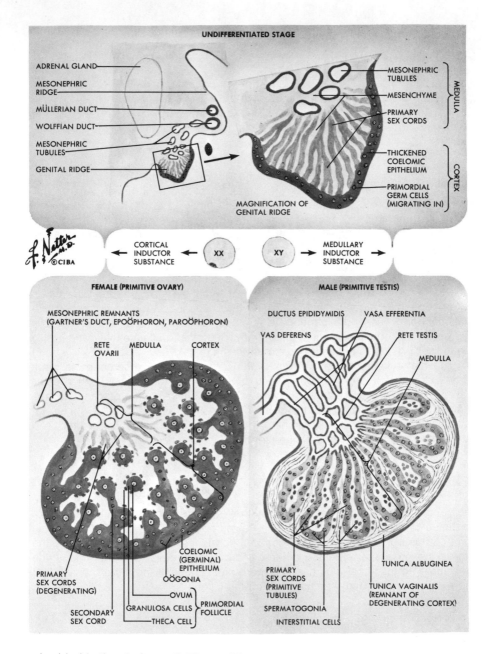

UNDIFFERENTIATED STAGE

ADRENAL GLAND

MESONEPHRIC RIDGE

MÜLLERIAN DUCT

WOLFFIAN DUCT

MESONEPHRIC TUBULES

GENITAL RIDGE

MAGNIFICATION OF GENITAL RIDGE

MESONEPHRIC TUBULES

MESENCHYME

PRIMARY SEX CORDS

MEDULLA

THICKENED COELOMIC EPITHELIUM

PRIMORDIAL GERM CELLS (MIGRATING IN)

CORTEX

CORTICAL INDUCTOR SUBSTANCE ← XX   XY → MEDULLARY INDUCTOR SUBSTANCE

FEMALE (PRIMITIVE OVARY)

MESONEPHRIC REMNANTS (GARTNER'S DUCT, EPOÖPHORON, PAROÖPHORON)

RETE OVARII   MEDULLA   CORTEX

PRIMARY SEX CORDS (DEGENERATING)

SECONDARY SEX CORD

COELOMIC (GERMINAL) EPITHELIUM

OÖGONIA

OVUM

GRANULOSA CELLS   PRIMORDIAL FOLLICLE

THECA CELL

MALE (PRIMITIVE TESTIS)

DUCTUS EPIDIDYMIDIS   VASA EFFERENTIA

VAS DEFERENS   RETE TESTIS

MEDULLA

PRIMARY SEX CORDS (PRIMITIVE TUBULES)

SPERMATOGONIA

INTERSTITIAL CELLS

TUNICA ALBUGINEA

TUNICA VAGINALIS (REMNANT OF DEGENERATING CORTEX)

embedded in the uterine wall. These differences are summarized in Table 2.2. Sex differences in the fetus begin to appear between the sixth and the tenth week. As long as there is at least one Y chromosome present—no matter how many Xs are also present—the fetal gonad begins differentiating in the male direction, as

TABLE 2.2 _____

SEX DIFFERENCES IN HUMAN FETAL DEVELOPMENT

Age	Male	Female
6–10 Weeks	The Y chromosome causes the medullary portion of the primitive gonads to change into testes.	Without any Y chromosome, the cortex of the primitive gonads change into ovaries.
3 Months	Androgens from the testes cause Wolffian structures to develop into male internal sex organs; MIS from testes causes Müllerian structures to degenerate.	Without androgens, Wolffian structures degenerate; without MIS, Müllerian structures develop into female internal sex accessory organs.
5 Months	Androgens from testes cause penis and scrotal sacs to develop.	Without androgens, vagina, clitoris, and labia develop.
3–8 Months	Presence of androgens leads to a male brain?	Lack of androgens leads to a female brain?

shown in Figure 2.4. This happens at around the sixth week. In the absence of any Y chromosome, the gonad begins to develop into an ovary around the tenth week.

The undifferentiated gonad consists of an inner part, the **medulla,** and an external rind, the **cortex.** Under the influence of the Y chromosome, the medulla develops into testes, one on each side, and the cortex on each side degenerates. If there is no Y chromosome, then the opposite happens: the medulla degenerates and the cortical portions of the fetal gonads develop into a pair of ovaries, already supplied with the lifetime supply of ova.

Thus, the Y chromosome in the human is the chromosome that determines gender. You will remember that Turner's women, with only one X, were still quite female in appearance and had normal ovarian development until the third month, whereas Klinefelter's men, even though they had a double X in addition to their Y, were male in external appearance and had testes.

The Effect of Sex Hormones

With the formation of the fetal gonads, the direct function of the chromosome is over; from this point on, sex differences in development are a function of the different sex hormones produced by the fetal gonads.

FIGURE 2.4 _____

FETAL GONADAL DEVELOPMENT

In the presence of a Y chromosome, the medullary portion of the fetal gonad develops into a testes; in the absence of a Y, the cortical portion develops into ovaries.

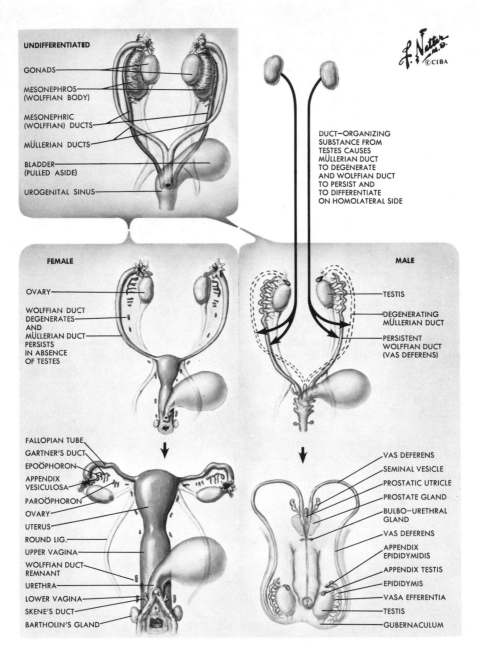

UNDIFFERENTIATED

GONADS

MESONEPHROS
(WOLFFIAN BODY)

MESONEPHRIC
(WOLFFIAN) DUCTS

MÜLLERIAN DUCTS

BLADDER
(PULLED ASIDE)

UROGENITAL SINUS

DUCT—ORGANIZING
SUBSTANCE FROM
TESTES CAUSES
MÜLLERIAN DUCT
TO DEGENERATE
AND WOLFFIAN DUCT
TO PERSIST AND
TO DIFFERENTIATE
ON HOMOLATERAL SIDE

FEMALE

OVARY

WOLFFIAN DUCT
DEGENERATES
AND
MÜLLERIAN DUCT
PERSISTS
IN ABSENCE
OF TESTES

MALE

TESTIS

DEGENERATING
MÜLLERIAN DUCT

PERSISTENT
WOLFFIAN DUCT
(VAS DEFERENS)

FALLOPIAN TUBE

GARTNER'S DUCT

EPOÖPHORON

APPENDIX
VESICULOSA

PAROÖPHORON

OVARY

UTERUS

ROUND LIG.

UPPER VAGINA

WOLFFIAN DUCT
REMNANT

URETHRA

LOWER VAGINA

SKENE'S DUCT

BARTHOLIN'S GLAND

VAS DEFERENS

SEMINAL VESICLE

PROSTATIC UTRICLE

PROSTATE GLAND

BULBO—URETHRAL
GLAND

VAS DEFERENS

APPENDIX
EPIDIDYMIDIS

APPENDIX TESTIS

EPIDIDYMIS

VASA EFFERENTIA

TESTIS

GUBERNACULUM

After the gonads are formed, both male and female internal sex organs, shown in Figure 2.5, begin developing. If the fetal gonads had differentiated into testes, they would begin secreting **androgens** (the class of male sex hormones, including testosterone) during the third month of development. One androgen causes the **Wolffian structures** to grow and differentiate into the male internal sex organs — the vas deferens, seminal vesicles, and ejaculatory duct (see Figure 2.5). At the same time, the fetal testes would also secrete another substance, often called the **Müllerian inhibiting substance (MIS),** which causes the **Müllerian structures** adjacent to that testis to atrophy and degenerate. In the absence of any sex hormones at all, the Wolffian structures will degenerate and the Müllerian structures will develop into the female internal sex organs — the uterus, the Fallopian tubes, and the upper portion of the vagina. Thus, hormones from the testes determine the sex of the fetus from the third month onward (Jost, 1961).

At around the fifth month, the external sex organs begin to develop, as shown in Figure 2.6. Again, if there is an androgen present, as in normal males, the external sex organs develop in the male direction. In the absence of androgens, or in the absence of any hormone at all as with Turner's girls, the external female sex organs develop.

In humans, somewhere between the third and eighth month, androgens may also affect the brain. In support of this hypothesis, the concentration of testosterone has been found to be higher in males than in females during critical periods of brain development in rhesus monkeys and rats (Resko, 1970; Resko, Feder, and Goy, 1968) and in the amniotic fluid of human infants (Dorner et al., 1973). The details of this effect will be covered in chapter 4.

Summary

The presence or absence of the Y chromosome — strictly speaking, the presence or absence of the proteins coded for on the Y chromosome or induced by the Y from an autosome — determines whether the fetal gonad will differentiate into testes or ovaries. From that point on, the presence or absence of androgens determines the sex of the internal sex organs, the external sex organs, and the brain. In a sense, the primary sex is female; you have to add something (androgens) to get a male. The more androgens there are, at least up to a point, the more male the fetus is.

FIGURE 2.5 _____

THE FETAL DEVELOPMENT OF THE INTERNAL SEX ORGANS

In the presence of an androgen, the Wolffian structures develop into the male internal sex structures; the fetal testes also secrete an inhibiting substance that causes the Müllerian structures to degenerate. In the absence of any androgens or inhibiting substance, the Wolffian structures degenerate and the Müllerian structures develop into the female internal sex organs.

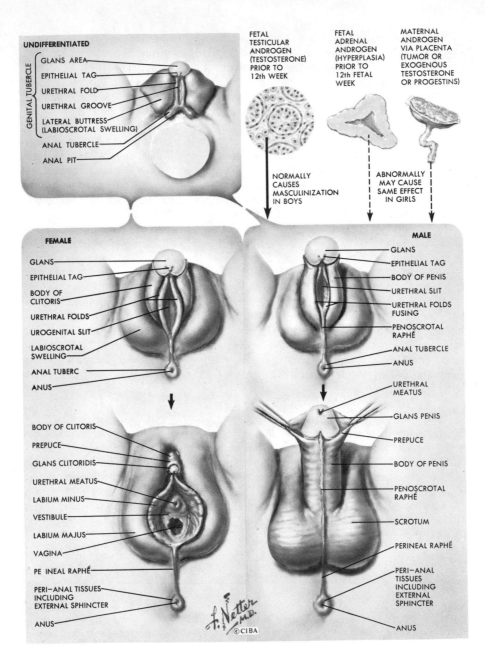

PUBERTY AND THE SEX HORMONES

At puberty, the presence or absence of a Y chromosome during fetal development, hence whether or not testes or ovaries had differentiated, again has a major impact on the organism. At this time, the concentrations of all three of the gonadal, or sex, hormones increases in both genders. The greater concentration of androgens from the testes leads to masculinization in the male. The greater concentrations of **estrogens** (one class of female hormones, the major one being estradiol) and **progestins** (the second class of female hormones, including progesterone) from the ovaries leads to feminization in the female.

Puberty is also significant because at this time the monthly hormone cycles begin in the human female. The male also has cycles, but they are smaller in magnitude. The cycles in the female are due to the effects that hormones secreted by the ovaries have upon the hypothalamus. During the first part of the female human **menstrual cycle,** the ripening egg **follicle** (the sac surrounding the egg cell or ovum) is secreting large quantities of estrogens; this part of the cycle is therefore called the **follicular phase.** During the later half of the cycle, the woman has ovulated (released the egg into one of the Fallopian tubes) and the empty egg follicle left behind secretes both estrogens and progestins. This part of the cycle is called the **luteal phase,** because the empty egg follicle is called a **corpus luteum.** Later, the hormones all decline, and the walls of the uterus slough off and are discharged in the form of menstrual blood. Understanding these hormone changes and the ways that they are controlled by the body will be very important to an appreciation of the implications of hormone changes described in later chapters.

Sources of the Sex Hormones

Glandular Secretion of Hormones. Both males and females have measurable quantities of all three of the major types of sex hormones. Thus, the sex difference in hormones is a matter of different concentrations and not a matter of which hormone is present in which gender.

In females, the ovaries secrete **estrogens** and **progestins** in amounts varying according to the phase of the menstrual cycle. The ovaries also secrete about 50 percent of the androgens present in the female. The outer portions of the **adrenal glands** are responsible for the other 50 percent of the androgens present in the female (Abraham, 1974). (The adrenal glands are better known for their secretion of epinephrine, or adrenalin, which is secreted in moments of stress from the inner, medullary, portion of the gland.)

FIGURE 2.6 _____

THE FETAL DEVELOPMENT OF THE EXTERNAL SEX ORGANS

In the presence of androgens, the organs develop or differentiate in the male direction; in the absence of androgens, these organs differentiate in the female direction.

Since the adrenals secrete approximately the same hormones in men as they do in women, the greater quantity of androgens, principally testosterone, in the blood of adult males (up to twenty times as much) is due to the testes. The testes also secrete some **estradiol** (the major estrogen) and **progesterone** (Lipsett, 1974) a major progestin. Before women reach menopause, men have about half as much estradiol as women have at the lowest monthly level (Hawkins and Oakey, 1974), and about the same amount of progesterone as women have at the lowest monthly level (Tea et al., 1975). After women reach menopause and their ovaries stop producing estradiol and progesterone, men of the same age actually have more of these hormones.

Interconversion of Hormones: Another Source.   Another source of sex hormones is the transformation of one into another in the adrenals, ovaries, and testes before secretion, and also in the blood stream after secretion. With the appropriate enzymes present, progestins can be transformed or converted into testosterone, and testosterone into estradiol. Thus, some estrogens in men come from their adrenals, but about half comes from their testes and the other half is created by conversion from testosterone (Calabresi et al., 1976). When pregnant women are given high doses of a progestin to maintain their pregnancy, their female fetuses can sometimes be masculinized because of conversion of progestins into testosterone.

Puberty

Before puberty, there are few or no sex differences in the quantity of sex hormones in the two genders; they are all at very low levels. At puberty, some part of the brain—perhaps the hypothalamus or the pineal gland—causes increased production of hormones by the pituitary, as shown in Figure 2.7. Under the influence of the pituitary hormones, both the gonads and the adrenals enlarge and increase their secretion of hormones.

Puberty occurs earlier in females than in males. The first sign of puberty in females occurs around age eleven, when the breasts begin increasing in size. Menstruation and ovulation usually start around age thirteen. The first sign of puberty in males is enlargement of the testes and scrotum, which occurs on the average at around age twelve. **Spermatogenesis,** the creation of sperm, usually starts between ages fourteen and fifteen.

The Roles of the Pituitary Gland and the Hypothalamus

The secretion of the sex hormones is controlled by the **pituitary gland.** In turn, the pituitary is controlled by the **hypothalamus,** as illustrated in Figure 2.8. The

FIGURE 2.7 ───

THE HORMONAL AND ASSOCIATED PHYSICAL CHANGES THAT OCCUR AT PUBERTY

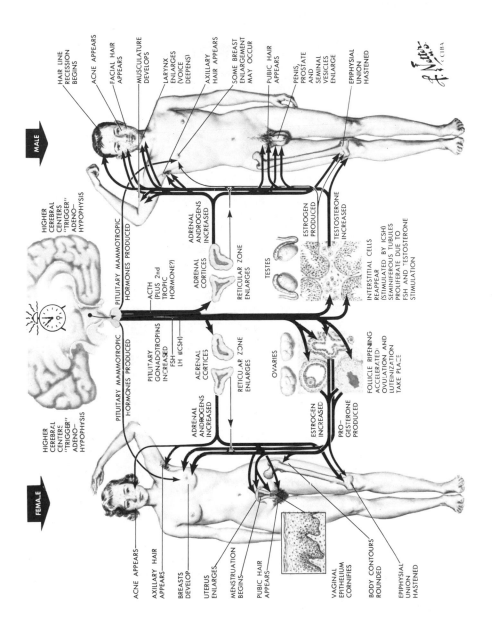

MALE

HAIR LINE RECESSION BEGINS
ACNE APPEARS
FACIAL HAIR APPEARS
MUSCULATURE DEVELOPS
LARYNX ENLARGES (VOICE DEEPENS)
AXILLARY HAIR APPEARS
SOME BREAST ENLARGEMENT MAY OCCUR
PUBIC HAIR APPEARS
PENIS, PROSTATE AND SEMINAL VESICLES ENLARGE
EPIPHYSIAL UNION HASTENED

HIGHER CEREBRAL CENTERS "TRIGGER" ADENO-HYPOPHYSIS

PITUITARY MAMMOTROPIC HORMONES PRODUCED

ACTH (PLUS 2nd TROPIC HORMONE?)

ADRENAL CORTICES

ADRENAL ANDROGENS INCREASED

RETICULAR ZONE ENLARGES

TESTES

ESTROGEN PRODUCED

TESTOSTERONE INCREASED

INTERSTITIAL CELLS REAPPEAR (STIMULATED BY ICSH) SEMINIFEROUS TUBULES PROLIFERATE DUE TO FSH AND TESTOSTERONE STIMULATION

PITUITARY MAMMOTROPIC HORMONES PRODUCED

PITUITARY GONADOTROPINS INCREASED FSH LH (ICSH)

ADRENAL CORTICES

RETICULAR ZONE ENLARGES

OVARIES

FOLLICLE RIPENING ACCELERATED: OVULATION AND LUTENIZATION TAKE PLACE

HIGHER CEREBRAL CENTERS "TRIGGER" ADENO-HYPOPHYSIS

ADRENAL ANDROGENS INCREASED

ESTROGEN INCREASED

PRO-GESTERONE PRODUCED

FEMALE

ACNE APPEARS
AXILLARY HAIR APPEARS
BREASTS DEVELOP
UTERUS ENLARGES
MENSTRUATION BEGINS
PUBIC HAIR APPEARS
VAGINAL EPITHELIUM CORNIFIES
BODY CONTOURS ROUNDED
EPIPHYSIAL UNION HASTENED

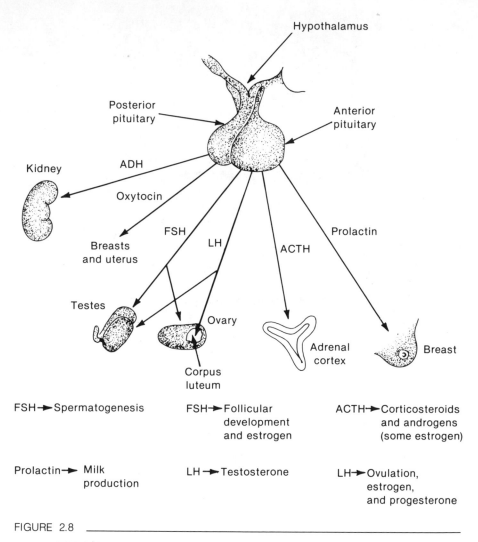

FIGURE 2.8 ──

EFFECTS ON SEX HORMONES AND SEX ORGANS OF THE HORMONES OF
THE ANTERIOR PITUITARY AND THE POSTERIOR PITUITARY

*The posterior pituitary hormones are manufactured in the hypothalamus but are
stored in the pituitary. The anterior pituitary hormones, manufactured in the anterior
pituitary, are released when the releasing factors from the hypothalamus, traveling
in the venous portal system, reach the pituitary. The other hormones of the posterior
pituitary are the growth hormones and thyrotropic hormone.*

human *pituitary gland* is divided into two sections: the anterior pituitary and the posterior pituitary. Each part secrets hormones that affect the gonads and other sexual organs, as well as most other organs in the body. The pituitary is sometimes called the "master gland" of the body.

Posterior Pituitary.   The **posterior pituitary** secretes only **oxytocin** and the **antidiuretic hormone,** or **ADH.** Both of these hormones are manufactured by the hypothalamus. After being produced there, they migrate along nerve cells into the posterior part of the pituitary, where they are stored. These hormones can be released from the pituitary into the blood stream by chemical or neural stimulation of the hypothalamus. Each hormone has the greatest influence on one organ, called the **target organ.** The target organ of ADH is the kidney; ADH decreases the output of urine. Since alcohol depresses ADH, that accounts for the fact that beer drinkers spend so much time waiting in line for the restroom. The target organs of oxytocin are the breasts and the uterus. Oxytocin may be part of the reflex arc that starts with nipple stimulation and ends with the release of milk by the breast; this occurs during nursing and even to some extent during intercourse, if the breasts are caressed. Oxytocin also increases the contractions of the uterus during childbirth, nursing, and orgasm (Newton, 1973). That may be one reason that some women report that nursing leads to such pleasant sensations.

Anterior Pituitary.   The major hormones of the anterior pituitary are manufactured by and stored in that organ. These hormones include: the **follicle-stimulating hormone (FSH);** the **luteinizing hormone (LH); prolactin;** the **andrenocorticotropic hormone (ACTH);** the **thyrotropic hormone;** and the **growth hormone.** The latter two have little or no known effect on the sex hormones, so we will not discuss them.

The hypothalamus controls all the hormones of the anterior pituitary by means of **releasing factors** or **inhibiting factors.** These factors are hormones that have more or less specific effects on one or another of the anterior pituitary hormones. So the LH releasing factor largely stimulates the release of LH, but it may also affect the output of FSH. These factors are manufactured by and in the hypothalamus, and are then carried by the so-called portal veins through the stalk of the pituitary to the anterior pituitary. These factors either increase or decrease the rate of secretion of the appropriate hormones from the anterior pituitary into the blood stream.

The target organ of ACTH is the outer portion of the adrenal gland, the adrenal cortex (hence the name of the hormone). ACTH increases the rate of secretion of all adrenal cortical hormones, including some sex hormones and the other corticosteriods, such as cortisol. These other steroids help to control the level of electrolytes, sugar, and antibodies in the blood, and they also have anti-inflammatory and antiallergic actions (useful in treating both arthritis and severe allegery reactions). Men tend to have higher levels of cortisol in their blood than women, and the difference increases with age (Zumoff et al., 1974); thus, women more often have arthritis (see Appendix B).

FSH has different but analogous effects in males and females; in both sexes, FSH leads to the production of mature germ cells, both sperm and eggs. In the female, FSH acts on the follicles that surround the egg cells, or ovum, in the ovary. FSH leads to the development of the egg in the follicle or egg sac. FSH, along with

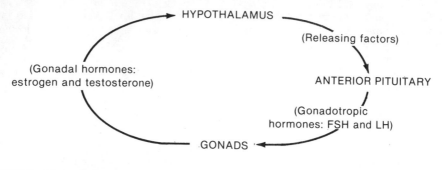

FIGURE 2.9 _____

INTERRELATIONSHIPS OF HYPOTHALAMIC, PITUITARY, AND GONADAL HORMONES

In the negative feedback loop, gonadal hormones inhibit the hypothalamus. Thus, the hypothalamus puts out less releasing factors, the pituitary puts out less gonadatropic hormones, the gonads release less sex hormones, and the hypothalamus is no longer inhibited. The positive feedback loop is initiated by very high levels of estrogen: those high levels stimulate the hypothalamus, and the resulting increase in releasing factors causes the pituitary to release very high levels of FSH and LH.

LH, also causes the ripening follicle to secrete estrogens; the larger the follicle gets under the influence of FSH, the more estrogens it secretes. In the male, FSH acts on the testes, leading to spermatogenesis.

LH also has analogous effects in males and females. In the male LH acts on the interstitial cells of the testes, leading to the release of testosterone, which is necessary for spermatogenesis. In the female, LH acts on the egg follicle, leading to the release of an egg from its follicle in one of the two ovaries. This is called ovulation. LH then acts on the ruptured follicle left behind by the egg on its way to one of the Fallopian tubes, turning it into a gland called the corpus luteum ("yellow body"). The corpus luteum, under the influence of LH and FSH, secretes both estrogens and progestins. In both males and females, then, LH increases the rate of secretion of all the hormones from the gonads.

Both sexes also have prolactin. In the female, prolactin causes milk production in the breast. Prolactin also aids in breast development during puberty and during pregnancy. In males, prolactin may affect spermatogenesis, and may also increase resistance to stress and cause the increase in androgen that occurs overnight in normal males.

Negative Feedback Control. All of the gonadal hormones exert a **negative feedback effect** on the hypothalamus. For example, increases in estrogens cause a decrease in the output of both FSH and LH, which in turn leads to a decrease in the secretion of estrogens. This relationship is illustrated in Figure 2.9. A useful analogy would be to the relationship that a thermostat creates between a furnace and the temperature of a room. When the room temperature (estrogen concentration) rises, the rise is sensed by the thermostat (in the hypothalamus), which then turns the furnace (gonad) off. Connecting the hypothalamus-thermostat and the gonad-furnace are the releasing and inhibiting factors and their associated pituitary hormones. With the furnace off, the room temperature (estrogen) will drop; this drop will be sensed by the thermostat, which turns the furnace back on.

This negative feedback loop describes the relationship between the sex hormones and the **gonadotropic hormones** (FSH and LH) most of the time, except during ovulation. A decreased sensitivity of the hypothalamus to circulating hormones, decreasing the effectiveness of negative feedback, may occur in both males and females at puberty (Critchlow and Bar-Sella, 1967).

Hormone Cycles and Positive Feedback. Because of the negative feedback loop, the hormones in males are kept relatively constant, just as the thermostat keeps the room temperature relatively constant. Although there are some hormonal cycles in the human male, they are smaller than the monthly changes that occur in the human female, who shifts from follicular secretion of estrogens before ovulation to corpus luteum secretion of both estrogens and progestins after ovulation.

The cyclic changes in female primates are accompanied by regular periods of uterine bleeding and are referred to as the menstrual cycle. Lower organisms have no regular periods of uterine bleeding, and the hormone cycle is referred to as an **estrous cycle.**

Hormonal secretion in the female occurs in a cycle partly as the result of a response of the hypothalamus to high levels of estrogen, a response seen only in females (at least in subprimates, or species lower on the evolutionary scale than primates). This sex difference has nothing to do with the pituitary itself, since the pituitary of a male rat, transplanted into a female, will start cyclic secretions leading to ovulation in an implanted ovary (G. Harris and Jacobsohn, 1952). Instead, at least in subprimates, the brains of males and females are different, probably as a result of the inductive effects of male sex hormones on the hypothalamus. In particular, there is a sex difference in the reactions of the hypothalamus to high levels of estrogen. Only in females does a very high level of estrogen, such as that seen just before ovulation caused by the ripening egg follicle, lead to a surge in the production of LH and FSH. This effect is called a **positive feedback effect,** since increases in estrogen lead to increases in the releasing factors from the hypothalamus, causing first increases in LH and FSH, then further increases in estrogen (S. Yen, et al., 1974, Figure 2.9).

The presence of this positive feedback loop in females leads to the large cyclical changes in hormones. During the first part of the cycle, the follicular phase, estrogen is high because of the effects of FSH on the egg follicle. But when estrogen reaches a certain critical level, positive feedback occurs and LH and FSH are increased. Then the high levels of LH lead to ovulation. Ovulation is accompanied by a temporary fall in estrogen, which brings its level down below the point required for the positive feedback effect. Then, as the corpus luteum develops under the influence of LH in the luteal phase, estrogen and progesterone both increase. Because of this increase, the wall of the uterus builds up and, from the negative feedback effect, the rate of gonadotropic hormone secretion drops. This decline in gonadotropins causes the corpus luteum to degenerate so that progesterone and estrogen levels decline. Because of this, the wall of the uterus begins to slough off and the menses begin.

Thus, the cycles in females are caused by regular changes in the ovaries and

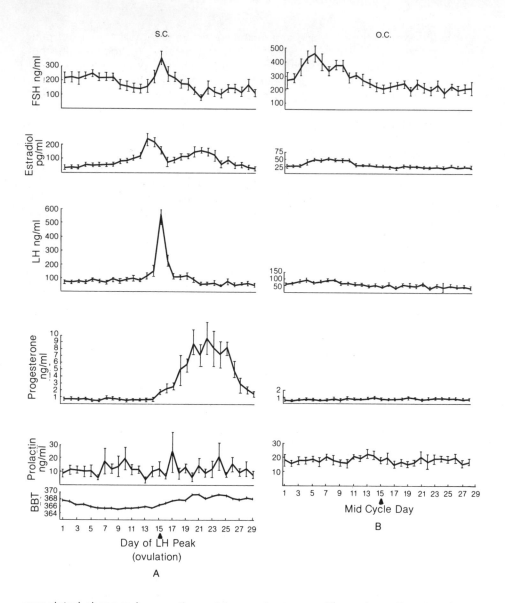

associated changes in secretions of the sex hormones. These then affect the pituitary secretions via negative and positive feedback loops acting through the hypothalamus. The hormonal events of the menstrual cycle in humans are presented in Figure 2.10. Only during the late follicular phase of the cycle (days thirteen to fifteen) is the estrogen level high enough to initiate the positive feedback loop. During the middle of the luteal phase (days twenty to twenty-five), estrogen does not reach that critical level again, so only during the late follicular phase does the positive feedback effect occur.

Whether or not males can show the positive feedback effect of estrogen on LH depends on the species. The hypothalamus of the male rat does not show as large an LH surge in response to very high levels of estrogen as does that of the female, and thus the male hypothalamus has a much less well developed positive feedback loop. But in primates, including the human male, both sexes will have a large LH surge in response to high levels of estrogen, or estrogen plus progesterone injections (Karsch, Dierschke, and Knobil, 1973; Knobil, 1974; Stearns, Winter, and Faiman, 1973a). In other words, the male primate hypothalamus is at least potentially cyclical since it can show strong positive as well as negative feedback effects.

SUMMARY: THE EFFECTS OF SEX CHROMOSOMES

The sex chromosomes apparently exert some indirect effect on behavior in view of the different characteristics exhibited by individuals with the various sex chromosome abnormalities. Not only is the sexual anatomy of these individuals often affected, their height, the level and pattern of their IQ, and their personality characteristics may also be altered. However, there is no reason to expect environment to exert any less effect on these people than on genetically normal people of either sex; sometimes individuals act completely differently from what is expected. One girl with Turner's syndrome we met reported that her favorite college subject, and the one in which she did best, was accounting.

Sex differences in development are caused first by the presence or absence of a Y chromosome. In the presence of a Y chromosome, the fetal gonad differentiates into testes and begins secreting androgens at about the third month. From that point on, the sex differences in development are caused by the sex differences in hormones secreted by the fetal gonads. In the presence of androgens and a Müllerian inhibiting substance, the internal sex organs, the external sex organs, and the brain are all differentiated in the male direction.

The differences in sex hormones after puberty are a matter of degree, with males having relatively more androgens and females more estrogens and progestins. These hormones are controlled by pituitary hormones that are, in turn, controlled by the hypothalamus either directly or indirectly by means of releasing or

FIGURE 2.10 —————————————————————————————

HORMONE PROFILES DURING THE MENSTRUAL CYCLE

The graphs show comparison of a spontaneously cycling group (A) with a group taking a combination oral contraceptive (B). Mean values are given along with standard deviations. BBT refers to basal body temperature. The menses would be from day 29 or day 1 to day 5. (n =16 for both groups.)

O. D. Creutzfeldt, et al., "EEG Changes During Spontaneous and Controlled Menstrual Cycles and Their Correlation with Psychological Performance." *Electroencephalography and Clinical Neurophysiology,* Vol. 40, 1976, p. 129.

inhibiting factors. Hormone secretion in the female subprimate occurs in a cycle because of the existence of positive feedback loop between the sex hormones and the gonadotropic hormones, combined with the sequences of changes in the ovarian follicles and their secretions. In primates, both sexes have a capacity for a positive feedback loop, but it does not cyclically influence hormone secretion in males. Except for around the time of ovulation in women, the concentration of both gonadotropic hormones and sex hormones in both genders is governed by a negative feedback loop working through the hypothalamus.

Of course, the major implication of the material in this chapter is that sex chromosomes do more than just determine the physical appearance of the body. In view of the data from the various genetic abnormalities, we can see the sex chromosomes may also affect behavior, although indirectly. The presence of only a single X chromosome may produce an exaggeration of the female stereotype, the presence of a double X in addition to a Y may produce a somewhat feminized male, and the presence of an extra Y may produce an exaggeration of the male sterotype. This suggests (but does not prove) that these chromosomes may also have some behavioral impact in genetically normal males and females. The existence of sex-linked and sex-limited traits provides more direct evidence of the effects of the sex chromosomes upon gender role; in particular, these genes may affect the sex differences in preparedness of the individual to respond in certain ways to certain experiences. There may be other traits, such as spatial ability, which are accurately described by using a multifactorial, sex-modified threshold model of heritability. Thus, one piece of the puzzle of why there are sex differences seems to be the influence of our chromosomal gender.

KEY TERMS AND CONCEPTS

Chromosome
Genes
DNA
Genetic induction
Genetic repression or inactivation
Geneotype
Phenotype
Sex chromosomes
Autosomes
Karyotype
Barr body and X-inactivation
Turner's syndrome
Performance and verbal IQs
Space-form intelligence
Klinefelter's syndrome
Hermaphrodite
Pseudohermaphrodite
EEG
Amniocentesis
Sex-linkage

Sex-limitation
Recessive and dominant
Multifactorial, sex-modified threshold
  model of inheritability
Medulla
Cortex
Androgens
Testosterone
Wolffian structure
Müllerian structure
MIS
Estrogens
Estradiol
Progestins
Progesterone
Menstrual cycle
Follicle
Follicular phase
Luteal phase
Corpus luteum

Adrenal glands
Spermatogenesis
Pituitary gland
Hypothalamus
Posterior pituitary hormones: oxytocin and
  ADH
Anterior pituitary hormones: FSH, LH,
  ACTH, and prolactin

Target organ
Releasing and inhibiting factors
Ovulation
Negative feedback loop
Gonadotropic hormones
Positive feedback loop

QUESTIONS ON KEY ISSUES

1. Why is the female human a genetic mosaic?
2. What are the major problems with interpreting data on people with chromosome abnormalities?
3. What are the physical, intellectual and behavioral characteristics of the following syndromes: 47, XXX; 45, X; 47, XXY; 47, XYY. What implications does this have for 46, XX and 46, XY people?
4. What are some of the general effects of changes in the number of sex chromosomes?
5. What evidence suggests that spatial ability is X-linked? How does the multifactorial, sex-modified threshold model explain sex differences in any behavior, including spatial ability, that is affected by genes?
6. What determines whether the following structures develop as male or female: gonads, internal organs, external organs, brain?
7. How does the hypothalamus control both the anterior and posterior pituitary hormones? What are the effects of each of those hormones?
8. What are the major events of the female human menstrual cycle, and how do negative and positive feedback loops fit in here?

_____

CHAPTER 3

Sexual Dimorphism in the Animal Kingdom

CONTRIBUTIONS OF AND PROBLEMS WITH THE COMPARATIVE APPROACH

Notwithstanding the hazards that are always present when we attempt to generalize from lower species to homo sapiens, researchers commonly agree that such risks are at times worthwhile. However, the risks must always be kept in mind if the comparative approach is to have any validity at all.

One risk is that the similar appearance of two behaviors in two different species will mislead us into concluding that those behaviors have similar causes and functions when in fact they do not. Altruism in humans and altruism in other animals may look similar, but could well have different biological meanings. In the context of the study of sex differences, a behavior may look to human observers to be an expression of a sexual motive but in fact be an expression of dominance or submission, or merely be an organism's request to be groomed.

Another problem with the comparative approach is that behaviors that seem unimportant to humans (or are imperceptible) may have extremely important functions for the animal involved. Ultrasonic communication in rats has recently been discovered to be very important in sexual and maternal behavior, but these are social signals that humans cannot even hear. As another example, until recently we thought that the most important aspect of sexual behavior in female animals was simply holding still, probably because of biased impressions that females are sexually passive and males are active. We now realize that the very active role of females is just as important as the more obvious aspects of the male sexual role. Thus, the Rosenthal effect is likely to exist in the comparative literature. That is, experimenters' expectations and values may lead them to misinterpret behavior, to ignore other behaviors that do not conform to their expectations, and possibly lead them to distort data inadvertently.

A final problem with comparative data is the large variability of sexual dimorphism that occurs across species, within a species, and across experimental techniques. For example, the male is not more aggressive than the female in all species. Even within a species, some strains may be more sexually dimorphic than others; shock often elicits aggression in rats, but this shock-elicited aggression may be dimorphic only in some strains of rats. Also, other ways of eliciting aggression and other types of aggressive behaviors might not show sex differences (Barr, Gibbons, and Moyer, 1976).

But that risks exist does not mean the comparative approach should be avoided. There are many advantages to the comparative approach, and perhaps more than usual in the area of sex differences. The comparative approach offers four major contributions to the study of sex differences.

1. Exceptions to and variations on the typical patterns of sexual dimorphisms found in most species may suggest new theoretical interpretations of sex differences in humans; this, in turn, may suggest ways of changing the traditional patterns.

2. Data from lower species may be less likely to be subjectively interpreted, or interpreted from a biased point of view, than human data.

3. Studies with lower species teach researchers to be more careful in studies with humans. Awareness of the relatively large individual within-sex differences in behavior—found even in the most inbred strains of rats and mice—suggests the importance of unbiased sampling procedures, or else the risk of reaching erroneous conclusions in human studies will be unacceptably large.

4. Observing lower species teaches us to not assume that sex differences are uniform. The comparative literature makes it clear that there are biologically successful species that exhibit both minimal dimorphism and others that exhibit great dimorphism. Thus, evolutionary pressures obviously do not exert a consistent pressure towards dimorphism or towards lack of dimorphism. And, since many species are **monomorphic** (exhibit minimal sex differences), monomorphy in humans could also be biologically advantageous. (Monomorphy in humans might be called **androgyny,** since an androgynous person is one who exibits both male and female traits with equal frequency.)

Because of the advantages of the comparative approach, this chapter will examine sexual dimorphism in lower species and will also describe the commonly used methods of measuring sexually dimorphic behaviors, which are referred to in later chapters. Infrahuman primates (primates below the human on the evolutionary scale) will be emphasized because they are the closest relatives of the human primate. Rodents are also emphasized in the sections on learning and activity, because most laboratory experimentation has used those species as subjects and because of the importance of the possibility of sex differences in learning.

This chapter will first examine the evolutionary utility of sex differences to try to determine how sex differences might have developed and why. Next, the common physical sex differences will be discussed. Finally, gender differences in the areas of sexual behavior, aggression, activity, and emotionality, social behaviors, and learning and sensory abilities will be examined from a comparative perspective. We will look for cross-species commonalities in sex differences and the evolutionary pressures that might have produced those differences.

EVOLUTIONARY DEVELOPMENT AND UTILITY OF SEX DIFFERENCES

Why have two sexes? And even if there are two sexes, why should they so often differ from one another in both appearance and behavior? What types of survival pressures might have produced sex differences?

Sexual Reproduction

In the beginning there were no sexes and no sexual reproduction. Asexual reproduction—fission and budding—proceeded for millions of years before there were sexes. While not all species have joined the bandwagon, division into sexes has become particularly popular in the animal kingdom today. There are male and female ants, spiders, fish, snakes, birds, mammals, and even plants.

The evolution of sexual behavior and its continuing success can probably be attributed in great part to the fact that the offspring of the combination of genetic material from two different sources (male sperm and female ovum) are a more variable product than are the identical daughters produced by asexual reproduction. This variability, coupled with **natural selection** (survival of the fittest) has allowed sexually reproducing species to adapt genetically to environmental changes more rapidly than asexually reproducing species. It appears that asexual reproduction is now most common in those species that inhabit a rather narrow biological niche, or biosphere, that has little variability. Parasites, for example, reproduce asexually and also live in a very stable environment (inside of other species), while sexual reproduction characterizes all the larger terrestrial animal species that inhabit a constantly changing environment.

Thus, sexual behavior increases flexibility, and this increased flexibility promotes species survival both over the long term and the short term (G. Williams, 1975). Populations evolve faster when they reproduce sexually, and thus they will prevail over the asexual populations in the same biosphere. Over the short term, sexual reproduction evolved because the genetic diversity of each parent's offspring was increased, and this diversity enabled them to cope with sudden, unpredictable environmental changes; despite the changes, at least some were likely to survive.

The Utility of Sex Differences

Given the advantages of sexual reproduction, why are there sex differences? What is the value of having the sexes differ in any way other than what is absolutely required for reproduction—having a penis and testicles or a vagina, uterus, and ovaries? There are several different, but not mutually exclusive, advantages to sex differences.

Sexual Recognition. First, it is advantageous for one sex to be able to recognize the other. It is uneconomical for organisms to spend most of their breeding life actively courting other animals of the same sex. Thus, sex differences promote sexual recognition. This is true for sex differences of all sorts, including territory claiming, mating calls, **pheromones** (sexual scents), courtship displays, and physical appearance. We humans also feel uncomfortable if we cannot identify the gender of the person with whom we are interacting.

Intersexual Competition.   Sex differences may also lead to decreased competition between the sexes for food and other resources, as well as to low intersex aggressive behavior. For example, the beaks of male and female birds of many species differ from each other such that different food supplies are sought by each sex (Selander, 1972). Behavioral and physical sex differences that reduce intersexual competition would also be adaptive, that is, would promote survival. The mane of the male lion, the canine teeth of the male primate, and the red belly of the male stickleback fish may all serve to elicit aggression; their absence in females may decrease intersexual aggression. The differential auditory sensitivities of the male and female tree frog also decrease intersexual aggression, since the female cannot even hear the aggressive call (Narins and Capronica, 1976).

Reproductive Roles.   Finally, in many species the sexes play different roles; each sex, to be maximally adapted for his or her own role, must be different— behaviorally and physically—from the other sex. For example, the male may arrive at the breeding ground first to fight with other males in order to claim and defend a desirable territory. Thus, the male, to be optimally suited for that role, needs to be large, strong, and have weapons of offense. He may also be colorful to attract the female when she arrives. In fact, the major male role of many species occurs before mating. The female's major role often appears only after mating, and it involves the care, protection, and feeding of the offspring. The more these reproductive roles are separated in the sexes, the more sexually dimorphic will be the species, in order that each sex will be maximally adapted to its own biological niche (Trivers, 1972; G. Williams, 1975).

Summary.   One reason there are two sexes involves the advantages sexual reproduction has over asexual reproduction. Sexual reproduction increases flexibility; sex differences in behavior and appearance will facilitate sexual reproduction and so increase biological adaptiveness. Sex differences promote sexual recognition, decrease intersexual competition and aggression, and—to the extent that the reproductive roles of the sexes differ—increase adaptiveness to the particular reproductive role played by each sex.

Sexual Selection, Natural Selection, and Sex Differences

According to Darwin (1874), in any given species, two distinct types of selection pressures operate on behavioral and physical characteristics, including sexual dimorphism. First, the organism must live until breeding age, or it will not contribute its genes to the next generation. Thus, the survival value of the individual determines which genes are likely to be available for the next generation. This type of selection pressure is called **natural selection.**

However, survival by itself is not enough. Organisms must also be attractive to the opposite sex for their genes to be handed on. This second type of selection pressure is called **sexual selection.** Sexual selection usually implies that one sex (most often the female) is more particular about the selection of a sexual partner than the other sex. This also implies that males are available in sufficient numbers to allow a choice. This means that some particular characteristic—behavioral or morphological (relating to body appearance)—will be selected for and occur only in one sex because of the choice exerted by the other sex. Of course, in some respects, this distinction between natural selection and sexual selection is arbitrary since the last step in both cases is the production of fertile offspring, but the distinction seems useful in understanding the role and effects of sex differences in evolution. As implied by what was said before, both sexual selection and natural selection can lead to sex differences.

Natural Selection. As Mayr (1972) points out, some sex differences have evolved solely through natural selection pressures. For example, if the male sex role includes competing with other males or defending offspring against predators (as in some social living primates), then horns or teeth would have appeared in the male through natural selection pressures, because such structures would have promoted survival.

The female's role also produces sex differences because of the work of natural selection. The female of most species must survive long enough to protect and care for her offspring. Therefore, any mechanism that facilitates a female's survival during that period would evolve only in females because of natural selection. Some such characteristics are drabber colors and smaller size, so that the female is not only less visible to predators but has a smaller food requirement as well.

Sexual Selection. Female preference, leading to sexual dimorphism through sexual selection, has been demonstrated in a wide variety of species (G. Williams, 1975). This strategy on the part of the female can lead to rapid improvement of the species, as animal breeders realize. All attempts to modify domestic animals are based primarily upon the selection of quality males, thus maximizing the genetic contribution of those males to the next generation.

There are many examples of female selectivity, a principle of great importance. Bertram (1975) reported that only 25 percent of male lions may ever have offspring, and LeBoeuf and Peterson (1969) found that 4 percent of the male elephant seals sired 85 percent of the offspring. Thus, the rest of the males were rejected by the females. Female fruit flies are more selective than male flies, and female flies seem to prefer whatever type of male fly is currently in short supply (Ehrman, 1972; McClearn and DeFries, 1973). Female mice prefer dominant males to nondominant ones (McClearn and DeFries, 1973). Female monkeys of several species also prefer dominant males, and males with an erect penis (Beach, 1976). In many primate species, the dominant male gets preferential access to the female when she is most fertile because of this female preference.

There are several other examples of females being more choosy than males. Female fish like brightly colored, dominant males (Weber and Weber, 1975). Female peacocks and pheasants evidently find large bright tails attractive, even though this also makes the male more highly visible to predators. Female rats do most of the sexual selecting (Doty, 1974), and female gorillas also have preferences (Nadler, 1975). Some females select not particular males but the territories held by the male (G. Williams, 1975).

Selection Pressures and Sexual Dimorphisms. Natural and sexual selection, then, predict the extent and nature of sexual dimorphism from species to species. As was pointed out previously, there is great variability in sexual dimorphism from species to species—and even some role reversal (G. Williams, 1975). In some birds, the male is responsible for the care of the offspring, so in this case the natural selection pressures are reversed. In this species, the female is larger and more brightly colored, engages in dominance battles, and even has more male sex hormone (Manning, 1967).

In some monogamous species parents care for offspring equally and thus have similar reproductive roles. In these cases there will be little sexual dimorphism, as is the case with many birds and with terrestial carnivores. Sexual dimorphism will also be reduced if female sexual preference is not a factor or if most members of the species have offspring. Sexual selection occurs only in species in which few males mate. Under these conditions, selection by females can produce sex differences. Some of the differences produced by sexual selection will then be maintained by natural selection if they represent body features and behaviors useful in social behavior, which thus serve to maintain the stability of the group in social living species (Crook, 1972).

Sometimes both natural and sexual selection will produce the same difference. For example, the male is usually larger both because females prefer larger, more dominant males, and because the size of the female is reduced by natural selection pressures in order to promote her survival after mating so that offspring can be successfully reared.

Summary and Implications of Evolution

Several behavioral and environmental characteristics of species promote sex differences. Hence, sex differences should be most visible in those species that have one or more of the following characteristics. First, we expect to find sex differences in appearance or behavior in those species that have a great deal of intraspecies (within the species) aggression and competition. Sex differences would tend to decrease aggression between the sexes and so could promote survival of the species. Second, we expect to find sex differences in those species in which rapid or accurate sexual recognition would be especially advantageous, as in species that mate only once per lifetime or those in which sexual activity exposes them to high levels of risk from the environment. Third, sexual dimorphism due to sexual selection should occur in species in which only a few males are responsible for most of the offspring and in species that have an unequal sex ratio during maturity. Fourth, sex differences should occur in those species in which males and females play very different reproductive roles. Fifth, sex differences will be maintained, and maybe even increased, in social species to the extent that these differences promote the survival of the group as a whole. Survival could be promoted either because sexual dimorphism in roles promotes group cohesion or because the social transmission of learned traits is more efficient when sexually dimorphic.

Sex differences arise through both sexual and natural selection pressures. Sexual selection will result in sex differences as long as one sex (usually female) is more particular than the other, giving certain males a reproductive advantage over other males or increasing their access to fertile females. Natural selection will produce sex differences as long as the differences promote sexual recognition or decrease intersexual competition, or if the sexes differ in their reproductive roles. However, whether produced by natural or by sexual selection, sex differences must be sex-linked or sex-limited. That is, the characteristic or trait must prove to be reproductively advantageous for only one sex—or mostly for one sex—such that that trait becomes sex-linked or sex-limited and thus appears mostly or solely in that sex.

In reading the rest of this chapter, you should keep the following five questions in mind:

1. What is the range of the magnitude of dimorphism across the phylogenetic scale, and how does social living affect it?

2. Does the amount of physical dimorphism correlate with the magnitude of behavioral dimorphism because selection pressures work on both in a similar fashion?

3. What behaviors are usually characteristic of the larger or the smaller sex, and what does size difference imply about the nature of the selection pressures?

4. Is a greater degree of sexual dimorphism found in those species in which only a few males father most of the offspring or those in which there is a large difference in reproductive roles?

5. What selection pressures might have led to each difference?

PHYSICAL SEXUAL DIMORPHISM

No simple rule predicts the direction and magnitude of dimorphism on the basis of a species' position on the phylogenetic scale. Many different kinds of characteristics may be involved in different species. In many species, such as rats and dogs, being male simply means being larger, and a small male is nearly indistinguishable from a large female. This is also true of *rapacious* (meat eating) birds, some fishes, and horses. In other species, pronounced sex differences in plumage and coloration appear only during the breeding season; this is the case with the hooked lower jaw of male salmon and the bright orange-red breast of male English robins. In still other species, males have larger implements of defense and attack, such as the rooster's spurs, the canine teeth of humans and baboons, and the horns of the billy goat, the elk, and the deer. Finally, physical sexual dimorphism sometimes means simply that the male is more conspicuous. Often the male mammal is the one with the greater hair growth, such as the mane of the male lion and the facial hair in male humans. In *precocial* birds (those in which the individual shows a high degree of independence from birth), the male is often the more brightly colored; this is also true of some fish and of certain primates, such as the mandrill.

Size

Sexual dimorphism in size is the most common physical difference. The direction of the size difference varies widely from species to species, however, depending largely on reproductive roles.

Subprimates. There seems to be a general trend among mammals for the male to be larger than the female, although exceptions do occur. In other classes of animals, either males or females may be larger. In species such as insects, spiders, and fish, the females are usually larger. In species in between mammals

TABLE 3.1 ──────────────────────────────────

SEXUAL DIMORPHISM IN WEIGHT IN SEVERAL PRIMATE SPECIES

Genus, Species, or Group	Approximate Female Weight Expressed as Percent of Male Weight	Range
New World Monkeys (based on eight genuses)	90%	78–100%
Old World Monkeys (based on ten genuses)	65	50–95
Baboon	50	40–55
Gibbon	99	93–105
Orangutan	48	43–54
Gorilla	50	38–52
Chimpanzee	92	90–93
Human	85	80–90

Source: P. van den Berghe, *Age and Sex in Human Societies: A Biosocial Perspective.* Belmont, Calif.: Wadsworth.

and insects on the phylogenetic scale—such as amphibians and snakes— *monomorphy* (similarity between the sexes) is common. The bird kingdom presents a rather complex pattern of size dimorphisms; in some species the sexes are equal in size, in some the males are larger, and in others the females are larger. However, even among birds, increases in paternal behavior often imply a reduction in sexual dimorphism. For example, in the *passerine* (perching) birds such as sparrows and doves, paternal behavior occurs as often as maternal behavior and sex differences in size are minimal.

The exceptions to the general rule that male mammals are larger provide very interesting examples to show that sex differences in behavior may be more related to relative size than to sex, per se. For example, the female hyena, which is larger than the male, is the dominant leader of the pack. Crook (1972) reports that among New World monkeys, the Saguinus female is larger than the male and is also more aggressive. The female hamster is also both larger and more aggressive than the male, even when tested in male-female fighting pairs (Payne, 1974a, 1974b; Payne and Swanson, 1973).

Primates. In primates, the magnitude of sexual dimorphism in size is greatest in the terrestial living species (where the male does not have to swing his greater weight from branch to branch) and in those species where group defense seems primarily to be the male role, as is the case with gorillas and baboons. As can be seen in Table 3.1, males tend to be heavier in most primate species. But these data on weight underestimate the sexual dimorphism in strength, since more of the male's mass is muscle and more of the female's mass is fat.

Development and Mortality

Usually if a species is dimorphic, the smaller member develops faster and reaches sexual maturity earlier (van den Berghe, 1973). Also full participation in sexual reproduction in the females of most species occurs as soon as the female is sexually mature, but in many dimorphic species the male reproductive life is relatively short, spanning only the period from acquisition of a territory or the attainment of high dominance status to the loss of that status or territory. Bertram (1975) reports that the heavier lion has a reproductive life of two to three years, whereas the smaller lioness has a reproductive life of nearly ten years.

Selection Pressures and Survival.   Because of the different roles, and thus the differing effect natural selection has upon the two sexes, and because sexual selection is usually exerted by the female on the male, the male will be less optimally adapted for survival than the female. The male must survive only until mating, whereas the female must survive at least until the offspring are independent. Of course, if there is no difference between the male and female reproductive roles, and if there is little male competition, as is the case with *monogamy* (one male mates with only one female), natural selection will not differentially operate on the two sexes, sexual selection will be minimized, and there will be little sexual dimorphism in survival and life expectancy. But as long as there are sex differences, the male would be expected to have the greater mortality rate.

The greater mortality rate of the male has in fact been demonstrated in a variety of species. Females are expected to live longer than males among rats, cats, lions, birds, reptiles, fish, several insects, and humans, in both protected and natural environments (Asdell et al., 1967; Gove, 1973; Hamilton, 1948; Hamilton, Hamilton, and Mestler, 1969; Hamilton and Mestler, 1969; G. Williams, 1975). Possibly the most extreme examples of this are found in the praying mantis and the A. Stuarlie, a tree-living marsupial. The male mantis is a more effective copulator without his head, so the female frequently obliges him by biting it off (Bermant and Davidson, 1974). From the female point of view, the best thing that the male shrewlike marsupial could do after intercourse, in order to reduce competition for food, would be to drop dead, which he does (Bradley, McDonald, and Lee, 1975).

Also, in many species the effect of sexual selection by the female acts in opposition to natural selection pressures on the male, producing morphological and behavioral traits that do not optimize the male's survival. The dominance battles among males for access to the females rarely end in fatal injury, but sometimes the male is too impaired to survive. The male lion's strength is useful to the female in the defense of the food she has killed against other predators, but that behavior in part accounts for the male's shorter life span (Bradley et al., 1975). The male peacock's tail delights the female, but it also makes him very visible to predators and slows him down.

Different reproductive roles also often lead to greater male mortalities. For example, in the wildebeest, the territory-defending male is most often the prey of lions' hunting (Estes, 1966). In many other species, mating itself or the preparation of the mating site involves tremendous expenditures of energy or body mass on the part of the male. Thornhill (1976) reported that the spermatophore produced by some male insects represents a loss of 25 percent of the male body weight, and this loss in turn may provide a source of protein for the female. In other species of birds and insects, females are commonly fed by males during courtship, again involving greater male stress and effort.

Summary.   Thus, dimorphic males tend to mature more slowly, are actively involved in reproduction for a shorter period, and die earlier. Both because of different reproductive role assignments and because of sexual selection, the males of many species will be less optimally adapted for survival. There is one nearly perfect summarizing example of this. One species of fish (*Nothobranchius guentheri*) is strikingly dimorphic; males are brilliantly colored in blue, red, and yellow and the females are a uniform brown (Haas, 1976). The brilliant colors of the male seem to be preferred not only by females, but also by predators such as the heron. The female fish do most of the sexual selecting and prefer brighter males; in the muddy waters in which these fish live, the color of the male is useful for rapid sexual recognition. Thus, natural selection (herons see and eat bright fish easier) led to drab females, while both sexual selection (females prefer to mate with the brightest males) and natural selection (bright males can be found and recognized easier in the muddy water) led to brighter colors in the male. Who then gets eaten by a heron?

SEXUAL DIMORPHISM IN BEHAVIOR

Sexual Behavior

Not all sexually mature males engage in sexual activity. This is particularly true of the males in dimorphic species, for reasons described earlier. However, both males and females engage in behavior designed to attract the opposite sex. The sexual behavior of both males and females depends on male and female activational hormones, but not even sexual behavior is always sexually dimorphic.

Types of Sexual Activity. Both males and females actively court the interest of members of the opposite sex. Females actively display various parts of their bodies to the male of their choice. The female primate may display her genitals to a male in the so-called female sexual presentation posture and may also orally stimulate the male's genitals (Beach, 1976). The female subprimate may actively engage in behaviors designed to attract males, such as the darting, ear wiggling, and hopping displayed by female rats. The female may then assume the posture of **lordosis** in front of the male in response to his stimulations. In lordosis, the female subprimate holds still, often with arched back, bent tail and splayed hind legs. So female sexual behavior is often measured as the frequency with which an active male can elicit lordosis, or the amount of time in an experimental period in which lordosis is maintained.

The sexually interested male then **mounts** or climbs on, the female. Male sexual activity is measured by the frequency of **intromissions** (insertions of the penis) and the frequency of **ejaculations** in an experimental session. Sometimes researchers measure male activity by a **mounting score,** or the number of mounts in a given time period.

Sex Differences. Surprisingly, the frequency with which these sexual behaviors are displayed in response to appropriate hormone injections is not sexually dimorphic in all species (Goy and Goldfoot, 1975). In rats, for example, mounting does not seem to be neurally dimorphic and so can occur equally in males and females given appropriate amounts of male sex hormones (Beach, 1947, 1968a).

But in at least some primates and in sheep, dogs, hamsters, and guinea pigs, mounting is shown more often by males than by females (Beach et al., 1972; Clarke, 1977; Goy, 1968, 1970). Thus, testosterone injections will not increase the mounting scores of the adult female rhesus monkey, but they can increase the mounting behavior of normal adult female rats to a level very close to that of normal male rats (Beach, 1968b). The other aspects of male sexual behavior—intromission and ejaculation—are dimorphic in all species, but maybe only because they require a penis. There is a possibility that in rats at least, the parts of the brain controlling male sexual behavior are the same for both sexes, but normal females simply lack the appropriate hormones and a penis. On the other hand, the female sexual presentation postures and lordosis are more dimorphic in subprimates than in primates. So these behaviors are exhibited more often by females than by males only in subprimates, regardless of hormones.

Still, in primates, male and female sexual behaviors occur for nonsexual reasons. Females may assume the female sexual presentation posture to solicit food or grooming, and both males and females assume that posture to indicate submission and to halt an attack by another animal. Mounting behaviors may be displayed by both males and females to indicate dominance.

Summary.   Males and females show different kinds of behavior in response to sexual stimuli. Males more often display male sexual behaviors, although in rats this may be due only to sex differences in activational hormones and in anatomy, and not to any sex differences in the brain. Females more often display female behaviors, but in this case primates may be less dimorphic than other species. Sexual behavior may also occur in primates for nonsexual motives, such as aggression and fear.

Aggression and Dominance

The measurement of aggression and dominance varies from species to species—with no guarantee of comparability. Sometimes researchers simply compute the frequency of fights or aggressive gestures. Sometimes researchers use indirect measures, such as measuring the intensity with which an animal bites a ball provided for that purpose. These aggressive behaviors may be observed in natural settings or as elicited by shock in the laboratory. However, all ways of measuring aggression do not show sex differences. Even within a species, some aspects of aggressive behavior may not be sexually dimorphic.

Dominance in subprimates if often assessed by having pairs of animals compete for food or water. With like-sexed pairs, the results of this competition are usually stable, but with mixed-sex pairs, sexual behavior sometimes interferes (make love, not war). In primates, dominance is usually assessed by noting the frequency of dominant and submissive gestures, or by noting who gets first access to a choice bit of food. The problem with research in this area is that dominance as assessed one way may not adequately predict dominance in a different situation.

In view of this problem, the consistency of findings across species is surprising. If the male is larger, he is also the more aggressive sex and dominates the female.

Size and Aggression. Almost without exception, the larger sex is the more aggressive sex. The large female hyena is the dominant sex, and the larger female hamster will even attack males (Payne, 1974a, 1975b). The female gibbon—very close in size to the male—is also quite aggressive. But usually the males are both larger and more aggressive. In some situations, however, even the smaller female can be very aggressive. Females with young are usually very protective of them. The sow bear with cubs and the bitch with puppies can be very dangerous. Even the female rat can be extremely bold in protecting her young.

Subprimates. Most aggressive behavior in lower species occurs between like-sexed animals, females against females and males against males. Rarely do males attack females and vice versa.

Experimental studies in rodents generally show greater aggression in males than in females. This is true for aggression in like-sex pairings, for aggression in response to shock and overcrowding, and for aggression directed towards other species (Baenninger, 1974; Butler, 1973; J. Gray, 1971b). Male rats are even more likely to attack and kill newborn pups than are females (K. Rosenberg & Sherman, 1975a, 1975b). Males are also more often attacked, perhaps because of the effects of androgens upon their pheromones (Payne, 1974a). However, even in rats, sex differences in aggression vary according to the strain, the situation used to elicit aggression, and which particular aggressive behavior is being measured (Barr, et al., 1976).

Despite the variability, when sex differences are seen, the male rodent is more aggressive, and this may in part reflect sex differences in preparedness to respond to certain situations with certain types of aggressive behaviors. For example, Thor, Ghiselli and Ward (1974) found not only that male rats showed more aggressive responses to shock then females did, but also that training increased the aggression of males more than that of females.

In spite of the consistent sex differences found in rodent aggression, it has been difficult to get reliable sex differences in dominance (J. Gray, 1971b). However, Masur and Benedito (1974a, 1974b) finally succeeded in getting such results. They had adult male rats compete with adult females for food in a straight runway, where the two animals came from opposite directions and the winner—the dominant animal—was the one who pushed the other animal back to the starting point. Males were consistently dominant over females, but only after they reached sexual maturity. The experimenters showed that this male dominance was not the result of males being larger and stronger. Also, this sex difference in dominance only appeared after the first trial and thus after sexual recognition had taken place.

In many other social-living species, such as chickens, cows, and wolves, animals compete for a position of high status in a **dominance hierarchy.** This dominance hierarchy ranks the animals; in a confrontation over food or over a female the hierarchy can be used to predict which animal will give way. In most species, the female and male hierarchies are separate, although the female hierarchy may not predict behavior as well. The larger males or females, or the males with the larger canines, or the females with larger horns, typically occupy the higher status positions, maintaining them by fights or by threats against other animals (Bouissou, 1972; Rabb, Woolpy, and Ginsburg, 1967; Scott and Fuller,

1965). But in most species, the females generally defer to the males without a confrontation, and the males occupy the highest ranks in any dominance hierarchy.

Rank in the dominance hierarchy often confers reproductive advantages—"rank hath its privileges." This is the case in many species because females prefer to select the more dominant, higher ranking, males. It is also possible for high status in females to be associated with reproductive success, as in wolves and lions. In chickens, high status females are also better able to care for their offspring.

Thus, aggression and dominance presumably became sexually dimorphic in many subprimate species because these traits improved the reproductive success of males more than females. In some species, females also form dominance hierarchies to facilitate their reproductive success and the survival of their offspring. But sexual and natural selection pressures may have produced dimorphisms in aggression and dominance for the same reasons that these pressures produced sexual dimorphisms in size: females preferred winners, and aggression facilitated the reproductive role of males more than that of females, except in the case of the female's defense of her young.

Primates.   The relationship of aggression, dominance, and reproductive success is also seen in many primates. Dominant animals have more reproductive success, and the female usually defers to the male.

Male primates usually dominate the female. Goodall (1965) observed thirty-three dominance interactions among adult chimpanzees and found that of the sixteen that occurred between a male and a female, the male dominated in all cases. In baboons, macaques, and gorillas, adult males also dominate over adult females, paralleling the dimorphism in size (Washburn, Jay and Lancaster, 1965). Harlow (1965) also stated that males never withdrew from females, but most females withdrew from threatening males. This sex difference was found even when the monkeys were reared with mother surrogates, so it could not be the result of being taught by the parent. Even high status females sometimes show subordinate gestures to their own male offspring (Mitchell, 1968).

However, in Washburn, Jay, and Lancaster's review (1965) of dominance interactions in primates, they showed that females can take an important part in the interactions within male dominance hierarchies. Some female macaques dominate some males, and some even dominate a whole troop. The position of a male in the male dominance hierarchy may even involve alliances between a male and a female. And although when new monkeys are introduced to a stable group, the greatest aggression occurs within a sex, males to males and females to females (Scruton and Herbert, 1972), the older female sometimes determines whether or not a new male will be accepted into the group (Lancaster, 1976).

Females may also dominate males when infants are involved. For example, in the patas monkey, although the male is much larger than the female, the female may successfully threaten him, especially when protecting an infant (K. Hall and Mayer, 1967). The female may even elicit the aid of other females in threatening the male (Lancaster, 1976). Also, females or males carrying an infant will not be attacked by the dominant male (Ransom and Ransom, 1971).

But these examples are exceptions; greater male aggression and dominance seem nearly universally observed in both natural and laboratory settings (S. Alt-mann, 1968; J. Gray, 1971b; Hamburg, 1971; Harlow, 1965; Harlow and Lauers-dorf, 1974; B. Rosenberg and Sutton-Smith, 1972; but for an exception see W. Mason, Green, and Posepanka, 1960). Nevertheless, environmental factors as well as species are important in determining the amount of dominance behavior dis-played by males relative to females (Lancaster, 1976).

But it must also be emphasized that female primates do form their own domi-nance hierarchies. As in lower animals, the female primate's position in the hierar-chy may depend upon the status of the male consort; a lower status female may achieve higher status if she wins the favor of the dominant male (Imanishi, 1960). A lower ranking female may also gain in rank when she is sexually receptive (Car-penter, 1942; Crawford, 1940; K. Hall and Devore, 1965; Zuckerman, 1932). The female langur's rank may decline with age and with low reproductive value (Hrdy and Hrdy, 1976). Also, unlike the situation in lower animals, the primate mother's status may determine the status of offspring, which benefit from the mother's de-fense and from the opportunity of modeling high-status behaviors (DeVore, 1963; Imanishi, 1960). Lancaster (1973, 1976) stated that males were more likely than females to deviate from this hereditary status, and thus the dominance hierarchies of females may be more stable than that of males throughout the individual's life.

Natural and sexual selection pressures can lead to dominance hierarchies in females and males. In male primates, for instance, dominance hierarchies in many species predict access to receptive females (Sugiyama, 1969; van Lawick-Goodall, 1968), and so the genes that promote dominance are passed on. The for-mation of a hierarchy is also favored by natural selection pressures. The formation of a dominance hierarchy decreases aggression within the group, and the domi-nant male promotes survival of the group by defending it. Both these factors en-sure the survival of the offspring of the dominant males who head the hierarchy. The dominant male may also chase off any male of lesser rank attempting to copulate with a female, and the female, preferring a more dominant male, may also reject the low ranking male, so that the genes of this male, who is less well adapted, will not appear in the next generation.

Dominance hierarchies may also lead to reproductive success among fe-males (Sugiyama, 1969; van Lawick-Goodall, 1968). In the gelada baboon, social groups consist of one male, up to ten mature females, and offspring. These fe-males form a stable and consistent dominance hierarchy. And the rank of the female predicts the mean number of offspring (correlation $= + .667$); the higher the rank, the more babies. However, the female differs from the male in that rank does not predict the frequency of sexual behavior. Instead, it seems that the lower birth rate is caused by the dominant females attacking those of lower ranks, which either impairs the fertility of the low ranking females or leads to abortions in them (Dunbar and Dunbar, 1977).

So even though males may dominate females, dominance rankings can exist in both sexes, and in both sexes rank correlates with reproductive success. Thus, similar selection pressures were at work on both males and females to form domi-nance hierarchies, but the frequent female preference for a dominant male and the reproductive role of that male (group defense) may have led to the sex differences in aggression and dominance.

Summary. The male is usually the more aggressive and dominant of the two genders, although most aggression is directed toward other males. The only clear exceptions to this seem to be situations where sexual dimorphism in size is reversed or greatly reduced. However, the female may occasionally dominate a male, particularly in defense of an infant or when she is defended by another male. Also, the dominance of female primates is more determined by hereditary caste than that of males, and thus the female status is more stable.

It should also be remembered that the gesture of subordination among primates is the female sexual presentation posture, and both males and females may mount other animals of either sex as gestures of dominance. The dominant male may even use the subordinate female sexual presentation posture to elicit grooming from a lower ranking male (Birch and Clark, 1946). Because of this dual purpose, researchers always risk confusing sexual and social interactions with dominance interactions in primates.

Activity: Emotionality and Curiosity

Activity in animals is measured in a variety of ways and has been taken to reflect a corresponding variety of motives, including the intrinsic pleasure of activity, curiosity, and emotionality, or anxiety and fearfulness. Activity levels can be measured by the size of the territory claimed by the animal, or the size of the range over which the animal commonly roams. Activity in a laboratory has usually been measured either in an activity wheel or in an open field. In the **activity wheel** the animal runs inside a cagelike ferris wheel causing the cage to rotate; the researcher records the number of revolutions per hour or per day. The **open field** is a box, often four feet square with sides two feet high, and with lines on the floor marking out a grid. To measure activity, the researcher notes the number of different lines on the grid floor the animal crosses in a given period of time—usually five or fifteen minutes. The open field has been used not only to measure activity, but also curiosity and emotionality. As will be mentioned later, curiosity is also assessed in ways other than activity levels.

In contrast to the relationship found between gender size and aggression, being the larger or smaller sex does not consistently lead to lesser or greater amounts of general activity. Among rodents, females are both more active and more curious, or exploratory. But we need caution in using activity studies to establish sex differences in other motives and other species; there is very little evidence available in species other than rats, and there is little consistency in the evidence with regard to sex differences in emotionality.

Activity Levels. In higher animals, the data usually suggest that males wander and explore new habitats more than females. Males, particularly during breeding season, may roam widely in search of receptive females. G. Mitchell and Brandt (1970) reported that infant male monkeys were more active than females, but only when stimulated to be so by the presence of other males. But there is really not much evidence of intrinsically greater activity levels in male mammals above the level of rodents.

The laboratory data of rodents in both the open field and the activity wheel consistently show sex differences. Female rats and mice are more active in the wheel (Dawson, Cheung, and Lau, 1973; Kransnoff and Weston, 1976; Manosevitz and Joel, 1973; E. Robinson, 1975), and female rats, mice, and hamsters are more active in the open field (Barrett and Ray, 1970; Blizard, Lippman, and Chen, 1975; Broitman and Donoso, 1974; Sjödén and Södderberg, 1972; J. Stewart, Skvarenina, and Pottier, 1975, Swanson, 1966, 1967, 1969).

Emotionality. The open field is also often used as a test of emotionality (Broadhurst, 1957). **Emotionality** is assumed to be directly related to the number of defecations and urinations and inversely related to activity. Fearful animals huddle in the nearest dark corner and defecate and urinate frequently.

Female rats not only have higher activity scores, they also have lower emotionality scores in the open field. Nevertheless, the sex difference in activity is more consistent across different strains and species than is the sex difference in emotionality (Archer, 1974a, 1975; J. Gray and Lalljee, 1974).

J. Gray (1971b) suggested that sex differences in other areas may also reflect sex differences in fearfulness in rodents. Male rats get ulcers more often than females when placed in a situation where they have to choose between either not getting shocked or getting shocked plus getting something to eat. Females also leave a familiar place faster to enter an open field, which may suggest lower levels of fearfulness (Archer, 1975; Swanson, 1966).

But greater fearfulness in subprimate females is not consistently observed. Females show a more complete conditioned emotional response, often interpreted as anxiety (Barrett and Ray, 1970), and females have a greater physiological and motor reactivity to shock (Archer, 1975). Also, female rats more often than males get ulcers when they are tied down or imprisoned in a tiny tube (J. Gray, 1971b). Finally, Scott and Fuller (1965) found no sex differences in emotional reactivity among dogs.

Because of this variability, Archer has concluded (1975, 1977) that there are no consistent cross-species sex differences in emotionality. The consistent sex differences observed in emotional behavior in rats are attributed to differences in the preferred types of response to fearful situations. The female rat more often becomes active and the male becomes immobile, or freezes, when frightened. Thus, females get ulcers when they cannot be active, when they are immobilized, and males get ulcers in a conflict situation, where freezing cannot resolve their problem.

J. Gray (1971b) has suggested that male primates may be less fearful than female primates. If subordinate postures in females are a valid measure of fear, all the studies reviewed earlier that showed female deference to males would also show that female primates were more fearful than males. However, these data seem to have more to do with dominance than with fearfulness. Thus, deference or withdrawal as a response to a male probably does not indicate greater fearfulness on the female's part, but is instead a well-socialized gesture used to reduce aggression. Also, some of the fearful gestures are very similar to the female sexual presentation postures, and so confusion can arise here.

Curiosity. Exploration—activity motivated by curiosity or boredom—should be considered separately, though it should be remembered that in general the female rodent is more active than the male. It is often assumed that the male is the more exploratory. Certainly, for example, the unneutered male cat explores a larger range than the female (Lorenz and Leyhausen, 1973), and the male primate may also have a larger range (J. Gray and Buffery, 1971). However, laboratory procedures do not often confirm this assumption that males have a greater exploratory tendency.

A number of laboratory procedures are used to assess an animal's preferences for novel or complex stimuli as a measure of exploratory tendencies. Often a novel object is introduced into a familiar environment and the time it takes an animal to approach the object or the time the animal spends in contact with it are measured. Another method is to give the animal a choice between entering a novel environment or a familiar one; in this experiment the proportion of times the novel environment is chosen or the proportion of time spent in that environment is measured. Finally, the animal may be given a lever to press that causes some environmental change, such as turning on a light, and the number of lever presses is tabulated (have you ever observed a young child who has just discovered how to work a light switch?).

Several such laboratory studies have suggested that the assumption of greater male curiosity is incorrect. Generally, female rats show more exploratory behavior than male rats (Hughes, 1968; Simmel, Cheney, and Landy, 1965; W. Thompson, 1953), although this difference is affected by the procedure used and the strain of rats tested (Wachs, 1974). Male rats do more exploring when hungry, but hunger can inhibit exploration by the female (W. Thompson, 1953). Females are more reinforced by simply being able to turn on a light (Inglis, as cited by Archer, 1975) and they also show a greater preference for a novel as opposed to a familiar environment (Russell, 1975). The tendency of males to freeze may inhibit their exploratory activities in some strains of rats in fearful situations (Wachs, 1974), but this cannot account for all the sex differences cited above. Though female rats can be said to be more exploratory than male rats, little data exists for any species other than rats.

Summary. Female rodents are more active in a variety of situations and also have a greater preference for novelty. Exploration may also have a somewhat different motivational basis in males than in females, a possibility that should be kept in mind when the effects of hormones are discussed. With regard to fearfulness, consistent sex differences have been taken to indicate greater fearfulness on the part of the male rat and female infra-human primate, but the generality and validity of these interpretations are in doubt.

Nurturance and Other Social Behavior

Perhaps more capital has been made out of this area of sex differences in animals than out of any other area. Data from this area have been taken as proving that females have incontrovertible and irresistible parental instincts and that males do not. The social structure of some primates has been pointing to as evidence that the most natural arrangement for all primates, including humans, is for the male to dominate over a group of females (a harem) and children. Also, it has often been assumed that the animal data prove that males engage in bonding but that females do not; that is, that males naturally form cooperative groups (clubs and teams) but that females do not. The observations cited below demonstrate that these conclusions are relevant only to a few primates, that there is no such thing as a single primate society, and that males often show a great deal of parental behaviors—sometimes even more than females do.

Primates. All primates live in groups, though the size and sex and age composition of the group is highly variable. However, the stability of most primate groups reflects the tendency of offspring, particularly young females, to remain with their mother. In many species, the juvenile males form their own group peripheral to the main one (Crook, 1966; K. Hall, 1966). It appears that social bonds are strongest between mothers and infants and among siblings; it is through these bonds that the primate groups retain their identity. Therefore, parental behavior is the major type of social behavior, and is the most important to maintaining group stability.

The maintenance of social groups is reinforced not only by mother-infant and sibling-sibling ties and by the dominance hierarchy—where the dominant male suppresses intergroup aggression—but also by mutual grooming, which increases group cohesiveness. In all primates, grooming behavior is more commonly exhibited by females, who direct it towards their young, towards other females, or towards males who solicit their attention. Males mostly limit their grooming to relatives (Lancaster, 1976). This is even the case without mothers needing to teach the behavior; females raised with surrogate-mothers spent more time in mutual grooming than did surrogate-raised males (Harlow, 1965).

There are also sex differences in parental behavior in primates. One study compared how preadolescent male and female monkeys reacted to a strange infant (Chamove, Harlow, and Mitchell, 1967). The females directed four times as much positive social behavior toward the infant as did the males, but the males exhibited ten times more hostility. One male even bit off the infant's fingertip. All but one of the fifteen females contacted the infant (the one exception was afraid of it), but only two (or three) males did so.

We cannot generalize from these examples to all primates, however, as there are considerable species differences in the parental behavior of both sexes among primates (Michael, 1969). Maternal behavior may vary from the specific and intense mother-infant bond seen in pigtail macaques to the general maternal care and interest exhibited by all lemur females to all infants (Jay, 1963; Lancaster, 1976). In the hamadryas baboon, both juvenile and adult males carry and defend young infants (Kummer, 1968), and young juvenile baboons are more likely to seek adult males than to seek their own mothers during times of crisis (DeVore, 1963). Even in the rhesus, adult males sometimes groom immature monkeys, especially siblings, cousins, and orphans, and the young of their female consorts (Michael, 1969).

Crook (1972) reports that of five species of New World monkeys that have minimal physical dimorphism, the male takes extensive care of the young. In fact, the greatest amount of paternal behavior is probably exhibited by the New World monkeys, including the tamarins and other marmosets, which have little physical dimorphism; infants of these species spend a great deal of time clinging to their fathers (Mitchell, 1969). In the titi monkey, the father holds the infant all the time, except when it is being fed (Michael, 1969). In primates, as in lower species, where there is little sex difference in parental role assignments, there is also little sex difference in physical appearance or in social behavior.

However, paternal behavior in primates has to have a different evolutionary (motivational) basis than maternal behavior. Since most primate females mate with many males during each menstrual cycle, paternity is very difficult for the male to determine, so selection pressures would not lead to much paternal behavior. But natural selection will increase paternal behavior in those species whose social organization makes it possible for that behavior to increase the survival of that particular male's offspring. Thus, in species that are monogamous and in species that have only one male in a group, males often show a great deal of paternal behavior; paternal behavior in other species is most often directed towards relatives. For example, the hamadryas baboon male adopts female infants, but these females later become part of his harem (Kummer, 1968). In species that form groups with only one male, upon taking over a new troop, the male attacks the infants (which were not his), but in a well-established troop a male is more tolerant of infants (which probably are his) (Sugiyama, 1966, 1967).

Thus, the role of males in most primate species is simply protective behavior directed toward the group rather than love directed towards any one infant. The male seldom provides the intense contact that the female does. Thus, the sex differences in parental behavior in primates are the result of differences in selection pressure that are caused by differences in reproductive roles. These differences are therefore innate and appear even in animals that have been reared in isolation from other members of their species.

Nevertheless, sex differences in social behaviors may also be affected by experience. Monkeys do treat their infants differentially according to the infant's gender. Macaque mothers hold their male infants more than they do their female infants (G. Jensen, Bobbitt, and Gordon, 1967). However, within a few weeks, this difference reverses, and mothers hold and carry male infants less and punish them more. Mitchell (1968; see also Mitchell and Brandt, 1970) found that rhesus mothers of females held their infants more than did mothers of males at all ages; however, mothers of males also spent more time in vigorous play with their infants, and even sexually presented to them. The only instances of aggression directed towards infants by mothers were seen in mothers of males. And adult males are also more protective of infant females than of infant males (Michael, 1969). Male infants become more independent of their mothers earlier than females do, both because of the greater tendency of males to move away from their mothers (Rosenblum, 1974), and because of the greater attention the male receives from other members of the primate troop (Boelkins, as cited by Mitchell, 1968).

Subprimates.   There are also large sex differences in the social behaviors of lower species. Some species, such as wolves and many species of birds, are not very dimorphic and the pair bond determines most of the social interactions among adults; in these species there are few sex differences. Other social-living species may be more dimorphic. Female rats, for instance, have been reported to do more social grooming than males (Barr et al., 1976). However, other researchers found that males remained closer together in an open field, interpreting that as indicating a greater sociability in males (Quadagno et al., 1972; Syme and Syme, 1974).

Parental behaviors are often dimorphic, but this varies widely across species. In monogamous species with relatively little dimorphism, both males and females care for the young. Males may also help feed (jackals, dogs, coyotes, wolves, and foxes) or defend the young (zebra, musk oxen) (Barash, 1976; Mackey, 1976). In other social living carnivores (lions, hyenas), males may actually be a threat to the young. A number of experiments have demonstrated that male rodents take more time to exhibit maternal behavior (retrieving or grooming) to continually present pups (Quadagno and Rockwell, 1972; Quadagno et al., 1973). However, in gerbils, paternal behaviors are quite extensive and appear even during birth, when the male often tries to sniff the newborn pups (Elwood, 1975).

Summary.   In primates, females of most species show more social and parental behaviors than males. However, those primates with little physical dimorphism (as is true of humans), also show less dimorphism in parental behaviors; males of these species may be extensively involved in the care of the young. Some but not all of these sex differences may be learned, since monkeys treat their children differentially according to their gender. Among subprimates, females generally show more parental behaviors, but sex differences in social behavior depend upon the species, the testing situation, and what particular behavior is being measured.

Learning

Males generally perform better in mazes, while females are better at avoidance learning and delayed response learning. The basis for the maze differences may be the male's greater spatial ability (ability to visualize the relationships among objects in three-dimensional space). Emotional reactions—the tendency to freeze when frightened—may impair the performance of males on active avoidance learning tasks. In this light, performance in mazes, which involves spatial ability, and tasks requiring active avoidance, which involve emotional factors, may well show sex differences.

Types of Learning Tasks.   Before sex differences in learning performances are described, it might be helpful to describe some of the common learning tasks.

In avoidance tasks, the organism is supposed to learn how to prevent the occurrence of some noxious or unpleasant stimulus. In **active-avoidance** learning, the subject must make some response to a signal (such as a light, a bell, or simply the passage of time); if no response is made, then the subject will be shocked. In **two-way active avoidance,** the apparatus is constructed so that the subject shuttles back and forth across a low barrier each time the warning signal occurs. The number of trials required before the animal avoids several times in a row (ten of ten times, or eighteen of twenty) is the usual measure of learning. In **passive avoidance,** the subject is given a noxious stimulus, such as a strong shock, in a given place or after a given response. In order to avoid the shock, the subject must avoid that place or avoid making that particular response. The usual measure of learning is the length of time it takes for the animal to learn to stay away from that place or refrain from making that response.

Maze learning involves a three-dimensional, rat-sized version of the mazes that often appear in puzzle books. The rat is to learn the route from the start box to the goal box, where some reward awaits. The measure of learning is typically the number of tirals required before the animal can do this without making a wrong choice; the measure can also be the total number of errors made in learning the maze. The time to **extinction** may also be measured. In this case, the reward is withdrawn, and the number of trials the animal persists in making the response in the absence of reward is measured. In **delayed-response** learning, the animal is required to inhibit a response for the duration of delay period. The animal may also be required to remember the last response or stimulus received previous to the delay period.

Avoidance Learning and Motivational Factors in Sex Differences in Rodents.   Female rats usually perform better than males in active avoidance learning tasks (Barrett and Ray, 1970; Beatty and Beatty, 1970a, 1970b; Ikard et al., 1972; Nakamura and Anderson, 1962; B. Powell, 1967; Wilcock and Fulker, 1973). This sex difference is seen even when the animals are escaping from frustration — a box where food was but is no longer (Wong, 1977). Despite the apparent consistency of findings, Barrett and Ray (1970) reported that the strain of rats used could affect sex differences, which may account for the reversals in results that are sometimes seen (see J. Gray and Lalljee, 1974; C. Stewart and Brookshire, 1967).

Although females are usually better at active avoidance tasks, males may be better at passive avidance learning. Not only has it been reported that males learn faster than females, but males may also remember the passive avoidance responses for a longer period of time (Beatty, Gregoire, and Parmiter, 1973; Denti and Epstein, 1972).

Some researchers report sex differences in the performances of other types of learning tasks that may also involve either inhibitory processes or motivational differences between the sexes. Kearley, van Hartesveldt, and Woodruff (1974), reported that females were better at a task that involved accurate timing of the response as well as the ability to withhold responding (Differential Reinforcement of a Low rate, or DRL). Beatty and O'Briant (1973) found slower extinction of food-rewarded running in females than in males, but there was no sex difference in the rate of extinction of pressing a bar and getting a reward of food. In light of the second finding, sex differences in exploratory activity may account for the difference in the extinction of the running response. Finally, Schulze (1976) reported better discrimination learning in male rats, but this difference was also attributed to motivational differences between males and females, rather than cognitive ones.

Maze Learning and Spatial Ability in Rodents.   Researchers have consistently found male rats to learn mazes faster than do females rats, and have usually attributed the difference to a greater spatial ability on the part of the male. A large number of studies have found faster maze learning in male rats, and these studies cluster in the 1930s and earlier (Hubbert, 1915; McNemar and Stone, 1932; Tomilin and Stone, 1933—though in only one out of their six mazes—; Tryon, 1931) and again in the 1970s (Barrett and Ray, 1970; Dawson, 1972; Dawson et al., 1973; Kransnoff and Weston, 1976; Stewart et al., 1975). Sex differences were not reported between 1940 and 1970 not because of changes in rats, but because no attempts to find sex differences were made.

Spatial ability can be even more dramatically demonstrated in a task where it is important to learn where in space the reward is, rather than what responses have previously led to that reward. Males have also been reported to do better at this task (Dawson, 1972, Tolman, Ritchie, and Kalish, 1946). Barnes and his colleagues (1966) also reported that males were better at spatial visualization in a water maze task than were females.

But these sex differences are not universally seen. This variability suggests that apparently minor differences in procedure and motivation may be critical, such that a small difference in procedure could create a large difference in results. For example, pretraining or increasing the amount of time allowed for the first trial might eliminate sex differences in exploration and so eliminate sex differences in learning scores (Tomilin and Stone, 1933). Reducing hunger might allow the curiosity motive to become even more important than the food goal, especially for the female (because of the greater incentive value of exploration for females), so that in this case, the females will do even better than the males (Corey, 1930). Thus, the sex differences usually found in mazes might not reflect spatial ability at all.

Other Species. Avoidance learning in cats gives the opposite results as in rats. One study reported that male cats learned an active avoidance task more rapidly than did the female ones (Andy, Peeler, and Foshee, 1967).

Several differences in learning performance have appeared in primates, and some appear to be fairly reliable. Female monkeys cease responding (habituate) to a repeated stimulus more rapidly than do males (Sackett, as cited by Phoenix and McCauley, 1974). The female rhesus monkey may be able to learn a cue discrimination task with fewer errors than the male (McDowell and Brown, 1963). Goldman and her colleagues (1974) and McDowell, Brown, and McTee (1960) found that females performed a delayed response better, and improved faster with practice. However, the difference may be caused only by the greater ease with which males are distracted.

Summary and Interpretations. Some reliable sex differences have been found in learning, but the interpretation of the differences is not clear. Female rats and male cats do better at active avoidance tasks, but male rats are better at passive avoidance learning. Male rats have better maze learning scores, but female primates are better at delayed response tasks.

At the present time, it seems quite possible that some of the differences are the result of differences in motivation. In fearful situations, male rats may be more apt to freeze; thus, males would be better at passive avoidance and females better at active avoidance tasks. The difference in maze performances may be attributable to differences in activity levels or exploratory tendencies, as well as to differences in the types of responses made to fear. And male monkeys may be more easily distracted.

On the other hand, differences in reproductive roles may have led to differences in learning styles. For example, Buffery and Gray (1972) have claimed that sex differences in emotionality and sex differences in spatial ability are both the result of natural selection pressures. For example, the male in his reproductive role wanders more, searching for females or food, and this would require good spatial ability.

Sensory Abilities

From what has aleady been said, it seems obvious that males and females do not produce the same visual, olfactory, or auditory stimuli. It is identifiably a cock pheasant, a bull frog, or a billy goat from the signals it produces, distinctively different from those of the females of the same species. Since the sexes produce or send out different stimuli, it might also be the case that they differ in their ability to receive stimuli. There may also be differences in **preferences.** That is, two organisms may be equally **sensitive** to color, but they each may prefer different colors.

Some sex differences in sensitivities have been reported. Pietras and Moulton (1974) found that male rats generally have lower olfactory sensitivity thesholds, thus being more sensitive to at least some types of scents. In addition, female rats have lower preference thresholds for the ingestion of salt and sugar solutions (Appendix B). Archer (1975) also reviewed several studies that suggested that females are more sensitive to shock, since they make escape responses to lower levels of shock than do males and also flinch at lower shock levels (Beatty and Beatty, 1970b; Fessler and Beatty, 1976).

One excellent study found sex differences in the auditory sensitivity of the tree frog (Narins and Capronica, 1976). The female tree frog can hear only one part of the male tree frog's vocal call, while the male frog can hear only another part. So the call that is a threat call to other males is not detected by the females at all.

A study involving sex differences in the color vision of squirrel monkeys (G. Jacobs, 1977) is even more interesting. When the monkeys were adapted to light (their eyes became adjusted to the brightness of the room) females were significantly more sensitive to red than males. This difference was so large that there was no overlap between the groups; one could determine the sex of an animal just by observing its response to a dim red light. When the animals were dark adapted (eyes adjusted to the dark), however, the sex difference disappeared. Therefore, either the retinas or the brains of these male and female monkeys must be differently organized.

Thus, some evidence suggests that in several species, males and females smell, taste, feel, hear, and see things somewhat differently. If this is also true in humans, what effects do you think the differences might have on behavior?

SUMMARY AND IMPLICATIONS FOR HUMAN SEXUAL DIMORPHISM

Looking over the phylogenetic scale, there are some interesting commonalities with regard to sexually dimorphic traits, and very great variability from species to species and even from strain to strain within a species. However, it is generally true that males are larger and stronger, more aggressive, and more concerned with dominance interactions than females. When reversals in aggression and dominance do occur, it is generally in species in which the female is larger than the male. However, even when not the larger sex, the female can at times be very aggressive, particularly to other females or in defense of young.

Female rodents are more active than male rodents, but differences in other species are not clear-cut, and there is not as yet convincing evidence of greater female or male fearfulness for any species. Females seem more often to be concerned with social interactions, and are more often nurturant than are males, even when it is clear that they did not learn that behavior from their mother.

There are consistent differences in learning performances. These differences may be related more to motivational differences than to cognitive differences, however. Some evidence suggests sex differences in sensory abilities, though few experiments have been done so far.

Thus, sex-linked and sex-limited traits in humans must have evolved because of differing sexual and natural selection pressures exerted on our human ancestors. Perhaps our female ancestors, by way of sexual selection, exerted pressure on males, preferring larger, stronger, hairier, and more aggressive males. Natural selection would also have had differential effects on the sexes as long as the roles they played were different. If males hunted and did more extensive gathering of food over a larger range, while females stayed closer to home while caring for children, then these differences in reproductive roles might have resulted in the development of sex-linked and sex-limited traits.

The cross-species similarities suggest that in humans sex differences might be particularly likely to appear in aggression and dominance, nurturance and affiliation, some sensory abilities, and in some types of cognitive performance that might be affected by spatial ability. However, since the physical dimorphism in humans is small, behavioral dimorphism is expected to be small. Furthermore, the more overlap there was in the reproductive roles of our ancestors, the fewer sex differences we should expect to see. For example, females may be particularly aggressive towards other females in those species in which the male exhibits much paternal behavior, because the female has more to lose in such species by the loss of the male (Barash, 1976).

But the cross-species data also suggest that what we owe to our ancestors may not be absolute differences, but biases; the sexes may differ in their preparedness to make certain responses in certain situations because of our evolutionary history. The data also suggest that sex differences are very much a function of the particular response measured, the situation, and the past experience of both sexes.

Returning to our closest relatives, the infra-human primates, it is obvious that there is no single primate society, but rather that all types of groups can be found. However, it is also obvious that whenever there is sexual reproduction, there are some sex differences in both behavior and appearance, and that these differences have utility both for the ability of the individual to produce offspring and for the survival of the social group. Is this true for humans in today's societies? And is this, therefore, one reason we have two sexes with different behaviors and appearances?

KEY TERMS AND CONCEPTS

Monomorphy and androgyny
Infrahuman
Natural selection

Pheromones
Sexual selection
Female choice or female preference

Rapacious
Precocious
Passerine
Lordosis
Mounting
Mounting score
Intromission
Ejaculation
Dominance hierarchy
Activity wheel

Open field
Emotionality
Active avoidance
Two-way active avoidance
Passive avoidance
Maze learning
Extinction
Delayed response
Sensitivity vs. preference

QUESTIONS ON KEY ISSUES

1. What are the advantages of sexual over asexual reproduction?
2. Why are sex differences so common— what utility do they have?
3. How can both natural and sexual selection pressures lead to sex differences?
4. What are the most common physical sexual dimorphisms?
5. What are the most likely conclusions to be reached (at least at this time) about the most typical sex differences found across species in each of the following areas: sexual behavior; aggression and dominance; activity, emotionality, and curiosity; nurturance and other social behaviors; learning; and sensory sensitivities and preferences?
6. How might sexual or natural selection lead to each of the differences listed in the previous question?
7. What implications do the data in this chapter have for sex differences among humans? (Note: The answer to this question is only partially covered in this chapter; you must also answer by saying what you think.)

CHAPTER 4

Inductive Hormones and Sex Differences in the Brain

THE NATURE OF THE INDUCTIVE EFFECT

Sex differences in sex hormones affect sex differences in the brain and behavior in two ways. The sex hormones can have both inductive and activational effects on the brain, both of which produce behavioral biases. The inductive effects of sex hormones occur early in the organism's life, usually before birth (**prenatal**) or just after birth (**neonatal**). The sex hormones present during this crucial **perinatal** period (both prenatal and neonatal) of an organism's life, when its brain is still developing, may actually determine the shape of and interconnections within and among brain cells. The activational effects of hormones usually occur after fetal development, including that of the brain, has been completed. Once the organism is developed, the level of the sex hormones circulating in the bloodstream has an activational effect on various parts of the brain and on other organs by either increasing or inhibiting their normal actions. Since the activational effects of the sex hormones depend upon the circulating levels of hormones, whenever the levels change, the behavioral biases will also change. Thus, the inductive effect is assumed to refer to relatively permanent or irreversible effects on the brain and behavior, while the activational effect can vary from moment to moment as the levels of hormones vary.

In this chapter, the evidence for an inductive effect of sex hormones upon the brains and behaviors of human and subhuman animals will be presented. The major purpose of this chapter is to show how sex differences may be affected by the differences in hormones present before and after birth. Male fetuses have relatively more androgens than do female fetuses—does this have any permanent effects on the brain and on behavioral differences between the sexes? Individual mothers also vary in the quantity of sex hormones present in the bloodstream. Could this be part of the individual variability in sexually dimorphic behaviors? If hormones affect developing brains, what might we be doing to our children by giving pregnant women artificial estrogens or progestins to prevent abortions?

Cautions and Implications of the Research

Conclusions based on the data presented in this chapter are the most controversial ones in the whole area of sex differences. Many researchers doubt that hormones can have any major effects on the brains of infra-human fetal organisms; these researchers often deny that hormones could have any effects at all on human brains. Instead, any apparent inductive effects of hormones on human brains are attributed by these researchers to experimental bias, misinterpretation of data, and insufficient control. Because of this controversy, and because the emotionalism can lead to inadvertent biasing of data (the Rosenthal effect), any conclusions in this research must be regarded as tentative. And even tentative conclusions are warranted only if there is some consistency across data from different species and different experimenters. Otherwise they must be rejected.

However, if perinatal hormones do in fact have inductive effects on the brain that are visible in behavior, the implications are tremendous. Since the sexes have different concentrations of perinatal hormones, the existence of inductive effects could lead us to conclude that the brains of males and females are permanently different. This means that if a behavior can be demonstrated to be affected by perinatal hormones, any sex difference in that behavior would have to be attributed, at least in part, to a biological bias. It might also mean that some degree of individual and species differences in sexually dimorphic behaviors might be due to variations in perinatal hormones. There are in fact large individual differences in perinatal hormones in humans. Might this have any behavioral consequences? And if male brains can be changed into female brains by manipulating perinatal hormones, then we can produce male animals who act feminine, or animals that are androgynous. The same might someday be true of the human animal. Would this be desirable?

One problem unique to this area is that inductive and activational hormones interact, and conclusions may depend upon the particular way the interaction is interpreted. As one example, Dawson, Cheung, and Lau (1973) castrated (removed gonads from) male and female rats on the first day after birth, thus depriving them of the normal neonatal and inductive hormones. In the next two days, estrogen was injected into the male rats and testosterone into the females, reversing the normal sex difference in neonatal hormones. The activity of these animals as adults in an activity wheel were then compared to that of intact (uncastrated), normal controls. Among the control subjects, the mean number of revolutions of the activity wheel in a twenty-minute period was 20.3 for the males and 90.6 for the females, a tremendous sex difference. The activity score of the males injected with estrogen was 27.0, and that of the testosterone-injected, or androgenized, females was 17.0. Thus, the two neonatally treated groups reversed the usual sex difference in activity.

But the procedure meant that both activational and inductive hormones were different for the various groups, since the controls still had their gonads to produce activational hormones and the experimental groups did not. How much of the difference between the experimental and control groups was the result of a change in neonatal hormones, and how much was the result of the presence or absence of gonads? Because of the procedure this is not clear.

The experimenters felt that these data showed that neonatal hormones affected the balance of activating (or arousing) and inhibiting processes of the brain, with testosterone inhibiting and estrogen permanently increasing the arousing processes of the brain. Whether or not their conclusion was warranted depends on how the interaction between the effects of activational and inductive hormones is interpreted.

Such problems as the one just described are common in this area of research because inductive hormones do interact with activational hormones. Even if the experimental animals had not been castrated, perinatal hormones will affect the gonads; therefore, the adult, activational levels of hormones will still differ from normal in these animals. Also, some inductive effects of hormones on behavior are visible only in the presence of appropriate levels of appropriate activational hormones. And some inductivelike effects may be exerted by pubertal hormones, so the timing of castrations of experimental and control animals can be crucial and the effects can be open to different interpretations. Finally, since humans are never castrated for the sake of research, these types of problems can make human data difficult to interpret.

Inductive Effects on the Brain and Other Organs

The effects of perinatally presented hormones on the brain are usually inferred from changes in behavior. Androgens introduced in the perinatal period, for example, permanently affect the brain, making some behaviors more likely to appear or easier to learn than would be the case for an animal whose brain had not been exposed to androgens during its development. The type and quantity of hormones present during the critical period when the brain is being formed seem to determine the way the brain is formed and thus affect behavior. These behavioral effects may be the result of permanent changes in the sensitivity of the brain to later activational effects of hormones; without perinatal androgens, for example, later injections of androgens are much less likely to increase aggression in the adult animal. The behavioral effects may also be the result of changes in the actual shape and interconnections of nerve cells in the brain, changes that have actually been seen by direct microscopic examination. The perinatal hormones may also exert permanent effects on the metabolism of the animal's brain. These three types of effects of hormones on the brain could obviously have dramatic effects on behavior, as will be seen.

Organs other than the brain are also affected by inductive hormones, and sometimes changes in these other organs affect our conclusions about how perinatal hormones might have changed the brain. Perinatal hormones can permanently affect not only the gonads and genital organs, but also the liver and the adrenal cortex (Gustafsson et al., 1974; Maüsle and Fickinger, 1976, Ramaley, 1974).

The Inductive Effect on Behavior: Chapter Survey

In this chapter, data relevant to four possible conclusions about inductive hormones will be presented. Both male and female neural systems are present in every developing brain. Our first conclusion, then, is that *the brain is not organized along a masculine-feminine continuum; instead, "every mammalian nervous system contains separate neural systems for the mediation of masculine and feminine modes of conduct"* (italics added) (Goy, 1972, p. 50). The inductive effects of these hormones upon the brain affects only the probability that certain behaviors will appear in a given set of circumstances. This means that both males and females will show both male and female behaviors, though with different frequencies or rates of occurrence. Also, this means that masculinity is obviously not the opposite of femininity; since both are separate response tendencies, one need not oppose the other.

Since inductive hormones affect only the probability of responding in one way or another, these effects of hormones are very likely to be specific to the particular stimuli present, and to the particular types of behavioral measures used. Also, since the effects of the hormones are specific to a situation, the effects may be altered by the animal's past experiences in that particular situation. Our second conclusion is that even though the brain may be permanently changed by hormones, *the effects are often situation specific and may be overridden by particular kinds of experiences.*

The effect of androgens is largely to suppress female behavioral tendencies, which leads to the third conclusion. *Perinatal androgen injections will **masculinize** females (make them more likely to show male behaviors): perinatal castrations will **feminize** males.* Whether they are supplied by an experimenter injecting hormones (**exogenous,** from the outside), or by the animal's own testes (**endogenous,** from the inside), androgens masculinize behaviors. However, dosage may be important; too much androgen can have effects similar to the absence of androgens—both may be feminizing.

The distinction between male and female behaviors implies the fourth conclusion. In general, *only if a behavior is dimorphic will it be affected by inductive hormones.* In other words, if a behavior is more likely to be exhibited by males than by females, neonatal androgens will increase the likelihood of any animal exhibiting that behavior. Perinatal hormones affect only sexually dimorphic behaviors, and most sexually dimorphic behaviors are masculinized by perinatal androgens. If aggression, for example, is exhibited more often by males than by females in a certain species, then perinatal androgens should increase the tendency of both males and females to be aggressive.

In order to allow you to evaluate these conclusions, this chapter reviews research on hormone-sensitive behaviors, behaviors whose frequencies may be altered by perinatal hormones. These behaviors include sexual gestures, aggression, parental behaviors, social behaviors, emotional responses, and learning. Taste preferences are also affected by neonatal hormones (food tastes differently to males and females?). But this data is presented separately, in Appendix B. If these behaviors can be shown to be sensitive to hormones in lower species, they may be dimorphic in humans also and the dimorphism may have some biological basis. Human data will be evaluated with that in mind.

INFRA-HUMAN RESEARCH

This type of research is typically done by either castrating male animals just after birth or by injecting hormones either into the mother before the organism is born or into the neonate itself shortly after birth. Sometimes researchers inject hormone antagonists, such as testosterone or estrogen antagonists. These antagonists seem to oppose the action of the hormones normally present, so their effect is usually similar to the effect of hormone withdrawal caused by castration. In species such as primates, dogs, and guinea pigs, the hormones or antagonists must be given to the mother in order to affect later adult behaviors, because after birth the brain can no longer be permanently changed by hormones. In other species, such as rats and mice, the brain is still developing for at least ten days after birth, so injection or castration during those ten days can still have permanent effects on later behaviors.

After changing the hormones, experimenters assess the effects of the perinatal hormones by comparing the behaviors of the altered animals to untreated controls. In order to control for any possible inductive changes in gonads that would change activational hormones—changes that may confuse the interpretation of the results—all the animals may be castrated some time before the behavioral testing. Sometimes all of the animals are then given a constant amount of activational hormones because some behaviors, such as sexual behaviors in subprimates, will not appear at all without activational hormones. In order to look for the effect of inductive hormones upon sexual responses, all animals must be given hormone injections for the behavior to appear and differences to be measurable.

In Tables 4.1 through 4.5, summaries of this research are presented. In these tables, the behavior of the various perinatally treated groups is compared to a group of normal animals of the same sex, usually when both groups have been castrated and given the same replacement (activational) hormones for the test. In reading these tables and the accompanying discussions, you should always keep in mind that the effects will depend upon the particular species involved, the testing situation, and the particular way that the behavior is being measured, and sometimes upon the chromosomal gender of the animals. Some details and conclusions, along with some specific examples of effects and implications, will now be discussed.

Sexual Behavior

As would be expected, the more dimorphic the sexual behavior, the greater the effect inductive hormones have on that behavior. Thus, inductive hormones have consistent effects on intromission and ejaculation, since these behaviors are dimorphic in all species. Inductive hormones also affect mounting behavior in most species and lordosis in most subprimates. However, mounting in rats and mice and female sexual presentation postures in primates are less neurally dimorphic in these than in other species, that is, these behaviors are less affected by perinatal hormone levels. Also, because both male and female sexual behaviors are used in dominance and other nonsexual social interactions in primates, changes in their frequency of appearance in those species may not always reflect changes in sexual motivation.

Androgens and Sexual Behaviors. As can be seen in Table 4.1, the species differences described above are clearly seen. Perinatal injections of androgens increase intromission and ejaculation in females of all species (which could be because their clitoris is increased to near penis size), and increase

TABLE 4.1

EFFECTS OF PERINATAL HORMONES ON VARIOUS SEXUAL BEHAVIORS

Behavior and Hormone	Species and Gender	Effect and Comments	References
Mounting and Androgens	Female rats and mice	Neonatal testosterone does not increase this behavior; it is not sexually dimorphic.	Carter, Clemens, and Holkema (1972); Sachs et al. (1973); Schoelch-Krieger and Barfield (1975); Ward (1969); Whalen et al. (1969)
	Male and female dogs and hamsters	Prenatal testosterone increases mounting in females, and neonatal castration decreases mounting in males.	Beach et al. (1972); Eaton (1970); Payne (1976)
	Female primates, ewes, and guinea pigs	Prenatal testosterone increases mounting.	Clarke, 1977; Goy, 1968, 1970; Goy and Goldfoot, 1974, 1975
Intromission, Ejaculation, and Androgens	Male and female rats	Neonatal castration decreases these behaviors in males and neonatal testosterone increases them in females.	Feder, Phoenix, and Young (1966); Grady, Phoenix, and Young (1965); Pfaff et al. (1974); Whalen and Edwards (1967)
Lordosis and Androgens	Female rats and mice	Neonatal testosterone decreases lordosis.	Brown-Grant (1975); Carter et al. (1972); G. Harris (1964); Pfaff et al. (1974)
	Male and female dogs	Prenatal androgen decreases lordosis in females and neonatal castration increases lordosis in males.	Beach et al., 1972
	Male and female hamsters	Neonatal castration increases lordosis in males, and neonatal testosterone decreases it in both.	Carter and Landauer (1975); Eaton (1970); Payne (1976, 1977)
	All females, including humans	Perinatal androgen delays puberty.	Brown-Grant and Sherwood (1971); Goy (1970); G. Harris (1964); Money and Schwartz (1976); Pfaff et al. (1974); Whitsett and Vandenbergh (1975)
	Male subprimates	Neonatal castration increases all types of female sexual behaviors; males may be able to ovulate if given ovarian transplants.	G. Harris (1974); Pfaff et al. (1974); Pfeiffer (1936)

Table 4.1 (*Continued*)

Behavior and Hormone	Species and Gender	Effect and Comments	References
	Female primates	Prenatal testosterone has no effect; this behavior is not sexually dimorphic in primates.	Goy and Goldfoot, 1975
Other Hormones Decrease All Types of Sexual Behaviors	Subprimates	Estrogen decreases male and female types of sexual behavior; progesterone decreases male sexual behavior in males.	Diamond (1966); Diamond, Llacuna, and Wong (1973); G. Harris and Levine (1965); Hendricks and Weltin (1976); S. Levine and Mullins (1964); Regenstein, Williams, and Rose (1975); Soulairac and Soulairac (1974); Vale, Ray, and Vale (1973); Whalen and Nadler (1963); J. Wilson and Wilson (1943)
More Androgens than Normal Male Levels		Decrease mounting and increase lordosis in male rats, but this decreases lordosis in male hamsters.	Diamond et al., 1973; Payne (1976, 1977); Pollack and Sachs (1975)

mounting in (masculinize) females of all species except for mice and rats. Perinatal androgen injections also decrease lordosis in (defeminize) subprimate females, but not primates. Neonatal castrations decrease all male sexual behaviors in (demasculinize) males of all species, except for mounting in mice and rats. Neonatal castrations of males also increase lordosis in (feminize) those animals. The earlier in life hormone injections or castrations occur—starting from the first hour of birth—the greater their effects (Pfaff et al., 1974).

However, the observation that has the most implications concerns sexual behavior in hamsters (Payne, 1976, 1977). In these animals, males display lordosis fairly readily, and androgen injections suppress lordosis in both males and females. This implies that, in some sense, the males' brains are normally not completely masculinized. But higher or more prolonged doses are required to suppress lordosis than to increase mounting. Thus, with low doses of perinatal androgens, a female can be masculinized (show more mounting) without being defeminized (reducing lordosis), thus producing an androgynous or at least a bisexual animal.

Inductive Effects of Hormones Other Than Androgens. Some difficulty arises in interpreting the inductive effects of androgens, such as testosterone, upon sexual behavior because many different hormones and drugs can have similar inductive effects. Also, in view of the effects of female sex hormones, it should not be assumed that the ovaries have no inductive effects on sexual behaviors (see Table 4.1). Still, the nature and details of their effects are not as yet clear.

Since so many types of hormones other than sex hormones and even drugs such as tranquillizers can exert inductive effects on sexual behaviors, these effects are obviously not specific to androgens or even to sex hormones.

Summary and Implications for Humans. Any alteration, whether an increase or a decrease, in the level of perinatal hormones that can change the developing brain can permanently affect sexual behavior. As would be expected, these hormonal variations have more effect on behaviors that are more sexually dimorphic. In species such as primates, sheep, and hamsters, mounting scores are more sensitive to perinatal hormones than lordosis scores, but in the rat and mouse, lordosis is more hormone-sensitive. In dogs, both types of behavior are dimorphic and both are hormone-sensitive. And in all species, intromission and ejaculation are dimorphic, so these behaviors depend upon inductive hormonal effects on the brain and the penis.

Although the species differences are puzzling, they must be interpreted before one can generalize to humans. For example, lordosis seems to be less dimorphic—and less sensitive to neonatal hormones—in hamsters than in rats. This difference may reflect the end point of the evolutionary process that made the female hamster more aggressive and larger than the male. This process may also have made the male hamster more feminine than the male rat. More androgens than normal can defeminize the male hamster (decrease lordosis), while high doses may actually feminize the male rat (increase lordosis; see Table 4.1). Will androgyny in animals always imply that the brain of the male was not completely masculinized in the perinatal period, as it seems to with the hamster? What about androgyny in humans?

Aggression

In most species the male is the larger and more aggressive gender, so perinatal androgens should increase aggression. The inductive effect of androgen in this case is apparently to *"sensitize* the central nervous [brain] structures which mediate aggressive behavior to the action of *testosterone* in adulthood" (J. Gray and Drewett, in press, italics theirs). For example, neonatal androgenization of male or female mice caused them to begin fighting sooner than mice not androgenized when both groups were given a series of testosterone injections (vom Saal, Svare, and Gandelman, 1976). Neonatal androgenization apparently increased the sensitivity of the brain to the aggression promoting effects of later testosterone injections.

But hamsters and primates are again exceptional. In these species, sex differences in aggression are more related to inductive than to activational hormones. Therefore, sex differences in these species involve more than just a changed sensitivity of the brain to the aggression promoting effects of androgens. This would imply that neonatal hormones caused physical differences in the brain of these animals, such that aggression is organized differently in male and female brains.

Subprimates. In rats and mice, castration of the male on the first day of life reduces aggression levels to below those shown by normal females. In these

TABLE 4.2 ⎯⎯⎯⎯⎯⎯⎯⎯⎯⎯⎯⎯⎯⎯⎯⎯⎯

INDUCTIVE EFFECTS OF GONADAL HORMONES ON VARIOUS AGGRESSIVE
BEHAVIORS

Behavior	Species and Gender	Effects and Comments	References
Within- Species Aggression	Male rats	Neonatal castration reduces aggression.	Baenninger (1974)
	Female rats	Neonatal testosterone and neonatal estrogen makes about 15 percent of subjects hyperaggressive.	K. B. Hoyenga and Hoyenga (1977)
	Female mice	Perinatal androgen and estrogen increase all types of aggression.	Bronson and Desjardins (1970); D. A. Edwards (1968, 1969); Erpino (1975); Quadagno, Briscoe, and Quadagno (1977); vom Saal et al. (1976)
	Male mice	Neonatal estrogen increases aggression.	Quadagno et al., 1977
	Male and female hamsters	Neonatal testosterone increases aggression and makes adult aggression more sensitive to activational androgens.	Carter and Landauer (1975); Payne (1974b, 1976, 1977); Payne and Swanson (1973)
	Female primates and sheep	Neonatal testosterone increases aggressive behaviors.	Clarke (1977); Eaton, Goy, and Phoenix (1973); Goy (1970)
Pup Killing	Male and female rats	Decreased by neonatal castration in males and increased by neonatal testosterone in females.	K. Rosenberg and Sherman (1974, 1975a, 1975b)
Territorial Scent Marking	Male and female gerbils and dogs	Decreased by neonatal castration in males and increased by neonatal testosterone in females.	Beach (1975); Turner (1975)

animals, testosterone injected during the aggression tests will have little or no effect on their behaviors, which is very different from what is the case with normal males. Thus, without neonatal androgen, adult androgen had no effects on aggression. Neonatal hormone injections also affect females. Both female rats and mice are made more aggressive by neonatal injections of either testosterone or estrogen. These effects and others are summarized in Table 4.2.

However, different types of aggressive behaviors in rats are differentially sensitive to neonatal testosterone (Barr et al., 1976). Neonatal androgen, endogenous or exogenous, affected the tendency of one animal to attack another, but neonatal castrations of males or injections of testosterone into females did not affect the frequency of aggressive or submissive gestures.

Hamsters and Primates. With the hamster, aggression seems to have a somewhat different hormonal basis than in the rat or the mouse, related perhaps to the high level of female aggression. Neonatally injected testosterone increases aggression in both sexes, even in the absence of activational androgens. In fact, the neonatally androgenized male hamster becomes as aggressive as the normal, sexually unreceptive female.

In rhesus monkeys, prenatal testosterone given to females increases the frequency of threat and rough-and-tumble play to a level intermediate between that shown by normal females and normal males, as can be see in Figure 4.1. When the females monkeys whose behavior is shown in Figure 4.1 reached adulthood, they were castrated and compared to a female control group. When the neonatally masculinized females were given estrogen, they were more aggressive than were the controls; this difference in aggression was even greater when both groups were given testosterone.

Summary and Implications for Humans. The effect of androgens on the brain seems even more powerful with respect to aggression than for sexual behavior. Surprisingly, aggression seems more sensitive to inductive hormones than is sexual behavior. In all species tested, perinatal testosterone, endogenous or exogenous, increased adult levels of aggression, usually in both genders. Estrogen may also increase aggression. This suggests that any sexual dimorphism in human aggression may also be partially the result of a biological bias and a sex difference in the brain due to the higher levels of prenatal androgens in males.

In most but not all species, neonatal androgens simply made the adult brain more sensitive to the aggression promoting effects of testosterone. But in hamsters, the normal male could be masculinized—be made even more aggressive—by neonatal hormones, just as the male could be masculinized in sexual behavior. And in normal and androgenized monkeys and in normal hamsters, sex differences in aggression do not require differences in activational hormones, implying that the brain got "wired" differently in males and females. Still, we must be cautious in generalizing; these effects are often very specific to the particular experimental situation used and the particular aggressive behavior measured.

FIGURE 4.1 _____

AVERAGE FREQUENCY OF PERFORMANCE OF STEREOTYPED THREAT EXPRESSIONS AND OF ROUGH-AND-TUMBLE PLAY

R. W. Goy, "Early Hormonal Influences on the Development of Sexual and Sex-Related Behavior." In F. O. Schmitt (ed.), *The Neurosciences: Second Study Program* (New York: Rockefeller University Press, 1970), p. 202. C. H. Phoenix, "Prenatal Testosterone in the Nonhuman Primate and Its Consequences for Behavior." In R. C. Friedman, R. M. Richart, and R. L. Vande Wiele (eds.), *Sex Differences in Behavior* (New York: Wiley, 1974), p. 23. Reprinted by permission.

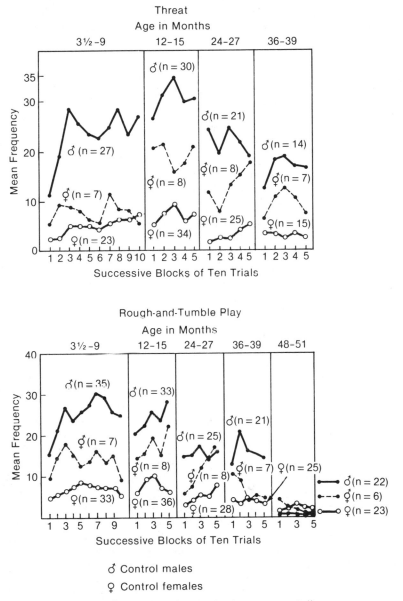

Threat

Age in Months

Successive Blocks of Ten Trials

Rough-and-Tumble Play

Age in Months

Successive Blocks of Ten Trials

♂ Control males

♀ Control females

♂̟ Females given testosterone prenatally

TABLE 4.3

INDUCTIVE EFFECTS OF GONADAL HORMONES ON VARIOUS PARENTAL
BEHAVIORS

Behavior	Species and Gender	Effects and Comments	References
All Parental Behaviors	Male rats and mice	Neonatal castration increases these behaviors, as do neonatal injections of a testosterone antagonist.	Lisk (1972); McCullough, Quadagno, and Goldman (1974); Neuman, Steinbeck, and Hahn (1970); Rosenberg and Herrenkohl (1976)
Nest Building	Female rabbits	Prenatal testosterone decreases this behavior.	Anderson, Zarrow, and Denenberg (1970)
	Female hamsters	Neonatal testosterone has no effect, even though the behavior is sexually dimorphic.	Richards (1969)
Retrieval of Pups	Female rats	Neonatal testosterone decreases retrieving; no effect on other types of parental behaviors.	Bridges, Zarrow, and Denenberg (1973); Quadagno and Rockwell (1972)

Parental and Other Social Behaviors

Social behaviors refer to nonaggressive interactions among members of the same species. The most frequently occurring type of social behavior is the interaction of parents with offspring. Since some aspects of parental behavior are dimorphic (see Quadagno and Rockwell, 1972), they also ought to be sensitive to perinatal hormones. The same may be true of some other social interactions.

Neonatal androgens, either endogenous or exogenous, seem to reduce the frequency of typical female behaviors, as shown in Table 4.3. Removal of androgens by castration from males should then increase female parental behaviors, and it does. Thus, some parental behaviors may be sensitive to inductive hormones, at least in rats, rabbits and mice. Other species have not yet been tested.

Some work on other social behaviors has been done with rats and primates. Quadagno, Shryne, Anderson, and Gorski (1972) found that neonatal androgenization increased at least one type of social behavior in female rats to a level above that of the normal male, reversing the typical sex difference, and neonatal castration

FIGURE 4.2

AVERAGE FREQUENCY OF PERFORMANCE OF PURSUIT PLAY AND PLAY INITIATION

R. W. Goy, "Early Hormonal Influences on the Development of Sexual and Sex-Related Behavior." In F. O. Schmitt (ed.), *The Neurosciences: Second Study* Program (New York: Rockefeller University Press, 1970), pp. 202 and 203. Reprinted by permission.

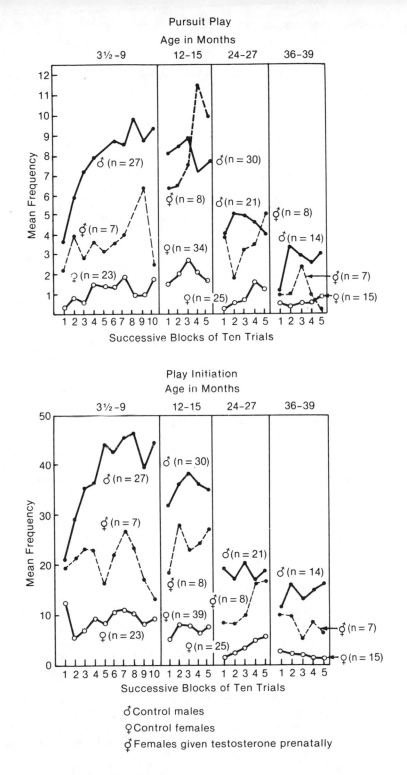

Pursuit Play

Age in Months

Play Initiation

Age in Months

♂ Control males
♀ Control females
⚥ Females given testosterone prenatally

TABLE 4.4

EFFECTS OF PERINATAL MANIPULATION OF HORMONE CONCENTRATIONS ON
ACTIVITY AND EMOTIONAL BEHAVIOR

Behavior	Species and Gender	Effect and Comment	References
Open Field Activity	Male and female rats and hamsters	Neonatal castration of males increases activity; neonatal testosterone or estrogen decreases activity in females; neonatal testosterone injections increase activity in intact male rats.	Archer (1975); Blizard et al. (1975); J. Gray (1971b); J. Gray, Drewett, and Lalljee (1975); Magalhães and Carlini (1974); Pfaff and Zigmand (1971); Phillips and Deol (1977); J. Stewart et al. (1975); Swanson (1966, 1967, 1969)
Wheel running	Male rats	Neonatal estrogen increases activity.	Dawson et al. (1973)
	Female rats	Neonatal androgen decreases activity.	Dawson et al. (1973)
Defecation in the Open Field	Rodents	Perinatal hormone changes have no consistent effects—effects depend on the situation and strain of animal tested.	Archer (1975); Blizard et al. (1975); J. Gray (1971b); J. Gray et al. (1975)

of the male decreased the sociability of male pairs. In the primate, Phoenix (1974), Goy, (1970), and Goy and Goldfoot (1974) have found that such sexually dimorphic behaviors as play initiation and chasing (pursuit play) were also affected by prenatal testosterone. As can be seen in Figure 4.2, the neonatally androgenized female showed these behaviors at a frequency in between that of normal males and normal females.

But the data are as yet too sketchy to warrant conslusions other than that some aspects of social behavior may be hormone-sensitive. There is a possibility, then, that some sexually dimorphic social behaviors in humans might be affected by sex differences in neonatal hormones.

Emotional Responses and Activity

As we saw in the previous chapter, only in some species is there any evidence of sexual dimorphisms in emotionality. Among rodents there is a sex difference in the type of response made when frightened—females flee and males freeze. Female rodents are also more active than males both in the open field and in the activity wheel. Since these behaviors are dimorphic, they should also be sensitive to inductive hormones.

Activity. As shown in Table 4.4, neonatal hormone injections can change open field and wheel activity. Dawson, Cheung, and Lau (1973) have interpreted this data to mean that normal male levels of perinatal testosterone permanently inhibit the brain, whereas perinatal estrogen permanently increases arousal levels.

While perinatal androgens seem to reduce activity in the open field and in the activity wheel, the effects of estrogen seems to depend upon the type of test employed. Estrogen decreases open field activity but increases wheel activity. Since hunger also increases wheel activity but has little effect on open field activity in a quiet environment, field activity may reflect emotionality and exploration, while wheel activity may reflect metabolic requirements. So the difference in the hormonal effects on these two types of activity may reflect different hormonal effects on energy balance and reactivity to external stimuli, rather than on the activation or inhibition of the brain.

Emotionality. Since behavior in the open field has been changed by inductive hormones, this has sometimes been interpreted as indicating emotional changes. For example, activity in the open field has sometimes been viewed as being inversely related to emotionality. In that case, the research indicates that both inductive estrogen and normal male levels of testosterone increased emotionality (decreased open field activity) in males and females. Defecation scores in the open field have also been sometimes been interpreted as measuring emotionality. However, the inductive effect of hormones here seems to be much less reliable and consistent than their effects upon activity scores, as indicated in Table 4.4.

In view of the lack of consistency, the inductive effects of hormones upon emotionality cannot as yet be reliably differentiated from inductive effects on curiosity, reactivity to stimuli, or food consumption. And yet, in view of the consistent effects of neonatal hormones upon open field activity, we must conclude that at least one of those motives or responses is being affected by those hormones.

Learning

Money (1971) reported positive effects of prenatal androgens on human IQ, and Buffery and Gray (1972) pointed out the superior maze performances of male rats, and the superior active-avoidance performances of female rats (but not cats). In view of these dimorphisms, some effects of inductive hormones would not be surprising, but remarkably little work has been done.

Avoidance. Several researchers, as Table 4.5 indicates, have found that avoidance learning varies as perinatal androgens are varied. There may be, however, dosage effects, with both very high levels and the complete absence of neonatal testosterone increasing active-avoidance performances.

One recent study has suggested that the behavioral effects of neonatal testosterone may not involve learning ability. Phillips and Deol (1977) found that neonatal testosterone facilitated active-avoidance learning in intact male rats, but had no effect on their passive-avoidance performances. However, these neonatally androgenized males were also more active than normal males, and were more reactive or sensitive to shock. So neonatal androgens may affect motivational responses rather than learning ability. In fact, comparing Table 4.4 to Table 4.5 reveals that neonatal hormones often have parallel effects on activity and active-avoidance performance.

Maze Learning. As can be seen in Table 4.5, maze learning appears to be affected by neonatal hormones in rats. The maze learning error scores of an-

TABLE 4.5 _____

INDUCTIVE EFFECTS OF NEONATAL HORMONES ON EXPLORATION AND ON PERFORMANCE OF LEARNING TASKS

Behavior	Species and Gender	Effect and Comment	References
Active Avoidance	Intact male rats	Either an androgen-antagonist or androgens increase the behavior.	Beatty and Beatty (1970a, 1970b); Phillips and Deol (1977); Scouten, Grotelueschen, and Beatty (1975)
	Female rats	Neonatal testosterone decreases performance, and makes adult performance sensitive to activational androgens.	Beatty and Beatty (1970a, 1970b); Phillips and Deol (1977); Scouten et al. (1975)
Maze Learning	Female rats	Neonatal testosterone increases performance.	Dawson et al. (1973); J. Stewart et al. (1975)
	Male rats	Neonatal estrogen decreases performance (two-choice maze).	Dawson et al. (1973); Kawashima and Shinoda (1972)
Exploration	Female rats	Neonatal testosterone decreases exploratory behaviors.	Gummow (1975); Quadagno et al. (1972)

drogenized females are not different from those of normal males, and both are significantly lower than the error scores of normal females. On the other hand, neonatal estrogen seems to depress maze learning.

Only one study directly compared the effects of neonatal estrogen and neonatal testosterone (Dawson et al., 1973). In this study, male and female rats were both castrated shortly after birth; females were then injected with testosterone and males with estrogen. Their maze-learning performances as adults were then compared to those of intact controls. Among the controls, the mean error scores after performing several different tasks on a difficult maze was 188.8 for the males and 266.5 for the females—a dramatic difference not very likely to be due to chance alone. For the neonatally androgenized females, the errors were significantly reduced, to 224.2. Neonatal estrogen significantly increased the error scores of the males, to 225.3. Unfortunately, these neonatal groups differed from their controls both in neonatal hormone conditions and in activational hormones. This double difference may not affect the validity of the data, since it was reported that adult injections of hormones had no effect on the maze-learning scores of the neonatally treated groups of rats. Thus, the authors concluded that the cognitive abilities of these rats had been permanently altered by the neonatal hormones.

Summary and Implications for Humans. Neonatal estrogen may decrease learning scores in adult animals, while normal male levels of neonatal testosterone decrease avoidance learning but improve maze learning. The interpretation of these results is uncertain, however.

Some of the problems with this research are dosage effects and lack of control over possible effects of these inductive hormones on motivational states. In avoidance learning, as was the case with activity scores, mounting scores, and weight gains (Appendix B), giving intact male rats extra testosterone affects them in the opposite way that normal levels of testosterone apparently affect normal males or females. Does this mean that there is an optimal level of testosterone, and that too much has the same effect on behavior as too little? Another problem with the research in active avoidance is that the effect of inductive hormones may well be a function of effects on motivation or on the types of responses made when frightened. The maze learning results could be contaminated with effects of both fear or exploration. And since exploration is also sensitive to neonatal hormones (Table 4.5), exploratory tendencies rather than cognitive capacity may have been altered. We cannot yet conclude that neonatal hormones affect cognitive processes in subhumans, even though there are dramatic and not easily ignored effects on behavior in learning situations.

HUMAN RESEARCH

To study the effects of inductive hormones upon human behavior, we have to turn to clinical data about people who have various congenital hormone abnormalities that might have affected their brains. These people have all been exposed prenatally to hormone levels not typical for their gender. The effects of prenatal androgens and progestins will be discussed by looking at the behavior of people who have the **adrenogenital syndrome,** those who were exposed prenatally to progestin, and those who have the **androgen-insensitivity syndrome.** The possible effects of prenatal estrogen in humans will also be discussed. As you read the description of the behavior characteristic of these people, keep in mind what animal studies show about the inductive effects of hormones on sexual behavior, aggression, parental and social behaviors, activity, and learning.

In all the research on humans discussed here, as was the case with the research on genetic abnormalities, the effect of parental expectations must also be kept in mind. That is, if your girl is born with a small penis, you may expect her to behave in a more masculine fashion, and these expectations may be subtly communicated. This could bias the child's behaviors—a Rosenthal effect in parenting. However, only some sex-role stereotypic behaviors appear to be affected in these syndromes, so it is unlikely that alterations of the sex-role expectations of parents will account for all the differences between the behavior of people with these syndromes and that of matched normal controls.

Adrenogenital Syndrome and Progestin-Affected Fetuses

The adrenogenital syndrome is an autosomal recessive trait that decreases production of cortisol by the adrenal cortex and causes masculinization of genetic females. The absence of cortisol leads to very high rates of secretion of ACTH, causing an increased output of androgens from the adrenal cortex. This happens around the third fetal month, leading to masculinization of the external genitals and—if not corrected by cortisol injections after birth—will lead to further mascu-

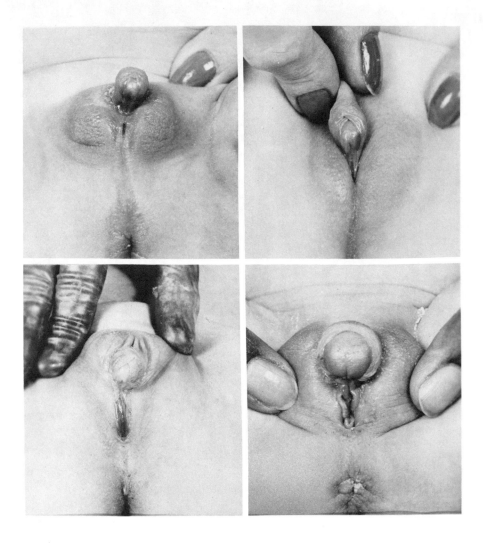

FIGURE 4.3

FOUR CASES OF ANDRENOGENITAL SYNDROME

*These four cases show varying degrees of clitoral enlargement and urogenital clo-
sure (displacement of the urethra)* that produce the ambiguous appearance of the
sex organs characteristic of the adrenogenital syndrome.

J. Money and A. A. Ehrhardt, *Man and Woman, Boy and Girl*, fig. 6.2. Copyright, Johns Hopkins University Press, 1973. Reprinted by permission.

linization after birth and an early puberty. Untreated females with this syndrome have normally functioning ovaries and normal internal female sexual organs, but have a masculinized external appearance. This can vary from a slightly englarged clitoris to a nearly normal-sized penis with an empty scrotum, as can be seen in Figure 4.3. If treated with cortisol from birth on, these girls will have a later menarche than normal but will be able to conceive, lactate, and deliver babies normally.

Most of our knowledge about the behavioral characteristics of people with the adrenogenital syndrome comes from two sets of studies. At Johns Hopkins University Hospital Money and his colleagues studied fifteen girls whose adrenogenital syndrome was detected and treated early; these girls were compared to a set of controls matched for age, socioeconomic class, and IQ (Ehrhardt, Epstein, and Money, 1968; Ehrhardt, Evers, and Money, 1968; V. Lewis, Money, and Epstein, 1968; Money and Lewis, 1966). Another set of seventeen girls whose adrenogenital syndrome was treated early was studied by Ehrhardt and Baker in Buffalo; these girls were compared to their unaffected siblings (Baker and Ehrhardt, 1974; Ehrhardt, 1973, 1975; Ehrhardt and Baker, 1973, 1974).

In both samples the behavior of adrenogenital girls who were treated early was studied and compared to that of normal controls. When the adrenogenital syndrome is detected and treated with cortisol shortly after birth, the behavioral effects of prenatal androgens can be evaluated uncontaminated by the effects of high levels of androgens that would be present after birth if the people were left untreated. The behavioral differences reported between the adrenogenital females and their controls seem to lie in three areas: tomboyism, maternal interests, and IQ.

Tomboyism in Adrenogenital Females.   In the Buffalo sample, 59 percent of the adrenogenital girls were identified by themselves and others as tomboys all during their childhood; this was true of none of their unaffected siblings, only 27 percent of whom were tomboys at any time. In the Johns Hopkins sample, eleven of the fifteen (73 percent) were always tomboys; none of the matched controls were.

Tomboyism appeared in a variety of behaviors. These girls usually preferred boys' to girls' toys, climbed trees, and loved outdoor sports. In the Buffalo sample, over 80 percent of the girls had little or no interest in dolls; only 10 percent of the unaffected female siblings did. The mothers of the adrenogenital girls often reported "that dolls as birthday or Christmas gifts get put on the shelf or in the closet and there they stay" (Money, 1974b, p. 250). These girls usually preferred clothes like shirts and shorts or blue jeans. The tomboy girls also played with boys more often than with girls; none of their siblings displayed that preference. Thus, these girls somewhat resembled the neonatally androgenized female monkeys who had high levels of rough-and-tumble play and pursuit play. However, since these girls did like perfume and dressing up, that might suggest that these preferences are not sexually dimorphic in humans—or at least are not the result of any biological bias.

Maternalism and Gender Identity in Adrenogenital Females.   These females gave some evidence of reduced maternalism. In the Johns Hopkins sample, ten of fifteen expressed aversion or indifference to infants; none of the matched controls did. In the Buffalo sample, over 50 percent of the adrenogenital girls expressed these attitudes, but only 10 percent of their normal siblings did. The adrenogenital girls preferred not to babysit and daydreamed significantly less often of pregnancy and motherhood or of weddings and marriage. Only one of the Johns Hopkins andrenogenital girls wanted to become a full-time wife and home-maker; all others wanted careers, with or without marriage. Of the matched controls, ten of fifteen preferred marriage over careers.

But it should be emphasized that relatively few of these girls showed any serious problems, including problems of identity, and they were not masculinized in all aspects of behavior. Although more of them than of the control group expressed ambivalence about the desirablity of being female, none had any doubts as to their gender identity and none seriously wanted to change it. Thus, these girls had a female gender identity even though they may have had some masculine gender role traits. They also did not tend to have homosexual experiences any more often than do hormonally normal women, and only three were bisexual. In Lev-Ran's sample (1974) of eighteen, none were homosexual. Finally, these girls in later life were, if anything, less aggressive than normal females, as Money and Schwartz (1976) demonstrated with a sample of fifteen adrenogenital females who were from fifteen to twenty-three years old. Instead, these women did not tend to be leaders, to be dominant over others, or to engage in many extracurricular activities.

Progestin-Affected Fetuses.   The behavioral differences between the adrenogenital girls and the control groups might be genetic rather than hormonal in origin, or result from some alteration in the uterine environment other than an increase in androgen levels. However, girls who were masculinized by the artificial progestins (which sometimes have androgenic properties) given to their mothers in order to prevent spontaneous abortions show many of these same effects (Ehrhardt and Money, 1967; Money and Ehrhardt, 1972). These progestin-masculinized girls were also tomboys. In one sample, the only one of these girls who actually preferred dolls to boys' toys was the only one who had a normal-sized clitoris. These girls also liked to compete with boys in sports, and they seemed to be self-assertive, independent and self-reliant. They, like the adrenogenital females, often put careers before marriage in their plans for the future. They also preferred males as playmates and preferred slacks to dresses.

Reinisch (1977) examined the effect of prenatal exposure to a synthetic progestin in twenty-six males and females by comparing these people to unexposed siblings. The progestin-exposed people, when tested between the ages of five and seventeen, were significantly more independent, individualistic, self-assured, and self-sufficient, as measured by the Cattel personality questionnaire. Since in this case the genitals of the females were not masculinized, an altered external appearance which could have affected parental expectations could not account for the hormonal effects. Males also were further masculinized by the prenatal hormone. Still, in both sets of studies—Reinisch's and those of Money and Ehrhardt—the artificial hormones were given to mothers with problem pregnancies, which leaves open the possibility that some aspects of the uterine environment other than the progestin could be responsible for the masculinization of both the females and males.

A prenatal progesterone can be feminizing. In the work of Dalton and her colleagues (Zussman, as cited by Dalton, 1976), children exposed prenatally to a progesterone were compared to a control group consisting of children from normal pregnancies and children from problem pregnancies who had not been exposed to artificial hormones. In this case, the females given progesterone were less likely to be tomboys than the controls. However, in this study neither the males nor the females had masculinity or femininity scores on either of two different inventories different from those of the controls. Two other studies looked at the effects of prenatal progesterone by comparing these children to controls matched for pregnancy problems, age, sex, race, and socioeconomic status (Ehrhardt, Grisanti, and Meyer-Bahlburg, 1977; Meyer-Bahlburg, Grisanti, and Ehrhardt, 1977). In these studies, males exposed prenatally to a progesterone did not differ from the controls, but the females were less often tomboys and more often preferred a feminine style of dress. The progesterone females also tended to be less active than the controls.

Adrenogenital Boys.   Adrenogenital boys are also exposed to high levels of androgens before birth, higher even than normal male levels. Nine males have been studied and compared to eleven unaffected male siblings, with ages ranging from 4.8 to 26.3 years (Ehrhardt, 1975; Ehrhardt and Baker, 1973, 1974). These males differed from their siblings in only one way: they were more often interested in sports and in rough outdoor activities, and were more often excellent athletes. However, like the adrenogenital girls, these children were *not* more aggressive.

Intellectual Abilities.   Some researchers claim that both adrenogenital and progestin-exposed males and females have higher than normal IQ (Baker and Ehrhardt, 1974; Dalton, 1968a, 1976; Ehrhardt et al., 1968; Ehrhardt and Money, 1967; Lev-Ran, 1974; V. Lewis et al., 1968, Money and Lewis, 1966; Money and Schwartz, 1976). The mean IQs or school performances of these groups have all been higher or greater than normal. Of the adrenogenital patients, 60 percent had an IQ above 109, as opposed to 25 percent in a normal distribution; the mean was 111 compared to 100 for the general population. The distribution of IQ scores of three samples of adrenogenital people is compared to the normal distribution in Figure 4.4. In the female progestin-masculinized group, the mean IQ was 125, with none having an IQ below 100, and six being above 130. In Dalton's study (1968a), the higher the dose and the earlier the progesterone was given, the greater the achievement in school in all subjects except physical education.

Dalton (1976), in an excellent, prize-winning study, recently reported a continuation of her investigation of thirty-four children of both sexes whose mothers had been given progesterone during their pregnancy to treat toxemia (a disease of pregnancy that can have severe consequences such as death or abortion). These children were compared to both normal controls and the children of toxemic mothers not given progesterone. The progesterone-treated children were significantly more likely to pass the level examinations given to children in England to gain entrance to a university. Their superiority was particularly marked in the areas of science. Social class may have caused differences among the three groups, with higher-class toxemic women being more likely to receive progesterone treatment. However, this is not likely to be the sole reason for the differences in academic achievement among the groups, since even within the treat-

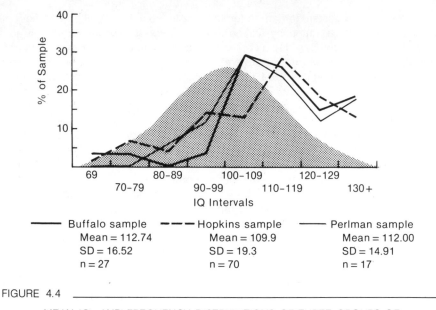

Buffalo sample	Hopkins sample	Perlman sample
Mean = 112.74	Mean = 109.9	Mean = 112.00
SD = 16.52	SD = 19.3	SD = 14.91
n = 27	n = 70	n = 17

FIGURE 4.4

MEAN IQs AND FREQUENCY DISTRIBUTIONS OF THREE GROUPS OF ANDRENOGENITAL PATIENTS

The shaded area shows the normal IQ distribution. The three groups are samples taken independently at different hospitals.

S. W. Baker and A. A. Ehrhardt, "Prenatal Androgen, Intelligence, and Cognitive Sex Differences. In R. C. Friedman, R. M. Richart, and R. L. Vande Wiele (eds.), Sex Differences in Behavior (New York: Wiley, 1974), p. 65. By permission.

ment group, the effects were found to be significantly related to the timing, dosage, and duration of the hormone therapy. Dosage effects were found for numerical ability and verbal reasoning, though the latter was true for the children only when they were younger; there were marginal dosage effects on spatial and mechanical ability.

However, it is not possible to conclude that neonatal androgen or masculinizing progestins increase IQ. Baker and Ehrhardt (1974) found high IQs in the unaffected siblings of the adrenogenital girls and in their mothers and fathers. Money and Lewis (1966) also found no differences in IQ between affected and unaffected siblings. Reinisch (1977) found no intellectual differences between progestin-treated people and their untreated siblings. All this suggests that the apparent effects of neonatal hormones upon IQ are seen only when the affected people are compared to nonrelated controls and not when they are compared to relatives. In a detailed analysis of the types of mental abilities shown by the adrenogenital people (Baker and Ehrhardt, 1974), only one significant difference between them and their siblings was found: adrenogenital patients did significantly poorer than their siblings on a test of number ability, and poorer on that test as compared to their own performances on verbal and spatial tasks.

Summary and Implications of Prenatal Hormones. The data from the studies of people exposed prenatally to higher than normal levels of masculinizing hormone—the adrenogenital males and females and the progestin-exposed males and females—suggest that these hormones may have had permanent effects on the brain. This implies that normal levels of hormones would also have some effect on the brains of normal men and women, although a lesser one. In particular, the adrenogenital and some progestin-exposed females are somewhat masculinized. These females were more often tomboys and were less interested in having or caring for babies than the control females. Both progestin-exposed males and females have been reported to be more independent, individualistic, self-assured, and self-sufficient. The females did not have to be physically masculinized to show these effects. These behaviors then seem to be hormone-sensitive, so we should expect sex differences in these areas among hormonally normal people, and these sex differences might be the result of a biological bias.

So some artificial progestins may masculinize both males and females, but progesterone may affect only females, making them less likely to be tomboys. Perhaps, as Ehrhardt and her colleagues (1977) suggested, the dosages of progesterone were too low to successfully counteract the androgens normally produced by the male fetal testes and so did not feminize the males, although the dosages might have been sufficient to counteract the smaller quantities of androgen produced in females by ovaries and the adrenals. Or maybe there is more pressure on the male to conform to his sex role than for the female, so environment provides stronger biases—overwhelming any possible hormonal bias—for the male than for the female.

As was the case with the feminizing effects of progesterone, the adrenogenital males seem to have experienced fewer behavioral effects from their high levels of prenatal hormones than did the adrenogenital females. These males were only said to be more often interested in and skilled at sports. These results make the human male more similar to a hamster than to a rat. That is, higher than normal doses of androgens do not seem to feminize adrenogenital men, as they did the male rat, but these men, like the hamster, were masculinized, at least in one respect.

It is also important to remember that other aspects of behavior were not affected by these neonatal hormonal abnormalities in any group. Gender identity, sexuality, and aggression were not affected. And we cannot safely conclude that these hormones affected intellectual abilities, though more work is needed here.

So it seems in humans, as in lower animals, that some aspects of behavior may be sensitive to neonatal hormones. Other syndromes involving neonatal hormonal abnormalities will provide further evidence relevant to this point.

Androgen-Insensitivity Syndrome

This is an X-linked, recessive syndrome in which body cells are insensitive to androgens. XY people with this syndrome are born phenotypic females. In such a person, since Müllerian inhibiting substances come from the testes, there are no female internal organs; but since the androgens from the testes have no effect on the body, there are no male internal organs either. The vagina is short, but the clitoris and breasts are of normal female size. Overall, the person is a very normal appearing woman, as can be seen from Figure 4.5. People with this syndrome are generally tall, however, with an average height of 5 feet, 7½ inches. They are, of course, infertile. They also have little or no pubic or axillary hair, since this depends on androgens.

Money and his colleagues have studied eighteen of these people, fifteen raised as women and three raised as men (Masica et al., 1969; Money and Ehrhardt, 1972; Money, Ehrhardt, and Masica, 1968). In their behavior, the patients raised as women clearly conform to the female gender role. Most of them strongly desired marriage and every one repeatedly had dreams and fantasies about raising children. They preferred dolls to other toys and enjoyed caring for infants.

The patients raised as females were normal to bright normal (mean IQ =108.3), with verbal IQ higher than the performance IQ in 80 percent of them (means of 111.8 and 102.3, respectively). In particular, these women showed a typical female pattern of poor spatial ability, in spite of having male chromosomes (Bock and Kolakowski, 1973; Masica et al., 1969). The three raised as males had a mean IQ of 118 with no consistent difference between verbal and performance IQs (means of 116.7 and 118.0, respectively).

Thus, the androgen-insensitivity XY people raised as females are quite feminine. In appearance, sex role, and intellectual abilities, they are normally female.

Variations in Estrogen

Two separate studies have used different techniques for trying to infer what effects, if any, prenatal estrogen might have on the brain and behavior of humans. One study looked at children of diabetic women. Since diabetic women do not produce normal amounts of estrogen and progesterone during pregnancy, they are often given supplemental doses of these hormones; these supplemental doses, particularly those of estrogen, may increase their level above normal. The other study looked at children of women had had been given estrogens during their pregnancy to prevent abortions.

Yalom, Green, and Fisk (1973) studied the male offspring of three groups of women: normal women, diabetic women given supplemental hormones, and diabetic women given no supplements. Thus, there are probably three different levels of prenatal exposure to estrogen represented by these groups, with fetuses of dia-

FIGURE 4.5 ————————————————————————————————

APPEARANCE OF AN ADULT XY WOMAN WITH ANDROGEN-INSENSITIVITY SYNDROME

Feminizing puberty occurs with no hormonal treatment needed, under the influence of estrogens normally secreted by the testes in males, since the body is unresponsive to the competitive effect of testicular androgen.

J. Money and A. A. Ehrhardt, *Man and Woman, Boy and Girl,* fig. 6.4. Copyright, Johns Hopkins University Press, 1973. Reprinted by permission.

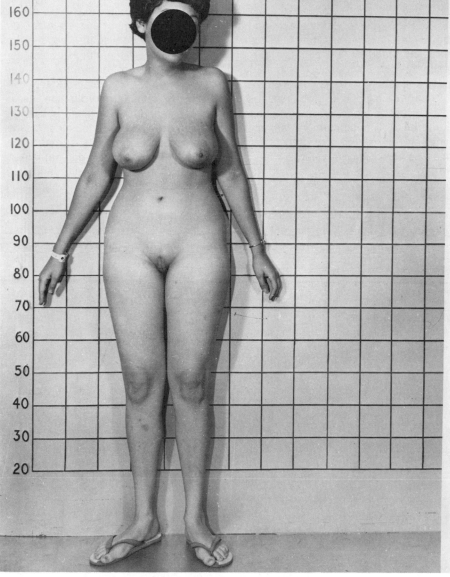

betics given supplemental hormones having the most estrogen, and those of diabetic mothers not given supplements having the least. Two such groups of boys were studied, one at six years of age and one at sixteen. The only differences found among the three groups of six-year-olds was that the children exposed to the highest levels of estrogen were rated by their teachers as being less assertive and less athletically able.

Several differences were found among the three groups of sixteen-year-olds, however. These groups may have shown greater effects because they were in fact exposed to higher levels of estrogen prenatally or because the effects of neonatal estrogen are exaggerated by puberty. Whatever the reason, for the sixteen-year-olds, the following behaviors were consistently, though weakly, related to the level of estrogen exposure: global ratings of masculinity, athletic coordination, assertive-aggressiveness, competitiveness, and success-orientation. In all cases, the children of diabetic mothers without supplemental estrogen were the most masculine, and the children of diabetics given supplements were the least masculine; the children of normal controls were intermediate. The boys exposed to high levels of estrogen were also more field-dependent (had lower spatial ability) and were shorter. But the most consistent difference among the groups was in aggression, with aggression being inversely related to the level of maternal estrogen.

Reinisch (1977) compared sixteen male and female children who had been exposed prenatally to estrogen to their untreated siblings. In this study, the children were exposed because of high-risk pregnancies; their mothers were given estrogen and progestin to maintain the pregnancy. Reinisch found that the children exposed prenatally to more estrogen than progestin, when compared to their siblings, were "significantly less individualistic, and therefore more group-oriented than their siblings and less self-sufficient and therefore more group-dependent" (p. 562). Reinisch did not find any differences among her groups— high estrogen, high progestin, and control—on any of the Wechsler IQ scales, including the spatial task.

In summary, both studies found that children prenatally exposed to higher than normal levels of estrogen were somewhat feminized. Still, these results must be interpreted with caution. First, the effects of estrogen were not entirely consistent in the two studies cited. Second, the effect of neonatal estrogen upon the aggression of the male children of diabetic mothers is surprising in view of the lack of effect of androgens upon aggression in the adrenogenital males and females and the fact that estrogen in infra-humans seems to increase aggression. Furthermore, part of these effects may be activational in these children, since their testes could have been affected (Zondek and Zondek, 1974; Jean, et al., 1975).

MECHANISMS OF THE INDUCTIVE EFFECT: SEX DIFFERENCES IN THE BRAIN

Since inductive hormones apparently have permanent effects on behavior, they must also have affected the brain, but how? Several possibilities have been suggested. Hormones, to have any effect on body cells, must first combine with receptors in the cells. The number of these receptors might be permanently altered by perinatal hormones; any change in number would permanently affect the sensitivity of the brain to the activational effects of hormones. The metabolism of brain cells might also have been permanently changed by inductive hormones. Perinatal hormones may actually change the connections and shapes of brain cells themselves. Finally, it has been suggested that all the masculinizing effects of androgens may actually be effects of estrogen, that is, that the brain of a male is masculinized by the female sex hormone. It is these possibilities we will now discuss.

Hormone Receptors

Some behavioral and physiological evidence suggests that experimental manipulations of perinatal hormones permanently affect **hormone receptors** in brain cells. For example, in most species neonatal androgens simply make the brain more sensitive to the aggression-promoting effects of activational androgens, which suggests that neonatal androgens could have permanently changed the number of hormone receptors available for androgens in the future. Perinatal androgen has also been reported to depress the sensitivity of the brain to progestins (Clemens, Shryne, and Gorski, 1970) and to estrogen (Pfaff et al., 1974; Whalen et al., 1969). Perinatal androgen has also been found to cause a reduction in the number of estrogen receptors in the brain (McEwen et al., 1974).

Nevertheless, these changes in receptors cannot account for all sex differences in normal animals. Some researchers have been unable to demonstrate a sex difference in normal animals in the number of estrogen receptors in brain cells, so the number of receptors may be a part of the inductive effect of hormone injections but not of normal sex differences in the brain (Cidlowski and Muldoon, 1976). Also, some sex differences—such as scent marking in dogs—are apparently independent of activational hormonal effects, so the inductive hormones must have had some effect on the brain other than producing a permanent change in its sensitivity to gonadal hormones (Beach, 1975).

Brain Structure and Metabolism

Another possibility is that the inductive hormones may have permanently affected the physical structure of the brain and so have produced permanent sex differences. For example, neonatal estrogens accelerate brain maturation (Timiras, 1971), and both estrogen and testosterone increase the branching of hypothalamic nerve cells in a laboratory culture (Toran-Allerand, 1976).

Infrahuman. There are sex differences in the structures and connections of cells in the brain in lower animals and these differences are the result of inductive hormonal effects. For example, Matsumoto and Arai (1976) demonstrated that neonatal estrogen in rats changed the synaptic structure of one of the hypothalamic nuclei. Raisman and Field also reported (1971) sex differences in the structure of neurons in the **preoptic nucleus** in rats, an area of the hypothalamus important for the sexual behavior of both males and females. The sex difference has to do with the location of the synapses of the incoming afferent fibers upon neurons of the preoptic nucleus. More recently, Raisman and Field (1973) found that this sex difference in the preoptic nucleus was affected in the predicted directions by neonatal castrations of males and by neonatal androgen injections in females. Similar sex differences, similarly affected by neonatal hormones, have been found in hamster brains (Greenough et al., 1977).

Other sex differences in the brain have also been found, and found to be sensitive to perinatal hormones. The size of the neuronal cell bodies (nuclear size) of anterior preoptic hypothalamic cells and of some cells in the amygdala (part of the emotional area of the brain) is larger in females and in neonatally castrated males than in normal male rats (Dörner and Staudt, 1968; Staudt and Dörner, 1976). In fact, the degree of femaleness in sexual behavior was positively correlated (+ .97) with the nuclear size of the preoptic area, and the degree of maleness in sexual behavior was negatively correlated with nuclear size (− .94). Male rats have heavier brains, with larger neocortical, brain stem, hippocampal, and amygdalar areas than females or neonatally castrated males, mostly because of differences and changes in cell size (Pfaff, 1966).

Sex differences in metabolic processes of the brain are probably also affected by perinatal hormones (Litteria, 1973a; Litteria and Thorner, 1974a, 1975, and 1976). For example, neonatal androgen injections permanently inhibit protein synthesis in the brain of the adult female rat (Litteria, 1973b). Also, when neonatal hormones were shown to significantly affect protein synthesis in the cerebellum (the area that controls motor coordination), there were also sex differences found in the brains of control animals (Litteria and Thorner, 1974b).

There are two very common methods for studying brain functions, both of which show sex differences in brain structure or function that are presumably caused by perinatal hormone differences. One method involves destroying (**lesioning**) a certain area or structure of the brain, and then looking for changes in behavior. Supposedly, if some type of behavior show changes after brain lesions, then the destroyed part of the brain was involved in the control of that behavior. The other method is to use electrical or chemical stimulation. If stimulating an area of the brain elicits or blocks a given behavior, then that part of the brain is assumed to control that behavior. If sexes show different behaviors as a consequence of lesions or stimulations, then there are probably sex differences in brain organization.

Particularly likely to lead to sexually dimorphic results are lesions and stimulations of the **limbic areas** of the brain, which are concerned with emotional behaviors. Hippocampal lesions have different effects on male than on female rats (Kearley et al., 1974). Hilger and Rowe (1975) also found that gender interacted with the effects of olfactory bulb removal in hamsters, with greater effects being seen in the male. Sex differences in the effects of lesions of the septal region on sexual behavior may be partly the result of sex differences in activational hormones and in part to sex differences in neonatal hormones (Nance et al., 1977; Phillips and Deol, 1973). The effects of hypothalamic lesions upon sensitivity to shock also interact with gender (Dennis, 1976).

Human.   There is also some evidence of sex differences in the human brain. J. Nash (1970) has claimed that the gray commissure is more often absent from male than from female brains. He also stated that the female brain has simpler and more regular convolutions.

There are also sex differences in the electrical activity of the brain. Adult females have larger amplitude (more voltage) EEGs than do males (Eeg-Olofsson, 1971; N. Ellis and Last, 1953; Matousek and Peterson, 1973). Females also have a larger amplitude and shorter latency in **evoked responses** (changes in brain electrical activity caused by the presentation of some stimulus) (Buchsbaum and Pfefferbaum, 1971; Rodin et al., 1965; Shagass, Overton, and Straumanis, 1972; Shagass and Schwartz, 1965a, 1965b). The sex difference in the evoked potential appears within forty-eight hours after birth (Molfese et al., 1975). However, this sex difference appears at all ages, and the evoked response in 45, X females is even larger than that in 46, XX females (Buchsbaum, Henkin, and Christiansen, 1974; R. Engel, Crowell, Nishiyima, 1968).

The Conversion Hypothesis

Finally, an idea with rather startling implications should be mentioned. Naftolin and his colleagues (Naftolin, Ryan, and Petro, 1971; Reddy, et al., 1974) have proposed that testosterone exerts its masculinizing effect on the brain by being changed into estrogen by the fetal brain cells of males. This is now being called the **conversion hypothesis.** If this hypothesis is correct, the brain of the genetic male is actually being masculinized by the female sex hormone, estrogen.

There is some evidence to support this hypothesis. Perinatal estrogen can, to a large extent, duplicate the effects of neonatal testosterone, as was presented in Tables 4.1 to 4.5. Androgens that cannot be transformed (**aromatized**) into estrogen do not masculinize the brain when injected in the same manner as those androgens that can be converted. Brain tissue from several species converts testosterone into estradiol. Work from the laboratory of Doughty and McDonald also strongly supports this hypothesis (Doughty et al., 1975a, 1975b; Doughty and McDonald, 1974). For example, injections of an estrogen antagonist will inhibit both the masculinizing action of estrogen and testosterone. Finally, estrogen is much more potent than testosterone in its masculinizing effect on the brain (suppression of lordosis in genetic females) (Brown-Grant, 1974). It does seem rather uneconomical, however, for the male fetus to secrete such large quantities of testosterone just so that 1 percent can be converted into estrogen to masculinize the brain and behavior.

Other investigators have found evidence to oppose the conversion hypothesis. Androgen that cannot be converted into estrogen may be able to masculinize or defeminize the brain when presented in sufficiently high and prolonged doses (Gerall et al., 1976; Gerall, McMurray, and Farrell, 1975; Payne, 1976; Whalen and Rezek, 1974). Furthermore, hypothalamic implants of an estrogen antagonist may not prevent the masculinizing effects of androgens upon female rats (Hayashi, 1976).

The conversion hypothesis cannot be regarded as confirmed, but it has received some very strong support, and it makes some sense out of the fact that so many hormones can have similar effects on behavior, particularly sexual behavior. It is possible that this hypothesis is true for rats but not for primates or other species.

SUMMARY AND CONCLUSIONS

Perinatal hormones may have permanent effects on brain structure and function that become visible in behavior. Fetal gonadal hormones not only affect internal and external sex organs, they also influence the brain's neural pathways, as seen by direct examination and by measuring postnatal behavior. The inductive effect of these hormones most likely works by means of direct effects on brain structures and connections, although hormone receptors and other metabolic processes may also be permanently affected.

Activity levels may be affected by neonatal hormones in both humans and lower animals. The data on rats suggest that both field and wheel activity are affected by both estrogen and testosterone, but often in different ways. In primates, including humans, rough-and-tumble play and similar behaviors may be increased by prenatal androgens in both males and females.

Some evidence suggests inductive hormonal effects on parental behaviors. In lower animals, neonatal androgens seem to suppress parental behaviors typical for females. In humans, Turner's females and androgen-insensitive women lack even normal female effects of inductive androgen, and both seem quite maternal (though infertile). Adrenogenital women, though fertile, were frequently indifferent or even hostile to babies.

Evidence for any influence of inductive hormones on sexual behavior in humans is seen only in people with Klinefelter's syndrome. In them, a decrease in sexual behavior is seen, a decrease that cannot be corrected by activational androgens and which may have been caused by their low prenatal levels of androgens. The sexual behaviors of people with the other hormonal abnormalities are almost always entirely congruent with their gender identity as determined by their gender of rearing. This suggests that sexual behavior of humans, in contrast to that of animals, is not sexually dimorphic. Instead, the differences often claimed to exist between the sexual behaviors of human males and females—particularly with regard to activity and passivity—may be solely a function of individual socialization and cultural expectations. This may even be true of the Klinefelter's male, in view of his somewhat feminized body appearance.

In humans, only people with Turner's syndrome and the male offspring of diabetic mothers gave any evidence of inductive effects on aggression. The adrenogenital males and females were assertive but were, if anything, rather nonaggressive. The effect of estrogen upon the male offspring of diabetic mothers was the opposite of that obtained with mice and rats. But, as Money and Schwartz (1976) pointed out, the adrenogenital girls preferred to play with boys, and "to be accepted among a group of boys, a tomboy girl usually must not be too assertively dominant" (p. 28). Thus, the clear inductive effect of hormones upon animal aggression is not paralleled by the human data, either because human aggression is not hormone-sensitive or because expectations and experience overrode the inductive bias.

With regard to learning and intelligence, some hormone effects have been seen. Estrogen may inhibit spatial ability in both rats and humans, and androgens have been associated with increased spatial performances in both humans and lower animals. However, in other types of learning tasks, the effects of hormones in animals upon responses prompted by fear, curiosity, reactivity, and emotionality have not yet been established. And the mechanism for the elevation of IQ and school performance in progestin- and progesterone-exposed children, in adrenogenital boys and girls, and in their parents and siblings remains obscure.

Also, the possible role of parental expectations and the effect they may have upon these behaviors should not be overlooked. The presence of even a very small penis could lead parents of monkeys and humans to treat those offspring differently from normal females, such that the children end up as tomboys (Quadagno et al., 1977). However, it should also be remembered that Turner's girls are less often tomboys than are matched controls, even though they are not really more feminine-looking. Furthermore, adrenogenital males also had higher levels of energy expenditure than did matched controls even though they looked the same. Finally, sexual and aggressive behaviors were not affected in females with masculinized appearances, although parental expectations might bias those stereotypic behaviors also. Still, the effect of parental expectations is undoubtedly important, and the contributions of those expectations to their children's behaviors cannot be satisfactorily estimated from the available data.

Most important, it must be emphasized that behavior is also a function of activational hormones, the stimulus situation, and the organism's past experiences with similar situations. Environment will affect the degree to which these perinatal, hormonal biases actually appear in behavior, since the biases only affect the preparedness of the organism to associate certain stimuli or to learn a particular type of behavior from a particular situation. For example, experience with sexually active males or the experience of exploring a particular open field may well override the neonatal effects of testosterone upon the lordosis and activity scores of genetic female rats. Therefore, with sufficient experience, these hormonally biased differences in preparedness would no longer be visible in behavior.

The other major conclusions of this chapter have to do with sex differences. First, masculine and feminine behaviors belong on different dimensions, not on opposite ends of a single dimension; an animal can be masculinized without being defeminized. So it seems quite possible for an organism to be both masculine and feminine, or to be neither. Second, one reason the sexes differ might have to do with the differences in hormones present before birth because these differences give them different brains.

KEY TERMS AND CONCEPTS

Inductive effect
Prenatal
Neonatal
Perinatal period
Endogenous hormones
Exogenous hormones
Adrenogenital syndrome
Androgen-insensitivity syndrome
Tomboyism

Inductive effects on hormone receptors
Preoptic nucleus
Lesioning
Limbic areas of the brain
Evoked response
Conversion hypothesis
Masculinize and demasculinize
Feminize and defeminize
Aromatize

QUESTIONS ON KEY ISSUES

1. What is the evidence that all brains have the capability of both masculine and feminine types of behaviors—that inductive hormones only change the degree of bias?

2. What sexually dimorphic behaviors in infra-human animals (Chapter 3) may be affected by perinatal hormones? Which dimorphic behaviors have not yet been tested? Which of these behaviors may also be affected by hormones in humans? Which behaviors are not affected in humans?

3. Can an organism's brain be masculinized without being defeminized? What are some examples of this? What are the implications?

4. In all species, masculinization increases as the amount of perinatal androgen increases. What evidence is there that this statement is *not* true?

5. In what three major areas do adrenogenital and progestin-treated females differ from normal females? Does neonatal androgen really affect intelligence?

6. How are the androgen-insensitivity people (XY people raised as females) similar to Turner's people, both hormonally and behaviorally? What conclusions could be reached from this?

7. Is there any evidence that neonatal estrogen can have similar effects on humans as on lower animals?

8. Given the data in this chapter, what sex differences would you expect to see between hormonally normal male and female humans? Could these differences be attributed, at least in part, to biological biases created in the brain prenatally?

9. What sex differences have been found in brain structures and functions? What evidence is there that perinatal hormones might be responsible for these differences?

CHAPTER 5

The Activational Effects of Gonadal Hormones

INTRODUCTION

The gonadal hormones may not only affect the way the brain is "wired," they may also activate the developed brain to make certain behaviors more or less likely to occur. This chapter will discuss possible activational effects of gonadal hormones upon the brains of humans and subhumans. How much of our behavior right at this moment might be subtly affected by our hormones in ways of which we are unaware? Can our hormones affect what we see, hear and feel? Whether we feel good or bad? How much of sex differences in behavior might be attributable to sex differences in activational hormones?

The Effect of Past Experience and Situation: A Model

Discussing the activational effects of hormones does not imply that they elicit behavior. Instead, it means that hormones may change the probability that a given stimulus will be noticed and will be responded to in a certain way. Past experience with that stimulus, however, also affects the probability of a given response, and the response will not appear without the presence of an appropriately stimulating environment. For example, castration in male cats, mice, and primates decreases sexual behavior, but the rate of decline depends upon the prior sexual experience of the male (Manning and Thompson, 1976; Michael, Wilson, and Plant, 1973; Rosenblatt and Aronson, 1958).

Similar situation-specific effects are also seen in humans. When humans are injected with adrenalin, they interpret the resulting emotional state as euphoria or anger according to how they interpret the situation in which they find themselves (Schachter and Singer, 1962). What emotional state was produced by a given hormone injection depends upon the individual's interpretation of the situation.

Given all this, the conceptual model for the activational effect of hormones might be best described as follows: *The behavior that occurs in any given situation is a complex function not only of the hormonally affected brain structures, but also of the way the present stimulus situation is sensed and interpreted in light of both past experience and the current hormonal conditions.* Stress might also affect the relationship between activational hormones and behavior. *Physical or*

117

psychological stress may also increase sensitivity to hormone effects in much the same way that it reduces resistance to disease (Selye, 1956). *Genetically affected susceptibility to hormone changes may also be a factor.*

It is clear then that a one-to-one relationship between either perinatal or postnatal hormones and behavior should never be expected. The model above shows that the situation obviously affects the relationship. Also, even behaviors biased by hormones will not always appear in situations for which they are biased; they may appear at other times for other reasons. Even behaviors that appear to be the same may have different causes at different times. A behavior might be more influenced by physiological factors in one person and by psychological factors in another. Death is physiologically caused, but it is not only disease that kills; psychological stress does also (Seligman, 1975). Obesity can be caused by many influences, from hormones to genetics to situational stress to lifetime habits of dealing with stress. Any given case of obesity is likely to be a complex combination of several factors; the importance of those factors will vary in different cases. The same is probably true of behavior, even of behavior with some type of hormonal bias; not all people will show the effect, and the same behavior will not have the same cause in all people.

Not everyone should be expected to visibly show the effects of activational hormone changes. Susceptibility will be a complex function of learned responses to stress and the situation, how much stress the person is currently experiencing, genetics, and the way the hormonal and environmental stimuli are interpreted. The behavioral biases produced by different levels and types of inductive hormones will also be important.

Experimental Techniques

Both correlational and manipulational techniques are used to explore the relationship between hormones and behavior. Both techniques present problems of interpretation.

One way of relating hormones to behavior is to inject hormones directly into the blood or the brain and then measure the resulting changes in behavior. The major defect of this technique is the tendency of these hormones to transform themselves after injection. Testosterone may be aromatized to estrogen, and the resulting change in behavior may be due to estrogen, not testosterone. Also, hormone injections may increase the adrenal output of other hormones, which are also likely to influence behavior (Gorzalka, Rezak, and Whalen, 1975; Kitay, 1963).

Another way of relating hormones to behavior is to measure the hormonal levels in the organism from time to time and try to correlate changes in them with changes in behavior. This technique suffers not only from the defects of the correlational technique (see the discussion in Chapter 1), but also from the difficulties involved in measuring hormone levels. Older studies using this technique measured the levels of hormone metabolites in urine, but these levels are only indirect and often misleading indicators of actual blood levels of the active forms of the hormone. Because their data are not sound these studies are generally not discussed here.

But more recent data are not completely unambiguous, either. Researchers now can determine blood levels of hormones directly from blood samples, but there are problems with this technique also. All three major gonadal hormones appear in several different forms, all differing in biological potency, and different areas of the body may vary in their sensitivities to the different forms. Another problem is that variability from study to study is introduced by variations in the chemical techniques used for analysis, meaning results may not be comparable. Also, since the levels of various hormones are often correlated with one another— for instance, the prefollicular ovary secretes high levels of both estradiol and testosterone—what hormone causes what behavior is obviously hard to determine from correlational data. Finally, stress and diet affect hormone levels. The effect of stress means that the very process of drawing blood samples may change the levels of the hormones being measured. Diet and situational stress may also contaminate the results if these factors are allowed to vary from group to group.

Chapter Overview

This chapter will review the activational effects of gonadal hormones upon the behaviors of human and lower animals. The activational effects of hormones upon infrahuman behavior is a much older and much less controversial field of research than the effects on humans. The major effects of circulating hormones upon infrahuman sexual, aggressive, parental, emotional, and learning behaviors will be briefly reviewed, to show the extent to which they are sensitive to hormones. The activational effect of hormones upon human behavior is considerably more controversial, so that research will be examined much more carefully. But first, the data concerning the effect of experience upon hormones—the reverse of the relationship under consideration—will be introduced, so that it can be used to interpret the effects of hormones.

Several general conclusions will be suggested by the data reviewed in this chapter. First, *sex differences in behavior are often greatly reduced, though usually not eliminated, if the sexes are given identical hormonal levels at the time of the test.* This means that some sex differences in behavior may be caused by activational hormones biasing the brain, making some behaviors more or less likely to occur. Thus, sex differences in activational hormones may produce sex differences in behavior.

Second, *a one-to-one correspondence between hormones and behavior should never be expected.* This is partly because of situational and individual variability, as was made clear earlier. But it is also true because of the unpredictable effects of varying hormone levels upon behavior, even upon a behavior which is sensitive to hormonal biases. For example, some behaviors seem to have a hormone threshold, such that their frequencies decrease or they disappear when the relevant hormone is completely removed. However, as long as the hormone level is above that threshold, variations in the hormone level might not correspond to any variations in behavior; both low and moderate levels have the same effect on behavior. As another example, sometimes very high levels of hormones can have opposite effects on behavior compared to the effects of lower hormone levels, similar to what was observed for inductive hormonal effects. Thus, variability is to be expected.

A third conclusion is implied by what was said before. *Only for some types of behavior, and then only in some individuals in certain environments and with certain past experiences, will activational hormonal biases be visible in behavior.* Only the sexually dimorphic behaviors described in Chapter 3 should be sensitive to changes in activational hormones, but even for these behaviors, some may prove more sensitive to hormones than others. The effects of the hormones will be influenced by species and by genetics, by the present situation, the past experiences of the organism, and by stress. Also, particular effects of activational hormones upon the brain might be behaviorally visible only in an individual whose brain had been exposed perinatally to either those or other hormones. For example, activational androgen may increase aggression most easily in those individuals perinatally exposed to androgen, whether from their own testes or by experimental injections.

Overall, it seems that *some sex differences in behavior, and some individual differences in sexually dimorphic behaviors within a sex, could be due to individual differences in activational hormones.* However, this may be *less true for humans than for lower animals.* This difference between species seems likely for two reasons: (1) the human brain is uniquely sensitive to the effects of experience; and (2) *relevant experiences make behavior relatively resistant to changes in activational hormones.*

ACTIVATIONAL EFFECTS ON THE BRAIN

Two Kinds of Effects

Before going any further, it will be useful to distinguish between two kinds of activational effects that gonadal hormones may produce. Both kinds of effects occur when these hormones enter a body cell, attach themselves to specialized receptors, and induce the genes of that cell. This causes specific proteins to be manufactured and thus changes cellular activity (Edelman, 1975). For the **specific activational effects,** the hormone changes cellular activity in a specific area of the brain, making one particular kind of response to a specific environmental stimulus more likely to occur. In this way estrogen increases lordosis in female rats in response to specific visual, vocal, olfactory, and tactile stimuli coming from a male.

Hormones also have **nonspecific activational effects** on the brain, apparently affecting a wide variety of behaviors. In fact, the areas of the brain affected by hormones are so extensive as to suggest that the whole nervous system is influenced by all three gonadal hormones (Kawakami and Sawyer, 1959).

Several effects that could be nonspecific have been reported, including the effects of the gonadal hormones upon **transmitter substances** (chemical agents secreted by one nerve that influence another nerve at a synaptic area). The concentration of one transmitter, acetylcholine, is affected by all three gonadal hormones (Kobayashi et al., 1966; Torda and Wolff, 1944). Broverman and his colleagues (1968) have presented evidence to suggest that in humans and lower animals both estrogen and testosterone inhibit monamine oxidase (MAO), which inhibits another transmitter substance, norepinephrine (noradrenalin). Since both estrogen and testosterone inhibit the inhibitor, both hormones would increase brain activity. Thus, the availability of transmitter substances throughout the brain is affected by the gonadal hormones. Sleep patterns and the electrical activity of the brain also seem to be affected in relatively nonspecific ways by gonadal hormones (Gorski, 1976; Gyermek, 1967; Kawakami and Sawyer, 1959, 1967; Kopell, 1969; Kubo, Gorski, and Kawakami, 1975). Overall, testosterone and estrogen seem to increase brain activity, while progesterone is a depressant.

Implications of the Two Effects

This distinction between specific and nonspecific activational effects has several important implications. The nonspecific activational effects may imply that the gonadal hormones have similar effects on a wide variety of behaviors. For example, if testosterone and estrogen increase brain activity, they may also increase responsivity to all kinds of stimuli. The animal influenced by these hormones may be more likely to be made anxious by fearful stimuli, elated by joyful stimuli, active by arousing stimuli. Progesterone, with its depressant properties, may decrease responsiveness to all kinds of stimuli, making the organism less likely to respond to anything.

Second, if there are both specific and nonspecific effects the design and interpretation of experiments becomes complicated. If estrogen increases activity levels in a given situation, is the increase due to specific or nonspecific effects? Does estrogen increase the likelihood of an exploratory response to a novel situation? Or does it increase the responsivity of the organism to all kinds of stimuli, and this increase becomes visible in behavior as an increase in general activity levels?

EFFECT OF EXPERIENCE UPON HORMONES

This section comes first to modify and interpret the later sections. The other sections will all emphasize the role that the gonadal hormones may play in determining our experiences, in affecting how we perceive stimuli and the probability of our responding to those stimuli in some particular way. But our experiences also determine our hormone levels. What actually happens, from moment to moment, is an interaction between biology and environment.

The range of stimuli that can affect hormones is astonishing, from lighting conditions to social stimuli (the sound, sight, and scent of other animals). In some species, environment even determines the gonadal gender. For example, in one species of fish living on coral reefs, the larger female dominates both one adult male and several smaller, preadult males that make up a particular social group. If, however, the female dies or is removed, then the adult male turns into a female, losing all testicular tissue (Fricke and Fricke, 1977). The absence of domination changes a male into a female—a fairly dramatic effect of experience.

The environmental factors that have been shown to affect hormones cover a wide range. Some of the more important effects deserve being discussed in greater detail. We will discuss the effects of stress, aggression, and various types of social stimuli.

Some Examples

The effect of stress upon the gonadal hormones has been the most completely investigated effect of experience. Usually stress depresses sex hormone levels (Mason, Brady, and Tolliver, 1968). In humans, a drop in testosterone level has been reported to occur following a stressful military situation, surgery and hospital admissions, and final exams in college (Mason, 1975; Rose, Gordon, and Bernstein, 1972). In human females, stress affects the menstrual cycle. Stress induces bleeding early (Dalton, 1968b) or increases the length of the cycle, presumably by increasing the duration of the follicular phase (Preston et al., 1974). Stress may also hasten puberty in humans (J. Whiting, 1965).

Testosterone is also affected by dominance and by fighting (Bronson and Desjardins, 1971). When a male rhesus monkey was exposed for two hours to a large group of males and was defeated in fighting, testosterone levels dropped by 80 percent in three to five days (Rose et al., 1972). When four males were put together to form a new social group, the male who became dominant showed a progressive rise in testosterone while the subordinate ones showed an 80 percent decrease. These changes occurred even when the animal had not been wounded, and so physical damage or stress did not cause the changes. When the four males were then introduced to a larger group, they all showed at least an 80 percent drop in testosterone, while the dominant male of the larger group who had successfully defended his dominance showed a 238 percent rise within twenty-four hours (Rose, Bernstein, and Gordon, 1975).

The detailed descriptions of these monkeys are even more impressive. One male rhesus with increased testosterone had successfully defended his rank, and he "became more confident and assertive, strutting around with his tail high in the air and curled" (Bernstein, quoted by Gair, 1975, pp. 8–9). One who had been defeated and whose testosterone levels had fallen "doesn't move around much and becomes depressed. He becomes submissive in encounters with others of his kind. In extreme cases, he quits eating. In the most extreme cases, he may go into shock and die without medical intervention" (Bernstein, quoted by Gair, 1975, p. 9).

Sexual activity may also affect hormones. Sexual activity may increase testosterone levels in male rhesus monkeys, in male rats and bulls, in male guinea pigs, and in male mice, but evidently not in male humans (Harding and Feder, 1976; Purvis and Haynes, 1974; Quadagno et al., 1976; Rose et al., 1972; Stearns, Winter, and Faiman, 1973).

Social interactions, even in the absence of actual sexual behavior, can also affect hormone levels in many lower species. For example, male rats, mice, and guinea pigs experience a rise of testosterone levels just upon being placed close to an unfamiliar female (Harding and Feder, 1976; Macrides, Bartke, and Dalterio, 1975; Purvis and Haynes, 1974). And lionesses living in a single pride tend to have synchronous estrous cycles (Bertram, 1975). Several other examples were supplied by a recent report in *Science* (Lombardi and Vandenbergh, 1977): for instance, olfactory stimuli from other mice can delay or hasten puberty in a juvenile mouse, or can block or produce estrous in females. At least among lower animals, then, the hormone levels of social-living animals can be very much affected by the size and composition of the group in which the animals live. Similarly, J. Gray (1971b) has summarized research with infra-humans showing that crowded conditions reduce testosterone levels in males, and can suppress fertility and lactation in females and increase the frequency of abortions.

Some of these effects may also appear in humans. Women who live together tend to have synchronized menstrual cycles and women who date more often have shorter menstrual cycles (M. McClintock, 1971). The amount of light or darkness may also affect the timing of puberty in humans (Altman, 1976).

Implications of the Effects of Experience

Thus, experience can have dramatic effects on hormones. Stress usually decreases the sex hormones, and both sexual and social stimuli can increase hormones (though apparently not in humans). But too much social stimulation—crowding—can also lead to a drop in hormones. Defeat or depression also leads to a fall in testosterone in male infra-human primates, while winning fights leads to a rise.

This data will profoundly influence the interpretation of the following sections of this chapter. In correlational data it is always hard to distinguish between cause and effect. However, correlational data comprise most of our knowledge about hormones and human behavior, and correlational data also appear often in animal research. Thus, it will often be difficult to decide whether a correlation means, for example, that aggression causes a rise in testosterone or that a rise in testosterone causes aggression, or both, or neither. Keep this in mind throughout the rest of this chapter. We will only be safe to infer cause and effect when hormonal injections lead to behavioral changes similar to those seen in the correlational research.

INFRA-HUMAN RESEARCH

Sexual Behavior

In order to understand sexual behavior, it is necessary to remember that sex is very obviously an interaction of organisms, so we must assess the behavior of both participants before we come to any conclusions about the sexual motivations of either. At least two things affect the incidence of sexual behavior: the attractiveness of the animal to the opposite sex and its own sexual interest or motivation (Beach, 1976; R. J. Doty, 1974; Michael, 1968). In all species, the active role of the female in soliciting sexual behavior should not be underestimated.

Of Males. Just as most normal males exhibit both typical male and typical female sexual behaviors at various times, each hormone also causes behavior of both kinds. There are, however, biases built into both the animal and the hormones. Males are more likely to show mounting than lordosis, and testosterone is more likely to activate mounting than lordosis. Thus, "testosterone treatment stimulates female sexual behavior in males only rarely and under rather special circumstances" (Bermant and Davidson, 1974, p. 182). While estrogen can increase all male sexual behaviors in male castrates (at least in some species), it may be less effective than testosterone (J. Davidson, 1969; but see Gorzalka et al., 1975). Both testosterone and estrogen facilitate lordosis in most males, but in long-term castrates estrogen is more effective at producing lordosis than intromission and ejaculation (J. Davidson, 1969). So, although the estrogen the male animal has normally may be important for complete activation of all aspects of his male sexual behavior, his testosterone may be even more important. There seem to be biases "built into" both the animal and the hormone. Various hormonal effects are summarized in Table 5.1.

Hormones also affect how attractive the male is to the female. Castrated male monkeys are less attractive to females, whereas an erect penis increases a male's attractiveness (Beach, 1976).

However, androgen levels are not always clearly related to variations in sexual behavior in males. Although castration decreases sexual behavior in males of all species, the rate of decline is not associated in any simple way either with the species' position on the phylogenetic scale (B. J. Hart, 1974) or with the level of androgen. Testosterone disappears from the bloodstream within a few hours after castration, but sexual behavior may last for days or months after that time (Bermant and Davidson, 1974). Furthermore, when animals are castrated and then each injected with exactly the same quantity of testosterone, the same differences in sexual behavior seen before castration will reappear; so individual differences in sexual behavior are not simply the result of individual differences in activational androgens (Bermant and Davidson, 1974; McCollom, Siegal, and Van Krey, 1971).

TABLE 5.1 ──

ACTIVATIONAL EFFECTS OF GONADAL HORMONES UPON THE SEXUAL BEHAVIORS

Gender	Types of Behavior	Effects and Behaviors	References
Males	Mounting, intromission, and ejaculation	Castration not only decreases behaviors, but also decreases penis size.	B. L. Hart (1974)
		Testosterone can restore all male sexual behaviors in castrated males.	Bermant and Davidson (1974)
		Estrogen also restores mounting in castrated males of some species, but not all.	Ågmo (1975); Alsum and Goy (1974); J. Davidson (1969); Feder, Naftolin, and Ryan (1974); Gorzalka et al. (1975); Nobel and Alsum (1975); Pfaff (1970); Sodersten (1973a)

Table 5.1 (*Continued*) _____

Gender	Types of Behavior	Effects and Behaviors	References
	Lordosis	Both testosterone and estrogen will facilitate lordosis, but estrogen facilitates lordosis more than mounting; progesterone can facilitate estrogen-induced lordosis in rats and hamsters; estrogen-induced lordosis is most likely to be seen in intact, sexually active males, not in castrated or inactive ones.	J. Davidson (1969); J. Davidson and Levine (1969); Nobel and Alsum (1975); van De Poll and van Dis (1977)
Females	Lordosis and sexual interest	Castration leads to prompt decline of lordosis and interest in subprimates.	Bermant and Davidson (1974)
		Sexual behavior varies during the estrous or menstrual cycles in infra-human females.	Bermant and Davidson (1974); Eliasson and Meyerson (1975); Michael (1969, 1975); Nadler (1975)
		Lordosis and interest can be produced by injections of estrogen at any time; whether or not progesterone will facilitate estrogen's effect depends upon the species involved.	Beach (1976); Bermant and Davidson (1974); J. Davidson and Levine (1969); Kow and Pfaff (1975); Nadler (1970)
		Progesterone in primates inhibits sexual attractiveness and sexual interest.	Bielert et al. (1976); Michael (1969, 1975)
		Testosterone increases sexual motivation in rats and primates.	Everitt and Herbert (1969); Herbert (1970); Herbert and Trimble (1967); Meyerson et al. (1973)
	Mounting	Mounting increases during estrous and decreases with castration.	Beach (1976); Michael, Setchell, and Plant (1974)
		Mounting is increased by both estrogen and testosterone in most subprimates, except hamsters; mounting behavior is not as dimorphic as lordosis.	Bermant and Davidson (1974); Noble and Alsum (1975); Söderstein (1973a)
		Testosterone has no effect on mounting in primates, although the behavior is dimorphic.	Peretz et al. (1971)

In summary, both testosterone and estrogen can stimulate both male and female types of sexual responses in male animals. However, testosterone is more likely to produce mounting than lordosis, and estrogen may be more effective at producing lordosis than male behavior. In infra-human males, then, sexual behavior is sensitive to activational hormones; at least some of the sex differences in sexual behavior in normal animals must be the result of sex differences in hormone levels. However, the relationship between hormone and behavior is neither simple nor direct, perhaps because very low normal levels of androgen are sufficient to produce the aspects of male sexual behavior that are typically measured. Variations in androgen would not necessarily cause variations in behavior, since the brain would be maximally activated by low androgen levels. More is not always better.

Of Females. In most subprimate females, the frequency of female sexual behavior depends completely on ovarian hormones. Therefore, castration (removal of ovaries) in these females nearly always produces a very prompt and complete disappearance of female sexual behavior. Even primate females are affected by hormones. The estrous or menstrual cycle therefore affects sexual behavior, especially in subprimates. This happens both because females lose interest in sex at certain times and because males lose interest in them. The extent of this variation depends upon the species, ranging from an almost total lack of sexual behavior in nonestrous rats (which have low estrogen and are not receptive) to a decline in receptivity in the luteal part of the menstrual cycle in rhesus monkeys and great apes (Michael, 1969, 1975; Nadler, 1975).

The effect of these hormones on the sexual interest of the female primate is very interesting because it might be generalized to humans. Michael (1969, 1975) gave female rhesus monkeys hormone injections that deliberately paralleled the doses given to women taking the birth control pill. All four mating pairs of monkeys that were tested showed a decline in sexual behavior when injected with either estrogen-progesterone or with progesterone alone. The progesterone-induced depression in sexual activity had two causes: in some pairs the female appeared as interested as before, but the male had lost interest in her; in other pairs, the female showed an increased tendency to reject the male. Thus, the low frequencies of sexual behavior that occur in the female primate during the luteal phase and during late stages of pregnancy may be the result of the high progesterone levels that exist at those times.

The effect of testosterone upon the sexual interest of female infra-humans is also provocative in view of Money's belief that androgens increase the sex "drive" of female humans (Money and Ehrhardt, 1972). In primates, androgen injections increase the sexual motivation of females (Table 5.1). In fact, in primate females, low doses of testosterone had more effect on their sexual interest than estrogen, even though testosterone did not increase their attractiveness to a male (Herbert and Trimble, 1967; Michael and Zumpe, 1977). And when the adrenals of the female primate are suppressed or removed, the female primate begins rejecting the male. Testosterone injections may reverse the effects of adrenal removal (Everitt and Herbert, 1969; Herbert, 1970).

In summary, hormones strongly affect sexual behavior in infra-human females; consequently, their sexual behavior fluctuates with the hormonal changes of their estrous and menstrual cycles. Both estrogen and testosterone facilitate either male or female types of sexual behavior in many subprimates (but not hamsters), but biases seem to be built into both hormone and animal. In primates, progesterone inhibits and testosterone increases female sexual interest, but male behaviors are affected only by female hormones. The data from primates suggest that similar hormonal effects might be found in humans. However, it is also important to note that many infrahuman primate females—unlike subprimate females—are at least somewhat sexually active all of the time, suggesting that activational hormones have less effect on sexual behavior in these higher animals.

Aggression

Aggression, like sexual behavior, is an interaction. Just as it takes two to make love, it takes at least two to make war. Hormones can affect the aggression of a pair of animals in one of three ways (Floody and Pfaff, 1977). First, the hormone may affect aggression by increasing or decreasing competing behavior. If, for example, you are making love, you are not making war; if a hormone increased sexual behavior, it might decrease aggression. (On the other hand, sex and aggression frequently go together, so that when one increases, so does the other—and one can shift suddenly and unexpectedly into the other.) Second, the hormone might have no effect on the injected animal, but change the degree to which that animal elicits aggression from another animal. Progesterone may generally change the olfactory stimuli, pheromones, produced by animals so as to reduce attack directed toward them. Third, the hormone may actually change the tendency of the animal to respond aggressively to an aggressive stimulus. Because aggression is an interaction, and because there are three possible effects, any conclusions about hormones and aggression should be based on a careful analysis of the behavior of both animals in the pair.

Aggression between males and that of females during lactation seem to be the only types of aggression strongly under hormonal control, and even this may vary from species to species (Hart, 1974). Generally, intermale aggression is controlled by androgen but female aggression is not; female aggression may reach its peak during lactation when prolactin levels are high (Moyer, 1974; Noirot, Goyens, and Buhot, 1975). However, experience is the critical determinant of the relationship between aggression and hormones in all species in any situation.

Testosterone and Aggression.   Several types of research support that idea that male aggression depends on testosterone. For example, the increase in aggression that occurs at puberty in male animals seems to parallel the increase in testosterone that occurs then (Hutchinson, Ulrich, and Azrin, 1965; McKinney and Desjardins, 1973; Rose et al., 1974). Castration decreases male aggression. This decline occurs in all species, though at different rates (Hart, 1974). In general, it seems as though species that live together socially, in which aggressive behavior has dominance functions—such as in wild dogs and in primates—are less influenced by castration than are other species, such as cats, rats, hamsters, and mice (Hart, 1974). But as can be seen in Table 5.2, castration and testosterone injections affect a wide variety of aggressive behaviors in the nonsocial species.

Not only does testosterone have less effect on aggression in social species, it

TABLE 5.2

ACTIVATIONAL EFFECTS OF GONADAL HORMONES UPON AGGRESSION

Gender	Treatment and Species	Behaviors Affected and Types of Effects	References
Males	Castration and testosterone injections in all species	Many types of aggression decline with castration, including dominance, shock- and isolation-induced aggression, territorial spraying, and pup killing; all are restored by testosterone injections.	Baenninger (1974); Bernard and Paolino (1975); Cochran and Perachio (1977); Gandelman and vom Saal (1975); Hart (1974); Heilman et al. (1976); C. Lee and Naranjo (1974); Lincoln, Guinness, and Short (1972); K. Rosenberg and Sherman (1974); Turner (1975)
	Progesterone injections in mice and hamsters	Progesterone inhibits androgen-activated aggression and inhibits the aggression of partners.	Erpino (1975); C. Lee et al. (1976); Moyer (1974); Quadagno et al. (1977)
	Estrogen injections in rodents	Estrogen inhibits aggression and dominance in intact male mice and rats, but it increases aggression in castrated male mice and increases intermale (but not intrasexual) aggression in castrated male hamsters.	Finney and Erpino (1976); Moyer (1974); Payne and Swanson (1973); Quadagno et al. (1977); Work and Rogers (1972)
Females	Testosterone injections in rodents and primates	Short-term treatments had little or no effect on aggression.	Hart (1974); Tollman and King (1956)
		Prolonged treatment can increase aggression in females: it increases pup killing in rats, aggression in mice, and dominance in monkeys.	Birch and Clark (1946); Brain and Evans (1975); Cochran and Perachio (1977); Herman and Hyde (1976); Joslyn (1973); K. Rosenberg and Sherman (1974); Svare, Davis, and Gandelman (1974); Trimble and Herbert (1968)
	Progesterone injections in mice	In combination with either activational or inductive androgens, progesterone inhibits aggression; otherwise, there is no effect.	Bronson and Desjardins (1968); Erpino (1975); Michael (1971); Moyer (1974)
	Progesterone injections in hamsters	Progesterone inhibits the aggression of partners.	Floody and Pfaff (1977); Quadagno et al. (1977)

TABLE 5.2 *(Continued)* _____

Gender	Treatment and Species	Behaviors Affected and Types of Effects	References
	Progestin in primates	Progestin has no effect by itself; it may inhibit estrogen-activated aggression.	Birch and Clark (1946); Clark and Birch (1945)
	Estrogen injections in rodents and primates	Estrogen had little effect on rats, hamsters and mice; it increases aggression in primates.	Birch and Clark (1946, 1950); Clark and Birch (1945); Floody and Pfaff (1977); Michael (1968, 1971); Quadagno et al. (1977)
	Prolactin injections in hamsters	Prolactin increases aggression.	Wise and Pryor (1977)
	Castration in rodents	Effects reported had little consistency.	Floody and Pfaff (1977); Michael (1971); Quadagno et al. (1977)

Note: Aggression was usually assessed in males with male opponents and in females with opponents of either sex.

does not affect all types of aggression even in the other species. Pup killing in hamsters or frog killing in rats by either sex does not seem to depend upon gonadal hormones (B. Bernard, 1976; B. Bernard & Paolino, 1975; Marques and Valenstein, 1976). And most important, as summarized in Table 5.2, testosterone has much less effect on aggression in females than in males, unless the females had been neonatally androgenized.

Prolonged Testosterone Treatment in Females. In the absence of neonatal testosterone (as in normal females), the adult animal is less sensitive to the aggression-promoting effects of testosterone. But it seems that high doses of testosterone continued for a sufficiently long period of time can increase aggression and dominance (Table 5.2). This is important because it implies that, at least in this case, the combination of activational hormones and the experience of aggression and dominance can override the biases created by inductive hormones.

Hormones Other Than Testosterone. As can be seen in Table 5.2, the effects of hormones other than testosterone upon aggression depend upon activational and inductive androgens and upon the species. Aggression in primates may be affected by estrogen. The menstrual cycle may change aggression: female-female aggression is highest during menstruation (Rowell, 1970, Sassenrathe, Rowell, and Hendrick, 1973), and female-male aggression highest at the time of ovulation (Michael, 1968). However, Clark and Birch (1945) found that the effect of estrogen upon the aggression of castrated animals depended upon gender.

Effects of Experience. The effects of castration and of hormone injections upon aggression depend upon the past experiences of the animal. Generally, experience decreases the relationship between hormones and aggression. Dominance interactions are particularly dependent on past experiences (see Lumia, Rieder, and Rynierse, 1973; Work, Grossen, and Rogers, 1969). For example, testosterone injections will not restore lost dominance in castrated male mice (C. Lee and Naranjo, 1974); this may be because the memory of the experience of having lost fights made these male mice keep on giving up even after hormone injections. The converse may also be true. Male mice and female monkeys with fighting experience continue to exhibit aggression even after castration, or after testosterone injections have been halted (Beeman, 1947; Bevan, Daves, and Levy, 1960; Herman and Hyde, 1976; vom Saal et al., 1976). Apparently the memory of winning has more important effects on behavior than the change of hormones.

Summary and Interpretation.   Generally, only testosterone has reliable effects on aggression, and then only on intermale aggression. Castration reduces aggression in all males studied, and testosterone injections restore many aspects of aggression lost after castration. However, the effects are highly variable, and all aggressions do not depend on testosterone. The aggression of social-living species—such as dogs and many primates—seems less controlled by androgen than that of other species. Apparently up to a point increased testosterone increases aggression—just as aggression and dominance increase testosterone.

Nevertheless, high and prolonged doses of testosterone permanently increase aggression and dominance in females of several species, including primates. The details of these changes suggest a very subtle interaction between the way the animal responds to the change of hormones, and the way other organisms react to the change in that animal's behavior. But, overall, androgens have their major effects on aggression in animals that have been exposed to perinatal androgens.

Finally, experience apparently decreases the sensitivity of many aggressive behaviors to hormones. Since the effects of hormone changes depend upon past experience, the durable effects of long-term testosterone treatments on female aggression are probably the result of learning.

Parental Behavior

Subprimates.   The activational hormonal factors underlying maternal behavior are complex and not well understood.

The technique that has produced the most dramatic evidence of the effects of hormones upon maternal behavior is that of cross-transfusions. In this research, blood samples are taken from one animal, usually one exhibiting maternal behavior, and then injected into another animal. Cross-transfusions of blood taken from a recently pregnant rat thirty minutes after giving birth, and producing an equal mix of blood from the donor and recipient, produce all maternal behaviors in nonpregnant female rats (Terkel and Rosenblatt, 1972). All maternal behaviors except nest building appear in virgins transfused with this blood within 14.5 hours. These activational effects presumably depend upon the ratio of prolactin, estrogen, and progesterone in the blood of recently pregnant rats (Lamb, 1975b).

Horomones can also inhibit parental behaviors. Long-term castrations of male rats can increase their parental behaviors (Leon, Numan, and Moltz, 1973; Quadagno and Rockwell, 1972), suggesting an inhibitory role for testosterone. Castration can even increase some aspects of parental behaviors in female rats (Leon et al., 1973; Wade, 1976).

In these activational hormonal effects, we should again remember that hormones interact with both environment and experience. Castration of pregnant rats (who then require cesarean births) will cause a reduction in the acceptance of the young by inexperienced females; only about 50 percent will ever accept their young. But this treatment will produce little change in the behavior of experienced mothers, 95 percent of whom will accept their babies (Moltz and Wiener, 1966).

Primates. Activational hormones appear to be even less important in the control of parental behavior in lower primates, since sex differences in infant care appear well before the pubertal increase in hormones (Chamove et al., 1967; DeVore, 1963). However, castrated male rhesus monkeys, unlike intact males, will sometimes adopt infants (A. Wilson and Vessey, 1968), again suggesting that testosterone inhibits parental behaviors. Also, retrieval of wayward infants by females increases toward the end of pregnancy in rhesus macaques, and this may be related to the increase in prolactin that occurs at that time (Van de Wiele, as quoted by Phoenix & McCauley, 1974).

Summary. Despite a fair amount of research in this area, the hormonal basis of parental behavior remains obscure. It seems very likely, though, that the ratios of estrogen, progesterone, and prolactin will prove critical for the activation of at least some kinds of parental behaviors. It is clear, however, that the effect of hormones upon parental behaviors of any kind is affected by the past experience of the animal and by the current situation. Finally, some parental behaviors in subprimates, and most of them in primates, may be relatively independent of hormonal control or modulation.

Emotional Behavior and Learning

The activational effects of hormones upon learning will be very difficult to disentangle from their activational effects on spontaneous activity, fearfulness, exploration, and motivation. All four of these probably affect behavior in learning situations, and all four are probably affected by nonspecific activational effects of hormones.

Activity. Hormone injections change the level of activity, though many effects are specific to the apparatus for measuring activity, to the hormone, and to the gender and species of the animal involved. Much of the research in activity is summarized in Table 5.3. That hormones and puberty have different effects upon open-field activity and upon wheel activity once again suggests different motivational bases for those activities. Wheel activity is probably related more to general metabolic levels and body temperature (hungry rats run to keep warm), while open field activity may be affected by emotionality and/or curiosity. So, for example, puberty decreases metabolic rate and so may also decrease wheel activity, but estrogen may increase open field activity because it increases responsivity to novel stimuli (curiosity). Other explanations are also possible.

Emotionality. Estrogen has been claimed to decrease emotionality or fearfulness. For example, estrogen increases open-field activity in female rats, and

TABLE 5.3 _____

ACTIVATIONAL EFFECTS OF GONADAL HORMONES UPON ACTIVITY LEVELS AND EMOTIONALITY

Behavior	Effects and Comments	References
Open-Field Activity	Endogenous and exogenous estrogen increase activity, as does puberty in female rats.	Birke and Archer (1975); Burke and Broadhurst (1966); J. Gray (1971b); Guttman, Lieblich, and Gross (1975); Quadagno et al. (1977); Valle and Bols (1976)
	Estrogen has no effect in female hamsters or in male rats.	J. Gray (1971b); Swanson (1966)
	Testosterone injections in males or females or castrations of males have no durable effect.	Bernard and Paolino (1975); Blizard et al. (1975); J. Gray (1971b)
Wheel Activity	Endogenous and exogenous estrogen increase activity, but puberty decreases activity in female rats.	Birke and Archer (1975); Burke and Broadhurst (1966); J. Gray (1971b); Guttman et al. (1975); Krasnoff and Weston (1976); Quadagno et al. (1977); Roy and Wade (1975); Valle and Bols (1976)
	Testosterone increases activity in male rats.	Roy and Wade (1975)
Open-Field Defecation	Endogenous and exogenous estrogen decrease this behavior in both male and female rats.	J. Gray (1971b)
Persistence	Androgen—up to some optimal level—increases this behavior in chicks.	R. Andrew (1975a, 1975b, 1975c); Archer (1973, 1974b); Rogers (1974)
Adrenocortical Responses to Stress	Androgen decreases size of this response but increases duration.	J. Gray (1971b); Levine (1974)

this activity has sometimes been interpreted as indicating decreased emotionality. But estrogen also increases wheel activity, which is generally not used as a measure of emotionality. Estrogen also decreases defecation in the open field (see Table 5.3), which also has been interpreted as indicating that estrogen reduces fear. However, this effect may result from estrogen depressing food intake (you defecate less if you eat less; see Appendix B). Estrogen also depresses the performance of an active-avoidance response, which is taken to indicate reduced fear (P. Gray, 1977). Still, it is hard to separate estrogen's effects on emotionality from its effects on general energy metabolism (Birke and Archer, 1975; Slater and Blizard, 1976), activity levels, and exploration.

Many important studies (see Table 5.3) have investigated the effects of testosterone on the emotional behavior and attention of young chickens. According to

TABLE 5.4 _____

EFFECTS OF VARYING THE LEVELS OF GONADAL HORMONES UPON LEARNING

Behavior	Gender and Species	Effects and Comments	References
Active Avoidance	Male and female rats	Castration and testosterone injections have no effect except in neonatally androgenized females; progesterone inhibits this behavior.	Beatty and Beatty (1970a, 1970b); Bengelloun et al. (1976); Gyermek (1967); Scouten et al. (1975); Telegdy and Stark (1973)
	Female rats	Estrogen combined with progesterone inhibits this behavior, as does estrous.	Banerjee (1971); Burke and Broadhurst (1966); P. Gray (1977); Ikard et al. (1972)
Extinction of Active Avoidance	Male and female rats	Estrogen and progesterone decrease the rate of extinction; testosterone decreased the rate in castrated males but increased it in neonatally androgenized females.	Telegdy and Stark (1973)
Passive Avoidance	Male rats	Progestins inhibit performance.	Greidanus (1977)
Bar Press Response	Male and female rats	Moderate doses of testosterone facilitate the rate of response; estrogen and progesterone increase bar press duration; estrogen increases the rate of pressing when pressing causes pleasurable brain stimulation.	D. Broverman et al. (1968); R. Moss (1968); Prescott (1966)
Maze Performance	Male rats	Castration had no effect; estrogen injections decreased performance.	Commins (1932); Dawson (1972)
	Female rats	Puberty increases error frequency; testosterone injections had no effect.	Dawson (1972); Krasnoff and Weston (1976)

this research, testosterone increases the behavior often termed **persistence.** Persistence is measured by the subject having a longer visual fixation time, showing an increased frequency of contact with an empty food dish, and taking a longer time to switch from a response no longer rewarded to a new response. Thus, persistence may be related to attention, with testosterone, either endogenous or exogenous, increasing the persistence of attention to particular stimuli. However, very high levels of testosterone have opposite effects, suggesting a curvilinear relationship between testosterone and attention (Cummins et al., 1974). Remember this important suggestion, because it will come up again.

Learning. The rate of learning of an avoidance response is not consistently affected by hormones, as can be seen in Table 5.4. However, the rate of extinction of that response may be affected by hormones, and neonatal androgenization also determines the effect of activational hormones upon avoidance. P. Gray (1977) found that while the estrous cycle did not affect active-avoidance learning in female mice, estrous did inhibit the performance of that avoidance response. So he concluded that hormones do not affect learning ability or memory, but that they change behavior, perhaps by affecting fear levels or the sensitivity of the animal to shock.

On the other hand, as can be seen in Table 5.4, both bar press behavior and maze-learning performances are fairly consistently changed by hormones. For example, D. Broverman reported (D. Broverman et al., 1968) that although moderate doses of testosterone facilitated the learning of a fixed-ratio bar press in rats, high doses had no effect.

Summary.   Open-field and wheel activity are clearly and consistently altered by activational hormones. However, the effects appear very specific and limited to species, gender, hormone, and apparatus. Partially because of changes in open-field activity, estrogens are assumed to decrease emotionality. Much evidence supports that conclusion, but not all of the other possibilities have as yet been eliminated. But the physiological responses of females to stress are clearly different from those of males, at least in part because of sex differences in activational hormones.

Performances in a variety of learned tasks—active avoidance, bar press and maze learning—are also altered by changes in hormones. However, these changes may reflect the effects of hormones on motivation, emotionality, activity, attention, exploration, or sensory sensitivity, rather than effects on cognitive capacity itself. But for both bar press performance in rats and persistence in chickens, there may be an optimal level of testosterone needed for its effects such that moderate levels facilitate performance but neither high nor low levels of testosterone do. With activational effects, as with inductive effects, we clearly see that something is being changed; it seems that the hormones have general and far-reaching effects on performances in these situations.

Summary and Conclusions from Infra-human Research

The behavior that occurs in any given stimulus situation is a complex function of the hormonally affected brain structures and of the way the present stimulus situation is sensed and interpreted in light of both past experience and current hormonal conditions. Past experience with the particular hormonal condition also affects the organism's responses; it can learn how to interpret the effect of its own hormones on itself. The data summarized here represent the biasing effects that the gonadal hormones have upon an organism's preparedness to associate certain behaviors with given situations or given consequences of responding. For example, although estrogen combined with progesterone increases lordosis in female rats, this behavior does not occur in a vacuum. The hormones simply increase the probability that the stimuli supplied by the male—smell and touch— will lead to lordosis in the female.

Sexual behavior, aggression, parental behavior, emotional behavior, activity, and performances in learning situations are all affected by hormones. Therefore, sex differences in those behaviors are at least partly the result of sex differences in activational hormones. It is also interesting to note how often the hamster differs from other species—since reproductive roles are partially reversed in hamsters, this difference implies that reproductive roles are important in predicting the effects of hormones upon behavior. But here we will review the data on lower animals with an eye to see what it predicts about hormone-behavior relationships in the human animal.

In subprimates, sexual behavior is very dependent upon hormones. But the nature of the hormone-behavior relationships are different in the infra-human primates, and primate data might better predict the human primate. Will progesterone suppress sexual interest in human females and testosterone facilitate it, as in other primates?

Only some types of aggression—that between males and that by females during lactation—are affected by hormones. Since humans are a social-living species, the relationships between hormones and aggression may be less clear-cut in them than in other species. It must also be emphasized that the effect removal and restoration of androgen has upon aggression depends upon experience: the effect of losing or winning can override changes in hormones. Similarly, hormones may not have as great an effect on male social relationships in well-established groups of primates as they have on the relationships in unstable groups (Cochran and Perorchio, 1977; Eaton and Resko, 1974). All this suggests that the relationship between hormones and aggression in humans is very subtle and hard to uncover, if it exists at all.

Emotional responses, activity levels, maternal behaviors, and learning scores have also been reported to be affected by hormone injections, and so some effects of hormones upon sex differences in these behaviors in humans should also be looked for. In particular, spatial ability and attention may depend upon current levels of hormones. Also, the hormonal conditions of mothers right after giving birth might be important for parental behaviors and interest in humans.

In general, sex differences in activational hormones in animals cause sex differences only in the tendency to make a response, not in the kind of behavior. And relevant experiences can make the behavior—and sex differences—relatively independent of hormones.

HUMAN RESEARCH

In the following four sections, some commonly cited effects of hormones upon human behavior are discussed, paralleling the topics discussed in the context of animal research on activational hormones. You may find it helpful to review the appropriate section on lower animals as you read each section on humans. These sections are followed by a discussion of the effects of the combination of hormones contained in the birth control pill. The remaining sections discuss naturally occurring cycles in males and females and the effects of pregnancy and age upon hormone-behavior relationships.

Before reading these sections, you may wish to review the section at the beginning of the chapter on the various problems with experimental techniques. Human research is vulnerable to distortion by both experimenter and subject expectations. Since experience is so important a modifier of hormone-biased behaviors, what the subject expects to happen might very well be what does happen— even if the hormone did not affect behavior, and even if it was exerting a bias in exactly the opposite direction.

Hormones and Sexual Behavior

Humans have sometimes been castrated for treatment of cancer. When this was done, the sexual activity and interest of castrated males decreased, but that of castrated females was usually not affected (Money and Ehrhardt, 1972). This suggests that changes in female hormones have little effect on sexual behavior in women, but changes in testosterone may affect sexual activity in men. Still, the animal research suggests that there is a threshold in males; if androgen levels exceed that threshold, adding still more androgens will not produce more sexual behavior. The data from infra-human primates also suggests that androgens are involved in female sexual behavior as well as male sexual behavior.

In Males. Androgens have been used to successfully restore the sexual behavior of castrated men and of men with abnormally low androgen levels (but not Klinefelter's men). There is little evidence that injections of androgens can affect impotence caused by anything else (Bermant and Davidson, 1974).

Some studies have measured blood testosterone levels in men in an attempt to correlate them with sexual activity. Fox and his colleagues (1972) collected sixty blood samples from one man and found that testosterone levels taken during and after intercourse were significantly higher than at other times. However, this study noted that intercourse frequently took place on days in which very low testosterone levels were seen and that the major testosterone peaks were never associated with sexual activity. In a report in *Nature* (Anonymous, 1970), a man said his beard grew faster when he was anticipating sexual activity. However, three other studies found little or no relationship between testosterone levels and intercourse frequency or timing (Monti, Brown, and Corriveau, 1977; Raboch and Starka, 1972; Stearns et al., 1973a).

Doering and his coworkers (Doering et al., 1974) found significant between-subject correlations between testosterone level and sexual activity, but, more important, they found no relationship between a subject's testosterone level and when his own sexual activity took place. The between-subject correlation of testosterone levels on the day before sexual activity with the number of orgasms was −.62; the correlation between orgasms and the level of testosterone on the day after sex was −.39. Thus, the sexual behavior of a given male could not be predicted by measuring his testosterone level from day to day, but his sexual behavior could be predicted by comparing his own testosterone level to that of other men.

Hormones other than testosterone have also been reported to affect male sexual interest. Treatment of men with testosterone antagonists decreases sexual behavior, so these drugs are sometimes used to treat sexual offenders (Bancroft et al., 1974; Blumer and Migeon, 1975; Laschet and Laschet, 1975; Sands, 1954). However, in none of these reports did the hormone manipulations change the direction of or the object of sexual desire, and in some cases the change in sexual behavior continued well past the end of the treatment (Laschet, 1973). Both of these results suggest the importance of experience in human sexual behavior.

In Females.   Androgens have also been related to sexual arousal in women. Salmon and Geist (1943) reported that they successfully treated frigidity with testosterone; the clitoris, in particular, became more sensitive in these women. Sopchak and Sutherland (1960) gave women both estrogen and androgen, but only androgen increased sexual interest. Waxenberg, Drellich, and Sutherland (1959; see also Waxenberg, 1969) have found that in women who have had both an adrenalectomy (which will reduce adrenal androgen) and an ovarectomy (reduces estrogen), only the loss of the adrenals was associated with a loss in sexual interest—even when the adrenalectomy significantly improved health. Also, the sex drive in women with a late treated adrenogenital syndrome declined once cortisol therapy decreased their adrenal androgen levels (Ehrhardt, Evers, and Money, 1968).

Summary and Interpretation.   Thus, androgen seems to be related to sexual interest in both males and females, but the nature of the relationship is far from clear. Even among lower animals, the relationships often were not clear and did not always seem to be direct, though they were often dramatic. Although suppression or removal of androgen reduces sexual behavior in the human male, sexual activity may occur following a period with a relatively low level of androgens. One can apparently predict sexual behavior more accurately by comparing one man's androgen levels to those of several other men, than by looking at the changes in levels that occur from day to day just in that man. Also, relatively low levels of androgen are probably sufficient for complete male sexual behavior. Thus, going above this low threshold would probably not produce any changes in sexual performances. Finally, there may be a time lag of unknown duration that occurs between testosterone changes and the correlated behavioral changes.

None of the studies on human females involved normal women, so it is difficult to generalize thse findings. However, the results are consistent with the effects of androgen and adrenalectomy upon the sexual behavior of infrahuman primate females. In view of the possibility that androgen increases sexual arousal, one wonders about the therapeutic value of the treatment of hypersexuality in women in Victorian times: these women were sometimes given androgens to cure them.

Both similarities and differences between human and lower animal data can be found. In both humans and infra-humans, experience can make behavior independent of hormonal changes, since temporary hormone therapy causes relatively durable change in behavior. But only the amount of sexual behavior—not the type—could be changed by changing hormones in humans, which was not the case with infra-humans. Humans do not seem to have any biases built into the hormones.

Hormones and Aggression

Most studies on human aggression have attempted to correlate testosterone level with aggressiveness of the individual, both within and between subjects. Testosterone level shows high within-subject correlations in men over days, weeks, or months (Ehrenkranz, Bliss, and Sheard, 1974; Kreuz and Rose, 1972; Meyer-Bahl-burg et al., 1974). Testosterone varies within a given male from morning to night and from season to season, and the level in men and women varies monthly, but people who have relatively high levels at one time will also have relatively high levels another time. Thus, it is possible to compare people to look for differences in behavior as a function of the relative difference in testosterone level. These data could help us decide what proportion of sex differences in aggression might be due to sex differences in the level of activational androgens; the more closely related aggression is to androgen levels, the more biological bias there would be for sex differences in aggression.

In Men. The first correlational study of testosterone and aggression in men was done by Persky, Smith, and Basu (1971). They studied two healthy groups of men, eighteen of whom ranged in age from seventeen to twenty-eight, and fifteen of whom ranged in age from thirty-one to sixty-six. All the men took a battery of tests, including the Buss-Durkee Hostility Inventory (BDHI), a paper-and-pencil test asking the respondent to mark aggressive statements that he thinks apply to himself. The questions cover such things as the likelihood of getting into a fight or losing his temper. Scores on the BDHI and the blood production rate of testosterone measured over a two-hour period were significantly and positively corre-lated in the younger men ($r = .66$); test scores and the concentration of testosterone in the blood were also correlated ($r = .49$). Testosterone level or production rate did not significantly correlate with aggression in the older men.

This study had a powerful impact on the field—as you can imagine—but such a correlation had been suggested before that study. For example, it was known that the testosterone level in males rises rapidly at puberty and that aggression also increases at that time. Sands and his coworkers (Sands, 1954; Sands and Chamberlain, 1952; Strauss et al., 1952) gave androgens to young men. One group of schizophrenic patients showed a decrease in fearfulness and apprehension and increased self-confidence and euphoria with androgen treatment; two men also showed increases in aggression and tension. In young men with "inadequate" personalities ("shrinking violets" as they were called), androgen therapy resulted in a decrease in inferiority, timidity, and apathy. An androgen also increased masculine activity and self-confidence, such that timid men became more confident, and hostile men were made even more aggressive. Hawk (cited by Moyer, 1974) described a large group of castrated men who were given large doses of testosterone. In some cases, the injections had to be discontinued because the patients become generally destructive; they "had reverted to all of their antisocial tendencies, were attacking small children, starting fights, breaking windows and destroying furniture" (quoted in Moyer, 1974, p. 364).

With this background, the next important study appeared. Kreuz and Rose (1972) studied twenty-one prisoners, selected because they exhibited both extremes of aggressive behavior, and over a two-week period, measured blood testosterone six times in each man. Neither the frequency of prison fights involving these men nor their scores on any paper-and-pencil test—including the BDHI—correlated with testosterone levels or with each other. However, those individuals with a history of violent crimes in adolescence had significantly higher levels of testosterone in prison. Also, there was a significant and positive correlation between the age at the first occurrence of the aggressive crime and the current levels of testosterone ($r = .65$). This study and the work by Sands and Persky and colleagues suggest a correlation between testosterone and aggression—but only in young men.

Ehrenkranz, Bliss, and Sheard (1974) measured testosterone levels on three successive days in thirty-six male prisoners: twelve who were chronically aggressive; twelve who were socially dominant without being physically aggressive; and twelve who were neither dominant nor aggressive. Although the aggressive group scored significantly higher on the BDHI than either of the other two groups, BDHI scores and testosterone levels did not significantly correlate. However, both the dominant and the aggressive groups had significantly higher testosterone levels than did the nonaggressive, nondominant group (8.36, 10.10, and 5.99 μg/ml, respectively). *dominant monkey syndrome*

Doering and his colleagues (Doering et al., 1975; Doering, Brodie et al., 1975) measured plasma testosterone levels in normal men over a two-month period. The mean of each subject's testosterone levels, averaged over all test days, was compared across subjects to the mean of each subject's self-rated hostility. The result was a nonsignificant correlation of +.348. The only significant correlation of testosterone with the BDHI was on the Indirect Aggression Subscore (+.415, uncorrected for alpha levels). Persky and his coworkers (1971) also found this subscale to be the one most strongly related to testosterone levels.

Finally, three recent studies failed to find any correlation between testosterone and either the various scales of the BDHI or aggressive behaviors (Meyer-Dahlburg et al., 1974; Monti et al., 1977; Persky et al., 1977). It may be important that none of these studies used adolescents or studied adolescent aggression in adult subjects.

In Women.   One attempt was made to correlate testosterone levels with aggression in women (Persky, 1974). Testosterone in women varies with the phase of the menstrual cycle. Persky found a small but significant relationship between BDHI scores and the average testosterone levels of women in the follicular phase. However, although testosterone levels significantly changed over menstrual phases, BDHI scores did not.

Aggression in women has also been related to the premenstrual syndrome, a time when estrogen, progesterone and testosterone levels are rapidly falling (see Moyer, 1974), although testosterone may decline comparatively less than the other two hormones. This possibility will be discussed later in this chapter.

Summary.   Although the research seems contradictory, some suggestions can be made. There does seem to be a small (and sometimes significant) correlation between testosterone level and aggression as measured by BDHI score; the correlations reported have ranged from .27 to .66. However, between-subject relationships seem stronger than within-subject relationships. In other words, a subject's change in testosterone level does not consistently predict a change in his or her own aggressive behavior, but the mean testosterone level often differentiates between groups of subjects with different levels of aggression, especially among adolescent males. This does not mean, however, that testosterone caused aggression or dominance; the reverse could just as well be true. Also, it might be the case that the correlation of androgens and aggression is very low or completely nonexistent among relatively unstressed people, since stress may increase the aggression promoting effects of testosterone.

If there is an effect of testosterone, it may not be due to any specific activational effect. Testosterone may nonspecifically increase brain activity, thus increasing responsivity to all stimuli. Aggressive stimuli would then be associated with stronger (more aggressive-looking) responses in the presence of testosterone.

Nevertheless, the data suggest that testosterone levels and aggression are more closely related in adolescents than in older males. This might reflect a durable, inductivelike effect of pubertal androgen. Such a possibility was suggested recently in a study of pubertal androgen levels and aggression in male mice (Selmanoff et al., 1977). Is this also true of humans? Perhaps experience with the effect of pubertal increases in androgen levels makes adult aggression relatively independent of androgen levels such that only adolescent levels of androgens can predict either adolescent or adult aggression. It certainly seems that adult aggression is independent of adult androgen. Castration or treatment with testosterone antagonists has little or no effect on aggression in adult males, except on sexual aggression, like rape (Moyer, 1974).

Hormones and Emotions

Most research on this topic has been done in women and has attempted to relate emotions to hormonal changes during the menstrual cycle or has looked at the birth control pill and postpartum depression. All these topics will be discussed later. That hormones do affect emotions is recognized, however. All three gonadal hormones are given, or once were given, to psychiatric patients (Glick, 1967). Progesterone has been used to treat anxiety (Kopell, 1969), and testosterone and estrogen have both been given to treat depression (Black, 1975; Klaiber et al., 1974; Sands, 1954).

Some studies have attempted to correlate testosterone levels and emotional-social behaviors in men, but these attempts have usually been peripheral to the main focus of the study (Doering et al., 1975; Ehrenkranz et al., 1974; Monti et al., 1977; Persky et al., 1971). They do not provide clear evidence for any relationship, however. Anxiety and depression (or negative self-description) have been reported to be both negatively and positively correlated with testosterone levels. Also, in most of these studies there were no corrections for alpha levels, and cause and effect relationships were not clear.

Hormones and Intellectual Ability

Hormones may affect learning performance, but this may be caused by nonspecific activational effects. Both testosterone and estrogen (at least in moderate doses) increase brain activity (D. Broverman et al., 1968), while progesterone is an inhibitor, and can even be used as an anesthetic (Kopell, 1969).

Kwashiorkor.   One of the first suggestions that hormones might affect cognitive processes in humans came from Dawson's study (1972) of West African kwashiorkor males. **Kwashiorkor** is a starvation-induced syndrome in which a male is exposed to high levels of estrogen from infancy onwards because his liver is unable to break it down, so estrogen accumulates. These men develop breasts and muscularity decreases. Dawson also reported that compared to other males they had significantly lower spatial ability and were more field dependent. They had lower numerical and higher verbal ability and were even more feminine as measured by a masculinity-femininity (gender role) scale. Some of these effects are probably not the result of an increase in estrogen, but of a decrease in androgens, since the testes of these men were shrunken. Some effects also may be the result of the man's own response to his altered appearance.

Progesterone Injections.   Progesterone, when given to normal men, significantly depresses reaction times (Little, Matta, and Zahn, 1974). This study also found a progesterone-induced decrease in the variation of the heart rate and in the rate of skin conductance changes (a measure of emotionality), suggesting a decrease in arousal.

Cognitive Ability and Body Type.   In one set of research reports, androgen levels were inferred from body appearance, and then the relative cognitive abilities of these people with either masculine or feminine body types were assessed on a variety of intellectual tasks. Androgen levels in males have been inferred from the degree to which the men were muscular and hairy. Androgen levels in women were inferred from their narrowness of hips, wideness of shoulders, smallness of breasts, and muscularity.

Androgen levels in men, as inferred from body types, have been found to be positively correlated with performances on such tasks as rapid reading and object naming, speed of tapping, and color naming, and tasks involving an individual's ability to resist fatigue (D. Broverman, 1964; D. Broverman et al., 1964). However, these men do poorly on tests of spatial ability. A. Peterson (1976) also found that by age eighteen (but not before) boys with a more masculine body not only had lower spatial scores, they also had higher verbal fluency scores than males with a less masculine body. For girls, those with the more masculine body had higher spatial scores; verbal fluency scores were not related to body type in females. Together, the results of the Broverman and Peterson studies suggest that moderate levels of androgen (as found in feminized males and masculinized females) may optimize spatial ability, but that verbal fuency may be best at very high or very low levels of androgen, and perhaps estrogen.

D. Broverman (1964. See also Blum and Broverman, 1967) has also related androgens, again inferred from body appearance, to persistence. Men with a good speed of tapping and low spatial ability who tended to have masculine body types were called *strong automatizers*. Strong automatizers achieved higher occupational levels. They also had a high level of persistence, maintaining an original response when the task called for a change in the response. The relation between androgens and persistence is somewhat similar to that found with chickens in the studies discussed earlier.

It is somewhat questionable to infer androgen levels from body types, because genetics, nutrition, and activity levels also influence the body. Also, the effect of androgens upon facial and pubic hair, for example, may be permanent even though the androgen levels had changed before the time of the actual experiment. Still, injections of androgens have confirmed some of these effects.

Androgen Injections. Androgen injections also increase persistence, at least up to a certain point. Androgen injections can prevent the fatigue-related decline in ability to perform serial subtractions over the course of a day (Klaiber et al., 1971, 1974). But this effect may be curvilinearly related to testosterone levels, since the greatest number of problems are solved with intermediate levels of the hormone. This result is again similar to the relationship found between testosterone and attention in chickens (Cummins et al., 1974).

Summary. The data suggest that spatial ability and verbal fluency may be somewhat hormone-sensitive in humans. Both masculinity of body type and kwashiorkor affect these cognitive skills. Moderate levels of androgens are associated with optimum spatial performances, while verbal fluency seems best at very high levels or very low levels of testosterone, or at high levels of estrogen. Testosterone may also increase attention and persistence in a variety of areas, and opposes fatigue. So some of the sex differences that occur in these areas may be related to sex differences in activational hormones.

The Birth Control Pill

Birth control pills contain artificial estrogens and progestins in various ratios. Two kinds of pills have been commonly used. Someone using the **combination** type takes twenty identical pills with both estrogens and progestins. Someone using the **sequential** type (which has been taken off the market because of its possible association with cancer) starts off by taking fourteen to sixteen pills containing only an estrogen, and then takes five or six pills containing both an estrogen and a progestin. Both pills render the woman temporarily infertile. This is not only because they inhibit ovulation, but also because the hormone-induced change in the vaginal and uterine chemistry decreases the motility and survival time of sperm. The combination pill also greatly suppresses the normal hormone cycles and seems to depress blood testosterone levels (Persky, 1974; see Figure 2.10).

Physical Side Effects. Some of the minor (either not life threatening or rare) side effects associated with pill use are summarized in Table 5.5. As can be seen, there are a number of them.

Some women have problems when they stop taking the pill hormones. Some women do not have a menstrual period, others have abnormal milk flow, infertility, and nonmalignant tumors on the pituitary (Sherman, 1971). Long-term pill use (two-and-a-third to nine years) sometimes results in a profound depression in pituitary gonadotropic activity (Marshall, Reed, and Gordon, 1976; Perez-Lopez, L'Hermite, and Robyn, 1975) even after the women stop taking the pill. Other studies have reported depression, fatigue, and decreased intellectual performance after sex hormone withdrawal in both males and females (Kutner and Brown, 1972; Little et al., 1974; B. Sommer, 1972). The most recent report concluded that hormone withdrawal was the sole culprit in half of the women who discontinued the pill and had problems, and that it contributed to the problems of the other half (Ingerslev, Jeppesen, and Ramsing, 1976).

There are also more serious side effects. These include an increased risk of heart attacks, especially in women over forty who smoke. The pill also increases the tendency to form blood clots, which may lead to an increased incidence of ce-

TABLE 5.5 ──────────────────────────────────────

MINOR SIDE EFFECTS REPORTED IN USERS OF A BIRTH CONTROL PILL

Effects	References
Enlargement and tenderness of breasts Shortening of menstrual cycles, with decreased bleeding Breakthrough bleeding in midcycle and vaginal discharges Weight gain and water retention; nausea and diarrhea Headaches, varicose veins, nose bleeds, leg cramps, sweating, and fatique	Bardwick (1972)
Thyroid depression	Weeke and Hansen (1975)
Lowering of systolic blood pressure, lowering of serum glucose levels, increase of white blood cell count, impairment of glucose tolerance (these are all effects of a combination pill)	Cathelineau (1976); Friedman, Richart, and Vande Wiele (1974); Pietarinen, Leichter, and Pratt (1977)
Decreased adrenal cortisol secretion	Durber, Lawson, and Daly (1976); Marinari, Leshner, and Doyle (1976)
Impairment of liver function, leading to jaundice	Hutt (1972b)
Slowness in metabolization of alcohol (causing user to stay drunk longer)	R. Jones et al. (1976)
Decrease in allergies	Smolensky et al. (1974); Suteri (cited by Petit, 1976)
Brain electrical changes that may last well past the time pill use is stopped	Creutzfeldt et al. (1976), Matsumoto et al. (1966); Struve et al. (1976)
Nausea (caused by estrogen-dominated pill); weight gain (caused by progestin-dominated pill)	Cullberg (1972)

rebral strokes. According to a review (Marx, 1976), the pill is also related to breast cancer. Both uterine and cervical cancer have also been linked to pill use (see McDonald et al., 1977; E. Stern et al., 1977).

However, past usage of the pill does not seem to be associated with a greater than normal frequency of genetically abnormal fetuses. Instead, it seems that women who can best tolerate the pill are also less likely to have fetuses with chromosome abnormalities (Boúe, Boúe, and Lazar, 1975). That is, the same physiology enabling a woman to tolerate the pill also makes her less of a risk to have a genetically abnormal fetus.

Psychological Side Effects. Any psychological side effects of pill use will provide further evidence of hormone-behavior relationships, and further evidence that sex differences may be affected by some hormonal bias. But although many physical changes are associated with pill use, remarkably few psychological effects have been consistently reported (Paige, 1971).

However, several problems of interpretation may have contributed to the lack of consistency (Leeton, 1973). Among the problems is finding an appropriate control group, since women who choose to take the pill may differ psychologically or physically from other women. Also, different pills contain different artificial hormones in different ratios, and the woman's own hormone levels might affect her responses to the pill. The major problem, though, is that different studies use different psychological measures, and many just used self-reports or researcher's impressions. These measures leave the door wide open for the preconceptions of the women or the biases of the researchers to determine the results. One way to eliminate some of these problems is to use a **double-blind procedure** (where neither the doctor nor the patient knows what pill is given to whom) and either randomly assign people to have the pill or the placebo or use a **cross-over technique** (where the same person will have the pill for one period of time and a placebo for another).

Five studies using the double-blind procedure gave no consistent results (Goldzieher et al., 1971; Grant and Pryse-Davies, 1968; Grounds, Davies, and Mowbray, 1970; Nilsson and Sölvell, 1967; Silbergeld, Brast, and Noble, 1971). Other studies allow us to reach some conclusions, though. The pill may cause depression in some women. Leeton (1973) used a double-blind, cross-over design with forty-five subjects to study pill-induced depression. There were no mean differences in depression between the combination pill months and the placebo months. But he found that four of his patients were definitely depressed by the pill; their depression increased when they took the pill and was promptly relieved when they stopped. However, the fact that three of these women were also quite depressed before they started on the pill and all four had severe side effects suggests that these types of women are particularly vulnerable to pill-induced depression. In support of this Winston (1973) found that the women most likely to develop depression with pill use either had a history of depression or had severe premenstrual tension or post-partum (after giving birth) depression. It could be that those women represent a particular biochemical group especially susceptible to the chemical changes associated with depression, or that those women have learned to attribute depression to hormone changes rather than to their own external experience and stress. Or else the stress associated with depression may also make women more susceptible to hormone-induced increases in depression.

Cullberg (1972) carried out one of the better designed and more complete experiments. He used a double-blind procedure and randomly assigned women to one of three different combination pills or to a placebo for two months. There were eighty women in each of the four groups. Overall, they had few adverse reactions, but significantly more of them were reported by women on the pills than by women on the placebo. Of the two groups of women given an estrogen-dominated pill, 14 percent more of them than of the control group complained of symptoms such as nervousness; whereas of the group given a progestin-dominated pill 18 percent more complained of symptoms like depression. These psychological changes were independent of physical changes.

In most of Cullberg's subjects, symptoms of premenstrual tension were not changed by the pill. However, in some women both premenstrual tension and reactions to the pill seemed hormone-related. The premenstrual symptoms of these women were improved by the progestin-dominated pill and made worse by the estrogen-dominated pill. And the pill's effects on the mental state of the woman was linked to its effect on premenstrual tension. The group without premenstrual tension reacted adversely only to the progestin-dominated pill; the group with premenstrual tension reacted adversely only to the estrogen-dominated pill.

Thus, most women do not seem to be affected psychologically by the hormones in the birth control pill. However, some effects may be reported even by psychologically healthy women (Bardwick, 1972). The women adversely affected by the hormones in the pill seem to form a particular subgroup; the adverse responses to pill use are related to the effect their own hormones have on these women. Progestin-dominated pills seem more likely to produce adverse reactions, particularly depression. These effects are most likely to occur in women who are already depressed (already stressed), in women who have genetically defective babies, and in women who do not have premenstrual symtoms. Women with premenstrual symptoms reacted more to the estrogen-dominated pill, most often with nervousness. Genetically determined susceptibility may also be a factor.

Correlates of the Menstrual Cycle

In Tables 5.6 and 5.7, physiological and behavioral correlates of the menstrual cycle are presented according to the phase in which they occur in a normal, twenty-eight-day cycle. Emphasis was given to those studies that measured the same women several times (preferably many of them) under controlled conditions, as well as to those studies that more accurately estimated the day of the cycle, either by measuring body temperature or by measuring hormone levels, particularly that of LH. Also emphasized were some more recent data that used more sophisticated statistical rhythm evaluation techniques (Ferin et al., 1974). If this technique was not used and phase is simply inferred by counting days since the last menstrual period, the chance for error is too great. Cycle length varies so greatly among women—and often even in the same woman from month to month—that any effect of hormones will be undetectable unless the phase is measured accurately.

Only some of the physiological changes that have been reported appear in the table; we selected only those that seem most likely to be related to behavior. The extensive review of Southam and Gonzaga (1965) was the source of many of the cyclical changes, and many of the changes that do not appear in the table can also be found in that review. However, Table 5.6 also contains many effects discovered or confirmed since 1965.

The tremendous variability in the data in both tables must not be overlooked. All of the effects are not seen in all women, and to find many of them requires testing and averaging data from a very large number of women. One of the best ways to gain an appreciation of the variability is to read the detailed individual daily records supplied by Altmann, Knowles, and Bull (1941). Variability is also created by the fact that many measurements fluctuate with the time of day as well as the day of the month. And the daily, or **circadian,** rhythms are altered by the monthly cycle, such that the daily peak depends on the phase of the cycle (see Smolensky et al., 1974) and may even depend upon the season of the year, as will be shown later in this chapter for testosterone cycles. Thus, disagreement among studies

TABLE 5.6

PHYSIOLOGICAL CORRELATES OF THE MENSTRUAL CYCLE

Effect	Phase and Day				
	Menstrual 1–5	Follicular 6–13	Ovulatory 14–16	Luteal 17–25	Premenstrual 26–28
Hormones	All low	Moderate FSH; highest estradiol; low LH and progesterone; high testosterone	High FSH and LH; moderate estradiol and progesterone	Moderate to high estradiol; high progesterone; low LH and FSH	Low LH and FSH; declining estradiol and progesterone
Temperature			Low (Altmann, Knowles, and Bull, 1941; Dyrenfurth et al., 1974; Little and Zahn, 1974; Southam and Gonzaga, 1965)	High (Altman et al., 1941; Dyrenfurth et al., 1974; Little and Zahn, 1974; Southam and Gonzaga, 1965)	
Weight				Lowest (Friedman et al., 1974)	Highest (Friedman et al., 1974; Southam and Gonzaga, 1965)
Heart Rate	Low (P. Engel and Hildebrandt, 1974; Friedman et al., 1974; Little and Zahn, 1974)		High (for older women) (Little and Zahn, 1974)	High (for younger women) (Friedman et al., 1974; Little and Zahn, 1974)	High (Friedman et al., 1974)
Heart Rate Variability		High (for young women) (Little and Zahn, 1974)		Low (Little and Zahn, 1974)	
Blood Pressure			Highest (P. Engel and Hildebrandt, 1974; Friedman et al., 1974)	Lowest (P. Engel and Hildebrandt, 1974; Friedman et al., 1974)	

Thyroid Action[1] (TSH response to TRH)	High (Sanchez-Franco et al., 1973)		
MAO Activity[2]		High in blood platelets (Belmaker et al., 1974)	Low in blood platelets; high in blood (Belmaker et al., 1974; Klaiber et al., 1974)
Plasma Electrolytes		Low potassium; high calcium (B. Bell, Christie, and Venables, 1975; Southam and Gonzaga, 1965)	High potassium; low calcium (B. Bell et al., 1975; Southam and Gonzaga, 1965)
Serum Glucose	Low, increased incidence of diabetic coma (Friedman et al., 1974; Southam and Gonzaga, 1965)	Highest (Friedman et al., 1974)	Low (Friedman et al., 1974; Morton et al., 1953)
Physiological Responses to Stress		Low (Marinari et al., 1976)	High (Marinari et al., 1976)
White Blood Cell and Red Blood Cell Counts	Low (Friedman et al., 1974)	High (Friedman et al., 1974)	High (Friedman et al., 1974)
Disease Resistance	Low (Southam and Gonzaga, 1965)		Low (Southam and Gonzaga, 1965)

[1] Thyroid action: pituitary release of thyroid stimulating hormone (TSH) more sensitive to stimulation by the hypothalamus (TRH).
[2] MAO activity: inhibition by MAO of the release of transmitter substances and therefore of part of the brain's activity.

TABLE 5.6 (continued)

| Effect | Phase and Day | | | | |
	Mentrual 1–5	Follicular 6–13	Ovulatory 14–16	Luteal 17–25	Premenstrual 26–28
Sensitivity to Allergens	Highest (Smolensky et al., 1974)		Lowest (Smolensky et al., 1974)		
Resting Skin Conductance[3]	High (older women) (Little and Zahn, 1974)			Low (older women) (Little and Zahn, 1974)	
Skin Changes	Easy bleeding (Southam and Gonzaga, 1965)				Darkening and acne (Southam and Gonzaga, 1965)
Migraine Headaches					High (Somerville, 1972)
Incidence of Seizures	High (Laidlaw, 1956; Logothetis et al., 1959; Southam and Gonzaga, 1965)			Lowest (Kopell, 1969)	High (Laidlaw, 1956; Southam and Gonzaga, 1965)
Alpha Frequency[4]		Lowest (Creutzfeldt et al., 1976)		Highest (Creutzfeldt et al., 1976)	
EEG Photic Driving Response[5]		Fewer (Klaiber et al., 1974)		Greater (Klaiber et al., 1974)	
Sensitivity to the Intoxicating Effects of Alcohol	Less sensitive (B. Jones and Jones, 1976)				Most sensitive (B. Jones and Jones, 1976)

[3] Skin conductance: a measure of emotionality; electrical resistance of the skin.
[4] Alpha frequency: the rate of cyclical brain activity in a relaxed, waking state.
[5] EEG photic driving response: a measure of brain electrical activity; the degree to which brain activity can become synchronous with regularly flashing (strobe) lights.

TABLE 5.7

BEHAVIORAL CORRELATES OF THE MENSTRUAL CYCLE

Effect	Phase and Day				
	Menstrual 1–5	Follicular 6–13	Ovulation 14–16	Luteal 17–25	Premenstrual 26–28
Positive Activation (vigor, elation, surgency, social affection, and centration)	Low (Little and Zahn, 1974)		High (Altmann et al., 1941; Little and Zahn, 1974)		Low (Little and Zahn, 1974)
Anxiety, Apprehension, Depression, Tension	Highest (Hamburg, Moss, and Yalum, 1968; Paige, 1971)	High (Benedek and Rubenstein, 1939a, 1939b; Patkai, Johannson, and Post, 1974)	Low or Lowest (Benedek, 1959; Ivey and Bardwick, 1968; Paige, 1971)		High (Altmann et al., 1941; Benedek, 1959; Beumont, Richards, and Gelder, 1975; Ivey and Bardwick, 1968; Paige, 1971; Shainess, 1961)
Restlessness				Lowest (Patkai et al., 1974)	Highest (Patkai et al., 1974)
Hostility	High (Paige, 1971)		Lowest (Paige, 1971)		Highest (Paige, 1971)
Aggression					High (Morton et al., 1953; Silbergeld et al., 1971)
Percent Volunteering for an Experiment	9 (Doty and Silverthorne, 1975)	53	91	19	25
Sexual Intercourse and Sexual Arousal			Highest (Benedek and Rubenstein, 1939a, 1939b;		High (Udry and Morris, 1968)

TABLE 5.7 (continued)

Effect	Phase and Day				
	Menstrual 1–5	Follicular 6–13	Ovulatory 14–16	Luteal 17–25	Premenstrual 26–28
Sleep			Hamburg et al., 1968; McCance, Luff, and Widdowson, 1937; Udry and Morris, 1968 Shortest (Patkai et al., 1974)	Rapid eye-movement sleep increased (Petre-Quadens and De Lee, 1974)	Rem sleep time longest, most disturbances (Altmann et al., 1941; Patkai et al., 1974; Petre-Quadens and De Lee, 1974)
Likelihood of Activity Peaks		Highest (Dan, 1976)	Lowest (Dan, 1976)		
Highest Auditory Frequency Producing Beats	High (Oster, 1973)	Low (Oster, 1973)	High (Oster, 1973)		
Visual, Auditory, and Touch Sensitivity		Highest (Henkin, 1974)	Perceived pitch as lower than it is (Wynn, 1972)	Lowest (Henkin, 1974)	Perceived pitch as lower than it is (Wynn, 1972)
Sensitivity to Pain and to Cold	Low (Kenshalo, 1966; Procacci et al., 1972)	Low (Kenshalo, 1966; Procacci et al., 1972)		Highest (Kenshalo, 1966; Procacci et al., 1972)	

Olfactory and Taste Sensitivity	Low (Good, Geary, and Engen, 1976; Henkin, 1974; Le Magnen, 1974; Schnieder and Wolf, 1955; Vierling and Rock, 1967)	High (Good et al., 1976; Henkin, 1974; Le Magnen, 1948, 1950; Vierling and Rock, 1967)	
Craving for Sweets		High (Good et al., 1976; Le Magnen, 1948, 1950; Pietras and Moultor, 1974)	High (Morton et al., 1953; S. Smith and Sauder, 1969)
Pleasantness of a Sweet Tasting Solution		Slowest change from pleasant to unpleasant following ingestion of a large quantity of glucose (Wright and Crow, 1973)	Least Pleasant (Wright and Crow, 1973)
Reaction Time and Calculation Time	Slowest (Creutzfeld et al., 1976)		Fastest (Creutzfeldt et al., 1976)
Rod and Frame Task (spatial ability)	More field dependent (Klaiber et al., 1974)		More field independent (Klaiber et al., 1974)
Time Estimation			Longer perceived elapsed time (Kopell et al., 1969)

should be expected and will continue to be seen until the nature of the daily, monthly, and annual rhythms have been identified and their interactions accurately characterized.

Physical Correlates.   The best substantiated physical correlates of the cycle are temperature and weight. The lowest body temperature is usually seen on the day preceding ovulation, and the premenstrual weight gain is largely attributable to water retention.

The changes in brain electrical activity (seizures, alpha frequency, photic driving) are usually attributed, directly or indirectly, to the suppressive effects of progesterone or to the arousing effects of estrogen. **Alpha frequency** is the rhythm of brain electrical activity associated with being in an awake but relaxed state, usually with eyes closed. These effects of the hormones may be mediated by their effects on transmitter substances or on MAO, or to their effects on electrolytes such as potassium and calcium, which also affect the excitability of nerve cells. Serum glucose could also affect brain excitability, as well as affecting taste responses. Thus, the general state of the brain may vary with the menstrual cycle.

Psychological Correlates.   Again, although there is tremendous variability, positive moods seem to predominate at ovulation, and negative moods (anxiety, restlessness, hostility, and aggression) seem to be high in the premenstrual phase. But it should be pointed out that all women do not show these emotional changes. Persky (1974) preselected a group of young, healthy women on the basis of a psychological test battery, a psychiatric interview, and a medical history. In this very select group of twenty-nine women, there were no cyclical changes detected in moods, no menstrual-related changes in anxiety, depression, or hostility. Thus, mood changes may occur only in some women. The women most likely to show mood changes overtly in behavior, as pointed out in the introduction to this chapter, may be those genetically most sensitive to hormone changes or those already under physical or psychological stress.

Perhaps the mood changes that occur in some women during the menstrual cycle affect the probability that they will volunteer to serve as a subject in a psychological experiment (Table 5.7). The differences in the rate of volunteering reported by Doty and Silverthorne (1975) could affect sex cycle research, since most women would volunteer while in the ovulatory phase, thus biasing the point of the menstrual cycle at which the research project begins. This volunteering cycle could also affect sex differences research.

These mood changes may also be related to the peak of sexual behavior that has occasionally been reported at ovulation; it might be that women prefer sex when they are not hostile, anxious, or depressed. The secondary peak in sexual activity sometimes reported in the premenstrual phase is usually attributed to the increased swelling of the sexual tissues that occurs at that time, making stimulation more easily arousing and pleasurable (W. Masters and Johnson, 1966). But many other studies found no cycle-related changes. Udry, Morris, and Waller (1973) also suggested that the increase of progesterone in the luteal phase decreased the sexual attractiveness of the wife to her husband.

The changes in perceptual sensitivity seem related to the ratio of estrogen to progesterone, with estrogen increasing and progesterone decreasing sensitivity to visual, auditory, and tacticle sensation. However, progesterone increases dilation of the blood vessels and sensitivity to cold, as seen both by the cyclic changes in cold sensitivity and by the effects of progesterone injections (Kenshalo, 1966). Sensitivity to pain parallels sensitivity to cold. Taste and olfactory sensitivity are often reported to increase in the high estrogen phases of the cycle, but the locations of the peaks and troughs may vary from study to study (see Elsberg, Brewer, and Levy, 1936; Good et al., 1976; Henkin, 1974; Le Magnen, 1950; Schneider and Wolf, 1955; Vierling and Rock, 1967).

The changes in performance of the rod-and-frame task are sometimes attributed to estrogen, with the individual being more feminine, and field dependent, when the estrogen level is highest, and being more masculine, or field independent, when estrogen is opposed by progesterone. According to this analysis, the greater sensitivity of women to all stimuli in the follicular phase makes them less able to ignore the irrelevant stimuli, making them more field dependent. It should be remembered that the kwashiorkor man, with a high estrogen level and low androgen levels, was also field dependent.

The Psychological Correlates and Their Implications.   One review of this literature was very properly critical. As B. Sommer pointed out (1973), most of the studies that claimed to have demonstrated behavioral changes throughout the menstrual cycle have used self-reports or other subjective measures. And, as Sommer pointed out, studies using self reports are particularly likely to be contaminated by the subjects' culturally conditioned expectations and by those of the experimenter, that is, the Rosenthal effect.

Other problems are associated with this type of data. One has to do with the publication biases described in Chapter 1. The studies finding no cyclical changes in any of these physiological or behavioral responses are not as likely to get published. Also, there is as yet no encompassing (or even several specific) and generally accepted theory explaining the causes and interrelationships of these effects. About all that can be concluded is that the data on menstrual cycles are consistent with the data reported earlier in this chapter for humans and animals: hormones may affect aggression, emotionality, and some intellectual activities, mostly those that are also affected by stimulants and depressants.

What implications do these cyclical changes have for sex differences? They demonstrate in another set of circumstances the ways in which hormones can affect our behaviors, in males or females. Thus, these data are relevant to the question of to what degree sex differences in hormones bias us towards sex differences in behavior, and for what types of behavior that is true.

Several types of behavior seem to consistently vary with the phases of the menstrual cycle. Moods vary, but only in some women. More consistently, well-controlled studies of psychologically and physically healthy women have found cyclical changes in vision, audition, touch, sensitivity to pain and cold, olfaction, and taste. The performance of some tasks, particularly spatial tasks, may also vary cyclically in some women. Women also vary in their reaction time. However, because these changes in individual women are small relative to the differences among women, they are most important in determining the effects that hormones may have on sex differences, rather than for predicting the performances of individual women relative to men.

TABLE 5.8

INCIDENCE OF PREMENSTRUAL SYMPTOMS IN PHYSICALLY NORMAL WOMEN

Symptom	Percentage Reporting Symptoms				
	Morton et al. (1953) (n = 249)	Pennington (1957) (n = 1000)	Coppen and Kessel (1963) (n = 465)	Sutherland and Stewart (1965) (n = 150)	Timonen and Procope (1973) (n = 748)
Irritability	63%	47%	32.3%	69%	67%
Nervousness	55	38	} 23.3		52
Anxiety					11
Depression	42			63	35
Restlessness					36
Fatigue	40				
Concentration Difficulties	20				
Headache	59	30	21.8	32	23
Nausea and Dizziness }	19	27		16	10
Vomiting					2
Loss of Appetite		2			
Increased Appetite	23				
Craving for Sweets	37			—[1]	
Weight Increase	28				30
Swelling of Abdomen	50	2	} 71.8	} 63	51
Swelling of Breasts	28	18			48
Constipation				27	13
Diarrhea				20	19
Acne		10		70	47
Insomnia		11		5	
Greasy Scalp and Hair				35	
Muscle Pain	43	19		24	
Circles under eyes				40	
Menstrual pain		62	57	83	92

Note: A blank indicates that the symptom was not measured in that particular study.
[1] Symptom reported by one person.

The Premenstrual Syndrome

The premenstrual period lasts from three to five days before menstruation up to the time of menstruation. During this period some women experience a variety of symptoms that may be relieved by menstruation or continue a couple of days into menstruation. These symptoms constitute the so-called **premenstrual syndrome.** Frank (1931) initially described this syndrome, stating that the symptoms consisted of tension, frequent severe headaches, swelling, and a "desire for foolish actions."

Incidence of Symptoms.   Table 5.8 presents the incidence of many of the premenstrual symptoms as reported by five different studies, all with large sample sizes. All these studies sent out questionnaires for women to fill out, so these symptoms and their rates of occurrence are as reported by the women themselves.

As can be seen, there is a large variability among the self-reported incidence of symptoms.

Not all women will have all symptoms, but most women are likely to report experiencing at least some. In Sutherland and Stewart's study (1965), only 2.7 percent of the young women reported having no symptoms. The incidence of symptoms may also increase with age (see Timonen and Procope, 1973). Premenstrual symptoms are also claimed more frequently by those women who had an early puberty (Kashiwagi, McClure, and Wetzel, 1976). The psychological symptoms tend to be reported by the same women who say they experience swelling and headaches (Coppen and Kessel, 1963; Timonen and Procope, 1973).

Aggression, Illness, and Death. The paramenstrual period (four or five days before to four or five days after the onset of the menses) may be a time of greater frequency of psychiatric admissions, psychopathological symptoms, illnesses, and crime. Figure 5.1 comes from a review by O'Connor, Shelley, and Stern (1974) of six different studies. As can be seen, the ovulatory period is at the mean (chance level) of these behaviors, the luteal and follicular phases are associated with decreases in the frequencies of these behaviors, and the frequency in the paramenstrual period is well above the ovulatory frequency. A study of prison inmates found 62 percent of those who committed crimes of violence did so in the paramenstrual week (Morton et al., 1953). Hatotani (Hatotani, 1973; Wakoh and Hatotani, 1973) also found that in women with periodic relapses of psychotic symptoms, 55.4 percent of the relapses were related to the menstrual cycle. Most of these cyclical relapses occurred in the premenstrual period. Many of these women were successfully treated by estrogen and progesterone given during that phase of the cycle.

Suicides also vary with the menstrual cycle, but deaths from suicide and other causes seem to occur in different stages of the cycle than do suicide attempts. In one study not included in Figure 5.1, MacKinnon, MacKinnon and Thompson (1959) examined the uteri of 102 women who had died from accident, suicide, or disease. As can be seen in Table 5.9, deaths by suicide and by accident were concentrated in the luteal phase of the cycle. Of the deaths by disease (primarily circulatory disease), over 84 percent occurred in the last half of the cycle. On the other hand, as shown in Figure 5.1, suicide attempts seem to occur in the premenstrual and menstrual periods, with a secondary peak at ovulation, and not during the luteal period (S. Smith, 1975; B. Sommer, 1972; Tonks, Rack, and Rose, 1968). So suicide attempts and successful suicides may occur at different phases.

In interpreting this data, it should be pointed out that the incidence of accidental deaths and suicides, as well as of crimes, when averaged over all phases, is considerably lower in women than in men. Thus, any luteal increase of these behaviors merely decreases the sex difference. However, the incidence of suicide attempts is higher in women than in men, and in women this may increase premenstrually. But in this case, women who have had children and who also admitted having premenstrual tension showed significantly fewer suicide attempts than did the mothers without premenstrual complaints. This suggests that admitting premenstrual symptoms helped to prevent more drastic consequences, at least in mothers (Tonks et al., 1968).

Objective Measures of Task Performance.   When performance is measured

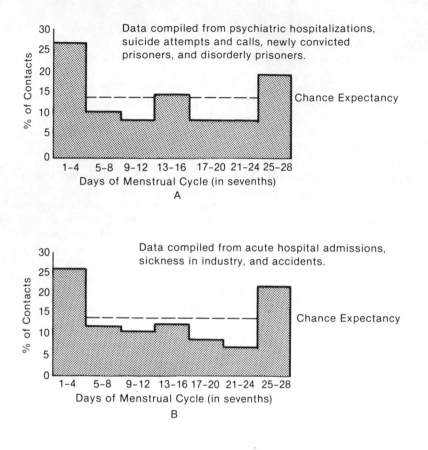

FIGURE 5.1 _____

INCIDENCE OF VARIOUS PSYCHOPATHIC AND EMOTIONAL BEHAVIORS AS A
FUNCTION OF MENSTRUAL CYCLE

*Part A presents the incidence of various psychopathic behaviors: psychiatric hos-
pitalization, suicide attempts and calls, prisoners acting in a disorderly manner,
and various types of morbidity: Part B shows the incidence of acute hospital admissions, sickness in industry, and accidents. Chance expectancy is the mean
frequency of the symptoms averaged over all of the days of the menstrual cycle.*

J. F. O'Connor, E. M. Shelley, and L. O. Stern, "Behavioral Rhythms Related to the Menstrual Cycle." In
M. Ferin, F. Halberg, R. M. Richart, and R. L. Vande Wiele (eds.), *Biorhythms and Human Reproduction*
(New York: Wiley, 1974), p. 316. By permission.

objectively rather than subjectively, almost no research has found significant premenstrual declines (Parlee, 1973; Ryan, 1975; S. Smith, 1975; B. Sommer, 1973).
The exceptions are the heavily criticized reports of Dalton (1960, 1968b), which
stated that the premenstrual period is more likely to be associated with a decrease
in school examination scores than with an increase. It is possible that with a very

TABLE 5.9 _____

INCIDENCE OF DEATHS BY SUICIDE, ACCIDENT, AND DISEASE AS A FUNCTION
OF THE PHASE OF THE MENSTRUAL CYCLE

	Phase and Day				
Incidence	Menstrual 1–4	Follicular 5–14	Ovulatory 15–16	Luteal 17–23	Premenstrual 24–28
Chance (102)	14.6%	35.7%	7.1%	25.0%	17.8%
Suicides (38)	2.6	7.8	10.5	64.4	10.5
Accidents (20)	0.0	10.0	20.0	40.0	30.0
Disease Deaths (44)	2.2	13.6	9.1	59.1	15.9

Source: I. L. MacKinnon, P. C. B. MacKinnon, and A. D. Thompson, "Lethal Hazards of the Luteal Phase of the Menstrual Cycle." *British Medical Journal,* 1959.
Note: The phase of the cycle was determined at autopsy. Chance refers to the number of deaths expected in their phase based solely on the number of days in that phase.

difficult task under highly stressful conditions, some women may have poorer performances in the premenstrual phase, especially if they deny having premenstrual symptoms (J. Rodin, 1976).

Maternal Behavior. Two researchers have reported that paramenstrual mothers are significantly more likely to bring their ill children to the hospital. Dalton (1970, 1975) reported on the incidence of mothers bringing children with coughs and colds to the hospital. Fifty-four percent of the mothers doing so were in the paramenstrual period, although that period is only 28.5 percent of the monthly cycle. Tuch (1975) selected 140 women randomly from over 1500 who brought their children to the Southern California Medical Center Pediatric Outpatient Department in a month. Of the ninety-five women who had regular cycles, 51 percent were in their paramenstrual phase, defined by Tuch to be 39 percent of the cycle. Also, 80 percent of the children of paramenstrual women were judged (blindly) by the doctors to be not sick or only slightly sick; this was true of only 58 percent of the children of intermenstrual women.

There are two possible reasons for the above effects, and both could be true. One is that the mother makes her children sick because of her own symptoms and the stress she applies to her children. The second reason is that the mother might be more anxious about relatively minor symptoms in her children at that point of her cycle.

The Premenstrual Syndrome and Personality. Much of premenstrual research has been concerned with the relationship of premenstrual symptoms to personality. Most studies have found that the self-reported incidence of symptoms is more common in neurotic or depressed women (Coppen and Kessel, 1963; Kashiwagi et al., 1976; Paulson, 1961; Rees, 1953; Schuckit et al., 1975; S. Smith and Sauder, 1969; Wetzel et al., 1975). In Persky's (1974) preselected group of psychologically and physically healthy women, there were no premenstrual increases in depression, hostility, and anxiety.

There is one exception to the studies cited above, and that study tested premenstrual anxiety and depression objectively by well-validated clinical questionnaires. Golub (1976) found that both state anxiety (temporary anxiety) and depression were significantly greater in women in the premenstrual phase, and the two were significantly correlated. However, premenstrual depression and state anxiety were not correlated with anxiety as a personality trait, suggesting that the more generally anxious women were not necessarily more likely to be premenstrually depressed and anxious. This study is particularly important because the results are reliable; not only did Golub disguise the purpose of her study, she also used more objective tests of premenstrual symptoms than self-reports.

Causes. As yet there is no generally accepted explanation for the causes of the premenstrual syndrome. Physiological causes have been proposed by several people. For example, Janowsky, Berens, and Davis (1973) have suggested that water balance, blood electrolytes, and brain changes, all associated with the premenstrual period, are related to negative emotions.

Estrogen-progesterone balance or estrogen withdrawal are also often cited as possible causes of the premenstrual syndrome (see Bäckström and Carstensen, 1974; S. Smith, 1975). Birth control pills (Hamburg et al., 1968) and both estrogen (Somerville, 1972) and progesterone alone (Dalton, 1964) have been reported to decrease symptoms. Cullberg's data (1972), from the study already described, suggest that a few women can benefit from hormones, but only from a progestin-dominated pill.

On the other hand, some people working in the field claim that the syndrome is entirely psychosomatic or the result of cultural conditioning (see Parlee, 1974). These people often point to the correlation between symptoms and neuroticism and depression, although the recent work of Golub makes this connection somewhat less likely. Still, the influence of mind on body should not be overestimated. Ruble (1977) found that if women were misled into believing that they were premenstrual, they actually reported more water retention, changes in eating, and even pain than did women in the same cycle phase who thought their periods were at least a week off.

Paige's work has been very influential in pointing out the influence of culture upon menstrual symptoms. She (1971) has claimed that menstrual anxiety is entirely the result of cultural conditioning and related to the duration and amount of menstrual flow. She (1973) has reported research showing that premenstrual symptoms vary with religious affiliation, supporting her cultural arguments. However, cross-cultural analyses have not supported this conclusion. Janiger (cited by Luce, 1971) studied premenstrual distress in Lebanese, Apache, Japanese, Nigerian, Greek, and American girls. The symptoms reported were more similar than different, and the results of a questionnaire sent to zoo keepers indicated that rhesus monkeys, chimpanzees, and gorillas sometimes suffer from premenstrual tension, too.

The cultural and psychosomatic theories seem to overlook the continuous interaction between biology and experience. As was said at the beginning of this chapter, it would be hard to disagree that the final cause of death is physiological, and yet psychological stress alone can produce death (Seligman, 1975) as well as reduce resistance to all sorts of different diseases (Selye, 1956). The relationship of personality to physiological diseases is also being recognized (see Buck, 1976). A better model for cyclical behavior changes and premenstrual problems might be the interactionist one. In this model, any stress—whether supplied by personality or by situational factors—makes a person more susceptible or likely to show the effects of hormonally induced changes. This does not deny the fact that in some women (maybe even a majority), menstrual and premenstrual distress may be largely or even entirely a product of culturally conditioned expectations. For other women, though, hormonal factors, especially when the women are under stress, may be more important causes.

Finally, since the effect of experience is so important, "forewarned is forearmed"; that is, a knowledge of symptoms and their source could lead to alleviation of the symptoms. Instead of a woman blaming outside situations and people or herself, she would blame the proper source. This could lead to better control over behavior and thus, paradoxically, to a decrease in menstrual symptoms. As was mentioned earlier, mothers admitting premenstrual symptoms showed significantly fewer suicide attempts (Tonks et al., 1968). J. Rodin (1976) also compared the performance under pressure of premenstrual women who did or did not complain of premenstrual symptoms; their performances were also compared to those of midcycle women. Rodin said her results "suggest that if menstruating women attribute task-produced arousal and frustration to symptoms of menstruation, they actually perform more effectively than equally aroused nonmenstruating women and about as well as women who are not distressed at all on a variety of measures" (p. 351).   *Outer_Inner causation - usually opposite*

Summary.   The premenstrual period may present problems for some women, but others show no effects at all of the premenstrual hormone decline. The majority of women report only minor symptoms, and even these are influenced by attitudes and expectations. Both physical and psychological symptoms have been reported and although they are more often reported by neurotic or depressed women, they do sometimes appear in healthy women. But for the woman who already has problems, the premenstrual period may make them worse. The causes of these premenstrual changes are as yet obscure, but are likely to involve very subtle interactions between genetics, personality, culture, hormones, and stress.

Pregnancy and Postpartum

Pregnancy is associated with very high levels of hormones. Estrogen reaches an initial peak during the first three months, then briefly declines, only to reach another peak just before birth. Progesterone increases steadily throughout pregnancy and prolactin increases in the last stages. In the **postpartum period** (after birth), hormone levels rapidly fall.

Emotional Changes During Pregnancy.   For the normal woman, pregnancy has sometimes been described as a time of stability and calm. Benedek (1970) has described pregnancy as an intensification of the luteal phase of the menstrual cycle: "A woman whose personality organization makes her a natural mother enjoys the narcissistic state with vegetative calmness." However, the incidence of physical and emotional problems even in planned pregnancies seems rather high for a state of "vegetative calmness." Depression and anxiety scores seem very slightly elevated in all three trimesters (three-month periods), making them close to the scores in premenstrual women (Golub, 1976; Lubin, Gardner, and Roth, 1975). Uddenberg (1974) estimated that from 15 percent to 20 percent of women become "severely functionally handicapped" during pregnancy. Compared to nonpregnant women admitted to a clinic, pregnant women in their third trimester had significant increases in hypochondria, social introversion, and depression, and even got significantly lower scores on a femininity scale (Treadway et al., 1969). There may be a decrease of major psychiatric symptoms, but neuroticism seems to increase during pregnancy (Kane, Lipton, and Ewing, 1969; Sherman, 1971). Tobin (1957) compared 1000 women who had had recent pregnancies to 500 controls. Sixty-one percent of the women said they had been irritable while pregnant, 84 percent said they had become depressed, and 68 percent said they had suffered from crying spells. The percentages for the controls were, in order, 8 percent, 26 percent, and 5 percent. Also, only 12 percent of the women who had been pregnant said that they had had such symptoms before pregnancy.

Changes in sexual behavior also occur during pregnancy. The frequency of sexual activity decreases over the course of the pregnancy. Orgasms are also reported to decrease in frequency and intensity. All sexual activity other than orgasm also decreases, suggesting that the decline in sexual activity is related to more than just comfort and fear for the baby (perhaps because of progesterone?) (Kane et al., 1969; Solberg, Butler, and Wagner, 1973).

However, to be completely free of symptoms during pregnancy is also not healthy. Women who had few physical symptoms during pregnancy are likely to become emotionally disturbed after birth. Some nausea during pregnancy is normal, and both excessive nausea and vomiting and none at all indicate a poor adjustment to pregnancy and motherhood (Uddenberg, 1974; Uddenberg and Nilsson, 1975).

Thus, some emotional changes, both pleasant and unpleasant, and symptoms such as nausea seem to be common and normal parts of the hormonal changes of pregnancies, even planned ones. This again shows that hormones bias a person towards emotional changes. However, more severe mental symptoms seem to be related to past and present problems, not to the hormonal changes (Uddenberg and Nilsson, 1975). More severe physical problems may also be related to psychological and situational stress (Bardwick, 1971; Sherman, 1971). Cultural attitudes toward pregnancy are also undoubtedly important, but are, as yet, insufficiently researched. An excellent qualitative study, "Psychological Changes Accompanying Pregnancy and Motherhood," written by Myra Leifer (1977), is highly recommended for those who would like more information in this area.

Postpartum Depression. The postpartum period is also a time associated with frequent disturbances. Uddenberg and Nilsson (1975) found that 47 percent of their randomly selected pregnant women became "mentally handicapped" in the postpartum period. Pugh and his coworkers (1963) have estimated that there is a fourfold to fivefold increase in serious mental illness in the postpartum period. And 67 percent of women experience crying spells in the first ten days after giving birth; 28 percent cried for at least one hour or more (Hamburg et al., 1968). **Postpartum depression** occurs more in women after their first or second childbirth and in women who have had great menstrual difficulties, long flow durations, and early puberty. Another study comparing postpartum women to unpregnant controls found that postpartum women were more depressed and more neurotic, although their test results were also interpreted as indicating a "pleasantly sluggish drowsy state" (Treadway et al., 1969). Although scores on intellectual tests did not change significantly, two women demonstrated temporary but dramatic cognitive impairments. One college graduate could not subtract, and she also sent out incorrect birth announcements. Another forgot an entire day (Treadway et al., 1969).

The incidence of more severe reactions was studied by Uddenberg (1974), Uddenberg and Nilsson (1975), and Melges (1968). Severe problems began on the first day after birth, and their appearance seemed to be associated with the women rejecting motherhood and their own mothers. The women with more severe reactions either had had previous menstrual difficulties, as had other members of their families, or menstrual problems had been completely absent. Few of them were eldest children. However, these women had not had poor mental health in childhood or adolescence, and their pregnancies were usually planned. They did worry more often about their child after the child was born, and they also felt more fatigue and more concern about their self-perceived maternal inadequacies, and were often obsessed by the thought they would hurt their child. In other respects, these women were like adrenogenital girls: 35 percent had played with dolls in childhood only slightly or not at all; 70.6 percent had had a "severe" (as defined by researchers) tomboy phase, often extending into high school; 8 percent said they would rather have been men; and 11 percent tried to get jobs within the first two months after giving birth, while others felt that the infant interfered with their career. Also, 63.8 percent reported feeling stress from feelings of entrapment.

Causes of Postpartum Depression. Melges felt that these problems were situational rather than hormonal, since three adoptive mothers also experienced severe "postpartum" difficulties. Both Melges and Uddenberg emphasized poor relationships between the women reporting these symptoms and their mothers. It is true that the arrival of a new infant creates large changes in one's life and entails a considerable loss of freedom, but hormonal factors have also been implicated. The severity of postpartum symptoms is related ($r = -.60$) to the level of trytophan in the blood; depression of the trytophan level is also seen in clinical depressive states (G. Stein et al., 1976).

As Uddenberg said, "an endocrine and a psychodynamic etiology of a paranatal disturbance, however, are not mutually exclusive. On the contrary, 'hormonal imbalance' may impair the woman's ability to tackle her conflicts, and thus facilitate the precipitation of mental disturbance" (1974, p. 100). In addition to this, the correlation of postpartum problems with menstrual problems in these women, as well as in the other female members of their family, suggests that women differ in their sensitivity to "hormonal imbalance" and that this difference could be due to genetic inheritance as well as environmental and cultural stress. However, lack of premenstrual symptoms and physical symptoms during pregnancy is also associated with postpartum disturbances.

Cycles in Males

Circadian Rhythms. Men have cycles too. Both men and women have circadian (twenty-four-hour) cycles in physiology, mood, and performance. Men have been shown to have some diurnal variations in mood (Taub and Berger, 1974) and in speed of color naming (Klaiber et al., 1974). Moods improved from morning to

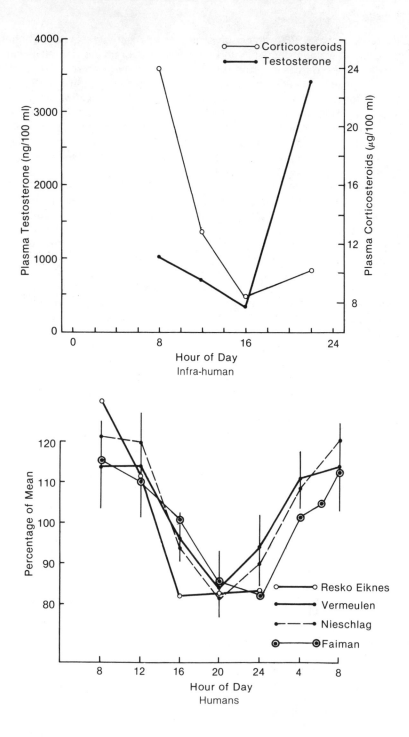

noon, but performance decreased. There have been some attempts to relate these changes to testosterone levels, but this is difficult to do in light of some new information that the time of the daily peak of testosterone depends on the season of the year.

Men may even have stronger circadian rhythms than women. Gonadal testosterone levels increase during the night in both male humans and monkeys, but not in premenopausal females (Southren and Gordon, 1975). As can be seen in Figure 5.2, the testosterone level of the primate male increases by about 40 percent overnight; other investigators have found up to a 50 percent increase over the night (Schiavi et al., 1974). Women may have weaker circadian rhythms of androgen because of the adrenals (Vermeulen, 1976). Men may also show a greater circadian rhythm in corticosteroid secretion (G. Curtis et al., 1968). Finally, only men have a circadian rhythm in tolerance of pain (Procacci et al., 1972).

Weekly and Monthly Rhythms. Longer cycles in men have also been found (Harkness, 1974). Doering and his colleagues (1975) found individually consistent cycles of testosterone, with the level varying from 9 percent to 28 percent. The cycles lasted from eight to thirty days, although most were between twenty and twenty-two days long. The mean cycle length may be even longer, however, since the technique used could not detect cycles longer than thirty days.

Behavioral cycles have also been found in men. The mean length of the testosterone cycle found by Doering and his colleagues matched the cycle length in sleep, anxiety, and anger in some of the subjects, and the cycle of sexual activity in one man. Hersey (1931) found that males had cycles of emotionality, varying from three-and-a-half to nine weeks in length. Biweekly to monthly cycles have also been found in beard growth (Harkness, 1974), grip strength and body weight (Kühl et al., 1974), and pain threshold (Procacci et al., 1972). Wynn (1972) also found that a man's ability to estimate absolute pitch varied cyclically, just as that of his female subjects had varied with the menstrual cycle; the cycle length for that man was about twenty days.

The most dramatic monthly cycles in males, however, were presented and reviewed by Richter (1968). Some of these cycles are presented in Figure 5.3. As can be seen, there are cycles in temperature, pulse, and white blood cell counts (just as in normal human females), as well as in mental state. Richter showed that monthly cycles in symptoms could exist in male catatonics, schizophrenics, epileptics, depressives, and manics. These cycles have three things in common: they appeared months or years after the onset of the basic illness; they are phenomena separate from the illness; they occur in only a small fraction of the patients (1 percent to 3 percent). He concluded that "it is likely that this monthly cycle has

---

FIGURE 5.2

DIURNAL VARIATIONS IN TESTOSTERONE LEVELS IN PLASMA OF MALES

R. P. Michael, K. D. R. Setchell, and T. M. Plant, "Diurnal Changes in Plasma Testosterone and Studies in Plasma Corticosteroids in Non-anesthetized Male Rhesus Monkeys (*Macaca Mulatta*)." *Journal of Endocrinology*, 1974, p. 332; A. Vermeulen, L. Verdonck, and F. Comhaire. "Rhythms of the Male Hypothalamo-pituitary-testicular axis." In M. Ferin, F. Halberg, R. M. Richart, and R. L. Vande Wiele (eds.), *Biorhythms and Human Reproduction* (New York: Wiley, 1974), p. 433. By permission.

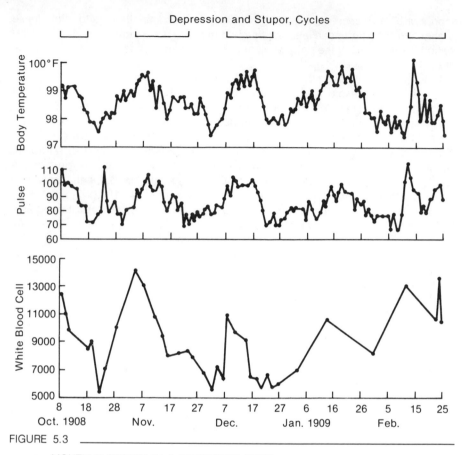

Depression and Stupor, Cycles

FIGURE 5.3

MONTHLY CYCLES IN A DEPRESSED MALE

These are the readings of a forty-six-year-old male patient with depression and stupor. The solid black bars show periods of depression and stupor; note that these states correlated with body temperature, pulse rate, and white blood cell counts. (A patient of Barnes, taken from Richter, 1968).

C. P. Richter, "Periodic Phenomena in Man and Animals: Their Relation to Neuro-Endocrine Mechanisms (a Monthly or Nearly Monthly Cycle)." In R. P. Michael (ed.), *Endocrinology and Human Behavior* (New York: Oxford University Press 1968), p. 290. By permission.

become submerged [in humans] but still plays a potentially important but hidden part in the regulation of behavior and other functions. It becomes visible under pathological conditions" (p. 307).

Annual Cycles.   Annual rhythms in testosterone have been identified in several species: red stags, bulls, stallions, drakes, male salamanders, male starlings, rams, boars, male reindeer, male caribou, and bull elephants (Berndtson, Pickett, and Nett, 1974; Krzanowski, 1974; Lincoln, Guinness, and Short, 1972; Reinberg et al., 1975). Not surprisingly, there are annual cycles in male primates, both human and infra-human. These primate cycles are presented in Figure 5.4. Notice that the highest levels of testosterone are from August through November, with a trough from February through March in both man and monkey. The details of the cycles cannot be compared since the one for humans is the best fitting model rather than the actual data. It should be noted, however, that in both species there was nearly a 300 percent increase in testosterone from March to September.

There is other evidence of annual behavioral cycles in male primates. The sexual behavior of the male rhesus follows the same annual cycle as the testosterone level (Michael and Wilson, 1975; J. Robinson et al., 1975). Gordon, Rose, and Bernstein (1976) found that the correlation across months between testosterone levels and the number of sexual mounts was + .898. Over the course of a year, there is also a positive correlation between testosterone level and noncontact aggression (+ .880) and a negative correlation between testosterone and play behavior (− .619) (Gordon et al., 1976). In humans, the frequency of rape also has an annual rhythm; the rate starts increasing in June, peaks in August, and remains high through September (Alford and Lewis, 1975). Other violent crimes show a similar rhythm. Halbery (cited by Luce, 1971) has also found that suicides peak in May, but deaths from arteriosclerosis peak around January.

It is tempting to relate these annual behavioral cycles to testosterone, but there are four problems involved in attempting to find such a causal relationship. First, the peaks and troughs of behavior frequency and hormone levels do not correspond: the peaks of one may follow the peaks of the other by hours or days. Second, there are highly variable within-subject correlations between testosterone and sexual activity (although there too the peaks rarely correspond). Third, much of the behavioral cycle may be due to brain cycles and thus not depend on the annual changes in testosterone (Michael and Zumpe, 1976). Fourth, often there are considerable delays between the hormonal changes and their effects, such as the discrepancy between the hormonal changes of puberty and the physical and behavioral effects.

The other major annual rhythm in male humans is the timing of the circadian peak of testosterone. In May, the level of testosterone peaks at around 8:00 A.M., while in November, the peak is found at 2:00 P.M., at least in Paris (Reinberg et al., 1975).

Thus, it seems clear that there are rather dramatic daily, nearly monthly, and yearly changes in testosterone levels and in the behaviors of human males. It is not yet clear that those changes are causally related.

Age and Menopause

Age and Hormones in Men. The older a male gets, the less testosterone he has (Vermeulen et al., 1974). These changes are nearly linear with age (Persky et al., 1971). These changes in testosterone are also paralleled by increases in FSH and LH, decreases in testes size, and decreases in facial, pubic, and axillary hair. Estradiol levels do not change in men with age, but estradiol levels do decrease in women so that after the age of sixty, levels are higher in men than in women (Greenblatt, Oettinger, and Bohler, 1976).

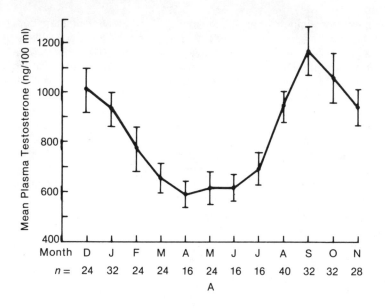

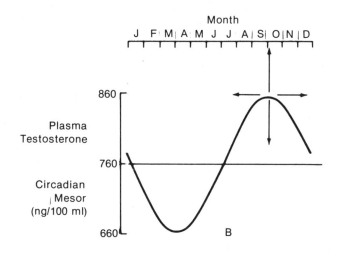

Menopause and Hormones.   The decline in hormones is sudden in women, coming when the ovaries stop functioning at **menopause,** which usually occurs between the ages of forty-five and fifty. The decline in estrogen in women may spread itself out over weeks or months, but not over years. At menopause, women have even larger increases in FSH and LH than men have when they age, and testosterone also increases (Greenblatt et al., 1976). Thus, with age, the sexes come to more closely resemble one another again, just as they did before puberty.

However, any relationship of menopause to mental symptoms such as depression has been questioned (Winokur and Cadoret, 1975). The greatest incidence of depressive illness is in the menopausal years, but there is no sharp increase from the incidence in women ages thirty-five to forty to the incidence in women ages forty-five to fifty. When compared to nondepressed menopausal women, depressed menopausal women more frequently had earlier symptoms, which implies that depression in menopause appears in women already susceptible to stress (Ballinger, 1976). The symptoms associated with menopause are highly variable; many women have no symptoms at all and only about 10 percent are seriously inconvenienced. Married women and women who have often been pregnant have more symptoms (Sherman, 1971). Bart (1976) has shown that postmenopausal depression is strongly affected by culturally defined sex roles, by religion, and by relative femininity. Women are more apt to become depressed if they live in an industrial society, are Jewish, and are very feminine. Problems associated with the menstrual period were also commonly reported by the women who later had menopausal symptoms. Women in lower social classes have more menopausal symptoms than those in higher social classes (Van Keep and Kellerhalls, 1975).

Age is associated with a decline in gonadal hormones in both sexes, with adrenal androgen increasing for women, while the menopausal ovary continues to secrete androgens. With age, then, the sexes become more similar in hormone levels, although as yet no one has definitely proved that there are any behavioral correlates of these hormone changes.

SUMMARY AND CONCLUSIONS

The activational effects of gonadal hormones are of two types: specific and general. For the specific effects, the circulating hormone acts on an already induced brain to make specific types of behavior—sexual, aggressive, or maternal—more probable. Hormones also exert more general effects; androgens and estrogens are arousing, and progestins are tranquillizing or inhibiting. These two types of effects operate jointly upon a variety of behaviors.

FIGURE 5.4 _____

ANNUAL VARIATIONS IN MALE TESTOSTERONE LEVELS

Part A represents the mean monthly plasma testosterone concentrations, sampled at 8:00 AM in eight adult male rhesus monkeys (n is the number of blood samples taken during that month). The natural mating season lasts from September to January. The vertical lines indicated standard deviations. Part B shows the annual changes of plasma testosterone in five healthy adult human male men in terms of the best-fitting individual curves.

T. M. Plant, D. Zumpe, M. Sauls, and R. P. Michael, "An Annual Rhythm in the Plasma Testosterone of Adult Male Rhesus Monkeys Maintained in the Laboratory." Journal of Endocrinology, 1974, 62, p. 404. A. Reinberg, M. Lagoguey, J. M. Chauffournier, and F. Cesselin, "Circannual and Circadian Rhythms in Plasma Testosterone in Five Healthy Young Parisian Males." *Acta Endocrinologica*, 1975, 80, p. 737. Reprinted by permission of the author and publisher.

Gonadal hormones have some specific effects on sexual behavior, with testosterone increasing mounting more than lordosis, and estrogen (with progesterone in some species) increasing female sexual behavior more often in females than in males. In humans and in infra-human primates, testosterone may have some specific activating effects on sexual behavior, increasing sex-typical sexual behavior in both genders. Progesterone may inhibit sexual behavior in primates. But sexual activity may also affect hormones (at least in lower species). In general, the relationship between behavior and hormone (in both directions) is stronger in lower species than in humans. Evolution may have worked to decrease the hormonal control of sexual behavior in humans, perhaps because of the long periods of social living.

Testosterone may also have specific activating effects on aggression and dominance in male and female animals, but the relationship is crucially affected by past experience and the current situation, and aggression in turn affects testosterone levels. The activational effect of testosterone on aggression interacts with the inductive effect of hormones such that in most species, testosterone increases aggression only in an androgen-induced brain. The relationship between androgen and aggression may be weaker in humans, again because of a long evolutionary history of social living, in which dominance and submission gestures increased social cohesion.

Hormones may also affect emotional behavior, but conclusions here are still very controversial, perhaps because emotions are so hard to measure. Though the conclusions are uncertain, it is true that there have been consistent reports of such an effect. Very low levels of estrogen and testosterone may be associated with depression and inactivity, and progestin may also be associated with depression and lethargy. However, cause and effect are not certain in most of these data; emotions could also cause changes in hormones. The strongest evidence for a connection between hormones and emotions comes from the cycles observed in human females. Some side-effects are associated with the withdrawal of hormones, as in the premenstrual period, pill withdrawal, the postpartum period, and menopause, and such withdrawal increases depression or neuroticism in some women (though not all) and may make an already predisposed woman more vulnerable to more serious psychological difficulties. On the other hand, the increase of hormones caused by pregnancy and the pill have also been associated with problems. There may also be cycles of emotionality in males, paralleling the changes in testosterone levels.

With two possible exceptions, there is no reason to believe that the effect of hormones upon cognitive abilities is due to anything other than nonspecific effects of hormones or experimenter bias. One possible exception is if a hormone had a specific activational effect on emotion, activity, or exploration, which might in turn affect performance in a learning situation. This might be the case with premenstrual changes in performance or those caused by the birth control pill. Another possible exception is spatial ability, which may be increased by testosterone, at least up to some point, or decreased by estrogen. There is also some evidence that hormones affect verbal fluency. However, most of the relationships that have been observed between hormones and learning or performance can be attributed to the arousing effects of estrogen and testosterone—counteracting fatigue, and increasing general activity, persistence, and attention—or to the depressing effect of progestins.

In conclusion, the specific activational effects of these hormones interact with a brain that has already been affected permanently by inductive hormones and by past experience; this determines the likelihood of perceiving and responding in a certain fashion to a specific stimulus. The response affects the hormones, which combine with the remembered outcome of all responses to exert biasing effects on what behavior will occur next time. Because activational hormones may bias some behaviors of humans and lower species, and because there are sex differences in activational hormones, there may be some biological basis for sex differences in dominance, emotionality, activity levels, and the performance of some cognitive tasks.

KEY TERMS AND CONCEPTS

Specific activational effect
Nonspecific activational effect
Transmitter substances
Persistence
Kwashiorkor syndrome
Combination pill
Sequential pill
Double-blind procedure
Cross-over technique
Menstrual cycle
Menstrual phase

Follicular phase
Ovulatory phase
Luteal phase
Premenstrual phase
Circadian rhythms
Alpha frequency
Premenstrual syndrome
Paramenstrual period
Postpartum
Postpartum depression
Menopause

QUESTIONS ON KEY ISSUES

1. What are the factors that determine whether or not a hormonal change will affect behavior, and what are some examples of the effects of androgen, estrogen, and progesterone?

2. What does it mean to say that there are sexual behavior biases built into both the animal and the hormone? What are some examples of these biases?

3. How does the sexual behavior of primates differ from that of the majority of subprimates?

4. What kinds of aggression are under hormonal control? What kinds of aggression are not affected by activational testosterone?

5. How can you increase dominance in females?

6. What evidence is there that parental behavior, activity, emotional behavior, and learning performance is hormone-sensitive in infra-humans? What can be concluded in each case about the nature of the effect?

7. Taking into account all the different ways of relating hormone levels to human behavior, what is the evidence that each of the following might be hormone-sensitive: emotional behavior and moods, sexual behavior, aggression, parental behavior, sensory responses, and cognitive processes?

8. What kinds of women are most likely to have unfavorable responses to the pill, and to what kind of pill.

9. If a woman wants to get drunk fast, what

time of the month should she go drinking?

10. Compare the symptoms reported to increase in the premenstrual period, the postpartum period and menopause. What are the similarities? What are the differences?

11. What are the three major cycles in men, as defined by length? What are some examples of each?

12. How can the effect of experience upon hormones modify many of the conclusions suggested by the data of this chapter?

PART 3

Environment and Sex Differences

_____

CHAPTER 6

The Development of Gender Identity and Gender Role

In this chapter, the effects that socialization, child rearing practices, and experience have on determining an individual's gender identity and gender role will be presented. First, we will show the overwhelming importance of gender of rearing in determining gender identity. We are what our parents said we were. But gender identity, socialization, and biological biases all interact in determining gender role, the way we behave.

Four influential theories of the development of gender role and gender identity will be described and compared. The ability of each theory to accurately predict sex differences will be evaluated. Freud's theory is probably the least accurate description of sex-role development; the other three theories have accurately described at least some aspects of sex-role development. Those other three all emphasize the importance of cultural sex-role stereotypes in influencing how people evaluate themselves and others differentially according to gender. A fifth theory will be used to summarize the data and ideas presented in this chapter.

GENDER IDENTITY

Gender of Rearing: Gender Identity and Gender Role

Money and his colleagues (Money, 1968, 1974a, 1974b; Money and Ehrhardt, 1972; Money, Hampson and Hampson, 1955) have done much of the work clarifying the relationship between gender of rearing and both gender identity and gender role. Money and his colleagues emphasize the experiential aspects of the development of gender identity, saying that gender identity and gender of rearing will usually be congruent even if neither agrees with any biological definition of gender (definitions based on genes, hormones, gonads, and internal and external sex organs). Children are born with the potential to develop the gender role and gender identity of either sex. Through experience, children learn both gender roles: "The ordinary child receives and responds to two sets of gender stimuli, one the behavior of females, the other the behavior of males. The child's response to one set is to imitate or identify with, and to the other, to reciprocate in a complementary manner" (Money and Ehrhardt, 1972, p. 179). So children of both genders learn both sex roles, but according to Money and Ehrhardt, one is "cleared for everyday use" and the other "is a template of what not to do or say, and also of what to expect from members of the other sex" (1972, p. 179).

However, it should be mentioned that Money (1974a, pp. 234–235) does not distinguish between gender identity and gender role as we do in this book. Although he does not deny (and even provides much evidence for) the prenatal influences that may make one or another gender identity and gender role easier for a given person to acquire, Money argues for the importance of environment in the development of both.

However, we prefer to keep the distinction, feeling that a person can behave in a very feminine fashion—as culturally defined—and still have a very firm male gender identity. From our point of view, gender identity may be entirely a matter of gender of rearing, but there may be biological influences on gender role. In the presence of certain specific environmental influences, these biological influences may produce discrepancies between gender identity as determined by the gender of rearing and gender role as culturally defined.

Pairs of Pseudohermaphrodites. Money presents his case for the importance of gender of rearing or experience in determining gender identity by describing groups of people for whom some aspects of biological gender are discrepant with their gender of rearing. These people develop a gender identity congruent with gender of rearing and not with their biological gender. However, their gender role may have been affected by prenatal hormones. One of Money's cases involved identical male twins, one reared as male and the other as female. The one reared as female had had his penis burned off flush to his abdominal wall when circumcision was performed. The baby was reassigned as a female at seventeen months of age, at which time the parents switched the child's clothes and hairdo. When the twins were four-and-a-half, the mother reported that her little girl did not like to be dirty, but that the boy did not even want his face washed. The daughter also helped around the house, but the boy did not. Toy preferences were also those appropriate to the gender. However, the girl had many tomboyish traits, such as an abundance of energy, stubbornness, and dominance over her friends, despite the mother's attempts to modify these behaviors.

In another case cited by Money (Money and Ehrhardt, 1972), a genetically normal boy was born with a small penis and was reassigned as a girl at seventeen months of age. Again, new clothes and new toys immediately followed the decision. Both the mother, the father, and the older son drastically modified their behavior and attitude towards the child. The daughter imitated the mother in her performance of household tasks and requested feminine toys such as glass slippers. However, at three the girl was a tomboy. She, too, had lots of energy, and seemed to be louder, more aggressive, and more dominant than other girls her age.

Money (Money, 1968, 1974a; Money and Ehrhardt, 1972) also presented "matched pairs of pseudohermaphrodites." These were people with similar biological definitions of gender but with different genders of rearing. One case was a pair of adrenogenital girls whose condition was detected at birth. The second pair were also adrenogenital but the syndrome was not identified until puberty, when the one reared as a girl was masculinized by increased adrenal androgens and the one reared as a boy was feminized by the increased ovarian output. A third case was a pair of XY people suffering from a partial form of the androgen-insensitivity syndrome; one was raised as a girl, with a diagnosis made at puberty, and the other was diagnosed and raised as a boy after age three-and-a-half months. In all three pairs, the gender of identity was the gender of rearing, regardless of chromosomes and hormones.

In another pair of pseudohermaphrodites, the parents were never certain what the gender of their offspring was, so gender of rearing was ambiguous; one was reared more or less as a boy, the other as a girl (with a boy's name on the birth certificate). When the children came to Money's clinic at around age twelve, both were unable to talk when the topic came to their gender identity; they became mute when asked what sex they were: they would have been unable to answer the question that started Chapter 1. However, through notes left under chairs and play therapy, Money was able to infer that both wanted a sex reassignment, and so this was carried out.

Money feels that the primary determinant of gender identity is gender of rearing, and that children acquire their gender identity from the age of six months to the age of three or four years. After that age—even much after 2 years of age—one cannot change the gender of a child without causing severe emotional upheavals and permanent damage. The only exceptions to this are cases where gender of rearing was ambiguous, as in the last example, or cases of many transsexuals. However, the gender role of all of the children described by Money, as was the case of the adrenogenital and androgen-insensitivity women, may have been affected by the prenatal hormones.

A Pubertal Change of Identity.   Mention should be made of a group of people in the village of Salinas in the Dominican Republic. These people were born with ambiguous genitals, with empty scrotal sacs and either an enlarged clitoris or a small penis. At puberty, their testes descended, the penis grew to four or six centimeters in length, and they became fertile and could ejaculate (Imperato-McGinley et al., 1974). Eighteen of the twenty-four people were reared as females, with both the children and their parents reporting no doubts concerning their gender identity; nevertheless, a successful shift to a male identity was made at puberty. This suggested to Imperato-McGinley and his coworkers that hormones before birth and after puberty may be more important to gender identity than gender of rearing is. They stated that in the first generation of these children, "the affected subjects were raised as girls and there was no ambiguity on the part of the parents as to the sex of the child at birth or in early childhood. They believed they were raising a little girl" (1976, p. 872). And yet these children successfully became males at puberty.

This interpretation was contrary to Money's insistence that hormones were relatively unimportant to gender identity. Money responded (1976) that even in the first generation, since the genitals were ambiguous, the parents could have raised the children ambiguously, and that this ambiguity allowed the shift in gender identity to be made. The issue can probably never be resolved, however, since the syndrome is now well-recognized, and even given a name at birth ("**guevedoce**," meaning penis at twelve). Because the syndrome is known and because a masculinizing puberty is expected, the way these children are reared is probably affected. Data on how the first generation children were reared—before the syndrome was recognized and a masculinizing puberty expected—depend upon the memory of their parents, which may now be colored by their experiences with later children. However, most evidence suggests that in most cases, hormonal factors are of minimal importance in the formation of gender identity.

Gender Conflicts

In some people, there are discrepancies among various aspects of the gender role or gender identity that they have adopted. Stoller (1968) differentiates among various types of conflicts within role and identity. **Transsexuals** deny that they are homosexual; instead, they insist that they desire to relate to a person of their own gender with themselves physically being the opposite gender. Most **homosexuals** retain their original gender identity and most aspects of the associated gender role, but choose a same-sex sexual object. **Transvestism** (dressing in opposite-sex clothes) occurs early in the life of most transsexuals, but the majority of transvestites cross-dress in a fetishistic fashion, with accompanying sexual arousal, and retain a clear concept of their gender identity congruent with their gender of rearing. And most transvestites are not homosexual. Thus, most transvestites do not have gender conflicts. Gender conflicts are more likely to be seen in transsexuals, who want their sex to be changed such that their body will be more congruent with their gender of identity.

Transsexuals. Person and Ovesey (1974) distinguished between three types of male transsexuals, each of which cross-dresses in childhood and requests sex-change surgery. The primary transsexual was not feminine as a child, but was withdrawn and gentle, having little sexual interest, loathing male characteristics, and having an increasing wish to be female. The two types of secondary transsexuals are homosexuals and transvestites. The homosexual transsexuals were effeminate at all times, were expressive and theatrical, and often desired to change gender because of some failure in homosexual adjustments or homosexual love affairs; they wanted to change their gender to keep or to attract a lover. The transvestite transsexuals were extremely masculine in childhood and adulthood, with fetishistic cross-dressing and decreased sexuality; the desire to change sex came with a stress that threatened both their masculinity and their security.

Considerably less is known about female-to-male transsexuals than about male-to-female transsexuals. There are many fewer female transsexuals, perhaps one-third to one-eighth as many as male transsexuals (Stoller, 1968). The possible reasons for the preponderance of male transsexuals include the greater likelihood of prenatal endocrinological problems with males, the greater latitude allowed to females with respect to cross-gender behavior, and the fact that boys and girls are both more involved with the mother than with the father during the critical early childhood years. Also, the surgery to transform a woman into a man is considerably less satisfactory than the procedures employed to change a man into a woman (Green, 1974).

However, one is struck by several aspects of both Green's (1974) and Stoller's (1968) description of female transsexuals. The female transsexual seems psychologically healthier even before the sex-change surgery than the male transsexual, and seems more likely to make a stable postoperative adjustment, including a secure marriage to a feminine woman. Female transsexuals after surgery usually adopt male, middle-class value systems, and they are reliable and responsible. Male transsexuals may become stage professionals, and are more likely to be financially undependable, have only transitory relationships with others, have no set goals, and move from rented room to rented room (Green, quoted by Friedman and Tendler, 1974).

Causes of Transsexuality.   Why do these people desire to change their gender? How does their sense of gender identity differ from that of people who would regard a change of sex with horror, and how did their gender identity get that way? Stoller (1968) finds certain common occurrences in the backgrounds of male transsexuals. Their mothers kept their infant boys close to their bodies for a long time after birth, often sleeping with them, and were permissive with regard to their son's cross-dressing, doll play, and feminine behavior. Their fathers were passive, distant, and did not intervene. The mothers themselves were somewhat bisexual—being tomboys and desiring to be males—and felt empty, and had themselves had empty, angry mothers. Green (1974) agrees with most of these statements and includes some other common aspects of their life history, such as physical beauty (33 percent), lack of male playmates (33 percent), repeated cross-dressing of the boy by some female (33 percent), maternal inhibition of masculine behavior, and a fear of castration. Person and Ovesey (1974) talk about the sense of being isolated, alone, and separate producing a fantasy of "symbiotic fusion with the mother," which evolves "into the insistent wish for surgical and hormonal sex reassignment" (p. 323). The female transsexuals were often close to and identified with their fathers (Green, 1974; Stoller, 1968). Most of them as children preferred boys' clothes and boys' toys and preferred boys as playmates; many even thought of themselves as boys.

However, none of these developmental factors appeared in all of the cases seen. Also, a family with an effeminate boy or a male transsexual may have one or more normally masculine children (Green, 1974). Thus, these developmental factors seem to contribute to the problem, but no one of them seems to be the sole cause of the problems in gender identity. Person and Ovesey (1974) say that their patients search for an identity, which is finally ended by coopting the "transsexual identity."

Thus, while hormonal factors must be of little or no importance in the development of gender identity, they may affect gender role. And if a particular gender role interacts with a rather special environment, like the ones just described, the person may eventually reject the environmentally determined gender identity. In Green's and Stoller's descriptions, one is struck by how, in some cases, the children persist in their opposite-sex behaviors despite attempts by their parents to make them stop. A boy who does not like rough sports, whether because of hormones or the environment, may reject his father's invitations to roughhouse and may be in turn rejected by his father; this paternal rejection could then lead to further feminization. So perhaps the child's own preferences are operated on by the environment, which either inhibits or supports those preferences, and in some cases the interaction results in a confusion of gender identity. But it must be emphasized that none of the adrenogenital girls with a male brain or the androgen-insensity people reared as men but with a female brain grew up to be transsexuals, so the biological biases in gender role, if present at all, must obviously interact with a very special environment before confusion of gender identity can occur.

Thus, our original conclusion seems to hold: gender identity is largely determined by gender of rearing, although certain biological biases affecting gender role may combine with certain types of environment to create discrepancies. For example, consider what would happen if the son of a diabetic mother given hormones had a father who demanded masculinity. His son's inability to be aggressive, dominant, and interested in rough sports could lead the father to reject his son, thereby making the acquisition of the male gender role very difficult for the son. But gender role is also a function of gender of rearing, with parents, teachers, and cultural stereotypes leading to certain roles on the parts of males and other roles for females. How do environmental factors create the identity and role? We shall now turn to these questions.

THEORIES OF THE DEVELOPMENT OF GENDER IDENTITY AND GENDER ROLE

The assessment of gender role preferences and gender identity in children is something of a problem since the validity of the usual tests is questioned. Tests commonly used include paper-and-pencil masculinity-femininity tests, where behavior appropriate to one gender is assumed to be the opposite of that appropriate to the other. Children are asked to draw figures, and the researcher notes which sex they draw first. Children may also be asked which games they prefer, or, being shown a set of pictures, asked which toys they prefer, or which activities, or which gender. A very common test is the "It" test, in which a child is presented with a picture of a stick figure and asked what toys, activities, or playmates the sexually neutral "it" prefers (Hollander, Slaymaker, and Foley, 1975).

Freud

Theory.   Freud's **psychoanalytic theory** (1927, 1959a, 1959b, 1965) emphasized the biological differences between the sexes, penis versus clitoris and vagina, in his approach to the development of gender role and gender identity. He said that these anatomical differences were ultimately responsible for sex differences in identity and role, hence his statement, "anatomy is destiny."

Freud postulated that both sexes go through the same developmental sequence, each stage being characterized by a concentration of reactions to a given area of the body. This area of the body was called an **erogenous zone.** An erogenous zone is an area of the body very sensitive to irritation, but certain kinds of stimulation can also produce intense pleasure. In each developmental stage, the child values, or **cathects,** a different part of the body, a different erogenous zone. In each developmental stage, stimulation of the particular body part provides the most pleasure to the child. These developmental stages are called **psychosexual stages.**

Freud's theory is essentially a drive theory, in which the organism strives to reduce tension to its lowest possible level. Tension is unpleasant and to be gotten rid of as soon as possible. Two mechanisms exist for the relief of tension: the Pleasure principle and the principle of Nirvana. In Nirvana, a state of complete nothingness is sought, a complete absence of stimulation or tension. In the Pleasure principle, the reduction of tension is accompanied by pleasure, as produced by the stimulation of an erogenous zone.

The child traverses each stage with ease or with difficulty, depending upon the child's interactions with his or her environment. Early childhood is a critical period, in the sense that irreversible changes in personality occur as the child goes through the stages. Social processes and parental influences affect the child differently than they can the adult. Thus, behavior changes as a function of maturation, and personality development is irreversibly determined by the child's experiences during that development. The child can regress—go back to an earlier stage—under the influence of later stress; however, the stage to which the adult regresses is also determined by the experiences of that person as a child during that particular stage. A child who did not experience an adequate satisfaction of drive during one of the psychosexual stages is likely to regress to that stage as an adult under stress; people who did not experience enough oral gratification as children are likely to chew on their fingers, smoke, or eat when under stress as adults.

In Freud's theory, there are few, if any, sex differences in the first two psychosexual stages of libidinal development. The **oral stage** lasts from birth to about one year of age, and is the stage in which the valued source of pleasurable stimulation comes from the mouth. In the **anal stage,** from one to three years of age, the pleasurable stimulation comes from retention and expulsion of feces. During the first two stages, both sexes identify with the mother, valuing her as a sex and love object and taking on some of her values and actions. At the **phallic stage,** from three to seven, sex differences begin. During the phallic stage both sexes increase their masturbatory behaviors. From seven until puberty, both sexes go through the **latent stage,** where ego and superego development continue until sexuality is reactivated by puberty. The last stage is the one of adult sexuality, the **genital stage.**

To return to the phallic stage, the boy in this stage begins sexually desiring his mother, beginning the so-called **Oedipus complex.** The Oedipus complex for the boy ends when he discovers the anatomical differences between the sexes. He begins to fear that his father will, out of jealousy, cut off the boy's penis the way that girls' penises have already been cut off. The boy reduces his fear by identifying with the father, thus vicariously enjoying the mother. This identification gives the boy his superego and his gender identity and gender role.

The phallic stage is considerably more complicated for girls. The female version of the Oedipus complex, the **Electra complex,** is begun (instead of ended) when the girl discovers that males have penises. She at once realizes her lack and blames her mother. She transfers her love to the father, who possesses the longed-for penis, and becomes very angry with and hostile toward her mother. In time, she gives up the wish for a penis, realizing that it can never be fulfilled, and replaces that desire with a desire for a child (preferably one with a penis) from the father. The girl gradually realizes that this also cannot be gratified. Then, she turns back to her mother, identifying with her out of fear of the mother's jealousy and the loss of her love, and also to vicariously enjoy the father.

At the end, both sexes identify with the same-sex parent and through this process of **identification** they acquire some of the parent's personality characteristics, behaviors, attitudes, and values, some of which form the child's conscience or superego. Also, through this process they acquire their own sense of identity, including gender identity and the appropriate gender role. The male's identification is much stronger and surer than the female's since his is caused by the powerful fear of castration. The fears that lead to the girl's identification with the mother are more diffused over time. These differences in development are responsible for the sex differences in behavior that Freud expects.

Predicted Sex Differences.   Females respond to the loss of a penis with an intensification of self-love; as a result, they will as adults chose to love someone who embodies what they would like to be themselves, their ego-ideal. The male never experiences the loss of a penis, only the threat of it, so the male looks for a mate similar to the woman he first sexually loved, "a girl just like the girl that married dear old dad." Also, because of this loss, women and men will perceive women to be inferior. Since the identification process is stronger in males, men will resemble their fathers more than women will resemble their mothers. Finally, these differences will lead to a sex difference in superego formation, as described by Freud in one of his most quoted passages:

> I cannot escape the notion (though I hesitate to give it expression) that for women the level of what is ethically normal is different from what it is in men. Their supero-ego is never so inexorable, so impersonal, so independent of its emotional origins as we require it to be in men. Character-traits which critics of every epoch have brought up against women—that they show less sense of justice than men, that they are less ready to submit to the great necessities of life, that they are more often influenced in their judgments by feelings of affection or hostility—all of these would be amply accounted for by the modification in the formation of the super-ego which we have already inferred. We must not allow ourselves to be deflected from such judgments by the denials of the feminists, who are anxious to force us to admit complete equality in the position and worth of the sexes: but we shall, of course, willingly agree that the majority of men are also far behind the masculine ideal and that all human individuals, as a result of their bisexual disposition and of cross-inheritance, combine in themselves both masculine and feminine characteristics, so that pure masculinity and femininity remain theoretical constructions of uncertain content (1927, pp. 141–42).

Freud postulated that both sexes went through the five stages of psychosexual development described above. Since the content of the Oedipal stage differed for the two sexes, so did their adult behaviors.

Data.   Some attempts have been made to validate Freud's theory of the development of gender identity and gender role. We will review some of the most cited, and most criticized, supporting evidence first.

G. Blum (1949) used a projective technique called the Blacky Test in an attempt to confirm some of the predictions of Freud's theory. In this test, male and female undergraduates were shown pictures of dogs—Blacky, Papa, Mama, and a spotted, sex-neutral sibling, named Tippy—involved in various activities. The subjects were then asked questions about the pictures, and Blum used Freud's theory to predict sex differences in some of their answers. After reviewing the responses, he felt that he found evidence that females are more orally sadistic, show more repression of anal-sadistic tendencies, show more pre-Oedipal attachments to their mothers, show more aggression to the same-sexed parent, and are more likely to search for a narcissistic love object (the ego-ideal). Finally, he inferred that females are less strongly identified with their mothers than are males with their fathers. To illustrate this research, this last conclusion will be described in more detail. The subjects were shown a picture of Blacky with an upraised paw, scolding a toy black dog. One question then asked who Blacky would rather pattern himself or herself after—Mama, Papa, or Tippy. Females chose Mama significantly less often than males chose Papa. In answer to the question of who Blacky is most likely to obey, both sexes chose Papa significantly more often than Mama. But much of this data could also fit other theories, and the connections to Freud sometimes seem tenuous. Also, Blacky itself seems more masculine than feminine making the test itself sex biased. Because of these problems this test is seldom used today.

Some other studies looked at another aspect of Freud's theory: the superego. C. Hall (1964) analyzed the dreams of young adults and found that females more often dream of being victims of aggression, while males more often dream of suffering misfortune; this was interpreted as meaning that the female has an externalized superego and the male an internalized one. M. Hall (M. Hall and Van de Castle, 1966) believed that men dream more often than women of male characters because women had Oedipal conflicts. However, this sex difference is reversed in Peru (Urbina and Gray, 1975). M. Hoffman (1971) found that, for middle-class boys at least, father identification correlated with internal moral judgments, rule conformity, and moral values. However, mother identification also predicted rule conformity in males, and the only correlation between the girl's moral behavior and identification was with her father, not with her mother.

Penis envy has also been investigated. D. Levy's (1940) semicontrolled observations of young children led him to conclude that the discovery of anatomical sex differences leads to castration anxiety in males and penis envy in females. Landy (1967) studied the way in which females and males opened cigarette packages. He found that females opening the flap more often left paper on, thus forming a cavity at the top. They then push the cigarette out from the bottom. Males tore off the paper and shook a cigarette out. Landy felt that this demonstrated penis envy in women. In our own classroom demonstrations of this experiment, conducted from 1975 to 1977, the only females out of about thirty who opened cigarettes the "female" way were those who kept them in a purse without a holder (leaving the flap on keeps tobacco crumbs from getting all over).

A last aspect of Freud's theory to be investigated was his contention that both males and females feel that females are inferior, and that males look for someone to love who is like their mother, while females look for an ego-ideal. MacBrayer (1960) found that women attributed significantly fewer unfavorable traits to men than men did to women. And, in response to the sentence "My idea of a perfect woman/man is . . . ," one of the top ten male answers was "like my mother," but answers by women emphasized maturity, stability, being a family man and a good provider, and being rich.

This illustrates the type of research often cited to support Freud. Sherman (1971) reviews a large number of other studies and concludes that little evidence supports Freud's view of the development of sex differences, and little supports the existence of the sex differences hypothesized to be the result of that development. There are sex differences before the age of three, and children also acquire a gender identity before the age of three. Genital sexuality appears in very young children, and the same may be true of anxiety usually characterized as Oedipal (Galenson and Roiphe, 1974). As Sherman pointed out, children of both sexes between the ages of three to five prefer their mother, even though according to Freud boys should be identifying with their fathers and females turning away from the mothers who are responsible for their lack of a penis. Both adult sons and daughters are more similar to their mothers than to their fathers (Hartley, 1959a; Sherman, 1971). In Heilbrun's surveys (1965, 1968b, 1974), femininity in females is often inversely correlated with mental health, although Freud would have predicted the reverse. The data on acquisition of gender identity already discussed suggest that the male, not the female, goes through the most torturous and complicated process to arrive at gender identity and gender role, since in the male this process most often goes awry and produces transsexuality, homosexuality, and transvestism.

With regard to the Electra complex, Freud may have misinterpreted the complaints of his female patients concerning sexual attacks by their fathers. He interpreted these statements as wish fulfillments, as desire for their fathers' penises. But Rosenthal and Klapper (1977) stated in the November, 1977 issue of *Mother Jones* that in the United States "twenty-five per cent of all women are sexually abused before they reach 18. Fully 75 percent of these sexual assaults are committed by men known to them, and 34 percent occur in the victim's own home" (p. 38). So maybe instead of expressing wish fulfillment or a desire for a penis, these women patients of Freud's were correctly reporting sexual assaults by their fathers.

Another piece of evidence contradicting Freud's theory is that awareness of differences in genitals is not as universal, as early, or as important for development as Freud predicted. In one study, children were given figures of a boy, a girl, a man, and a woman, each cut into three pieces. The children were told to assemble the four figures from the twelve pieces given. In one condition, the figures were all dressed in sex-appropriate clothes; children over three made no mistakes. In another condition the figures were undressed; 88 percent of the three-year-olds made at least one error, 69 percent of the four-year-olds made an error, and even 31 percent of the six-year-olds made errors (Katcher, 1955). Also contradicting this part of the theory is that men without penises or testicles and women without vaginas can develop normal gender identities (Meyer-Bahlburg et al., 1974; Stoller, 1968).

Finally, Freud seems to have mistaken women's sex-role envy for penis envy. That is, women often envy the roles men play in society but do not in particular envy their penises. Sherman (1971) cites an impressive amount of evidence supporting the notion of greater sex-role envy among women. More women than men (five to twelve times as many) wished that they had been born the other sex, and a majority of women feel that men have an easier time of it. Both sexes prefer male children, at least as first or only children. Even lectures were not able to change the belief of both sexes that the male was superior. Boys prefer the male role more than girls prefer the female role (Minuchin, 1965; Sherman, 1971), and this increases with age (Baruch, 1975). While boys and girls rate their own sex-appropriate activities as being the most fun, this tendency decreases with age for females (Sigalow and Reuter, 1975). This sex difference in the evaluation of the sex-appropriate roles increases at adolescence (Nash, 1975; Simmons and Rosenberg, 1975). According to Sherman, Oetzel's bibliography (1966) listed twenty studies showing that boys and men have greater sex role acceptance, and this acceptance apparently increases with age. I. Broverman and her colleagues (1972) have also cited supporting data. Mothers of daughters are happier about a new pregnancy than are mothers of sons. The interval between children is shorter when the first child is a girl, and the likelihood of having a third child is greater if the first two are both girls than if they were both boys. Thus, women may envy the more valued male role.

But males may also envy the female role. Men in many cultures apparently envy the ability of women to give birth (Bettelheim, 1962), and the origin of babies elicits more questions among children than does the function of the sex organs (Hattendorf, 1932). Reik (1960) also discusses the possibility that the myth of creation was originated to deny the reality that man was born of woman.

Thus, much of the research cited in support of Freud's theory rests on somewhat dubious assumptions. Researchers have also developed a wealth of evidence that does not fulfill Freud's predictions of sex differences. In particular, Freud seems to have mistaken sex-role envy for penis envy. On the other hand, Freud's theory has had an undeniably great impact both on our theorizing and on our culture. Freudian theory has also been reanalyzed and reformulated by other theorists, bringing it more into agreement with current data (see reviews by Bardwick, 1971, and by Sherman, 1971).

Mischel and Bandura

Theory. Mischel (1966) and Bandura and Walters (1963) have been identified with a **social-learning theory** of the development of gender role and gender identity. This theory emphasizes differential reinforcement, modeling, and generalization as the most important developmental mechanisms. According to this theory, **sex-typed behavior** is behavior that, once it occurs, receives different rewards from the environment as a function of the gender of the child exhibiting that behavior. Thus, there are sex differences only because people in the environment consistently react to, interpret, evaluate, and reward behavior differentially based on the gender of the person involved. So there will be sex differences as long as we think men and women ought to act differently.

In social-learning theory, **differential reinforcement** (reward and punishment) is largely responsible for sex differences in behavior. A reward for a particular response increases the frequency or probability of that response. Giving a girl attention or approval for playing with a toy stove increases that play. Punishment decreases the frequency or probability of the behavior it follows. Scolding a boy, or withholding approval and love, for playing with a toy stove decreases the frequency of the behavior. If the frequency of these rewards and punishments for particular behaviors is affected by the gender of the child, then sex differences are likely to result. Girls, but not boys, will play with toy stoves.

Generalization and **discrimination** can also lead to sex differences. Once a behavior has been associated with a given reward or punishment in a given situation, that behavior will tend to occur in similar situations. This is called generalization. A boy who does not play with a toy stove at home will not be likely to play with one at school, and may be less likely to want to use a real stove as an adult. Children can also discriminate between two different situations in which the same behavior receives different rewards or punishments. Mother may not punish a little boy for playing with a stove, but his father, teachers, and peers may laugh at him for it. As a result, he will play with a stove only when his mother is present and never in anyone else's presence.

Modeling, or **observational learning,** can also produce sex differences. This concept is similar to identification in Freud's theory. Children copy the behavior of adults and of other children around them, particularly the behaviors of people of the same gender as the child. This tendency to model others' behaviors is also called observational learning. If people around the child show consistently gender-related differences in behavior, then the child's modeling will reproduce those differences in the child's own behavior. If only the mother and not the father is observed working over a stove, daughters, but not sons, will display the same behavior.

There are three stages of development in this theory, but they overlap greatly, and are apparently not closely tied to age norms. It should be noted that this theory views children as acquiring sex-role stereotype behavior before they acquire gender identities. The first stage is learning to discriminate between appropriate and inappropriate sex-typed behavior. That is, the child learns which behaviors get reinforced and which are punished or ignored, based on the gender of the person exhibiting the behavior. The child also learns to copy the appropriately sex-typed behavior of a model, particularly of a model of his or her sex. The second stage is to generalize these behaviors to new situations beyond those in which reinforcement originally occurred. Finally, these behaviors are performed in all situations with the aid of an internalized label (gender identity) as a discriminative stimulus. Thus, the girl would say to herself, "I am a girl, and girls are supposed to be [get reinforced for] cooking."

Data. Mischel (1966) cites much evidence in support of the social-learning theory. As stated earlier, the behavior of parents toward their sex-reassigned children changed immediately and dramatically after the surgery. Also, five-year-olds are able to view a series of pictures and verbalize what activities mothers would most like them to do. Observational learning and modeling do occur, in lower animals as well as in humans. And differential reinforcement is an extremely powerful means of behavior control. Children imitate nurturant models and models with social power more than other models, and children and adults do pay more attention to a same-sex model than to an opposite-sex one (Slaby and Frey, 1975).

A study by Bandura and McDonald (1963) illustrates some of these effects. Children from five to eleven were asked to make moral judgments. They were then exposed to modeling or reinforcement procedures designed to change these judgments; that is, either the model demonstrated moral judgments contrary to those of the child or the experimenter reinforced the child for judgments contrary to the child's original one. Both boys and girls shifted their moral judgments in the direction of the model or the reinforcement. Another study (Bandura, Ross, and Ross, 1961) found that aggression was imitated more if the aggressor was a same-sexed model, which is again consistent with the theory.

A rare but important experiment actually studied the frequency of environmental reinforcement in a natural, behavioral setting, looking for differential rewards for sex-typed behaviors (Fagot and Patterson, 1969). The behavior of nursery school children was analyzed, and those play patterns that showed consistently different frequencies of occurrence in males and females were called sex-typed. Then, the number of rewards offered by both peers and teachers for sex-typical and sex-atypical behaviors were counted. Overall, the female teachers rewarded feminine behaviors more in both sexes. But in the peer group, where most of the rewards occurred, boys mostly rewarded boys and girls mostly rewarded girls, and reinforcement by peers for opposite-sex behaviors was almost nonexistent. The one boy who exhibited mostly feminine behaviors was criticized more and played with less than any other boy. So apparently both sexes overall got more reinforcement for sex-typical behaviors, just as predicted by social-learning theory.

The greatest strength of this theory is that it does not require consistency in behavior. Trait theories imply stable predispositions to behave in certain ways across all situations, whereas social-learning theory says that what behavior occurs in what situation depends upon the reinforcement history for that particular behavior in that particular situation. Generally, the correlations among behavioral data on sex role measured either in different ways or in different situations are, in fact, quite low (Domash and Balter, 1976; Hetherington, 1965; Mussen, 1969).

There may be some problems with the social-learning model, however, some of which were pointed out by Maccoby and Jacklin (1974). Children do not most closely resemble their same-sexed parent, although social-learning theory like Freud's says they should. Children engage in sex-typed behaviors several years before they favor a same-sex model more than an opposite-sex model. Much of children's sex-typed behavior is never performed by adults, so it cannot be acquired by modeling adults. Also, the evidence indicates that sex differences in aggression are not caused by more reinforcement of or less punishment for aggression in boys; instead, aggression may be more often punished in male than female children. Also, it is unclear from this theory why girls should imitate the behavior of both parents more than boys do (Hetherington, 1965).

Other problems with this theory have also been pointed out. B. Rosenberg and Sutton-Smith (1972) criticized the theory on three bases: the lack of field studies, case studies, and naturalistic observations to get away from the artificiality of the laboratory; the emphasis on the ways that behavior is acquired, ignoring the factors that influence the performance of that behavior after it is learned; and the fact that social-learning theorists can study only those behaviors that can be systematically reinforced. Perhaps the most damaging evidence in opposition to the theory comes from experiments in which children were offered reinforcements (or bribes) to change their sex-typed behavior. In many studies, children, particularly boys, will not change their behavior, despite the change in reinforcement. Such results have been seen, for example, in toy preferences (Kohlberg, 1966). According to social-learning theory, however, behavior should change when reinforcement does.

The theory also does not allow for any biologically biased sex differences in preparedness. For example, boys may be more prepared to learn aggressive acts, and may do so in spite of greater frequencies of parental punishments. Several studies (Bandura, 1965; Bandura, Ross, and Ross, 1963a, 1963b), exposed children to an aggressive mdoel or reinforced them for aggression; both exposure and reinforcement increased aggression in both sexes. However, in all conditions, the boys were still more aggressive than the girls. All the data on genes, inductive hormones, and activational hormones also implies some biological biases in sex differences.

In summary, social-learning theory has without doubt correctly pointed out some of the most important factors involved in sex-role development. Modeling occurs, and there are differential rewards for behavior depending upon gender, a fact of which children seem to be quite aware. However, the theory ignores the possibility of biological biases, and cannot account for those situations in which sex-role stereotypic behavior seems to take on a life of its own, occurring independently of the reward currently available, as though being appropriately male or female were more important than a reward. Still, this theory has had a tremendous impact not only upon psychology but also upon feminism, because it says that sex roles can be changed if we just change the reinforcements.

Kohlberg

Theory.   Kohlberg's **cognitive-developmental theory** (Kohlberg, 1966, 1969; Kohlberg and Ullman, 1974) proposes that gender identity and gender role develop through stages that parallel Piaget's stages in cognitive development. In other words, Kohlberg emphasizes the cognitive aspects of gender identity and role, and points out that children's conception of their identity and the appropriateness of their behavior changes and matures as their intellectual capacity grows.

In general, cognitive theories of learning, including Kohlberg's, state that learning consists of the formation of cognitive structures rather than the acquisition of particular responses or particular associations between stimuli and responses. Reinforcement does not have to occur in order for learning to take place, although some sort of motive is necessary for the learned response to be performed.

Kohlberg proposes that developmental learning consists of changes in the mental structure of the child. Structure refers to the shape, pattern, or organization of responses, rather than to the rate or intensity of a response or to how it is paired with a particular stimulus. **Cognitive structures** refer to rules for processing information or for connecting experiences. "Cognition . . . means putting things together or relating events, and this relating is an active connecting process, not a passive connecting of events through extensive association and repetition. In part this means that connections are formed by selective and active processes. . . . More basically, it means that the process of relating particular events depends upon prior general modes of relating developed by the organism" (Kohlberg, 1969, pp. 349–50). Thus, contrary to social-learning theory, experience permanently changes organisms, because it changes their way of perceiving new experiences. The child's motive for performance and development is to increase the competence of the self, a motive Freud (1959a) also recognized. The cognitive structure develops as the child becomes more cognitively complex. Due to the motive for competence, as the child matures, there are qualitative changes in modes of thought and this developing mentality interacts with the structure of the outside world. The cognitive structure is "the result of an interaction between certain organismic structuring tendencies and the structure of the outside world, rather than reflecting either one directly" (Kohlberg, 1969, p. 352).

Intelligence determines the rate of progress through the cognitive-developmental stages, but has no effect on what the final stage will be. In turn, the effects experience have upon the child are determined by the child's stage of cognitive development, and experience is more important than intelligence in determining the final stage. Thus, cognitive development is necessary but not sufficient for sex-role maturity; for a given stage, a given level of cognitive maturity must first be attained, but experience (or the lack of relevant experience) can prevent development. As in Freudian theory, regressions to an earlier mode of development can occur. Kohlberg says these regressions occur when the person encounters a world structure at odds with his or her cognitive structure, but that this regression will be somewhat unstable and will be accompanied by generalized distress. The inclusion of the possibility of regression makes cognitive-developmental theory quite different from social-learning theory, but Kohlberg, like social-learning theorists, does not expect high correlations among different tests of stereotyping or sex-role preferences, since the environment of children varies so greatly.

Kohlberg has cited five mechanisms by which gender role and gender identity are acquired. There are different age norms for each mechanism; we will present them as stages of development and give the approximate age ranges. The first stage of development, from birth to three years of age, is the *consistency stage,* during which the child responds to new interests in a way consistent with past interests and behaviors. In this stage, sex differences in behavior might be the result of innate differences between the sexes, in strength, for instance, or of differential treatment by parents.

In the second stage, from three to four, the child begins to *label himself or herself by sex and to value the self as good.* In this stage, same-sex peers and sex-typed activities are preferred, because the self and things similar to the self are valued. For example, by age four children already know which toys are appropriate for their own sex, although they may be unsure of what toys are appropriate for the opposite sex (J. Masters and Wilkinson, 1976). There is no further increase in the sex typing of toy preferences between three and eight (Rekers and Yates, 1976). In this stage, older and more powerful models are imitated by the child. Sex differences are equated by the child with physical differences in size and strength. The tendency to imitate adults increases over this period, especially if an adult does something interesting that the child wants to be able to do also. However, the child has not yet developed **gender constancy**; that is, a boy may label himself correctly as a boy, but still say he's going to grow up to be a Mommy, or, as one boy told his mother, "When you grow up to be a Daddy, you can have a bicycle too [like his father]" (Kohlberg, 1966, p. 95). The child reports that he can change his sex by wearing a wig, or by changing into a dress (Kohlberg's examples were all of boys). At this age, children do not have object constancy either.

In the third stage, from four to six, the children acquire both *object and gender constancy*. After age four, the child sees gender as a constant, not as something that can be changed by changing clothes or hairdos. This parallels the development of object constancy, the ability to recognize that objects remain the same despite differences in orientation; a plane receding into the distance is no longer seen as shrinking. At this age, prestige, competence, and goodness become associated with the male sex-role stereotype, and niceness and attractiveness become associated with the female stereotype. Fathers are seen as bigger, stronger, and more aggressive than mothers, and both boys and girls show increasing imitation of the father.

In the fourth stage, from five or six to seven, *conformity to the sex role* is seen as moral and performing out of role as immoral. As one boy of five told Katharine Hoyenga, with great disgust, "You can't be a real mother. You work." Imitation of same-sex peers increases steadily during these ages. Also, this is the age of good boy morality, when the child is concerned with external social definitions of correct, good, or moral performance, including the way those definitions affect his or her sex role. Girls adopt this morality sooner, but may keep it longer because of the conflict between sex typing and power in the next stage.

In the last stage, which also starts at age five or six but continues thereafter, there is an *increasing tendency to model adults who have prestige, power, and competency, and who are in some way, such as gender, like the self.* The tendency of the child to imitate any adult decreases from ages five to eight, and after this stage, imitation only occurs when the child perceives the behavior to be relevant to his or her own competence. The child then selectively models the good and the skillful. Parental dominance increases sex typing in boys at this age because of the tendency to imitate power, but the sex typing of adolescent males is more correlated with the father's occupational prestige than with his dominance over the mother (Kohlberg, 1969). After the age of seven, both sexes become oriented to authority and to the maintenance of the social order, but boys do sooner. Sex typing occurs because that is the way things are. By this age, the child has established an abstract, constant definition of gender, based on anatomy. Sex typing does not increase after this age, at least according to Kohlberg (1969).

The application of this theory to sex differences has to be inferred, since Kohlberg has not yet published the application of his theory to women (1966, p. 124). However, it seems reasonable to assume that sex differences in development would appear mostly in stages three and five, since prestige and power, which become important in those stages, are associated more with males than with females in this society. Children of both sexes start off knowing that fathers are bigger and stronger, next they learn that fathers are smarter and better, and finally, that fathers have more social power and are the boss. By five or six, all children agree that males are more physically powerful and invulnerable, and that fathers are more powerful, punitive, aggressive, fearless, and competent and less nuturant. These concepts are derived from physical differences and from sex-role differences observed outside the family—males are policemen, soldiers, robbers, and presidents.

These sex differences will cause adjustment difficulties for girls. The female will have difficulty valuing her role in stage three because prestige and competence are male attributes; a four-year-old girl whose mother was a doctor still insisted that only boys become doctors. The girl will also feel conflict in the last stage, because the models most like herself are not the ones who have the most prestige. Girls judge their own sex to be better less often than boys, and sex typing occurs earlier and more completely in young boys than in young girls. At five years of age, although both sexes are equally sex-typed, according to figure drawing, girls showed significantly less sex-role preference than boys on the It scales (Domash and Balter, 1976; Minuchin, 1965; Mussen, 1969). Another study showed delayed sex-role preferences in girls (Hetherington, 1965).

Kohlberg and Ullman (1974) also looked at developmental changes in sex-role concepts in children older than those covered by the five stages. The six-year-old conceives of sex roles as classes of activities and physical characteristics and defines the roles in terms of their morality. The six-year-old decides what males and females ought to be by seeing what they are, judging from physical attributes and gender identity. Eleven-year-olds see sex-role expectations as defined by socially shared expectations of behavior. There are differences in sex role because they serve social functions for other people or for society; conforming to sex roles helps other people. Gender identity is determined by what it ought to be. By age fifteen, boys see sex differences as occuring independent of and prior to the social sex roles. Sex differences are described by the stereotypic psychological traits, and the stereotypes are seen as almost completely due to social expectations and to the choice of the individual. College students still talk about psychological differences between the sexes, but do not believe they are innate; instead, the college student rejects conventional standards and tries to operate on a principle of equity (rewards proprotional to behavior, regardless of gender). All these attitudes describe only the development of sex-role concepts in boys; data on girls have not yet been supplied.

Data. Much data is consistent with this theory, although very little evidence can be interpreted as directly confirming it (Kurtenes and Grief, 1974). Kohlberg and Zigler (1967) compared bright and average children of both sexes on several measures of sex-role preference. Their results indicate that bright children have more advanced gender concepts than the average child of the same age. Thus, IQ and sex typing are positively correlated in children from four to ten, which evidence supports the theory, although this relationship reverses at adolescence (Maccoby, 1966).

Kohlberg (1966) cited other data to support his theory. Children's preferences among toys and activities, and children's imitation of same-sex adults undergo developmental changes. Unlike both theories discussed earlier, in this theory the father is not necessary as a model for masculinity because the child models many different adults; the development of sex-role preferences is in fact only slightly retarded in boys in father-absent homes. Contrary to Freud and in support of Kohlberg, paternal warmth (not fear) is most strongly correlated with father identification and with masculine preferences for boys. In homes with a dominant mother, girls imitated her more but did not become more feminine, and sex typing is positively correlated with father identification in girls and women. Kohlberg would have expected this, since the daughter can acquire the father's conception of the female sex role, and both boys and girls model powerful or dominant parents. Boys who are more sex-typed show more same-sex modeling than boys less sex-typed, and after age five or six, reinforcements of opposite-sex preferences in toys did not change the toy preferences of boys; this is contrary to social-learning theory, which predicts that sex-typed behavior changes whenever reinforcement changes.

Other studies on modeling have also obtained results consistent with Kohlberg's theory. By the age of seven, boys will not play with sex-inappropriate toys, even after watching a male model play with them; however, girls, although they played more than boys with opposite-sex toys, also were not affected by what the model had done (Wolf, 1976). In fact, when Heilbrun (1974) reanalyzed a similar experiment done by Wismar (1974, unpublished), both modeling and reinforcement suppressed play with opposite-sex toys in boys aged from three to six. This is inconsistent with social-learning theory but quite consistent with Kohlberg, who believes that the child's internalized concept of gender identity and gender role will determine behavior, even in the face of a conflicting environment. Also supporing Kohlberg is the fact that the age of gender constancy correlates well with the differential observation of a male as opposed to a female model by boys; that is, the higher the level of gender constancy in children, the greater the extent to which they will observe a same-sex as opposed to an opposite-sex model (Slaby and Frey, 1975). But overall, the boys spent more time watching the male model than the female model. Kohlberg would have predicted this because of the greater power and prestige associated with male models.

Other data on gender role development is also consistent with Kohlberg. Preschool children (aged three-and-a-half to five-and-a-half) choose sex-typed occupations for themselves when asked what they will "really be" when they grow up (Papalia and Tennent, 1975). The behavior of children also shows an increasing similarity to that of the dominant parent as the children grow older (imitation on the basis of power and prestige), and neither girls nor boys will identify with a passive father (Hetherington, 1965). The cognitive-developmental theory is also consistent with Money's observations of children undergoing sex changes, including his assertion of an inability to change gender after age three.

Another study was done explicity to test Kohlberg's theory and got mixed results (Blakemore, La Rue, and Olejnik, 1976). Boys from two to six show stronger sex-appropriate toy preferences than girls do. Cognitive development paralleled toy preferences, but the only cognitive skill found to be directly related to sex-appropriate toy preference was the ability to sort toys on the basis of a sex-typed division (putting boys' toys in one stack and girls' toys in another). Two-year-old boys showed strong sex-appropriate toy preferences; two-year-old girls showed no preference at all. But, contrary to Kohlberg, the two-year-old boys, in spite of their preferences, did not have the cognitive capacity to sort toys into piles of boys' toys and girls' toys. Thus, at this first stage of development, either only boys showed behavior predicted by the consistency stage, or girls weren't being differentially reinforced for toy preferences.

In another study, not all children imitated a same-sex model (Zimmerman and Koussa, 1975). Three- to four-year-old children were exposed to either a same-sex or an opposite-sex model who was playing in a way either gender-appropriate, gender-inappropriate, or gender-neutral. Males imitated masculine behavior most, regardless of the sex of the model. Females imitated models most when the models demonstrated sex-typed play appropriate to the model's gender, whether masculine or feminine. Overall, models displaying masculine behavior had the most impact. The subjects in this experiment were younger than the age of gender constancy, so same-sex imitation would not have been expected by Kohlberg, making the sex differences in the pattern of results difficult to incorporate into his theory.

Kohlberg's theory incorporates an impressive amount of data, and he did place a much needed emphasis on cognitive factors, However, he may have neglected emotional factors (B. Rosenberg and Sutton-Smith, 1972). His theory, like social-learning theory, also does not accurately predict all of the available data, and it as yet neglects sex-role development in females. Still, his ideas deserve to have, and probably will have, a great impact on theory and research, and may even have an impact on childrearing.

Parsons and Bales

Parsons and Bales (1955) generally accept the psychoanalytic model of development, but they add to it a discussion of the role of the family in the context of society. They generally agree with the psychosexual stages described by Freud, but add to them the concept of socialization, whereby children internalize cultural norms.

Parsons and Bales distinguish between the roles that each parent plays in society. The father is high on power and instrumentality, but low on expressiveness; the mother is also high on power, but is low on instrumentality and high on expressiveness. **Instrumentality** refers to a particular emphasis for tasks, an orientation towards more distant goals and relationships between the family system and the outside world. **Expressiveness** refers to behavior that emphasizes social-emotional interactions, that is concerned with the internal affairs of the system and the keeping of harmony. Thus, the possession of expressiveness or instrumentality is assigned according to gender. The concern of the mother with childrearing gives her the expressive roles, which frees the father for the instrumental roles. The other major role division, between leaders and followers, is divided along age lines.

In the first phase of development, the oral-dependent phase, the mother plays all the power roles with regard to her infant. During the anal stage, the mother assumes an instrumental orientation with regard to the child. As part of the Oedipal-phallic phase, not only is the conscience acquired, but the emphasis shifts from the mother-child role system to the nuclear family role system. Now the mother becomes mostly expressive and the father takes on the instrumental role. At this stage also, the child internalizes the sex role. Because the male child has to shift his identification from mother to father, he absorbs the masculine role as a defense against being feminine. Both boys and girls learn not to become their same-sex parent, but to take on the roles of that parent as defined by that culture. Thus, identification is with a socially defined role rather than with a person. The latency period and the genital period represent times in which sex-role behaviors are continuously acquired and refined by exposure to school and to people outside the family. The major sex difference is the defensive nature of the boy's masculine sex-role identification, which defensiveness is not seen in the girl's feminine sex-role identification.

SUMMARY AND CONCLUSIONS

Lynn's Theory

A brief look at Lynn's theory of sex role development (1966) will serve as a useful review of the data and ideas presented to this point. Lynn described his theory in terms of thirteen developmental principles, some of which are at odds with the evidence we have seen so far.

First, "*males tend to identify with a culturally defined masculine role, whereas females tend to identify with their mothers*" (p. 467). This is probably because the mother is the one who is usually at home (or is responsible for home and family) and is the parent with whom both sexes have the most contact; the male child's relative lack of familiarity with his father requires that a more impersonal role model be provided. Also because of this difference, children may perceive their father in more instrumental roles, as culturally-defined, and perceive their mother, who is more involved in their day-to-day problems, in more expressive roles. However, Parsons and Bales (1955) said that both sexes identified with a cultural role rather than with a person, instead of just the boy, as in Lynn's theory. Kohlberg's theory and Mischel and Bandura's theory emphasize the role of modeling, which can include models other than the parents, but they also do not make this particular sex distinction. Still, contrary to Lynn, neither sex is very similar in sex role to either the mother or the father (Maccoby and Jacklin, 1974).

The second principle is that, because both sexes have more contact with the mother, "*both males and females identify more closely with the mother than with the father* (Lynn, 1966, p. 467). Earlier cited research suggests that children of both sexes resemble the mother more than the father. Lynn himself cites research showing that both men and women are more similar to their mothers in test scores on semantic similarity, anxiety, childrearing values, and other values. This is also consistent with cross-cultural data showing that the more boys become involved in feminine chores around the home, the less sexual dimorphism there is in behavior (see Chapter 7). Freud also believes that both sexes start out with a mother identification, but he says that females keep this attachment much more strongly than do boys. The third principle qualifies the second: *"the closer identification of males with their mothers than with their fathers will be revealed most frequently in personality variables which are not clearly sex-typed"* (Lynn, 1966, p. 467). This is because males to some extent acquire a stereotype rather than the specific behavior and value of their fathers.

Sex differences in learning styles would also appear because of these differences in identification. The fourth principle states: *"in learning the sex-typical identification, each sex is thereby acquiring separate methods of learning which are subsequently applied to learning tasks generally"* (Lynn, 1966, p. 468). Since females identify with their mothers, their learning method revolves around personal relationships and imitation. Males identify with the cultural stereotype, so their learning methods involve defining the goal, restructuring the field, and abstracting principles. As we have seen, females are more often field dependent and may be more involved with social stimuli, such as faces. This principle may account for the sex differences found in the relationships between the cognitive-developmental stages and the associated sex typing. Some evidence indicates that girls in some situations (for example, with parent models) may do more imitating than boys, especially of cross-sex behavior. Much of the research on cognitive differences will be discussed in Chapter 8, but we can say here that contrary to Lynn's theory, abstracting principles and restructuring fields are not traits employed by men more than by women.

Since males do not have a same-sex model before them as often as do females, Lynn proposes the fifth principle, *"males tend to have greater difficulty in achieving same-sex identification than females"* (Lynn, 1966, p. 468), and the sixth, *"more males than females fail more or less completely in achieving same-sex identification, but they rather make an opposite-sex identification"* (p. 468). It is true that there are more male than female transsexuals, transvestites, and homosexuals, and Green (1974) used a similar explanation for the fact that there were fewer female than male transsexuals. However, both Freud and Kohlberg predict more difficulty for the female in gender role acquisition, and Mischel and Bandura do not make any distinctions here.

The seventh principle derives from the sixth: *"consequently, males are more anxious regarding sex-role identification than females"* (Lynn, 1966, pp. 469). This establishes the eighth *"males tend to hold stronger feelings of hostility toward females than females toward males"* (p. 469). Men are more concerned than women about doing sex-inappropriate tasks, as we have already mentioned. Girls are more willing to imitate opposite-sex behavior and to play with opposite-sex toys. By adolescence, girls are less likely to think it is important to avoid acting like the opposite sex (63 percent of girls thought so, but 74 percent of boys did) (Simmons and Rosenberg, 1975). Hartley (1959b) has postulated that the male anxiety over sex-inappropriate behavior may be created by the fact that most of his sex role is defined in terms of "don't" rather than "do." It may also be passed on from father to son. Lansky (1967) presented a situation to parents of preschool children in which a child chose either a sex-appropriate or sex-inappropriate activity. When girls chose a masculine activity, neither mothers nor fathers were concerned. When the boy chose a feminine activity, the parents reacted very negatively, especially the father. One father, when asked whether or not he would be disturbed by feminine characteristics in his son, "Yes, I would be very, very much. Terrifically disturbed—couldn't tell you the extent of my disturbance. I can't *bear* female characteristics in a man. I abhor them" (as quoted by Goodenough, in Maccoby and Jacklin, 1974, p. 328).

With age, these differences in identification become incorporated into the adult personalities, establishing the ninth principle—"*with increasing age, males become relatively more firmly identified with the masculine role*" (Lynn, 1966, p. 469). and—the tenth—males "*develop psychological disturbances at a more slowly accelerating rate than females*" (p. 469). The sex typing of boys increases with age consistently more than the sex typing of females, as was mentioned earlier. Adult males, significantly more often than females, will answer the question "Who am I?" by responding with their specific gender identity; women will specify their gender more indirectly, saying they are wives or mothers or sisters (Mulford and Salisbury, 1964). Hartley (1959b) has also pointed out that (perhaps because of the earlier difficulties with sex-role acquisition) demands that boys conform to their sex roles "come much earlier and are enforced with much more vigor than similar attitudes with respect to girls. These demands are frequently enforced harshly, impressing the small boy with the danger of deviating from them, while he does not quite understand what they are" (p. 458).

The slower sex typing of women may be explained by the eleventh principle: "*a larger proportion of females than males show preferences for the role of the opposite sex* (Lynn, 1966, p. 469). This is based on the data that Freud thought meant penis envy, and is consistent with the greater power, prestige, and competence associated with the male role, as pointed out by Kohlberg, and the greater instrumentality of the male role, as pointed out by Parsons. This sex-role envy of women may be a function of the universally lower status of women. Males who come from a family in which household tasks were assinged according to gender more often responded with their gender when asked "Who am I?" than did males from less dimorphic families. For females, the reverse was true, indicating probably that dimorphic role assignment underlined the inferior status of women and led women to less often identify themselves by their gender (Couch, 1962). Another piece of evidence in support of this principle is that father preference in girls increases from the fifth to the tenth grades (Baruch, 1975).

In conclusion, we have the twelfth principle, "*males will tend to show same-sex role preference with underlying opposite-sex identification*" (Lynn, 1966, p. 470). Females show the reverse. The thirteenth principle states that because of this, "*a higher proportion of females than males adopt aspects of the role of the opposite sex*" (p. 470). Heilbrun (1974) found that identifying both the primary and the secondary sex-role identifications of men improved his ability to predict their behaviors and mental health, but women showed little evidence for a secondary sex-role identity. (Primary sex-roles are behaviors mediated by modeling after the gender-appropriate behaviors of the same-sex parent; secondary roles are behaviors mediated by modeling gender-inappropriate behaviors of the same-sex parent.) Overall, girls are less sex-typed and more flexible than boys (Minuchin, 1965). The role behaviors that led up to this flexibility could be acquired through imitation and differential reinforcement (social-learning theory) as modified by the child's own cognitive abilities at each state (cognitive-developmental theory).

One problem with Lynn's theory is its deemphasis of the role of the father (Lamb, 1975d). All of the other theorists explicitly emphasize his role, with Kohlberg and Parsons emphasizing the importance of the father for normal female development as well as that of the male.

Comparisons Among the Theories

It may be helpful to compare the four theories on a few major issues. The major difference between social-learning theory and the cognitive-developmental theory is in regard to when and why gender identity occurs. In cognitive-developmental theory, identity comes first and makes the performance of sex-typed activities differentially reinforcing. In social-learning theory, differential reinforcement of gender role (sex-typed behavior) leads to gender identity. In Freud's theory, identification leads simultaneously to gender role and to gender identity. In social-learning theory gender role precedes gender identity, then, whereas in Kohlberg's theory, gender identity comes first. But most research has not differentiated between gender identity and gender role and so cannot test among these three different predictions. Lynn's theory also distinguishes between role and identity, using sex-role adaptation to refer to overt behavior, and holds that both are acquired simultaneously.

Identification is also conceptualized differently by all the theories. Identification in social-learning theory simply involves imitation of same-sex models, which results in acquiring their behaviors. For Freud, identification—at least during the Oedipal phase—occurs out of fear, and includes the child's incorporation of the same-sex parent's qualities, as the child sees them. Thus, children acquire the values and behaviors of the same-sex parent and this leads to their gender identity. In Kohlberg's theory, acquiring the behaviors of the same-sex parent is part of a more general process of imitation of any same-sex adult model, and this identification is facilitated by parental warmth, not fear. Kohlberg sees gender identity as preceding parental identification and not resulting from it, as Freud sees it. However, the imitation of social-learning theory also differs from identification in Kohlberg or Freud, in that identification involves irreversible changes in underlying personality or cognitive structure, whereas imitation is reversible or extinguishable by a change in reinforcement. In identification, modeling occurs even in the absence of the model and is motivated by a desire for competence (Kohlberg and Freud) and out of fear (Freud). Identification is a transitory stage in Kohlberg's theory, leading to attachment and dependency, but is a more continuous process in Freud's theory. Parsons differs from Freud mostly in terms of the societal factors in development and in seeing identification as the acquisition of the culturally defined role of a mother or father, not the acquisition of the traits of the child's own parents. Lynn also emphasizes the cultural aspects of male sex role identification, and says that the male acquires that identification through rewards and punishments. In Lynn's theory, the female acquires her identification largely through modeling, and thus Lynn makes a unique distinction between male and female processes of identification.

It should be pointed out that none of these theories has yet explained all of the mechanisms of sex typing. Modeling on the basis of sexual similarity is far from universal and occurs well after sex typing has begun. Also, children seem not very similar to either parent (Maccoby and Jacklin, 1974), suggesting the importance of cultural rather than parental stereotypes in sex typing. Thus, modeling may lead to acquisition of behaviors, but not to the sex-typed performances of that behavior once learned. Still, as Mischel, Lynn, Parsons, Bandura and Kohlberg have all pointed out, differential socialization and cultural stereotypes must be the most important aspects of sex typing in humans. So most of the answer to the question of why there are sex differences (at least in humans) must come from the culturally defined stereotypes that are imitated and incorporated by children differentially on the basis of their gender identities, the stereotypes that lead people to reinforce and evaluate behavior differentially based on gender. It is the relationship between culture, stereotypes, and sex roles that we will examine in the next chapter.

KEY TERMS AND CONCEPTS

Transsexuals
Transvestites
Homosexuals
Psychoanalytic theory
Erogenous zone
Cathect
Psychosexual stages: oral, anal, phallic, latent, and genital
Oedipus complex
Electra complex
Identification

Social-learning theory
Sex-typed behavior
Differential reinforcement
Generalization
Discrimination
Modeling or observational learning
Cognitive-developmental theory
Cognitive structures
Gender constancy
Instrumental
Expressive

QUESTIONS ON KEY ISSUES

1. Is biology or experience the major cause of gender identity, and what is the relevant evidence?
2. What are the three types of male transsexuals? How are they similar? How are they different?
3. What sex differences did Freud expect to see, and in each case, why?
4. What kinds of evidence support Freud? What kinds contradict his predictions?
5. What are the major strengths and weaknesses of social-learning theory?
6. What are the five mechanisms described by cognitive-developmental theory?
7. Compare and contrast each of the four major theories with each other on each of the following issues: when and in what order was gender identity and gender role acquired? What are identification and imitation? What is the role, if any, of biological biases?

CHAPTER 7 _____

Sex Typing and Sexual Stereotypes

In this chapter, some of the more general effects of culture and experience on sex typing will be examined. **Sex typing** refers to the degree to which culturally defined stereotypic gender role traits are exhibited by a person. In modern American culture, nearly everyone agrees what women and men are really like. What about other cultures?

Much of the agreement on the stereotypes seems to have been formalized and perpetuated by Freud's theory. Many of the sex differences predicted by Freud are found in the sexual stereotypes of today. So it would be helpful here for you to review the sex differences that Freud predicted. Freud had an incredible impact upon the world because many of his insights were so devastatingly true; the sex stereotypes gained validity in a sort of halo effect.

The other theories—those of Parsons, Mischel and Bandura, Lynn, and Kohlberg—all described how stereotypes can be transmitted from generation to generation. Parents subscribe to the stereotype and so treat their children differentially on the basis of gender. The models that the child imitates and the culture that the child internalizes all present the same stereotype. These stereotypes are found in books, in magazines, and on television.

There are certainly large cross-cultural commonalities in sex stereotypes and sex typing, which could consistently bias sex differences in particular ways. For example, males are usually assigned the more aggressive roles and traits, and girls are raised to be more nurturant. Still, there are really only two cultural universals: women have a lower status than men, and traits and jobs are assigned on a sexually dimorphic basis in all cultures. Why?

The sex-role stereotype that children internalize from their culture then form the basis against which the self and others are judged. So the cultural stereotypes have taken on an artificial reality, a dimension with masculinity and femininity on opposite ends, a dimension which is then used to measure, classify, and evaluate people.

Some people, however, seem to acquire the traits of both sexes, which would be impossible if masculinity and femininity were really opposites. These people are the **androgyns.** How did they successfully resist the sex typing? How do they differ from sex-typed people in behavior and in personal histories?

Sex typing, combined with the lower cultural status of women, may also lead to sexual prejudice. Why and when and how? And is there prejudice against men?

SEX TYPING ACROSS CULTURES

Introduction and the Logic of the Research

This section surveys cross-cultural commonalities in sex-role stereotypes and in the differential treatment of children according to gender. It has often been assumed that this research is most appropriate to proving the existence of biological biases for sex differences. That is, it is assumed that if men are more aggressive than women in all cultures, this sex difference must be caused by genes and hormones. However, this implies complete biological determinism, which is simply not true of any species; in fact, biological determinism is a myth in the sense that biology alone doesn't determine or cause any behavior. Instead, cross-cultural surveys can tell us about commonalities in childrearing practices and in stereotypic assignment of traits, tasks, and behaviors to males and females that could produce cross-cultural commonalities in sex differences, that is, a cultural bias.

Cross-Cultural Variability in Sex Differences. Several examples can be given of the lack of universality of sex differences, even biologically biased ones. Although the greater height of males relative to females is related to both chromosomes and androgens, cultural factors have their impact even here. The difference in height between the sexes can vary from two inches, as among the Klamath Indians of North America, to eight inches, as in the Shilluk of the Sudan (D'Andrade, 1966). Another study found that sex differences in height varied from 4.8 inches in American Indians to 3.6 inches in the people of New Guinea (Eveleth, 1975). Also, sex differences in both body hair and strength vary among racial groups (van den Berghe, 1973).

Margaret Mead (1969) has studied three New Guinea tribes, and her work dramatically illustrates that sex differences in behavior are not universal. In the Arapesh tribe, both sexes are usually peaceful, cooperative, and passive; both are concerned and involved with the growing of things, including children. The role of an authority figure is so disliked that the tribe has institutionalized ways of selecting an individual male to train him from birth to be more aggressive, and then the tribe seems to pity him. In the Mundugumor tribe, both sexes are described as "violent, competitive, aggressively sexed, jealous, and ready to see and avenge insult, delighting in display, in action, in fighting" (p. 213). And children are hardly cared for by anyone. In the third tribe, the Tchambuli, the males are artistic, sensitive, nervous, emotionally dependent, and susceptible to petty jealousy. These men are prudish and flirtatious, fearful of sex, and yet preoccupied with love magic and cosmetics. The females are efficient and competent and they are the sexual aggressors. Thus, looking at these three peoples from the point of view of our society, we see that culture can create men and women who are both feminine, who are both masculine, or whose gender roles are reversed. When we look across cultures, then, we should not expect to see all assigning the same role, occupation, and trait according to sex.

Two Cultural Universals. There are two universals, however. One is the lower status of women. As Mead said, "In every known human society, the male's need for achievement can be recognized. Men may cook, or weave or dress dolls or hunt humming-birds, but if such activities are appropriate occupations of men, then the whole society, men and women alike, votes them as important. When the same occupations are performed by women, they are regarded as less important" (1949, p. 159). Even the cross-cultural connotations of the words man and woman confirm this; in general, the connotation of man is more active, powerful, and aggressive than that of woman (Triandis and Osgood, 1958). "The secondary status of women in society is one of the true universals, a pan-cultural fact. . . . The universality of female subordination, the fact that it exists within every type of social and economic arrangement and in societies of every degree of complexity, indicates to me that we are up against something very profound, very stubborn, something we cannot rout out simply by rearranging a few tasks and roles in the social system, or even by reordering the whole economic structure" (Ortner, 1974, pp. 67–68).

There are many examples of the lower status of women. Women may contribute the bulk of the diet in hunting-gathering societies, but the food supplied by the male is always valued more (Rosaldo, 1974; Sanday, 1974). In Stephens' (1963) study of thirty-one societies, only five of them had an equal sharing of authority between husband and wife in the domestic sphere, and males were dominant in the public sphere in all of those societies. Even in societies in which the husband is not dominant, the wife is often under the authority of some other male relative (Gough, 1971).

And even among the three very different societies studied by Mead, women seem to have lower status. In the Arapesh, the wife is the "child" of the husband, and it is always a male who is raised to be the leader. Fortune (1939) provided other examples of the lesser value the Arapesh place on women. Perhaps the most dramatic is illustrated by the following quotes: " 'She pisses a goodly urine' they say of a woman who bears male children to replenish the clan, but 'She pisses a bad urine,' of a woman who bears female children only" (p. 26). High praise for an Arapesh woman is to say "she had in her a man's heart" (p. 37). Tchambuli women have to participate in rituals that give them inferior roles, and both Tchambuli and Arapesh men are free to beat their wives. Among the Mundugumor, wives are bought by a transfer of a sister of a daughter to the bride's family. In this society, male offspring are also more culturally prized, and female infants may be killed.

Several different kinds of social structures can predict (or covary with) the status of women. Women have a much lower status in those societies in which they are isolated from every one but their own children (Rosaldo, 1974). A rating of seventy-one different societies found that the relative inferiority of women's status is correlated $+.21$ with herding, $+.25$ with living with the husband's father, $+.44$ with reckoning descent through the father's line ($-.34$ with tracing descent through the mother's line), $+.51$ with father-son descent of authority, and $+.58$ with father-son property inheritance (Gouldner and Peterson, 1963). Sanday (1974) found a curvilinear relationship between the percent of the total food supplied by women and their relative status; when women contributed about as much as men, their status was higher. She also found that the more balanced the division of labor by sex, the higher the status of women ($+.416$). The more female deities there are with powers over both men and women, the higher the status of women ($+.300$). The relationship between technology and the status of women also seems to be curvilinear, though with many exceptions (see van den Berghe, 1973).

Thus, societies with paternal descent of authority and property, those in which the contributions of the two genders to food supply and labor are very uneven, those in which women are isolated, and those with moderate technological development have the lowest relative status of women.

Ortner (1974) proposed that the universal second-class status of women results from cultures perceiving women as closer to nature than men are. And culture, with its emphasis on control and achievement, transformation and mastery, is perceived as superior to nature, nature being uncontrolled and often polluting. Women are perceived as closer to nature for three reasons. First, the body of the woman and its functions—birth, lactation, and menstruation—are closer to nature; men create lasting objects and technology, while women create perishable, and imperfect, humans. Second, the woman's body and its functions place her in a lower social role. It seems natural for the birth-giver and lactater to care for and thus remain in contact with children, and children are closer to nature (further from culture) than are adults. Finally, these social roles give women a personality that is closer to nature. Being the one to care for children, a woman never really leaves the home (Chodorow, 1974). Thus, she develops weaker "ego boundaries" (D. Guttman, 1965), has more **communion** (being one with others, being open) than **agency** (self-assertion, separation, mastery) (Bakan, 1966), and is defined by others, her family, rather than by herself.

Thus, in Parsons's terms (Parsons and Bales, 1955), the mother takes on expressive roles, emphasizing social intercourse, cooperation, and nurturance, rather than the instrumental roles played by the man outside the home. According to Chodorow (1974), this difference in role assignments results from girls having a physically present model, while boys have only a stereotype with which to identify, and from boys being the ones to leave the home. Because in all societies women are second-class citizens, there are cross-cultural commonalities in the sex differences in personality.

The second cultural universal is that traits and roles are sexually dimorphic in all societies. Every society divides its tasks and specifies who does them according to gender to some extent. Thus, every child need not be trained in all activities, and socialization for roles can begin early (Dornbusch, 1966). "Despite great variability between cultures in the prescription of gender-dimorphic behavior in childhood, adolescence and adulthood, the existence of gender dimorphism of behavior is itself invariant. The options are not limitless. In the final analysis, culturally prescribed (or prohibited) gender-dimorphic behavior stems from the phyletic varieties of menstruation, impregnation, gestation, and lactation" (Money and Ehrdardt, 1972, p. 152).

Conclusions.   There are wide cultural variabilities in sex differences in both physical and psychological roles and traits. Almost every trait that has been assigned to women in one society has been given to men in at least one other society. In fact, there seem to be only two true universals: the lower status of women and sexual dimorphism. So what we will look for in the following discussions are cross-cultural commonalities in assignments or roles and traits that might produce consistent cultural biases.

TABLE 7.1 _____

THE DIVISION OF LABOR BY SEX IN 224 SOCIETIES

Activity	Percentage of Societies		N
	Men (usually or always)	Women (usually or always)	
Pursuit of Sea Mammals	100%	0%	35
Hunting	100	0	179
Trapping	95	2	148
Herding	84	9	55
Fishing	84	4	158
Gathering Fruits and Berries	14	72	106
Preservation of Food	9	81	108
Gathering Roots, Herbs, and Seeds	8	80	101
Cooking	3	92	201
Carrying Water	5	91	138
Grinding Grain	4	92	138

Reprinted from "Sex Differences and Cultural Institutions," table 1, p. 177, by Roy G. D'Andrade, in *The Development of Sex Differences*, edited by Eleanor E. Maccoby, with the permission of the publishers, Stanford University Press. © 1966 by the Board of Trustees of the Leland Stanford Junior University.

Note: N shows the number of societies scored on the particular activity. Percentages may not add to 100 because the activity may be performed by both sexes equally in some cultures.

Roles Assigned on the Basis of Gender

Tables 7.1 and 7.2 present data based on Murdock's (1935) survey of 224 different societies (cited by D'Andrade, 1966). The objects and activities presented in Tables 7.1 and 7.2 were the ones most consistently assigned to one sex or the other; for other objects and activities, such as preparing the soil or net making, the cultures varied more in which task was assigned to which sex. However, that does not mean that the activity was not assigned on the basis of sex. The activity most often assigned to neither sex was the bearing of burdens, which was done by both sexes in 27 percent of the societies. The other societies assigned that role on the basis of sex, and assigned the other activities and objects on the basis of sex even more often. Note that there is no task usually done by women that is not at least somewhere assigned to men, whereas the pursuit of sea mammals, hunting, metal work, and weapon making are always predominately male activities. Note, too, that many role assignments, such as the making of musical instruments, do not relate in any clear fashion to any genetic or hormonally biased sex difference.

One occupation not included in the tables, care of infants and children, is almost always assigned to women, or is at least mostly their job. However, little cross-cultural work on paternal behavior has been carried out. One study that has been done (Mackey, 1976), studied three contemporary cultures (the United States, Spain, and Mexico) and found adult females in the presence of children more often than males were. Nevertheless, a high level of contact between males and children was also seen, with from 8.5 percent to 17.7 percent of the children observed being with men. Older boys were often seen in groups of men only,

TABLE 7.2 _____

THE DIVISION OF MANUFACTURE OF OBJECTS BY SEX IN 224 SOCIETIES

Activity	Percentage of Societies		N
	Men (usually or always)	Women (usually or always)	
Metalworking	100%	0%	78
Weapon Making	100	0	122
Boat Building	95	1	100
Making Musical Instruments	98	2	48
Working in Wood and Bark	95	2	129
Making Thread and Cordage	21	70	119
Basket Making	22	70	126
Mat Making	20	73	89
Weaving	22	76	96
Pottery Making	14	80	106
Making and Repairing Clothing	12	82	127

Reprinted from "Sex Differences and Cultural Institutions," table 2, p. 178, by Roy G. D'Andrade, in *The Development of Sex Differences,* edited by Eleanor E. Maccoby, with the permission of the publishers, Stanford University Press. © 1966 by the Board of Trustees of the Leland Stanford Junior University.

Note: N shows the number of societies scored on a particular activity. Percentages may not add to 100 because the object may be made equally often by both sexes in some cultures.

though older girls were not more often seen in all-female groups. Thus, maturing boys are incorporated into all-male groups, but this does not occur for girls.

These divisions are found even in the most primitive and most egalitarian societies. The Tasady, the recently discovered tribe in the Philippine rain forest, may represent the most primitive culture extant today (they didn't even hunt or trap before discovery), and even they divide labor by sex (J. Nance, 1975). Although decisions are made after discussion by both sexes and the tribe leaders include a woman, in gathering the women do not go as far from the cave-home as the men do, and women are more preoccupied with child care. The men of the tribe dominated the first contacts after discovery, and the men were the ones to take over the newly demonstrated techniques of trapping, tattooing, and playing musical instruments. Even in Finland and Sweden, where sex roles have been deemphasized, feeding the family, cleaning and washing, and child care are done by the wives in over 70 percent of the families; husbands pay the bills and do household repairs (Haavio-Mannila, 1971). In the Israeli Kibbutz, founded on sex-egalitarian terms, 91 percent of the men are in agricultural, industrial, and technical roles, while 80 percent of the women are in services or in education (Mednick, 1975).

In all cultures, housework is overwhelmingly feminine. Even in countries like Russia, where about 90 percent of the women work, and work in usually masculine occupations such as medicine, law, and mathematics, women still have the primary responsibility for the household tasks and child care. Only in Scandinavian countries are any appreciable number of men becoming househusbands.

Most societies discourage women from marrying younger men. In van den Berghe's view (1973), women marrying younger men would be an unusual reversal since husbands dominate over wives not only because of the relative status of women, but also because the husbands' greater age confers dominance. Age reinforces the lower status. In Safilios-Rothschild's analysis of fifteen societies (1971), the percentage of women participating in the labor force is positively correlated with the proportion of women who marry younger men ($+.68$).

In summary, in most cultures, men provide the meat and women the other food. Men also perform most of the occupations that take people out of the house, especially for aggressive roles, while women work closer to home. This is seen even in highly primitive and egalitarian cultures, where more men than women work outside the home and both child care and housework of most types is seen as feminine. More equality of sex-role assignments is seen in those societies in which women are freer to marry younger men.

Survey of Traits Ascribed to the Sexes

Love, sex and emotions. Ford and Beach (1951) surveyed two hundred societies and reported that the majority label sex as something to be initiated by males. They found that if women dress to cover their genitals, so do men in the society, but the reverse is not true. Societies are more concerned with—have more proscriptions against and penalties for—the behavior of married women than that of married men. However, love charms are more often employed by men. Females are less likely to be transvestites (cross-dressers) or to be homosexuals. And in all of the societies, males were more apt to masturbate. From all this, Ford and Beach concluded that females have a more easily inhibited sexuality. Still, it should be noted that sexual restriction of females is strongly increased by such cultural factors as civilization (Stephens, 1963) and polygamy (D'Andrade, 1966).

Another recent study examined sexual attitudes and behaviors in twenty-one U.S. colleges and universities in the United States and four in other countries (Luckey and Nass, 1969). In general, the females were more sexually conservative. In all but one country (Norway), females more than males felt that marriage was important for a satisfying life, and both men and women thought the husband should be slightly older than the wife. Women (except in England) more frequently supported the double standard for sexual intercourse outside marriage, allowing it for men but not for women, but men were more concerned that their prospective marital partner be chaste. Women were less likely to sanction sex before marriage, while males were more likely to consider it appropriate to have sex with a good friend. Women reported less participation in all categories of sexual behavior, and petted and had intercourse for the first time at older ages. Men were also more in favor of coed living arrangements in college dormitories.

Some consistent sex differences in sex-role stereotypic traits also appeared in Block's analysis (1973) of six modern cultures. She had college students in each of the six cultures describe the "kind of person I would most like to be." The characteristics that were chosen significantly ($p < .10$) more often by men than by women in at least four of the six cultures included being practical, shrewd, assertive, dominating, competitive, critical, and self-controlled. Cross-culturally, women were more likely to describe their ideal selves as loving and affectionate, impulsive, sympathetic, and generous.

J. W. Berry has extended and expanded on these cross-cultural commonalities of sex differences in personality traits. In one study (1976), he looked at cognitive skills, conformity, self-disclosure, and the frequency of psychosomatic symptoms in seventeen different cultures (largely hunting-gathering groups). In a majority of the cultures, males showed greater spatial ability and better visual acuity. Males also conformed less to social pressure, and talked less about themselves. Women were more likely to show psychosomatic symptoms. But more important than the fact that these differences were found is that they were far from universal, and in some societies the reverse sex differences were found. Overall, agricultural societies were more complex and stratified—having social classes, formal political organizations, and strong conformity pressures—and in them, the sex differences were largest and most similar to those seen in the United States. The hunting-gathering societies were more loosely organized and in them, the sex differences were minimized, and sometimes reversed.

Sex-role stereotypic attitudes also show some cross-cultural commonalities. Luckey and Nass (1969) examined attitudes in their sample of university students described earlier. Most students supported the idea that "individuals and society function best if male and female roles in life remain essentially different though equal"; the percentage of students agreeing with this was highest in the United States and Canada. When asked whether or not "a four-year college education generally [is] as essential for the personal fulfillment and life satisfaction of *girls* as it is for *men* of comparable intelligence" (italics ours), many more women than men agreed, although a majority of both sexes did agree with that statement. Women also indicated a greater need for guidelines and limits for behavior from parents, adults, peers, schools, and especially from churches. In general, both men and women in North America emphasized sex-role differences, including restricting women to work in the home, and did so more than did students in England and Norway.

So there is some cross-cultural consistency in personality traits ascribed to the sexes. Men are seen as more sexually active, women as more conservative (less active sexually). Women are often more likely than men to show conformity to social pressure, to talk about themselves, and to have more psychosomatic or emotional symptoms. These data may be misleading, however, as fewer differences are actually observed between the sexes than are seen in descriptions of the ideal self or implied by the sex-role stereotypes prescribed by culture. Culture may be more sexually dimorphic than behavior. Also, complex cultures to some extent may maximize differences.

The Behavior of Children. The stereotypic differences in personality are also seen in the behaviors of children and reflected in socialization.

Blurton-Jones and Konner (1973) compared the sex differences in the behavior of twenty-one London children and twenty-three Australian Bushman children. In both groups of children, the males were more often aggressive, and in both groups, the boys showed more rough-and-tumble play. The sex difference in rough-and-tumble play was much smaller in the Bushman group, however, because Bushman girls engaged in such play more than London girls. In this study, mothers were present during the observation periods, and boys interacted more with other children than girls did, whereas girls interacted more with adults. But,

again, although this sex difference was found in both cultures, culture had more
effect on this behavior than gender did. The greater importance of culture was also
shown in two other measures, activity level and sex preference in playmates. London
boys were more active than London girls, but there was no sex difference in activity among the Bushman children. And boys preferred boys to girls as playmates
only in the London sample.

Several others have used cross-cultural studies to analyze children's behavior. One study analyzed the behavior of 134 children, aged three to eleven, from
six different cultures; trained field workers observed each child for an average of
seventeen different five-minute periods (B. Whiting, 1963; B. Whiting and Edwards, 1973). Among the younger children (aged three to six), girls sought help
more often, sought or offered physical contact more often, and were less dominant
than the boys. In the older children, boys sought attention more often, were less
compliant, offered less help and support, and were more likely to respond to
aggression with counter-aggression; the older girls were more compliant to their
mothers' commands and suggestions. Among both age groups, boys engaged
more often in rough-and-tumble play, were less often interrupted by others,
boasted and praised themselves more often, and were more verbally aggressive.
Boys also interacted more with peers, especially male peers.

Whiting and Edwards (1973) also found that tasks were assigned to children
on a sexually dimorphic basis. Older girls more often took care of children and did
domestic chores such as cleaning and cooking, whereas the older boys fed animals or took them to pasture. Both younger and older grils interacted with female
adults more than boys did, and older girls interacted more with infants than boys
did. This division supports Ortner (1974) and Chodorow (1974), who both hypothesize that many sex differences are a consequence of girls never leaving home.
Whiting and Edwards did find that girls even remained physically closer to home
than did boys.

The sex differences in chores and patterns of interpersonal interactions affect
sex roles, since sex differences in behavior are fewer in those societies in which
boys also care for infants and do domestic chores inside (but not outside) the
home, thus again supporting Ortner and Chodorow. And, in the one group of
children in which the females did not do many feminine tasks (the group from
Orchard Town, in New England), they showed more masculine behavior and less
feminine behavior than the other groups of girls. However, the sex differences
were only reduced by these cultural variations, and not eliminated. (This study is a
very important one, so perhaps you should frequently review its major findings.)

Some of these differences also appeared in Spiro's study (1958) of children in
an Israeli kibbutz, where sex differences are deemphasized. Boys more often
engaged in acts of conflict and aggression and girls were more likely to give aid,
to share, and to be affectionate and cooperative. Girls also all showed more signs
of regression such as thumbsucking and regressive play. These differences are at
least partly the result of the continued existence of sex-role stereotypes in the kibbutz (Rosner, 1967).

Another study analyzed dominance hierarchies and social interactions in
young children in three different cultures (Omark et al., cited by Maccoby and
Jacklin, 1974). Boys were more frequently involved in aggression and in all types

TABLE 7.3 _____

CROSS-CULTURAL SEX DIFFERENCES IN CHILDHOOD SOCIALIZATION IN 110
SOCIETIES

Socialized Behavior	Cultures with Sex Difference in Favor of			N
	Boys	Neither	Girls	
Nurturance	0%	18%	82%	33
Responsibility	11	28	61	84
Obedience	3	62	35	69
Achievement	87	10	3	31
Self-reliance	85	15	0	82

Source: H. Barry, III, M. K. Bacon, and I. L. Child, "A Cross-cultural Survey of Some Sex Differences in Socialization." *Journal of Abnormal and Social Psychology*, 1957, 55, p. 328. Copyright © 1957 by the American Psychological Association. Reprinted by permission.
Note: N shows the number of societies scored on a particular dimension.

of other physical interactions. Boys also moved around more and maintained a greater distance between themselves and others. Both boys and girls agreed that boys were tougher than girls, and there was more agreement among children about the boys' relative dominance positions than about those of the girls.

With fair consistency across cultures boys show more of the following behaviors; aggression, dominance, rough-and-tumble play, same-sex peer interaction, and boasting. Girls commonly show more of the following behavior: interactions with adults and younger children, seeking help, and offering help or cooperation. Boys were also less often interrupted. Task assignments paralleled these differences, with boys doing jobs outside the homes and girls engaging more in housework and child care.

Socialization patterns seem to enforce these differences. Barry, Bacon, and Child (1957) examined socialization practices in over one hundred societies, and Table 7.3 presents some of their data. As can be seen, boys are raised to achieve and to be self-reliant; girls are not. And girls are trained to be responsible, obedient, and nurturant. No culture rated on nurturance raised boys to be the more nurturant sex; no culture rated on self-reliance raised girls to be more self-reliant. Sex differences in socialization were greater in societies emphasizing male strength or having large families. In the latter case, the effect was attributed to the potential of losing the marital partner in small families, where both boys and girls must therefore be socialized to be able to assume some of the roles of the opposite sex.

Interpretation of Cross-cultural Data

There are many cross-cultural commonalities, with men being more often concerned with obtaining meat and producing weapons, and women most often being concerned with activities closer to the home: caring for children, preparing food, and making clothes. The behavior and socialization of children reflects these differences, with boys being more active and aggressive, and girls being more supportive towards other people. But which is cause and which effect? Did sex differences lead to differences in role and task assignment, or did differences in task assignment lead to sex differences in experience and socialization?

These sex differences could all have arisen from the two cultural universals, the lower status of women and the fact that women raise the culture's children, which implies much about role assignments and sex differences in personality (Chodorow, 1974). Evidence that sex differences derive largely from those two universals is provided by the character of the societies in which sex differences are exaggerated: those that are highly structured societies (G. W. Berry, 1976), those that practice polygamy (Barry et al., 1957), and those in which children had much more contact with their mothers than with their fathers or with male models (Chodorow, 1974; Romney, 1965).

DIFFERENTIAL TREATMENT ON THE BASIS OF GENDER

In Early Childhood

Sex typing starts at birth, and perhaps even before — mothers usually interpret active, kicking fetuses as male (M. Lewis, 1972). Even monkey mothers may sex type their offspring. As was mentioned in Chapter 3, differential treatment by parents occurs even among infra-human primates, as females are held more, while males are rejected and threatened more, and, in turn, reject contact themselves. Monkey mothers play more vigorously with male infants, and made sexually submissive gestures to them.

Parental Ratings of Their New Born. Parents immediately impose their sterotypes upon their newborn infants. Within a day after birth, daughters of first-time parents are rated as softer, smaller, more inattentive, and having finer features than the sons of first-time parents (Rubin, Pravenzano, and Luria, 1974). Daughters but not sons were also called little, pretty, beautiful, and cute by both parents. However, fathers were more dimorphic than mothers in their rating of all attributes. In addition to the traits already listed, fathers of boys rated their infants as being better coordinated, stronger, and hardier than did fathers of girls. The mothers' ratings were in the same direction but were less dimorphic. The difference between the parents is consistent with research cited in the previous section in which fathers were found to be more concerned with sex typing than mothers (Goodenough, 1957) and to be more dimorphic in their childrearing patterns and practices (Block, 1973). Thus, stereotyping begins at birth, particularly for fathers.

Unfamiliar Chidren. Parents also show sex-typed behavior towards infants who are strangers and even towards videotapes and voice recordings of children, where past interactions or expected future interactions could not have affected the parents' behaviors. In one experiment, mothers were introduced to an unfamiliar infant who was labeled as a male for one group and female for another; the subject was asked to interact with the infant. Mothers presented dolls more to an infant they thought was female, and gave a train more to the one they thought was male; mothers also tended to smile more at the apparently female infants (Will, Self, and Datan, 1976). In a similar experiment using adults who were not parents, men and women were introduced to a single infant labeled as male, as female or who wasn't labeled at all (Seavey, Katz, and Zalk, 1975). Again, both men and women used a doll more frequently for female infants, but touched the male infants more. Both of these effects were stronger in the men than in the women. Men also rated videotapes of children in a more stereotypic fashion than women did (Meyer and Sobieszek, 1972). These studies corroborate the finding of other studies, that men do more sex typing than women.

Parental Interactions with Their Own Infants.   Other research recorded interactions of parents with their own infants in a laboratory or at home. At three weeks of age, males were held closer, were attended to, stimulated, aroused, and looked at more, and had their musculature stretched more. None of these sex differences in infant treatment were significant at three months. But by three months of age, female infants were more often verbally imitated. Mothers of male infants vocalized more to their infants at three weeks of age, but mothers of females vocalized more to their infants at three months of age (H. Moss, 1967).

M. Lewis (1972) and his colleagues (L. Cherry and Lewis, 1976; S. Goldberg and Lewis, 1972) have confirmed many of these effects. In their work, males received more contact before six months of age, but after that females were held and touched more. Lewis also reported that mothers spent more time looking at and talking to female infants over the entire first two years of their life. Similarly, E. Thoman, Leiderman, and Olson (1972) found that first-time mothers of females talk to and smile at their infants during feeding more than first-time mothers of males, whereas mothers of males spend more time feeding their infants. These studies had different results for three-week-old infants than did Moss's study partly because the "talking to" behavior was scored differently.

Female infants may receive more verbal stimulation from their mothers, but fathers apparently reverse this sex difference. One study found that although fathers vocalized less to their infants than mothers did, fathers of two- to six-week-old female infants spent more time vocalizing than did fathers of male infants of those ages. This difference reversed by the time the children were eight to twelve weeks old (Rebelsky and Hanks, 1971).

Levenis, Fishman, and Kagan (cited by Repucci, 1971) found that the degree to which mothers verbally imitated their four-month-old daughters varied with the mother's education. Mothers with more education imitated daughters to a greater extent than mothers with less education, but education had no effect on mothers' imitation of their sons—the rate remained constant (and always lower than the rate of imitiation of daughters).

H. Moss (1967) found that the interaction of maternal contact and irritability varied with infant gender. Irritable females three weeks and three months old received more contact from mothers than did less irritable females of the same age. For male infants, irritability and contact were unrelated at three weeks and were negatively related at three months—fussy males received less contact.

Taken together this research suggests that there are more verbal interactions between mother and daughter and more physical interactions between mother and son, at least up to three months of age. Fathers of younger female infants also vocalize more, although as the infants grew fathers of males vocalized more. Still, since fathers spend less time at home, this probably means that female infants get more vocal stimulation overall, especially if their mothers are educated. The fact that fussy girls receive more contact than fussy boys suggests that fussiness is differentially encouraged.

H. Moss (1974) continued his study of parent-infant interactions to prove that females receive more social training. He had both parents of seven-week-old infants come into the laboratory where they were to try to get their infant to perform certain tasks. Parents of females spent more time trying to get their infants either to smile or to vocalize than did parents of males; parents of females, especially mothers, also spent more time overall with their infants. Both fathers and mothers of females used more terms of endearment ("honey," "precious," "angel") when addressing their infants. At the same time, Moss also went into the home to observe mothers. He found that when female infants fussed, the mothers responded by talking to them, imitating them, looking at them, or giving them a pacifier. When males fussed, mothers tried to distract them with auditory or visual stimulation (rattling keys), or else they picked them up.

Summary. Maccoby and Jacklin (1974) summarized many of these and other studies. They concluded that there were no sex differences in parental treatments, but their summarized results showed some trends consistent with those described here. Twelve studies showed no sex difference in parental contact, but eleven others found more parental contact with boys and only four found results favoring girls. Nineteen studies found no sex difference in verbal interactions with infants, but eleven found a difference favoring girls and only two did for boys. Stimulation of gross motor behavior is even more consistent; only two studies showed no sex difference and four others found a difference in favor of boys. Thus, sex differences in parental treatment are far from universal, but we cannot conclude that they are absent. Instead, the next task seems to be to determine under what conditions of testing, education, and social class, sex differences in parental treatment are most reliable, and to what extent they also appear in the home environment. More longitudinal investigations of parent-child interactions would also be helpful.

We must remember, however, that the infant is affecting the parent, just as the parent affects the infant, so cause and effect in this research can seldom be disentangled. Another problem with data on the sex differences in the interaction between parent and child is the different developmental rates of males and females. The female is developing faster, both physically and psychologically, throughout the time period of these studies. Thus, the extent to which differential treatment is based on differences in infants, cannot be determined. Still, the response of nonparents to unfamiliar infants would seem to partially control for these problems, and studies using that technique did find sex differences: female infants were smiled at and given dolls and males were held more.

Sex Typing and Social Factors

The degree to which the behavior and preferences of the child are sex-typed is affected by parental variables like dominance and warmth, social class, and education, and by family structure. Some general comments should be made first. The research indicates that the same factors do not always affect men and women in the same way. Also, keep in mind that women are often less clearly sex-typed than men (they are less feminine than men are masculine), although men receive more social pressure than women to take on traits of the opposite sex, to become both masculine and feminine. Angrist (1969) made the excellent point that women may be less sex-typed because they need to be socialized for many different contingencies. Most women are socialized for marriage, but even this implies flexibility, since women wish to be desirable to a wide variety of men. Also, marriage and family, even though planned for, may not be achieved, or the husband may die; so women must also be prepared to be self-supporting. In fact, as Stoll points out, most people living alone are women (1974).

Other factors that influence the degree of sex-typing are as yet insufficiently researched, but should be kept in mind when evaluating the following research. One is that sex roles, like most of the sexually dimorphic behaviors discussed previously, are affected by the situation. For example, the sex composition of the group being tested often affects the sex-role stereotype of its members (Ruble and Higgins, 1976). Also, the role of the child's peers in promoting sex-typed behavior may be critical. Very little research has been done in this area, but Fagot and Patterson's work (1969) suggests that peers supply more differential rewards for sex-typed behaviors than adults. And it seems that peers punish deviations more cruelly than adults. So, what follows should not be regarded as a complete list of social factors that affect sex-role development, other factors are also at work. Further light on the effect of social factors will be shed by studying the development of the people who resisted sex-typing pressures, the androgyns. These people will be discussed later in the chapter.

Parental Variables. Parental expectations and traits clearly affect the sex typing of their children, presumably because these expectations and traits affect the extent to which the parents treat their children differentially on the basis of gender. Another way in which they affect children is by making parents into different identification figures or models for their children. This is the effect described by the theories of Kohlberg and Mischel and Bandura.

Parental warmth is one factor that affects sex typing. As Kohlberg (1966) pointed out, paternal warmth (interest, affection, attention) tends to masculinize boys, while maternal warmth has little or no effect. Paternal warmth also masculinizes girls and, unlike boys, maternal warmth feminizes them (Mussen 1969; Sherman, 1971). Maternal restrictiveness and punishment feminizes both sexes (Sears, Rau, and Alpert, 1965). It seems, then, that parental warmth increases the value of the parent as a model and so affects sex typing, while restrictiveness may involve punishment of behavior called masculine in children of either sex.

Parental dominance (masculinity) may have different effects on the two sexes (Hetherington, 1965; Heilbrun, 1974; Kohlberg, 1966; and Williams, 1973). Boys can be masculinized by identifying with a masculine, or dominant, father or mother, and can be feminized by identifying with a feminine mother. Parental power is also important for girls, but femininity can come from identification either with a masculine father or with a mother who is either masculine or feminine. Perhaps, as Heilbrun (1976a) suggested, the girl who identifies with a masculine father vicariously enjoys the male sex role and so can behave in a feminine fashion and still experience the rewards of being male, at least second hand. So, overall, parental dominance increased identification in both sexes, although identification did not necessarily affect feminine sex typing in females. No one seems to identify with a passive father. These data are predicted by Kohlberg, since parental power would lead to increased modeling of that parent, and since females can acquire a feminine gender role by identifying with their father and his concept of femininity.

Other Variables.   Social class, timing of puberty, education, geographical location, and family structure have all been reported to affect gender role. Education may decrease sex typing, and in the United States sex typing may be more exaggerated in the South than in the Northeast (Constantinople, 1973). Early puberty may also be associated with increased sex typing (Terman and Miles, 1936). Also, children coming from the lower classes may show sex-typed behaviors and preferences earlier and more completely than do middle- or higher-class children (Kohn, 1959; M. Lewis and Weinraub, 1974; Minuchin, 1965; Mussen, 1969). Girls from traditional schools or home backgrounds were more strongly sex-typed in play, in fantasy, and on "It" tests (Minuchin, 1965). This relationship was weaker or absent for boys except in aggressive fantasy themes, which occured more among boys of a traditional background. However, it should be pointed out that these studies used a sex-role definition derived from white middle- and upper-class society; this definition may be inappropriate for use with other groups (Pleck, 1975). For example, the middle class considers intellectual competence to be masculine whereas the lower class stresses physical prowess (Biller, 1974).

Family structure also affects sex typing. Firstborn girls may be more traditionally feminine than only girls (B. Rosenberg and Sutton-Smith, 1974), but there are few differences between firstborn and only males. Once again we see that the family has more impact on the female than on the male. Rosenberg and Sutton-Smith also found that firstborn females with younger sisters and secondborn males with older brothers were both masculine, while firstborn males with younger brothers or secondborn females with older sisters are more feminine. Males with one sister appear very feminine in childhood, but this reverses at college age; males with two sisters are masculine throughout life.

Children affect the masculinity of the father, but not of the mother. The more males in the family, the more feminine is the father; the more females, the more masculine the father (B. Rosenberg and Sutton-Smith, 1974). Thus, sex typing between parent and child may be a continual interaction process, with the father perhaps being more strongly involved than the mother in sex typing the children, but with the children in turn affecting the father.

Sex typing changes with age. Older man and women may be more tolerant of their own opposite-sex impulses (Neugarten, 1968), meaning men and women may become more similar with age in terms of both hormones and sex roles. Adolescence seems the age with the most complete sex typing (Baruch, 1975; Coates, 1974; Hakstian and Cattell, 1975; Kohlberg and Ullman, 1974; Nash, 1975; Pleck, 1975; Vroegh, 1975).

Summary.   Overall, children identify more with warm, dominant parents of either gender. For boys, identification with a masculine parent of either gender can lead to a masculine gender role, but girls are feminized or masculinized by identification with parents exhibiting many different traits. The masculinity and femininity of both of the parents makes more difference for boys than for girls. Other factors, from social class to geographical location, also affect sex typing, perhaps because many of these factors are interrelated. Birth order and family structure are also important, probably because they make different models available in the family and because they affect the parents. Sex typing seems strongest, or at least most salient to the person, in adolescence. All of this points to the great impact that culture, society, and the family have on sex differences, perhaps because the sex-role stereotypes of different groups are, at least to some extent, incorporated by socialization into the attitudes of children. It is those stereotypes that will now be discussed.

PREVALENCE OF SEXUAL STEREOTYPES

Introduction to Stereotypes

As was mentioned earlier, the existence of sex-role stereotypes in the models of young children will perpetuate those stereotypes; the mechanisms of this perpetuation differ slightly from theory to theory, but Mischel and Bandura, Kohlberg, Parsons, and Lynn all agree that children will model themselves after cultural stereotypes.

These stereotypes do exist. I. Broverman and her colleagues (I. Broverman et al., 1972) constructed a list of pairs of traits, each pair consisting of traits representing opposite ends of a continuum of masculinity and femininity. For a trait to be considered stereotypic for a particular sex at least 75 percent of the 154 college men and women sampled had to agree on which end, or pole, of the pair was more characteristic of the average man and which more characteristic of the average woman. These traits are listed in Table 7.4. As can be seen, when each pole was rated for its general social desirability, there were more desirable masculine traits than there were desirable feminine traits. This is entirely consistent with the idea that women envy the male sex role.

Broverman and her colleagues have also given this list to other groups of people, aged from seventeen to sixty, and varying in education from elementary school to advanced graduate degrees. All groups generally agreed on which traits were masculine and which feminine. Factor analyses of these traits produced clusters of items, one group of male-valued items and one group of female-valued items. The male cluster included **competency behaviors,** whereas the female cluster included **warmth and expressiveness behaviors.**

People apply the stereotype to others, but do not think it applies as much to themselves. The Broverman stereotypic traits were given to men and women who were asked to use them to describe themselves (I. Broverman et al., 1972). Though there were significant sex differences in self-descriptions, women and men in general perceived themselves as conforming less to the stereotype than what they perceived as typical for men or women. When the men and women were given the traits and asked to indicate which ones were ideal for men and which for women,

TABLE 7.4

STEREOTYPIC SEX-ROLE ITEMS NAMED BY COLLEGE STUDENTS

Feminine	Masculine
Competency Cluster: Masculine Pole Is More Desirable	
Not at all aggressive	Very aggressive
Not at all independent	Very independent
Very emotional	Not at all emotional
Does not hide emotions at all	Almost always hides emotions
Very subjective	Very objective
Very easily influenced	Not at all easily influenced
Very submissive	Very dominant
Dislikes math and science very much	Likes math and science very much
Very excitable in a minor crisis	Not at all excitable in a minor crisis
Very passive	Very active
Not at all competitive	Very competitive
Very illogical	Very logical
Very home oriented	Very worldly
Not at all skilled in business	Very skilled in business
Very sneaky	Very direct
Does not know the way of the world	Knows the way of the world
Feelings easily hurt	Feelings not easily hurt
Not at all adventurous	Very adventurous
Has difficulty making decisions	Can make decisions easily
Cries very easily	Never cries
Almost never acts as a leader	Almost always acts as a leader
Not at all self-confident	Very self-confident
Very uncomfortable about being aggressive	Not at all uncomfortable about being aggressive
Not at all ambitious	Very ambitious
Unable to separate feelings from ideas	Easily able to separate feelings from ideas
Very dependent	Not at all dependent
Very conceited about appearance	Never conceited about appearance
Thinks women are always superior to men	Thinks men are always superior to women
Does not talk freely about sex with men	Talks freely about sex with men
Warmth-Expressiveness Cluster: Feminine Pole Is More Desirable	
Doesn't use harsh language at all	Uses very harsh language
Very talkative	Not at all talkative
Very tactful	Very blunt
Very gentle	Very rough
Very aware of feelings of others	Not at all aware of feelings of others
Very religious	Not at all religious
Very interested in own appearance	Not at all interested in own appearance
Very neat in habits	Very sloppy in habits
Very quiet	Very loud
Very strong need for security	Very little need for security
Enjoys art and literature	Does not enjoy art and literature at all
Easily expresses tender feelings	Does not express tender feelings at all easily

Source: I. K. Broverman, S. R. Vogel, D. M. Broverman, F. E. Clarkson, and P. S. Rosenkrantz, "Sex-role Stereotypes: A Current Appraisal." *Journal of Social Issues,* 1972, table 1, p. 63. Copyright © 1972 by the Society for the Psychological Study of Social Issues. Reprinted by permission.
Note: Seventy-four men gave ratings and eighty women.

they again gave descriptions very close to those of the typical man and woman. But where does this extensive stereotypic agreement come from?

Cultural Stereotypes

Stereotypes in Literature.   Children's books contain extreme versions of stereotypes. In one study, prize-winning children's books were analyzed (Weitzman et al., 1972). First of all, females were nearly invisible. For every picture of a female, there were eleven of males. The ratio of male to female animals was ninety-five to one. The ratios of titles featuring males to females was about three to one, and in a third of the books there were no females at all. As to how the sex roles were depicted, males (children and adults) were active and females passive; boys led and girls served; boys rescued and girls were rescued and then served as the prize. Adult men were pictured in many more varied roles and occupations than adult women. Fathers even played more interesting games with their children than mothers did. Hallmark published matched pairs of books: *What Boys Can Be* and *What Girls Can Be.* None of the female occupations listed required being out-of-doors, while eleven of the fourteen male occupations implied outdoor activities. Only two (not one, as Weitzman and her coauthors stated) of the females' occupations required having a college degree, nurse and nursery school teacher, but, then, only three (not four) male occupations required college degrees—doctor, zoo manager, and astronaut, although it is true that most pilots and presidents have degrees. The pinnacle of achievement for men was being president; the pinnacle for women was being a mother.

Key's (1975b) review of the studies of children's books confirmed most of these observations. Boys do, and they invent; girls just are, and they use the inventions of boys. In some children's textbooks recently adopted or recommended in California, 75 percent of the main characters were male. In another series, there were five times as many males in the titles as females (Fisher, cited by Key, 1975b). The absence of females inside the books was also a common finding of these studies. Even inanimate objects were male. In one college course concerned with writing for children, the instructor said: "the wise author writes about boys, thereby ensuring *him*self a maximum audience, since only girls will read a book about a girl, while both boys and girls will read about a boy" (Key, 1975b, p. 68, italics ours). In the books surveyed, the pronoun "he" occurs three times as often as "she," even though the reverse is true of adult literature (Key, 1975b). And many of the studies Key reviewed found no book including a mother who worked outside the home (even though over 40 percent of mothers actually do work). Males were pictured as interacting with each other more than females did and as being more competent.

The stereotypes persist in the mass media addressed to adults. Women in women's magazines are often pictured as passive, especially in middle-class, as opposed to lower-class, magazines (Flora, 1971; Franzwa, 1975). Ambitious women either come to a miserable end or else give up their ambitions for a man in order to live happily ever after. The female often reforms a male by being passively virtuous and standing by him. Women are also portrayed in popular songs as deceitful, domestic, passive, flirtatious, idealistic, dependent, emotional, sentimental, illogical, frivolous, and sensitive, while males are sexually aggressive, nonconforming, rigid, egotistical, nondomestic, rational, and adventuresome (Chafetz, 1974; Reinartz, 1975). The stereotypes even appear in art (L. Brown, 1975).

Television.   One very interesting occurrence of sex-role stereotypes turned up on television shows about doctors (McLaughlin, 1975). Twice as many female as male patients were bedridden. With male patients, 70 percent of the treatments were successful, while for female patients only 23 percent were. What does that communicate to steady viewers of those shows?

The stereotypes are also on children's television shows. One study of televised cartoons found males outnumbering females by three to one; another put the margin at over two to one (Levinson, 1975; Sternglanz and Serbin, 1974). Animals were mostly male, as were adult humans (81 percent were male, and 19 percent female). Only with teenage characters were there more females (66 percent to 34 percent). Most stars were males; women were seldom the superheroes or the archvillains. Males had the greater variety of occupational roles, and married women never worked (Levinson, 1975). Males were more often portayed as aggressive and constructive, while females were deferent. Males were more often rewarded, but the only consistent consequence of behavior portrayed for females was punishment for high levels of activity (Sternglanz and Serbin, 1974).

Television commercials are also a prime source of sex role stereotypes. One study of 199 commercials (McArthur and Resko, 1975), found males to be the central figure in 57 percent. Women were pictured in the home much more often than men. The implied rewards for product use for men were approval of friends and the advancement of career or social life; the rewards for women were approval from the family and the opposite sex. Males were usually the product authority, and were pictured in more varied occupational roles.

In our laboratory (K. I. Hoyenga, unpublished data), 300 different prime-time commercials from the spring and fall of 1975 were analyzed. A total of 387 men or boys and 386 women or girls appeared in these commercials, including off-the-screen announcers (mostly male) and hands. When more than ten people of the same sex appeared, only ten were counted, in order to reduce errors. A role analysis, similar to those done by anthropologists, was performed on all occupations pictured five or more times; the data appear in Table 7.5. As can be seen, the role assignments are surprisingly consistent with cross-cultural data. There are more exclusively male than exclusively female occupations, just as was seen cross-culturally. In only three cases was the product expert a female when a man also appeared in the commercial, and two of these commercials were for medical products. Overall, females are more often pictured using medical products (64 percent were females) and products designed to enhance the user's appearance or smell (75 percent). Only a few commercials included any type of sexual interaction (kissing, caressing), but the male was always the aggressor. If commercials were the only basis for inferring behavior and role assignments, the person watching them would conclude that women must stay at home, that they are allowed out of the house only in the company of men, and, rarely, of children, and that they are rarely allowed to drive cars.

That the stereotypes exist wherever you look is clear from these studies, even though they are a small sample of the research that has been done. The study of

TABLE 7.5

GENDER ROLES IN 300 TELEVISION COMMERCIALS

Role or Occupation	Percentage Male	Percentage Female	N
Baby and Infant Care	—	100	12
Inmate in Nursing Home	—	100	7
House Cleaning	3	97	35
Washing Clothes and Dishes	3	97	32
Shopping	3	97	32
Cooking and Serving Food	6	94	80
Store Owner	50	50	8
Salesperson	71	29	14
Product Expert	74	26	82
Builder	80	20	25
Riding Motorcycle	88	12	8
Farmer	90	10	10
Engaging in Sports	93	7	72
Driving a Vehicle	94	6	32
Office Worker (not secretary)	100	—	15
Soldier	100	—	25
Service Station Worker	100	—	11
Miscellaneous Occupations (secretary, nurse, doctor, etc.)	51	49	57

Notes: N is the total number of people participating in that particular role. People not performing a particular task (those standing or walking, for instance) were not counted. The only overlapping role was "product expert"; those people sometimes had another role.

sex-role stereotypes is such a large field that a rather long book is needed just to analyze stereotypes in readers, in grade school and high school textbooks, and on television (Gersoni-Stavn, 1974). So if the sex role developmental theorists are correct, this proliferation of the stereotypes will make behavior sex typed. In fact, it is amazing that there is not more sex typing than there is.

Internalization and the Effects of Stereotypes on Behavior

I. Broverman and her colleagues (1972) have also looked at some behavioral correlates of these stereotypes. Catholic mothers who felt they were high in competency traits had significantly fewer children than others who perceived themselves to be low in traits of that cluster; the warmth-expressiveness cluster was not related to family size. Catholic college students with a self-concept high in competency gave an ideal family size smaller than that of those low in that cluster; women who rated themselves high in competency planned to combine a career with childbearing.

Goldberg (1972) presented an interesting example of the effect of sex-role stereotypes. He presented the following riddle to fifty college students who had not read it before:

A father and his son were driving along the highway when the father suddenly lost control of the car and crashed into a telephone pole. The father was killed instantly and his son was badly injured. The boy was rushed to the local hospital where it was found that he was suffering from serious internal injuries. A prominent surgeon was immediately summoned. When the surgeon arrived and went to the boy, there was a gasp from the surgeon. "I can't operate on this boy," the surgeon said, "he is my son."

Of the fifty students to whom Goldberg gave that riddle, 86 percent could not solve it. Can you?

Effects of Stereotypes on Children.   Hartley (1959a) presented some quotes from eight- and eleven-year-old boys illustrating how well they had internalized the stereotypes. According to these young boys, men are strong, have to be able to make decisions, protect women and children, and are bolder, more restless, and more courageous than women. Men and boys also mess up houses. Women are indecisive, afraid, fussy, need help, do not like adventure, and do not know what to do in an emergency. They cannot do dangerous things, probably because they are more easily damaged than men, and they die more easily. Women are also more often sad, easily become jealous, and envy their husbands. Women stay home most of the time. They are the ones who have to keep things neat and tidy and clean up household messes. One boy said, "women do things like cooking and washing and serving because that's all they can do." These boys sounded like television commercials.

Parental stereotypy can also affect the sex-role stereotypes of their children. One study (Perloff, 1977) tested the degree to which mothers and fathers and their children perceived other people in sex-role stereotypic ways, using a modified version of Broverman's sex-role stereotypic traits. The more stereotyped the parents were, the more stereotyped the children tended to be. Perhaps even more important, the results of I. Broverman and her colleagues (1972) on the effect of maternal employment were replicated by Perloff. Both studies found that children whose mothers worked outside the home had less stereotyped sex-role perceptions than did the children of mothers not employed outside the home.

In view of the stereotypes that television presents, it is not surprising that television viewing can affect sex roles. Children who were heavy viewers of television have been found to be more sex typed in some studies (Beuf, 1974; Freuh and McGhee, 1975), but not all (Perloff, 1977). On the other hand, exposure to counterstereotypic television characters (like the title character in "Police Woman") changed children's perceptions (M. Miller and Reeves, 1976).

A particularly dramatic effect of the stereotypes was described by Beuf (1974). Children were given pictures with sex-role reversals and with incongruous elements on them (a bird flying upside down). The children, aged between three and six, were to tell the experimenter what was "not OK" with each picture. Sex-role reversals were very often not OK. For example, 20 percent said it was not OK for men to cook for women, and 49 percent said it was not OK for a woman to repair a telephone line. However, the most interesting results came when these children were asked what they would be when they grew up if they were of the opposite sex. Overall, more girls than boys had an answer to that question; many of the girls had thought of the possibility before. One girl said, "When I grow up I want to fly like a bird. But I'll never do it because I'm not a boy." A boy who, when pressed, finally did have an answer, said, "A girl? Oh, if I were a girl I'd have to grow up to be nothing."

Effects of Stereotypes on Adults. Adults also change their sex-role behavior in order to conform to the stereotypical expectations of those around them. In one interesting application of this principle, Zanna and Pack (1975) introduced female college students to a male partner who was either attractive or unattractive and whose concept of the ideal woman supposedly conformed or did not conform to the feminine stereotype. When the man was attractive, the women presented themselves as being more or less traditionally feminine, depending upon what the man supposedly wanted in women. If the partner was desirable and had a untraditional view of women (women should be competent), the female subjects unscrambled more anagrams (presented to the subjects as an "IQ" test) in his presence; with the attractive, traditional man, women did less well. This study is interesting, but for these results to be meaningful it must be redone, using both male and female subjects and partners.

These stereotypes take a toll on those who hold them. Both men and women pay the price physically and mentally in trying to live up to or cope with impossible stereotypes (Balswick and Peek, 1971; Bem and Bem, 1971; Chesler, 1972; David and Brannon, 1976; King, 1973; Mundy, 1975). College girls who step out of role meet with quite severe reactions (Weitzman, 1975). Komarovsky (1946, 1973) has written about the cultural contradictions associated with the roles of both sexes in our society. In these two articles, she presented the problems faced by women who pursue careers, the way that men respond to that pursuit as a threat, and the resulting conflict. Livson (1976) has also found that nontraditional people who try to conform to the stereotypes pay a price in stress and psychological health. The feminine adolescent male who had become a self-controlled and striving adult also became power-oriented, hostile, and anxious. The adolescent woman who gave up career interests for family roles became depressed as an adult. However, by the age of fifty both of these people went back more to their original desires and became healthier.

Sex Typing and Likability

One area of sex stereotypes that has received a large amount of attention is their effect on **likability**. How does a person's sex-role attributes affect how likable other people will find him or her? One of the first studies done in this area was done by Spence and Helmreich (1972), who showed students videotapes of a female being interviewed. The female was depicted as either competent or incompetent (for example, having a high or low grade point average, or participating or thinking about participating in student activities) and as either masculine or feminine. Surprisingly, both male and female subjects found the competent, masculine woman the most likable and the most desirable as a work partner, and the males found her most desirable as a date. Both sexes also preferred competent feminine women to incompetent ones, although the males liked the incompetent feminine person more than the incompetent masculine person.

However, Spence, Helmreich, and Stapp (cited by Deaux, 1976) redid the study, trying to get at more subtle attitudes by changing the technique. They then found that only the most liberal women preferred the masculine and competent woman to the feminine and competent woman. This result is consistent with other research showing that feminine women are liked more than masculine women, especially by women, whereas both women and men dislike feminine males (Seyfried and Hendrick, 1973; D. Shaffer and Wegley, 1974). Interestingly, though, D. Shaffer and Wegley (1974) found that while the feminine woman was liked more and the feminine, non-success-oriented woman was more desirable as a work partner, the masculine woman might be more likely to be hired.

Failure to conform to the appropriate sex-role often results in lower likability ratings. In one study, subjects rated videotaped men and women as to their intelligence and likability (Lao et al., 1975). Men and women of moderate assertiveness were liked better and were rated as the most intelligent, but high levels of assertiveness depressed the intelligence and likability ratings of women more than of men. Ratings of intelligence and likability were also significantly correlated for both male (+ .492) and female (+ .621) subjects: that is, for these colleges students, the more intelligent they rated the subject, the more they liked him or her. Costrich and her colleagues (1975) also demonstrated the penalties attached to cross-sex behavior by both men and women. Male subjects rated both passive males and aggressive females as unpopular; female subjects rated passive men as unpopular, but rated passive and aggressive females equally. Overall, the more submissive the man, the less popular he was; the correlation between submissiveness and popularity for women was not significantly different from zero, but was significantly different from that for males (− .06 for women and − .62 for men). Both dominant, aggressive women and passive men were also seen as being more in need of therapy and were liked less then their stereotyped counterparts.

Finally, Spence and her colleagues redid their original study again (Kristal et al., 1975), this time supplying half the subjects with masculine or feminine personality descriptions of a competent woman with either masculine or feminine interests. While men and women still found the woman with masculine interests more likable, they did so only if she was not described as having a masculine personality. In fact, the person with both masculine interests and a masculine personality was not liked. On stereotypic adjective traits, the feminine person with masculine interests came out as being the most feminine of all the women being rated.

One would have to conclude that feminine men and masculine women are not liked as well as more stereotypic counterparts, that people do not want to be around such people, and see them as needing therapy to cure them. However, masculine interests are tolerated, and even encouraged, in women by most male and female subjects.

TYPES OF SEX ROLES

Much of the sex-role research reviewed up to this point has assumed that to be masculine is to be unfeminine, and vice versa. Thus, researchers have puzzled over how women can identify with, and be similar to, their masculine fathers and still be feminine. As this section points out, however, masculinity and femininity—if they have any usefulness at all as cultural descriptions of expected behaviors—must be seen as separate dimensions, and not opposite ends of the same dimension. Unfeminine is not the same as masculine, it does not specify the same behavior.

Masculinity versus Femininity?

Constantinople (1973) has provided an extensive review and critique of existing scales of masculinity and femininity. According to her, these scales are not useful. Contrary to the assumptions underlying their construction, they all seem to measure more than one dimension. And even if they could be perfected to measure one dimension, that would not help; masculinity and femininity are separate dimensions, not just opposite ends of the same dimension. As we shall see, separating masculinity from femininity improves the ability to predict many personality traits.

Another approach to masculinity and femininity has been taken by Bakan (1966) and extended by R. Carlson (1971, 1972) and Block (1973). According to Bakan, agency is a male principle and communion is a female principle. "Agency manifests itself in self-protection, self-assertion, and self-expansion; communion manifests itself in the sense of being at one with other organisms" (p. 15). Agency is also separation, isolation, mastery, and repression; communion is lack of separation, contact, cooperation, and removal of repression. R. Carlson (1971) reviewed Oetzel's bibliography (1966) of sex differences, classifying the outcomes of the studies in terms of sex differences in agency and communion. Of two samples of one hundred abstracts each, Carlson found that this distinction was relevant to 81 percent of the studies in one and 84 percent in the other. Of the relevant abstracts, 15 percent were nonconforming because of a lack of significant sex differences; of the studies with significant sex differences, 97 percent confirmed the agency-communion principle. These differences have even been found in the content of the dreams of young adolescents (Trupin, 1976).

Block (1973) applied these two principles of agency and communion to four separate samples studying childrearing practices in the United States. Looking only at the sex differences significant in at least three out of her four samples, she found that girls were more often held, kissed, and hugged by their fathers. Boys were taught more often to control their feelings by their mothers and were not allowed to question their father's decisions. From this, she concluded that agency is more often developed in boys and communion in girls.

These theorists all insist that the healthy adult has to combine both agency and communion, although they admit that current socialization practices may make that easier for men than for women (Block, 1973; Block, van der Lippe, and Block, 1973). But keep in mind that agency and communion can be combined, that the presence of one does not imply the absence of the other.

Masculinity and Femininity: Androgyny

Other researchers have investigated sex roles without assuming that masculinity is the opposite of femininity, believing that a person can be both masculine and feminine, or neither masculine nor feminine. Some researchers have defined **androgyny** as occurring when a person attributes to himself or herself masculine and feminine traits in equal numbers (Bem, 1974); others define it as when a person attributes to himself or herself large numbers of both kinds of traits (Bem, in press; Spence, Helmreich, and Stapp, 1975). The latter seems the preferred definition (Bem, 1977). In using these definitions, Bem and others have found few sex differences in their research; instead, behavior was best predicted by gender role (masculine, feminine, or androgynous) rather than gender identity.

The Bem Sex-Role Inventory.   To identify androgynous people, sex-typed people, and opposite-sex-typed people (masculine women and feminine men), Bem (1974) constructed an androgyny scale, called the **Bem Sex-Role Inventory.** This scale consists of a list of traits such as independence, forcefulness, compassion, and affection. Based on the responses of college students, these traits were divided into equal numbers of masculine traits, feminine traits, and socially desirable traits that have no particular sex-role. Subjects are asked to rate themselves on a scale of one to seven on a series of traits; the average of all ratings on feminine traits constitutes the femininity score. The masculine score is similarly derived. A masculine sex-typed person is one whose masculinity score exceeds his or her femininity score; the reverse is true for a feminine sex-typed person. Androgyny was defined in earlier research as being inversely related to the size of the difference between masculinity and femininity scores (for an androgynous person those scores are very close together). In later research, the preferred definition of androgyny is achieving a high femininity score and a high masculinity score. The person who is neither masculine nor feminine would be androgynous according to the first definition but not according to the second; the second definition may better predict behavior (Bem, 1977).

Correlates of androgyny.   Using this scale, Bem found androgynous people were less conforming. In one study, both masculine and androgynous subjects were significantly more independent, having their judgments less influenced by the opinions of those around them, than feminine subjects (see Table 7.6). There was no effect of gender itself upon conformity in this study (Bem, 1975).

Bem has also measured nurturance. In one experiment (1975), the willingness of subjects to play with a kitten was tested. As can be seen in Table 7.6, both feminine and androgynous men played more with the kitten than did feminine women. A later study found women and men who were neither masculine nor feminine ("undifferentiated") also played very little with the kitten (Bem, 1977). The feminine females were not expected to show so little nurturant behavior. They may have disliked or been frightened of the kitten, or they may simply have been unwilling to take sufficient initiative to actually open the cage in order to take the kitten out to play with it. Another possibility, pointed out by D. Ford is that feminine women may have been more concerned about the possible effects of kitten fur and claws on their clothing.

In later experiments on nurturance (Bem, in press; Bem, Martyna, and Watson,

TABLE 7.6

SOME EFFECTS OF GENDER ROLE AND GENDER IDENTITY UPON SEX-ROLE
STEREOTYPIC BEHAVIORS

Gender	Masculine	Androgynous	Feminine
A. Conformity			
Male	15.8	16.8	22.7
Female	18.2	19.3	23.7
B. Nurturance (kitten)			
Male	9.6	22.9	23.8
Female	28.4	30.8	12.5
C. Nurturance (lonely college student)			
Male	−.43	−.04	.05
Female	−.16	.11	.43
D. Sex-role stereotypy			
Male	6.83	5.13	4.13
Female	−.13	.08	1.29

Note: In all cases, the higher and more positive the number, the more that behavior was displayed.

1976), the interactions of subjects with a human baby and a college student said
to be lonely (Table 7.6) were measured. This time, androgynous subjects and both
feminine males and feminine females were more nurturant than were masculine
subjects of either gender. But females were also significantly more nurturant to the
lonely college student than were males, averaged over all gender roles.

Androgynous subjects may also be more flexible in other sex-role behaviors.
Bem and Lenny (1976) gave male and female subjects a list of pairs of activities
and asked them to indicate which one of each pair they would rather do. They
were told that they would have to perform the activity just long enough to be photo-
graphed, and that the photographs would be used in another experiment at another university. The pairs varied in sex-role appropriateness, with higher rewards
(money) given for the performance of an inappropriate activity (baiting a fish line
for females and making baby formula for males). If both activities were sex-role
neutral (peeling an orange and playing with a yo-yo), males selected the higher-
paying activity significantly more often than females. But, as can be seen in Table
7.6, when the higher-paying activity was sex-role inappropriate, females more
often chose that activity and so were less stereotyped. Again, as pointed out before, females are more willing than males to engage in cross-sex behaviors, but in
this case, the men even lost money by doing so. Compared to the masculine men
and feminine women, androgynous subjects, masculine females, and feminine
males were all more willing to perform the sex-role inappropriate activities, and
were more comfortable performing them.

Using the Bem Sex-Role Inventory, Allgeier (1975a, 1975b) found that androgyny in women was correlated with preferred family size and achievement
strivings. Sex-typed (feminine) women wanted larger families and had a greater
perference for sons, just as Freud would have predicted. The correlation of androgyny with family size is similar to the relationship that I. Broverman and her col-

leagues (1972) found between family size and the masculine, competency cluster of sex-role stereotypes, with the more competent woman preferring smaller families. Allgeier also found that androgynous women were more open about sex and had begun their contraceptive education earlier than sex-typed women. Finally, these women placed more importance on education and competence for themselves than sex-typed women did.

Spence, Helmreich, and Stapp (1975) found that compared to sex-typed people, androgynous people who were both very masculine and very feminine had higher self-esteem, received more honors in school, dated more, and were sick less often. Heilbrun (1976b) also found that androgynous people were more consistent in saying what their behavior would be in various situations, showing they were more independent of the situation and psychologically healthier.

From this research, it seems as though the androgynous person is physically and psychologically healthier than the more sex-typed person and has greater self-esteem. Androgynous women are more interested in education and achievement and less interested in having larger families, characteristics that, as described earlier, are also associated with being less sex-typed.

Developmental Correlates. But how did androgynous people resist pressures to conform to sex-role stereotypes? Very little research has been done on this question, and much more is needed to verify and extend the little that has been done. Allgeier (1975a, 1975b) found that androgynous women moved more frequently in childhood, were raised in larger communities, and had parents with relatively more education than feminine women. These past experiences seem to have promoted sex-role flexibility.

Kelly and Worell (1976) also examined the possible developmental correlates of androgyny, using a measure of androgyny other than Bem's. They asked college students to remember how their parents had treated them at the age of sixteen. Perceived maternal warmth was associated with feminization in males, whereas parental involvement in cognitive and intellectual activities masculinized males. For females, encouragement of achievement strivings was again associated with masculinity, but maternal concern and being under relatively strict parental control was feminizing. Androgynous people perceived their parents as engaging in both types of behavior, thus both masculinizing and feminizing them. Overall, the authors concluded that "the likelihood of an androgynous orientation is especially enhanced when the *same-sex* parent exhibits cross-typed characteristics" (p. 843). So warmth in fathers and encouragement of curiosity by mothers promoted androgyny in same-sex children.

Some Problems. These relationships between androgyny and behavior must be interpreted with some caution. All the predicted results have not been found, and androgyny may be too simplistic a concept to successfully predict the behavior of people. For example, a study by Garske (1977) suggested that identification with feminine traits, such as nurturance, on Bem's Sex-Role Inventory may be able to predict behavior only in females, and identification with masculine traits, such as decisiveness, may predict behavior much better in males than in females. But to be androgynous a person would have to endorse both sets of traits; does that mean only the sex-role appropriate traits can predict that person's behavior? Garske's research is important and needs to be replicated.

The results of studies that attempted to find predicted correlations between androgyny and scores on other scales have also been mixed. In our laboratory (K. I. Hoyenga, Wallace, and Mathes, unpublished data), we carried out an extensive set of correlations between androgyny and other traits measured on well-validated paper-and-pencil tests. We used twenty-one males and forty-two females. We found that androgynous people tended to be more dominant, more autonomous (breaking away from restraints and restrictions), and more concerned about other people, all as measured by the Personality Research Form. Androgynous people, at least androgynous females, were also less concerned about there being negative consequences to their success (they did not fear success). Because of the small sample size we only examined correlations that were significant at the .005 level (to correct for alpha levels), but the conclusions should still be treated conservatively. However, androgyny did not correlate with some traits it might be expected to, such as locus of control, rigidity, and social insight. Also unexpectedly, Ginn (1975b) found that androgyny was not related to self-actualization.

In other studies (Waters, Waters, and Pincus, 1977; Whetton and Swindells, 1977), Bem's Sex-Role Inventory was subjected to a factor analysis. These studies found that there were more than just the three factors (masculinity, femininity, and social desirability) Bem said the scale was measuring. Instead, one study found that the test measured five independent traits or factors: empathy, power, honesty, autonomy, and neuroticism. On each of these five factors, sex differences have been proposed at one time or another. The other study found four similar traits or factors: biological sex, expressiveness (empathy), dominance-aggressiveness, and independence (autonomy). These analyses indicate that although using two separate dimensions of masculinity and femininity may provide a less simplistic and more accurate way of predicting behavior than simply assuming that there is only one, bipolar dimension of masculinity and femininity, peoples' performances are still even more complex. Masculinity and femininity may each involve several independent clusters of factors, and being high on one masculine factor does not necessarily mean that the person will score high on another.

Thus, androgyny scales predict behavior better than scales that assume a single, bipolar, masculine-feminine dimension of gender role, but peoples' behaviors may be even more complex. Also, not all of the predicted relationships have actually been found, suggesting that further refinements of measuring gender role are needed. Still, androgyny has been one of the most important concepts ever to appear in gender-role research, and it has led to the discovery of some very important relationships between sex role and mental health, achievement, preferred family size, nurturance, independence, and sex-role flexibility.

SEXUAL PREJUDICE

Sexual prejudice exists whenever judgments of a person are based on that person's gender rather than behavior. Even in areas where sex differences do exist, it is still prejudice to judge a person as, for example, aggressive or poor at spatial ability just because of gender, in the absence of any other knowledge about that person. So prejudice is pre-judgment—judgments made in the absence of relevant information about that particular person.

Evidence of Sexual Prejudice

Sexual prejudice is easy to document through the personal experiences of women and men, but it is becoming increasingly difficult to demonstrate in the laboratory. One of our female undergraduate research assistants applied to a graduate school in psychology but was told that although she was extremely qualified, that school did not take women. One of us, Katharine, was told by her fellow faculty members that she could not serve on a planning committee "since women don't understand finances." When she tells people she works for the university, they usually assume that she is either a grade-school teacher in the University Lab school or a depart-mental secretary. Once one of her male students told her that although he did not know anything about electricity himself, he did not see how a woman could teach him anything about it. This was particularly interesting since it is Kermit who lacks knowledge of laboratory circuitry. So the stereotypes exist in everyday life, and Freud seems right when he said that both men and women consider women to be inferior in all cultures.

Prejudice in the Laboratory.   Laboratory research on sexual prejudice was brought into prominence by P. Goldberg and his colleagues (P. Goldberg, 1968, 1972; Pheterson, Kiesler, and Goldberg, 1971; Pheterson, cited by Pheterson et al., 1971). P. Goldberg (1968) had female college students rate on several dimensions articles written on a variety of topics. He varied the gender of the author and found that there was a general bias by women against women that was most strongly seen in articles written about traditionally male topics, but was present in traditionally female topics as well. Articles written by women were rated lower on all dimensions. Pheterson, using middle-aged uneducated women, was unable to replicate this (Pheterson, cited in Pheterson et al., 1971). Later (Pheterson, et al., 1971), the prejudice of women against women was demonstrated in works of art that were said to be by male or female artists, though the prejudice was present only if the art works were said to be contest entries rather than contest winners. Thus, uneducated women might view writing an article as a significant ac-complishment, as college women would view creating prize-winning art; in these cases the prejudice is not seen.

Even when both sexes succeed, subjects are apt to attribute different reasons for the success of men and of women. When asked to give the probable reasons for a woman's success in a given task, subjects are apt to say that it was luck, that she tried harder, or that the task was easier for her (only male subjects gave the latter reason), while the success of males was attributed to their skill and ability (Deaux and Emswiller, 1974; Feldman-Summers and Kiester, 1974). In another study, female success in graduate school was attributed to good luck, an easy course of studies, and cheating; male success was attributed to ability. On the other hand, female failure was due to a lack of ability and lack of hard work, while an unfair accusation of cheating might have been responsible for the male failure (Feather and Simon, 1975). So if a woman succeeds, it is not because of her abil-ity, but if she fails, it is due to the lack of that ability.

Prejudice in Real Life.   There is evidence of occupational sex-role bias and sexual prejudice. Rosen, Jerdee, and Prestwich (1975) looked at the prejudice of managers and executives against female managerial job applicants and em-ployees. Women were felt to be inappropriate for jobs requiring extensive travel.

Males who desired to spend time with their families were favorably regarded for promotion, whereas females with that same desire were regarded as lacking in loyalty or commitment. Wives were obliged to attend business social functions for the husbands, but the reverse was not true. Wives were also expected to give up their own jobs if required for their husband's careers.

There is an even more dramatic area of sexual prejudice: the preference for male children (Norman, 1974; Westoff and Rindfuss, 1974). In China, ninety-nine women had their fetuses genetically screened during early pregnancy and the gender of their fetus was determined. Of the forty-six women carrying normal females, twenty-nine elected to have an abortion. Of the fifty-three carrying normal males, only one chose to abort (Leff, 1975).

Even in the supposedly egalitarian atmosphere of academia there is sexual prejudice. Students of both sexes perceive a lecture delivered by a man as having more authority than the same lecture delivered by a woman (Bernard, 1964). Lewin and Duchan (1971) sent out curricula vitae varying in gender and level of qualifications to 179 colleges, asking department chairmen to rate the applicant as to qualifications and state whether or not they would hire him or her. Of those questionnaires, 62 percent were returned. The chairmen favored the average male candidate over the average female candidate; this was especially true for higher-ranking schools, younger and newer chairmen, and schools in the east and the west. In most cases, the superior female applicant was favored over the average male applicant, especially in lower-ranking, midwestern, and southern schools; however, young chairmen and chairmen from higher-ranking schools preferred the average male if the applications came in without the recommendation of a trusted colleague. The chairmen also sent back questions asking what the woman's husband and children would do if she were hired, and asking what her personality was like, which suggests that different standards were being used for male and female applicants.

Males also meet with discrimination because of their sex roles. Women requesting a leave to take care of children because their husbands could not leave their jobs were evaluated much more favorably than men making the same request (Rosen et al., 1975). Females arrested for public drunkenness are treated more leniently than males (Fraser, 1973). Levinson (1976) had males and females making job inquiries in response to want ads for someone of the opposite sex (sex-listed want ads still appear, even though they are illegal). There was sexual discrimination against both sexes when applying for opposite-sex jobs, but more males than females experienced this discrimination. Some males had their masculinity questioned. However, in the more ambiguous cases of discrimination, females were told how hard the job was but males were told that the job was too "simple, dull or low-paying" and were sometimes spontaneously offered a better job. When college students pretended to be jurors in a murder trial, they gave males longer sentences than females (McGlynn, Megas, and Benson, 1976). There are also some legal discriminations against men, as well as against women (Haymen, 1976). For example, in many states, the legal age for marriage is higher for men than for women.

Some Contradictory Findings. However, discrimination is not universally seen. Sometimes the ratings of the performance of males and females interact with the rater's gender. In rating the personality and ability of a three-year-old child, males rated the girl more favorably while females rated the boy more favorably (Gurwitz and Dodge, 1975). Another study had students evaluate male or female teachers based on personality descriptions that contained stereotypic feminine or masculine traits. Masculine teachers were seen as superior by more male than female students, whereas feminine teachers were seen as superior by more female than male students (M. Harris, 1976).

Some studies have failed to find any evidence of discrimination at all. Several students in our laboratories have failed to replicate Goldman's work. Other studies have found no effect of teacher sex upon students' ratings of teaching ability, although female teachers who rated themselves low in warmth were seen as more effective than male teachers who rated themselves low in warmth (Elmore and La Pointe, 1974, 1975). No discrimination was seen in the evaluation of librarians' job performance (Brief and Wallace, 1976) or in the evaluations of job applications (Soto and Cole, 1975). Some studies even found that in some situations, such as helping to capture a robber, females performing well are rated higher than males performing equally well, perhaps because females are perceived as having more to overcome to succeed (Bigoness, 1976; Taynor and Deaux, 1973). The unsuccessful male may also be rated lower than the unsuccessful female (Deaux and Farris, 1975; Deaux and Taynor, 1973; Feather and Simon, 1975). And although the work of professionals who are males may be rated higher than that of professionals who are females, the reverse was true for the work of students (Panek et al., 1976).

Conclusions. Perhaps the feminist movement is having an impact and people are actually becoming less prejudiced. Or perhaps this has only happened in the artificial situation of the laboratory. This second conclusion is suggested by several of the studies just cited that found discrimination in a more real life situation; in these cases, people could have been behaving more in accordance with their actual beliefs because these were seen as more important situations. Sexual discrimination is hard to demonstrate in the laboratory, but it does exist—for both men and women—outside of that rather artificial situation.

Hacker (1951), several years ago, presented an analysis of the status of women and blacks in our society. She noted many similarities, including ascribed characteristics (scarcity of genius in both groups), rationalizations of status (both are content in their place), and types of discriminations. Because of these similarities, Hacker said, both groups acquired common attitudes and behavior, such as supplicatory voices, deference, and the appearance of ignorance or helplessness. In other words, some of the sex differences in behavior could have been a result of that cultural universal, the lower status of women. But that means that white males will meet with discrimination when they try to step out of their role as boss.

Social Utility

Why is sexual prejudice so common? What function does this prejudice serve that makes it so durable? Little research has been done on the social utility of prejudice, but some functions of prejudice can be suggested. First, as pointed out earlier in this chapter, sex typing means that everyone need not be trained for every job, which increases cultural efficiency (at some cost of flexibility). Furthermore, categorizing people and then responding to them on the basis of those categories reduces the information needed by everyone in society, which considerably simplifies life. As pointed out by Lynn (see Chapter 6) and others, males may be taught to devalue the female role to make their acquisition of the male role easier. This is not necessary for females; since they never have to give up their attachment to home and mother, they don't need to learn to devalue the male sex role.

Discrimination against women also reduces competition. Both men and women see the women's movement as threatening the jobs of the male breadwinners. Our own research using the Spence Attitudes toward Women Scale (Spence, Helmreich, and Stapp, 1973), indicates that both men and women have the least liberal attitudes on the economic questions (for example, "there are many jobs in which men should be given preference over women in being hired or promoted"). Economic questions also elicited negative attitudes in the study of Ross and Walters (1973). The reduction of competition becomes even more important in times of economic hardship. The following quotation from the hearings on the Equal Rights Amendment in the House of Representatives illustrates the role of prejudice in reducing competition:

> When a woman does enter the labor market, it would seem consistent with Biblical principles that she avoid situations that would place her in competition with and ascendancy over men. As noted earlier, the man is already under a curse to work hard for his livelihood. To compete with women and to be subordinate to women would make his burden even greater. It is generally psychologically (consciously or subconsciously) distasteful to a man to have to compete with a woman. On the one hand, he would not appreciate winning out over a woman either. For there is no satisfaction in winning out over a woman, because, after all, she is a woman.

There is also some social utility on the other side of the sexual barrier. As Hacker (1975) has pointed out, the movements for black and female liberation meet some similar resistance from blacks and women. Those few who are privileged and in power have their own vested interests; it provides some pleasure to be unique (and uniquely protected against discrimination) and receive the rewards and special recognition that such a special status provides (Laws, 1975; Staines, Travis, and Jayaratne, 1973). Thus, some blacks and women who have achieved success are undecided about helping others do the same, since that would remove their unique, special, and protected status.

There are also advantages to keeping the dependent role. "Unless one is stirred by a spark of divine discontent, it is difficult to resist the enormous appeal of being given social approval for a dependent, secure status protected from competition. . . . The child in all of us enjoys being lazy and slothful, savoring the present moment, and being treasured for ourselves rather than having to pit our achievements against those of others" (Hacker, 1975, p. 108). Nash's girls (1975) who preferred to be girls rather than boys gave as their reasons the lack of pressure to be independent and the freedom from competitive obligations. Being free means being free to fail, and fear of that keeps many housewives at home.

Finally, having been in a subordinate status for so long may make women especially jealous of women who have succeeded (Bardwick, 1977). These successful women may become the target of the aggression and anger of the other women, because they almost represent an accusation of failure to the women who did not succeed, who are made guilty over having not done so. And guilt leads to hostility—"even though *they* made it and *I* didn't, they are really terrible people so I needn't feel guilty." The successful women may even stop succeeding then, to halt the attacks of other women, attacks they usually do not understand.

SUMMARY AND THE IMPLICATIONS OF STEREOTYPES

The data in this chapter suggest that the only cultural universals are the lower status of women and the fact that all cultures differentiate between male and female traits and roles. However, there are some commonalities, which could suggest some consistent cultural biases. Men and boys engage more often in aggressive roles and behaviors and are more sexually active. Women and girls are more often nurturant and more often care for young children. These cross-cultural commonalities may reflect biological or cultural biases.

Differential treatment on the basis of gender begins at birth, with mothers giving their daughters more social and verbal stimulation and their sons more physical stimulation. Fathers may engage in more sex typing than mothers. Sex typing continues throughout development, although different parental and cultural factors affect the two sexes differently. Both sexes identify with warm, dominant parents (using identification loosely, to mean any of the uses to which the major theorists put it). But while boys are feminized by identifying with a feminine mother and masculinized by identifying with a masculine father, girls can be feminized by identifying with either parent. Seldom does any child identify with a passive father.

Sex typing decreases with education; it is stronger in the lower classes and in the South. Whether their backgrounds are traditional or nontraditional affects girls more than boys, perhaps because boys partially identify with cultural stereotypes, whereas girls derive their sex roles from within the home. Age may also affect sex typing, with the greatest sexual dimorphism in behavior occurring during adolescence.

Sex typing is reinforced by our culture's omnipresent stereotypes. The stereotypes can be seen in children's readers, in textbooks, in magazines, and on television programs and commercials. The stereotype of men is more favorable than the stereotype of women. These stereotypes often are internalized, and some people pay a large price for this internalization in terms of mental and physical health. Stereotyping also affects the likability of people, with the masculine, competent, woman and the feminine, expressive, male being less liked than the feminine woman or the masculine man.

Contrary to the assumptions underlying most of the tests, masculinity and femininity are not opposite ends of a single dimension, but separate traits that have different implications for behavior, depending on the gender of the person having those traits. Unfeminine does not equal masculine in personality, any more than it did in the inductive effects of hormones. Bakan's approach to masculinity and femininity was in terms of agency and communion, which were defined as polar opposites. However, Bakan and the researchers who have extended his ideas conclude that for optimal health and ability both men and women should have both kinds of traits. As implied by the costs of sex typing, androgynous people seem healthier and more flexible, and have greater self-esteem.

Sexual prejudice was originally demonstrated in the laboratory but now it only appears reliably in field studies. Laboratory research has found evidence for same-sex preferences. Competent women may be rated more highly than competent men, and incompetent men receive the lowest rating of all. Sexual prejudice serves useful functions for society by increasing the efficiency of socialization and decreasing the information needed to function. Men benefit from decreased competition; women benefit from being protected from having to compete. But sexual prejudice has costs to society as well as benefits: cultural flexibility decreases and society loses valuable womanpower. Men pay a price for their status also; they suffer earlier deaths. If prejudice is to be eradicted, the costs must be emphasized to make them seem more important to people to eliminate than the benefits are to preserve.

Across all cultures stereotypes and sex typing may create sex differences where none exist, and exaggerate those that do have some noncultural basis. Men and women evaluate themselves and others according to these stereotypes, with often unfortunate consequences both for their own self-image and for their treatment of others. The durability of the stereotypes should not be underestimated, and the reasons for that durability must be clearly understood before changes can occur. Until then, one major reason that the sexes differ in behavior must simply be because of cultural stereotypes.

KEY TERMS AND CONCEPTS

Sex typing
Androgyny
Agency
Communion
Competency behaviors

Warmth and expressiveness behaviors
Likability
Masculinity and femininity
Bem Sex-Role Inventory
Sexual prejudice

QUESTIONS ON KEY ISSUES

1. What are the two cultural universals, and why might they be universal?
2. What are the most common sex differences found across cultures? What types of cultures may exaggerate these differences?
3. What kinds of sex differences might be created or exaggerated by the different ways parents treat girls and boys?
4. What are the major parental and social variables that affect sex typing?
5. What examples of the Broverman sex-role stereotypic traits can be found in literature, in schools, and on television? What are some of the costs and effects of these stereotypes?
6. How do sex-role stereotypes affect how a person is evaluated by other people?

7. How is the concept of androgyny an improvement over concepts used in earlier sex-role research, and how does the androgynous person differ from sex-typed and opposite sex-typed people?

8. What are some problems with androgyny as currently defined and measured?

9. What functions does sexual prejudice serve for both men and women? Why is understanding these functions important?

PART 4

Sexually Dimorphic Behavior: The Interaction of Biology and Environment

CHAPTER 8

Sex Differences in Intellectual Ability

This chapter reviews evidence about sex differences in the preparedness to learn in particular ways. That is, because of differences in genes and inductive and activational hormones, the sexes may differ in their relative preparedness to learn particular tasks or to learn in particular ways. However, preparedness is only a bias, biology provides only predispositions; it is the developmental experiences and socialization of women and men that determine the degree to which this bias becomes visible in behavior, and even if it becomes visible at all. One can inherit a predisposition to alcoholism or to schizophrenia, but environment determines whether or not that predisposition is ever expressed in behavior. Systematic differences in environment, such as the sex differences in cultural status, role assignment, and socialization, can create differences that are not biologically biased.

INTRODUCTION

Chapter Overview

Data relevant to sex differences in performances on intellectual tasks will be presented here. No sex differences are expected in full-scale IQ, but some sex differences are commonly found in the pattern of intellectual skills. Women more often than men score higher on verbal tasks, while men score higher on spatial and mathematical tasks. Other tasks that show sex differences can usually be related to one of these three major areas. Sex differences in the correlations among those skills may be even more common and important than sex differences in the skills themselves. And, generally speaking, all these sex differences are most likely to appear after puberty; there seem to be few reliable sex differences among children.

As would be expected if we are dealing with sex differences in preparedness, both experience and biology provide biases. In what ways do genes and inductive and activational hormones affect intellectual capacities? To what extent does sex-role typing affect abilities?

In evaluating the biological-environmental interaction, several things should be kept in mind. First, cause and effect relationships among these variables are hard to disentangle. Second, different experimental procedures affect the likelihood of seeing sex differences. Third, the past history of the individual and the particular testing situation employed provide a better basis for predicting performance than does knowing the person's gender.

Developmental Sequence and Differential Vulnerability of the Sexes

Maccoby and Jacklin proposed a developmental sequence for sex differences in verbal abilities (1974, pp. 84–85). Since the sequence seems relevant to many other sex differences, not only in cognitive abilities but also in other areas, it will be summarized here. Maccoby and Jacklin point out that few studies of children younger than three show sex differences in cognitive abilities. The sex differences that do appear can often be related to the generally more advanced development of girls at those ages. From three until adolescence, boys catch up in development, and the sexes have similar levels of cognitive abilities. This is true except for populations that are in some way disadvantaged, where the girls will be less affected and therefore will show superior intellectual skills to the boys in the same population. At adolescence (ages eleven to thirteen), the adult pattern of sex differences in intellectual performance appears. These developmental patterns should be looked for in the data in the rest of this chapter, and in later chapters as well.

Males are More Severely Affected by Disadvantages?. According to Goy and Goldfoot (1974), "several researchers have found the male to be more susceptible than the female to traumatic environmental effects during infancy" (p. 572). For example, Levine (1974) found male rats to be more affected by early handling and by prenatal maternal adrenal tumors. In humans, if physical development is delayed by adverse conditions, females return to normal faster than males (Hutt, 1972a).

Males may also be more susceptible to social stress. J. Gray (1971a) reported that males were more likely to be adversely affected by the stress of overcrowding than were females. Male sexual behavior may be more affected by pathological environments than that of females (Arling and Harlow, 1967; G. Jensen, 1973; Michael, 1969). Male monkeys who were socially deprived during development displayed more self-directed aggressive attacks than females (Sackett, 1974). In this latter experiment, behaviors such as exploration, social fear, and motor activity were also less adversely affected in females than in males. Social isolation in these monkeys even impaired the ability to survive in a natural environment, but it did so less in females than in males. Overmothering may also retard male monkey development more than that of females (Mitchell et al., 1966).

This differential vulnerability means sex differences before puberty may be exaggerated in stressed populations or appear only in stressed populations.

Puberty and Sex Differences. Sex differences in many different kinds of behavior are increased after puberty. This is time when the activational hormones become different for the sexes, and may also be a time when sex roles are exaggerated. For example, sex differences in self-esteem, self-consciousness, sex-role attitudes, and attitudes towards personal appearance all appear at, or are exaggerated by, adolescence (Simmons and Rosenberg, 1975). It seems that sex differences in most behaviors are most likely to appear after puberty.

The differences in intellectual ability that appear at adolescence may appear because of different rates of development, because only one sex continues to improve, or because the performance of one sex actually begins to decline. The latter is true at least sometimes; females' achievement test scores in mathematics, science, social studies, and citizenship begin to decline at thirteen, and the decline continues into adulthood (Maeroff, 1975).

Thus, the increase in sexually dimorphic behaviors at adolescence is likely to be a complex function of the hormonal changes of puberty and the changes in sex role that occur then.

VERBAL ABILITY AND IQ

Sex Differences

As far as full-scale IQ is concerned, there are no sex differences (Maccoby and Jacklin, 1974). In fact, when the tests were constructed, items that showed a large sex difference were removed or were balanced with items showing the opposite sex difference. Although there are generally no sex differences, girls may have a slight advantage in IQ under the age of seven, especially in disadvantaged populations.

However, a declining pattern of IQ after grade school is seen more often in women than in men (Bayley and Oden, 1955; Kagan et al., 1958; Terman and Oden, 1947). In fact, males with a high pre-adolescent IQ also showed the largest IQ gains with age up to forty-one, while females with a high IQ before becoming adults showed the least IQ gain (Kangas and Bradway, 1971). Females with high IQ may somehow have their intellectual ability suppressed.

Overall, women more often show a verbal superiority, especially on measures of verbal fluency. This has been the conclusion of several large and recent reviews (D. Broverman et al., 1968, Buffery and Gray, 1972; Garai and Scheinfeld, 1968; Haketian and Cattell, 1975; Jarvik, 1975; Maccoby and Jacklin, 1974). The verbal superiority of women includes vocabulary, listening, speaking, ability at verbal analogies, comprehension of difficult material, creative writing, fluency, and spelling.

These differences in verbal ability are first reliably seen at age ten or eleven (Maccoby and Jacklin, 1974). They may last well into old age (Cohen, 1977; Jarvik, 1975). One study matched older people for verbal IQ, and still found that old men (aged sixty to seventy-nine) of average verbal ability performed a fast-paced serial rote-learning task much more poorly than did old women (Wilkie and Eisdorfer, 1977). The men of average ability simply did not respond quickly enough to be able to easily learn the fast-paced verbal material. There were no sex differences among older people of high verbal ability.

Males may also have more speech and reading problems. Boys have a greater incidence of speech defects, including stuttering. More boys than girls have difficulty in learning to read, although by age ten a difference in reading performance is no longer present (G. Thompson, 1975).

The sex difference in verbal ability affects scores on standardized tests, which can in turn affect the careers of people taking the test. American College

Test (ACT) scores and Scholastic Aptitude Test (SAT) scores show a higher mean verbal score for females, and the sex difference is the same for high school students in general and for college-bound seniors only (K. Cross, 1971). Even among a highly selected group, such as medical students, the mean verbal score was 554 for women, 531 for men (Notman and Nadelson, 1973).

The Graduate Record Exam (GRE) is taken by many college students planning on attending graduate school. In 1973–74 (the last year that sex differences were reported by the Educational Testing Service), the mean for women on the verbal portion of the aptitude test was 503 while the mean for men was 493. This difference is obviously very small but it is statistically significant ($p < .001$).

Recently, the sex difference in verbal scores has been reversed on the SAT (Dwyer, 1976). Beginning in the 1950s, the content of the verbal portion of the SAT was balanced by including items from areas other than the humanities, items in which males might be more interested. This was done so that there might be a better balance of scores between the sexes. However, the even larger sex difference on the mathematical portions, which favored males, was not balanced.

Buy why are the sexes different in verbal ability? Do some biological biases produced by genes or inductive and activational hormones contribute to this? And what kinds of developmental experiences and socialization pressures create or exaggerate this difference?

Biological Factors

Sex chromosomes have only one known effect on either verbal ability or IQ: the more extra Xs and Ys there are, the more depressed the IQ score is. There is certainly no reason to think that either verbal ability or IQ is sex-linked (DeFries et al., 1976).

Inductive hormones have been claimed to affect performances in learning situations in both humans and lower animals. Androgens given to female rats after birth reduce active-avoidance learning scores, making them more similar to the scores of normal males. Adrenogenital men and women, and men and women whose mothers were given an artificial progestin or progesterone before birth, often have verbal and total IQ scores higher than normal, but so do their parents and siblings. But the effects of perinatal hormones on avoidance learning in animals can be accounted for by differences in emotional responses or motivation, and the effects in humans are too complex to interpret. We cannot conclude that excess androgen before birth increases IQ or verbal ability in humans.

Activational hormones affect learning performances in lower species in some but not all situations. Adult hormones do not affect active avoidance in lower animals, at least as determined by the effects of castration. However, in female rats, active avoidance may change with the estrous cycle or be depressed by injections of estrogen and progesterone combined, or by progesterone alone (see Table 5.4). Bar press performances may also be hormone-sensitive.

Verbal ability has also been reported to be affected by estrogen and testosterone levels in humans. Both Broverman's (1964) and Peterson's (1976) masculine-appearing males, who may have had high testosterone, had high verbal fluency scores. Body type was not significantly related to verbal fluency in females, and the kwashiorkor males—with both high estrogen and a feminized body appearance—also had high verbal fluency scores. These effects seem inconsistent, but the answer may be to assume that there should be an optimal ratio of estrogen to testosterone: too much or too little estrogen combined with normal male levels of androgen might inhibit verbal fluency.

But in many cases in both humans and lower animals, the activational hormones could affect performances either by specifically activating other types of behavior—emotional, exploratory, activity—or by having nonspecific effects on the brain. Both estrogen and testosterone in normal levels increase brain activity, whereas progesterone is an anesthetic and a depressant. There may also be optimal levels of hormones for various effects, with both higher and lower levels producing effects different from, or even opposite to, those of moderate levels.

Environmental Factors

Earlier, it was stated that females more often than males show a declining pattern of IQ. Sex roles may be part of the reason for this difference, as one study recently showed (P. Campbell, 1976). In this study, between the seventh and twelfth grades, boys increased in IQ (+1.62), while girls declined (−1.33). The author then compared the males whose IQs declined to the females and concluded that "girl decliners appear to be accepting of the feminine stereotype including that it isn't feminine to be smart. Boy decliners however, seem *less* accepting of the masculine stereotype" (p. 634). So perhaps both males and females who accept masculine traits, including those involving academic achievement and intelligence, are more likely to show increases in IQ with age.

Several other sex-typed personality traits are associated with IQ changes in both genders. Passivity in girls was associated with a decline in IQ from ages six to ten, while aggression in boys was associated with an increase in IQ in those ages (Kagan et al., 1958). Girls with a nontraditional, masculine orientation had higher IQs or higher academic performances than more traditional girls (Doherty and Culver, 1976; Kagan and Moss, 1962). Thus, male sex role traits may promote intellectual development in both sexes during childhood.

Parental variables may affect verbal ability and IQ in quite different ways in the two genders. For example, maternal overprotection in middle-class boys was associated with particularly high verbal scores, as were maternal protection and warmth. However, these relationships did not exist, or the variables even had opposite effects, for girls. Lack of maternal intrusiveness seemed to facilitate the development of IQ in girls (Bayley and Schaefer, 1964, as cited by Maccoby, 1966). Also the more reading fathers did at home, the higher the verbal ability of the daughter, although this had no effect on the son (Bing, 1963). Biller (1974) also reviewed evidence suggesting that good relationships with fathers may facilitate verbal abilities, and fathers' absence from home may inhibit them, more in boys than in girls. The effect of fathers' absence on boys, however, may appear only among the lower class. In general, both the fathers' and the mothers' behavior may have more effect on boys' than on girls' verbal skills (Biller, 1974; Maccoby and Jacklin, 1974).

Bing (1963) found differences when she compared the behavior of mothers of children who had verbal skills higher than their spatial and quantitative skills to the behavior of mothers of children who had the reverse pattern of intellectual abilities. In general, mothers of children who had higher verbal abilities gave their children more help in an experimental situation (maternal intrusiveness). These mothers also gave their children more verbal stimulation, criticized them more for poor academic performance, restricted them more, and aroused more anxiety in them. Many of these relationships were found only in boys or only in girls; however, in this particular study sex roles were not related to the verbal or spatial abilities of either gender. Still, many of the maternal behaviors found by Bing to be associated with relatively higher verbal skills seemed more characteristic of mothers with daughters than of mothers with sons. Bing could not investigate this possibility; since she selected the children to be studied on the basis of their pattern of intellectual abilities, she did not select them at random, so any data on sex roles would have been suspect. But it seems that maternal behaviors increase the verbal skills of daughters relative to their own spatial and mathematical skills and also to the verbal skills of males.

Conclusions

There is some evidence for a biological bias for sex differences in verbal ability, but as yet it is very weak and inconsistent. Sex differences in experiences seem much more important. The greater verbal stimulation that female infants often receive may give girls a head start. The data of Bing and others suggest that treating children in female-typical ways may increase their verbal skills. Overall, it appears that different frequencies of parental behavior towards girls and towards boys causes sex differences in verbal performances and in IQ declines.

MATHEMATICAL ABILITY

Sex Differences

Males show a mathematical superiority (Bieri, Bradburn, and Galinsky, 1958; Maccoby and Jacklin, 1974). Stafford (1972), in his review of the hereditary and environmental components of quantitative reasoning, found a bimodal (see Appendix A) frequency distribution for pairs of twins. He found 42.5 percent of the males in the upper mode and 33.4 percent of the females in the upper mode. This difference appears after age twelve or thirteen, when boys' skills begin increasing faster than those of girls; before this age, there are few differences, except in disadvantaged populations.

The standardized tests mentioned earlier show a sex difference in mathematical ability that is the reverse of the difference on verbal scales. Among medical school students, women had a significantly lower quantitative aptitude scores (512 for women versus 541 for men) (Notman and Nadelson, 1973). The ACT and SAT scores also show a mathematical superiority for males, among both high-school seniors in general and college-bound seniors only (K. Cross, 1971). The sex difference in math ability is not related to the number of math courses taken, but the

TABLE 8.1

SCORES ON QUANTITATIVE APTITUDE, 1969–72

	Males	Females
99th Percentile	800	760
75th Percentile	650	560
50th Percentile	556	470
1st Percentile	260	220
Mean Score	545	468
Standard Deviation	133	122
Number Taking Test	483,121	368,769

difference is reflected in performance on the mathematical portions of science courses (Maccoby and Jacklin, 1974). Even in mathematical exercises related to food buying and household situations, males do consistently better (Lanouette, 1975).

Table 8.1 presents some data from the mathematical section of the GRE; the scores are the percentile norms based on scores obtained over four years. In this case, the difference between the sexes is not only significant, it is also relatively large. Males are also significantly more variable. The sex difference is largest in the sections of average ability and is smaller for both high and low levels of ability.

Wood (1976) analyzed the pattern of sex differences in mathematical performance on the standardized exams given in England, reviewing data from 1000 boys and 884 girls. He found that the same sex differences appeared regardless of the type of school the child went to. He pointed out that "none of the items on which girls out performed boys require what could be termed problem-solving behavior: instead they call for recognition or classification, the supplying of definitions, application of techniques, substitution of numbers into algebraic expression and so forth, just the kind of operations which are most susceptible to drilling" (p. 156). Thus, females did better with Venn diagrams, sets, real number line graphs, vectors, functions, and matrix multiplication. Males did better on problems involving spatial ability (interpreting graphs) or the ability to cope with proportions (for example, "the length in kilometers represented by one centimeter on a map whose scale is 1:100,000 will be __" (p. 149). Wood concluded that the sexes may differ in learning style and preferences, and that these differences might be removed by different styles of instruction. But why do these differences occur?

Biological Factors

There is only meager evidence for any biological bias for sex differences in mathematical performances. Stafford (1972) suggested that an X-linked gene may affect mathematical ability, but this suggestion has not received much attention or support. Turner's girls—with only one X and so no inductive gonadal hormones—often have poor mathematical performances; this may imply a role for inductive hormones. Dalton (1976) also suggested that the more prenatal progestin the mother was given, the higher the mathematical ability of the son or daughter. Dawson (1972) found depressed numerical performances in his kwashiorkor males, perhaps suggesting a role for activational androgen or estrogen. A biological bias cannot be completely ruled out, but one should not be assumed to exist. Differences in socialization probably account for most, if not all, of the sex differences in mathematical performances.

Environmental Factors

Environmental factors are critical in sex differences in mathematical performances and here again sex-role socialization may be the most important cause. Father-absence decreases mathematical aptitude scores in both genders, but may have more of an effect on males than on females (Biller, 1974). Birth-order may also affect mathematical ability. Second- and thirdborn girls, especially those with male siblings, did better on quantitative tests than firstborn girls (Stafford, 1972); this may reflect girls' modeling of older brothers. Masculinity (at least as measured by one scale) was found to be positively correlated with mathematical problem solving in both sexes (A. Stein and Bailey, 1973).

But in males, high quantitative ability is also associated with decreased male sex typing. The male with high ability is characterized as being low in dominance, low in aggression, low in masculinity, low in autonomy, and high in need for affiliation. Girls with high quantitative ability were more likable (Stafford, 1972). Thus, mathematical ability may be curvilinearly related to sex typing, at least along some dimensions (see Figure 8.1).

Finally, at all levels of schooling in which students choose courses, females are less likely to choose math courses than are males; this may be especially true for students of relatively lower ability levels (Sherman and Fennema, 1977). This means that at a very early age females are permanently tracked into occupations that do not require mathematical background. This difference may be largely a function of sex-role socialization and the prevalence of the impression that it is feminine to be poor in math, or at least that lack of math ability is more appropriate for females than for males.

Other sex differences that have been identified could lead to differences in mathematical preferences and performances. For example, both males and females perceive math as difficult, but perceived difficulty affects the choices and preferences of females more than of males (Keys and Ormerod, 1977). Thus, females may stay away from math simply because it is hard, but males take math courses even though they are hard because math is sex-role appropriate or because they perceive it to be more relevant to their career plans. This difference in preference would obviously be reflected eventually on standarized tests of performance.

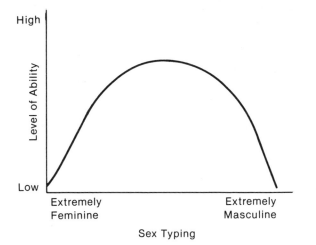

High

Low

Level of Ability

Extremely
Feminine

Extremely
Masculine

Sex Typing

FIGURE 8.1

MACCOBY'S CURVILINEAR RELATIONSHIP BETWEEN SEX TYPING AND
COGNITIVE ABILITY

*Highest ability is associated with moderate amounts of sex typing on any given sex-
ually dimorphic trait dimension; being either extremely masculine or extremely feminine is associated with the lowest ability.*

Conclusions

Most evidence suggests that the most important cause of sex differences in mathematical performances are related to sex-role socialization. Sex typing may be
curvilinearly related to mathematical ability. Because of socialization, females
stay away from math and don't perceive it to be relevant to their lives. They may
also feel that it is feminine to do poorly in math, or at least that it is unfeminine to
be very good in math.

SPATIAL ABILITY

Spatial ability involves the capacity to visualize objects in three-dimensional
space, such as the ability to look at a drawing of a three-dimensional figure and
mentally rotate it to visualize how it would look from another angle. This ability correlates highly with tasks of field independence, suggesting that a common factor
is involved (Kagan and Kogan, 1970; Sherman, 1967). **Field independence** is indicated by such things as the ability to tilt your body to be vertical even in a room
with tilted walls, the ability to adjust a rod to a true vertical even when it is sur-
rounded by a tilted frame (the rod-and-frame task), and the ability to find a simple
figure embedded in one of a series of more complex figures (like the puzzles that
ask children to find ten animals hidden in this picture).

Spatial ability is also correlated with performances on other tasks. Spatial ability is highly correlated with performance IQ (ability to apply information supplied in a question) in both younger children (+.51) and older ones (+.65); spatial ability is also correlated with verbal IQ, but only for older children (+.62) (Crandall and Sinkeldam, 1964). Spatial ability is positively correlated with performance in science and math courses, and with such skills as drafting, working with machines, and watch repair; but spatial ability is negatively correlated to performance in languages courses, and is not related to general school success (Bock and Kolakowski, 1973; A. Peterson, 1976).

Spatial ability increases with age up to late adolescence, but at any given age a person's ability is highly correlated with his or her relative ability at other ages. It is usually assumed that spatial ability and performance IQ decline with age after adolescence but this is not always so (Cohen, 1977).

Sex Differences

In all the tests of visual spatial ability just described, postpubescent males scored higher than females (Bieri et al., 1958; Hakstian and Cattell, 1975; Maccoby and Jacklin, 1974; McGee, 1976; Sherman, 1967; Vaught, 1965). In fact, only about 25 percent of the females scored above the median of the males (Bock and Kolakowski, 1973). The sex difference in spatial ability is seen cross-culturally in most groups tested. One notable exception is for Eskimos, where women are not socialized to be more dependent than men (Kagan and Kogan, 1970; Maccoby and Jacklin, 1974; Pande, 1970; Parlee and Rajagopal, 1974). Girls are more variable in spatial ability (Bieri et al., 1958).

The sex difference in spatial ability is also a function of age. Girls may be superior to boys among preschoolers (J. W. Berry, 1966; Coates, 1974), but this difference may then disappear and the sexes are equal until adolescence. Then males begin doing better than females (Wolf, 1971), and this sex difference may last well into old age (Cohen, 1977).

Males also do better in cross-cultural studies of maze performances, which may also reflect differences in spatial skills (Porteus, 1965). Porteus found that males were better at his maze test at all ages and across nine different cultures. The sex difference was greatest, however, in more primitive cultures. It is also interesting to note that among all of the studies Porteus reported, only six found that females did better, and all of them were conducted in the last four years of the testing period, which lasted from 1916 to 1959. There was some bias in Porteus's testing procedures, however. Males were sometimes systematically tested first because they would have been "insulted" to have to follow their wives.

Other tasks that also have a spatial component usually show male superiority. Among ten-year-olds, boys are better than girls at discriminating between various two-dimensional shapes (Etaugh and Turton, 1977). At all ages between six and nineteen, males do better at moving a spot of light over which they have control to intersect a moving target on a screen (Dorfman, 1977). Keogh (1971) also found that when nine- and ten-year-old boys and girls were asked to reproduce a visual pattern by walking it out on the floor, boys did better in all conditions. Finally, college-age males and females were asked to mentally search the alphabet, either for a given shape (those whose capital letters had a curve) or for a given sound (containing the sound "ee"). Males were faster and made fewer errors than females on the task involving the shape of the letter; females were faster and made fewer errors than males on the verbal task (Coltheart, Hull, and Slater, 1975).

Biological Factors

The evidence for a biological influence on sex differences in spatial ability is greater than for any other area. Some of the relevant evidence comes from data gathered on lower animals. Commonly, male animals (at least rodents) do better in mazes than do females. Since the learning performances are dimorphic, neonatal hormones affect maze performances. Androgens given to female rats after birth increased scores for complex mazes, and male rats given neonatal estrogen had poorer scores for maze learning requiring discrimination. Activational hormones also affect maze learning. Estrogen given to adult male rats depressed maze learning, and puberty also increased maze-learning errors in females; so in lower animals, neonatal androgen—endogenous or exogenous—may facilitate maze learning, while adult estrogen may inhibit it. The effects of hormones upon maze-learning performances may not be direct, but may be the result of changes in emotionality, exploration, activity, or energy balance.

Genes or hormones may also affect spatial ability in humans. Stafford (1961) suggested that spatial ability might be associated with an X-linked, recessive gene. However, recent evidence has not fit the predictions of an X-linked model of heritability, and so a multifactorial model may do better. In this model, spatial ability in humans is affected by a complex interaction of genes, hormones, and experience. Support for this model is found in Turner's women, who have very poor spatial and numerical ability, perhaps because of their lack of fetal androgens. Androgen-insensitive women have normal female spatial ability in spite of their being genetic males, suggesting that spatial ability may be androgen-sensitive. Both of these groups of women have normal to good verbal ability. Sons of diabetic mothers given estrogen also had a reduced spatial ability, being more field dependent than the control males. However, this effect of neonatal estrogen could not be replicated by Reinisch (1977).

There may also be some activational hormone effects in humans. Kwashiorkor men, with reduced androgen and increased estrogen, show lower spatial ability, but have good verbal fluency. Spatial ability has also been reported to decline slightly during the high estrogen phases of the menstrual cycle. The masculine-appearing males studied by Broverman and his colleagues (1964) and Peterson (1976) had low spatial ability and may have had high androgen levels. If androgen does affect spatial ability, then, there presumably must be an optimal level present; any higher or lower levels would lead to poorer spatial ability, as in masculine males. Adolescent females with a masculine body type have higher spatial skills than feminine adolescents, suggesting that the masculine females were closer to the optimal level of androgens. Maturation rate may also affect spatial ability, with faster maturers of both genders having relatively lower spatial ability; verbal fluency was not related to rate of maturation (Waber, 1976).

Thus, spatial ability in humans may be affected by a variety of factors, including genes and hormones, but some evidence is contradictory. For example, A. Peterson (1976) found no correlation between rate of maturation and spatial ability. Also contradictory is the pattern of abilities of the adrenogenital people: they sexually mature late, and their verbal scores as well as their spatial scores are higher than normal, and their spatial skills are lower than would have been expected based on their verbal scores. The spatial and verbal scores of their unaffected siblings are as high as those of the adrenogenital patients.

Environmental Factors

Cross-Cultural Studies. Cross-cultural research suggests that sex-role development plays a large part in the pattern of cognitive skills that develop in both genders, and spatial ability has often been found to vary with culture type. As was mentioned earlier, Eskimos show no sex difference in spatial ability. This could be because both sexes are socialized to be independent in that culture, or because there are differences in the gene pool, or because of some interaction of both processes. Cross-cultural analyses have also shown that spatial ability correlates positively with socialization of independence and negatively correlates with conformity (Kagan and Kogan, 1970; Maccoby and Jacklin, 1974). Dawson (cited by Dyk and Witkin, 1965) cross-culturally analyzed spatial ability; he found that field dependence (low spatial ability) was associated with parental strictness and severity of discipline and with father's having a greater number of wives (polygyny).

J. W. Berry (1976) carried out a cross-cultural analysis of variations in spatial ability. He found that nomadic, hunter-gatherer groups, which socialize both sexes to be assertive and independent, have minimal sex differences in spatial ability. He also found that it is precisely these groups that had the greatest levels of spatial ability, compared to that found in stratified, complex, agricultural communities (J. W. Berry, 1977). Thus, in societies in which spatial ability is relatively high, sex differences in that ability are decreased, absent, or even reversed. This means that even if there are sex differences in the preparedness to learn spatial skills, some societies may promote spatial abilities in such a way that everyone has ample opportunity to learn and the initial differences are overcome. Data on children in such societies may provide more information relevant to these ideas, and studies with children need to be done.

Parental Variables. The father may play an important role in the development of spatial ability in both his daughter and son. Having the father absent from the home for a prolonged period of time is associated with decreased spatial abilities in both boys and girls (Biller, 1974). Barclay and Cusumano (1967) also found that although the absence of the father had no effect on the masculinity scores of boys (as Kohlberg would have predicted), it did decrease spatial ability. Boys with a high level of spatial ability perceive themselves as more similar to their fathers than did boys with low spatial ability, and also saw themselves as having a warm father-son relationship (Biller, 1974). If spatial ability of girls is also affected by how close they feel to their fathers, the sex difference in spatial ability could be the result of fathers being closer to and more involved with their sons than with their daughters.

However, Bieri (1960) found that along with father-identified women, mother-identified men had greater field independence, when identification was measured by perceived similarity to the parent. But whether or not mother-identification produced greater field independence depended upon the man's acceptance of authority. Only mother-identified men with a low acceptance of authority had higher field independence scores than father-identified males. Only mother-identified males with a high acceptance of authority were significantly more field dependent than the comparable female group; in fact, they were the most field-dependent group of all. This probably accounts for the difference in the results of Bieri and Biller. Bieri found that perceived parental similarity was the most important determinant of women's spatial scores, while acceptance of authority was the best predictor of men's scores.

Sex-role Stereotypic Traits and Spatial Ability. Field dependence and independence (which are highly correlated with spatial ability) are often associated with differences in sex-role stereotypic traits. Witkin and Goodenough (1977) recently reviewed the rather extensive literature that makes this connection. Field-dependent people may pay more attention to social cues, such as facial expressions and social words (such as *party, dating,* and *dancing*). Field-dependent people may also be more sensitive to the opinions of others and more conforming, but only in situations in which they are unsure of what to do. On the other hand, field-independent people may be more concerned about achievement and mastery. Field-dependent people prefer to be closer to those with whom they are interacting than do the field independent and the field dependent are more willing to reveal intimate details about themselves to friends. The task performance of the field dependent may be facilitated by working in a group. These two groups prefer and do better in different kinds of occupations—writing and psychiatric nursing for the field dependent, architecture for the field independent, for example. Field-dependent people like other people more, rate them more highly, and try to avoid expressing hostility. The field dependent are also liked more by other people, especially if they are females: the perceived femininity of field-dependent males may lessen their likability.

In all of these areas, sex differences have been either claimed to exist by the stereotypes or have actually been found to exist. Perhaps being feminine is associated with being field dependent, associated with using all the available information to make a decision rather than ignoring the irrelevant. Two quotes from Bieri's review (1960) illustrate this connection. "Field independent people are likely to be rated high on such attributes as autonomy, showing initiation, responsibility, self-reliance, and ability to think for oneself" (p. 668). "In general, field dependent people tend to describe themselves and to be described by others in such terms as friendly, considerate, warm, affectionate, polite, tactful, accommodating, nonevaluative and accepting of others, like people and are liked by others, and make others feel comfortable with them" (p. 678). These lists of traits sound as though they came from Broverman's list of sex-role stereotypic traits (see Table 7.1). It would not be surprising to find that sex roles predict differences in field independence or spatial ability within each gender, as well as between them.

Sex Roles and Sex Differences in Spatial Ability. Sex roles can affect sex differences in spatial ability. Coates (1974) studied preschool children and found that feminine girls were field dependent (had poorer spatial ability), while field-independent girls were uninterested in dolls and preferred to paint, do puzzles, and make collages. Field-dependent boys, on the other hand, were rated by their teachers as being the toughest and most aggressive boys. However, if boys had extreme cross-sex interests, primarily dolls and house play, they were also field dependent. Aggression was highly and negatively correlated with field independence and achievement striving for boys, but was not correlated with the spatial ability of girls. In this group, girls were more field independent than boys, but Coates's research suggests that even at this early age, sex typing is related to spatial ability.

Several other studies have specifically related sex-role traits and attitudes to spatial ability in children. Ferguson and Maccoby (1966) found spatial ability greatest in children with cross-sex typing. On the other hand, the degree to which a three-year-old child engages in masculine activities was positively correlated with spatial ability both three and seven years later (Fagot and Littman, 1976).

Sex roles are also related to spatial ability after puberty. Vaught (1965) looked at spatial scores and the masculinity and femininity of college students. Males and masculine students of either gender did better on spatial tests, but both tendencies interacted with ego-strength (self-esteem). For males, high ego-strength was correlated with high spatial ability, regardless of sex role. For females, high ego-strength was associated with good spatial ability only in low to moderately feminine women. For highly feminine women, high ego-strength was associated with poor spatial ability. Nash (1975) also found that the more masculine an adolescent boy or girl viewed himself or herself, the better his or her spatial performance. If a person of either gender preferred to be a girl, his or her spatial score was lower. The spatial ability of the girls who preferred to be boys was equal to that of boys, and these girls described themselves as having more masculine traits than did other girls.

Some of these results may appear inconsistent. One reason may be the varying ages of the subjects involved; perhaps the relationship between sex typing and spatial skills varies with age. Another reason for the differences may have to do with the degree of sex typing; extreme sex typing may have a different relationship to spatial ability than moderate sex typing. For example, the adolescent boys who preferred to be girls in Nash's study are probably most similar to the doll-playing, preschool boys in Coates's study (Green, 1974), and both of these groups of males were very low in spatial ability. Perhaps extreme sex typing will decrease the spatial ability of both males and females.

Conclusions

Spatial ability may be curvilinearly related to sex typing, with extreme masculinity and extreme femininity in either males or females associated with lower spatial scores. If the typical socialization of males moves them closer to the optimal level for spatial performance than does the typical socialization of females, then most of the results cited above could be explained. Sex typing may be more related to spatial ability in girls and women than in boys and men; in males, spatial ability may be more affected by ego-strength and acceptance of authority. And if fathers are closer to sons than to daughters, this might also increase the spatial ability of males relative to females. So experience and socialization probably interact with the biological bias, if there is one, to either increase or decrease spatial ability. Therefore, the sex difference in spatial ability must be regarded as variable, depending critically upon socialization, and as reversible.

This section suggests that in some cases biological biases interact with environment. However, many of these studies do not allow us to disentangle cause from effect. For example, did the preference of Nash's field-independent girls for the male sex role give them their better spatial ability? Or did their better spatial ability lead them to reject femininity? Or did unusually high levels of androgen lead to a preference for the male role because those levels produced a more masculine body (or because of some more direct activational or inductive effect on behavior) and did these higher hormonal levels then also lead to better spatial ability? Are the cultural differences in spatial ability caused by socialization differences or different selection pressures on genes? Remember that correlation does not mean causation. These questions cannot as yet be answered.

WHY ARE THERE NOT MORE WOMEN GENIUSES?

This is a perennial question in the study of sex differences. We will evaluate four of the most commonly given reasons for the relative lack of women geniuses. Perhaps more men are geniuses because men are more cognitively developed than women are. Or perhaps it is because men can better ignore the irrelevant in arriving at new ideas. Perhaps it is because men are more analytic and creative and better able to break old patterns of thinking. Finally, perhaps it is because IQ in men is more variable than it is in women.

In this section, genius means not only a fairly high IQ, but also high levels of creativity; IQ alone will be far from enough. **Creativity** implies producing something unique, whether it be a novel, a scientific theory, or a painting. But as can be seen, there are problems with this definition. Some people with high IQs do unique things that are called bizarre rather than creative. Therefore, cultural evaluations must also play a part in the recognitive of genius.

Four Hypotheses

The Cognitive-Development Hypothesis. Garai and Scheinfeld (1968) said that since males develop more slowly, they reach a more complex level of development than do females. But Maccoby and Jacklin (1974) found no differences in the development of concept formation or reasoning. The only developmental task in which women have been reported to do dramatically poorer is in realizing that the level of still water is horizontal regardless of how its container is tilted. H. Thomas, Jamison, and Hummel (1973) reported that 87 percent of college men understood this principle, but only 50 percent of college women did. Even training did not improve the performance of women. These results were contradicted by a more recent study, however. Out of 130 males and 130 females, only eighteen males and twenty-two females did not know the principle, and the females improved more with practice than the males (Munsinger, 1974).

In some pilot work, we presented the horizontal water problem to women we knew, and found that even Ph.D.'s did not generally know the principle; intelligence seemed related only to the quality of the reasoning given for the wrong answer. In our own laboratory, we have used a forced-choice procedure and have found that out of three separate samples of forty-two to forty-five subjects, men did somewhat better than women. The percent of men and women, respectively, who answered the question correctly was: 85.7 percent and 83 percent; 93.8 percent and 75 percent; 83.3 percent and 80.9 percent. Also, women less frequently gave correct answers to a question from Piaget's stage of formal operations (adult): "What determines whether or not a given object will float on water?"

Thus, though there may be some sex differences in these areas, they are much too small and variable to account for the lack of women geniuses. Also, the differences may reflect differences in educational background, such as whether any physics was taken, and differences in spatial ability, rather than anything like cognitive development.

Disembedding.   Another hypothesis is that men are better at **disembedding,** ignoring the irrelevant in arriving at conclusions or perceptions. Maccoby and Jacklin (1974) found that the only tasks men did better that involved disembedding were those that correlated with spatial ability. There are no sex differences in nonspatial tasks, such as selective listening tasks that involve the ability to ignore irrelevant voices.

Creativity.   Hutt (1972a, 1972b) found some evidence to suggest that men were more creative and "more able to break a set, to restructure and to reorganize their concepts . . . even if the sexes were equated for IQ, verbal ability, and education" (Hutt, 1972a, p. 111). With regard to toy play, more "creative explorers" were boys rather than girls (25 percent as opposed to about 7 percent). But even among the creative explorers, boys got the higher mean scores on creativity tests. On the other hand, Maccoby and Jacklin (1974) found that verbal creativity tests favored females and that nonverbal tests showed no consistent differences. They concluded that "girls and women are at least as able as boys and men to generate a variety of hypotheses and produce unusual ideas" (p. 114).

Two abilities related to creativity are analytic abilities and set breaking. Neither of these show consistent sex differences. **Analytic abilities** require classification of a set of objects on the basis of isolated features, such as shape (balloon, ball, sun) or number of legs (cat, chair, table). There are no consistent sex differences in the performance on such a task (Maccoby and Jacklin, 1974).

There are two types of **set-breaking** tasks. On the solving of anagrams (unscrambling a list of words whose letters are in scrambled order), females do very well, but on other problems, men do better. Those set-breaking tasks on which men do better include the horse-trading problem and Luchin's water-bottle test. The horse-trading problem is as follows: "A man bought a horse for $60, sold it for $70, bought it back for $80 and then sold it for $90. How much money did the man make in the horse business?" In this problem, in one experiment, 43.7 percent of the men and 25.3 percent of the women solved it. One question from Luchin's water-bottle test asks how you can bring exactly six quarts of water from the river, when you have only a four-quart and a nine-quart pail to measure with (Maccoby and Jacklin, 1974).

There are sex differences in creativity, then, but again they are too inconsistent, too dependent on the task, and too small to allow us to say that men have more creativity than women.

Variability.   The last hypothesis is that of variability. If men are more variable, they will be overrepresented at both the upper and the lower ends of the IQ range. Since there would be more extremely bright (as well as extremely dull) men, men would more often be geniuses.

Maccoby and Jacklin (1974) found that while men were more variable in verbal ability, it was because more men than women were in the lower ranges of ability, not because there were more in the upper ranges. More males had reading difficulties, for example. One review of ten studies on the incidence of mental retardation analyzed sex differences, concluding that "the overall trend suggests a somewhat higher rate in male children. The age-specific breakdowns show that this sex difference persists at all ages" (Abramowicz and Richardson, 1975, p. 30). Thus, there are probably more males at the lower IQ range, but not at the upper. For quantitative ability, males were also more variable, as was indicated by the GRE norms (see Table 8.1). Males are more frequently found both at the upper and the lower ranges of mathematical ability.

However, genius and IQ are not highly correlated (D. MacKinnon, 1962), so the greater number of males found at the upper ranges of mathematical and spatial abilities cannot be related to sex differences in creativity. Since there is no such correlation, and since there are not more verbally bright men than bright women, variability cannot account for the lack of women geniuses either.

Conclusions

None of these hypotheses are sufficient to account for the relative lack of women geniuses, nor would all of them taken together be sufficient. The answer is more likely to be the action of prejudice and stereotypes and sex differences in achievement motivation and reasons given by people for succeeding or failing; both of these will be discussed in the next chapter.

SEX DIFFERENCES IN OTHER AREAS

Sex Differences in the Correlations of Abilities

Kagan and Kogan (1970), in their survey of intellectual abilities in children, concluded that although there were sex differences in the level of performance on some intellectual tasks, these differences were less common than were sex differences in the patterns of relationships among performances. For example, on a timed reaction task, IQ was related to the number of errors made by girls but was related to the response or reaction time of boys. Reaction time (impulsivity) was more strongly and inversely related to reading errors in girls than in boys. Thus, the patterns of correlations among cognitive abilities, and correlations of those abilities with personality, suggest that even similar scores on the same test indicate different abilities for males and females.

Hutt (1972b) also found some sex difference between her male and female creative explorers that suggested somewhat different personality correlates. Both boys and girls who were creative (as assessed by their use of toys) were independent and assertive, but only the boys were considered by their teachers to be disruptive influences in the classroom. The correlations between inventive play in early childhood and creativity scores in later childhood were significant only for boys, who scored much higher on these later tests. There were also sex differences within the nonexploring group. Nonexploring boys (who did not contact novel toys) were apathetic and inactive, while nonexploring girls were tense, anxious, and timid. Thus, both exploration and the lack of exploration occurred for different reasons in males and in females.

One impressive study rather dramatically demonstrated this type of sex difference (Chiang and Atkinson, 1976). This study investigated the relationships among different cognitive factors such as verbal ability, mathematical ability, and the time required to search one's memory to see whether or not something had just been said or presented. The sex differences were so large that the relationships found for a group of people vanished when the group was separated into males and females. For example, high verbal and mathematical abilities in females were associated with a slow memory search rate, but these abilities in males were associated with a fast search rate. Large sex differences were seen in the pattern of relationships among cognitive abilities, even though there were no significant sex differences in mean scores on any of the tasks.

Spatial ability frequently shows significant sex differences in correlations with other abilities. Spatial ability and numerical ability are correlated in both females and males (+ .50 for females and + .40 for males) (Bieri et al., 1958); this means that male spatial superiority could contribute to male numerical superiority. However, verbal ability and mathematical ability were significantly more strongly correlated in adult males (+ .66) than females (+ .31) (Bieri et al., 1958), although the reverse may be true for young children (Repucci, 1971). Moreover, different tests of spatial ability may be positively correlated for males and either not correlated or negatively correlated for females (Corah, 1965; Harley, Kalish, and Silverman, 1974). The scores of females on Porteus's maze test were more related to their IQ than were the scores of males (Porteus, 1965). Finally, although there were no sex differences in one test of logical reasoning or problem solving (syllogistic reasoning), male performance was positively correlated with spatial ability (+ .49), but female performance was not correlated significantly (+ .16) (Shaver, Pierson, and Lang, 1974).

Sex Differences in Other Types of Tasks

There are very few consistent sex differences found in the performaces on tasks other than verbal, spatial, and mathematical tasks, and what differences there are can usually be related to the sex differences in those three areas. According to Maccoby and Jacklin (1974), there are no sex differences in concept mastery and reasoning, in paired-associates learning, in discrimination learning that involves changing the initial response tendency, in learning with partial or delayed reinforcement, in incidental learning, or in learning through imitation (see also Dusek,

Mergler, and Kermis, 1976). Hakstian and Cattell (1975) found some sex differences in the 280 older adolescents they studied, but overall the sexes were more similar than different. There were no sex differences for speed of closure, memory, flexibility, ideational fluency, originality, and representational drawing. However, Hakstian and Cattell also found no sex differences in verbal ability (except verbal fluency) or numerical ability.

The sexes do differ in eyelid movement under classical conditioning—females learn faster—but when a masking procedure disguises the purpose of the task, so that anxiety is no longer positively related to speed of conditioning, the sex difference disappears. Thus, the sex difference in eyelid conditioning was probably due to sex differences in anxiety (Maccoby and Jacklin, 1974).

Females after the age of seven do better on memory tasks, at least on those involving verbal context (Arlin and Brody, 1976; Maccoby and Jacklin, 1974). Females are generally more accurate observers of people being interviewed than are males, but again the difference may be limited to recalling the verbal content and style of the interaction (Mazanec and McCall, 1975).

Males have usually been reported to be better at problem-solving tasks (Hutt, 1972a, 1972b) but this difference may be related to sex differences in spatial or mathematical skills. One study found that if the sex difference in mathematical ability were controlled, the sex difference in problem solving became insignificant (L. R. Hoffman and Maier, 1966). Boys in one type of listening task accurately identified more nonverbal sounds (phone dialing, washing machine) than girls, but this ability may be related to spatial skills (Knox and Kimura, 1970).

Summary

There are few reliable sex differences in ability other than those in verbal, spatial, and mathematical ability. Those differences that have been found can usually be attributed to something other than cognitive capacity or to the difference in the verbal, spatial, and mathematical ability. For example, women learn eyelid conditioning faster and men do better in problem solving probably because of sex differences in anxiety scores and spatial abilities, respectively.

But sex differences in correlations suggest a very important type of sex difference. The relationships among intellectual skills, or the relationships between these skills and personality, are often different for the two genders. This suggests that the cognitive structures of females and males may take somewhat different forms, and that this difference is both more important and more common than sex differences in mean scores. Do women and men think the same way?

EXPERIMENTAL MANIPULATIONS OF SEX DIFFERENCES

If the sexes do differ in their cognitive ability because of biological biases, then experience ought to improve abilities in both sexes, although at a faster rate in one than the other. And with sufficient training—more than that required for the best performance of the less well-prepared gender—the sex difference should be eliminated. For example, Bing (1963) suggested that early verbal stimulation may be more important for the verbal ability of boys than that of girls, which could be because boys have less verbal preparedness. Motivational factors should also affect the sex differences in cognitive performances.

Gender of Experimenter

Both sexes do better with a same-sex tester. In a study by Pederson, Shinedline, and Johnson (1968) on quantitative test performance, males and females tested by opposite-sex testers had scores of 34.75 and 33.00, respectively; when they were tested by same-sex examiners, males and females had scores of 35.75 and 41.67, respectively. Though both sexes benefited by having same-sex examiners, only females benefited significantly. Also of note is that the sex difference was reversed in the same-sex condition. L. R. Hoffman and Maier (1966) studied problem solving in men and women. They found that the percentage of women who solved the horse-trading problem with a female experimenter was not significantly different from the percentage of males who solved that problem with a male experimenter present, meaning that having a tester of the same sex benefits women greatly. However, this effect was not replicated with another series of eight similar problems.

Item Content and Practice

Changing the content of questions also changes performance. Milton (1959) gave male and female college students twenty math problems to solve, half with masculine content (measurement in a laboratory) and half with feminine content (measurement in a kitchen). Overall, men solved more of both types of problems, but the sex differences were decreased, although not eliminated, by feminine content: men solved fewer and women more of those problems than of masculine ones. However, L. R. Hoffman and Maier (1966) could not replicate this. This latter study also found that men did better overall, but both sexes seemed to find the feminine problems the more difficult ones.

Practice has been found to reduce sex differences. On verbal creativity tests, women usually produce more responses, but having a warm-up before the test improved the performance of males to equal the females' level; the performance of females was not significantly affected by this change (J. Freedman, 1965). On an extended series of embedded-figures items, males started out better, but the sex difference disappeared with practice (Goldstein and Chance, 1963). However, another investigator found that the sex difference on an embedded-figures task increased with practice when unique figures were used for each trial (Wolf, 1971).

Even discussion sessions may affect sex differences. Carey (1958) improved the problem-solving ability of college women by first engaging them in a discussion emphasizing the social acceptability of excellence; the performance of males was not so affected. Torrance (1963) tested grade-school girls and boys by having them figure out the principles of some science toys, and the boys did better. He then had a series of conferences with parents and teachers to emphasize that it was not inappropriate to the female sex role to be scientifically creative. The performance of girls improved to equal that of the boys, although the girls themselves still rated what they had done as inferior to the boys' work.

THREE THEORIES OF SEX DIFFERENCES

There have been three well documented attempts to explain and integrate the patterns of sex differences in cognitive performances. Two of them attempt to relate biology to sex differences: that of Buffery and Gray (Buffery and Gray, 1972; J. Gray, 1971b; J. Gray and Buffery, 1971), and that of D. Broverman and his colleagues (Blum and Broverman, 1967; D. Broverman, et al., 1964; D. Broverman et al., 1968; Klaiber et al., 1971). The third theory, originally proposed by Maccoby (1966), relates sex differences in cognitive performances to sex-role socialization.

Maccoby

The Theory. Maccoby has suggested that extreme sex typing, being either an extremely masculine male or an extremely feminine female, is associated with poorer levels of ability. Masculinity in females and femininity in males (opposite-sex typing), on the other hand, may facilitate the acquisition of cognitive skills. According to her theory, if the sex-role socialization of either gender moves one of them on any given trait dimension closer than the other to the optimal point for the development of any cognitive ability, then the performance of tasks involving that ability will show consistent sex differences. This hypothesis is illustrated in Figure 8.1.

For example, suppose that the optimal amount of sex typing associated with spatial ability involved being moderately aggressive, or moderately masculine on that particular masculine trait dimension. This trait is found more often in males than in females, so males would, on the average, have higher levels of spatial ability than females. But males who were even more masculine and aggressive than the majority of other males would have lower levels of spatial ability. On the other hand, masculine females—females who were very aggressive for women but only moderately aggressive overall—would have high levels of spatial ability.

Data. This chapter has already provided evidence in the areas of spatial, mathematical, and verbal ability, that extreme sex typing inhibits performance. Here, we shall simply summarize, extend, and evaluate these data.

The data generally support the idea that cross–sex typing facilitates cognitive development. Maccoby and Jacklin (1974) have cited several different correlations that support this idea; in all cases, the higher the score on a same-sex trait, the lower the cognitive performance. Aggression was positively correlated with IQ for girls (+ .41) and negatively correlated for boys (− .74) (Coates, 1974; Kagan and Freeman, 1963). Internal **locus of control** (a male trait, meaning belief in one's own power to control one's life) was positively correlated with spatial ability only in girls. The higher a score is on an *opposite*-sex trait, the *higher* the performance.

Other studies also provide support for Maccoby's hypothesis. Intelligence may be negatively correlated with masculinity among lower-class boys (Biller,

1974). Girls who reject the traditional female sex role score higher on IQ tests (Kagan and Freeman, 1963), and masculine adolescent females also have higher IQs (Doherty and Culver, 1976). Opposite-sex parental identifications are associated with higher spatial scores, at least as long as the men also had a low acceptance of authority and the women a high self-concept (Bieri, 1960; Vaught, 1965). Extreme sex typing, even opposite–sex typing, may depress spatial scores (Coates, 1974; Nash, 1975).

Creativity and professional achievement may also be related to cross–sex typing. Women mathematicians identified more with their fathers than their mothers (Plank and Plank, 1954). Creative women mathematicians differed from their less creative counterparts not in relative masculinity or femininity, but in identifying more with their fathers, in having a dominant father with strong intellectual and cultural values, and in not having any brothers. Creative male mathematicians and architects score high in femininity (Helson, 1971; Kanner, 1976; D. MacKinnon, 1962). Another study found creativity in air force officers to be positively correlated with three different measures of femininity (Barron, 1957)

There are also results inconsistent with Maccoby's theory. One review found that masculinity was negatively correlated with verbal ability in girls (A. Stein and Bailey, 1973). And several studies, as described earlier, have found that in boys and men their perceived similarity to their father is associated with greater spatial skills.

Summary and Evaluation. Overall, Maccoby's ideas provide a good summary of the effect of sex-role socialization on cognitive development. Both women and men need some of both Parson's instrumental and expressive roles for optimal cognitive development. And, in Bakan's terms, unmitigated agency, or instrumentalism in the absence of expressiveness, inhibits development.

However, sex-role research now suggests that those people who are both masculine and feminine, the androgyns, will be those in whom cognitive abilities become maximally developed. Alternatively, it may simply be that the more intelligent and creative people rejected the stereotypes; correlations of androgynous traits with performance do not establish the direction of causality.

Buffery and Gray

The Theory. According to this theory, evolutionary pressures produced the sex differences in spatial and verbal abilities. Just as anthropologists have told us, "the sex differences in emotional and cognitive behavior among mammalian species . . . are all remote but necessary consequences of the same overriding fact: the division of labour between the sexes in reproductive behavior" (J. Gray and Buffery, 1971, pp. 106–7). With regard to spatial ability, "it seems likely that, among rodents, this male superiority is connected with the fact that, in the wild, this sex has a larger home range than does the female. . . . The exploratory activity which is reflected in measurements of the home range clearly involves the exercise of spatial ability" (p. 95). Part of the reason for the superior spatial ability of the male primate may be his greater concern with dominance interactions, which may result in the throwing of objects: accurate throwing requires good spatial ability. "Another feature of primate behaviour which is similar to that of rodents is that the male . . . explores more than the female; this may have the same significance as the rodent sex difference in home range size. . . . A further reason, at the primate level, for the sex differences in spatial ability may be the male's role as protector of the group both against predators and against other groups of conspecifics" (p. 95). The male primate has greater spatial ability because of his greater exploratory tendencies and his roles in dominance and group protection. But females have a verbal superiority. "Thus, for language to evolve among primates, it must have been necessary for *females* to be particularly adept at the newly developing linguistic skills so that they would be likely to use them in the presence of their offspring. It seems probable that this is the selection pressure which resulted in the existing human sex difference in verbal ability" (p. 96).

Buffery and Gray have suggested that because of these evolutionary pressures, differences in brain organization appeared between males and females over the course of time. These sex differences appear in part because of an X-linked recessive gene that favors good spatial ability. Obviously more males than females will exhibit a trait controlled by a recessive X-linked gene. However, Buffery and Gray apparently also think it is likely that for this gene to be fully expressed, the organism must be exposed to optimal amounts of androgen, both before birth and during puberty.

According to Buffery and Gray, the difference in brain organization responsible for sex differences in verbal and spatial abilities is one of cerebral asymmetry. **Cerebral asymmetry** refers to the fact that different sides of the brain are specialized for different functions. The left cortex is **dominant** for, or controls, verbal functions; it controls the right hand and receives most of its input from the right ear and the right visual field (the right half of what you see). The right cortex is usually dominant for nonverbal functions, such as perception of rhythm and spatial relationships. The right cortex controls the left hand and receives most of its input from the left ear and the left visual field.

Buffery and Gray (1972) hypothesize that **lateralization,** the left hemisphere's dominance for language, occurs earliers and more completely in female brains than in male ones. This, they say, explains female superiority in verbal skills and male superiority in spatial skills, since linguistic skills "could benefit from being subserved by specific structures with a clearly lateralized and localized cerebral representation. . . . Spatial skill, however, which is usually exercised in a three dimensional and completely enclosing world, may benefit from a more bilateral cerebral representation," as that in the male (p. 144).

Evaluation.   Some data relevant to this theory has already been discussed. For example, we have seen that spatial ability is probably not X-linked, but both activational and inductive hormones may have some effects on both spatial and verbal abilities. According to these authors, verbal and spatial abilities are neural opposites, since verbal ability comes from greater lateralization and spatial ability comes from less lateralization. The two traits may, in fact, be negatively correlated, once the effect of IQ upon both of them is factored out (A. Peterson, 1976).

But the major premise of Buffery and Gray's theory is the idea of sex differences in lateralization, so much of the data relevant to their theory comes from sex differences in brain asymmetries as inferred from behavior. For example, differences in the reaction times to verbal and spatial stimuli presented to the left or right visual field or to the left or right ear are often assumed to reflect differences in lateralization. Significant sex differences have been found in such research.

Evidence on Lateralization. Buffery and Gray predict that there will be sex differences in brain lateralization of verbal and nonverbal functions. In fact, under some conditions, females do show greater activation in the right hemisphere when asked to visualize emotional stimuli (R. Davidson and Schwartz, 1976), and women show more difference between EEGs recorded from the left and right side of the brain (more cerebral asymmetry) then men do when asked to perform cognitive or emotional tasks (R. Davidson, et al., 1976).

Most of the data that Buffery and Gray cited in favor of their theory came from studies of children. They interpret these data to mean that girls lateralize earlier than boys do. These data included right-left ear differences in latencies of responses to verbal stimuli (Geffner and Hochberg, 1971; Kimura, 1963) and both in right-left differences in tactile sensitivity (Ghent, 1961), and in drawing ability of blindfolded subjects (Buffery, cited by Buffery and Gray, 1972). In all cases, females showed these differences at earlier ages than males.

The degree of lateralization is more complete for right-handed than for left-handed people. Almost all right-handed people (98–99 percent) and a majority of left handers (53–75 percent) will have left hemisphere verbal dominance, but many more left handers than right handers have mixed verbal dominance and more left handers (from 24 to 47 percent) have right hemisphere verbal dominance. Consistent with Buffery and Grays' hypothesis, more men than women are left-handed (Hicks and Kinsbourne, 1976; Hudson, 1975; Oldfield, 1971). Some data are contradictory, however. Left handedness indicates lower levels of lateralization only in those people whose families also include left-handed people (Zurif and Bryden, 1969). And sex differences in handedness are much smaller than sex differences in spatial skills (Hardyck, Goldmann, and Petrinovich, 1975).

One problem with the Buffery and Gray theory comes from their analysis of the sex differences in the effects of the removal of portions of the right or left brain in epileptics (Lansdell, 1961, 1962, 1968). Lansdell concluded from his data, contrary to Buffery and Gray, that there is more lateralization in the *male* brain. When Buffery and Gray cited Lansdell's work in support of their own, opposite, hypothesis, they tried to incoporate it into their theory by saying, "Lansdell's data could still be explained by considering the disruptive influence of the lateralized epileptogenic lesions," and even if the differences were opposite to those they would have predicted, "their very existence increases the likelihood of sex differences in the asymmetric functioning of the healthy cerebral hemisphere of the normal human adult" (p. 138–39).

There are other problems with their theory. One study found that the most verbally lateralized group of girls showed less spatial lateralization (Marcel and Rajan, 1975), suggesting that lateralization of functions is not always reciprocal. And even handedness may not be consistently related to spatial ability, as it was predicted to be by the theory. McGee (1976) found that left handedness was associated with decreased spatial ability in females, and increased spatial ability in males, when both were compared to right-handed females and males, respectively. Thus, the patterns of abilities associated with different lateralizations and handedness proposed by Buffery and Gray are not supported by these data.

Finally, it does not seem that verbal lateralization is associated with high verbal but low spatial ability, as proposed by Buffery and Gray. In fact, left-handed women with left-ear superiority, who presumably have bilateral speech and verbal ability, are the poorest of all groups on a spatial task (McGlone and Davidson, 1973). And verbal lateralization may be associated with superior spatial skills (Waber, 1976).

Conclusion: Females Are Less Lateralized Than Males. Most of Buffery and Gray's data on lateralization came from children, but more and more evidence from adults suggest that contrary to their theory, females are less lateralized than males (L. J. Harris, in press; J. Levy and Reid, 1976). There is some evidence for this. For instance, more females than males show a reversal of the typical pattern of physical symmetry in the temporal lobe, and a trend in that direction appears in infants' brains (Wada, Clark, and Hamm, 1975; Witelson and Paille, 1973).

Lake and Bryden, in reviewing (1976) the literature on right versus left ear superiority, stated that "the studies dealing with sex differences in dichotic listening [a task to test ear superiority and hence verbal brain asymmetry] are virtually unanimous in showing greater laterality effects in men than in women" (p. 275). They too gathered data of their own on sex differences in dichotic listening, and also found that males were more lateralized.

Some developmental data also suggest that lateralization is less complete or comes later in females than in males. Witelson (1976) analyzed lateralization for spatial processing in 200 normal right-handed boys and girls between six and thirteen years of age. She found no sex differences in verbal lateralization, but the boys had spatial processing more completely lateralized to the right hemisphere, and girls lateralized for spatial ability later than the boys did. Waber (1976) found that early maturers (which in an unselected sample would be mostly females) showed both less lateralization and better verbal than spatial ability after puberty, while later maturers had higher spatial than verbal scores and were more verbally lateralized after puberty. However, Waber's data were not replicated by A. Peterson (1976), and Waber found that only spatial ability and not verbal skills varied with the rate of maturation. Nevertheless, there seem to be lateralization changes with age that are related to spatial abilities.

Thus, there may be sex differences in lateralization; but it seems that males are more lateralized than females, and develop spatial lateralization faster than females. These differences may partly explain sex differences in spatial and verbal skills. Since Waber (1976) found that verbal lateralization was associated with superior spatial skills, this may be part of the reason for male superiority in spatial skills. The greater flexibility of the female brain early in development—the fact that lateralization of spatial skills occurs later—might lead women to suffer less often from the brain damage that leads to speech and hearing disorders and to autism (Witelson, 1976). This would account for some of the verbal differences between the sexes.

Although the hypothesis of Buffery and Gray was not strongly supported by more recent data, it did summarize and integrate a truly impressive amount of data. Their theory stimulated even more research. Thus, their theory was highly successful—even if not correct. And it probably could be corrected to explain most of the data.

Broverman

D. Broverman and his colleagues attributed the sex differences in spatial and verbal skills to the different effects of estrogen and testosterone upon neural functioning. Both hormones increase brain activity, and Broverman presented evidence to support his view that they do so by inhibiting MAO activity. But according to Broverman, estrogen is a stronger MAO inhibitor than testosterone, and so females have more brain activity. Because of this, females will do more poorly than males at tasks requiring some inhibition of responses such as spatial tasks. Even men with high androgen levels (automatizers) will be highly activated and so do poorly at spatial tasks. Speech, which becomes automatic with practice, does not require as much inhibition, so females are better than males in this area.

In evaluating this theory, several ideas can be suggested. One is that, a priori, it does not seem likely that spatial ability requires more inhibition than speech. In an earlier chapter, evidence was cited indicating that both estrogen and testosterone do increase brain activity. But the hormones may not work quite the way that Broverman suggests (Parlee, 1972). More importantly, even if estrogen were a stronger activator than testosterone, women also have more progesterone than men do, and progesterone inhibits brain electrical activity. However, the idea that there is an optimal level of androgen for cognitive functioning, as inferred both from body type and from the effects of injections, is consistent with some of the data.

SUMMARY AND INTERPRETATION

The sex difference in spatial ability, and perhaps that in mathematical ability, are due to a variety of genetic, hormonal, and environmental factors. Males may have a lower threshold than females for the expression of good ability. Or males may more often have favorable factors in their fetal and childhood development than females do.

It often seems that opposite-sex socialization—masculinity in females and femininity in males—facilitates cognitive performance, though there are exceptions to this. It is true that the same environment does not always have the same types of effects upon females as males, but it should never be overlooked that males are expected by society to be better in math and science, and females are expected to be more verbal. These expectations could influence performance.

The sex differences in verbal ability are probably solely due to environmental and stereotyped differences. Verbal ability has a genetic component, but the genes are not sex-linked. To determine the relationships between lateralization and verbal and spatial ability, one would have to measure all three traits in individuals whose cerebral dominance for verbal and nonverbal functions has been determined and who also vary in their family backgrounds for handedness. Until then, the most conservative conclusion is that sex differences in verbal ability are the result of sex differences in rearing practices, starting at birth, where a mother more often imitates and verbally stimulates her female than her male infants.

The causes of sex differences in other areas are even more obscure. Some differences can be attributed to sex differences in spatial, verbal, or mathematical abilities or in anxiety levels. The sex difference in genius seems to be solely a function of socialized differences in achievement motivations and in society's different evaluations of the achievements of women compared to men. Important sex differences in cognitive abilities are those in the correlations among the different kinds of ability. The sexes may not think the same way about a given type of problem, and a given level of ability may be associated with different behavioral traits in males than in females.

One of the major implications of this chapter is that sex differences should not be ignored. The mathematical portion of the National Merit Scholarship Test is so heavily weighted with the types of items on which males do better that almost no girls could become finalists in equal competition (Garai and Scheinfeld, 1968; Jarvik, 1975). So a quota was set—the final group had to be 25 percent female. Is this the fairest solution? Obviously the long-term solution is to identify and eliminate the factors that make some questions easier for one sex. But until then, what do we do?

KEY TERMS AND CONCEPTS

Spatial ability
Field independence
Creativity
Disembedding
Analytic abilities

Set breaking
Locus of control
Cerebral asymmetry
Cerebral dominance
Lateralization of function

QUESTIONS ON KEY ISSUES

1. What is Maccoby and Jacklin's suggested timetable for sex differences in development, and why?
2. What are the major sex differences in intellectual performance?
3. What are the four hypotheses proposed to explain the relative lack of women geniuses, and what is the evidence relevant to each?
4. What evidence is there that the father is important in the development of sex differences in all areas of intellectual ability? And what does the mother do that creates sex differences?
5. What evidence suggests that androgyny may facilitate creativity and intellectual development?
6. Evaluate the evidence that there are biological biases for sex differences in

spatial ability, mathematical ability, and verbal ability.
7. What are the major cultural and parental variables that affect verbal, spatial, and mathematical abilities, and in what way are each of them affected?
8. How can sex differences be experimentally manipulated and what are the implications of this?
9. If sex differences exist in verbal, spatial, and mathematical abilities at this time (regardless of their origin), how could this be fairly taken into account in evaluating aptitude and achievement test scores?
10. What is the evidence indicating that the typical man and the typical woman think differently from one another?
11. What was Buffery and Gray's hypothesis

about sex differences in lateralization, and what evidence suggests that they might be wrong?

12. Judging from the available data, how might sex differences in lateralization be related to sex differences in verbal and spatial skills?

13. Compare Broverman's theory to Maccoby's theory of sex difference in cognitive performance—similarities and differences. Are males better at inhibition?

CHAPTER 9

Achievement and Motivation for Success and Failure

There are some consistent sex difference in abilities, but they are small and highly variable. They are much too small to account for the sex differences in achievement that have been recorded across time and among nations, including differences in professional achievements, differences in Nobel and Pulitzer prize winning, and differences in the incidence of genius. To account for these differences we must turn to some socialized differences in motivation. There may also be some sex differences in the expectations and evaluation of behavior by society, as summarized in the section on prejudice. Perhaps women achieve less often because they are socialized to value some types of achievement less than males value them. It has also been hypothesized that females actually fear success. Differences in achievement may also be explained by different expectancies for success and different explanations for failure; both tendencies do affect performance. This chapter will evaluate these possibilities.

NEED FOR ACHIEVEMENT AND FEAR OF SUCCESS

Perhaps men and women have been socialized to differentially value achievement, or to differentially value different kinds of achievement. In view of the data presented in Chapter 7 on differences in sex roles and sex typing, it seems reasonable to hypothesize that women have been socialized to view achievement outside the home as less important for them, or less appropriate for them, than men do. Or it could be that women direct their achievement efforts toward different goals; women might value being good parents more than men do, while men might value academic and occupational achievements more highly than women do. Or it could be that women have been taught to fear success because of what succeeding might do to their own self-concepts or the opinions held of them by others.

Introduction to the Achievement Motive

The Logic, Reliability, and Validity of Some Common Tests of Achievement. McClelland, Atkinson, and Clark (1949) developed a system for scoring achievement motivation in men. They used the **Thematic Apperception Test (TAT),** a projective test that consists of a series of pictures depicting situations open to interpretation in which people are shown in a variety of settings that might have something to do with achievement. The subjects were asked to write stories about the pictures, describing what the people in the pictures were doing and thinking, and what would happen next. The logic of this test is that the subject's motivation would influence the themes of his or her stories. The experimenters verified this logic in research in which food deprivation was found to increase the number of food-related themes in the TAT stories (Atkinson and McClelland, 1948).

McClelland and his colleagues (McClelland et al., 1949) gave different instructions to different groups of men and evolved a system for scoring themes of achievement motivation based on differences in the effects of the various conditions. In this experiment, the TAT was given at the end of a series of seven paper-and-pencil tests of perceptual-motor ability, and was in no way differentiated from them. The different conditions under which these tests were given ranged from relaxed, where the men were told that the tests were being tested, to success-failure, where the men were told that the tests measured IQ and leadership and that while they had passed the first of the eight tests, they had failed all of the others. Telling subjects that the tests measure IQ and leadership has since become called an *achievement* or **intellectual arousal condition,** that is, an arousal relevant to the achievement motive. The scoring system was then used to test the need for achievement(**n-ach**) of people not given arousal instructions.

Other projective tests have been devised to measure n-ach. These include French's Test (1958) and Crandall's method (1963), which use incomplete sentences and doll play. In general, all three of these projective tests predict behavior better than the paper-and-pencil tests that have also been devised (Buck, 1976).

The man with a high need to achieve on all of these tests is one who is disposed *"to find gratification in successful competition with standards of excellence through one's own efforts"* (Veroff, McClelland, and Ruhland, 1975). These men are persistent in the solution of moderately difficult tasks, set realistic task aspirations, and continually set higher and higher goals. These men are entrepreneurs, who emphasize concrete feedback and like to assume personal responsibility; they show more initiative and exploratory behavior (McClelland and Winter, 1969). McClelland (1961) even related the n-ach of the men of a society to the productivity of that society as measured by electricity consumption, number of patents granted, and extent of trade. Even the decline and fall of the Roman Empire was claimed to result from the drop in the n-ach of the men of that society when they began to be raised by slaves.

Sex Differences in the Achievement Motive.   The major sex differences in need to achieve are present in Table 9.1. There are three points to be made with regard to this table. First, *under neutral conditions, females got the higher score,* but under aroused conditions, there was no sex difference. Second, *both men and women get higher n-ach scores with TAT pictures of males than with those of females.* Is achievement a male thing? If n-ach is a stable personality disposition, why is it aroused only by male cues? Other research has also found that females' n-ach scores are higher than males' under neutral conditions (McKeachie, 1962).

TABLE 9.1

MEAN NEED FOR ACHIEVEMENT IN HIGH SCHOOL STUDENTS

	Subjects	
Conditions	Males	Females
Neutral instructions		
Males in pictures	1.94	5.76
Females in pictures	1.72	1.77
Arousal instructions		
Males in pictures	4.93	5.22
Females in pictures	1.57	1.92

Source: D. C. McClelland, J. W. Atkinson, R. A. Clark, and F. L. Lowell, *The Achievement Motive* tables 6.2 and 6.4, pp. 167, 172. Copyright 1953, © 1976 by Irvington Publishers, Inc., New York. Reprinted by permission.

But in using Mehrabian's male and female paper-and-pencil tests of need to achieve (1968), males get higher scores than females.

However, the sex difference that has received the most attention is that arousal increased the scores only of males; because of this finding, it was concluded that *the achievement motive has only been validated for males*. So when McClelland (1961) reported the results of testing men from at least thirteen different societies, he never mentioned women. In fact, until recently most achievement research has ignored women. But why these sex differences in n-ach? As McClelland and his colleagues stated, if women have a higher need to achieve, "why don't women's scores increase under experimental arousal? This is the puzzler" (McClelland et al., 1953, p. 178).

Sex Differences in Adult Need to Achieve: Three Hypotheses

There are several possible reasons for the sex differences in the need to achieve. One is that the difference really reflects differences in **fear of failure**; if women fear failure more than men, they will avoid achievement situations, they will give up after failure, and their achievement scores will not be increased by arousal instructions because of this conflict between achievement approach and failure avoidance (O'Leary, 1974). In fact, it has been found that girls are more likely than boys to avoid situations of probable failure and to give up or withdraw after failure (Crandall and Rabson, 1960).

Another possibility was proposed by Horner (1972a, 1972b, 1973) who found evidence that women have a higher **fear of success.** This fear of success would not only inhibit TAT scores, but would also prevent women from seeking achievement in the real world, because of their anticipation of negative consequences following their success. Thus, women are defeated by success, whereas men are defeated by failure.

The last hypothesis combines and extends the ideas of L. W. Hoffman (1972) and of A. Stein and Bailey (1973). Perhaps females have been socialized in such a way as to fuse **affiliation and achievement** motives. This idea includes more than Hoffman's statement that women often achieve because of their affiliation motives, and more than Stein and Bailey's idea that achievement in women is directed toward a social area. Instead, this hypothesis states that achievement and affiliation are the same motives for some women (though not all), because women are taught to achieve by affiliating. A successful woman is one who marries a successful man and who raises successful children. Thus, traditional methods of measuring achievement or affiliation may not adequately tap or measure the form these traits take in many women.

Sex Differences in Fear of Failure

Do women have a greater fear of failure than men do? The direction of the sex difference in fear of failure depends on how it is measured. Sometimes fear of failure is assessed by measures of test anxiety; when this is done, there are frequently no sex differences found, though when differences do appear, women score higher (Maccoby and Jacklin, 1974). Using a questionnaire to measure sex differences in fear of failure, Horner (1972a) found no sex difference, but L. W. Hoffman's replication found that females received higher scores (L. W. Hoffman, 1974). In projective measures of fear of failure, males or females can score significantly higher (Berens, 1972; Veroff et al., 1975; Vollmer and Almås, 1974). Berens also found that high n-ach boys were significantly lower in fear of failure than were high n-ach girls, but low n-ach children did not differ in fear of failure scores.

Thus, there is no consistency in the data; fear of failure cannot explain sex differences in n-ach.

Sex Differences in Fear of Success

Horner's Original Research.   In 1965, Horner presented the following sentence stem (based on French's test of achievement) to men: "After first-term finals, John finds himself at the top of his medical school class." Women were given the same stem, but with Anne in place of John. Both sexes were asked to write stories about these people, receiving instructions similiar to those for the TAT n-ach test. According to Horner's scoring of these stories, 65 percent of the women, but only 10 percent of the men, told stories that showed evidence of a motive to avoid success (Horner, 1972a).

There were four types of fear of success (FOS) themes (Horner, 1973). The most frequent female FOS theme reflected *fears of social rejection*. As one story went, "Anne is an acne-faced bookworm. She runs to the bulletin board and finds she's at the top. As usual she smarts off. A chorus of groans is the rest of the class's reply. . . . All the Friday and Saturday nights without dates, fun . . .—she wonders what she really has' " (Horner, 1973). As another example: "Anne doesn't want to be number one in her class . . . she feels she shouldn't rank so high because of social reasons. She drops down to ninth in her class and then marries the boy who graduates number one." Or: "Anne is pretty darn proud of herself, but everyone hates and envies her." Another common theme reflected *concern about the definition of womanhood*. "She is worried about herself and wonders if perhaps she isn't normal." "Anne feels guilty. She will finally have a nervous breakdown, quit medical school and marry a successful young doctor." The third type involved _denial._ "Anne is a code name for a non-existent person." "Anne is really happy she's on top, although Tom is higher than she." "It was luck that Anne came out on top because she didn't want to go to medical school anyway." (This last story is especially typical of women, as we shall see in the last section of this chapter.) The last type reflected _bizarre stories:_ "Anne starts proclaiming her surprise and joy. Her fellow classmates are so disgusted with her behavior that they jump on her in a body and beat her. She is maimed for life."

Horner (1972a, 1972b, 1973) also talked about the effects and correlates of FOS in women. Each subject in her experiment was tested twice on a number of achievement tasks, once alone and once with a large, mixed-sex group. Thirteen of the seventeen women high in FOS did worse in the competition situation; twelve of the thirteen low-FOS women and 67 percent of the men did better in the competition situation. Eleven of twelve women high in FOS who were interviewed later changed their career plans in college to a more traditionally female occupation, but only one of the four low in this fear did so. The girls high in FOS reported A's as C's to their boyfriends, although high-FOS women were more likely to be honors students. Those girls who were low in FOS and those who were high in FOS but were still interested in pursuing masculine careers had boyfriends who encouraged them academically; however, the assumption among both boyfriends and girlfriends was that the male was the smarter of the two. Women high in FOS also responded with bizarre or hostile stories to a sentence meant to measure need for affiliation: "Gun in hand she is waiting for her stepmother to return home."

However, the research since Horner's study has not strongly supported her conclusions or results (see the September, 1976, issue of _Sex Roles,_ which was devoted to fear of success). When L. W. Hoffman (1974) redid Horner's experiment, she found that while 65 percent of the women wrote stories with FOS imagery, so did 77 percent of the men; thus, the sex difference in FOS had disappeared. One study found that FOS increased with education (Caballero, Giles, and Shaver, 1975), as Horner would have predicted, since one fears success only if success is a real possibility. However, another study found that both men and women in law school with high FOS had gotten lower scores on the law boards (R. Curtis, Zanna, and Campbell, 1975). Both Spence (1974) and Eme and Lawrence (1976) found that FOS did not correlate with SAT scores or with grade point averages. Finally, while females may be less willing than males to tell other people of their good grades, this tendency was not related to FOS for law school students (R. Curtis et al., 1975). Thus, not all of Horner's original results have been replicated.

Type of Occupation and Gender. The sex differences in the incidence of FOS imagery depend upon the type of occupation contained in the sentence stem, the sex of the stimulus figure, and the nature of the competition, as can be seen in Table 9.2. The greatest number of FOS themes are told by both males and females in the context of success in opposite-sex occupations. Overall, males were more anxious about Anne's success than females, especially if all of her classmates were men. Another study found that a single female elicited more FOS imagery than a married male or female in both men and women (Spence, 1974).

The type of FOS theme that appears in the stories is also affected by the sex

TABLE 9.2

SEX DIFFERENCES IN FEAR OF SUCCESS IMAGERY

	Sex of Subject	
	Males	Females
Medical School		
John	40%	20%
Anne	70	50
Nursing School		
John	63	65
Anne	50	13
Half of Anne's Medical School Classmates are Women	46	35
All of Anne's Medical School Classmates are Men	72	40

Sources: F. Cherry and K. Deaux, "Fear of Success vs. Fear of Gender-Inconsistent Behavior: A Sex Similarity." Paper presented at the Midwestern Psychological Association, Chicago, May 1975. M. E. Lockheed, "Female Motive to Avoid Success. A Psychological Barrier or a Response to Deviancy?" *Sex Roles,* 1975, 1, pp. 41–50.

of the subject and the sex of the stimulus person. Male stories about John, compared to female stories about Anne, more often questioned the value of achievement (30 percent versus 15 percent), attributed success to luck (9 percent versus 1 percent), and were cynical (18 percent versus 4 percent). Women writing stories about Anne are more often concerned with affiliative losses, such as losses of a boyfriend or girlfriend, brought on by success (42 percent versus 15 percent) (L. W. Hoffman, 1974). However, many of these studies confounded sex of subject with sex of stimulus person. The original studies had males write only about males and females about females. The sex differences in stories were attributed to the sex of the subject. But when later studies had both males and females write about both Anne and John, it became clear that the difference in results was due to the sex of the stimulus figure, and not the subject. For instance, when both women and men wrote about Anne, the frequency of fear of affiliative loss was the same (Spence, 1974; Winchel, Fenner, and Shaver, 1974).

However, even in studies in which both males and females write about both Anne and John, some differences caused by gender of the subject do appear. When men wrote stories about Anne's success in a medical school class where she was the only female, they wrote that she succeeded because she distracted everybody else, or that men helped her cheat, or that men helped her succeed in return for sexual favors, or that she found herself turning into a man (Lockheed, 1975). These themes are common attributions made by both females and males when asked to explain the success of a female. Also, in their stories male subjects more often killed the females off (Spence, 1974).

Social Class and Sex Roles.   FOS may be affected by social class, but the data are inconsistent. In some studies, neither social class nor the sex of the examiner had any effect on women's FOS (R. Curtis et al., 1975; Weston and Mednick, 1970). This is inconsistent with Horner's earlier research, which found that most high-FOS women had come from the middle or upper class (1972a).

Type of education may affect FOS. Having attended a coeducational school affected FOS, but only in females (in this case FOS was measured by summing over John and Anne cues) (Winchell et al., 1974). Females who attended a non-coed grade school had a very low incidence of FOS imagery. Coed grade schools increased FOS imagery, especially if the high school was also coed. This latter result may partly explain why women achievers have usually attended women's colleges (Tidball, 1973; Tidball and Kistiakowsky, 1976).

Sex roles also do not seem consistently related to FOS in either women or men (Depner and O'Leary, 1976; Tresemer, 1976; Zuckerman and Wheeler, 1975). Still, the relationship of sex roles and FOS in males has been little studied. However, FOS affects the behavior of women differently, depending upon their sex roles, even though women with different sex roles may not differ in the degree of FOS. For example, FOS may decrease competitiveness only in women with traditional sex roles (Peplau, 1976). Tangri (1972, 1975) divided college women into a traditional group (those going into an occupation in which 50 percent or more of the people were women) and a role-innovator group (those choosing occupations with fewer than 28 percent women in them). These two groups did not differ in mean FOS scores, but FOS was associated with lower n-ach scores only in the traditional group. On the other hand, the absence of FOS in the role innovators was associated with those women's stressing the importance of advancement, leadership, and salary to their future occupations, job aspects that usually do not seem very important to women.

Predictive Validity and Reliability of Horner's Measure of FOS. Can FOS accurately predict behavior (is it valid)? And does FOS represent a stable personality trait, with a person who got a high score tending to get a relatively high score on that test on a different occasion (is it reliable)?

L. W. Hoffman (1977) had the same coders rate different stories from the same people in 1965 and again in 1974, partially to check on the reliability of scores over time. In this study, both men and women wrote stories only about same-sex stimulus figures. The 1965 stories were the same ones Horner had analyzed in her original experiments. Hoffman got questionnaires, including new stories, back from 158 out of the original 177 subjects.

In 1965, women showed more FOS than men, but by 1974, men showed more. This was because scores for women decreased significantly; men's scores did not change significantly over time. Individual men's scores, however, showed little consistency with time; a man who had high FOS in 1965 was just as likely to have low FOS in 1974 as he was to score high again. But most women who had high FOS in 1974 had had high FOS in 1965 (thirty out of thirty-three). This study found that FOS scores remained reliable for the same person only for females, and only for females did FOS decrease with age. However, most reviews of FOS have concluded that there are few consistent effects of age on FOS scores (Baruch, 1975; Zuckerman and Wheeler, 1975).

The validity of Horner's measure of FOS is also in some doubt. The FOS scores for men have not been successfully validated (L. W. Hoffman, 1977). Perhaps, as Hoffman suggested, FOS scores in men represent not a fear of success, but some questioning of the value of success. If this is true, FOS would not be related to the same behavior in men as in women.

For women, Horner's original research found some evidence for validity, suggesting that FOS did in fact lead to avoidance of success. Hoffman found that women who showed high FOS in 1965 were by 1974 more likely to have gotten married, especially to older men. They were also more likely to have had children, and to have had more children than women who had had low FOS in 1965. The most dramatic effect of FOS was in the case of women who got pregnant just after the success of their husband or lover declined relative to their own success (for example, the woman got promoted, the man lost his job). Of the fourteen "success-anticipation" pregnancies, thirteen occurred in women who had had high FOS scores in 1965. The fourteenth woman was unmarried, and aborted the baby. Thus, women who fear success may use affiliation (having a baby) to avoid it, at least if their success is greater than that of their men.

There are problems with the validity of this research, however. All this research used same-sex stimulus figures, and different results may be obtained if, for example, men write about both Anne's and John's successes. It is true that the sex difference in types of FOS themes and in overall levels of FOS often disappears under those conditions. Other research has found only limited evidence for the ability of FOS to predict women's performances in achievement situations (Patty, 1976; Tomlinson-Keasey, 1974; Tresemer, 1973; Zuckerman and Wheeler, 1975). It could be that FOS only measures culturally prescribed attitudes towards success and that FOS women will withdraw from competition only on masculine tasks, and only when competing against men; this is exactly the pattern of results that Makosky (1976) found. As mentioned before, FOS may also lead to success avoidance only in traditional women. Only under these conditions will FOS predict behavior and so have validity.

Conclusions.   FOS does not seem to be a motive that generally subtracts from need to achieve and decreases achievement strivings, as measured by achievement themes written under arousal conditions on the TAT. FOS may predict performance under certain kinds of achievement conditions, but there are too few reliable sex differences in FOS to enable us to use the concept to explain sex differences in n-ach. For example, sex differences either in the incidence of FOS or the kind of FOS are rare, when both sexes write stories about the same stimulus figure (Zuckerman and Wheeler, 1975). Instead, as Spence and Zuckerman and Wheeler have pointed out, FOS seems to measure cultural attitudes towards the achievement of men and women in our society, and FOS and achievement behavior thus reflect the same underlying attitudes.

However, the importance of Horner's innovative contribution should not be underestimated. Because of her, researchers have begun to investigate why women fail more often than men. Also because of Horner, researchers have dramatically demonstrated the existence of negative sanctions that our culture imposes upon achievement in areas traditionally belonging to the opposite sex. Women expect to be punished for achieving in male areas, such as medical school; men expect to be punished for achieving in female areas, such as nursing school.

Sex Differences in the Development and Effects of Need to Achieve

This section will examine, first, some socialization practices and their effect on n-ach, and second, their effect on the achievement patterns of adolescents. (The next section will review the differences in the adult patterns of n-ach.) This section will focus on the idea that women are often socialized to achieve by affiliating, and explore some ways this would make n-ach affect men and women differently. Also, we will look at some ways women deal with the equation of affiliation and achievement: their choices are to accept it, reject it, or try to achieve in both the male and the female way at the same time. Lest there be any doubt that achievement is equated with affiliation for women, consider this. A man is evaluated as more intelligent and richer and has higher status if he has an attractive rather than an unattractive wife; but the attractiveness of her husband does not affect the evaluation of a women. This could mean that people believe an attractive woman will be more likely to succeed as evidenced by a prestigious affiliation, but men succeed in other ways (Bar-Tal and Saxe, 1976).

Socialization of Children and Need to Achieve. In young children, it appears as though socialization to be feminine reduces n-ach in girls (Alper, 1974; L. W. Hoffman, 1972; Lesser, 1973; Maccoby and Jacklin, 1974; A. Stein and Bailey, 1973). Thus, girls feel they should not try too hard, and women feel it is unfeminine to compete vigorously, especially against a man. Also, being dependent, passive, illogical, unadventurous, gentle, and quiet—stereotypic female traits—would not seem likely to promote achievement strivings.

Maternal behavior may differentially affect boys and girls. Kagan and Moss (1962) reported that maternal protection of children from birth to age three predicted adult male achievement (the correlation for females was nonsignificant but negative), but that maternal hostility predicted female achievement. In general, the relationships between achievement and both restriction-protection and hostility are probably curvilinear, with maximal n-ach produced by moderate warmth and restrictiveness (Berens, 1972; A. Stein and Bailey, 1973). Though moderate warmth and restrictiveness produce maximal n-ach, Lesser (1973) and A. Stein and Bailey (1973) agree with Kagan and Moss that that relationship is more true in males and that in females maternal distance and hostility are more effective in increasing n-ach. Only those females who have failed to affiliate with their parents seem to develop a high need to achieve, perhaps because they are trying to affiliate through their achievements.

In addition to sex differences in socialization, there are sex differences in the behavior associated with n-ach. In the achievements of girls, affiliative factors keep appearing. For girls, n-ach scores do not correlate with achievement test scores, but they do correlate with the adequacy of their social relations; for boys, the reverse was true (L. W. Hoffman, 1972; Lesser, 1973). Social approval may have a greater effect on girls' than on boys' achievement efforts, while appeals to mastery increase the efforts of boys (L. W. Hoffman, 1972). One study looked at the academic performances of fourth graders as a function of both student type (ability and motivation) and classroom type (open and traditional) (Solomon and Kendall, 1976). Overall, boys did best in classes that were controlled and orderly and emphasized student-initiated activities; girls also did better in orderly classes, but only in those that emphasized warmth and friendliness (affiliation) rather than achievement.

Though socialization to be feminine—to be passive, affiliative, dependent, and nurturant—inhibits achievement in both sexes, girls are also encouraged to do well in school in order to win parental approval. The net effect of socialization of girls might be to fuse achievement and affiliation. For many girls achievement becomes the same as successful affiliation (or successful affiliation is achievement), particularly for those who do not feel close to their mothers. And this may later lead to conflict.

Socialization can also affect IQ scores. For grade-school boys who are low in anxiety (meaning anxiety will not interfere with either n-ach or with the way they take tests), achievement-oriented instructions (being told the test measures how smart and clever they are) significantly increased their IQ scores, from below 104 to over 109. On the other hand, girls with low anxiety did worse with achievement instructions; their IQ scores dropped from 112 to 105 (F. Young and Brown, 1973).

The above results are important because they demonstrate conditions that can produce a drop in IQ in girls. The increase in boys' IQ scores with achievement instructions is characteristic of males with a high n-ach. The drop in girls' scores under the same conditions was not due to anxiety, but must be due to a feeling that females are not supposed to be particularly smart and clever. Females may learn to achieve in order to affiliate, particularly if they cannot affiliate through other methods, but they may see too much achievement as inappropriate.

This implies that sex-role stereotypes have an impact. As discussed earlier, active, achieving boys are much more common in children's books than active, achieving girls. McArthur and Eisen (1976) verified that the sex of a storybook character who achieves affects task persistence in nursery-school children. Both sexes persisted at a task longer if they read a story about the achievement of a same-sex character than if they read about the achievement of an opposite-sex character. However, the effect was more dramatic for boys, and boys showed more persistence when the scores were averaged over all conditions. This sex difference may be due to the cumulative effect of reading about achievement by same-sex characters, which males do more often than females. Thus, the cultural stereotypes may result from and reflect differences in achievement behavior that result from differences in socialization.

Adolescence and Patterns of Achievement. Adolescence represents a time when differences in socialization begin to crystallize into adult patterns of achievement. This is the time when both sexes begin to abandon opposite-sex characteristics (Kagan and Moss, 1962). For example, boys abandon, deny, or sublimate dependency, and girls do the same for aggressiveness. And this is the time when the fusion of achievement and affiliation for girls will affect their career and life plans; this is also the time when the possibility of achievement hindering affiliation for women will begin to provide real conflicts for them, conflicts that should not appear in men.

Simmons and Rosenberg (1975) studied males and females in grades three through twelve and found striking sex differences in achievement and affiliation desires, which were exaggerated by adolescence. Females were less likely to expect to attend college and rated being popular as more important than doing things well; these differences were largest for the adolescents. F. Rosenberg and Simmons (1975) also found that adolescence is the time that girls begin to say more often than boys that they care about what people think of them and about being well liked. Adolescent boys were more concerned than girls about being at the top of their chosen profession, being successful, and being the best. Douvan and Adelson (1966) also found this age-related shift of boys to concern with occupational success and of girls to concern with social and marital success. Thus, in adolescence, boys are more concerned about personal success and girls about social success (Maccoby and Jacklin, 1974). As Douvan (1957) pointed out, identity for a male adolescent is defined by external achievement ("What is my work?"); identity for a female adolescent is defined by affiliation-achievement ("Who is my husband?").

However, school achievement is one way to achieve social success, or affiliation-achievement, for adolescent girls, although it is a route which can later lead to conflict. One measure of affiliation, popularity, is positively related to IQ for girls but not for boys, although the correlation decreases with age (Kagan and Freeman, 1963). Coleman (1961) found that for girls being a brain was almost as sure a route to popularity as was being a beauty. For boys, the athlete-scholar was the most popular. The boy who was just a scholar was considerably less popular, and he was generally less popular than was the brainy girl. But for boys, academic values increase in importance from adolescence on, while for girls, academic values decline in importance. Also, in an effort to increase popularity, girls try to avoid being better than boys all during adolescence (Maccoby and Jacklin, 1974).

Because in early adolescence the girl may achieve in order to win popularity, female achievement will often take different forms from male achievement. For example, in males from age nine to seventeen, the more prestige an occupation has, the more it is preferred, and the correlations between prestige and preference increase with age (from +.39 to +.72). For girls, the correlations of occupational prestige with preference are close to zero, while the correlations of occupational prestige with ratings of aversion for the job are positive for girls at all ages (Barnett, 1975). Instead, the achievement concerns of the adolescent female are directed more to the social-affiliation sphere. Field (as cited by Lesser, 1973) found that while giving instructions appealing to intelligence and leadership increased the n-ach scores of adolescent boys, the same instructions had no effect on the n-ach scores of adolescent girls. Instead, experimental conditions that aroused concerns about social acceptability increased the scores of girls, but not those of boys.

Lesser, Krawitz, and Packard (1962) gathered data on n-ach of a select group of high-school girls. The girls were from Hunter High School, which had highly competitive admissions criteria and accepted only about 150 of 4,000 applicants, 99 percent of whom went on to college. Even in this group of girls, instructions emphasizing IQ and leadership did not increase overall n-ach scores. The girls were also matched for IQ and classified as achievers or underachievers, based on whether their grades were in the first or the fourth quartile. Overall, achievers had higher n-ach scores on the TAT than did the underachievers. Under neutral conditions, n-ach scores were higher in stories written about pictures of men than pictures of women for both groups of girls. However, with arousal instructions, underachievers' scores increased only for pictures with males in them, while scores of achievers increased only for pictures with females. In fact, the highest n-ach scores were produced by aroused underachievers in response to pictures of males.

Thus, achievement scores mean different things for male and for female adolescents. Only for the high IQ and highly achieving girls of Hunter High School was n-ach associated more with female than with male pictures, and that was only under aroused conditions; but even for them higher scores were seen for male pictures under neutral conditions. For males, n-ach scores positively correlate with academic performance (Lesser et al., 1962), while high-scoring females are less likely to go on to college and are more likely to get a job or to marry immediately after high school (Lesser, 1973). This could mean, paradoxically, that the less feminine girls would do worse in school because they would be less oriented towards the affiliation-achievement motive. Doherty and Culver (1976), in fact, found when they matched for IQ, that these masculine girls got poorer grades.

Parental roles also affect the form of achievement strivings in adolescence, which may then affect adult achievement. Identification with the mother by females decreases their n-ach scores, unless the mother herself has atypical role aspirations, such as working and enjoying it (A. Stein and Bailey, 1973). This may well be part of the reason for McCall's results (1977). He found that the education of the mother was a much better predictor of adult occupation and adult education for females than for males. Paternal education predicted achievement in males and females equally well. Thus, whether or not the mother works, her attitude towards her job, and her educational level may be a relatively important part of the development of achievement in females, but not in males.

ACHIEVEMENT IN ADULTS

Sex Differences in Correlates of Need to Achieve

The conflicts just described can dramatically affect the correlations of n-ach and the behavior of females and males of college age and older. For example, one study found that 65 percent of the males stayed in college to become seniors, but only 59.9 percent of the females did (Brabant and Garbin, 1976). This is in spite of the fact that females tend to get higher grades in college (Maccoby, 1966).

As was mentioned earlier, women in college are more likely than men to tell their friends about C's than about A's and more likely to report A's as C's. This may be a quite realistic response, in view of the often conflicting ideas that college males and females have about females' roles (Yorburg and Arafat, 1975). Males espouse egalitarian standards for women in general, but expect that their wives will be traditional wives and mothers (Komarovsky, 1973). Also, while men value intelligent women, they are in considerable conflict about having wives who may be more intelligent than they are. Men also think that women should not have a career that interferes with childrearing, and that women should not work when they have young children at home (Rossi, 1965). Most married women without children agree that women should stay home when they have young children, but there is less agreement with this statement among married women with children.

These conflicts appear in other research with college students. Field (as cited by Lesser, 1973) found that female college students' n-ach scores were increased by instructions appealing to social acceptability but not by those aimed at intelligence and leadership. French and Lesser (1964) sampled women from six different colleges that varied in their emphasis of role values for women. Two of the colleges valued intellectual achievement and not women's role achievement; two others did not value intellectual achievement but valued women's role achievement, endorsing statements such as "college is to prepare women for marital social responsibilities"; and the last two valued both types of achievements. Using French's test with male and female stimuli combined, they found that the n-ach scores of the intellectual-achievement group increased only with intellectual arousal, whereas the n-ach scores of those that valued women's roles increased only with social arousal. However, just as Lesser and his coworkers found (1962), French and Lesser found that under intellectual arousal, the n-ach scores of all groups were higher for sentences with male subjects than for sentences with female subjects.

Friedrich (1976) recently tried to replicate the French and Lesser study, using students from just one university. Although all of the differences between groups were in the same direction as those found in the French and Lesser study, none were significant. In fact, Friedrich found very few correlations between either type of value system and achievement behavior. Even when the achievement test was scored so as to indicate women's role n-ach, the results were unimpressive; women's role n-ach scores correlated significantly but unimportantly (+.12) with college grade point average. Thus, whatever is being tapped in women by need to achieve tests of either kind, it does not predict achievement behavior.

In general, achievement behavior in college has different associations in women than in men. College classes that emphasize warmth (the teacher takes a personal interest in students or calls students by name) produce higher grades in women and lower grades in men; women also prefer warm classes, regardless of how they do in them (McKeachie, 1961). Need for power (social influence over others) affected only the grades of men. Classes also differed in competitiveness; women with a high n-ach do better in noncompetitive psychology classes while men with a high n-ach do best in more competitive psychology classes. However, overall, class competitiveness has more effect on the grades of men than on the grades of women (McKeachie, 1961).

Thus, the typical tests may not adequately measure the form that achievement takes in most women because of the fusion of affiliation and achievement. For example, Bardwick (1971) found that college women usually gave interpersonal (affiliative) responses to the questions: What would make you happy? Or sad? Or angry? In our laboratory (K. B. Hoyenga, unpublished data), when those questions were put to 130 men and women, women more often fused achievement and affiliation ("I'm happiest when I can succeed at something that will also make other people happy") than men did (50 percent versus 15 percent). But men more often than women mentioned achievement by itself ("Being the best at something makes me happiest") (32 percent versus 24 percent). Alper (1974) also found that feminine women often wrote TAT stories combining affiliation and achievement.

There is other evidence that adult women equate achievement and affiliation, and that equation may produce conflicts. Walker and Heyns (1962) explicitly put affiliation and achievement in conflict for college men and women by placing them in a contest and then having a good friend send them a (bogus) request to slow down so that the friend could win their contest. Almost all of the men did not slow down, but most of the women did. The only women who did not slow down were those whose n-ach scores were higher than their scores on a test of a need to affiliate. Perhaps because of this conflict between achievement and affiliation, women honor students have a lower self-concept than male honor students, and a lower one than males and females who are not honor students (M. McEwen, 1975). The same was found to be true of high school girls with an A average (O'Leary, 1974). These women were evidently not able to let male achievement give them a good self-concept, perhaps because they felt they were failing in affiliation.

Many women apparently resolve this conflict by deciding to achieve solely through affiliation, no longer trying to achieve affiliative success through other kinds of achievement. Davis and Olsen (1965) asked female nursing students to rank the importance of the following qualities in their future lives: beauty, devotion to family, activity in community affairs, and dedication to work and career. Over 87 percent put home and family first. Although in one group, 82 percent gave career second place when they entered school, this was reduced to 61 percent by the time of graduation. A. Rossi (1965) found that while recent college graduates admired professional women more than other types of women, the type of success they preferred for themselves was to be the "mother of several highly accomplished children" and the "wife whose husband becomes very prominent."

Affiliation is a common theme throughout the literature on the achievement strivings of adult women. Affiliation is often fused with achievement, but the fusion often brings conflicts of its own. Affiliation is less often a factor in men's achievement desires, probably because they do not expect family and career to be in conflict. As we will see, however, this may be somewhat unrealistic on their part, especially in these times of changing sex roles.

Three Groups of Women

By adult life, women seem to take one of three courses: they deny the women's role achievement, they try to achieve in both women's role and in men's role areas, or they continue to fuse achievement with affiliation, evidently losing something with each.

The Traditional Woman. Women who have fused affiliation and achievement are in the majority, and they are commonly called **traditional**. They may look for an occupation, but only in a traditional area, and they do not work while their children are young except out of economic necessity. This group of women would therefore include two of A. Rossi's groups (1965), homemakers and women with traditional occupations. As Rossi said, the traditionals were much more similar to the homemakers than to those women with untraditional careers.

Traditional women do not look for success in order to increase their own self-esteem; they look for vicarious achievement by their husband or future husband achieving—his success (and failure) becomes theirs. There is a stronger relationship between family income and the n-ach scores of wives than of husbands (Lesser, 1973). These women want to achieve primarily through highly accomplished children and prominent husbands (A. Rossi, 1965). These women probably correspond to the unambivalently feminine girls, described by Douvan and Adelson (1966), who had low educational goals and who preferred security to success. These traditional women are also likely to come from a home in which the mother did not work (Birnbaum, 1975; Tangri, 1972, 1975).

Traditional women show unique relationships between both n-ach and FOS and behavior. FOS is associated with lower n-ach scores, although the FOS scores of these women may be lower than those of unmarried women or women without children (Makosky, 1976; Tomlinson-Keasey, 1974). Perhaps choosing to achieve through affiliation gives them less cause to fear success. White women who fear success may have more children, though this is not true for black women (Moore, cited by C. Smith, 1976). This is not surprising in view of L. Hoffman's (1977) finding that most of the women who got pregnant in the face of impending success relative to their men's success had had FOS as college students. N-ach is even associated with liking housework for the traditional woman. For women without a college education, n-ach scores, measured by pictures of women in both domestic and career situations, correlated positively with favorable attitudes towards housework (Lesser, 1973).

Another study looked at traditional women as those who were planning to enter a traditional field and for whom being married and having children was very important. These women, compared to less traditional ones, had a lower need to achieve and a higher need to affiliate (Trigg and Perlman, 1976). In fact, need to affiliate seemed one of the most important determiners of what career they chose.

However, the adult homemaker—at least if intellectually gifted—may have the lowest self-esteem of all the groups of women, even in the area of child care (Birnbaum, 1975). Housewives married to professional men also report more life pressures and worries than do working wives, and are less happy with their marriages (Burke and Weir, 1976a). These relationships may be less true for women lower in IQ or for women married to nonprofessional men.

So many women fuse achievement and affiliation, seeking achievement for themselves, if at all, only in traditional areas and only so long as the search does not interfere with what they regard as their primary responsibilities and interests. Their primary sense of achievement comes from their affiliative roles and success in those roles and also, vicariously, from their husband's success. But their primary doubts about themselves may also come from those areas, almost as if secondhand success were not quite enough.

The Doubly Achieving Woman.   Women who try to achieve in both masculine and feminine ways often show evidence of strain. They want to be good wives, good mothers, and competent professionals, but there are only so many hours in a day.

The **doubly achieving women** often come from homes in which mothers were educated and had worked (Birnbaum, 1975; Tangri, 1972). As children, they were tomboys—competitive, active, and even aggressive. These women might correspond to Douvan and Adelson's (1966) ambivalently feminine adolescent girls, who were interested in both family and achievement. These adolescent girls often modeled themselves after nonfamily women or after masculine figures. In fact, the personality of working wives, as a group, was more similar to the personality of men than to the personality of housewives (Burke and Weir, 1976b).

But these doubly achieving women often place jobs and career plans second, behind their families. In a projective exercise, husbands and children were placed in conflict with career goals for women just beginning to try to combine family with career (Halas, 1974). The women met the family's needs first, even if it meant sacrificing a career goal. These women are likely to say that their husband's careers are more important to them than their own (A. Rossi, 1965). They also say they pursue their own career only because they perceive that their husbands could do still better (Birnbaum, 1975). They value their achievement, but they perceive that their husbands achieve even more. For example, college women choosing a nontraditional career (medicine or dentistry) had boyfriends or families who supported their choices (Trigg and Perlman, 1976). So these women may need the approval, as well as the success, of people important to them before they feel free to achieve on their own.

The doubly achieving women, even though they placed their families first, still worried about their affiliation achievement. They felt tied down by their children, but they worried about being a good mother (Birnbaum, 1975) and about having enough time for their family (Burke and Weir, 1976a). It is also interesting to note that divorce is two and half times more likely for a female scientist than for a male scientist (*New Scientist,* 1976). These women may have to achieve affiliative success—a successful husband and healthy children—before they can feel free to attempt achievement in other areas.

The Role Innovator.   The single professional woman denies women's roles and affiliative achievements for herself (Birnbaum, 1975; A. Rossi, 1965). Instead, she tries to succeed only in the male way. The background of these women is quite different from that of women in the other two groups. The role innovator often comes from a lower-class background, with a nonworking mother. Her parents were traditional and somewhat distant. She dated less than the other two types of women, and was a tomboy, although she did not play with all-girl groups at all (doubly achieving women were tomboys, but also played in all-girl groups). These women might develop from Douvan and Adelson's (1966) achievement-oriented adolescents. They often think about marrying, just as the achievement-oriented girls did, but marriage is not central to the plans of either group. Some of these women might also come from Douvan and Adelson's "antifeminine" group, adolescent girls who said they did not want to marry, who had traditional, restrictive, and punitive parents. These adolescents also wished that they had been born boys, and even menstruated later than the other groups.

The role innovator rates herself as more dominant and occupationally aggressive than do women in the other two groups. However, the conflict over affiliation still remains in these role innovators. They do not react positively to children. They agree that husbands' careers are more important than those of their wives, and so feel conflict over marrying because they expect their own careers to be the most important source of satisfaction to them and do not want to give them up. Furthermore, unlike the married professional, who often finds the intrinsic aspects of a job the most satisfying, the most important part of the single professional's job is the interpersonal gratification it provides (Birnbaum, 1975). These women are also in conflict over dependency, seeking to affiliate with students, patients, and colleagues, but perhaps they end up needing too much and actually keep people away. They often feel lonely. However, they still find themselves busy, happy, satisfied, competent, productive, and worthwhile. These women place achievement for themselves first, but may feel doubts about themselves because of their lack of affiliative success.

So all three groups of women show the conflict over the equation of affiliation and achievement. This conflict does not exist for men, at least not in the same form. Men expect family relationships to be important to their satisfaction, but they do not anticipate conflict (A. Rossi, 1965). However, this expectation may be somewhat unrealistic.

Achievement and Affiliation in Men

Men also differ in the degree to which they value and attempt to integrate family and career, and the way they value affiliation affects the happiness of their marriage (Bailyn, 1970). In one sample of 217 married men, 58 percent said that they derived more satisfaction from their families than from their careers, whereas 27 percent reported that their careers were the most important aspect of their satisfaction with life. The success of the marriage was related to which type of woman these men married. Not unexpectedly, if a doubly achieving woman married a career-oriented man, the marriages were generally unhappy. But, surprisingly, in the case of traditional couples (career-oriented men and traditional women), the more children they had, the less happy the marriage. Also, the greater the family income, the less happy was the traditional marriage. Both of these relationships suggest that achieving traditional success by neither the husband nor the wife necessarily leads to a happy marriage. When a family-oriented man married a doubly achieving woman, however, marital happiness increased with family income and was not related to the number of children.

The way a man deals with achievement and affiliation interacts with the way his wife deals with them in determining marital happiness. But, overall, the husband's orientation is more important than the wife's in determining marital happiness.

Just as women try to succeed vicariously through the achievement of their husbands, men try to experience emotions vicariously through their wives' reactions. If the woman expresses fear, the husband may vicariously experience that fear, and thus be able to express it without feeling unmasculine. This may also be true for the emotions involving closeness and love (Tresemer and Pleck, 1973). Burke and Weir (1976a, 1976b) have looked at husbands of working wives and those of nonworking wives, and have found some effects that might be explained by saying that the husbands have only a vicarious emotional life. The husbands of housewives were more concerned with authority and dominance and were less concerned with affiliation, perhaps because their wives were affiliating for them. Husbands of working wives reported greater job pressures and were more dissatisfied with their job and with their marriage. There were also indications that husbands with working wives were in poorer psychological and physical health than the husbands of nonworking wives. Husbands of working wives also worried more about communicating with and showing affection to their wives. On the other hand, another study indicates that husbands of working women find their own jobs more intrinsically interesting, whereas husbands of nonworking women or of women with more traditional jobs emphasize the monetary and authoritarian aspects of their jobs (Winter, Stewart, and McClelland, 1977).

Finally, men have an impact on whether their wife is a traditional woman or a doubly achieving woman, which depends as much on her husband as on her own attitudes, aspirations, and background. Winter and his colleagues (Winter et al., 1977) measured motivation in college men in 1960 and then looked at their marriages and the working roles of their wives in 1974. Men who had had a high need for power in 1960, a need for having an impact on others, tended not to have working wives. But men who had had a high need to affiliate tended to have professional wives. This difference could be the result of different criteria for mate selection used by these men or by the women. But the difference also seems to be the result of pressures applied by the man. These pressures affect whether or not his wife has a career, and if so, what kind of career. Men with a high need for power may find having a working wife to be very aversive since that increases her power relative to his; men with a high need to affiliate may be more supportive.

Conclusions and Implications

The pattern of socialization for achievement creates a conflict between affiliation and achievement that can lead to problems for both men and women. For men, the problems may occur when their wife cannot or will not live their emotional life for them. A woman without a man may be viewed by herself and others as somehow being a failure. Also, women may need the approval of a successful man before they can feel free to achieve on their own. Socialization has also left each sex dependent upon the other for complete expression of its capabilities. The husband may depend upon the wife for his social-emotional success; thus, if she fails (makes a social error), he may feel that he also failed, become extremely angry, and claim that she has let him down, a feeling that may be shared by the wife. The wife, in turn, may feel as proud of her husband's occupational success as she would her own, because, in a way, it is hers. And his failure may also damage her self-esteem.

The people, single and married, who try to live out some other role patterns often find that they must overcome their own socialized evaluations and dependencies. The woman who tries to suceed in both male and female ways and the single career woman are both concerned about their affiliative success and failure. Husbands of working women may also experience role strain for similar reasons; they have not learned how to take on part of the social-emotional burden of house and family. But as difficult as those paths are, following the traditional pattern is no guarantee of fulfillment either.

Men may question the value of success for themselves and value their family more than their career, but they still (perhaps unrealistically) expect that only women will suffer affiliative loss as a consequence of success. However, the man with a high n-ach who cannot succeed in the traditional male role has no other socially sanctioned road to achievement, and so must come to terms with that failure. He may stop trying, saying that success was not worth it anyway, so that failure is attributed to the lack of effort on his part rather than to any intrinsic defect within him. Or he may say that he was plagued by bad luck or the ill will of others. In the next section, we will see that men claim just that.

OTHER ACHIEVEMENT VARIABLES

Another sex difference in the area of achievement has to do with the way men and women view their own performance. This includes their expectation of success, who they perceive controls their life (themselves or others), and the reasons they give for success or failure. In all of these areas there are sex differences, and they all affect performances in achievement situations.

Expectation of Success

In most ages tested and for almost any task, women have a lower expectation of success and lower personal standards for performance than men (Crandall, 1969; Frieze, 1975; Nicholls, 1975; A. Stein and Bailey, 1973). And, generally speaking, people who expect to do better, actually *do* better, including in school (Crandall, 1969). First-grade girls have higher occupational aspirations than boys, but this is reversed by the fifth grade: the fact that the parents of both first- and fifth-grade girls have lower aspirations for their children than do the parents of boys may have caused the girls' aspirations to decline. (Brook et al., 1974). This sex difference in expectancy of success is also seen in Norway (Vollmer, 1975). And cross-cultural surveys show that boys boast and praise themselves more often than girls (Whiting and Edwards, 1973).

Several hypotheses as to the causes of sex differences in the expectancy of success seen from first grade on were examined and rejected by Crandall (1969). She found that IQ scores and actual performances could not account for this difference. She also ruled out both the possibility that achievement had different values for girls and boys, and the possibility that different social pressures made women more hesitant to boast. Crandall found that males and females were not differentially sensitive either to positive or to negative feedback (reward and punishment) in the laboratory, and so either rewarding correct responses or punishing errors (as with bad grades) produces equal performance in females and males. She also suggested that different reinforcement histories are probably not involved, even in school. But in fact, not only do girls get better grades, Biller (1974) also cited evidence indicating that boys receive more negative reactions and criticisms and more often have their performances underrated by teachers, both of which would certainly not produce a higher expectency of success in males.

However, Crandall found that contradictions within the environment (for example, having the lowest class standing in a high-ability class), produce the largest sex difference in hope of success. When the feedback is mixed, boys focus more on the positive and girls on the negative aspects of their aspects of their situations. Crandall had also found earlier (Crandall and Rabson, 1960), that boys return to tasks at which they had failed, especially as they grow older, but girls of all ages withdraw after failure. Girls also withdraw from threat more often, and more often ask for help and approval from adults rather than peers. The expectancy of success of girls and women is lower than that of males because females focus more on negative feedback and thus are more affected by it.

Women do not have a lower expectancy of success than men in all areas of achievement. As Crandall (1969) concluded, females might have a lower expectancy of success only in situations of mixed feedback, where females focus more on the negative aspects than males do. In one review of this area, Lenney (1977) identified other aspects of a situation most likely to produce a lower expectancy of success in women than in men. First, the type of task is relevant. Lenney said that the more appropriate the task is to the female sex role, as in the case of verbal or interpersonal tasks, the less likely women are to devalue their chances of success. Second, the less explicit the feedback for performance is, the more likely it is that women will have a lower expectancy of success. Third, when women expect to have their work evaluated by others, they are more likely to have lower ability estimates. Finally, a woman's satisfaction with her work depends more upon her partner's success or failure than does a man's.

Locus of Control

Women also feel that external factors control their lives to a greater extent than men do. Boys see themselves as having more strength, dominance, or power than girls see themselves having. Rotter's locus-of-control scale (1966) was used to test people from college age on. Women were found to perceive themselves as having a more external locus of control, as having a lack of personal control over their lives (Maccoby and Jacklin, 1974; Nisbett and Temoshok, 1976). One study looked at locus of control in people from five different countries and found that women believed they had a more external locus of control in all of them (McGinnies et al., 1974).

Achievement is related to locus of control. Mehrabian (1968) found that a high n-ach score for both males and females was associated with having an internal locus of control ($r = .64$ and $r = .41$ for males and females, respectively). Maccoby and Jacklin (1974) reported that an internal locus of control was more associated with school achievement in boys and men than in girls and women. Also, FOS may be associated with having an external locus of control, especially for males (Tresemer, 1976; K. B. Hoyenga, Wallace, and Mathes, unpublished data). Believing in an external locus of control seems to inhibit achievement in men, but does not have as strong an effect for women; so here, as in the case of most of the achievement research, men's achievement behaviors are easier to predict and are more consistent than those of women.

In interpreting this data, we should realize that much of the locus-of-control scale is made up of sex-role stereotypic items (Hochreich, 1975). Consequently, sex differences in scale scores might reflect the stereotypes rather than sex differences in locus of control. In support of this idea, sex-role stereotyped people have a more external locus of control based on the scores from that test than those who were less stereotyped (Minnigerode, 1976).

Problems with the Rotter scale, including its use of sex-role stereotypic traits, may account for its relatively low correlation with academic achievment in adults. Using a different locus of control scale, Duke and Nowicki (1974) found that an internal locus of control was related to high achievement for males (+.50), but that an external locus of control predicted achievement for females (+.39). They replicated this on three different samples. This is not surprising if women do in fact achieve in order to affiliate; affiliation depends on other people, on external factors.

Although locus of control shows consistent sex differences, some may be more related to the female stereotype than to achievement. An internal locus of control does facilitate achievement in males, and an external locus of control may be more important for females. Again, this is entirely consistent with the hypothesis that achievement equals affiliation for women, since successful affiliation depends upon external factors—other people—even though that affiliation may be sought through academic achievement. So achievement seems to be a more complex motive in women than in men.

Attributions

Sex differences also appear when women and men are asked to explain why they think they succeeded or failed at some task (Deaux, 1976; Frieze, 1975; A. Stein and Bailey, 1973). When men succeed, they attribute the success to their ability. However, women who suceed say that their sucess was due to hard work or to luck. The reverse is true for failure. Men more often than women attribute their failure to lack of effort or to bad luck, while women attribute failure to lack of ability. Even in a group situation, when the group fails, women feel more personal shame than men (Frieze, 1975). If there are sex differences in attributions, failure will obviously have different effects on men and women. Women would tend to give up after failure—if failure is due to lack of ability, they feel that they could not do it anyway—while men would redouble their efforts, since their failure was due to lack of effort, not lack of ability. In fact, the energizing effect of failure is often seen in the man with a high n-ach. For example, failure on an exam increased the hope of success of men but not of women (Vollmer and Almås, 1974).

Nicholls (1975) explicitly tested the relationship between aspiration level, performance, and attributions. He subjected fourth-grade girls and boys performing a task to either two successes, a success followed by a failure, or a failure followed by a success. Girls, but not boys, attributed failure to poor ability more often than they attributed success to good ability. Boys more than girls attributed failure to bad luck. In line with these attributions and in support of Crandall's theory (1969), girls had a lower expectancy of success than boys when success was later followed by failure, but not in the other two conditions. Similarly, boys but not girls increased their efforts after failure feedback (since for boys failure was due to bad luck, luck might change). Thus, the attributions of girls exaggerated negative feedback, lowered their aspirations, and decreased their performance. Similar effects have also been seen by other researchers (Dweck and Bush, 1976; Dweck and Repucci, 1973).

The sex difference in the attribution of causes of success and failure also appears when both sexes explain the success and failure of other people. In one study, the success of a male graduate student was attributed to ability, and the failure of a male was attributed to an unfair allegation of cheating (bad luck). A woman's failure was seen as caused by lack of ability, but her success was due to luck, such as having easy courses or getting away with cheating (Feather and Simon, 1975). When subjects were given descriptions of people performing various activities, males were seen as having greater ability than females, even if neither of them had been pictured as doing anything. But if a female performed well on a masculine task (such as helping to capture a robber), she received a high rating in effort, but not in ability (Taynor and Deaux, 1973). And many of the fear of success stories told by women and men about Anne's succeeding in a male field also followed these patterns of attributions. For example, it was claimed that she succeeded because she had good luck, or cheated, or used her sex appeal as a bribe.

This sex difference in attributions affects the sort of games that each gender prefers to play. Deaux, White, and Farris (1975) found that task preferences, both at a county fair and in the laboratory, were consistent with this sex difference. Males preferred games of skill while females preferred games of chance. If you go to Las Vegas, you can see that poker players are almost exclusively males, while the slot machines are played mostly by women. Most poker players see their game as involving more skill than luck, whereas very little skill is required to play the slot machines.

However, in the attribution of causes of success and failure as in expectancy of success, the nature of the task may be crucial. Only on masculine tasks (where, for example, subjects either believe or are explicitly told that a task is one which males generally do better or do more often) is there a large and consistent sex difference in attributions (Deaux and Farris, 1977). And as Deaux and Farris suggested, the attributions may be related to the expectation of success. Men expect to succeed, and so attribute success to a stable, internal trait, ability; women expect to fail, and so attribute failure to a stable, internal trait, lack of ability. When confronted with the unexpected—failure for men and success for women, particularly in masculine tasks—both men and women invoke luck to explain away their surprise. These attributions then affect later performances, such that the performance may come to be more in line with expectations. Thus, a vicious cycle is set up.

SUMMARY AND CONCLUSIONS

The sexes differ in the patterns of their achievement-related behavior, but more than any other factor, the reason for the differences seems to be an underlying difference in the socialization of the two genders. Common threads run through much of the data cited in this chapter. Fear of success, the need to achieve, and locus of control are interrelated, although the relationships are often stronger for men than for women. People with a high fear of success have a different pattern of attributions than do those with a low fear of success. Even fear of success and fear of failure are positively correlated in both males (+.42) and females (+.57) (Jackaway and Teevan, 1976).

The most typical effect of socialization seems to be that women try to combine achievement and affiliation (sometimes with notable lack of success) more often than men. This leads women to devalue their success—because they cannot succeed more than their man does—and, paradoxically, to attribute their failure to lack of ability, for the same reason. But women also have more routes to success than men do. A woman who fails a class can still succeed at dating, or at being a good wife and mother, and thus not experience a great loss in self-esteem. But a man has to live with that failure—no one will respect him just for being married to a competent and successful female. A man may cope with failure by attributing it to lack of effort, to bad luck, or to the ill will or lack of ability of others. However, since achieving through affiliation involves more social interaction—external factors—than does intellectual achievement, women have a more external locus of control.

All this means that need to achieve scores will reflect different behaviors and motives for men and women. All through their adult life women will attempt to come to terms with the notion that somehow for them, achievement equals affiliation; they come to terms with this either by denying that affiliation equals achievement for themselves, by trying to succeed in both masculine and feminine ways, or by accepting the equation and seeing affiliation as achievement. Generally, putting the job before the family has different outcomes for women and men. Women are expected to put their family before their job and so will often get a leave of absence if they need it to care for their children. Prospective employers who are told that the family is very important to a job applicant view the male favorably but perceive the female as lacking commitment and loyalty to the job. Yet women are also punished if they are committed to their job. Women less often receive support—and more often receive anger—if they put the job before the family, because that is not what people expect of them, and anger is frequently the result of unfulfilled expectations.

So men emphasize their careers (and get heart attacks?—see Appendix B) but do not expect that their families will suffer from that commitment, and women put their families first, and then worry that both job and family may suffer and be cheated. Women support their men and derive pleasure from their careers, but the reverse is rarely true. And men depend upon their wives for part of their emotional life. There are bound to be some consequences of this dependence in terms of happiness and mental health.

Another, more personal implication of the data in this chapter has to do with the ability of men and women to achieve their own personal goals. Societal prejudices and differential evaluations operate against achieving goals that are not sex-role appropriate, such as emotional closeness for men and occupational success in a "male" field for women. But with goals that are inappropriate to a person's sex role, the more failure to achieve that goal is attributed to external forces, the less likely the person will achieve that goal. Only when people take a personal responsibility for their own behavior, and attribute failure to lack of effort, will they be able to persist in the face of prejudice, and manage not only to achieve their own goal but also to change society's evaluation of that goal. Ironically, then, prejudice should be understood as contributing to the failure of others, but prejudice must not be used to explain one's own failure, if change is ever to come.

The data presented in this chapter also suggest that sex differences in cognitive abilities—in spatial performance, in mathematical performance, in verbal tasks—are a very complex function of the interaction of biological biases with socialized differences in expectations, motives, and values. For instance, the sex difference in mathematical performance undoubtedly has several different bases. There may be differences in biological preparedness, as suggested by the high correlation of math reasoning with spatial ability. But more important than that, there may be differences in the style of thinking, the method of approaching problems; this is implied by the sex differences in the correlates of math ability. Also, women may not see math as useful, as relevant to their own personal experience or to their motives to affiliate. Women may perceive themselves as much more different from the stereotype of a mathematician than males do; in fact, the self-description of the woman is quite different from the self-description of the creative mathematician, even though feminine traits are high in both. More females than males have math phobias, meaning they respond to quantitative concepts with debilitating levels of anxiety. Women may become nauseated when trying to balance their checkbook. Since females more often attribute failure to lack of ability—especially in a male area like math—and concentrate more on past failures as opposed to past successes than males do, past failures would have much more severe consequences for the self-concepts of women and could well lead to math phobias. Females may also perceive, correctly, that people expect them to do worse than males in math, that it is appropriate for women to do poorly in math. All these factors undoubtedly play a part in the sex differences in math performance. Parallel analyses can be made for sex differences in verbal and spatial performance, but these analyses will be left as an exercise for the reader.

There are sex differences in achievement behavior largely because society evaluates behavior differentially according to gender. Whether someone succeeds or fails in medical school or nursing school or in capturing a criminal, the way that person and others evaluate the performance depends upon the gender of the person responsible for the behavior. As long as performance is differentially evaluated according to gender, the two sexes will exhibit different behavior in achievement situations, especially in situations related to sex roles.

KEY TERMS AND CONCEPTS

TAT
Intellectual arousal condition
Need to achieve (n-ach)
Fear of failure
Fear of success (FOS)

Affiliation equals achievement
Traditional women
Doubly achieving women
Role innovators
Locus of control

QUESTIONS ON KEY ISSUES

1. What are the three major sex differences in the need to achieve?
2. What are the three hypotheses advanced to explain these differences? How has each of those hypotheses been evaluated?
3. What evidence indicates that FOS does not measure fear of success in either men or women? What does it measure?

4. What are the three ways women deal with the equation of affiliation and achievement, and in what ways does each lead to conflict?
5. How does the conflict between affiliation and achievement affect adult men?
6. What are the sex differences in each of the following areas, and how might each lead to sex differences in achievement:

expectancy of success; locus of control; attribution of causes of success and failure?

7. Using the data presented in this chapter

and in Chapter 8, how might sex differences in verbal ability and spatial ability be affected by n-ach, attributions, and expectation of success?

_____

CHAPTER 10

Personality Traits

In this chapter, some of the sex differences in the way people act, move, speak, and view the world will be discussed. Go to a bus station, a train station, or an airport and watch people. Note the sex differences in facial expressions, in vocal intonations, in the ways people hold packages or books, in the ways people move through crowds or react to others, and in the ways people stand and sit. There is obviously much to being feminine or masculine in this society. As Money points out in many of his writings, few men or women can mimic the opposite sex well enough to fool even casual observers.

There are some consistent sex differences in behavior that presumably reflect underlying motivational differences or differences in personality traits. We need to exercise caution in using the word traits, however; several current theorists (for example, Mischel) question the validity and usefulness of the concept, pointing out that people show few consistencies in behavior in different situations. But as we will see, some sex differences do seem to transcend this lack of consistency and appear in a variety of situations. We will look for such consistency in the following areas: aggression, dominance, competition, cooperation, and compliance; childhood dependency and passivity; affiliation; nurturance and help giving; physical attractiveness; and communication styles and preferences. In each area we will look for differences in socialization that might lead women and men to value different things or the same things to different degrees.

AGGRESSION AND DOMINANCE

Review of Biological and Cultural Biases

The evidence strongly supports the idea that a biological bias affects sex differences in aggression. This bias may be an indirect effect of the Y chromosome. Although both XXY and XYY men end up in prisons more often than the XY men, only the men with two Y chromosomes, not the XXY men, are more impulsively aggressive than XY men, that is, have poor control over their impulses. Also, the Y chromosome is associated with aggression in most species. Male animals usually show more aggression than females, at least with other males, and show more interest in aggression. Dominance hierarchies, when they do occur, are more salient in male animals, and males more often dominate females than females do males. There are some exceptions, however. When the female is larger than the male, she is generally more aggressive and dominant. And females can be very aggressive, especially against other females, in defense of their young, or in repulsing the unwanted sexual advance of a male.

The evidence from the effects of perinatal hormones on aggression and dominance is also quite consistent with the hypothesis of a biological bias. Perinatal castration of males reduces their aggression and perinatal androgen increases female aggression. A prenatal androgen given to female monkeys increases the incidence of threats and rough-and-tumble play. Prenatal androgens and estrogens may also affect humans, but that is not as clear as with lower animals. Genetically and hormonally normal human males reared as females are more dominant and aggressive than other females, but andrenogenital males and females and progestin-masculinized females are not more aggressive than their same-sex peers or siblings. They were, however, assertive, independent, and self-reliant. Boys prenatally exposed to less than normal levels of estrogen (those who had diabetic mothers who were not given estrogen) were more aggressive, assertive, and competitive than both males with a normal prenatal environment and sons of diabetic mothers who were given estrogen during their pregnancy.

Androgens also activate aggression, particularly with a male-induced brain (except in hamsters). Castration decreases and testosterone injections restore aggression in males of most species, but the change caused by castration is slower and not as likely to occur in social-living species such as dogs, monkeys, and humans. Estrogen injections depress dominance in males of several species. High doses of an androgen given over a long time also increase aggression in female mice, rats, and monkeys.

In human males and females, some correlations of blood testosterone level with aggression and dominance have been found, but as yet the experimental results are highly variable and unreliable. But aggression does increase with adolescence in males, when testosterone increases. For human females, estrogen and progesterone withdrawal—or some correlate of that withdrawal—may increase the likelihood of criminal behavior and self-directed aggression (attempted suicide). However, successful suicides may be more likely during the luteal phase of the menstrual cycle when all sex hormones are at high levels.

Cross-culturally, males are assigned the more aggressive roles of fighting wars, making weapons and hunting. Boys are generally socialized to be more dominant and generally are. Boys have a more clearly developed dominance hierarchy than do girls, and in boy-girl pairs, boys are rated as tougher. Cross-cultural surveys show that boys engage more often in rough-and-tumble play, are more verbally aggressive, and more often respond to attacks with aggression. Very few assaults were observed in one study (Whiting and Edwards, 1973), but boys more often did the assaulting. Husbands are usually dominant over wives in the domestic sphere and men are always dominant over women in the public sphere.

Thus, males of most species, including the human species, seem more prepared to associate reinforcing consequences with aggressive acts. But this bias is also operated on by experience, such that the effect of hormones is never to elicit behavior; hormones may merely facilitate the appearance of aggression in an environment that also supports the behavior. The cross-cultural data suggest that most societies, in socializing their children, reinforce any bias created by the Y chromosome and inductive and activational androgens, to make males even more aggressive relative to females.

Human Aggression

The male is more aggressive. This conclusion was reached in two recent exhaustive reviews (Deaux, 1976; Maccoby and Jacklin, 1974). The latter review cited ninety-four studies. Only in five of these studies were girls and women more aggressive; boys and men were more aggressive in fifty-two, while no sex difference was found in the others.

Boys and men are usually both more physically and more verbally aggressive, although the sex differences in verbal aggression are not found as often as in physical aggression (Maccoby and Jacklin, 1974). Boys are aggressive physically as often as they are verbally, while girls are more often verbally than physically aggressive (McIntyre, 1972). Sex differences in aggressive doll play appear even before children reach three years of age (Sears, 1951, 1965). Masculine examples of doll play include the boy who pretended to flush the baby doll down the toilet and the boy who, at the end of the scene of play, said, " 'And so he puts mommy on the stove and fries her in the frying pan till she's all burned up' " (1965, p. 140). Girls, on the other hand, use more prosocial or disciplinary aggression, such as spanking.

The aggression of males is not limited to interesting but nondangerous laboratory experiments. Men commit more murders and more assaults. The crime rate of women is increasing faster than that of men, but so far the increase in the rate of crimes involving personal aggression is still greater in the male. Newsweek (1975) reported that from 1960 to 1973 the percentage of women committing robbery, burglary, larceny, auto theft, fraud, and narcotic-related crimes increased more than that of men, but the percentage of murders and aggravated assaults committed by men increased more than that by women. Only in the case of child abuse are women more often aggressive; the battered child is most often a victim of her or his mother. Child abuse may not be like other forms of aggression—it may be more due to the frustrations of the female role—or the greater frequency for women may simply result from the fact that the mother is usually the one responsible for the child.

Conditions That Produce Aggression. Observation of violence increases aggression more in males than in females. Boys show more aggression after observing an aggressive model, as well as without observing such a model (Bandura, 1965; Bandura, Ross, and Ross, 1961, 1963a, 1963b; Bandura and Walters, 1963). Boys, more than girls, show both imitative aggression (mimicking the model's behavior fairly accurately) and nonimitative aggression (aggressive acts other than those demonstrated by the model). This is true whether the model was observed in person, on film, or in a cat costume. Sex differences in modeled aggression can be affected by other variables. For instance, they are most likely when the child was frustrated first and when an adult was present during the test (Caplan, 1975).

Reinforcement for aggression may also have sexually dimorphic effects on modeled aggression. In Bandura's experiments, punishing the model for his or her aggression decreased imitative aggression in both sexes, but girls' aggression was even more suppressed than that of boys. Bribing the children with pictures and fruit juice to perform aggressive acts, however, increased the aggression of girls more than that of boys. In this last condition, then, explicit reinforcement for aggression reduced the sex difference in aggression though it did not eliminate that difference. The bribe increased the aggression of girls in all three conditions but increased the aggression of boys only when the model was punished. But in all conditions, boys were more aggressive. All this suggests that boys' aggression requires less to elicit it, and that girls' aggression is more easily suppressed.

The surgeon general's report on the effects of television violence supports this research (Buck, 1976). Boys whose facial expressions showed pleasure when they observed violence were more aggressive than the boys who expressions had shown disinterest; this effect was not seen in girls. Among boys but not girls, high exposure to televised violence was related to aggressiveness at age eighteen. Thus, exposure to aggressive models may increase aggression in both sexes, but the effects seem stronger in boys.

Males are also more aggressive under other conditions (Deaux, 1976; Maccoby and Jacklin, 1974). When a subject is placed in the role of a teacher in an experiment and told to shock another student, the learner, for his or her mistakes, males give more shocks and more severe ones than females. Males give a disabled subject more shock than one not disabled; females give the disabled one less. In fact, females feel emotionally drawn to victims of somebody else's attack, whereas males develop a dislike for someone they overhear being harshly treated. Male drivers also more quickly honk their car horns when blocked at an intersection that has a green light.

Much of this research used male experimenters, however, which may overestimate the sex differences in aggression. One study, which unfortunately used only female subjects, found that insulted women were much more aggressive in the presence of a female experimenter than in the presence of a male one (Larwood, et al., 1977). Perhaps men inhibit aggression in women, or women facilitate aggression in other women.

There may also be some sex differences in the conditions that produce aggression (Frodi, 1977). When men and women were asked what was the most anger-provoking behavior that could be displayed toward them, 54 percent of the women said it would be condescension—being treated as if they were no good or being criticized—regardless of the sex of the provoker. For men, 52 percent were also most provoked by condescension, but only if done by a female. Forty percent of the males said they would be most provoked by physical or verbal aggression by another male. Many sex differences in aggression, then, might be due to sex differences in the stimuli that provoke aggression, rather than sex differences in the tendency to respond with aggression.

Delinquency in girls and boys is often related to different types of backgrounds (J. Andrew, 1976), suggesting different causes of aggression in males and females. Broken homes are found more frequently in the backgrounds of female delinquents than in the general population, but large families were more common in the backgrounds of delinquent males. Large families may make it harder to control the more aggressive boy, whereas disrupted affiliative relationships may prove more of a problem for a girl. But it should be remembered that what is called delinquency in a girl—sexual acting out—may not be called delinquency in a boy.

Males and females show different correlates of aggression, also suggesting different causes or developmental processes. Temper tantrums at ages six to ten were significantly correlated with arousal of anger for adult men (+.42) but not for women (+.13) (Kagan and Moss, 1962). Early maturing girls are more verbally aggressive than later maturers, but early maturing boys are both more physically and verbally aggressive (M. Jones and Mussen, 1958). Frequency of verbal and nonverbal interactions was recorded, producing an index of social activity, which was also positively correlated with verbal aggression for both sexes (+.72 for boys and +.74 for girls) (McIntyre, 1972). However, social activity was negatively correlated with physical aggression for boys (−.76) but was positively correlated for girls (+.62). Furthermore, verbal aggression was not related to physical aggression, or to other types of direct or indirect aggression for boys (−.36, −.32, and −.37), but these behaviors were strongly intercorrelated for girls (+.83, +.89, and +.82).

Males are more often the victims of aggression (Deaux, 1976; Hutt, 1972b; Maccoby and Jacklin, 1974). Males do more murdering, but men are more often murdered, especially single men. Female learners are given milder and fewer shocks than male learners by both sexes. The greater aggressiveness of males is thus directed largely towards other males, although males also more often direct aggression to objects, as can be seen in Figure 10.1. The only exceptions to this rule found so far are that women drivers who do not start their cars promptly when the light changes elicit more horn honking than do male drivers, and that women who push into a line ahead of other people may elicit more indirect aggression such as glares from other women than do men who push ahead (M. Harris, 1974).

Types of Aggression and Responses to Aggression. Even the physiological responses of men and women to an aggressive attack may be different (Hokanson, Willers, and Koropsak, 1968). Male and female subjects were shocked and then allowed to give their aggressors either a reward, a shock, or no response in return. Even under these conditions of explicit provocation, females were significantly less aggressive than males. Systolic blood pressure of both sexes was increased by receiving a shock, but males showed a faster recovery of normal blood pressure when they shocked their aggressor, while females recovered faster if they rewarded their aggressor. These sex differences could be reversed by explicitly rewarding females for shocking their aggressors and rewarding males for rewarding their aggressors. However, when the trials using rewards ended, the original sex differences began to reappear. This sex difference is subject to change by conditioning, but without conditioning females seem to find that aggressive responses increase their arousal rather than decrease it, as aggression had done for males. Thus, males may be more prepared to be reinforced for aggression, or females may have learned that rewarding other people is a more effective response for them to use.

Perhaps women find more indirect outlets for aggression than men do. Maybe some of the sex differences in mental health, such as the greater frequency of

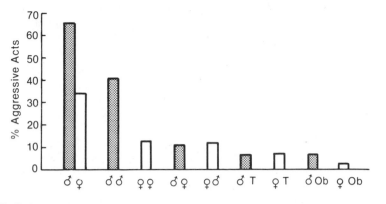

FIGURE 10.1 ———————————————————————————————————————

AGGRESSIVE BEHAVIOR BY BOYS AND GIRLS

The first two bars show the proportion of all aggressive acts committed by boys and that by girls. The other bars show to whom these acts were directed: boys to boys, girls to girls, boys to girls, girls to boys, boys to teachers, girls to teachers, boys to objects (toys, furniture), and girls to objects.

With permission from C. Brindley, P. Clark, C. Hutt, I. Robinson, and E. Wethli, "Sex Differences in the Activities and Social Interactions of Nursery School Children." In R. P. Michael and J. H. Crook (eds.), *Comparative Ecology and Behavior of Primates* (New York: Academic Press, 1973), fig. 1, p. 807. Copyright by Academic Press Inc. (London) Ltd.

female suicide attempts, could be best understood as indirect aggression; since women do not show aggression against others, they use it against themselves. Women also more often use the glare as an aggressive response to people who push in line ahead of them (M. Harris, 1974). And in graffiti writing, safely anonymous, the graffiti in women's toilets may be more hostile than is that in men's toilets (Solomon and Yager, 1975).

Summary. Aggression in girls carries over into different types of behavior, but it seems more channeled in boys. Childhood aggression predicts adult aggression only for males, suggesting that males are more consistently reinforced (or less consistently punished) for aggression than are girls. But Maccoby and Jacklin (1974) concluded from their review that, if anything, males were more often punished than females were for being aggressive. Aggression in the two genders seems to have taken different developmental courses, so we expect it to be expressed in different ways and in response to different provocations or in different family situations.

The aggression of males seems to be elicited in more situations (though each male seems to have his own preferred aggressive response), and aggression in females is more easily suppressed and more indirect and generalized. Modeling and being attacked increases aggression more in males than in females, though the sex of the experimenter (or attacker) and, for children, the presence of an adult, may have an effect: the presence of males or adults may inhibit aggression in females. Males are more often the victims of aggression.

Overall, males seem more biologically prepared to associate reinforcing consequences with aggressive acts, but the cross-cultural data suggest that society has suppressed aggression in women. Perhaps this suppression has succeeded only in making the aggression of females more indirect, or in directing it towards the self (women have more suicide attempts) or towards people who cannot punish them for being aggressive, such as their own children.

Competition and Cooperation, Dominance and Compliance

To what extent are the sex differences in aggression carried over into other areas of human interactions? Sex differences in competition and dominance are less clear-cut than those in aggression. What data there are indicate that men are more often dominant, while neither sex is more conforming.

Conformity. Both Deaux (1976) and Maccoby and Jacklin (1974) concluded that females are not necessarily more compliant, suggestible, or submissive than males are. Young girls are more apt to comply with an adult's directions than are boys, but girls are not more compliant with their peers.

Adult women have often been reported to be more suggestible than men, but this difference may have resulted from using masculine tasks. Both sexes apparently do more conforming when the task is not sex-role appropriate, or involves something that they assume they know relatively little about. Thus, when the conformity task involves judging line length, and the measure of conformity is the extent to which subjects change their judgments to agree with those of stooges surrounding them, women might assume that they know less about judging length and so be more conforming or suggestible. But in another study using a male spatial task as a measure of conformity, Gingrich (1973) found that while conformity decreased with age, gender had no significant effect and did not interact with any other variable, so sex differences, even on masculine tasks, are far from universal.

However, as discussed in Chapter 7, women—regardless of gender role—are more willing than men to conform when the task involves performing sex-role inappropriate behaviors. Women are more willing to step out of role than men are. But Bem's work in this area also suggests that gender role may be even more important than gender identity in determining whether or not conformity will occur. Feminine people of either gender are more conforming than are masculine or androgynous people (Table 7.6).

In one important area of conformity, men might be expected to be more compliant. Men and boys might be expected to be more likely to comply with instructions or orders to be aggressive, to shock another person. Some such research has been done: subjects were told to punish other subjects for incorrect behavior by giving painful shocks (this is the Milgram paradigm, 1963). But in two separate studies (Goldman, cited by Sheridan and King, 1972; Sheridan and King, 1972), adolescent females were more willing to inflict shock than males, even though Milgram got no sex differences in his original work. Females were more willing to inflict shock on a puppy, even when the puppy was immediately present and being visibly hurt by their shocks. But, college-age females are less likely to be obedient in the Milgram paradigm when human subjects are being shocked. This was especially true when the females actually had to deliver the shock and when the shock level was high; at the lowest shock levels, females were slightly more obedient than males (Kilham and Mann, 1974). Perhaps whatever motive is responsible for obedience in this paradigm (and it is probably not aggression) comes into conflict with affiliation for females when humans and higher shock levels are involved; under these conditions, affiliation wins out, and women are less obediently aggressive than men.

Competition versus Cooperation. Much of the research into competition and cooperation has dealt with strategies of game playing, which may have little or nothing to do with actual competitiveness (Deaux, 1976; Maccoby and Jacklin, 1974). What most studies found, however, is that neither sex is necessarily more competitive (McClintock et al., 1973), although women are more frequently concerned with the social aspects of the situation than men (Deaux, 1976). To illustrate this conclusion, we shall examine in detail two studies that did show a sex difference, to illustrate how social concerns sometimes produce a sex difference in competitive situations. Peplau (1976) had dating college couples solve anagrams, competing either with each other or together against another couple. Only women who had traditional attitudes about women's role and a high FOS score performed worse against their dates than against the other couple. Men who wrote hostile stories about Anne being at the top of her medical school class performed better against their date than against the other couple.

Walker and Heyns (1962) had pairs of friends compete at forming anagrams, to see who could scramble the most words according to specific rules. The subjects were also told (erroneously) that their friend was in another room and in another contest to see who could unscramble the greatest percentage of words that they had just scrambled. After a few trials, each subject received a bogus request from his or her partner to slow down so that the partner could win her or his contest. Most men refused the request, but many women complied. All but a few men had higher need for achievement scores on the TAT than need to affiliate scores; the only women who did not slow down, like the men, had higher need for achievement scores than need to affiliate scores. Here, as in achievement, women may succeed in the competition by achieving different goals than the men (and different ones from those the experimenter had in mind) by following different strategies.

Dominance and Assertiveness. Assertiveness and dominance are related to aggression but are not the same as aggression. Dominance is trying to impose opinions and desires upon other people, trying to influence other people; aggression and threat are ways of expressing dominance, but there are other ways. Assertiveness is a forceful but not aggressive (not hostile) response to a situation.

It is generally assumed that men are more assertive, but college women can be as assertive as college men, or even more assertive, depending on the scale used (Tolor, Kelly, and Stebbins, 1976). Even though sex-role stereotyping for either sex was not significantly related to assertiveness, assertiveness was also associated with a favorable self-concept for both genders.

Men and boys seem more concerned with dominance, more concerned with knowing just who is boss, who is the major influence in a group. This difference starts early in life and is reflected in and reinforced by sex differences in patterns of play. Lever (1976), studying fifth-graders, found that boys played outdoors more often, played in age-heterogeneous groups more often, and played competitive games more often. This suggests that dominant-submissive, win-lose relationships are more salient for boys than for girls, while interpersonal characteristics, unstructured by game rules, are more salient for girls. Given this difference in play patterns, it is not surprising that males are more concerned with dominance and with competition; this concern leads males to learn to be more skilled at dominance attempts, and more sensitive to them, which means they will more often dominate and exert leadership.

The cross-cultural work of Omark and his colleagues on dominance in children (Maccoby and Jacklin, 1974) has been replicated and extended by research in this country (Omark and Edelman, 1975). Omark limits dominance to interpersonal behavior (attacking and fleeing), and states that object possession (females, food, toys) may be a secondary benefit of a dominant position but is not an essential part of the dominance hierarchy per se. He cites research by himself and others showing that preschool children develop and maintain stable dominance hierarchies as he defines them. This research shows not only that boys are dominant over girls, but also that there is greater agreement about who is tougher in boy-girl pairs than in same-sex pairs. The largest increase in agreement on toughness occurs between kindergarten and first grade; both males and females are aware of the male dominance hierarchy that forms then. However, Omark and Edelman point out that girls may develop a more stable dominance hierarchy when there are no boys in the group, which may have something to do with the effects of coeducation upon achievement in girls (see p. 269).

Other evidence indicates that there are sex differences in dominance. Young boys make more attempts to dominate adults than do young girls (Maccoby and Jacklin, 1974). And both sexes are more nonverbally anxious when interacting with men than with women, suggesting an awareness of a dominance interaction when a male is involved (Weitz, 1976). Many of the sex differences in nonverbal behavior that will be reviewed later also suggest a greater dominance, and a greater interest in dominance, in males. Even on paper-and-pencil tests, adolescent boys and adults may score higher on dominance in both Canada and England (Hakstian and Cattell, 1975) and in the U.S. (Jackson, 1967).

Dominance relationships even affect sex differences in humor. Both males and females find jokes funnier when the male dominates the female, compared to those in which the female dominates the male; in general, jokes with female victims were found to be funnier (Cantor, 1976). Male subjects also liked jokes in which a male enemy is put down, but females found these jokes the least humorous. Instead, females enjoyed more those jokes in which a person put down themselves (Stocking and Zillmann, 1976; Zillmann and Stocking, 1976).

Men are also more likely to be elected as leaders, from the presidency of a high-school club to the presidency of the United States. In studies involving decision-making groups or decision-making games using high-school and college-student subjects, men were four to seven times more likely to emerge as group leaders than females (Lockheed and Hall, 1976). When leadership assignments were experimentally manipulated, males showed more leadership behavior (and females more emotional, affective types of behavior) and females were less likely to choose themselves to be a future leader than were males (Eskilson and Wiley,

1976). This last study also found more leadership challenges were made by males, especially in a mixed-sex group led by a male.

Megargee (1969) measured dominance as it related to leadership in same-sex and opposite-sex pairs of subjects, with one member of the pair being high and one low in dominance. About 60 percent to 75 percent of the time, the high dominant person, as assessed previously by a paper-and-pencil test, became the leader in same-sex pairs. In opposite-sex pairs, a dominant male became the leader when paired with a less dominant female about 90 percent of the time, and even when the female was dominant, the male became the leader 80 percent of the time. In the other pairs, the leader was the one who made the decision to lead, but in the dominant woman, less dominant man pairs in 91 percent of the cases it was the woman who decided that the man should be the leader.

Blood and Wolfe (1960) studied the correlates of the dominance of the husband over the wife as perceived by the wife. The husband is more often involved in decisions about the wife's job than is the wife about the husband's job. Husbands also are more likely to make decisions about cars or insurance than are wives, but wives make decisions about food purchases. Decisions about whether or not the couple will become swingers are also usually reached by the husband (Henshel, 1973). Blood and Wolfe also found that the greater the husband's occupational prestige, income, and education, the more relative power he had. Husbands in the suburbs were more dominant than those in the city. The wife's power declined with the more children she had at home. In general, "there is a strong reservoir of attitude on the part of the American male generally, that he has a *right* to tell his wife what to do. This attitude is given more overt expression, and is more frequently backed by force, in the lower [socioeconomic] strata" (p. 122). The wife can gain in power by working, by being more educated than her husband, and by belonging to more organizations than he does. Also, the longer the marriage lasts, the relatively more dominant the wife becomes (Maccoby and Jacklin, 1974).

Thus, dominant-submissive relationships seem pervasive, and men are more often the dominant gender. This difference starts very early in life, and colors much of later interpersonal relationships, including humor and marriage. Men are more often leaders, both because they seem more willing to assume that role and also because women seem to push them to assume it. These differences in dominance may be affected by a biological bias, as was the case for aggression; much of the data indicating a bias for aggression is relevant for dominance. Children's play patterns reinforce and extend any biological bias, making sex differences in dominance even greater.

Need for Power. A concept closely related to dominance is that of **need for power.** Need for power is concern for having an impact on others, either by persuasion or by force. Tests for this have been developed and are scored in ways very similar to those described for need for achievement. Men usually have higher average need for power scores than women, although arousal instructions affect women the same way they do men (A. Stewart and Winter, 1976), unlike the case with need for achievement.

However, the correlations of need for power are so different in the two sexes that different motives may be involved. In men, need for power was correlated with recall of dreams, frequency of arguments, having sleeping and drinking problems, and disliking child care (McClelland, 1975). For women, it was correlated with dieting, number of credit cards, concern about the appearance of clothes, playing tennis, number of organizational memberships, and trying new foods. Need for power was significantly correlated with need to affiliate in women (− .32) but not in men (−.11), though McClelland did not state whether the correlations were significantly different.

There is other evidence that need for power correlates with different behavior in men and women. Need for power has gender-specific effects on a dating relationship (A. Stewart and Rubin, 1976). If the man had a high need for power, the couple was likely to break up; over a period of several years, few of these couples got married. The woman's need for power was not related to the future of the dating relationship, perhaps because her power was being expressed through the relationship. McKeachie (1962) found no correlation of grades with need for power in women, but intelligent men with a high need for power did better in classes in which there was a great deal of student volunteering than in classes with little student participation. That need for power is related to different behaviors suggests either that women's need for power expresses itself in different ways than men's, or that the test measures different motives in men than in women.

One very interesting study done with children suggested that the sexes may acquire different power or dominance strategies at a very early age, and find these strategies differentially effective. (This type of research needs to be replicated with adults.) This research studied **Machiavellianism,** the "use of exploitive and manipulative behaviors in interpersonal relations" (Braginsky, 1970, p. 77). Braginsky gave ten-year-old children a child's version of a Mach (Machiavellianism) scale to divide them into high and low Mach groups. All children were then offered five cents for every one of a bad-tasting cracker that they could get another child of the same sex to eat. High Mach children were more successful than low Mach children in getting another child to eat bad-tasting crackers, but the sexes found different strategies effective. High Mach boys succeeded by directly lying. Low Mach girls also tried lying, but that strategy did not work for them. High Mach girls were successful using a strategy of indirect lies (answering questions with statements that contained the answer to a question not asked—classic bits of misdirection) or else offering to split the five cents with their target (though they did not offer to share the cracker), or else blaming the whole thing on the experimenter ("She says they taste good"). Overall, the high Mach girls' strategies would seem more effective over a longer period of time and a wider range of situations than those of the high Mach boys. Braginsky compared high Mach boys to used car salesmen and high Mach girls to insurance salesmen. However, sex roles may have affected behavior even in this study, because postexperimental distress was greatest for unsuccessful boys and successful girls. Also, low Mach boys liked their target more than did the high Mach boys, but high Mach girls liked their target more than low Mach girls.

Rosen and Jerdee (1973) also showed that the sexes have differentially effective dominance or power strategies. They had subjects rate how effective certain supervisory styles would be. The threat approach was perceived as more effective for male than for female supervisors, while the reward style (bribing for good performance) and the friendly-dependent style (asking employees to help the supervisor by improving) were perceived as more effective for female than for male supervisors.

Average need for power scores are usually higher in men than in women. However, since the scores correlate with such different behaviors in women and men, this suggests that need for power tests are measuring different motives or traits in the two genders. Still, men and women seem to find different power strategies differentially effective; men and boys find lies and threats more effective, while women and girls find misdirection and rewards more effective.

Review and Evaluation

Men are more aggressive and more concerned with dominance relationships in our society, just as male infra-human primates are more concerned about dominance in their societies. Although boys may be more frequently punished for aggression than are girls, there are enough aggressive models in our society for even the slowest boy to learn his aggressive lesson. It is only surprising that with the pervasiveness of aggressive models girls have not completely caught up. Men thus seem more prepared to learn to become aggressive.

Sex differences in preparedness are suggested by several behavioral studies cited by Maccoby and Jacklin (1974). In the Bandura experiments, even with explicit bribes for aggression, girls remembered less of the aggressive model's behavior than boys did. Maccoby also cited one of her earlier studies in which girls remembered less of the aggressive content of films than boys did. When two pictures are presented together in a stereoscope (one picture to each eye such that only one at a time can be seen), boys more often reported the violent scene than girls (Moore, 1966). Kagan and Moss (1962) used a tachistoscope to present pictures to children, and measured how long the exposure time had to be before the child recognized what was in the scene. Girls took longer than boys to recognize aggressive scenes.

Thus, the Y chromosome and inductive and activational androgens may make males more likely to initiate and respond to aggression, particularly with other males, and also make them more likely to be concerned with dominance. Females can be extremely aggressive, but they are less often directly aggressive. These biological biases are then accentuated by socialization patterns and by internalization of the sex-role stereotypes, so that women are even less aggressive compared to men than would be expected on a biological basis alone.

Sex differences in cooperation and suggestibility depend even more strongly upon sex typing than do sex differences in aggression. In these areas, sex differences appear only when the task is sex-role appropriate, when one sex or the other would stereotypically have the best knowledge or ability, or when affiliative goals conflict with the experimenter-defined goals. There is no biological bias.

CHILDHOOD DEPENDENCY AND PASSIVITY

Dependency refers to a great variety of behaviors that are probably not highly interrelated. Dependency includes both **emotional** and **instrumental** behaviors, with the goal of the first being affection, reassurance, or approval (succorance), and the goal of the second being to get help for the performance of some task. Bardwick (1971) adds **aggressive dependency,** "in which the objectives are negative and manipulative" (p. 119). Dependency may also include attachment behaviors. Attachment behaviors involve both **proximity** (being close to a parent or other adult) and **proximity seeking** (searching for, following, and approaching the parent). These two types of proximity behaviors are highly correlated ($r = +.80$) (Lamb, 1976). Attachment behaviors have been divided into **proximal attachment** (touching and remaining close to a parent) and **distal attachment** (looking at or talking to a parent) (M. Lewis and Weinraub, 1974).

Correlates of Dependency

Kagan and Moss (1962) reported that dependency behavior at ages six to ten was positively correlated with adult dependency for females (.30), while the correlation was essentially zero for males. The correlation between dependency at the age of three with that at the age of fourteen was $+.64$ for girls and $-.33$ for boys. Sears (1963) also found that different measures of dependency were more interrelated for preschool girls than boys; the median correlation was $+.61$ for girls and $-.45$ for boys. And for girls, but not for boys, exploration and attachment tend to be inversely related (Willemsen et al., 1974).

So dependency behaviors may reflect a more stable and pervasive trait for females than for males, but are females more dependent than males? Sherman (1971) suggests that this is the case: "On the whole, the evidence suggests that females, combining all ages, are more dependent, passive and conforming than males" (pp. 27–28). However, as we shall see, this conclusion depends on how dependency is defined and measured.

Proximity

People generally rate girls as being more dependent or valuing proximity to parents more than boys, although most observational studies show no sex differences (Maccoby and Jacklin, 1973). Some studies, however, have found sex differences in this area. Lewis and his colleagues (Brooks and Lewis, 1974; M. Lewis and Weinraub, 1974) found that one-year-old females remain closer to their mothers than boys do. Lamb (1976) reviewed research on proximity and concluded that boys are more likely to follow their mothers than girls, but that proximity seeking declined more with age in boys than in girls.

But more important, several authors have specified conditions that made sex differences more or less likely to occur. According to Lewis, sex differences in proximity behavior are more likely to appear if observations are continued for at least fifteen minutes and if lower-class children are studied. Also, being separated from the mother affected boys but not girls, such that the attachment behavior of boys increased to the female level. Lamb (1976) concluded that sex differences appear only in a stress-free situation under conditions of extended observation. Finally, Brookhart and Hock (1976) found that sex differences in proximity and proximity seeking depended on rearing condition. Boys reared at home showed more attachment to a stranger than did girls, but the reverse was true for girls and boys who had regularly gone to a day-care center away from home.

There may also be some developmental differences in dependency (S. Goldberg and Lewis, 1972; M. Lewis and Weinraub, 1974). The more the mother touched her male infant at the age of six months, the more he would touch her at thirteen months of age. For girls, the most proximity behavior occurred after having experienced either high or low levels of maternal contact earlier in life. Boys may move from proximal to distal attachment between one and two years of age, but girls remained in proximal contact with their mother at both ages one and two.

The implications these differences have for adult behavior are unclear. Attachment, strictly speaking, is not dependency, since attachment is specific to parents (Sears, 1963). M. Lewis, in several of his writings, related children's attachment behavior to adult touching, noting that for females touch is more likely to occur and is more socially acceptable than it is for males.

Emotional, Aggressive, and Instrumental Dependency

Sex differences have generally not been reported in these areas—in fact, it seems that emotional dependency is equally often punished in both sexes (Marcus, 1976)—but some researchers have found differences in other types of dependency. Crandall and Rabson (1960) reported that first-grade girls more often showed instrumental dependency than boys; the same was reported for one-year-old, firstborn girls (Rothbart and Rothbart, 1976). Mothers would reinforce this instrumental dependency in girls by offering more emotional encouragement and instrumental help to daughters than other mothers did to their sons (Rothbart and Rothbart, 1976). This difference in treatment giving girls more help upon request than boys—was also seen in a study that paired college women with seven- to ten-year-old girls and boys (Cantor and Gelfand, 1977).

One implication of this difference in adult responses to requests for help by children is illustrated by Bing's work (1963). She found that greater maternal help-giving was associated with high verbal ability in children. In turn, high verbal ability facilitates instrumental dependency, asking for help. Thus, if daughters are encouraged to do well and are reinforced for seeking help, affiliation is combined with achievement for girls, and separated for boys.

Passivity

Whether there are sex differences in passivity depends upon how passivity is measured and defined. **Passivity** can refer to sexual behavior, to being dominated, to being manipulated, to withdrawal from the world, to lack of activity, to helplessness, to lack of aggression, or simply to being quiet (Bardwick, 1971). Men are more dominant and aggressive, but sex differences in the other measures of passivity are not consistent.

There are no consistencies in cross-cultural analyses of passivity in children (Whiting and Edwards, 1973), or in other types of data. Sex differences in helplessness should be seen only in so far as girls and women attribute their failure to a lack of ability and men attribute their failure to a lack of effort; that research has already been reviewed. Females tend to withdraw more after failure because of these attributions, but this tendency seems specific and does not reflect a general trait of passivity. Maccoby and Jacklin (1974) concluded that boys are more active than girls only when stimulated to be so by the presence of other boys; a similar result was seen in lower primates. Thus, boys may be more reactive to certain kinds of social stimuli, but they are not more active than girls when by themselves. Kagan and Moss (1962) reported that childhood and adult passivity are more strongly related in females (.48) than in males (.27).

Conclusions and Implications

Sex differences in dependency and passivity seem minimal. The sex differences reported in childhood are not easily related to adult behavior, although there is more consistency across ages and across different situations for females than for males.

Kohlberg (1969) feels that attachment does not mean dependency. In fact, according to Kohlberg, the child imitates the adult out of a desire for competence, and this imitiation leads to attachment (it is easier to imitate a model you are close enough to see), and to dependency, or the need for the model to give feedback on the adequacy of the imitation. Even the dependency of the infant is not passivity, but a desire to use the parent to gain control over the world. Kohlberg also suggests that experiencing many failures (or, as with women, a greater emphasis on failure) increases imitation and suggestibility, and that both sexes will therefore be more suggestible and imitative—and dependent—when they feel incompetent. Thus, attachment and dependency come from a desire for competence, not from passivity, and are an end point of mature ego development. The greater consistency of these behaviors in females might indicate that females more consistently take the social route to competence and achievement.

We shall now look at some behaviors in adults that may or may not be related to these childhood differences in dependency and passivity: affiliation, nurturance and help giving, and communication style and preferences.

AFFILIATION

Affiliation usually means the desire to be near other people and the reinforcing value of being around other people. It is not directly related to proximity, because one can be close to people for reasons other than preference. For instance, boys play in larger groups than girls, but as Maccoby and Jacklin (1974) said, boys are often involved in game playing where the particular affiliative relationships are not as important as conforming to the rules, written and unwritten, of the game. Girls, on the other hand, form smaller groups that depend more upon affiliative preferences.

Need to Affiliate

The **need to affiliate** in adults is usually scored on paper-and-pencil tests or by responses to the TAT. The conditions used to derive the TAT scoring are analogous to those used to derive scoring for the need for achievement.

Women generally score higher on both paper-and-pencil and TAT tests of need to affiliate (Exline, 1960; Maccoby and Jacklin, 1974; McKeachie, 1962; Walberg, 1969). Women also score higher on scales that measure need for social approval, or the desire to respond in culturally sanctioned ways (Clancy and Gove, 1975). So women may more often claim that they are concerned with affiliative relationships than men do.

This sex difference may be particularly striking during adolescence. Simmons and Rosenberg (1975; see also F. Rosenberg and Simmons, 1975) have reported that adolescent females are more concerned than males about social relationships, at least according to self-reports. Females more often value popularity and more of them worry about what other people think of them and about being well-liked. They smile when they are not happy and act nice to people they do not like. More adolescent girls would like to be well-liked (38 percent) than to be the best in things that they do (33 percent). For boys, more of them wanted to be best (45 percent) than well-liked (27 percent).

Affiliative Behavior

These differences in test scores and self-reports seem to be validated by similar sex differences in affiliative behavior. For example, McClelland (1975) reported that women belonged to more organizations than men did. Booth (1972), based on his interviews of 880 adults, found that women had more weekly contacts with their close friends, engaged in more spontaneous activities with them, and confided in them more often. Latané and Bidwell (1977) studied social interactions in a college cafeteria by counting people at tables or by interviewing people as they left. Females were considerably less likely to eat alone than males; in fact, females were almost twice as likely as males to leave the cafeteria rather than eat alone. Women do not affiliate more than men under conditions of fear or shock (misery loves company equally in both sexes), although in these situations, affiliation reduced the anxiety of women but not that of men (MacDonald, 1970).

Self-disclosure (the willingness to reveal oneself to close friends) probably facilitates affiliative relationships, so we should expect this behavior to appear more often in women than men. Cross-culturally, women do seem more willing to reveal themselves than men do, though there are tremendous cultural differences in the size of that sex difference (J. W. Berry, 1976). One review found more self-disclosure among females than among males in half the studies cited, and found no study reporting a reverse sex difference (O'Neill et al., 1976). This sex difference in self-disclosure seems greatest for the most intimate items that could be revealed, such as emotionality, anxiety, and dependency (B. Morgan, 1976; O'Neill et al., 1976). Another study (Bender et al., 1976) found that self-disclosure was greatest among both females and feminine people of both genders.

Other research suggests that females are more sensitive to affiliative stimuli. Females seem more able than males to remember names associated with faces, and this sex difference begins at a very early age (see Chapter 11). Women (but not young girls) may also more accurately convey emotions with facial expressions than men (Buck, 1976), and females of all ages are better at reading emotions in people's body language, including facial expressions (Rosenthal et al., 1974), although males in social occupations (clinical psychologists) also show high levels of this ability. Females have better memories for the personal characteristics and feelings of others depicted in films (Turner, cited by Falbo, 1975). Falbo (1975) had her subjects write descriptions from memory of what had just been shown to them on a slide. Women wrote more often about how the people in the slide felt.

A study of interpersonal interactions with a stranger found that the personality characteristics of an opposite-sex partner affect the nonverbal behaviors of women in the first minute of contact, but do not affect men (Weitz, 1976). The nonverbal dominance behavior of females was inversely related ($-.57$) to the dominance scores of their male partners, and the females' nonverbal warmth behavior was also negatively related ($-.72$) to their partner's need for affiliation. These relationships were not significant for men (the correlations were not presented), so only women were sensitive to and affected by the dominance and affiliative needs of their partner.

This greater sensitivity of women to other people may occur in other situations, where the difference may have far-reaching consequences. Male college students asked to teach a "child" a particular task by rewarding correct responses, tried to do so with relatively little regard for what the child was actually doing (there was no child present; responses were feigned by an experimenter in another room). In fact, the child was teaching the subject by performing a correct response only when one particular reward (out of the two the subject had) had been given on the last trial. Only 27 percent of the male college students succeeded in teaching the child, but 67 percent of the females did, demonstrating a greater responsiveness to what the child was actually doing (Arenson and Bialor, 1976).

Most of this research suggests that women are more sensitive to social stimuli. This sensitivity is very useful for successful affiliation (not to mention successful manipulation, as the high Mach girls showed), and affiliation seems more important to females than to males, since they are socialized into viewing successful affiliation as achievement. It is also possible that the lower status of women makes them more sensitive to interpersonal stimuli.

Sex Differences in Correlates of the Affiliation Motive

Need to affiliate scores probably have different meanings for women and men. Need to affiliate more often correlates with achievement behavior (but not with the need to achieve) in women than in men. Need for power and need for affiliation are negatively correlated to a greater degree in women than in men. Women's scores on need to affiliate tests are not related to popularity (Fishman, cited by Boyatzis, 1973), whereas men's scores are negatively related to popularity (Atkinson, et al., 1954; Shipley and Veroff, 1952). More early maturing girls than later maturers have a high need for affiliation, but the reverse is true for early and late maturing boys (M. Jones and Mussen, 1958). All these correlations suggest that need to affiliate tests measure different behaviors in men and women.

In our own recent work with the Personality Research Form (K. B. Hoyenga, Wallace and Mathes, unpublished data), we found sex differences in correlations with the affiliation scale that exceeded the sex differences found in the normative group for that test (Jackson, 1967). Men's affiliation scores were correlated with exhibitionism, whereas women's scores were not. This may be related to the sex differences in the correlation of affiliation and popularity—perhaps exhibitionists are not well liked. Women's scores were negatively correlated with autonomy and positively correlated with nurturance.

Conclusions

Affiliation in men may be related to unpopularity and exhibitionism, while in women it may be inversely related to autonomy and the need for power and directly related to nurturance. Affiliation scores have different meanings for men and women, as was predicted in the section on achievement. Women's greater concern with social stimuli and affiliation may reflect their fusion of achievement and affiliation. They are sensitive to faces and to body language because those abilities are needed for successful affiliation, which leads to achievement.

NURTURANCE AND HELP GIVING

We will define **nurturance** to include care taking directed towards children younger than the subject being observed. **Help giving** refers to aid directed towards peers of the subject or towards people older than the subject. This would include data on **bystander Intervention,** which measures, for example, the subject's willingness to pick up a dropped package or to intervene to prevent a murder. The distinction between help giving and care taking may seem arbitrary, but helping someone younger, helping children, may reflect different motives than helping a peer.

Some evidence suggests there are biological and cultural biases for sex differences in nurturance and help giving. There are consistent sex differences in nurturance in most primates, though not all, and many primate males do show relatively large amounts of parenting behaviors. The adrenogenital females show a lack of interest in infants—or an actual aversion to them—much more often than control females, and they also have very little interest in babysitting. On the other hand, androgen-insensitive women (with XY genes) and Turner's women are very interested in children, perhaps because they are not exposed to the inductive effects of ovarian or testicular androgen. Some of these effects, however, may be due to parental expectations and biases in rearing these children.

Hormones also activate some components of maternal behavior. Hormones may be related to maternal behavior shortly after giving birth in humans, as they are in rats. That the period just after birth is important for human maternal behavior is indicated by the lasting bad effects of separating mothers and infants at this period (Greenberg, Rosenberg, and Lind, 1973; Leifer et al., 1972). Another indication that hormones affect nurturance is the fact that mothers in the premenstrual period take their children to the hospital more often than at any other time of the cycle.

Cross-culturally, child care is assigned to females, and females are more often reared to be more nurturant. By the time they reach older ages (seven to

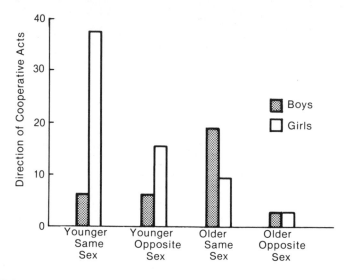

FIGURE 10.2 _____

COOPERATIVE BEHAVIOR OF NURSERY SCHOOL CHILDREN TOWARD OTHER
CHILDREN

*The first pair of bars shows the proportion of all cooperative acts that boys directed
toward younger boys and girls directed toward younger girls; the second pair
shows those directed by boys toward younger girls and girls toward younger
boys. The last two pairs show cooperative behaviors directed toward older children.*

With permission from C. Brindley, P. Clark, C. Hutt, I. Robinson, and E. Wethli, "Sex Differences in the
Activities and Social Interactions of Nursery School Children." In R. P. Michael and J. H. Crook (eds.),
Comparative Ecology and Behavior of Primates (New York: Academic Press, 1972), fig. 4, p. 815. Copy-
right by Academic Press Inc. (London) Ltd.

eleven), girls offer more help and support and more often suggest that someone
do something for his or her own good or because the rules suggest that he or she
do something (Whiting and Edwards, 1973). In view of all this, it is surprising that
so few sex differences are reported in our own society.

Nurturance

On paper-and-pencil tests, women score higher than men in nurturance (Jackson,
1967), but behavioral data show few sex differences. Hutt (1972a, 1972b; see also
Brindley et al., 1972) reported that girls directed cooperative behavior toward
younger children much more than boys, as indicated in Figure 10.2. The cooperative behavior of girls was primarily of a care-taking and protective nature; boys
tried more often to join in the activities of older boys. Similarly, O'Bryant and
Brophy (1976) found that two and a half times as many girls as boys (seventeen of
thirty-five, as opposed to seven of thirty-five) helped a younger, same-sex child
who requested aid.

Sears (cited by Maccoby and Jacklin, 1974) reanalyzed his data on nurturance in children to see if having younger siblings, thus having the opportunity to learn by observation of the mother, had an effect. Girls were nurturant to a baby doll whether or not they had younger siblings, but boys were nurturant only when they had younger siblings. This data could mean that girls are more prepared to learn to be nurturant and so require fewer trials (fewer observations of nurturant adults) to learn this behavior. Other than these observations, few sex differences have been reported.

Observations were made of both fathers and mothers of newborn infants. In one study (Parke and O'Leary, 1976), when both parents were present, mothers smiled more but fathers did more looking, touching, rocking, and holding. When each parent was alone, however, fathers were nurturant as much as mothers or more. Despite this, Lamb's research (1977) suggests that the types of parental interactions may differ. He found that mothers held infants most often to take care of them, while fathers held them mostly to play with them. Thus, there may be no sex difference in the amount of parental interest, but perhaps the ways of expressing that interest show sex differences. What might it mean to the child if the mother is the care taker, but the father is the one who plays?

Bem's research on androgyny also suggests a lack of sex differences in nurturance. Androgynous people of both sexes play with a kitten, although a feminine woman does not (Bem, 1975). But both feminine and androgynous people interact with an infant and with a lonely college student. However, overall, women were more nurturant toward the lonely college student than men, even androgynous men (Bem et al., 1976).

Helping Behavior

Deaux (1976) reviewed studies of sex differences in the incidence of helping behavior and concluded that none were consistent. Women more often receive help, but whether or not help is given depends upon several factors. Women may be less likely to take the initiative in a helping situation, but they are not less likely to respond to requests for help or to mail a stamped letter found lying on the ground by a mailbox. If all else is equal, people seem more willing to help a person of the opposite sex. Both men and women are not likely to help if the task involves sex-inappropriate behaviors, such as tire changing for women or purchasing a hair remover for men, but they do help if the behavior is sex-role appropriate. Men are more willing to intervene to help stop a fight than women (Borofsky, Slotlack, and Messe, 1971), and females use more nurturant types of behavior in helping people with problems (Haccoun, Allen, and Fader, 1976). Although either gender may volunteer to help equally often, females continue to help for a longer time (Pandey and Griffitt, 1974).

Two behaviors related to help giving and nurturance are empathy and sympathy. **Empathy** means recognizing emotions and feelings in other people, a skill women may more often develop than men, as reviewed earlier. **Sympathy** means experiencing the emotion that another person does, feeling joy or anger when he or she does. In L. Hoffman's review (1977) of the literature, he concluded that women more often than men have emotions induced in them by viewing the emotions of someone else. He believed that this difference appeared very early in life, perhaps even in infancy, and was due both to socialization and to biological biases. If this is true, women might be more motivated to be soothing and nurturant, to children as well as to adults, since they might be experiencing the other person's distress. Males would be more likely to take an instrumental, problem-solving approach to alleviate the problem.

Summary. There do not seem to be any consistent sex differences in the likelihood of exhibiting nurturant or helping behaviors. That does not mean that sex differences will never appear, but only that the occurrence of differences depends upon the task, the situation, and the other person or persons involved. There is little evidence of sex difference in any personality trait of nurturance, despite the biological evidence. There seem to be sex differences in the way nurturance is expressed, though. Women may more often experience a similar emotion when viewing someone else's joy or pain, and thus may more often express their concern or use nurturance to solve the problems of another person. Men may more often take instrumental problem-solving approaches. Men may also more often use playfulness to express nurturance.

SEX DIFFERENCES IN COMMUNICATION STYLE AND IN VALUES

Verbal Style

Women and men use language differently (Deaux, 1976; Key, 1975a). Even cross-culturally, females are more correct in their use of grammar, which Key attributes to their aspirations to higher status. Also, men sometimes equate nonstandard usage with masculinity. Women apologize more often, and also use hyperbole more often, giving phrases strong emphasis ("I'd just *die!*").

The intonation of females more often indicates surprise, hesitancy, cheerfulness, and politeness. Women are more likely to end a sentence with a rise in pitch, making the sentence sound tentative. Another tendency also makes women sound more hesitant: they use tag-questions instead of statements when they speak. A woman says, "The cake I baked was good, wasn't it?" Men would be more likely to say, "I baked a good cake today." Men also give commands more often, especially to females, whereas women make the same request more indirectly: "While you're up, dear, would you mind getting me a cup of coffee?"

Subjects associate male and female language forms with stereotypic traits. For example, a person using a female language form rather than a male form is seen as neat, dependent, easily influenced, less decisive, more submissive and passive, and less confident (Edelsky, 1976). And not only are female language forms more often attributed to females, they are also rated as indicating less intelligence, even when the speaker's gender is not specified (Siegler and Siegler, 1976).

In conversations between women and men, women are more often interrupted and men more often initiate topics or communications (Key, 1975a; Michelini, Passalacqua, and Cusimano, 1976). This particular sex difference is often large and dramatic, and may be related to dominance. Willis and Williams (1976) analyzed conversations of groups of women and men in natural settings. Women and men interrupted others in equal amounts (although men talked more overall), but women interrupted men and women equally, whereas men interrupted women more than four times as often as they interrupted men. Also, women agreed with men more often than they disagreed with them, but men disagreed with women more than four times as often as they agreed. In fact, when women interrupted men, it was usually to agree with them.

Thus, there are recognizably male and female patterns of speech. Women sound more tentative than men—they use apologies and tag-questions and end statements with a rise in intonation. Female speech is seen as indicating submissiveness, passivity, and less intelligence. That may be part of the reason that women are more often interrupted by men, although speech patterns probably simply confirm the other data on dominance interactions.

Nonverbal Communication

The sexes also differ from each other nonverbally. Boys and girls and women and men keep varying distances from each other and they stand, sit, and carry objects differently. There are also differences in smiling, touching, and eye contact.

Personal Space.   Personal space is defined as that area around the body that is defended. You can approach another person to be only so close, and no closer; if you approach too closely, that person will step back. There are both individual and cultural differences in personal space.

Sex differences have been found in the use of personal space by children. As mentioned earlier, some studies have shown that girls display more proximal attachment behaviors at one year of age, and that the shift from proximal to distal attachment is more likely in the male than in the female. Personal space was also measured by having children adjust figures representing themselves and others, and then measuring the distance between the figures (Guardo, 1969; Guardo and Meisels, 1971; Meisels and Guardo, 1969). Girls placed themselves closer to best friends (but not to friends in general) and further from strangers and people they disliked or feared. Where girls placed these figures was more affected by the emotional tone of the relationship; where boys placed them was more affected by the gender of the stimulus figure.

Among adults, males less often directly face each other than do females (S. Jones, 1971). This difference affects the way people react to different approaches from others (Fisher and Bryne, 1975; Krail and Leventhal, 1976). Males reacted more negatively than females when a stranger approached them face to face, and females reacted more negatively to approaches from the side. In observations in a library, students of both sexes erected barriers of books and personal effects, but males did so against a frontal approach, whereas females erected them against an approach from the side. Another study found that males oriented directly towards someone they disliked, while females oriented directly towards someone they liked (Mehrabian, 1968). The quickest reaction to an invasion of personal space was seen when males sat down facing other males; females also reacted faster to an invasion by same-sex intruders (Krail and Leventhal, 1976). When people are told to get together for a discussion with a stranger, females prefer to sit closer to a female stranger than a male one, and males prefer to sit further away from or opposite to a stranger, regardless of gender (Sommer, 1974). Thus, whether or not interactions are anticipated seems to affect the direction and closeness of an approach. Men seem to prefer to sit opposite a stranger with whom they expect to interact, but do not like to sit opposite a man with whom they are not interacting; the reverse seems true of women.

Other research found that male-male pairs kept a greater distance from each other than female-female pairs; male-female pairs stood closest of all (Baxter, 1970; Evans and Howard, 1973). Women are also approached more closely than men; the differences in personal space for women are more affected by their relationship with the other person, just as with girls (Willis, 1966). Finally, female pedestrians are more often disturbed or pushed from their path by motorists than are male pedestrians (Henderson and Lyons, 1972).

It seems that women have a smaller personal space than men, and that their space is invaded more often. These differences, like those in speech patterns, may simply reflect the sex difference in dominance interactions.

Body Language. **Body language** refers to nonverbal communication. It includes gesture, facial expression, and posture. This is a subtle area of sex differences, but one that is very important in interpersonal relations. Women can be labeled as masculine or men as feminine because they exhibit too much of the body language of the opposite sex. Earlier we suggested that women should be more sensitive to these types of communication than men (the evidence will be reviewed in Chapter 11); here we will review sex differences in the frequency with which these behaviors occur.

It is possible to identify gender on the basis of posture alone. Women and, men can correctly identify the gender of a figure or an outline copy of a magazine photograph by posture alone, with all other cues to gender removed. Male postures included standing with legs apart and hands on hips and sitting with legs spread, often facing the back of a chair. Females stand with arms crossed in front of them, and sit with their legs closer together. Some sex differences in posture are seen cross-culturally; in many cultures, males assume open-leg standing or sitting positions (Hewes, 1957). Figure 10.3 illustrates some sex differences in posture, showing how people who changed their gender learned to adopt the postures of their new gender.

Sex differences in gesture start rather early in life. Boys and girls in two different age groups (four to five and eleven to twelve) were observed at play. Limp wrists, arm flutters, and flexed elbows were observed more often in girls than in boys, regardless of age (Rekers, Amaro-Plotkin, and Low, 1977). Same-sex modeling of stereotypic behaviors must occur early and must be pervasive.

There are also sex differences in the way people carry things. Females carry parcels closer to their bodies than males, often clutching books to their breasts. This sex difference was found in three colleges and two high schools in the United States, and also in colleges in Canada, Costa Rica, and El Salvador (M. Jenni, 1976). From 68 percent to 92 percent of all females used the female carrying pattern for books, and from 91 percent to 100 percent of the males used the male pattern. This sex difference was largest among adolescents, and appeared to decrease with age. Young children of both genders used the male carrying pattern, but the sex difference began to appear before the body proportions began to differentially change during adolescence (D. Jenni and Jenni, 1976).

The reasons for this sex difference in carrying patterns are not at all clear. The female pattern may indicate more tension or anxiety, and females may use the books to defend the body. The difference also probably results from the different hip width of male and female adults. The difference in hip width causes adults to carry differently, and children then model the adults. Still, it is not clear why children do not copy this difference even earlier, or why the difference fades with age.

There are also sex differences in eye contact, which may be another result of differences in dominance. Females use more eye contact than males (Exline, 1972), and females find eye contact more important. In one study, males found women who looked at them more attractive and interesting than women who did not look at them; on the other hand, women preferred men who looked at them less (Kleinke et al., 1973). This probably reflects an awareness of the sex difference in eye contact. Wives may look more at husbands than husbands do at wives (Key, 1975a). In another study, women were less talkative and more uncomfortable and men more talkative when they could not see to whom they were talking (Argyle, Lalljee, and Cook, 1968). If women are more sensitive to interpersonal cues than men are, and affiliation is more salient for them than for men, then the greater importance of eye contact to women seems understandable. The lower status of women might also make a difference here; women may find it more important to be able to read men through eye contact than men do to read women.

Sex differences in touching may also have overtones of dominance. Females do more same-sex touching than males (Mehrabian, 1971), which M. Lewis attributed to a continuation of sex differences in children's attachment behavior. But contact between opposite-sex pairs shows a different kind of sexual dimorphism. Males touched females more frequently than females touched males, especially when interactions occurred out-of-doors (Henley, 1973). Dominant males also touched their subordinates more than the reverse occurred, as though touching was a dominance gesture (Henley, 1973). When members of the same sex greeted each other, or when a man greeted a woman, the more physical contact the greeter made, the more favorably evaluated the greeter was (Silverthorne et al., 1976). However the more physical contact a female greeter initiated with a male subject, the less favorably she was evaluated. Again, touch seems to have overtones of dominance.

Women also smile more (Deaux, 1976; Key, 1975a). Adolescent females, for instance, say they smile even when they are not happy. As mentioned earlier, mothers of newborns also smile more than fathers. Beekman (cited by Weitz, 1976) found that females smiled more, but also found that the sexes smiled for different reasons. Females smiled when anxious, uncomfortable, or out of deference or abasement; men's smiling was correlated with need for affiliation and with sociability. Again, females' smiling seems to be connected to dominance. Men reportedly smile only when they say positive things, while women smile when they say negative things as well (Bugental, Love, and Gianetto, 1971).

Summary. Many of the differences in nonverbal communication seem to reflect dominance and submissiveness, with men more often making the dominant

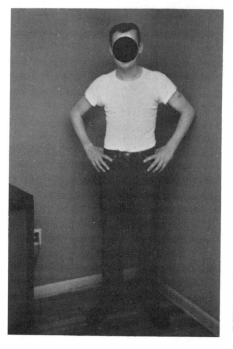

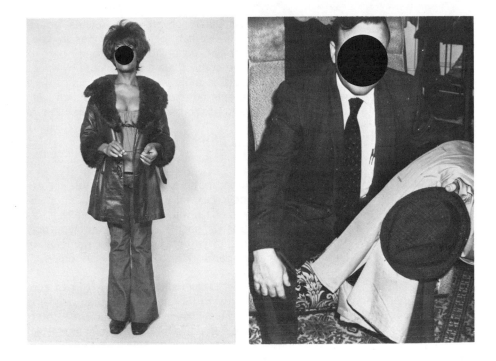

FIGURE 10.3 _____

GENDER DIFFERENCES IN POSTURE SHOWN BY PEOPLE WHO CHANGED
THEIR GENDER

*In A an adrenogenital female of ambiguous rearing and male gender identity who
switched to male legal status at adolescence shows stereotypic masculine stance
and expression. In B two pictures taken on the same day show the alternation of a
male transvestite and his feminine alter ego. C shows a male-to-female transsexual,
D a female-to-male transsexual, each showing postures appropriate to their reassigned status. Note especially the differences between open leg and closed leg
postures.*

Reprinted from the *Nebraska Symposium on Motivation, 1973,* edited by James K. Cole and Richard
Dienstbier. By permission of the University of Nebraska Press. Prints courtesy of Dr. John Money.

gestures and women the submissive ones. Other nonverbal differences are attributed to greater anxiety on the part of the woman, or to differences in body shape. Men more often assume dominant, open-leg postures, and carry parcels further from their body. Women use more eye contact, are touched more by males than they touch males, smile more, and adopt more submissive postures. The cause of these differences probably represents an interpersonal interaction, with dominant gestures eliciting submissive gestures, and submissive gestures in turn encouraging dominant gestures.

Physical Appearance

Another possible area of sex differences that may be based on sex-role stereotypes is what qualities people of the opposite sex associate with physical attractiveness. There is a stereotype that beauty is good, with attractive people rated as happier and more intelligent than less attractive people. But this stereotype may be true especially for women, because affiliation is more important for women than for men, and successful affiliation may depend more on physical attributes for women than it does for men.

Some data suggest that this is the case. M. Hill and Lando (1976) had subjects rate photographs of people; subjects rated the attractive woman as being happier, more intelligent, and more competent than the less attractive woman. There were no such effects for men. In fact, attractive males are sometimes perceived as having lower ability than unattractive males (Bar-Tal and Saxe, 1976). An attractive woman can make her male escort be perceived as more successful. Unattractive women are rated lower than unattractive men by both males and females (A. Miller, 1970). In Coleman's study (1961) on adolescents cited earlier, being attractive was the most certain way to gain popularity for the adolescent female. So beauty may only be good for females, because women succeed by affiliating.

The differences in the evaluations made by other people affect the evaluations made by the self. Self-rated attractiveness predicted self-esteem better in adolescent females than in males, but self-rated physical skill predicted the self-esteem of males significantly better than it did the self-esteem of females (Lerner, Orlos, and Knapp, 1976). Attractiveness in college women was associated with high self-esteem, low neuroticism, and happiness, whereas attractiveness in men was associated with low self-esteem and higher neuroticism (Mathes and Khan, 1975). The stereotypes may cause people to think it is more important for a woman than for a man to be physically attractive and so influence the person's self-esteem.

Morality

Men and women may also differ in their evaluation of social rules and principles of conscience. In one study concerning the internalization of moral values females showed more consideration for others, although no sex differences in the ability to make moral judgments were found (M. Hoffman, 1975).

However, females more often associate transgressions with guilt (internal locus of control) while males more often associate transgressions with fear (external locus) (M. Hoffman, 1975). This difference corresponds rather closely to the sex differences in the attributions of causes of failure: lack of ability for women (internal locus) and luck for men (external locus). These sex differences are more reliable and pronounced among adults than among preadolescents. Gross (1972) found that if subjects found money when they were alone, 45 percent of the women returned it, but only 23 percent of the men did. When the subjects found the money with someone else present, the sex difference disappeared. This also suggests that males were more externally controlled and females more internally controlled. Douvan (1957) found that adolescent boys were more apt to consider rules as external controls rather than internalize them as being morally correct.

contrary to freud

Other evidence indicates that males may be more willing to bend the rules and females to judge transgressions more severely. For example, Mathews and Cooper (1976) instructed subjects in a teacher-learner experiment to lie. They found that males were more likely to do so, especially to female learners. Female jurors seem more likely to vote to convict defendants (East, 1973), and to judge social violations more severely (Oetzel, 1966; Sherman, 1971).

There seems to be little reason to believe in a sex difference in morality (or superego). Instead, the sex differences that do appear seem to be caused by different variables affecting the sexes differently. The moral judgments and behaviors of females are affected by having an internal locus of control for transgressions, by consideration for others, and by guilt; the judgments and behaviors of males are affected by fear of getting caught or fear of the consequences.

Values

Given the sex differences we have discussed so far, it would not be surprising to find that women and men value events and objects differently. Based on the evidence we have seen, it would seem that men value competition, scientific toys and principles, prestige, power, dominance, and freedom, and women value interpersonal relationships and security.

In fact, when people rate the values of different interests or pursuits, women rate aesthetics and social and religious areas higher than men do, while men rate theoretical, economic, and political areas higher (Allport, Vernon, and Lindzey, 1951). A more recent study replicated Allport's results. Walberg (1969) tested 705 girls and 1,369 boys taking a high-school physics course. Girls rated social, aesthetic and religious values higher, while boys rated economic, political, and theoretical values higher. Job values and desires also show these sex differences (Singer and Stefflre, 1954). Women value having an interesting experience or being of service to society, while men value power, profit, and independence; but although these sex differences do appear, women and men do have very similar ratings of job values. Still, men do value prestigious jobs, while women are more likely to show an aversion to them (Barnett, 1975).

However, these sex differences may vary with sex role. Nontraditional women rate intellectual curiosity, ability, and creativity higher than traditional women; nontraditional women also rate moral values, emotional maturity, happiness, conscientiousness, and interpersonal skill lower than traditional women (Lipman-Blumen, 1972). This suggests that these sex differences are solely a function of sex-role socialization.

SUMMARY

The sexes may differ in many personality traits, but most of these differences seem to reflect different socialization pressures for the two sexes. Women are socialized to achieve in order to affiliate and to achieve by affiliation. Thus, they will more often pay attention to and value social stimuli. Because of this emphasis on affiliation, women may believe that they have less control over their lives, that they succeed by luck and fail by lack of ability, and are unable to do anything about either condition. These differences may also enter the area of moral behavior, with both failure and guilt being internalized more by women. Men may conform to moral rules out of fear, women out of guilt.

The sex differences in verbal styles and personal space, in cooperation and competition, also seem to result from the greater male interest in dominance interactions, with adult females somewhat more often taking the submissive postures with respect to men (Goffman, cited by Hochschild, 1973). These particular differences are a product of socialization, added on to the male bias for aggression and dominance. As a result, the differences will most likely appear where the different sex stereotypes are in greatest evidence or are most free to operate; for example, sex differences in conformity and in helpfulness appear when the task is stereotyped, or when motives are assessed by ratings rather than by observation of behavior.

Aggression and interest in dominance interactions may reflect biological bias, but sex-role socialization affects the way men and women express aggression. In fact, socialization undoubtably exaggerates the sex difference; human aggression seems more dimorphic than human size differences. Nurturance may also be biologically biased, but conclusions about sex differences in nurturance can only be tentative. They have not often been looked for, and even when they have, they have not often been found.

A Summarizing Study

One study not discussed earlier rather dramatically summarizes and confirms much of the data cited in this chapter. Aries (1977) studied interpersonal interactions in six experimental discussion groups that met together for five ninety-minute sessions. There were five to seven people in each group; two groups were all male, two all female, and two were mixed.

Sex differences in dominance were seen in the groups' discussions. In the mixed groups, males both initiated and received more interactions than the females. Also, the all-male groups formed more stable dominance hierarchies, while a female who dominated an all-female group in one session tended to withdraw later, saying she had felt uncomfortable. Male groups also talked more about subjects in which they had expertise (dominance through knowledge), or about subjects that involved sports and hostility. Thus, the male groups were more often concerned with competition and leadership while the women more often expressed affection and concern for others.

Women also revealed more of themselves than did men. "Men in the all-male groups talked very little of themselves, their feelings, or of their relationships with persons of significance to them. In the all-female groups, on the other hand, members shared a great deal of information about themselves, their feelings, their homes, and their relationships with family, friends and lovers. . . . Women referred more frequently to self, feelings, affiliation, home and family" (Aries, 1977, pp. 295–96). However, men in mixed groups revealed more about themselves, while females in mixed groups revealed less and talked less, especially to other females. Thus, the presence of women encouraged androgynous behavior in men, but the presence of men inhibited women. Does this also happen in coeducational schools?

Implications for Other Chapters

Some of the data of this chapter can help to explain material from earlier chapters, such as that on achievement, affiliation, and intellectual abilities. Dominance may be related to ambition and drive in men, and these all may in part be affected by androgen. The greater help given by mothers to girls as opposed to boys and the greater early verbal stimulation of girls would exaggerate (or create) a sex difference in verbal ability (Bing, 1963). Sex differences in spatial and mathematical ability may be in part genetic or hormonal, but socialization increases these tendencies in men by preventing the conflict between affiliation and achievement; masculine sex-role preference, independence, and the need to achieve are positively correlated to spatial ability in both sexes. The female's socialization to be affiliative makes her achievement dependent upon other people, giving her an external locus of control. Thus, she may become an **externalizer** (a person able to reveal emotions to other people), while the male responds to other people internally, or physiologically (Buck et al., 1972). Women also reveal more about themselves. Thus, the male may be less accurate in sending emotions to other people and at reading the body language of others.

The sex differences in the attribution of causes of success and failure lead to lowered expectation of success for girls, because they think they fail from lack of ability and because lower dominance levels may lead them to emphasize past failures (Maslow, 1937, 1939). This, combined with the option of achieving through affiliation, leads more often to decreasing IQs, because girls emphasize affiliative traits—low aggression and high passivity are often associated with declining IQ (Kagan et al., 1958). This could partly account for the relative lack of women geniuses. High IQ girls are popular, and girls with a high need for achievement get married early; high IQ men have successful professional careers, and men with a high need to achieve become entrepreneurs. But the male, who has no other route to success than achievement, has to live with his failures by projecting the cause for the failure to something outside of himself. In the last chapter, we will look at some possible consequences these socialization pressures have on the mental health of men and women.

KEY TERMS AND CONCEPTS

Dominance
Assertiveness
Need for power
Machiavellianism
Emotional dependency
Instrumental dependency
Aggressive dependency
Proximity
Proximity seeking
Proximal attachment
Distal attachment

Passivity
Need to affiliate
Self-disclosure
Nurturance
Help giving
Bystander intervention
Empathy
Sympathy
Body language
Externalizers

QUESTIONS ON KEY ISSUES

1. What evidence indicates there is a biological bias for sex differences in aggression and dominance?

2. Where, and under what conditions, is the male human more aggressive than the female? What part do socialization pressures play in this sex difference?

3. What is the evidence from behavioral experiments that the human male may be biologically more prepared to learn to be aggressive?

4. How do socialized sex roles affect sex differences in each of the following areas: conformity; competition and cooperation; dominance; helping behavior.

5. What are some implications of childhood differences in dependency and passivity? What do these differences *not* imply?

6. If affiliation equals achievement more often for women than for men, what implications does this have for sex differences in affiliative behaviors, in characteristics associated with physical attractiveness, and in values and morality?

7. In what ways are sex differences in dominance behavior mirrored by sex differences in the following areas: verbal styles; personal space; and body language?

_____

CHAPTER 11

Sex Differences and Dimorphic Response to Stimuli

The sexes may differ in responses to many different stimuli. There may be sex differences in response to drugs, to stress, and to stimuli such as lights, sounds, faces, and scents. Some people claim that the male is more adapted for responses involving intense expenditures of energy. Some theorists propose that the sexes differ in their response to erotic stimuli, such as pornography. Do men have a greater sex drive? The data relevant to these kinds of sex differences will be presented in this chapter.

This chapter, then, will look at differences in sensitivities, skills, and responses. These sexual dimorphisms are obviously affected by experience, training, and expectations, but many are also affected by biology. For example, visual and auditory sensitivities vary with the menstrual cycle, which suggests that if there are any sex differences in such sensitivities, they may be due in part to biological biases created by sex differences in inductive or activational hormones.

PERCEPTUAL-MOTOR SKILLS

Strength, Drugs, and Stress

It has been claimed that men are stronger than women, and that women are stronger than men. In the first case, muscular strength is usually being discussed, while in the second case, the ability to withstand stress is usually what is meant. To what extent are both claims true?

Males: "An Engine Operating at Higher Levels of Speed and Intensity"? At birth, the male is heavier and has a larger head circumference (Palti and Adler, 1975; Yang, Federman, and Douthitt, 1976). The male grows faster before birth and after birth for about seven months. After that, the female grows faster until about four years of age, but remains shorter and lighter until about eight years of age (Tanner, 1970). From the age of two on, the male has a higher basal metabolic rate.

The sexes also differ in strength, and in the relative amounts of muscle and fat in the body. From infancy on, girls have more fat (Hutt, 1972a; Palti and Alder, 1975), but boys have larger and stronger muscles and seem to be more adapted to vigorous activity. By college age, female bodies are 25 percent fat, while male bodies are 15 percent fat (Wilmore, 1975). This sex difference in muscle and fat means that men have more body water, since muscle tissues have more water than fat tissues; total body water constitutes 60 percent of men's weight and 50.2 percent of women's weight (Edelman and Liebman, 1959). Men can carry more oxygen in their blood because of an increase in red blood cells at puberty. Boys and men also have a lower heart rate when resting (though they have a higher blood pressure) and can more effectively neutralize the metabolic byproducts of exercise and work. Paralleling the sex difference in muscle tissue, the sex difference in strength increases from age eleven to age seventeen (Tanner, 1970; Wilmore, 1975), and may even be present at birth (Korner, 1974).

These differences are largely the result of differences in activational hormones, but they are also caused by experience. Androgens that increase muscle mass are the so-called **anabolic steroids** (meaning they promote protein synthesis). Estrogens increase fatty tissue, and both estrogens and progestins are referred to as **catabolic steroids,** (meaning they promote the breakdown of protein). Still, experience obviously plays a part in strength. Starting almost at birth, male children may be more physically stimulated than female children are, which would increase the difference. Recent research on female athletes suggests that the physical differences in strength and cardiovascular (heart, lungs, and veins) fitness are largely the result of life-style, since training greatly reduces—though it does not eliminate—sex differences in strength, especially in the leg muscles (Drinkwater et al., 1975; Wilmore, 1975). Training increases muscle strength in both sexes, but the increase in muscle size is much greater in the male (Wilmore, 1975).

Responses to Drugs.   The different effects gonadal hormones have on metabolism (see Appendix B), along with the sex difference in the percent of body water, probably accounts for most of the sex differences in the response to drugs. Antidepressants (such as tryptophan and imipramine) are less effective in females than in males (Kline and Shah, 1974; Raskin, 1974). Pentobarbital has a greater depressive and fatiguing effect in women (Slánská et al., 1974). Chlorpromazine is more likely to disturb motor control in female humans and rats than in males (Mislow and Friedhoff, 1973), and males are better able to resist the toxic effects of drugs (Selye, 1971a, 1971b). Female rats are also more affected than males by marijuana (Carlini and Masur, 1969; Cohn, Barratt, and Pirch, 1972).

Alcohol also affects women more than men. Given equal amounts of alcohol on the basis of body weight, women still reach higher blood levels of alcohol than men, metabolize it faster than men do, and more often rate the whole experience as unpleasant (Myrsten, Hollstedt, and Holmberg, 1975; B. Jones and Jones, 1976; B. Jones, Jones, and Paredes, 1976). Hormones may be involved in this difference since women have also been reported to get most intoxicated premenstrually and at ovulation, and to get least intoxicated during menstruation (B. Jones and Jones, 1976).

Thus, women are more likely to get depressed (and less likely to get undepressed) and to get drunk, given equivalent dosages of drugs. In general, males metabolize a drug more rapidly than females (except alcohol), due to estrogen effects on the liver in females; for example, females will sleep longer after a given dose of barbiturates (Gram and Gillete, 1969) because estrogen retards the breakdown of that drug by the liver and so the effect of the drug lasts longer.

Responses to Stress. The sexes differ in their responses to stress. J. Gray (1971b) states that males are more often adversely affected by stress; this difference may be the result of differences in adrenal responses. Although the normal adrenal level of corticoid, a hormone released by stress, is higher in women than in men, and although the corticoid response to stress is more intense in women, corticoid returns more quickly to normal levels in females than in males (Erskine, Stern, and Levine, 1975; J. Gray, 1971b). This means that stress affects females sharply but briefly, while it bothers males for a longer time. Females also discriminate more among different levels of stress (Erskine et al., 1975). Although there is no difference in the rate of excretion of adrenaline and noradrenaline from the adrenal when at rest, males show a greater increase with exercise (Johansson, 1972) and with stress (Frankenhaeuser, Dunne, and Lundberg, 1976). However, in the partially sex-role reversed hamster, the female is the more aggressive and the male has the higher normal level of corticoid secretion, thus reversing the human and rat sex difference (Zieger, Lux, and Kubatsch, 1974).

In humans, the sexes also differ in their responses to electric shock. The **galvanic skin response**, or **GSR,** is the change in electrical resistance of the skin caused by sweat gland activity; it is used as an index of emotional arousal. In one study, the GSR of females was more variable between tests, although basal GSR was lower in women than in men (Montagu and Coles, 1966). J. L. Berry and Martin (1957) found greater female GSR responses across all experimental conditions. They also found that classical conditioning of the GSR works best in males who are aroused and in females who are relaxed. Another study showed that females exhibit a greater response to stress than males and reach their highest levels of GSR at lower levels of stress (Kopacz and Smith, 1971). The sexes also differ in the type of reaction. Males respond to shock with changes in blood pressure; women respond with changes in respiration rate (Liberson and Liberson, 1975). This may be related to the greater frequency of heat attacks in males (see Appendix B).

Summary. As Hutt points out, the male "has been likened to an engine operating at higher levels of speed and intensity and which therefore needs more fuel than the less energetic female" (1972a, p. 79). However, the female of most species, including the human, seems more capable of coping with stress, although she may react more to it. These differences may be the product of selection pressures operating differentially upon the genders because of their different reproductive roles. As detailed in Appendix B, the male role adapted men to handle peak expenditures of energy, whereas the female role adapted women to survive in times of short food supply. Different selection pressures led to sex differences in strength and response to stress. Hamsters, a species that reverses much of the reproductive role, also reverse many of these differences. With this in mind, it might be helpful to reread the first parts of Chapter 3.

Many, if not most, of these differences are due to differences in activational hormones. Testosterone and estrogen have different effects on the body, including the liver, the adrenal gland, and muscle mass. Still, experience undoubtedly plays a role. Males are encouraged to engage in sports and to develop their strength.

Also, sex-role socialization probably affects both responses to drugs and responses to stress. Women may believe themselves to be more emotional than men, which could affect their responses.

Differences Present Shortly after Birth

Hutt (1972a), Korner (1973), and Garai and Scheinfeld (1968) all reviewed the literature and concluded that there are several perceptual-motor sex differences in neonates. Since these differences appear shortly after birth, they presumably are not due to learning.

Sex Differences in Neonates.   Male neonates are said to be more active and more reactive to stimuli, while females are more sensitive to touch and to pain. Males may have more gross body movement (movement of the whole body); the movements of female infants tend to be finer, often directed toward the mouth region (Korner, 1974). Garai and Scheinfeld reported that "female neonates obtained significantly higher ratings on irritability" (p. 191) but Hutt said that "boys are found to sleep less than girls; they are also more fretful and irritable" (p. 82). Korner (1973) reported that female neonates spent more time in reflex smiles, rhythmical mouthing, and moving the mouth to objects, whereas males showed more startle responses. However, she observed no sex differences in fussiness.

Thus, there is great inconsistency in the data reported, suggesting that if there are sex differences among newborns, they are very small and depend very much upon the experimental situation and the particular response being measured. One study of 137 newborns found no sex differences in crying, arousal, activity, sleep, or any other behavior (Yang et al., 1976).

Causes of Sex Differences in Neonates.   Differences in neonates are usually said to be innate, since experience cannot have had much impact. However, it was recently suggested that some of the variability in the observations of sex differences may be the result of whether males were circumcised (Korner, 1974). Richards, Bernal, and Brackbill (1976) reviewed the literature on gender differences in neonatal behavior and pointed out that these differences are usually seen only in studies in America, where males are almost always circumcised, which creates a dramatic difference in experience between males and females. Circumcision has been found to decrease sleep and increase wakefulness, fussiness, and crying, so it could lead researchers to conclude, incorrectly, that there are sex differences in those behaviors.

Differences in neonates may also be caused by developmental differences. The female infant at any given age is more advanced than the male. Behavioral sex differences may then be a function of developmental stage rather than gender.

Summary.   Discrepancies in data are very common in research on neonates. If neonatal sex differences do exist, they are likely to be very small and to be found only in certain situations. Circumcision may lead to differences in behavior; these differences would be caused by the operation, not gender itself. Other differences may be the result of the fact that females develop faster than males. And differential effects of maternal behavior cannot be ruled out—even with neonates—since their treatment varies with infant gender.

Sensory Sensitivities

According to several reviewers, from birth on, women have lower touch and pain thresholds, and men are more sensitive to visual stimulation and females to auditory stimulation (Bardwick, 1971; Garai and Scheinfeld, 1968; Hutt, 1972a). The sex differences in auditory and visual ability are supposedly paralleled by the ability of those stimuli to be reinforcers; girls learn to increase visual fixation more when reinforced with soft tones, while boys learn better when reinforced by the presentation of a face (Watson, 1969). However, Maccoby and Jacklin (1974), in reviewing this literature, did not find much support for sex differences in audition, vision, or tactile sensitivity, although most of the studies they reviewed involved very young children. They found that the sex difference in auditory and visual reinforcement found in some studies was not replicated by later research. Differences among children, then, may be minimal, as they were for neonates. Among adults, however, some fairly consistent sex differences in responses to various types of skin sensations, in audition, in vision and in olfaction have been found.

Skin Sensation. Under some conditions, women are more sensitive to some types of skin sensations. One study, using a sophisticated and well-controlled technique for measuring pain sensitivity, found women to have lower thresholds, to be more sensitive (Procacci et al., 1972). Woman may also have lower pain tolerance. The tolerance level for men in one study was found to be 28.7 pounds per square inch of pressure, while that for women was 15.9 pounds (Woodrow, et al., 1972). In another study of eighteen men and eighteen women, six men and only one woman could tolerate the maximum shock level (Liberson and Liberson, 1975).

Sensitivity to stimuli other than pain may also show sex differences. Weinstein (1968) investigated the skin sensitivity of forty-eight adults and reported that women had a significantly greater sensitivity to pressure than men. But for all three measures of skin sensitivity—pressure, two-point discrimination, and point localization—gender significantly interacted with body part. Thus, Weinstein could get a significant sex difference in either direction, depending on which part of the body was used for the measurement. Still, women were more sensitive than men to pressure on all parts of the body.

Kenshalo, Nafe, and Brooks (1961) reported sex differences in sensitivity to cold. The threshold for cold sensation increases as the temperature of the environment to which the subject was adapted increases (difference thresholds increase when the intensity of the standard increases), but this increase occurred at higher adapting levels in females than in males; thus, females were more sensitive to cold at moderate adapting temperatures.

Sensitivity to Auditory and Visual Stimuli. Compared to males, females may have a lower auditory threshold—they may be more sensitive to sounds—but only for high frequency sounds (Corso, 1959; McGuinness, 1974). Boys from five to ten years old and men tolerate louder noises than women and girls (Elliott, 1971; McGuinness, 1974). Males reportedly have better visual acuity from ages eighteen to seventy-four (Burg, 1966; McGuinness, 1976; and Roberts, 1964). Women are more tolerant of bright lights than men, and when men and women of

TABLE 11.1

SEX DIFFERENCES IN TASTE SENSITIVITY

Taste	Effect	References
Quinine and Acid (bitter)	Females more sensitive	Nisbett and Gurwitz (1970); Soltan and Bracken (1958)
Salt	Males more sensitive	K. Jensen (1932); Nisbett and Gurwitz (1970)
	Females more sensitive	Pangborn (1959)
Sucrose (sweet)	Males more sensitive	Nisbett and Gurwitz (1970)
	Females more sensitive (but difference not significant)	Pangborn (1959)

Note: Differences in taste sensitivity do not imply differences in preference.

equal acuity were tested, the women were more sensitive to lights during all stages of dark adaptation (McGuinness, 1976). McGuinness and Lewis reported (1976) that a visual image (as in an afterimage) persisted longer in males but that females were probably more sensitive than males to red and orange. As mentioned earlier, the same was found to be true for one lower primate species, where the males had a defect of color vision in the red range but the females did not. These latter results suggest that there may be sex differences both in the eye and in the way that the brain processes visual information.

Taste and Olfactory Sensitivity. There have been relatively few attempts to measure sex differences in human taste sensitivity. As can be seen in Table 11.1, the few studies that have been done have not found consistent sex differences. However, this is not surprising, as we will see.

Several studies have not found any olfactory difference among newborn humans (Maccoby and Jacklin, 1974). However, Le Magnen (1948, 1952a), and Köster and Koelega (1976) found that adult women were more sensitive than men to the odors of musk as well as to the scent of some of the urinary hormone metabolites. Adult women seem to have greater sensitivity to other odors as well (Köster and Koelega, 1976; Schneider and Wolf, 1955).

Olfactory sensitivity is also at least somewhat hormone sensitive, so the sex differences may be partly the result of activational hormones. The sex difference in the sensitivity to the smell of musk appears only after puberty; before puberty, neither males nor females are sensitive to that odor (Köster and Koelega, 1976). Olfactory sensitivity to musk in women declines after the removal of the ovaries, but it may return with estrogen injections. Also, some women experience a decline in olfactory sensitivity at menopause (Le Magnen, 1950). However, these effects vary from species to species; in rats, puberty decreases the olfactory sensitivity of the female, although estrous (with its high estrogen) increases olfactory sensitivity (Good et al., 1976; Le Magnen, 1949, 1950, 1952a, 1952b; Pietras and Moulton, 1974; Schneider et al., 1958). Also, sensitivity to different odors is affected in different directions by estrogen and testosterone injections (Le Magnen, 1952b).

Thus, sex differences in taste and olfactory sensitivities are probably specific to the substance, the hormone, and the species involved. It is difficult to assert the existence of sex differences in odor and taste sensitivity at the present stage of research. Systematic studies, comparing species, hormones, and substances, simply have not been done; such research is badly needed.

Summary. There may be sex differences in pressure and cold sensitivity and in pain tolerance and pain thresholds. Sex differences in olfaction, taste preferences, and visual and auditory sensitivities may be seen, but only under some conditions. However, sensitivity to these stimuli varies in both men and women; that is, there are rhythms in which the sensory sensitivity of individuals varies. Until these rhythms have been identified and adequately characterized, comparing men and women with a single measurement for each remains a dubious endeavor. For example, there is apparently a circadian rhythm in pain sensitivity for men, but not for women (Procacci et al., 1972), so sex differences might vary according to the time of day of the test. Sex differences are also likely to be related to the day of the week and the month of the test. These differences in sensitivity may also be related to differences in socialization, a possibility that has been relatively neglected. Women might expect themselves to be more sensitive to taste and smell since they are expected to cook and clean, and since flowers are considered to be feminine.

Social Stimuli

Sex differences have also been reported in responses to social stimuli, sometimes called **social intelligence**. According to Garai and Scheinfeld's review (1968), during the first year of life, girls pay more attention to faces and to facial stimuli than to other visual stimuli; this differentiation in attention between social and nonsocial visual stimuli was not seen in boys. However, Maccoby and Jacklin (1974) found no evidence in their review that girls look more at social stimuli than boys, and even the sex differences in the distribution of attention between the social and nonsocial stimuli was not replicated by later research; thus, "there is no evidence that girls are more interested in social [and] boys in nonsocial stimulation" (p. 37).

However, H. Ellis (1975) reviewed studies involving the recognition of photographs of faces by adults and concluded that most studies find women have better facial recognition, particularly (or only) for female faces (J. Cross, Cross, and Daly, 1971, H. Ellis, Shepherd, and Bruce, 1973; Goldstein and Chance, 1970). Witryol and Kaess (1957; see also Kaess and Witryol, 1955) found that women more often than men remembered the names associated with photographs of men and the names associated with people interviewed, although both sexes did better at remembering the names associated with people of their own gender. In one names-and-faces task, females did so well that only 21.7 percent of them were below the male median (Witryol and Kaess, 1957). Both men and women have also improved with time on this task, possibly reflecting such social changes as the rise of feminism, and the increased value placed on typically feminine traits.

This sex difference may appear early in life. A sex difference in facial memory was seen in five- and six-month-olds. However, this sex difference was not seen when opposite-sex twins were compared to one another, perhaps because twins are less sensitive to faces (Fagan, 1972). The sex difference also was not found when the task was made easier, either by increasing the exposure time or by presenting the face twice, indicating that the sex difference only appears when the task is relatively difficult (Fagan, 1973). M. Lewis and Weinraub (1974) also found the sex difference appearing early. They reported sex differences in attention to faces of other infants in ten- to eighteen-month-old intants. Males looked more at males, and females looked more at females. But females began to do so earlier than males and did so to a greater extent.

Feldstein (1976) found that girls had better social memory. He gave children in a day-care center pictures of their classmates to identify. Even though the boys had attended the center on the average of three months longer than the girls, girls were more accurate at identifying the pictures (the mean errors were 4.83 and 7.29 for girls and boys, respectively). This difference could not be accounted for by differences in age, or differences in verbal, perceptual or memory ability.

Whatever the origin of this difference, contrary to Maccoby and Jacklin's conclusion, girls and women do seem to have a better memory for faces, starting at a very early age.

Motor Ability

Many researchers have reported sex differences in motor ability. Males exceed females at paper-and-pencil tests of mechanical ability (Garai and Scheinfeld, 1968; Hakstian and Cattell, 1975). On the Mechnical Aptitude Test, only 5 percent of the women and girls exceed the median score for the men (Tyler, 1965). The sexes also differ in the types of solutions they try to use for mechanical problems (Garai and Scheinfeld, 1968).

In speed and coordination of gross body movements, males tend to do better than females at all ages (Garai and Scheinfeld, 1968; Maccoby and Jacklin, 1974). Boys and men have faster reaction times, and men also have a greater tendency to slow the heart rate during the period just before the response (Coles, Porges, and Duncan-Johnson, 1975; Garai and Scheinfeld, 1968).

However, females do better at coordination of small-muscle movements and have greater finger dexterity (Garai and Scheinfeld, 1968; Hakstian and Cattell, 1975; Hutt, 1972a; Maccoby and Jacklin, 1974). The sex difference in manual dexterity is most strongly seen in finger tapping; females tap a small target faster, while males tap a larger target faster (Majeres, 1977 and private communication). Females from the ages of five to sixteen are also more accurate in maintaining a steady beat with finger tapping and do better at matching an external beat (Wolff and Hurwitz, 1976).

Females also do better at tasks involving **perceptual speed.** This includes tasks that require rapid identification of colors, whether the identification is communicated verbally or by finger tapping (Dubois, 1939; A. Jensen and Rohwer, 1966). Sex differences favoring females have also been found with finger-tapping recognition of words and line orientations, but not for recognition of shapes (Majeres, 1977). These differences seem to involve more than motor coordination or perceptual speed. Perhaps, as suggested by Majeres, females can more efficiently use verbally encoded material or information.

Again, though, we see the male engaged in more vigorous and skilled whole body movements. In physical sports, men's records have always exceeded the records set by women (although the gap is steadily closing). But females have greater control over their small muscles; this, combined with their greater pressure sensitivity, gives them the edge on tasks requiring fine coordination. Garai and Scheinfeld (1968) said that, in general, women were better at **clerical skills**—finger dexterity and word recognition; only 16 percent of males exceed the female median on these skills. Perhaps the androgen that stimulates the growth of large muscles affects both types of sex differences; before puberty, girls have faster reaction times than do boys (Fairweather and Hutt, 1972).

SEX DIFFERENCES IN SEXUALITY

This topic has generated much heat, but unfortunately little light. The argument has centered on two points. First, who has the stronger sex drive, men or women? Second, is each sex aroused by different stimuli?

We will illustrate the controversy on the first question by presenting the ideas of three theorists: Freud and Morgan, who both believe that the male sex drive is stronger, though each gives different reasons, and Sherfey, who believes that the female sex drive is stronger. We chose Freud because of the great impact his ideas have had, E. Morgan because of the novelty of her ideas and the interest they have generated, and Sherfey because she supports her view with recent data on female sexuality.

The second question, that the sexes may be differentially aroused by different stimuli, has been stated, for example, by Money and Ehrhardt (1972): "feel and touch require body contact, which are essential to a woman's arousal, whereas a man is more responsive to distant stimuli, especially visual stimuli, to initiate erotic arousal" (p. 155). According to these authors, both a male and a female can be aroused by visual imagery, but in both cases, the resulting fantasy is focused on the man wanting the woman in the picture. The man reacts to the figure as a sexual object, while the woman "is projecting herself into the picture and identifying with the female to whom men respond. She herself becomes the sexual object." Neither sex responds to a picture of a nude male. They make an important distinction about women: "whether in a movie or any other form of erotica, the romantic story leading up to the embrace of the penis in intercourse is important to a woman's fantasy. There is evidence of this in the circulations, among adolescent girls and women, of magazines and stories of the true romance, true confession type. These narratives are indeed woman's pornography" (pp. 262–63). We will look at recent evidence to evaluate these statements.

Three Different Points of View

Freud. Freud thought males develop the stronger sex drive or instinct. In early writings Freud equated masculinity with activity and femininity with passivity, and said that for both sexes the sex drive was masculine (Sherman, 1971). During the phallic stage, the girl discovers her clitoris and gains pleasure by masturbation; she becomes a "little man" (Freud, 1965). However, masturbation of the clitoris is a masculine activity and must be given up in order to achieve adult feminine sexuality (Freud, 1927). "We have long realized that in women the development of sexuality is complicated by the task of renouncing that genital zone which was originally the principal one, namely, the clitoris, in favour of a new zone—the vagina" (Freud, 1959a, p. 252). The little girl notices the differences between the sexes and feels cheated because she has no penis; since she cannot compete with boys here, she gives up the active masculine sexuality and replaces it with a wish for a child (Freud, 1927).

The young girl must give up the pleasure she feels in her clitoris and desire pleasure from the vagina, switching from an active, masculine mode to a passive, feminine mode. Therefore, a girl may never mature as much as a boy will. Some women never traverse the "very circuitous path" to normal female development and instead become homosexual or completely repress their sexuality (Freud, 1959a). Some also keep their clitoral sexuality and become masculine. Males, on the other hand, never have to give up their penis-centered pleasure; their shift is from the pleasure of masturbation to the pleasure of intercourse.

These ideas suggest that Freud felt that women would never develop as complete or as natural a sex drive as men. Instead, women would always remain in some conflict between clitoral and vaginal sexual pleasure. As Freud said, "very often when the little girl represses her previous masculinity a considerable part of her general sexual life is permanently 'injured' " (1959a, p. 263). Since Freud (1959b) felt that civilization was built up because of frustrated, sublimated sex drives, this difference would have far-reaching consequences; because the women's sex drive is injured, civilization is done by men. (Men are only frustrated by women; women are so frustrated by life that their sex drive disappears.)

Morgan. E. Morgan's (1972) theory represents a dramatic break from the tradition that saw male-female differences in sexuality as evolutionary inheritance of hunter-gatherer society (Ardrey, 1961; D. Morris, 1968; Tiger, 1969). Basically, the traditional idea was that man hunted and woman gathered. Man hunted because his greater size and strength made him better suited for that role, which involved traveling long distances (which, incidentally, represents a very interesting reversal of cause and effect). A woman who was carrying a child could not hunt very well, so she stayed home and cooked and gathered and sewed. All physical and psychological sex differences evolved from that distinction, including the breasts of women, which increased the hunter's attachment to his woman.

Morgan proposed, instead, that during the Pliocene drought, women took to the oceans to escape predators and the heat and became, in part, aquatic. Men simply stayed by the seashore, while women and children went into the water; the only function of men was to provide sex and some meat. Women became hairless (except for hair on the head, for a baby to hang on to) and developed breasts (again, for a baby to hang on to). Over many generations, the vagina moved forward to keep sand out. Since the vagina moved forward, the male had to develop a larger penis to reach it from the rear, the usual position among lower animals. But the vagina kept moving (over centuries) and the penis could not grow that much, so the male finally turned the female over and approached her from the front instead. So she was "flung down on the shingle on her soft wet hairless back and mounted the wrong way up. . . . She thought he had gone beserk and was aiming to disembowel her. . . . Dizzy with terror, she was only aware that at the hands of this absolute beginner her viscera were being squashed and the air compressed out of her lungs" (p. 72).

The female vagina was designed for stimulation from the rear, so when the frontal approach was begun the female **vaginal orgasm** was no longer triggered. At that point, the **clitoral orgasm** began to develop, but unfortunately for women, it has not yet developed completely. To substitute for having no orgasm, females developed love (not to be confused with sex). Female sexual desire began dying out because it was no longer being satisfied and was therefore no longer adaptive. Thus, Morgan reverses for women as a whole the development Freud postulated for women individually. In Morgan's theory, women went from a perfectly good vaginal orgasm to a frequently malfunctioning clitoral orgasm; Freud said that each woman develops away from the immature clitoral pleasure to the mature vaginal pleasure.

Sherfey. Sherfey (1966, 1973) used the data of W. Masters and Johnson (1966) on human sexual response as a basis for her theory. According to Sherfey, since the female is the only sex capable of multiple orgasms, the female is sexually insatiable. "The rise of modern civilization, while resulting from many causes, was contingent on the suppression of the inordinate cyclic sexual drive of women because (a) . . . women's uncurtailed continuous hypersexuality would drastically interfere with maternal responsibilities; and (b) with the rise of the settled agricultural economies, man's territorialism became expressed in property rights and kinship laws. Large families of known parentage were mandatory and could not evolve until the inordinate sexual demands of women were curbed" (1973, pp. 139–40). "If the conclusions reached here are true, it is conceivable that the *forceful* suppression of women's inordinate sexual demands was a prerequisite to the dawn of every modern civilization and almost every living culture" (1973, p. 151). Thus, Freud attributed civilization to the suppression and sublimation of the male sex drive whereas Sherfey attributed civilization to the male suppression of the female sex drive.

As you can see, vigorous arguments have been made on behalf of each sex having the stronger sex drive. The question begins to seem like the classic question about the chicken and the egg. Vigorous as these theories are, they all have problems: Freud was criticized in Chapter 6; Morgan has as little real data as the hunter-gatherer theorists; and Sherfey made several serious errors in fact concerning hormones, embryology, and ethology in the derivation of her theory (Money, Athanasiou, and Tobach, 1973). In any case, a sex difference in the *satisfaction* of the sex drive is different from a sex difference in arousability. Which is the real sex drive question?

Some Recent Data

For some time it has been claimed that the male of all species is more sexually aroused by smell, sight, and sound, whereas the female, though less arousable overall, is more affected by touch and (in the case of humans) by romance. Is this true?

Responses to erotic stimuli. Several studies have looked at the responses of human males and females to various types of erotic and pornographic material. The Kinsey survey of sexual behavior (Kinsey et al., 1965) found that women were less responsive than men to a variety of visual, narrative, and fantasy-produced stimuli. Women were as aroused as men only by commercial motion pictures (not pornographic ones), literature (not erotic stories), and by being bitten.

However, this sex difference may be disappearing, at least in some cultures. This may be because women are becoming more arousable (Schmidt, 1975), or because they are becoming more willing to report arousal (A Rossi, 1973). This disappearance of the sex difference would not be surprising since the sexualities of men and women are so similar. For example some research has found that the orgasms of men and women are much more similar than different, both physiologically and in terms of self-descriptions (W. Masters and Johnson, 1966; Proctor, Wagner, and Butler, 1973). Some recent data from the United States, however, suggest that in some places at least sex differences in arousability are still prominent. Stauffer and Frost (1976) studied students at Babson College and found that men were more aroused by the female nude pictures in *Playboy* than women were aroused by the male nude pictures in *Playgirl*. Izard and Caplan (1974), working at Vanderbilt, found that men were aroused more than women by a sexually explicit narrative passage.

Despite these findings, much recent data suggests that women can be aroused as much as men by slides, pictures, and narratives of explicitly sexual material (see Byrne and Lamberth, 1971, with data from Purdue and Oklahoma; Griffitt, 1973, 1975, with data from Kansas State; and Schmidt, 1975; Schmidt and Sigusch, 1970, 1973; and Schmidt, Sigusch, and Schäfer, 1973, all with data from the University of Hamburg, West Germany). But even among these equally arousable students, there are some differences in sexuality. Women more often respond to this material with feelings of disgust as well as arousal (Byrne et al., 1974; Izard and Caplan, 1974; Schmidt, 1975; Schmidt and Sigusch, 1973; Stauffer and Frost, 1976). Females are also more likely to report an increase in sexual intercourse after exposure to this material.

The sexes also differ in terms of what stimuli they find arousing. Males, not females, are more aroused by visual than by narrative stimuli (Schmidt, 1975). Both males and females are aroused more by opposite-sex stimuli than by same-sex stimuli, though females are more aroused than males by same-sex stimuli. Males are more aroused than females by more unusual sexual activities (Griffitt, 1973; Schmidt, 1975; Schmidt and Sigusch, 1970). Overall, there is little support for Money and Ehrhardt's assertion than romance is **woman's pornography;** an affectionate context to stories is not necessary for women's arousal, nor did men and women react differently to affectionate versus nonaffectionate stories (Schmidt, 1975; Schmidt et al., 1973). Also contrary to Money and Ehrhardt, both men and women were aroused more by opposite-sex stimuli, and the sexes can be equally arousable under some conditions.

Effect of Culture and Social Class.   This does not mean that sex differences in sexual arousability do not still exist. Surveys in many areas of the world still consistently show sex differences in the person's age when having first intercourse and the amount of sexual activity; though the difference is declining, men still have sex for the first time at a younger age, and have sex more often. This difference may account for the sex differences in arousability that are still being seen, since experience increases arousal, and experience is very much a function of cultural sanctions. And, as mentioned earlier, the sexual behavior of women is more culturally controlled than that of men. Interestingly enough, experience in masturbation made the most difference in the arousability of males, while experience in all types of sexual behavior increased females' arousability (Griffitt, 1975). And females more than males still emphasize the importance of romance (Steele and Walker, 1976).

The sexual behavior of women also seems somewhat more affected by IQ, education, age, class, religion, and marital variables than the sexual behavior of men (Hariton and Singer, 1974; Maslow, 1942; Sherman, 1971). Both intelligence and education are associated with increased sexual activity in women.

Conclusions

Thus, women can be aroused as men are, by both visual and narrative stimuli, in the absence of romance. The fact that sex differences can be found does not mean that there is any biological basis for these differences. Also, the material in Chapter 4 strongly suggested that in humans, different inductive hormones did not have an effect upon sexual behavior, which also implies that there is no biologically biased sex difference in sexuality. The differences must be understood in terms of sex differences in experience and in cultural sanctions that vary with social class, education, and religion. Cross-cultural similarities in sexual behavior—such as males being more active—must be due to similarities in socialization rather than biology. And certainly, contrary to Freud, there is no biological difference between orgasms triggered by clitoral and by vaginal stimulations; most orgasms of women involve at least some clitoral stimulation (W. Masters and Johnson, 1966).

The only biologically biased sex differences in sexuality seem to be the capacity for multiple orgasms in women and the different effects of age; men reach their peak in late adolescence and women reach their peak in their thirties and forties (W. Masters and Johnson, 1966; Morgan, 1972; Sherfey, 1973; Sherman, 1971). The most frequently cited sexual complaint of older women is lack of sex (L. Harris, 1970). Erotic dreams appear in adolescence for males and for late-treated adrenogenital females, but not in hormonally normal females until they reach their twenties and have masturbated or had some coital experience (Money and Ehrhardt, 1972). This may be related to the greater incidence of fetishism (use of objects, such as shoes, for sexual arousal) in males (Bermant, 1972).

SUMMARY

The data in this chapter suggest that there are some consistent sex differences in responses to or sensitivity to stimuli. Women seem more sensitive to various types of skin sensations and to sounds, whereas men have better visual acuity. Women may be somewhat more sensitive to olfactory stimuli and facial stimuli as well.

The types of responses made are also sexually dimorphic. Men, with more muscle and less fat, are stronger, have greater mechanical ability, faster reaction times, and better coordination of gross body movements. Females, on the other hand, have better coordination of small-muscle movements and greater perceptual speed, making them better at the so-called clerical skills. Females also respond more to stress, although they are better able to withstand its effects. And most drugs seem to affect women more than they do men.

The contributions of biological and developmental biases to these differences are unclear. The sex difference in responses to facial stimuli is probably affected by the socialized differences in the value of affiliation and achievement. Since more women are socialized to equate affiliation with achievement, faces might seem more important to them. The causes of other sex differences are not as well understood. Certainly hormones affect body composition (fat and muscle) and they probably also affect sensitivities to various stimuli other than facial. The role of experience and expectations is less clear, however. In any case, given the biological evidence, it makes little sense to continue to compare women and men on any of these perceptual-motor dimensions until a complete analysis of the cycles in behavior and sensitivity has been carried out.

Despite the theories, the stereotypes, and the cross-cultural consistencies, there are few biologically biased sex differences in sexuality. Women are as arousable as men, and in response to very similar stimuli, and have similar sexual climaxes. The only differences that may be affected by biology are the capacity for multiple orgasms in women and the different effects of age upon sexuality. But in view of social restrictions and sanctions, the latter difference may not be the result of biology either.

KEY TERMS AND CONCEPTS

Anabolic steroids
Catabolic steroids
Adrenal corticoid stress response
Galvanic skin response (GSR)
Social intelligence

Perceptual speed
Clerical skills
Clitoral and vaginal orgasm
Women's pornography

QUESTIONS ON KEY ISSUES

1. In what ways is the male "an engine operating at higher levels of speed and intensity" and the female more capable of withstanding stress?
2. What are the directions of the most typical sex differences found in sensitivity to pain, pressure, and cold, and auditory, visual, taste, and olfactory stimuli?
3. What are the directions of the most typical sex differences found in each of the following areas: social stimuli; mechanical ability; gross body coordination; reaction time; perceptual speed; finger dexterity. And, whenever possible, why?
4. What are the two major issues of debate about sex differences in sexuality, and what does the recent data suggest about each?

5. What differences in sexuality may have some biological basis?
6. Given the biological utility of sex differences discussed in Chapter 3, what do you think might have led to sex differences in sensitivities and skills in humans? How could you test your hypothesis?

CHAPTER 12

Sex Differences in Mental Health

In this chapter, some of the sex differences in mental health will be evaluated. Mental health will be very broadly defined to include not only anxiety, depression, neuroses, and psychoses, but also self-esteem and satisfaction with life. As has been demonstrated in earlier chapters, the sexes are socialized to take different roles. Women are socialized to achieve through marrying a successful man and rearing successful children, and men are socialized to be financially responsible for themselves, and, eventually, for their families. What consequences do these roles have for men and women? Are people happiest when they conform to society's expectations and socialization pressures?

SEX DIFFERENCES IN SURVEYS OF GENERAL MENTAL HEALTH

This section will examine sex differences in the likelihood of people saying they are happy or satisfied with their life. We will also look at sex differences in the incidence of various kinds of depressive and neurotic symptoms. Sex differences in more serious disturbances will be examined later. Here we will try to answer the question, are men or women happier?

Before going any further, we must consider whether sex differences in self-reports of neuroticism and anxiety, for example, might be the result of sex differences in the willingness to report symptoms, rather than the result of sex differences in the actual incidence of those symptoms. Clancy and Gove (1975) investigated this question by controlling for any possible sex differences in the perceived social desirability of symptoms and in the need for social approval. They found that these factors could not account for the larger scores of women on a psychiatric symptom checklist. In fact, they found that the sex differences were largest when both males and females are high, or both were low, in the need for social approval or the perceived undesirability of symptoms.

However, this is but one study, and much more research is needed in the area of gender biases in symptom checklists. Sex biases in the diagnoses of professionals will be examined later in this chapter, but several sex differences discussed in earlier chapters would suggest that women are more willing to admit symptoms than men. Women go more often to doctors, and the frequency of these visits is affected by the number of children they have and their employment status, suggesting that this difference is largely due to differences in sex-role expectations (see Appendix B). Women are also more willing than men to disclose intimate aspects of their behavior and emotions. Admitting emotions is perceived as more appropriate to the female than to the male sex-role stereotype (Chapter 7). Because women are socialized to value affiliation more, they may be more cooperative when an experimenter asks them to be honest in filling out a mental health questionnaire. Also because of this socialization, women may be more sensitive to their emotions in the first place, and thus be more capable of accurately reporting them. Women might also be more inclined to focus more on the negative than on the positive aspects of their life (see chapters 9 and 10), and this would lead them to report more symptoms. Given all of these tendencies—and you can undoubtedly think of more—it is not surprising to see sex differences in questionnaire surveys of mental health. But given all these tendencies, these differences may not be real at all.

But what we should look for in the following data is the different effect male and female sex-role achievement has on reported happiness and emotional symptoms. That is, we should look for differences in correlates and causes, rather than differences in means. According to the hypotheses presented in chapters 9 and 10, affiliation should be more important to the well-being of females, and failure in that area should more often lead to problems for women than for men. For males, achievement failure cannot be compensated for by affiliative success, so problems related to achievement may be relatively common for males. For example, men usually get on skid row because of occupational failure; women end up on skid row because of failure with the men in their lives (Garrett and Bahr, 1976). But remember that this would be a matter of degree; both males and females will be disturbed by both social rejection and career failures.

Anxiety, Emotionality, and Self-Esteem

According to Maccoby and Jacklin's (1974) review, the sexes do not differ in self-esteem. These reviewers also found no differences in emotionality in children, although girls more often cried because of injury and boys because of frustration; also, after eighteen months of age, boys more often became angry. There did appear to be some circumstances more likely to elicit fear in girls than boys, such as being around strangers and being in strange situations. Although several studies found no sex difference, women generally get higher scores on anxiety tests than men do; no study has found the reverse sex difference (Ekehammar, 1974; Maccoby and Jacklin, 1974). Since in other areas sex differences are more consistent among adults than among children, this section will look for sex differences among adults in anxiety, emotionality, and self-esteem and in their correlates. Do different things upset men and women or make them happy?

Sex Differences in Incidence. J. Gray (1971b) surveyed emotionality in humans and concluded that women are more often phobic and more often have neurotic symptoms, psychosomatic symptoms, and depressive disorders, or at least that they more often claim to have or admit having these symptoms. Eysenck and Eysenck (1973) also found that females had higher neuroticism scores, but they found that males had higher psychoticism scores. Two surveys of general practices in London (one of two practices, the other of fourteen) also found that women scored higher on a neuroticism scale (Shepherd et al., 1966; Silverstone, 1973)—from 14 percent to 15.6 percent of the men could be classified as neurotic, whereas from 34 percent to 35.2 percent of the women could be.

Other surveys using self-reports show a greater incidence of emotional symptoms in the general female population than in the male population (Clancy and Gove, 1975; Levine, Kamin, and Levine, 1974). Atchley (1976) found that retired women were not only more likely than retired men to report that they were anxious, they also said they were more lonely, sensitive to criticism, and depressed. In general, men adjusted to retirement more rapidly and more completely than women, which is surprising in view of the socialized importance of the man's job for him. Maybe he is relieved at being able to abandon that job in a socially-approved fashion, retirement.

Most surveys have found no sex differences in self-esteem (Helmreich and Stapp, 1974; H. Kaplan, 1970, 1973; H. Kaplan and Pokorny, 1972; Maccoby and Jacklin, 1974). One study found female undergraduates to have a more favorable self-concept than males (Tolor et al., 1976), but Simmons and Rosenberg (1975; see also F. Rosenberg and Simmons, 1975) found female adolescents to have lower self-esteem. In their study, 26 percent of the fifteen-year-old or older girls had low self-esteem; 19 percent of the boys did. The girls were also more self-conscious, and said that they felt more vulnerable to the opinions of others.

Sex Differences in Causes and Correlates. Surveys have found different correlates of anxiety and neuroticism in the two sexes. Women and men do not become equally upset by the same things, and being upset does not have the same effect in men as in women.

Ekehammer (1974; Ekehammer, Magnusson, and Ricklander, 1974), using data from 116 sixteen-year-olds, did a factor analysis on self-reported anxiety. Of the eighteen different responses indicating anxiety (sweating palms, faster heart rate, and so on), females reported experiencing twelve of them significantly more often than males. Of the anxiety-producing situations studied, females reported experiencing significantly more anxiety than males reported in fourteen of them. The three exceptions where boys' scores were closer to those of girls, included three of the four achievement situations: an important examination, starting a new job, and giving an oral report. The girls were also significantly more variable than the boys.

Other research found evidence that the sexes worry about different things. One study found that the aspects of life that worried adolescent boys the most, gave them the greatest difficulties and most fearfulness, were school, sex, low marks, and vocation (Meissner, 1961). On the other hand, for girls, being field independent (having good spatial ability) increased anxiety (Iscoe and Carden, 1961). This may be because these girls were also unpopular (Kagan and Kogan, 1970), perhaps because of having a more masculine body type (A. Peterson, 1976). As pointed out before, women honor students in both college and high school have a lower self-concept than women nonhonor students, perhaps because they worry about their success. The self-concept of male students was not affected by their honor status (M. McEwen, 1975; O'Leary, 1974).

Affiliative relationships—their quantity and quality—may be more important to the well-being of women than to that of men. In college females, low anxiety was associated with significantly higher scores of popularity, respect from others, and self-esteem. These correlations were not seen in males (Mathes and Edwards, unpublished data), so popularity was related to anxiety only for females. Gibson and Corcoran (1975) found sex differences in the relationship of neuroticism to extraversion and introversion. They found no sex differences among the neuroticism scores of extroverts, but among introverts, females were more neurotic, probably because an introvert might find it difficult to be socially successful.

These data suggest that anxiety and neuroticism have different correlates in females and males, thus they have different meanings. A neurotic female may have different behaviors and a different past history than a neurotic male. Affiliation concerns seem more likely to worry women, and achievement concerns to worry men.

Females who achieve by affiliating may evaluate themselves according to their attractiveness and other traits that facilitate social acceptability. Research suggests that attractive females have more self-esteem, but that the relationship between attractiveness and self-esteem was reduced or even reversed in males (Lerner et al., 1976; Mathes and Kahn, 1975). Men may become popular by having athletic ability and may even achieve occupational success based on that attribute. As a result, self-esteem in males may depend more on the effectiveness of their bodies than on their appearance (Lerner et al., 1976).

In summary, adults may not differ in their level of self-esteem, but they do seem to differ in what decreases or increases self-esteem. Females may be more affected by attributes and external factors relevant to affiliative success, whereas males may be more affected by physical ability and occupational success.

Happiness and Depression

Happiness and satisfaction in women and men seem to depend upon different aspects of their lives, as is suggested by much of the data already cited. For example, Wills, Weiss, and Patterson (1974) studied married couples and found that men and women did not differ in the degree of reported happiness or marital satisfaction—just as men and women did not differ in self-esteem—but their ratings were correlated with different behaviors. Men's marital happiness was related to the performance of services (the degree of submissiveness?) by the wife, such as looking attractive, cooking, and shopping; women's ratings of material satisfaction were correlated with how affectionate their husbands had been on the day they responded. Similarly, in Law's review (1971), the husbands' satisfaction was related to their relative autonomy and dominance, whereas the wives were happier when there were egalitarian role definitions. Both studies imply that wife-dominated marriages might be less happy, because of the effects this would have on the husband. This corresponds to the preference among dating couples for the male to be dominant (Curran, 1972).

Happiness in women and men may be affected by different things outside marriage as well as inside it. As Constantinople concluded from her own research, happiness in men was "closely associated with their own estimates of how they

[were] performing relative to their own standards and to what they [thought] others expected of them. In women, happiness was more closely associated with feelings of receptivity towards the world and sociability vs. withdrawal" (quoted by Gump, 1972, p. 80). Also, attractive women may be happier than unattractive women, though this seems not to be true for men (Mathes and Kahn, 1975). Affiliation and affection, then, may more often be associated with greater happiness in women; dominance and success may more often lead to greater happiness in men. Keep these differences in mind when you read the surveys described below.

Two Studies of Happiness.   Two studies used self-reports to survey the satisfaction and happiness of a wide cross-section of people; both found very similar results. A. Campbell, Converse, and Rogers (1975) studied 2,164 adults; and Spreitzer, Snyder, and Larson (1975) studied 1,536. In both studies, women reported greater happiness than men from age eighteen through sixty-four, at which time this sex difference reversed. Men were happier than women from sixty-five to seventy. Of all ages, women were the least happy from sixty-five to seventy. The decline in attractiveness with age seems to have more of an impact on women than on men, as the sex differences were reversed with age. The reversal may also be caused by men's greater happiness in retirement, which generally begins at 65.

Depression.   Women say that they are more depressed than men do (Winokur, 1973), leaving us with the apparent paradox that there is no sex difference in happiness, but women are more depressed. Radloff (1975) gave 876 whites in Kansas City and 1,639 blacks and whites in Washington County, Maryland, a well-validated depression scale to fill out (see Table 12.1). Depression scores were highest among the young, among those with lower levels of education, and among those with lower incomes. Within each of these subgroups, women were more depressed than men. Radloff supplied a summary rule for depression: an average male worker happy with both job and marriage gets a depression score of 5.72; add 2.5 if the worker is unhappy with the job, add 4.0 if the person is unhappy with the marriage, and add 2.0 if the person is female.

The Effect of Children

Many women feel pressured to succeed by raising successful children, and women also say that they highly respect mothers of successful children (for example, Rose Kennedy, the mother of John, Robert, and Edward Kennedy, perennially is listed as among the nation's ten most admired women). As mentioned earlier, the success most preferred for recent college graduates was to be the "wife whose husband becomes very prominent" and the "mother of several highly accomplished children" (A. Rossi, 1965). Therefore, children ought to make women happy. But in fact they do not, at least not always.

The surveys just discussed included data suggesting that children do not make women or men more happy or less depressed. Both men and women, and particularly women, are less satisfied with life after the birth of children and are more satisfied and less depressed after the children have left home. Depression of parents correlates negatively with the age of the youngest child at home.

Laws (1971) reviewed data relevant to the effect of children upon marital hap-

TABLE 12.1

ITEMS FROM RADLOFF'S DEPRESSION SCALE

Instructions for Questions: Below is a list of the ways you might have felt or behaved. Please tell me how often you have felt this way during the past week:

Rarely or none of the time (less than 1 day)
Some or a little of the time (1–2 days)
Occasionally or a moderate amount of time (3–4 days)
Most or all of the time (5–7 days)

During the past week:

1. I was bothered by things that usually don't bother me.
2. I did not feel like eating; my appetite was poor.
3. I felt that I could not shake off the blues even with help from my family or friends.
4. I felt that I was just as good as other people.
5. I had trouble keeping my mind on what I was doing.
6. I felt depressed.
7. I felt that everything I did was an effort.
8. I felt hopeful about the future.
9. I thought my life had been a failure.
10. I felt fearful.
11. My sleep was restless.
12. I was happy.
13. I talked less than usual.
14. I felt lonely.
15. People were unfriendly.
16. I enjoyed life.
17. I had crying spells.
18. I felt sad.
19. I felt that people dislike me.
20. I could not get "going."

Source: L. Radloff, "Sex Differences in Depression: The Effects of Occupation and Marital Status." *Sex Roles,* 1975, table 1, p. 251.

piness and satisfaction with life. Becoming a parent is taking on a lifelong, irrevocable responsibility for the life of another person. In one study, 83 percent of the couples reported a severe crisis at the birth of their child; mothers with professional training and work experience were particularly affected. Laws cited several other studies showing that marital satisfaction declined with the birth of children, particularly for women, and that marital satisfaction was an inverse function of the number of children and the time between children (child density). Another review (Glenn, 1975) concluded the same. Middle-aged women were happier, enjoyed life more, and were more satisfied with their marriage after all children had left home.

Even the incidence of severe psychological problems in men and women may be related to the number of children a couple has. In one study of large numbers of white men and women, as the number of children increased from three to six, so did the incidence of severe psychological problems (this relationship was not seen among blacks) (Pollack, et al., 1968). Since androgynous women have fewer children, though, this increase may really be the effect of aging upon more completely sex-typed people, rather than an effect of children.

However, some women become clinically depressed when their children leave home (Bart, 1976). These women are likely to be very feminine and probably overidentified with their children. They perceive their children as their success to such an extent that when the children leave home, the women no longer experience life as worthwhile.

Thus, neither men nor women should expect children to make them happier. Children may increase stress on both men and women, even when they are planned and having them is not regretted. And it seems that even if women value the achievement of successful children more than men do, having children will not make women happier, maybe because no mother has complete control over the success or failure of her children—she cannot force them to be successful in the way she wants them to be.

Summary

Surveys using self-reports show few sex differences in self-esteem or happiness, but there may be different correlates of these in men than in women. In women, social relationships and personal attractiveness may be more important to their happiness and self-esteem, while for men achievement may be more important. Despite their greater emphasis on occupational success, men adjust better to retirement. Women more often report feeling anxious in more situations than do men, except in achievement situations. Women also get higher scores on neuroticism and depression scales. But cause and effect are unclear. Women may score higher on these scales because they tend to answer more honestly than men, or because they tend to focus more on the more unpleasant aspects of their life than men. There are also sex differences in the correlates of anxiety, neuroticism, and depression in men and in women. Unattractive women are high in these measures; perhaps they feel they are less likely to achieve through affiliation, and so they devalue themselves. Though children decrease happiness and increase depression in both sexes, the effects seem stronger in women.

These differences in means and correlations, although reasonably consistent and significant, are not rigid boundaries predicting behavior; there is always a great deal of overlap between the sexes. Not all unemployed men are unhappy, and not all beautiful women are happy. Success in any area does not guarantee happiness for either gender. But these data suggest that sex roles may be related to mental health, although not quite in the way that might have been expected. It is to this relationship that we shall now turn.

SEX ROLES AND MENTAL HEALTH

As has already been suggested, conformity to sex role may not be the quickest road to mental health. Women, to fulfill their sex role, should get married and have children. But children decrease their happiness and increase depression. What about other aspects of sex roles and mental health?

Masculinity, Femininity, and Mental Health

Parental Identification and Sex Typing. Male identification with a masculine father seems to lead to better mental health (Heilbrun, 1968b, 1974). However, female identification with either parent does not. Heilbrun (1974) analyzed parents as sex-role appropriate (masculine father and feminine mother) and sex-role inappropriate (feminine father and masculine mother). For both sexes, identification with the masculine parent—regardless of biological gender—seemed more likely to be associated with mental health. And, in fact, adult males and females identified with a masculine father more than with any other type of parent. Well-adjusted males and females saw themselves as similar to masculine fathers; those who saw themselves as most similar to feminine mothers were more often maladjusted. More maladjusted males identified with a feminine mother than with any other type of parent. Intermediate levels of adjustment were associated with identification with a masculine mother in both sexes.

Analysis of sex-role identification into primary and secondary components improved the ability to predict adjustment levels only for males; females' mental health was determined by the interaction between their sex role and that of the parent with whom they had identified. Of the males with both a primary and secondary feminine sex role, 73 percent were maladjusted. Thus, maladjusted males were more feminine and more similar to their mothers and adjusted males were more similar to their fathers. These relationships did not exist for females. However, girls can be either masculine or feminine as a result of identification with either parent of either sex role (Heilbrun, 1968a). Still, a feminine girl was better adjusted if she identified with a feminine mother rather than any other type of parent. A masculine girl was better adjusted if she identified with a masculine father.

There is also evidence that well-adjusted people of either sex will combine traits of both sexes. Although both the well-adjusted feminine girl and the poorly adjusted masculine girl were low on instrumental traits, well-adjusted masculine girls were both instrumental and expressive (Heilbrun, 1968b). For postadolescent men (ages twenty to sixty), high masculinity (low expressiveness) was slightly but significantly correlated with anxiety (+.157) and with neuroticism (+.176) (Harford, Willis, and Deabler, 1967). Heilbrun (1976b) found that the people who were lowest on both masculinity and femininity were the least well-adjusted of all; those high in both sets of sex-role traits received the highest adjustment scores.

Other research suggests that although a combination of sex-role traits is desirable, masculinity may be especially desirable for both sexes. Both masculinity and femininity are positively correlated with self-esteem in both college women and men, but the correlation between socially desirable male traits and self-esteem was stronger for both sexes. The correlations for male traits were +.77 and +.83 for males and females, respectively; the correlations for female traits were +.42 and +.30 (Spence et al., 1975). Deutsch and Gilbert (1976) found masculinity on the Bem Sex-Role Inventory to be positively correlated with mental health for both sexes; that is, the degree to which masculinity scores exceeded femininity scores predicted mental health for both women and men.

Femininity in women may be part of either good or poor adjustment, although femininity in the absence of masculinity for men does not seem advantageous. Similarly, Heilbrun's low masculine-high feminine women (1976a) had nearly as high an adjustment score as did the women who were high on both types of traits. But of those students who requested help at a campus mental-health center, nearly half of the males (41.8 percent) and the highest percentages of females (38 percent) were low in masculinity and high in femininity. However, the next largest group of women (35.6 percent) were well-adjusted and had the same levels of sex-role traits, low masculinity and high femininity.

Thus, it seems as though extreme sex-typing and sex-role conflicts may both be often associated with poorer mental health among adults, especially among feminine males. This may not be true for early adolescents, where appropriate sex typing may increase mental health (Constantinople, 1973). Early puberty seems to be correlated with greater sex typing in both boys and girls (Terman and Miles, 1936), and early maturing adolescents have more favorable self-concepts and better levels of adjustment (M. Jones and Mussen, 1958; Mussen, 1961). But in order to maintain mental health after adolescence, both males and females must acquire some characteristics of the opposite sex. Mussen (1962) followed his high and low masculine boys into adulthood. After twenty years, the high masculine group, which had been well-adjusted at puberty, still had more ego control, self-sufficiency, and stress resistance; but this group did have some symptoms of poorer health, such as low dominance, lower self-acceptance, lower sociability, lower self-assurance and a greater need for abasement than the low-masculine group.

Adjustment in adolescence may be facilitated by sex typing, but being a healthy adult implies possessing traits of both sexes. In view of this, and in view of the fact that self-fulfillment brings conflict more often for women, severe mental illness should occur with different frequency according to sex and sex role.

Sex Roles in More Severely Deviant Behaviors.   Chesler (1972) says that "what we consider 'madness,' whether it appears in women or in men, is either the acting out of the devalued female role or the total or partial rejection of one's sex-role stereotype" (p. 56). Society punishes these role deviations by labeling the behaviors madness. When women fully act out the female sex role, they may get labeled as neurotic, or else they are likely to suffer from an anxiety neurosis, or depression, paranoia, frigidity, or promiscuity, or they may attempt suicide. When women who reject their sex role get labeled and so diagnosed as mentally ill, they are called schizophrenic, or lesbians, or promiscuous. Males who act out the female role become labeled as neurotic or become hospitalized as schizophrenic or as homosexuals; men who fully act out the male sex role become criminals or sociopaths.

Problems with one's sex role have been said to contribute to serious behavior problems such as schizophrenia and hysteria. McClelland and Watt (1968) hypothesized that schizophrenia involves sex-role alienation. They said that male schizophrenics were less masculine and female schizophrenics less feminine than normal controls, perhaps because the schizophrenics never developed stable gender identities. There are more female than male schizophrenics (Chesler, 1972); perhaps more women envy the male role than men envy the female role. There are also remarkable similarities between the feminine stereotype and both masochism and the so-called hysterical personality, all of which are characterized by flamboyance, exaggerated concern for others, and overreaction to criticism (Belote, 1976).

Alcoholism in either sex may also reflect sex-role alienation (Badiet, 1976). Women alcoholics were said to fall into three types (W. Fraser, 1976), according to their sex roles. "Lace curtain" alcoholics, the most common, are usually housewives whose children have left home. The other two types of women alcoholics are the single career woman, who drinks when she comes home to an empty house, perhaps because that emptiness signifies affiliative failure, and the woman on skid row who trades sex for money, food, or wine. Fraser found that the reasons alcoholics give for drinking may be sex-role related. Women say they drink to feel more warm, loving, sexy, and sensuous; men say they drink to feel stronger and more aggressive.

Implications of Sex Roles. Sex roles are a recurrent theme in research on mental health. Extreme sex typing, or extreme opposite–sex typing, may be associated with problems. The former leads to problems because of the virtual impossibility of living up to a sex role. The person who tries to is bound to fail, and may suffer as a consequence. Masculine men may suffer because of a lack of an emotional life, and the woman who sacrifices career for family may become depressed, perhaps over the opportunities she gave up. Even if a woman somehow manages to become the perfect homemaker, society does not attach much value to her success. Extreme opposite–sex typing may also cause problems, because both society and the individual punish out-of-role behaviors and label them as deviant. The single or childless woman who is successful in a male occupation, and the warm, expressive man who values his family more than his job may often be forced to wonder if they are normal.

Much research associates androgyny with increased well-being and satisfaction with life. However, the data are essentially correlational, and cause and effect are uncertain. The data have usually been interpreted to mean that androgyny promotes mental health. But it could be the reverse. Androgyny and mental well-being may be related because some people refuse to believe that out-of-role behaviors are inappropriate and so they do not feel guilty at displaying them. Perhaps androgynous people were more healthy in the first place, and because of that were more able to accept their own out-of-role behavior and select which sex-typed behavior they will exhibit. Thus, being more healthy and secure in the first place may enable people to acquire the useful traits of both sex-role stereotypes and become androgynous.

Employment and Marital Status

The surveys discussed in this chapter also found some evidence concerning the effects of employment and marital status upon happiness and depression in women and men. Being married makes men happier than it makes women, and marriage gives women more problems than men. Employment may have more of an effect on men than on women, but there are also some provocative findings about how employment affects mental health in women.

Happiness and Depression. Marriage and employment affect self-ratings of happiness (A. Campbell et al., 1975; Spreitzer et al., 1975). Married people were happier than divorced people, widowed people, and people who never married. Though this was true for both sexes, females who had never married were happier

TABLE 12.2

MEAN DEPRESSION SCORES BY SEX AND MARITAL STATUS

	Kansas City		Washington County	
	Male	Female	Male	Female
Married	7.33	10.03	7.33	9.26
Divorced/Separated	6.96	12.99	8.51	14.19
Never Married	10.16	9.59	10.05	10.20
Widowed	15.09	10.08	11.28	10.46

Source: L. Radloff, "Sex Differences in Depression: The Effects of Occupation and Marital Status." *Sex Roles,* 1975, table 3, p. 255, by permission of Plenun Publishing Corporation.

Notes: There were 876 subjects in Kansas City; 1,639 in Washington County. Psychiatric inpatients get an average score of 24.42 on this test.

than males who had never married, despite females' affiliative failure. Divorce may affect women more than men, since divorced women were unhappier than divorced men. Widowhood, on the other hand, may affect men more; widowed men were unhappier than widowed women. Perhaps divorce is perceived by women as affiliative failure, and widowhood, naturally enough, is not. Employment status had no effect on the happiness of women, although unemployed women reported experiencing the greatest marital satisfaction. However, among women with a higher level of education, those who were employed part-time reported the greatest happiness and the most excitement in life. Also, the greatest percentage of women who reported low happiness were full-time homemakers. For men, employment status had a great impact on reported happiness.

Radloff (1975), in her depression survey, found that married people were less depressed, but again the effects of marriage were greater for men than for women (see Table 12.2). Marriage increases life expectancy—more for males than females (Gove, 1973)—so it could be that the stress of depression caused by being unmarried, divorced, or widowed, decreases life expectancy particularly for men. Radloff found the same results as other surveys: divorced women were more depressed than divorced men, but widowhood had a greater impact on men than on women.

Radloff also found that employment status was generally related to depression only in men. Women were more depressed than men regardless of their employment status; only unemployed men were more depressed than women. This sex difference was seen even when both the women and the men were retired, supporting Atchley's (1976) findings that retired women more often reported feeling depressed than retired men. Radloff tried to control for the fact that working wives were also responsible for the children and house (it might depress them to have to do two jobs) by having women rate how often they did housework. For every category of time spent in housework, married female workers reported more symptoms of depression than did married male workers. But regardless of how much the husband helps, the house is still regarded as the woman's responsibility in most marriages. That may be important to the sex differences, as Radloff pointed out.

Radloff did find some evidence for an effect of employment on women. If happiness is held constant, housewives were significantly more depressed than the married working woman, implying that happiness is not the inverse of depression. Thus, the housewife reports herself to be more happy, but if two wives are equally happy, the housewife will report more depression than the working woman.

Burke and Weir (1976a) found somewhat different effects of employment on happiness. They sent a twenty-page questionnaire to 300 working and nonworking wives and their professional husbands; 63 percent responded. Housewives described themselves as being the worrying type and as having lower spirits more often than the working wives. Housewives also reported more life pressures and worries, especially over feeling in a rut, and were less satisfied with their marriage and with life in general. But it may be important that all of these women were married to men who were professionals. Women married to nonprofessionals may be more likely to regard not working as desirable, beneficial, and even a privilege. The husbands of these working women reported themselves as physically and mentally less healthy than did the husbands of housewives. Perhaps men are even less well prepared by socialization than women to assume both instrumental and expressive roles; certainly the expressive, caretaking roles that the husband of a working woman may assume do not add prestige to his life.

Incidence of More Severe Problems.   Marriage may decrease the incidence of more severe mental problems in women less than it does in men. Gove (1972) analyzed sex and marital status as related to the incidence of mental illness. Women had a higher rate of mental illness than men did, almost entirely because of married people. Married women had a much higher rate of severe mental problems than married men. Similarly, more female patients in private practice and in mental hospitals are married than males (Koskiner, Zalcman, and Ruppert, 1973; Weintraub and Aronson, 1974). Among the widowed, divorced, and retired, Gove found little or no sex difference in the incidence of mental problems; if anything, the single woman was less vulnerable than the single man. So although marriage decreases the incidence of severe psychiatric problems dramatically for both sexes—just as it decreased depression and increased happiness—this effect is greater for males. Married women have more severe psychological problems than married men.

The sex difference in overall mental health is a reversal of the difference found prior to World War II, suggesting that the recent marital role of women may be a cause. Gove points out that women only have one social role (wife) while men have more than one (husband and worker). Housekeeping as a role is frustrating (it keeps getting undone as fast as you do it), unstructured, and socially invisible. There are also no clear standards or rewards for being a housewife and mother. And job training for being a housewife is often haphazard, leaving the woman feeling helpless and inadequate. In addition to all this, even when a married woman works, her job is usually of lower status and income than that of her husband, and she is still given the responsibility for the house. Finally, the role expectations confronting the married woman may be unclear; they have been socialized to view achievement as leading to affiliation and so are not prepared for the resulting conflicts.

Work may lead to a lower incidence of psychiatric depression, for women as well as men, even if employment status is not clearly related to women's happiness or depression. Mostow and Newberry (1975) raised the possibility of the therapeutic role of work for women, and their own data point out that although the working woman was more symptomatic than the nonworking woman on admission to the hospital, the working woman recovered faster and more completely.

Each gender clearly has peculiar role strains or role conflicts that, when exaggerated, can lead to problems. Both employment and marriage benefit both men and women, but there are sex differences. Being married to a working woman may present some problems for the husband, and marriage seems far more beneficial to the mental health of men than of women. But, at least some of the sex differences among married people could be the result of the lesser marriageability of unstable men compared to unstable women, perhaps representing another instance of sexual selection by females. That is, as in lower animals, maybe women do most of the sexual selecting and prefer or marry stable males; males may be less selective.

SEX ROLES, DIAGNOSIS, AND TREATMENT

Before we analyze the incidence of types of mental illness as a function of age and sex, we should consider what biases might exist in that data. Women may be more willing to admit themselves to mental institutions because their greater expressiveness allows them to acknowledge mental discomforts more readily than men do (Phillips and Segal, 1969). Since women less often play an economic role than men, they may be admitted more often than men simply because that causes less economic disruption—the family does not lose its sole source of income. Finally, the sex-role stereotypes of the diagnosing clinicians may lead to differential rates of admission and different types of treatment. It is this latter factor we will discuss first.

The Healthy Adult

The first major study in this area was done by I. Broverman and her colleagues (1970); this study serves as an introduction to the methodology of later research. The researchers used a list of stereotypic traits similar to those presented on page 213. The list consisted of a series of twenty-seven traits for which the masculine pole was socially desirable, and eleven traits for which the feminine pole was socially desirable. Clinicians, forty-six males and thirty-three females, were given the trait list and told to use them to describe either "a healthy adult man," "a healthy adult woman," or just "a healthy adult." The researchers found that the **healthy adult** had a description nearly identical to that of the healthy adult male, whereas the healthy adult woman was described very differently. The healthy woman was submissive, dependent, suggestible, less competitive, less aggressive, more excitable, more vulnerable, more emotional, more conceited, less objective, and disliked math and science. Thus, a woman who possessed several healthy adult traits might be seen as a less healthy adult person than would a man with those same traits, and so she would be more likely to be diagnosed as unhealthy and admitted to a hospital. Evidently one can be a healthy adult and an unhealthy woman. Broverman's study was later replicated with a group of 120 Australian psychologists (M. Anderson and the Feminist Psychology Group, 1975), so the results are not specific to this culture.

Ratings of Mental Health

Given the biases Broverman discovered, what evidence is there that people use sex-role stereotypic traits in their evaluations of the mental health of other people? Several studies have found that sex-role inappropriate behaviors are perceived as evidence of maladjustment by college students (Costrich et al., 1975; Seyfried and Hendrick, 1973; Zeldow, 1976).

Coie, Pennington, and Buckley (1974) looked at attributions of disorder as a function of the gender of the person with the symptoms and of the type of stress that produced the symptoms. They found that students perceived both aggressive women, and males complaining of headaches, nausea, shortness of breath, and heart pounding to be more maladjusted than aggressive males and nauseated females. When a male had symptoms supposedly as a consequence of an impending examination, less pathology was attributed to him than to the woman with the same symptoms under the same conditions. Thus, a male with achievement-related stress was seen as less in need of mental health services. On the other hand, females who had symptoms as a result of being rejected by their fiancé were not rated as less disturbed than males with the same symptoms who had also been rejected, but the females were seen as less in need of hospitalization than the males. Thus, it is appropriate (less pathological) for males to be upset by examinations and for females to be upset by affiliative losses; the reverse is not true. This judgment is, in fact, incorrect; a study of dating couples showed that males were more severely affected by a breakup than females (Hill, Rubin, and Peplau, 1976).

When clinicians rate mental health, bias can affect the ratings, as the Broverman study showed. But the problem goes beyond the clinicians themselves; some of their diagnostic instruments may have a built-in sex-role bias. Potkay and Merrens (1975) found some effects of sex of figure in the Thematic Apperception Test (TAT) cards. Females' pictures on the cards were perceived as more mentally healthy, but men's pictures were perceived as being more favorably portrayed compared to other people in society. Possibly because of this difference in cultural favorability, males could not identify well with female figures, although females could identify with male figures. If this difference in cross-sex identification were used for diagnostic purposes, some sex bias is bound to result.

Despite this, and despite the findings of the Broverman study, several studies found no sexual bias in clinicians' ratings, or found a reverse sex bias, with masculine women being rated as more healthy (Chasen, 1975; Gomes and Abramowitz, 1976; Zeldow, 1976). Even when biases appear, they are small. There may also be a same-sex bias in ratings of mental health (Lewittes, Moselle, and Simmons, 1973). Only politically conservative clinicians attributed more psychopathology to a left-oriented, politically active female than to a comparable male or to a politically inactive female (Abramowitz et al., 1973). The feminine patient (whether of male or female gender) may not be rated as more or less healthy, but they may be rated as being better liked (Gomes and Abramowitz, 1976).

One study did find differences, finding that parents, clinicians, and graduate students in psychology attributed more psychopathology to children exhibiting sex-role inappropriate behavior than to those exhibiting sex-role appropriate behavior (Feinblatt and Gold, 1976). Identical behaviors were evaluated differentially based on the gender of the child. Even when the same behavior was seen as pathological in both males and females, it was considered pathological for different reasons. Aggression was a problem for a female because it meant she did not interact with her friends; aggression was a problem for a male because it might affect his school work. These different interpretations reflect the relative value of affiliation and achievement. It may be that people who fail to achieve in the sex-role appropriate fashion (affiliation for women and careers for men) are seen as more pathological than when they fail to achieve in a less inappropriate fashion.

Treatment and Diagnosis

Some evidence indicates bias in psychiatric practice and treatment. Female neurotic depressives may receive more therapy treatments (L. Stein, del Gaudio, and Ansley, 1976), maintaining dependency longer. Male depressives may receive electroconvulsive shock therapy more often than women (38 percent for men, 22 percent for women), even though slightly more women than men may benefit from this therapy (Winokur, 1973). Middle-aged females are most likely to be treated with psychosurgery; that is, women are more likely to have parts of their brain removed for the treatment of behavioral problems, such as obsessive-compulsive behavior, depression or dissatisfaction with life, aggression, and abnormal sexual behaviors.

Sex roles may also be relevant in getting out of hospitals. When psychiatric patients can be released to cooperating families in the community, females were released more often than males (Keskiner et al., 1973). Males were released only if they could be employed, even though only two of the sixty women accepted into the outpatient program had had regular jobs. And feminine people (those who are docile and conforming) are released sooner from institutions than masculine people (those who are assertive, adventuresome, leaders) (Distler, May, Tuma, 1964; Doherty, 1976).

Hysteria is another behavioral problem in which sex differences in diagnosis and treatment are often seen. **Hysteria** is usually characterized by complaints of bodily ills that occur without known physical causes. Female and male hysterics differ very little in personality characteristics—flamboyance, exaggerated concern for others, overreaction to criticism (Luisada, Peele, and Pittard, 1973). Despite this, there are large differences in diagnostic frequency (Weintraub and Aronson, 1974). Male analysts diagnose hysteria significantly more often than female analysts. In one study, males diagnosed 26 percent of their patients as hysterics, and 48 percent of their female patients were so diagnosed. Women analysts in that study diagnosed only one patient, a male, as a hysteric. Weintraub and Aronson also found that female patients were more likely to be treated by inexperienced analysts than were male patients.

Women are more often given **psychotropic,** or mood-altering, drugs. Female neurotic depressives receive more drugs, and more potent ones, than males with the same symptoms (L. Stein et al., 1976). Cooperstock (1971) found that 69 percent of the prescriptions for psychotropic drugs in Canada were for women. Brahen (1973) found that 54 percent of the habitual users of barbiturates and 58 percent of the frequent users of the major tranquilizers were women. Women also comprised 60 percent of the pep pill users, 63 percent of the noncontrolled narcotic users, 70 percent of the minor tranquilizer users, 66 percent of the sedative users, and 80 percent of the psychotropic diet pill users. Cooperstock (1976) later looked at the frequency of repeat prescriptions of drugs in Canada. More women (5 percent) than men (3.3 percent) received ten or more prescriptions during the year from 1973 to 1974. For all psychotropic drugs except sedatives, two women received prescriptions or repeat prescriptions for every man who did. The greater frequency of women receiving prescriptions was most striking for married people; the number of women who had never married taking drugs was very similar to that for men (C. Chambers, Inciardi, and Siegal, 1975; A. Thompson, 1973). Even on television commercials, women are the pill takers (Chapter 7).

Summary

Because sex role affects diagnosis and treatment, figures on the incidence of various problems in men and women are probably contaminated by these biases. Out-of-role people may be seen as more deviant, and as more in need of help. The distinction between affiliation and achievement also appears. Affiliation failure may make others see problems of women and girls as more severe; achievement failure may magnify the way others perceive problems of men and boys. Even the same problems may be treated differently, with men receiving more electroconvulsive shock treatments and getting more experienced therapists, and women receiving more therapy, more psychosurgery, and more drug therapy. These differences are based on very few research reports, and much more work is needed in this area, but if they can be confirmed, these differences strongly suggest that the perception of problems and appropriate treatments is colored by the gender of the person being evaluated.

SEX RATIOS AMONG PERSONS IN INSTITUTIONS OR UNDERGOING THERAPY

There is evidence of bias in diagnosis and treatment, and it will be very difficult to evaluate how much that factor contributes to the differential incidence of mental illnesses in men and women. The most conservative conclusion is that there are few sex differences in disturbances and the incidence of deviant behaviors per se, but that the sex role of the patient, the stereotypes of the society, and the biases of the diagnostician interact to produce sex differences in the types of behaviors exhibited. Women will more often be hospitalized as hysterics, depressives, and schizophrenics. Men will more often show aggression or sexually deviant behavior, and so are more often sent to prisons or drug treatment centers, or are hospitalized for personality disorders.

Incidence of Problems

Surveys of inmates in mental hospitals, of people treated as outpatients, and people treated in private practice all show more females than males being treated (Chesler, 1972; Gove and Tudor, 1973; Levine et al., 1974; Weintraub and Aronson, 1974). One review article pointed out that the rate of increase from 1955 to 1968 of female use of psychiatric resources was greater than the rate of increase for males, ending with a usage rate of outpatient facilities of 444 for males and 542 for females, per one hundred thousand population (Levine et al., 1974).

Chesler's data (1972) are the most extensive available, and she shows more women than men in six types of psychiatric facilities. But she did not correct for population frequencies of men and women: in 1968, approximately 52 percent of the institutionalized population was female, but in 1970 53 percent of the total population was female. When the admission rates were corrected for population frequencies, the results showed that in 1969, 623.5 white women and 498.7 white men were admitted, per one hundred thousand people. The rate is even higher for nonwhites, but the sex difference remains.

Gove (1973) corrected his data for both population and age frequencies, and still found more females were reported as having poor mental health in community surveys, were in mental hospitals, were treated in private practice, and were treated for psychiatric disorders by general medical practitioners. However, Gove did not include personality disorders, and most people treated for personality disorders are male.

Neither Gove nor Chesler included prison inmates in their surveys, most of whom are male and many of whom have psychiatric disorders. In view of this, and in view of the other problems with their data, it could be that the sex difference in the total incidence of all mental disorders is very small or nonexistent.

Types of Problem and Gender

The type of deviant behavior, however, does interact with gender (Chesler, 1972; Gove, 1972; Weintraub and Aronson, 1974). More females than males are diagnosed for the following illnesses: depression, psychophysiological disorders (stress-induced diseases), psychoticism, schizophrenia, paranoia, and self-poisoning. There are also more female than male hysterics, perhaps because most diagnosticians are male (Chesler, 1972). Depression begins earlier in life for females than males, and females have more depressive episodes and longer episodes (Winokur, 1973). Even impermanent, stress-induced personality disorders are exhibited more by women. Males predominate in the following types of disorders: alcohol addiction and intoxication, drug addiction, and personality disorders, **psychopathic** and **sociopathic.** (These disorders are often combined today into one category because both refer to a person who seems to feel no remorse or guilt, or who lacks the ability to empathize with others, though these people may be very socially skilled, and appear warm and charming.) Male psychoanalytic patients are more likely to be homosexuals, exhibitionists, voyeurs, fetishists, transvestites, or sadomasochists, all problems in sexual behavior. Although suicides are attempted more by women, most successful suicides are men (Chesler,

1972; Weissman, 1974), though this difference is reversed in a few countries, such as India and Poland.

Men and women also show different ages at admission for hospitalization. Psychotic men are hospitalized at a younger age than psychotic women, perhaps because the male's symptoms are responded to faster by the family or the community (Gove, 1973). But as mentioned earlier, the symptoms of female depressives begin earlier than those of male depressives (Winokur, 1973). In 1969, the rate of people receiving outpatient care was higher for white males than white females between the ages of eighteen and twenty-four, but this difference reversed for people older than twenty-four (Chesler, 1972). In the same year, there were more white male than white female psychiatric admissions for all ages; the same was true for nonwhite admissions, except for ages fourteen to seventeen, when females predominated (Chesler, 1972).

There is also a sex difference in the types of complaints among college students. Winer, Dorus, and Moretti (1974) found no sex difference in the mean number of complaints of students at the University of Chicago Student Mental Health Clinic (150 males and 130 females were seen). However, the types of complaints differed in frequency as a function of gender. Females more often complained about interpersonal adequacy (largely with family and boyfriend) and self-adequacy; females also more often had gastrointestinal complaints (stress illness) and unspecified affective complaints. The males were more often homosexuals or drug users. In another study, men complained more of concentration difficulties and women of overeating and of crying (Ginn, 1975a).

Sex differences in types of disorders appear even among institutionalized children. Between ages five and twelve boys more often than girls had an antisocial or a mixed antisocial-neurotic disorder (40 percent of fifty-three boys; 25 percent of thirty-nine girls) (Wolkind, 1974a, 1974b). Girls more often had a purely neurotic disorder (50 percent, 30 percent for boys). Even the background of the disorders differed for boys and girls. Boys with an antisocial disorder had large numbers of siblings and a lack of contact with their father. Girls with the same disorder had been institutionalized for a long time. In another study, it was found that more boys than girls were referred to a child-guidance clinic for being emotional or passive, while more girls than boys were referred for being defiant and verbally aggressive (Feinblatt and Gold, 1976). Thus, even children have psychological problems differentially, based on their gender; this could be related, as Chesler suggested, to either sex-role rejection, extensive acting out of the sex role, or differential diagnosis of psychopathology based on sex-role expectations.

As was mentioned earlier, more prison inmates are male. In 1972, for example, 95 percent of all people in local jails were male (U.S. Department of Justice, 1972). However, males and females in prison may also differ. Mitchell and Murphy (1975) compared male and female patients at Carstairs State Hospital, which receives mentally ill patients from prisons. Female patients had more previous psychiatric admissions and also showed more aggression, both self- and other-directed. Eysenck and Eysenck (1973) also found more psychiatric disorders among male and female inmates of Holloway Prison, London, than in the general population. Although males in the general population received higher psychoticism scores than females, female prisoners got higher scores than male prisoners. Thus, it may be that women must be more severely disturbed than males before they commit a crime, or at least before they are incarcerated rather than hospitalized for committing one.

INTERPRETATION: THE INTERACTION OF GENES WITH ENVIRONMENT

Many of the deviant behaviors discussed in this chapter have a biological component. Sex differences in types of mental illness could be the result of sex-linkage, sex-limitation, or sex differences in environmental pressures or in resistance to those pressures. These possible interactions will now be discussed, to see how those interactions could produce sex differences in the incidence of various mental illnesses.

Both depressive and manic-depressive psychoses have genetic components. Though the genetic component of the first seems autosomal, some people have proposed that some of the manic-depressive psychoses may be affected by an X-linked dominant gene as well as an autosomal gene (Helzer and Winokur, 1974; Loranger, 1975; Mendlewicz, Fleiss, and Fieve, 1972; Pardue, 1975; Reich, Clayton, and Winokur, 1969; Winokur, 1973; Winokur and Tanna, 1969). A **manic-depressive** is a person who alternates between periods of elation with high activity levels (mania) and periods of depression. Researchers also say that some manic-depressive psychoses may be sex-limited, and related to female hormones (Buchsbaum et al., 1973; A. Powell et al., 1973); examples include depression sensitive to the birth control pill, premenstrual depression, postpartum depression, and, maybe, menopausal depression. However, much of the data supporting the theory of X-linkage can also be predicted by a sex-modified threshold model of heritability, with females having a lower threshold for depression than men given the same combination of contributing factors: genes, hormones, and their interaction with the person's environment.

Alcoholism also has a genetic component (Reich, Winokur, and Mulhaney, 1975), and there are more male than female alcoholics. However, the sex difference in alcoholism is most probably the result of sex differences in environmental stress or the amount of exposure to alcohol, because genetic factors predict male better than female alcoholism. This indicates that environmental factors play a larger part in female than in male alcoholism (Reich et al., 1975).

Fathers who are alcoholic may have manic-depressive children. Perhaps both syndromes are different expressions of the same autosomal gene; when this gene is combined with an X-linked gene, manic-depressive behaviors may be likely to occur (Reich et al., 1969; Winokur, 1973). For example, females with an early onset of depressive disease often have depressed female relatives, and both alcoholism and sociopathy are common in their male relatives (Winokur, 1973). Thus, there may be both genetic and environmental commonalities between manic-depressive behaviors and alcoholism, though females more often show the former and males the latter behavior. This difference in behavior could be the result of the interaction of genes with environmental stress and of differences in vulnerability to stress.

Sociopathy and hysteria may also be liked to the same gene or genes (Cloninger et al., 1975a, 1975b), with hysteria being a less severe form of sociopathy. Neither behavior will appear in an environment without stress, even in a genetically predisposed person. Less severe forms of stress produce hysteria; more severe stress produces sociopathy. The sex differences in these traits seem the result of different resistance to stress, so that the stress that produces sociopathy in men produces only hysteria in women, who need much more stress to be sociopathic. In fact, sociopathic women seem to have a much more deviant home environment than sociopathic men. Montagu (1970) also reported that under equal stress (bombing raids), more men than women suffered not only from shock and psychoneuroses, but also from hysteria.

One of the most provocative, and in some ways alarming, discussions of sex differences in inherited susceptibility to stress came from a series of studies of adoptees from psychiatrically disturbed biological parents (Cadoret et al., 1975, 1976; Cunningham et al., 1975). In these studies, 114 adoptive parents of children from twelve to twenty-four years of age were interviewed. The children were divided into those whose biological parents had had a psychiatric condition (fifty-five) and those whose biological parents had had no record of symptoms or treatment (fifty-nine). These two sets of children were then matched according to gender and according to the age of the biological mother. In both groups, the children had had no contact with their biological mothers after birth.

The researchers found different problems among the female and male adoptees. Among the male adoptees, those whose biological parents had had psychological problems showed a significantly greater incidence of childhood behaviors requiring professional care, when compared to the control group. These problems included hyperactivity, antisocial traits, and either withdrawal from new situations or a violent reaction to changes. None of these differences between experimental and control groups were found to be significant for female adoptees. On the other hand, female children of psychiatrically disturbed parents showed a significantly increased number of somatic traits, such as complaints of aches and pains without an apparent cause, nervous stomach, and menstrual difficulties. This sex difference should be treated only as suggestive, but it is in agreement with the cause of sex differences in hysteria and sociopathy proposed above. It should be noted that not all of the children of disturbed parents had problems, so the environment provided by the adoptive parents was obviously also extremely important.

We close this chapter as we began Chapter 1: proposing that the existence of any sex difference in any behavior is the result of the interaction of the sex chromosomes and the prenatal and postnatal environments, including the effects of hormones. The relative importance of each factor in a behavior will depend upon genetic variability and environmental variability, and will vary from trait to trait. Any sex differences in a mildly or severely deviant behavior are likely to be a very complex interaction of the genes and hormones of the individual; that person's susceptibility to different stress as determined by sex role (affiliation stress for women and achievement stress for men, generally); the person's sex-role traits; and the sex-role stereotypes of the person doing the diagnosing. Any sex difference in the total incidence of deviant behaviors, if present at all, is likely to be very small.

KEY TERMS AND CONCEPTS

The healthy adult
Hysteria
Psychotropic drugs

Psychopathics and sociopathics
Manic-depressives

QUESTIONS ON KEY ISSUES

1. In what areas of mental health are there no sex differences?
2. Why might sex differences in mental health largely be limited to causes and correlates (rather than there being differences in mean scores or frequencies of symptoms)? What are some examples of this?
3. What major biases — both on the part of the subject and on the part of the person doing the diagnosing — can affect sex differences in this area?
4. How do children affect the mental health of their parents?
5. What are some examples of the effects of sex roles upon mental health? What could you suggest to parents of young children based on this?
6. How do employment and marital status affect various psychological problems, including depression and happiness?
7. What are some of the most dramatic differences in the mental health of the sexes in terms of the types of treatment they receive and the types of symptoms they show?
8. How do genes, hormones, environment, and sex role interact to contribute to sex differences in various behavioral problems?

CHAPTER **13** _____

Retrospect and Prospect

LOOKING BACK

Looking back over the previous chapters, it seems obvious that sex differences have a developmental timetable. They are most marked when fertility is highest and the chance of a genetically abnormal offspring is lowest for both females and males, that is, just a few years after puberty. This is seen in both humans and lower animals, and it is undoubtedly the result of a combination of hormonal changes and cultural pressures to take on adult sex roles. In lower animals, the peak sexual activity of the male is often delayed relative to fertility because the male needs to establish dominance or a territory. Perhaps this contributes to the fitness of offspring, by having the male prove his fitness before he reproduces. But in the human, female sexual activity, or at least peak sexual interest, is also delayed until well past puberty and the greatest period of fertility. The function this delay in human females might have had, if indeed it had any, is unknown. But it seems relevant that most societies encourage women to marry older men and that more females marry younger males in societies in which females have relatively greater status. So power and dominance relationships may be a part of the relationship among sex differences, sexual activity, and mate selection.

The increase in sexual dimorphism at puberty is seen in a wide variety of physical and behavioral characteristics. For example, sex differences in dominance, maze learning, and activity appear in rats and hamsters only after puberty. Sex differences in food preferences (see Appendix B) and olfactory sensitivities also appear after puberty in rats; the female rat decreases the percentage of the diet that is protein and increases her sweet tooth; the female also shows a decreased olfactory sensitivity after puberty, perhaps because of increases in progesterone.

In humans, sex differences in food preferences, olfactory sensitivity, and mortality are also greatest after puberty (see Appendix B). Adult sex differences in intellectual skills, including spatial, mathematical, and verbal skills, appear just before or during puberty. The greater female use of prescription drugs also begins just after puberty (Appendix B). Sex differences in self-esteem, sex-role attitudes, moral attributions, attitudes towards personal appearance, and self-consciousness are exaggerated by adolescence, as are sex differences in how books are carried.

355

Adolescence also increases the aggression of the male relative to the female, and increases the ability of the female to send emotions to other people by means of facial expressions. Also, under the influence of the change in hormone levels that occur at puberty, sex differences in the ratio of muscle to fat, in strength and height, in the number of red blood cells, in metabolic rate, and in body water content are increased. Even the timing of puberty may be related to sex differences. Early puberty is associated with higher verbal than spatial scores (and with a decreased spatial ability relative to a more delayed maturation), with increased sex typing, and even with greater frequencies of premenstrual and postpartum symptoms. Early puberty is also associated with increased aggression, although both early maturing girls and late maturing boys have a higher need to affiliate.

For the human particularly, puberty represents a time when socially defined sex roles are exaggerated, and this exaggeration undoubtedly contributes to the appearance of many sex differences at puberty, though it is certainly not the only cause. With age, the sexes become more similar, in hormones and other physiological characteristics and in some behaviors. Age seems associated with an increased tolerance for opposite-sex impulses, and with a decrease in sex differences in spatial ability, food preferences, usage of doctors and drugs, and in ways of carrying books. Thus, adolescence is the age in which the sexes are more likely to differ. This makes sense when you remember that the functions of sex differences include sexual recognition and the reduction of competition; these functions are the most important for the species when fertility and the chance of producing genetically normal offspring are high. These functions may be partly atavistic and anachronistic for the modern human—if, as some believe, humans are no longer evolving—but placing sex differences in this context makes them seem less arbitrary and whimsical.

But sex differences appear before puberty as well as after puberty, in both humans and lower species. Juvenile monkeys play in sex-typed ways, whether or not a mother is available to teach them appropriate behavior. Sex differences in aggression, with the larger male (or the larger female in some species) generally being the more aggressive, appear at all ages. This sex difference in aggression may be a function of both chromosomes and androgens, but it is also a secondary consequence of the greater muscle strength of the male in humans as well as other animals; girls tell experimenters that they do not hit boys because boys are stronger than they are. Some sex differences appearing before puberty are reversed after puberty. In humans, male reaction time is faster than that of females after puberty but slower before puberty, perhaps because the female develops faster. Spatial ability is another example; preschool girls may have greater spatial ability, but postadolescent males do better than females. Sex differences in the rate of going to the doctor also reverse at puberty. In these cases, maturation rates, sex roles, and differential socialization are probably responsible for the preadolescent differences and also contribute to the reversal that occurs at puberty. As we discussed earlier, differential treatment on the basis of gender starts at birth in all primates, so from birth on, socialization interacts with genes and inductive hormonal effects to produce the sex differences that are observed before puberty. After puberty, the experiences of the person and the activational effects of the hormones become part of the interaction.

Just as the increase in hormones at puberty affects sex differences, so does the rapid decline in hormones that women experience at various times. Women may experience this decline, at various rates and to various degrees, four times in their lives: in the premenstrual phase, after withdrawal from the birth control pill, after giving birth, and at menopause. It has been said that at these times women are more at risk for emotional problems, but this is far from certain. The commonality of these four experiences ought to be kept in mind in future research on this question, as should the tremendous effects of women's culturally conditioned expectations and attributions. Research may show that only some women are particularly susceptible to these changes, while most women do not respond to them at all.

Another type of sex difference seen in all of the chapters was in the interactions or correlations of one variable with another. Aggression, achievement, affiliation, intellectual abilities, neuroticism, and anxiety all have different patterns of correlations in men and women. An aggressive man should not be expected to have the same developmental history, or even exhibit the same behavior, as an aggressive woman. In other words, these behaviors mean different things depending on the gender of the person exhibiting them. This may account for much of the difficulty in seeing reliable sex differences across different tests; if the behavior in question has different correlates in men and in women, the behavior—and the sex difference in that behavior—will be situation-specific. Masculinity in men refers to different behavior than masculinity in women, and achievement, affiliation, neuroticism, and anxiety refer to different behavior in men and in women, even if the sexes receive identical mean scores on an appropriate test. The mean self-rated scores of self-esteem seldom show any sex differences, yet men and women are made happy and unhappy by different events. Thus, sex differences in the means of distributions may well be the least common sex difference that can be reliably observed. Sex differences in correlations and in variability, in gender interacting with other variables, will be more common experimental outcomes. But these outcomes are difficult to interpret.

However, the preceding makes it clear that the typical criteria for deciding that a behavior is affected by a biological bias cannot legitimately be applied to sex differences (see Maccoby and Jacklin, 1974, for a description of the traditional view). Biologically biased differences are most likely not at birth, as is most often assumed, but during and after puberty, when the sexes are the most biologically different. Nor can universality (appearing in all samples and all cultures) be required to establish the existence of a biological bias for a sex difference. Both human and infra-human behavior are sensitive to the situation; what behavior will appear depends upon the current stimulus context and how that context is interpreted by the organism in light of past experience. A rush of adrenalin may be interpreted as an expression of fear, anger, or euphoria, depending upon how the person perceives the situation. Correlations between a person's behavior across situations and across time are low, also suggesting that sex differences are very situation-specific. So biologically biased sex differences should not be expected to appear in all contexts.

More fruitful research will probably involve attempts to identify the stimuli that allow and do not allow a sex difference to appear. Some attempts have been made in this direction by several researchers, including primate ethologists (Lancaster, 1976). For example, living on the open ground or the plains, as opposed to in the forest, exaggerates primate sex differences in dominance and aggression, but reduces sex differences in parental behavior. Similar variations are seen in humans. Sex differences in aggression in children depend upon the presence of an adult and upon prior frustration (Caplan, 1975). Identification of the situations that do and do not produce sex differences will perhaps give us far more control over those differences.

On the other hand, though behavior varies with the situation, the consistencies in sex differences should not be overlooked. For example, as mentioned earlier, women who have premenstrual symptoms are also more likely to have postpartum and menopausal symptoms. Thus, some women have reactions to these three periods of hormone reduction. The reason for this consistency is unknown—it may be the result of genetic predisposition, personality factors, cultural factors, or all together. But the question certainly needs to be studied. As another example, researchers working with human females and with infra-human primate males found evidence suggesting that some of the monthly and annual cycles of behavior may be the result of cycles in the brain, and not directly the result of hormones at all, although hormonal changes undoubtedly increase the magnitude of the behavioral cycles. The research on cycles in men and women and hormone reduction in women suggests that many biorhythms, if not most, are directly due to changes in the brain itself, rather than to indirect effects of hormone cycles on the brain, so that the hormone changes are correlates and not causes. Other consistencies should be watched for, and possible reasons for them tested.

The presence of biorhythms in both men and women has tremendous implications for sex differences, only some of which are now realized. Many sex differences in perceptual-motor ability depend upon the time of day of the test, as well as the stage of the cycle in which the subjects are located. Since the phase of the menstrual cycle affects volunteering for experiments, consistent biases might be expected on that basis alone. Many perceptual-motor behaviors show consistent rhythmic changes, although more often males than females may show circadian changes. But the presence of biorhythms means that in order to establish a sex difference, it is first necessary to specify the rhythm of the behavior in each sex—the effect of the time of day and the season, and the possible effect of annual rhythms upon circadian and monthly rhythms. Unless this is done, small sex differences are meaningless—they can be reversed if the subjects are tested at a different time of day, on a different day, or in a different season. Thus, more research into these cycles must be carried out, with more sophisticated analysis. For now, at least, the menstrual cycle of women can be placed in its appropriate context: it is but one of many rhythms of varying magnitudes and durations affecting both behavior and physiology in both men and women.

The distinction between environmental and biological factors seems overdrawn, for two reasons. Feminists deemphasize and devalue biological factors in sex differences for essentially political reasons. "Feminist leanings would tend to make one seek for environmental etiologies" (Unger and Denmark, 1975, p. 605). This tendency has been a useful antidote to the earlier emphasis on the biological differences between the sexes, which was used to justify differential role assignments and such discriminatory practices as the denial of the vote to females. For example, Filene (1974) quoted some antisuffragist arguments: " 'Doctors tell us . . . ,' wrote one man, 'that thousands of children would be harmed or killed before birth by the injurious effects of untimely political excitement on their mothers.' And, indeed, Dr. Charles L. Dana explained that, because of the female neurological structure, women who led masculine lives [as by voting] would risk a 25-percent higher rate of insanity" (p. 37).

But feminists may be making a mistake in deemphasizing biology; biological biases may be easier to modify than environmentally produced biases. Recall that women who claimed premenstrual symptoms had a lower incidence of suicide attempts and also had better task performances; by attributing behavior to the proper cause they were more able to control behavior. Changing behavior to combat environmental biases seldom has results as rapidly as does changing what a person attributes to biological bias. Changing attributions (explanations for one's own behavior) to make them correct gives one greater control over behavior. The people who study memory have the explanation: we enter any situation already possessing extensive beliefs and value systems set up to deal with environmental biases, and behavioral change means changing attitudes and attributions. The more prior, incompatible learning there has been (the greater the proactive interference), the slower the new learning or the change will be. To be sure, menstrual attitudes, for example, have also been culturally created and must be slowly unlearned (if they are false, which most are), but many other biological biases do not have such large cultural incrustations, so their effect on behavior can be more rapidly modified because there are fewer attributions and attitudes that have to be changed.

The other reason the environmental-biological distinction seems overdrawn is illustrated beautifully by a question from one of our introductory psychology students. I (K. B. Hoyenga) had just completed a lecture on the nervous system and endocrine system, illustrating each part of the anatomy-physiology lesson by explaining the role each structure and gland played in behavior. I also emphasized my belief as a physiological psychologist that all behavior has a biological basis. When I asked for questions, there was complete silence. After class, one girl came up—with a very puzzled expression on her face—and plaintively asked, "Don't you believe in learning?" Learning is also biological, learning also involves changes in glandular secretions and in the activity of nerve cells. Experience creates physiological changes in the brain. In fact, if some of the current theories on memory are correct, experience affects genes in much the same way gonadal hormones do. Both hormones and experience may de-repress or induce a gene permanently; we see this in the inductive effects of hormones and the creation of long-term memory stores and traces in the brain. Both hormones and experience can also have less permanent effects on the brain, as we see in activational hormonal effects and short-term memory. And the biological learning process and the biological hormonal process interact, so that learning affects hormones and hormones affect learning. Thus, the distinction between biology and environment is, in many respects, spurious. It seems more important to be able to recognize the environmental and biological biases that affect behavior so that correct attributions can be made, and more accurate control of the self be possible.

Perhaps the most controversial issue in the field is the sex difference in achievement. If the research is correct, males achieve for achievement's sake, for the intrinsic satisfaction associated with accomplishment. Females achieve by affiliation in grade school, and even to some extent in high school; after that, many women feel the conflict between affiliative achievement and other achievement. But at the very earliest ages this difference has implications beyond those pointed out earlier. Not only do women learn to attribute failure in math or in other areas to a lack of ability—thereby becoming helpless and feeling a lack of control over their own future success—when they do achieve, it is for reasons extrinsic to the task and its mastery. That is, when men achieve, the goal of achievement for many of them is intrinsic, mastery leads to and supplies its own rewards. Women more often achieve for extrinsic reasons, to please others, and extrinsic motivation interferes with intrinsic motivation for the same task. A girl who memorizes an answer to an addition problem in order to win the approval of the teacher is never likely to learn the intrinsic satisfaction that comes from understanding the idea or the concept of addition. This means that achievement in women is likely to be much more fragile than achievement in men, because women's achievement is extrinsically motivated, and thus dependent upon the whims of the environment supplying the motives, and because the extrinsic motivation interferes with the operation of the independent, intrinsic motive for accomplishing the same task.

Truth is relative, which unfortunately precludes neat, simple packaging of conclusions about sex differences. Truth is whatever a majority of the relevant peer or reference group agrees to at any given time, so scientific truth is whatever a majority of scientists believe at any given time. Thus, truth is relative to the cultural-political environment of the time. The history of science has taught us that politics can determine the truth, and that the fate of the truth of any given time is very difficult to predict. A scientific fact discovered at one time might later be discovered to be founded on incorrect assumptions related to the cultural-political environment of the time. Or the fact might later be seen to be true only in a very limited and restricted sense, as Einstein's theory superseded Newton's. And some facts remain as such for succeeding generations, other facts simply being built on their foundation. From our point of view, influenced by our own culture, we cannot predict which of these fates will befall the observations in this book. But we can always recognize that their truth may be transitory, and keeping an open mind about these observations will gradually evolve into a different framework for the study and understanding of sex differences.

LOOKING FORWARD

We might ask ourselves what our schools have been doing to our children. In some respects, schools represent a feminine environment. Obedience, neatness, and social and verbal skills are emphasized. And most teachers are female, though their bosses are male. But that may be what boys need most to optimize their development. They are weaker in verbal skills, and so need extra time, help, and effort in that area. And socialization in the school is more apt to create communion in boys than agency in girls. If androgynous people are really healthier and happier and more effective, the femininity of the school benefits males. But it does so at an awful price. Boys pay by having greater failure rates because some cannot cope with constant drills in the skills that they most lack and that are the most foreign to them. Girls pay by growing up to avoid achievement, to have math phobias, to thank luck for their success, and blame lack of ability for their failure. But some masculinization of the schools seems very likely to occur as part of the change in sex roles, and it is interesting to speculate on the possible consequences of this masculinization. What if activity and coordination, dominance and independence, and math and spatial skills were emphasized for both men and women? What might be the outcome of this?

Ethology will contribute more and more to our future knowledge of sex differences. For example, Barash (1976) found that when men and women crossed the street with infants present, men made significantly more head turns than women. The sex difference vanished in the absence of infants. Barash attributed this to parental defense behavior, which is exhibited more by males than by females in many primate species—the male human has simply "substituted Chevrolets for cheetahs" in his vigilant watch for harm to his infants. Ethological techniques seem to promise the discovery of unexpected sex differences, which may, in turn, lead to a better understanding of the evolutionary history and function of these differences in humans and to greater specification of the conditions under which sex differences are likely to appear. This is particularly true now that ethologists begin to make their data more reliable by admitting that their own culture can bias their observations, even those of animals in the wild (Lancaster, 1976).

One direction ethology research may take is to determine if sexual selection still operates for humans. This question is being debated theoretically and studied experimentally (B. Campbell, 1972). Several experimenters, including Margaret Mead, feel that women select men who are brighter, more dominant, and more competent then themselves, and that the more sexually attractive the female, the more success she will have in her selection. But this means that many bright, dominant, competent women will be left over. Is this one reason for the lower rate of marriage among professional women than among professional men? To what extent does preference exist in both women and men? To what extent do women prefer brighter mates and men less bright ones? What were the origins of this particular selection and what are its effects? Will the women's liberation movement change this? Will feminists more than nonfeminists select men who are less intelligent, dominant, and competent than themselves? Can men learn not to devalue themselves if their wife is more intelligent, more aggressive, and more dominant?

More data will also appear on the interactions or impact of one animal's cycles upon those of another. As was mentioned earlier, female humans who live together tend to have synchronized menstrual cycles. Female monkeys may also affect the annual sexual cycles of male monkeys (Gordon et al., 1976; Michael and Zumpe, 1976), and the female cycle may determine the copulatory effectiveness of the male primate (Michael and Bonsall, 1977). Exposure to an inaccessible estrous female will increase the aggression of a male rat (G. Taylor, 1976), perhaps because of the increase in androgens produced by that exposure. Dan (1976) even found some suggestions of a synchronization of monthly activity between a woman not on the pill and her husband; there was no evidence of such synchronization between women on the pill and their husbands. More of such research will undoubtedly appear.

We must keep in mind that all sex differences can be eradicated. The theory of evolution concerning the effects of sexual and natural selection and the data from anthropological and cross-cultural surveys tell us that the only way to remove sex differences is to remove all sex differences in role assignments and role evaluations. This does not mean just that women would work, or would be just as likely to work as men, because for most women working means that they have simply added some aspects of the male role to their female role requirements, housekeeping and child care. If differences are to disappear, men must be just as involved in child and home care as women. Children must be raised by males as well as by females. There must be as many househusbands as housewives. Any biologically biased sex differences, once identified, can be eliminated with special training, as by emphasizing spatial skills for females and suppressing aggression in males.

But is this the most desirable thing to do? If we could eliminate sex differences (unlikely as that may sound), would we try to make everyone masculine or everyone feminine or everyone androgynous? What effects might this have on children and their development? Feminists have pointed out another possible approach to the "woman problem." Instead of eliminating sex differences, we could stop devaluing the female role in relation to the male role—but that may be even harder to do. And if it is desirable to eradicate sex differences, the job will be a long one. Perhaps we should begin by removing a major obstacle, one of the few cultural universals—the lower status of women. But even so obvious a problem has no obvious solution. Certainly the current status and role of women does not correspond closely to the stereotype. Women work. In 1970, about 43 percent of all women were working, and women were 38 percent of the total work force (Filene, 1974). Of the working women, 60 percent work out of economic necessity, and 90 percent of all women work at some time in their lives. But women are largely in low-paying, low-status, dead-end jobs. Legislation can remove the discrimination against both men and women in overt public behavior by making it illegal, and this might lead to some attitude changes, if dissonance theory is correct (Buck, 1976).

But change of any sort, whether it is to remove sex differences or to remove differential evaluations of behavior as a function of gender, will produce uneasiness. The fight against the Equal Rights Amendment is a perfect example. As pointed out earlier, prejudice serves useful functions for both the group on top and that on the bottom. These functions must be dealt with directly so that their importance can be deemphasized and devalued; otherwise change will not occur. Once we get past those obstacles and roles are no longer assigned from birth, there may still be a price to pay. To be sure, there will be benefits, including increased flexibility, since men and women could perform both roles; this flexibility is particularly important in a society of nuclear families, not extended families, where a person of either gender may be suddenly called on to play either role as a consequence of death or divorce. Women who outlive their husbands will be able to pay the bills and change the furnace filters and in general feel competent, not helpless, in dealing with the outside, instrumental world. And men may live longer if they are more in contact with their own feelings and more able to admit weakness. But what may the price be? During the transition period, people will be in doubt as to what is appropriate and in the face of too many options, decisions become harder and more stressful. People may thus respond with anger and aggression, directed outward or towards themselves, in the form of depression, because of their inability to define themselves and others on the basis of sex roles. Part of people's identities will be removed. People are aware of these costs, and reluctant to pay them. The greatest resistance to the change in the definition of women's roles comes not from men, but from women (L. Harris, 1970).

Role assignments and restrictions cannot be logically made if the only criterion is gender, except for impregnation, parturition, and lactation (and even these may change in the future, since female monkeys have already successfully served as foster mothers for someone else's fetus, and primate males may someday be able to do the same). The variability within each gender is large, especially in comparison to the typical size of any sex difference. Both females and males show relatively large and consistent cycles in hormones, moods, and sensitivities. Thus, one can never argue that the best assignment of a person to a task has been made, if the only basis for that assignment was gender.

> . . . and there was a certain excitement
> when after midnight you came home
> and we had coffee
> and i had a day of mine
> that made me as happy
> as yours did you
> —Nikki Giovanni*

*Last stanza of "A Certain Peace—9 Jan 72" from *My House* by Nikki Giovanni. Copyright © 1972 by Nikki Giovanni. By permission of William Morrow & Company, Inc.

———————————

A Guide to Statistics

When a researcher wishes to report the results of an investigation, the communication must be as unambiguous and condensed as possible. Researchers most commonly use statistics to achieve these goals in presenting their data. Three basic questions usually elicit a statistical answer. The first is, how did this group score on a certain measure? The second, do the scores on this measure relate to or predict the scores on a second measure? And thirdly, do the scores of this group differ from the scores of another group?

FREQUENCY DISTRIBUTION AND CENTRAL TENDENCIES

With respect to the first question, we can construct a figure that graphically represents the scores. This figure is called a frequency polygon. If you weighed each person in a large group of college-aged men and then plotted on a graph how many men achieved each weight (rounded off to the nearest number of pounds) you would have a frequency polygon (see Figure A.1). If the group consisted of college women rather than college men, the curve would be shifted towards the left. How could we most accurately describe the tendency for men to be heavier? If the number of people sampled were large, then the shape of that frequency polygon, regardless of what is being measured—height, weight, IQ, level of sex hormones in the blood—will approximate that shown in Figure A.1. This particular shape is called a normal curve, or a normal distribution. It can easily and accurately be summarized by specifying its mean ($\bar{X}$) and its standard deviation (σ).

There are three ways of expressing or describing the typical score in a distribution of scores. The mode refers to the most frequently achieved weight or score, the one score that more people get than any other score. The median refers to the score that divides the group exactly in half, with half of the group getting higher scores and the other half getting lower ones. However, the most frequently used method for expressing the typical score is the *mean,* or arithmetic average, which you get by adding up all the scores of the group and dividing by the number of people or scores in the group. In our example, looking for sex differences in weight, we would most likely compare the mean weight of the male group to the mean weight of the female group.

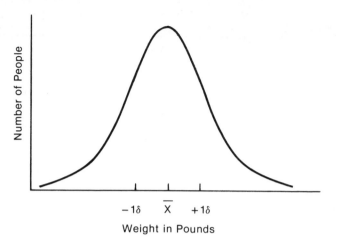

FIGURE A.1 _____

A SAMPLE OF A FREQUENCY DISTRIBUTION

The number of people at each particular weight (rounded off to the nearest pound) is presented. This particular distribution is called a normal distribution, which is a symmetrical curve with 68 percent of the people getting scores in between plus one and minus one standard deviation (σ) from the mean. In this particular sample the scores are normally distributed, so the mean ($\overline{X}$), median, and mode are all the same.

However, not all distributions of scores are normal. There may be more than one very frequently occurring score, in which case the distribution has more than one mode. For example, if we weighed males and females of a given age, we would see two unimodal normal curves. But if we combined those two distributions and simply looked at the number of people at each given weight without specifying gender, we would find that two scores occurred more often than any other, which is called a bimodal distribution. When we looked at our sample, we would see one mode corresponds to the most frequently occurring weight for females and the other to the most frequently occurring weight for males. Obviously, mean weight is not as good a description of a typical score in a bimodal distribution as in a unimodal distribution.

VARIABILITY

Variability is usually expressed or measured in one of two ways: the range or the standard deviation. The range refers to the difference between the highest score and the lowest score achieved by members of some group on some variable. For example, if four men weighed 140, 150, 160, and 170 pounds, then the range of weights for that group of men would be the difference between the highest and lowest scores, or thirty pounds. This is often expressed as range: 140–170 pounds, and means that the weight varied thirty pounds from heaviest to lightest.

The average deviation is another way to express the same concept, but it is less affected by one extreme score. For example, adding just one score—say, a 200-pound man—to the group doubles the range of the new group, making it sixty pounds. To determine the average deviation of a sample, we would find out how much each individual differs from the group mean, then add up all those differences (disregarding the sign) and divide by the number in the group. The average deviations for the two groups with the ranges of 30 and 60 would be 10.0 and 16.8, respectively; thus, the one score that doubled the range increased the average deviation only by 6.8.

Actually, the average deviation is not often used, but a variant of it, the standard deviation, is. The standard deviation is computed similarly to the way the average deviation is, except that all the differences from the mean are squared before they are added together. After adding the squares, find the average by dividing by the number of scores in the group. Finally, take the square root of the average squared deviation, which is then called the standard deviation. The standard deviations from the above two groups are 11.2 and 20.6 pounds, respectively. The standard deviation is preferred to the average deviation because of its relationship to the normal curve. For example, one standard deviation from the mean is always the point of greatest slope on the normal curve, and 68 percent of all scores always lie between plus one and minus one standard deviation from the mean (see Figure A.1). Since much of the data of psychology fit a normal distribution, the standard deviation is a very useful, standardized description of variability. Variance is a related concept of variability; it is simply the square of the standard deviation.

Thus, when the data from an experiment fit a normal distribution, a complete description of that data can be given by stating the mean and the standard deviation. From just these two pieces of information, the curve could be redrawn. Theorists proposing that the sexes differ in variability are suggesting that male variance is significantly greater on some measure than female variance, or vice versa.

CORRELATIONS

The second question that statistics may answer is: can a subject's score on one measure be used to predict the score of that same subject on another measure?

For example, height and weight are positively correlated; that is, taller people tend to be heavier, or being taller generally also means that you are heavier. Thus, we could predict that a person who is above average in height would also be above average in weight. An example of a negative correlation would be the relationship between miles traveled and gas remaining in a car's gas tank. The degree of the relationship is expressed in terms of a correlation coefficient, which can range in value anywhere from -1.0 through 0 to $+1.0$. Correlations of $+0.1$ and -1.0 are called, respectively, perfect positive correlations and perfect negative correlations. A correlation less than perfect falls somewhere closer to zero.

One way of visualizing correlations is by means of a scatter plot. In a scatter plot, the values of each of two variables are plotted, with one point representing one person's score on each variable. Often, the variables are first transformed into standard scores, which simply means that you replace each score with its distance from the mean measured in units of standard deviation. Figure A.2 presents six different scatter plots of different correlations between pairs of hypothetical variables. The scatter plot is circular when the correlation is zero. If there were a zero correlation between performance on a given test and grade point average in college, for example, knowledge of someone's score on that test would not enable us to predict that person's grade point average. As the correlation increases, the shape becomes more and more elliptical; the diagram narrows to a straight line when the correlation is perfect. When standard scores are used, the perfect correlation will be a straight line on a 45° (+1.0) or a 135° (−1.0) angle. When a correlation is close to perfect, close to either +1.0 or −1.0, one score can easily be predicted from another; when the correlation is zero or close to zero, you cannot predict one score from the other.

To evaluate a correlation, you must look at the probability that the particular correlation, based on the size of the sample, was due to chance factors alone and at the probability that the true correlation was in fact zero and that the variables were not related at all. That is, you need to establish that the correlation is true, and not the result of chance, and that it is significant. Significance is determined by the distance between the correlation you obtain and zero, and by the sample size.

When evaluating correlations, however, even significant ones, you must remember that the amount of variability in behavior that the correlation can reliably account for is related to the square of the correlation, not to the correlation itself. A correlation coefficient of +.70 between two different behaviors actually means that less than 50 percent ($.70^2 = .49$) of the variability in those behaviors can be accounted for by the relationship between the two. This gives a better idea of how risky it is to use one variable to predict the value of another. And in research on sex differences, correlations of .20 and .30 are much more common than correlations of .70, so conclusions based on such correlational data are obviously only tentative.

A special use of correlations is to determine the reliability and validity of some psychological test. Reliability means a person would get approximately the same score if she or he took the same test at different times. The simplest test of reliability is to give the test twice to the same group of people and calculate the correlation coefficient between the two sets of scores. A test should have a reliability of more than +.80 before it could be considered useful. (What might a reliability of −.80 mean?) Validity refers to the ability of the test to measure what you want it to. Naming a test "A Creativity Test" does not guarantee that it actually measures anything we could call creativity. To determine the validity of a test, correlate test scores to scores on some task, trait, or job that people generally agree is related to creativity; again, the closer the correlation is to +1.0 or −1.0, the more valid the test.

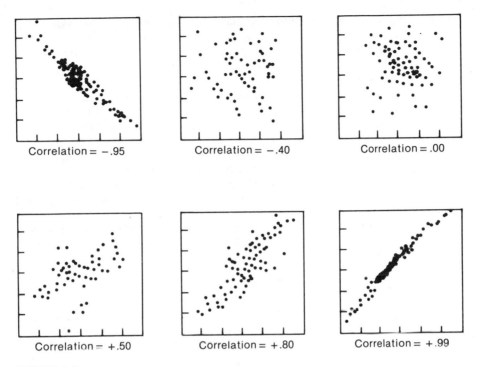

FIGURE A.2

HYPOTHETICAL SCATTER PLOTS OF DIFFERENT CORRELATIONS FOR
STANDARDIZED PAIRS OF VARIABLES

*Suppose that the −.95 correlation represents the relationship between miles trav-
eled and gas remaining in the tank. To get a scatter plot, measure miles traveled
and gallons remaining many times, marking a dot on the graph for each measure.
One axis of the graph represents the miles traveled, and the other represents the
number of gallons remaining. The +.80 correlation might represent the relationship
between weight and height for a group of college males; in this case, each dot represents one person, with one axis corresponding to their weight and the other axis
corresponding to their height. These two scatter plots and the high correlations
show that taller people weigh more, and the further you travel, the less gas remains
in your tank.*

TESTS OF SIGNIFICANT DIFFERENCES BETWEEN GROUPS

Testing the significance of differences between groups is most important. Research reports contain information that because *t* exceeded a certain value, or
because the F ratio was of a certain magnitude, we can reject the null hypothesis
with a certain degree of confidence. This means that the researcher has tested the
significance of the difference between groups. The null hypothesis is the statement that the independent variable had no effect and differences are solely the

result of chance. If it is rejected, the results are meaningful. While t-test and F ratio are the most common tests, chi square, U, the Wilcoxon and other tests are also performed, to determine if the groups being compared differ. In the t-test and F ratio, statistical significance results when the numerator of the fraction is larger than the denominator.

The numerator size increases as differences between the groups increase, while the denominator size is proportional to the variability of scores within a group. The value obtained by forming the ratio will be approximately 1 if the scores were randomly assigned to the groups being compared and there are no differences between the groups. When the value becomes larger, such as 2, 4, or 10, it suggests that there is a difference between the groups. The precise value needed for each test to feel confident that differences are real and not due to chance is usually found in a table near the end of a statistics book. One important point to remember in reviewing statistical tests is that these tests only determine the degree of confidence we have in rejecting the null hypothesis, and that data only support or do not support theories. Data never prove or disprove a theory.

TYPE 1 AND TYPE 2 ERRORS

The decision to reject or accept the null hypothesis on the basis of data analysis could be wrong. In inferring population characteristics from samples, sampling errors may occur even if the rules of good random sampling were strictly followed. Statisticians classify these errors often as the Type 1 (or alpha) error and the Type 2 (or beta) error.

The Type 1 error is defined as rejecting the null hypothesis when it is tenable or true. In the area of sex differences research, this would mean concluding that there was a difference between males and females on a dimension, when in reality there was none (reality in this sense simply means that results have been consistently replicated). This error could have serious implications if the sexes were treated differently because of this incorrectly assumed difference. Two strategies are followed to reduce the probability of making this error. The easiest is to simply adjust the alpha level. That is, before rejecting the null hypothesis, demand that chance alone could account for the observed differences extremely rarely, for example, one time in one hundred or one time in a thousand, rather than five times in a hundred, the level commonly used in sex difference research. The other strategy is to suspend judgment until the results are replicated, which simply means do the experiment again. Failure to replicate results suggests that a Type 1 error was made the first time.

The Type 1 error may be more serious in research into sex differences, but the Type 2 error should also be avoided. This error is to assume that the data suggest no basis to reject the null hypothesis when in reality that is not the case, and it should be rejected. As a result of making this error, you would treat males and females as equals on some dimension where they really differ, which could result in increasing the sex difference. To reduce the probability of making this error, repeat the experiment with a larger sample size or employ better experimental controls.

While our examples of these two errors involve tests of differences between males and females, the same two errors can occur in deciding whether a correlation coefficient is or is not statistically significant. These errors can also occur in determining whether two correlation coefficients are different, in trying to see, for example, if the correlation between anxiety and performance is the same for males and females. There is no way to determine in a given experiment if one of these errors has been made; but in a rapidly developing area such as sex differences, where the data appear to move rapidly from the laboratory to the journals with few replications, the literature may contain many of these errors. Experimenter bias may also be a particularly potent variable in this socially sensitive research, but again there is no simple way to detect its presence.

A problem not unique to sex difference research is the probability of making the Type 1 error when many comparisons are made between two groups. For example, if we compared males and females on ten dimensions or attributes and found they differed on one, what would it mean? Could we be certain that this was a reliable difference, that would occur only five times in a hundred if chance factors alone were operating? The answer is no. By making ten comparisons our chance of finding a significant difference at a given alpha level has increased ten times. Therefore, when we do ten comparisons we should expect to find a significant difference at least half the time ($10 \times .05$), even if only chance was operating. Since in this hypothetical instance there was only one significant difference found, it clearly was not reliable.

Statisticians tell us how to maintain a constant alpha level even though we make many comparisons, but often in our search for significant differences their warnings are ignored. Moreover, readers of a research report often have no idea of how many comparisons were made in addition to the ones specifically mentioned. Readers, even readers sophisticated about alpha levels and repeated comparisons, cannot protect themselves from an experimenter who seeks widely, if not wisely, for significant differences.

Sex Differences in Death, Disease, and Diet

There are sex differences in death (or life span), disease, and diet in many species, including humans. However, since these are peripheral topics, not necessary to understand other areas of sex differences (though the conclusions of this appendix are presented in the rest of the book), data on these differences are presented in an appendix as an optional area for study. These topics are peripheral, but they are also fascinating. It is remarkable that gender makes a difference in when you are likely to die and from what cause, that gender affects what you like to eat. Also, the data in these areas illustrate the complexity of the interaction between inductive hormones, activational hormones, life-style (personality and reproductive roles), and experience.

These topics are treated together because they are related to one another; eating patterns affect longevity and disease. Therefore, sex differences in food preference may partly cause sex differences in disease and life expectancy. For example, the more you eat and drink, the more you will be exposed to carcinogens in food and water. Also, the type of diet affects longevity. Finally, because of differences in the effects of selection pressures, weight levels may have different impacts upon disease and longevity in males and females. Data on disease and mortality will be discussed first to establish the nature of the sex difference, and then diet and its relationship to those differencs will be discussed.

In many species, the female has the longer life expectancy. This is partly because of the greater aggressiveness of males, increasing the incidence of wounds that cause death or weaken the animal. Also, the larger male requires more food than the smaller female, and so may be more susceptible to starvation. Other aspects of the male sex role, in infra-human as well as human animals, may lead to different stresses that leave the male particularly vulnerable to certain diseases. This means that sex differences in diet and disease will be related to life-styles, inductive and activational hormones, and genes.

Since taste also affects food intake, sex differences in this area will also be evaluated. Responses to taste are obviously very strongly affected by past experience and, at least in primates, by culture. The fact that taste varies with the menstrual cycle suggests that it is sensitive to hormones as well.

DISEASE PATTERNS AND MORTALITY RATES

Females live longer. In humans this difference starts before birth. The sex ratio (the number of males per hundred females) at conception has been estimated to be 120:100 (M. Ounsted, 1972). This imbalace at conception is true only of very few species. It may be that a Y-containing sperm is smaller (because the Y chromosome is smaller) and so can swim faster and get to the ovum sooner than an X-containing sperm. By the time of birth, however, the sex ratio has decreased to 105 or 106 males for every 100 females. This means that most spontaneous abortions are male. Male fetuses may provoke more of an immune reaction from the mother than female fetuses since the male is more genetically dissimilar to the mother than the female. Male fetuses may also be more sensitive to drugs, and genetically abnormal males may be more frequently spontaneously aborted than genetically abnormal females (Damon et al., 1966). Even schizophrenia in pregnant women is associated with a decreased sex ratio (Astrup, 1974; M. Ounsted, 1972), implying better prenatal survival of females.

After birth, males die more often of most diseases, of accidents, of suicides, and of homicides. Men suffer more often from inherited disorders, many of which are connected to X-linked recessive genes (Childs, 1965). For these reasons, the life expectancy today for men in the United States is about 68.7 years; for women it is about 76.5. Even among people living a cloistered existence, who are relatively free from disease and the societal stress that often causes death in men, Catholic nuns lived longer than Catholic brothers, and the sex difference in life expectancy increased with age (Madigan, 1959). Because of the greater male mortality rate, the sex ratio, which was about 105:100 at birth, reverses between ages twenty and twenty four, and by the seventies there are over twice as many women as men (Stoll, 1974). The largest sex ratio for mortality may be just after puberty (Childs, 1965).

The Sex Ratio of Particular Diseases

Not only do men have a shorter life expectancy, men and women tend to suffer from and die from somewhat different diseases.

In 1969 in the United States, more males than females died of tuberculosis (a sex ratio of 3:1), syphilis, leukemia, diabetes (though more women died of this between sixty-five and sixty-nine years of age), cardiovascular disease, hypertension (though the sex ratio reverses after sixty), influenza and pneumonia, and cirrhosis of the liver. At all ages, men are more susceptible to infections (Washburn, Jay, and Lancaster, 1965). Syphilis manifests itself more severely in male victims (Hamilton, 1948). In 1969, males also died more often of homicides and of accidents in general and car accidents in particular. Men even have more fatal accidents in the home. Thus, of the major sources of death in our society, males are more vulnerable to all but one (more females died of cerebral hemorrhage, at least between the ages of twenty and fifty, and again after seventy), although the vulnerability of women increases after menopause, when their androgen levels increase. In fact, the sex ratio of death by any disease increases when the total death rate from that disease declines (Gadpaille, 1972; Hamilton, 1948; D. Taylor and Ounsted, 1972; Washburn et al., 1965).

Diseases of Males.   During all of childhood, boys more often suffer from autism, stuttering, reading disorders, epilepsy, cerebral palsy, and hyperactivity (D. Taylor and Ounsted, 1972). Boys are also more vulnerable to asthma (Meijer, 1975). Among 15,000 babies born in one year, the boys were born in worse condition; many more boys had one of the 187 abnormalities listed on neonatal summary sheets. This sex difference in the frequency of abnormalities remained at another testing at four years of age (S. Singer, Westphal, and Niswander, 1968). This study also found that males did worse on all scales—mental, fine-motor, gross-motor—except the social-emotional, where female one-year-olds did worse. At four years of age, boys had more speech and hearing defects, more abnormalities of IQ, motor coordination, and concept formation, and did more poorly on all scales of the Stanford-Binet IQ test. In fact, the higher the mean IQ of several samples, the worse boys did relative to girls. Males are also more often subject to abnormal delay of puberty (Money and Clopper, 1974). And males are more subject to "biologically inappropriate sexual behavior" (Bermant, 1972).

Males die more frequently of most types of cancer. One study found a fatal cancer to be caused by drinking carcinogenic water; the death rate per one hundred thousand was 192 for white and nonwhite males, and 117 for white and nonwhite females (Page, Harris, and Epstein, 1976). (This may be the result of males drinking more of that water). Breast cancer is rare in men, but cancer of the lungs and bronchial tubes occurs in three times as many men as women. However, the difference in respiratory cancer is largely the result of more males smoking cigarettes, so it may decrease as more and more women smoke (Berge and Toremalm, 1975b; Vessey, 1972). Cancer of the stomach and small intestine also occurs more frequently in men (Berge and Toremalm, 1975a), which may be related to the quantity and type of food ingested and to activity levels (Vessey, 1972). As was mentioned, leukemia is also more common in men. Bone cancer strikes females at a younger age than males, but it affects more males altogether (D. Taylor and Ounsted, 1972). Men more often have cancer of the mouth, skin, and pancreas. Of course, only women get uterine and cervical cancer, but women also are more likely to get cancer of the gall bladder. The sex difference in the incidence of these and other diseases are listed in Table B.1.

Stress Illnesses.   Some disorders are called stress or psychosomatic illnesses. Sheldrake, Cormack, and McGuire (1976a, 1976b) tried to determine what affected the percentage of college students who reported experiencing a stress illness. In addition to finding that reporting varied as a function of birth order (only children reported more illnesses) and college major (art majors reported more illnesses), they found sex differences. Women reported more nervousness, more nervous exhaustion, more migraines, more arthritis, and more eczema. Men, on the other hand, reported more insomnia, more cases of high blood pressure, more ulcers, more asthma, and more hay fever.

Diseases of Women.   Women get some diseases more often than men (see Table B.1). One disease ought to be added to the list in the table: the cold. Other diseases that affect females only, or at least mostly, include a congenital failure of the callosum (the connection between the two hemispheres) to develop, result-

TABLE B.1

SEXUAL DIFFERENCES IN SUSCEPTIBILITY TO DISEASE

Males		Females	
Diseases	Preponderance	Diseases	Preponderance
Acoustic Trauma	Almost exclusively	Acromegaly	More often
		Arthritis Deformans	4.4–1
Acute Pancreatitis	Large majority	Carcinoma of Genitalia	3–1
Addison's Disease	More often	Carcinoma of Gall	
Amebic Dysentery	15–1	Bladder	10–1
Alcoholism	6–1	Cataract	More often
Angina Pectoris	5–1	Chlorosis (anemia)	100%
Arteriosclerosis	2.5–1	Chorea	3–1
Bronchial Asthma	More often	Chronic Mitral Endocar-	
Brucellosis	More often	ditis	2–1
Cancer, Buccal Cavity	2–1	Cleft Palate	3–1
Cancer, Gastrointestinal Tract	3–1	Combined Sclerosis	More often
Cancer, head of Pancreas	4.5–1	Diphtheria	Slight
Cancer, Respiratory Tract	8–1	Gall Stones	4–1
Cancer, Skin	3–1	Goiter, Exophthalmic	6–1 or 8–1
Cerebral Hemorrhage	Greatly	Hemorrhoids	Considerable
Cerebrospinal Meningitis	Slight	Hyperthyroidism	10–1
Childhood Schizophrenia	3–1	Influenza	2–1
Chronic Glomerular Nephritis	2–1	Migraine	6–1
Cirrhosis of Liver	3–1	Multiple Sclerosis	More often
Coronary Insufficiency	30–1	Myxedema	6–1
Coronary Sclerosis	25–1	Obesity	Considerable
Diabetes	More often*	Osteomalacia	9–1
Duodenal Ulcer	7–1	Pellagra	Slight
Erb's Dystrophy	More often	Purpura Haemorrhagica	4 or 5–1
Gastric Ulcer	6–1	Raynaud's Disease	1.5–1
Gout	49–1	Rheumatoid Arthritis	3–1
Harelip	2–1	Rheumatic Fever	Considerable
Harelip and Cleft Palate	More often	Tonsillitis	Slight
Heart Disease	2–1	Varicose Veins	Considerable
Hemophilia	100%	Whooping Cough	2–1
Hepatitis	More often		
Hernia	4–1		
Hodgkin's Disease	2–1		
Hysteria	2–1**		
Korsakoff's Psychosis	2–1		
Leukemia	2–1		
Meningitis	More often		
Mental Deficiences	2–1		
Muscular Dystrophy	Almost exclusively		
Myocardial Degeneration	2–1		
Myocardial Infarction	7–1		
Paralysis Agitans	Greatly		

TABLE B.1 (continued)

Males		Females	
Diseases	Preponderance	Diseases	Preponderance
Pericarditis	2–1		
Pigmentary Cirrhosis	20–1		
Pineal Tumors	3–1		
Pleurisy	3–1		
Pneumonia	3–1		
Poliomyelitis	Slight		
Progressive Muscular Paralysis	More often		
Pseudohermaphroditism	10–1		
Pyloric Stenosis, Congenital	5–1		
Q fever	More often		
Sciatica	Greatly		
Scurvy	Greatly		
Syringomyelia	2.3–1		
Tabes	10–1		
Thromboangitis Obliterans	96–1		
Tuberculosis	2–1		
Tularemia	More often		

Source: A. Montagu, The Natural Superiority of Women (New York: Collier, 1970), table 3, pp. 87. Copyright 1952, 1953, © 1968, 1974 by Ashley Montagu. Used by permission.
  *According to Waldron (1976) diabetes is slightly more common in females.
  **Refers to stress-induced hysteria; otherwise, hysteria is diagnosed more often in females.

ing in spasms and eye inflammations, and an infection of the brain and spinal cord that results in muscle pain (benign myaligic encephalomyelitis). Females also get more varicose veins and more endocrine disorders (Hamilton, 1948).

In general, females are more prone to autoimmune diseases (diseases where the body attacks itself), such as systemic lupus erythematosis and arthritis (D. Taylor and Ounsted, 1972). In systemic lupus erythematosis the body develops antibodies that attack connective tissue, meaning it can affect any organ in the body. Though more females have lupus, males are more severely affected by it. The greater incidence of autoimmune diseases in females may be the result of the lower female level of corticoids, which oppose inflammations. For example, female mice have a stronger immune response to allergens (Terres, Morrison, and Habicht, 1968) and female rats reject tissue grafts sooner (Hinsull and Bellamy, 1974); both of these results suggest higher levels of immune responses and so immune diseases in females. Female rats and mice, like human females, all have lower corticoid levels than males do.

The sex difference in obesity shown in Table B.1 deserves further comment. This difference does not appear for younger people in the upper socioeconomic classes. The incidence of obesity is inversely correlated with socioeconomic class for both sexes, but the relationship is much stronger for women than for men (Burnight and Marden, 1973; Goldblatt, Moore and Stunkard, 1973): The percent of people who are thin is greatest for females in the upper classes, while the relationship for men is either weaker (Goldblatt et al., 1973) or reversed (Burnight and Marden, 1973). Obesity increases with age, again particularly for women (Silverstone, 1973). Thus, obesity in women is more a function of age and of class than it is in men, suggesting that socio-cultural factors have more effect on women than on men. But, overall, more women than men are at least 20 percent overweight (Widdowson, 1976).

Women go to the doctor more often. A national survey in the United States (U.S. Department of Health, Education, and Welfare, 1975) found that 60 percent of all patients' visits were made by females. Cooperstock (1971) found that 56 percent of the people visiting doctors in Ontario were women; in a more recent study (1976) it was 54 percent. When the later figures were broken down by age, they showed that up until age fifteen, more males saw physicians; from ages fifteen to sixty-four, more women visited doctors; and after age sixty-five there was no sex difference. Women also report more symptoms, especially mental, digestive, and rheumatic symptoms, and are more likely to take prescribed or nonprescribed medicines (Dunnell and Cartwright, 1972; Wadsworth, Butterfield, and Blaney, 1971). These statistics mean either that women are more subject to minor disorders than men or that women are more likely to admit symptoms or to seek help because of their sex role. Supporting the latter theory is Cates's finding (cited by Cooperstock, 1976) that even when people perceived themselves to be "on the edge of a nervous breakdown," women were twice as likely as men to seek professional help for that condition.

Hormones, Disease, and Mortality

The cure, at least in part, for the disparity in death rate and disease types is the same as the cure for male baldness: castration. Hamilton and his colleagues (1969a, 1969b) reported that castration increased the life expectancy of male cats and of male institutionalized mentally retarded humans. Castration also increased the life expectancy of some strains of male rats (Asdell et al., 1967; Drori and Folman, 1976). In cats, castration of males significantly increased life span, especially if the surgery was done before puberty, though castrated females also tended to live longer. However, castration increased the risk of dying of cancer in cats.

White male humans who were castrated, had a longer life span than intact males regardless of the age of castration; however, life span was significantly greater if the operation occurred before puberty than if it occurred after. Males castrated early even outlived intact females. The effect of castration upon the survival of nonwhite males and white females was lesser. In all groups, castration decreased the number of deaths from tuberculosis and pneumonia and slightly increased deaths from cancer. It did not affect deaths due to heart attacks in white males. Castration probably has these effects because it changes the levels of testicular and ovarian androgen. Castration of human males and removal of androgens decreased the risk of dying from infections. The relationship between androgens and infection is supported by data in germ-free mice; more males than females died after exposure to disease (Outzen and Pilgrim, 1967). Testosterone injections reduced the life span of castrated male and female rats, but estrogen increased the life span of male rats, though not that of females (Asdell et al., 1967). This suggests that estrogen suppresses the production of testosterone in the male testes. Testosterone may decrease life expectancy by increasing metabolic rate or by changing dietary preferences, as we will discuss shortly, but that cannot completely explain the difference in life span. Some male diseases appear only with age, when androgens decline (Hamilton, 1948), and the greatest increase in life expectancy caused by castration is in older males. On the other hand, hormones clearly have an effect. Testosterone injections reduce both the median survival age and the average age at death in rats.

As we will see later, males have more exposure to carcinogens because they engage in different occupations, they smoke more, and they eat and drink more. These differences account for most of the sex difference in humans in the incidence of various types of cancer. However, here too hormones may be involved. Male rodents given a lesser exposure to a carcinogen may develop cancer more often and die sooner than females. The difference in sensitivity to a carcinogen may be caused by hormones; testosterone decreases resistance to at least some types of tumors (Balish et al., 1977). Thus, while Hamilton said that castration increased the risk of dying of cancer in cats, this may have been the result of changes in life-style rather than the result of a drop in testosterone. Cancerous tumors of the reproductive system in both sexes (breasts, uterus, prostate, and so on) are often hormone-sensitive. Castration decreases the rate of growth of these tumors, so it is often part of the therapeutic procedure.

Both estrogen and testosterone increase resistance to toxic doses of drugs, but testosterone is evidently more potent, since "males are more resistant than females against a large number of poisonous substances" (Selye, 1971b, p. 338; see also Selye, 1971a). As a result, while testosterone generally decreases longevity, it does protect against poisons better than estrogen.

Other hormone-sensitive behaviors are also related to longevity. Sexual activity increases the life span of male rats (Asdell et al., 1967; Drori and Folman, 1976), but sexual activity and the associated pregnancies may decrease the life span of female rats (Asdell et al., 1967). Pregnancies may decrease life span by increasing arteriosclerosis, which is caused by a suppression of the body's immune responses during pregnancy (Lattime and Strausser, 1977). Also, the rate of tissue aging is accelerated during pregnancy in the rat; but later in life, female rats who have had litters may age more slowly than either the virgin female or the castrated female. Similar effects may exist in human females (Árvay and Takács, 1966; Philippe and Yelle, 1976). Having one or two babies may be associated with the greatest life expectancy. Exercise also increases the life span of male rats, and so it may be that the estrogen-activated greater activity levels of the female rat contribute to her longer life expectancy (Drori and Folman, 1976).

As implied by Hamilton's data, hormones may not be related to the sex difference in heart attacks. The sex difference in the frequency of heart attacks decreases with age, but is still visible at all ages (Vessey, 1972). Some evidence suggests that removal of the ovaries in females before menopause increases heart attacks by increasing the hardening of the coronary arteries. Removing the uterus alone and leaving the ovaries also increases hardening of the arteries of the heart, however, suggesting that the first results were affected by subject selection (Waldron, 1976). But no clear conclusion can be reached because no one can do a double-blind, randomized ovariectomy study. There is no alteration in the rate of heart disease at menopause, when hormone levels change, and the sex difference is much smaller in nonwhites than in whites, though the hormones of the two groups are the same (Furman, 1971). Thus, the sex difference in heart attacks does not seem related in any simple way to hormones; in fact, giving estrogen to male heart attack victims increased their death rate (Furman, 1971), just as the pill increased heart attacks in older women. However, since cigarette smoking increases heart attacks in both men and women (Miettinen, Neff, and Jick, 1976), the sex difference in smoking could account for the sex difference in heart attacks (Retherford, 1974; Waldron, 1976). As we shall see, sex roles are also undoubtedly part of this sex difference.

It seems that hormones are part of the reason the sexes differ in mortality rate. Testosterone may protect against poisons better than estrogens, but it seems also to increase the rate of deaths from infections. Hormones may also affect susceptibility to carcinogens and the rate of growth of tumors of the reproductive system. The hormones of pregnancy may affect tissue aging and the body's immune responses. Testosterone may more indirectly affect survival by affecting sexual activity, aggression, activity levels (compared to estrogen), and, as we shall see, eating habits. This means that mortality rates should show monthly and annual rhythms, paralleling the changes in hormone levels. This in fact happens, as was discussed in Chapter 5. However, hormones may not be related to the greater frequency of heart attacks in males, since estrogens, not androgens increase heart attacks.

Sex Roles, Disease, and Mortality

However, the sex difference in hormones accounts for only a small part of the sex difference in mortality and disease rates. For example, it seems that women go to doctors more often and take more medicine solely because of differences in sex roles. Working women are less often sick than housewives; they have fewer symptoms, take fewer disability days, and suffer less anxiety. Taking care of preschool children in the home is also associated with fewer illnesses in women (Nathanson, 1975). Nathanson found that sex differences in the rate of illness appeared only after age sixteen, and that the sex differences remained even when illnesses associated with reproduction (childbirth and pregnancy) were excluded. Thus, she concluded that role assignments were the most likely explanation for sex difference in illnesses, which is the opposite of the sex difference in mortality. Those women who can afford to be ill, those who have fewer obligations, have more illnesses.

Gove (1973) analyzed mortality as a function not only of gender but of marital status. Overall, being married was beneficial—married people live longer than single people—but this was more true for males than females. In other words, the difference in mortality rates for married and unmarried people was much greater for males. Single men are more apt to commit suicide, are more apt to get murdered (especially if divorced), and are more apt to be killed in a car accident.

Married women also showed fewer suicides and accidental deaths than single women, but the difference that marital status makes for them is less than that for men. However, married women are more likely to be murdered than single women. Marriage also decreased deaths due to cirrhosis of the liver, tuberculosis, diabetes, and lung cancer in both sexes, but again the effects are smaller for women than for men. Averaging over all causes of death, the unmarried have a higher mortality rate, with the differences being significantly greater for men than for women. The order of mortality rates for men, from highest to lowest, was: divorced men, widowed men, single men, and married men. For women, married women have the lowest mortality rate, but the differences between the single, divorced, and widowed are very small.

The greater benefit of marriage to men than women is undoubtedly the result of the different roles prescribed by society for married men and women. The sex difference in the rate of heart disease, cirrhosis of the liver, and accidents can be related to sex differences in cigarette smoking, alcohol consumption, the occurrence of the aggressive-dominant syndrome associated with heart attacks, and the greater male recklessness in driving, that is, to male roles or male traits (Waldron, 1976; Waldron and Johnston, 1976). Because of their care-giving role, woman may protect their husbands, leading married men to seek help for serious illnesses more often and sooner than single men.

Summary

Men die earlier than women, and more men than women die of almost all causes. Some of these differences are based on genes (X-linked diseases) and some on hormones; the most dramatic evidence of the latter is the longer life expectancy of castrated males. In most other cases, sex differences in mortality and in types of diseases are associated with sex differences in behavior, such as the level of activity, the amount of carcinogenic food eaten or water drunk, smoking, drinking, willingness to admit minor symptoms, and care-giving wives. There must also be cultural factors involved—more women than men had ulcers in the nineteenth century, reversing the present sex ratio (Bernard, 1973). And among the Amish, there are more old men than old women (Ounsted and Taylor, 1972a), which reverses the proportion in the general population. It also seems that the sex that is less likely to get a disease is more severely affected by it once it occurs. This is true of convulsions associated with fever (more common in boys but more severe in girls) and with systemic lupus erythematosis (D. Taylor and Ounsted, 1972).

ENERGY METABOLISM AND FOOD PREFERENCES

There are sex differences in energy metabolism and food preferences, which seem to result from the inductive and activational effects of hormones and from their interactions with each other and the environment. Sex roles also probably play a part in causing these differences in humans. These sex differences may affect longevity.

The gonadal hormones have widespread effects on metabolism and basal metabolic rates. Androgens facilitate the synthesis of proteins, whereas estrogens increase fatty tissues. Androgens, estrogens, and progesterone all increase body temperature in rats, although in humans progesterone increases body temperature but an estrogen decreases it (Little et al., 1974; Marrone, Gentry, and Wade, 1976).

The following sections will present evidence to support the hypothesis that, even in humans, there are hormone-sensitive sexual dimorphisms in food preferences. And, in some cases, these differences are related to mortality rates. Differences in energy balance—body weight, the amount of food eaten, and the activity level—also affect mortality. When generalizations are made from rats to humans, remember that both species are omnivores, with very similar taste sensitivities and preferences.

Infra-human Sex and Age Differences and Mortality Rates

In most lower species, the male is larger. In the rat at least, this is a result of the combined effects of males eating more and exercising less (Wade, 1972, 1976). Males also eat more protein, but females seem to have a greater preference for sweets and a greater aversion for bitter taste than do males.

Taste Preferences.   Mature female rats have more of a sweet tooth than males. Female rats consume more of a slightly sweet 3 percent sucrose solution and of a highly sweet .25 percent saccharin solution. Females also prefer (drink more of than water) saccharin or sucrose solutions that are sweeter than those males will prefer (Gabric and Saljačic, 1975; Valenstein, Kakolewski, and Cox, 1967) For postpubertal rats, age increases the sex differences in sweet preferences (Nisbett, et al., 1975).

These sex differences in sweet tooth have been replicated in several strains of rats and hamsters, but not much seems to have been done in other species (Wade, 1976). Itani (1958), however, studied the responses of a free-living troop of Japanese macaques to novel foods. Initially, they did not like candy. Only 10 percent of the adults ate candy upon the first presentation, even though 50 percent of the monkeys younger than three did. A year after initial introduction, all of the one-year-olds were eating candy, 32 percent of the adult and young males were, and 51 percent of the adult and young females were. Thus, in primates there also seems to be a sex difference in sweet tooth.

There is also a sex difference in rats' response to quinine and protein. Females are more reactive than males to the taste of quinine. When the only water or food available is adulterated with quinine, males will drink or eat more of it (Nisbett et al., 1975). Males have a greater protein preference. When placed in a cafeteria situation allowing choice among foods, male rats select a greater percentage of their diet as protein and since their carbohydrate consumption also remains high they end up with a greater proportion of their bodies as fat than females do (Leshner and Collier, 1973). This reverses the human difference, where females have more fat. The male preference for protein is also found in primates. Among chimpanzees, males do most of the monkey killing and, although they will share the meat with the females, they eat most of it themselves (van Lawick-Goodall, 1968). Male baboons also do most of the meat hunting (Lancaster, 1976).

Energy Balance and Mortality. Food preferences may also affect life expectancy. When male rats are put into a cafeteria situation, their life span is affected by what foods they choose to eat (Ross and Bras, 1975). Life span is inversely related to the amount of food eaten and for adult rats to the amount of protein eaten. It may be, then, that male food preferences are associated with shorter life span. Asdell and his colleagues (1967) found that the body weights of their eleven groups of rats (different combinations of sex, castration, and hormone injections) were roughly, but negatively, correlated with survival. Partial starvation may reduce sex differences in mortality (Hamilton, 1948) and may increase male survival (Drori and Folman, 1976).

But females survive starvation better than males (Widdowson, 1976). This was shown in experiments on rats and pigs, and may also be true of humans. After the food supply is restored, the female is more likely to return to a normal weight than the male, and may even become extremely fat. The cause of the sex difference in resistance to starvation, whether partial or complete, is apparently that males lose twice as much body protein as females while females lose almost twice as much fat. Thus, males lose more of vital body tissue than females, and become even more susceptible to infection.

As was mentioned earlier, female humans are more likely to become obese, and the same seems true for rats (Sclafani and Gorman, 1977). This fact, combined with the data described above, lends support to James and Trayhurn's (1976) theory of obesity. They stated that a "propensity to obesity in animals and man identifies those individuals who are genetically favored to survive when food supplies are scarce" (p. 770). These particular individuals may allow body temperatures to fall during cold or during starvation, thereby conserving body tissue. In fact, human females are more reactive to cold than males. Thus, humans may still carry the metabolic processes developed because of natural selection. The sex role of the female animal, care of infants, led to the development of a physiology best adapted to survive in times of short food supply, rather than one adapted to peak expenditures of energy. Today this is expressed as a greater sensitivity to cold and a greater tendency towards obesity, and, perhaps, in some differences in food preferences. This is highly speculative, but at least two aspects of this line of thought seem well established: (1) food preference affects mortality rates, and there are sex differences in food preferences among lower animals; and (2) females survive starvation better than males.

Activational Effects of Hormones

The effects of hormones upon energy balance and metabolism are summarized in Table B.2. As can be seen, the sex differences in weight, activity, and food preferences may well be the result of biasing effects of the sex hormones.

Variations in Hormone Levels and Energy Balance. Many sex differences in food preference do not appear until puberty, when the gonadal hormones increase, suggesting that the differences are affected by hormones. Sex differences in the saccharin preference of rats appear only after puberty, when the female rat dramatically increases her preference (Wade and Zucker, 1969a). And both male and female rats before puberty select an equally high percentage of their diet as

TABLE B.2 _____

ACTIVATIONAL EFFECTS OF HORMONES UPON ENERGY BALANCE

Behavior	Gender and Species	Effects and Comments	References
Wheel Activity	Subprimate males and females (except hamsters)	Estrogen and testosterone increase activity; progesterone decreases it.	Gentry and Wade (1976); Longuski, Cudillo, and Stern (1976); Roy and Wade (1975, 1976); Slater and Blizard (1976); Stern, Cudillo, and Longuski (1976); Wade (1976)
Food Intake	All males and females (except gerbils)	Estrogen decreases food intake and testosterone increases it; progesterone opposes both types of effects; the effect of estrogen may be seen only in animals that are gaining or have already gained weight and are above normal levels.	Asdell et al. (1967); Czaja and Goy (1975); Gerall and Thiel (1975); Gilbert and Gillman (cited by Czaja and Goy, 1975); Joslyn (1973); Kakolewski, Cox, and Valenstein (1968); Marks (1974); Roy, Maass, and Wade (1977); Wade (1972, 1976)
Salt Intake	Male and female rats	Both estrogen and progesterone increase salt intake.	Fregly (1973)
Rejection of Quinine; Intake of Sweets	All species, both sexes	Estrogen and progesterone combined increase finickiness, testosterone has very little effect.	Gabríc and Soljačíc (1975); Zucker (1969)
Protein Intake	Male and female rats	Estrogen and progesterone may decrease protein intake; testosterone has little effect.	Leshner and Collier (1973); Leshner, Siegel, and Collier (1972)
Conditioned Aversions	Male and female rats	Estrogen and progesterone have little effect; testosterone decreases intake of a sweet-tasting substance that was previously associated with illness.	K. Chambers (1976)

protein (Wade, 1976), though males eat more protein afterwards. Finally, sex differences in open-field and wheel-activity appear only after puberty; puberty increases open-field activity more and decreases wheel-activity less in females than in males.

Food preferences and energy balance often seem to vary with the changes of a female's hormones during the estrous or menstrual cycle. During the peak of sexual receptivity (estrous), just after the estrogen peak, activity levels in female hamsters and rats increase. Also, in guinea pigs, rhesus monkeys, ewes, pigs, goats, and cows, but not in hamsters, food intake and weight decrease at estrous (Czaja, 1975; Czaja and Goy, 1975; Drewett, 1974; Nance and Gorski, 1975; Wade, 1976). Estrous also decreases the female rat's willingness to work for food (Jennings, 1973). Taste preferences do not fluctuate with the estrous cycle (Jennings, 1973; Leshner, Siegel, and Collier, 1972; Wade, 1976), though conclusions about taste sensitivity cannot be made, as it has not been tested.

There are also changes in food intake during pregnancy and pseudopregnancy (changes in hormones and weight paralleling pregnancy but without a fetus). In some species, such as the rat, because these states are dominated by progesterone, food intake and weight increase, saccharin preference and quinine aversion decrease, and the percent of diet that is protein increases (Lesher et al., 1972, Wade and Zucker, 1969a, 1969b). In some species—such as the rhesus monkey or the human, during the first trimester—estrogen dominates; these species show an increase in food aversion and rejection at this time (Czaja, 1975).

The results of castration also reflect the effects that gonadal hormones have on energy balance, consistently with the effects reported in Table B.2. Castration of adult males removes testosterone, leading to decreases in food intake, in wheel activity, and in the percent of the diet that is protein (though this is mostly because the proportion of carbohydrates increases); slight decreases in saccharine and glucose preference; and except in hamsters, slight changes in weight (either decreases or increases, depending on the kind of food available and the species and age of the animal). Castration of females removes estrogen, so activity decreases, but food intake increases and weight increases dramatically. The spayed female cat and dog are likely to become quite overweight. Castration of females also increases their protein preference, bringing it close to the male level, but decreases their saccharin preference.

But as in many other effects of hormones, experience affects the results of castration. Female rats' experiences with saccharin drinking apparently causes them to acquire a taste, or drive, for it (K. T. Hoyenga and Hoyenga, 1973); once females have tasted it, castration has no effect on their saccharin preference or consumption (Wade and Zucker, 1969a). We see once again that experience can make a behavior independent of hormonal changes.

Summary.   As Table B.2 shows, testosterone and estrogen increase activity, whereas progesterone depresses it. Testosterone increases food intake and body weight, while estrogen decreases both; progesterone opposes the effects of both hormones in both cases. Estrogen and progesterone together determine the taste responsiveness and preferences of animals to foods that taste sweet or salty, and to protein.

There is some controversy over the mechanisms of these effects. Progesterone may exert a direct effect on eating and body weight (see S. Roberts, Kenney, and Mook, 1972), or it may simply act in opposition to estrogen, either by decreasing the level of estrogen or by interfering with the uptake of estrogen by brain cells (Wade, 1975). There may be two mechanisms for the effects of the other hormones. One possible mechanism is for the sex hormone directly to affect metabolism. The other possibility is for the hormone to affect the brain, which then has an effect on eating, hunger, or the taste of food (Södersten, 1974; Vilberg et al., 1974).

Inductive Effects of Hormones

Inductive hormones have permanent effects on weight, activity level, and food preference. Even so, the effects of neonatal hormones often interact with genetic gender. For example, neonatal androgens decrease the weight of intact males, but increase that of intact females; this effect may be related to the sex difference in levels of hormones that occur either shortly after the hormone injection or after puberty.

Energy Balance. The energy balance of rats can be permanently affected by perinatal hormones. Neonatal injections of testosterone permanently reduce the weight of intact males (J. Gray, Leon, and Keynes, 1969; K. B. Hoyenga and Hoyenga, 1977), but permanently increase that of intact and neonatally castrated females (D. Bell and Zucker, 1971; J. Gray et al., 1969; K. B. Hoyenga and Hoyenga, 1977; Magalhães and Carlini, 1974; Slob and van de Werff ten Bosch, 1975; Södersten, 1973b; Ward, 1969). However, this effect is larger in intact female rats than it is in castrated ones, probably because neonatal androgenization inhibits sensitivity to the appetite-suppressing effects of estrogen (Tarttelin, Shryne, and Gorski, 1976). The weight increase in neonatally androgenized females reflects growth of the whole body; it is not a type of obesity (Dubuc, 1976a, 1976b). Neonatal estrogen also greatly increases the adult weight of neonatally castrated male rats, even above that of normal males (B. L. Hart, 1977). Neonatal androgenization also reduces open-field activity and wheel running in females to the male level, and neonatal castration increases open-field activity in males (see Chapter 4) (Broitman and Donoso, 1974; Wade, 1976).

The permanent effect of neonatal hormones upon the energy balance of animals also interacts with activational hormones (Gerall and Thiel, 1975; G. Harris, 1964; Wade, 1976). For example, castration of males and females at birth eliminates the sex differences in food intake, activity level, and weight gain, whereas castration at twenty-one days of age (before puberty) only decreases the sex differences (Wade, 1976), indicating prepubertal hormones make a difference. Thus, given a similar environment and no sex differences in inductive or activational hormones, there will be no sex differences in energy balance, suggesting that these differences normally are controlled by the gonadal hormones.

Taste preferences. Neonatal hormones also affect taste preferences. Wade and Zucker (1969a and 1969b) found that neonatal androgenization of females suppresses their saccharin preference as adults. They also found that estradiol combined with progesterone elevated saccharin consumption only in adult castrated females, not in adult castrated males. Shapiro and Goldman (1973) studied the saccharin preference of the male rat pseudohermaphrodite. This rat has an XY karyotype but its body tissues are unresponsive to androgens, as was the case with humans with androgen insensitivity. This pseudohermaphrodite male rat shows the female pattern of a strong preference for saccharin.

We looked for the effects of neonatal injections of androgen and of a testosterone-antagonist upon taste preferences of adult male and female rats, comparing them to oil-injected controls (K. B. Hoyenga and Hoyenga, 1977). These data are presented in Table B.3. The saccharin was presented first for two seven-day periods, with a seven-day interval between presentations. The saccharin was pre-

TABLE B.3

TASTE RESPONSIVENESS OF RATS TO SACCHARIN AND QUININE EXPRESSED AS MEAN PERCENT OF BASELINE WATER DRINKING

Saccharin was paired with water, but quinine was presented alone. TP refers to the neonatally androgenized groups, CPA to the groups given neonatal injections of a testosterone-antagonist; the control group was given neonatal injections of oil. The number of each group is indicated in the parentheses.

		Test Solution				
	16% Saccharin Solution			Quinine Sulphate Solutions		
Subjects	First Exposure (2 days)	Second Exposure (2 days)	Difference	.0075% (3 days)	.01% (3 days)	Difference
TP Males	2.39 (8)	3.29 (8)	+.90	.84 (8)	.82 (8)	−2
CPA Males	2.95 (3)	2.94 (3)	−.01	.77 (5)	.66 (5)	−11
Control Males	2.56 (5)	3.11 (5)	+.55	.96 (9)	.80 (9)	−16
TP Females	3.50 (13)	4.26 (13)	+.76	.73 (13)	.73 (13)	0
CPA Females				.87 (2)	.60 (2)	−17
Control Females	6.87 (3)	6.21 (3)	−.66	.98 (10)	.64 (10)	−26

sented simultaneously with water, but very few rats drank water as long as saccharin was avilable. The quinine sulphate was then presented for three days, with the weaker solution presented first, followed by three days of water alone, followed by three days of the second, stronger solution. Since saccharin consumption declined over days and group differences decreased, the mean for only the first two days of each seven-day period is presented. The quinine data represents the mean for all three days.

As can be seen, control males drank less saccharin and more of the .01 percent quinine solution than control females, replicating the results of earlier research. High neonatal death rates made the number in each group small, but the direction of the differences is as predicted. Neonatal testosterone depressed the saccharin preference of females. The testosterone-antagonist eliminated the increase in saccharin consumption usually seen after animals have been deprived of saccharin for seven days (K. T. Hoyenga and Hoyenga, 1973). Control females did not increase saccharin consumption either, but that was undoubtedly because of ceiling effects; they were already drinking over six times as much saccharin as water. Neonatally androgenized males and females were not affected by changes in quinine concentration, although all other groups decreased their drinking when the concentration was increased. The difference in intake with the different quinine concentrations was particularly striking for normal females.

Summary. Neonatal hormones clearly have permanent effects on taste preferences, weight gain, food intake, and activity levels. Neonatal androgen, at least in normal male levels, permanently increases body size (but not obesity) and permanently decreases activity. Neonatal androgen may also permanently decrease finickiness, defined by overeating food with good taste and undereating food with bad taste. Thus, male rats may be less inclined than female rats to become obese when fed a wide selection of good-tasting foods (Sclafani and Gorman, 1977). Could the same mechanism be part of the reason for the sex difference in the incidence of obesity in humans?

The mechanisms for the effects of these inductive hormones seem obscure, especially in view of the possibility that higher than normal male levels of androgens have opposite effects on body size. Androgens may permanently depress the areas in the brain that respond with pleasure to good-tasting food. Or androgens may permanently increase the responsiveness of the brain to estrogens, with estrogens having a more important and more immediate impact on the pleasure associated with food. Or androgens may permanently affect metabolism and energy balance by affecting the liver, which regulates levels of food metabolites in various areas of the body, or the fat cells of the body. The relevant data is not yet available, in part because generally acceptable theories of hunger and obesity in hormonally normal organisms do not yet exist. But in view of the data that are available, some sex differences in energy balance and food intake among humans might be expected.

Sex and Age Differences in Human Food Preferences

That both olfactory and taste sensitivities vary with hormone levels during the human menstrual cycle (see Chapter 5) suggests that food preferences are affected by hormones. The pleasantness of a sweet taste also varies with the menstrual cycle; sweet solutions are least pleasant during the high progesterone luteal phase (Wright and Crow, 1973). Other findings are contradictory. S. Smith and Sauder (1969) found that depressed women "often developed a peculiar craving for sweets in the premenstruum" (p. 281). Morton and his colleagues (1953) also found that of their patients who complained of premenstrual tension, 37 percent had a craving for sweets and 32 percent had an increased appetite.

Hormones and Energy Metabolism. The hormones of pregnancy affect food preferences. During the first trimester of pregnancy, when estrogen is high relative to progesterone (Mishell et al., 1973), women frequently report nausea; as was pointed out in Chapter 5, not to experience nausea is pathological. The decline in nausea after the first trimester could be the result of either adaptation to estrogen (the effect of estrogen upon appetite in rats is temporary even when the high estrogen levels continue) or the steadily increasing progesterone level.

Exogenous manipulations of hormones also affect appetite and weight. In Cullberg's (1972) extensive study of the side effects of the birth control pill, estrogen-dominated pills were more likely to produce nausea and progesterone-dominated pills were more likely to produce weight gain. These hormones may have the same effects in males. Blumer and Migeon (1975), who treated aggressive males with a progestin, said that "all patients gained weight, from .9 to 6.7 kg (average of 3.3 kg) after six months of therapy. . . . In almost every instance the patients noted a marked increase in appetite" (p. 133). But an artificial estrogen, stilbestrol, produces weight gains in human males (Sands, 1954) as well as in cattle. Another exogenous hormone change, castration, decreases muscle and increases the proportion of body fat in human males, which usually results in a net loss of weight (Hamilton, 1948). The effects of hormones seem very similar in humans and lower animals. Estrogens usually increase food rejection and nausea, while progesterone leads to weight gains.

Food Preferences and Oral Differences. Some studies found sex differences in food preferences among newborns. Nisbett and Gurwitz (1970) reported that female newborns were more responsive to sweetness than male newborns. Females drank 24 percent more of a sweetened than of an unsweetened formula, while males consumed only 6 percent more of the sweetened formula. Females also drank less with a nipple that was harder to work (one with a much smaller hole). These sex differences parallel the differences produced by infant weight; females show the same responses as fatter infants. That is, females acted like fatter infants in drinking less with the hard nipple, suggesting sex differences in energy regulation even at this age.

Korner (1973) also said that female infants were more oral. She said that the female infant was more sensitive to oral stimulation and that from the age of one onward female children are more frequent and persistent thumbsuckers. Korner related these differences to oral differences in the adult. For example, females may be less likely to be able to give up smoking (though this may be changing: see Bossé and Rose, 1976), and females may also be less able to give up eating despite being overweight.

Two studies, however, failed to find sex differences in the consumption of sugar in newborns. The methodology of these studies differed from that of Nisbett and Gurwitz, however. Both studies offered a sucrose or dextrose solution mixed in water, rather than in milk, and offered the solution for a fixed period of time, rather than until the infant rejected it (Desor, Maller, and Turner, 1973; Dubignon et al., 1969). Shorter times of availability also remove sex differences in the sweet tooth of rats (Chambers and Sengstake, 1976). Thus, males and females do not differ in how soon after presentation they will drink a sweet solution, but females will drink it longer than males.

Other data suggest a greater female responsiveness to taste, especially to sweet tastes, though males eat more protein. Adult females show more eating disorders (such as anorexia nervosa or voluntary self-starvation, and obesity) and more food aversions than do males (Byrne, Golightly, and Capaldi, 1963; W. Smith, Powell, and Ross, 1955a, 1955b). According to a national survey conducted by the Department of Health, Education and Welfare (cited by Bender, 1976), males ate 24 percent less sucrose than females, in terms of grams per total calories eaten. Bender found no consistent differences in protein consumption, though one large Canadian survey found more females than males eating inadequate amounts of protein, particularly among Eskimos. Bender concluded that women have a greater preference for fruit, a lesser preference for milk, and "a more adventurous palate."

Desor, Greene, and Maller (1975; see also Greene, Desor, and Maller, 1975) looked at age and sex differences in the preferred concentrations of sucrose, lactose, and salt solutions. They found that younger people (ages nine to fifteen) preferred sweeter and saltier solutions than older people; this was especially true for salt solutions among young blacks. Both younger and older males preferred sweeter solutions, although the sex difference was significant only in the younger group. As the researchers pointed out, this corresponds to estimates that after the age of nine, males consume more sweets than do females.

But these results are surprising in view of the sex differences in food preferences in animals, the effects of hormones, and other data, so we carried out a survey on food preferences (K. T. Hoyenga and K. B. Hoyenga, unpublished data). This seemed appropriate because the relationships among preferences and percent of total intake on the one hand, and total intake and preferred concentrations on the other hand, do not seem entirely clear.

Our food preference questionnaire consisted of two sections. The first listed sixty foods that male and female college students say they commonly eat. The subject was to indicate his or her preference for each food on a five-point rating scale. The second part of the questionnaire asked the subjects to list their ten favorite foods. The questionnaire was given to fifth graders (43 males and 35 females), college freshmen (101 males and 58 females), and people over sixty (42 males and 36 females).

Chi squares (tests for significant differences in frequencies of behaviors among different groups) were calculated on the frequency of different categories of food being listed among the ten most preferred; that is, different red meats could be listed among the ten favorite foods either not at all, or one, two, three, or more times by the same subject. Then we analyzed age and sex differences in the number of times a particular type of food was listed. There were several significant age differences (differences at the .01 level), including the fact that fifth-grade boys preferred sweet foods more than college males, which confirms the Desor study. Only four significant ($p < .02$) sex differences were found, three of them among college students. Old men liked sea food more than old women. College men more often listed red meats and poultry among their ten favorite foods, whereas college females more often listed sweet desserts. In all three age groups, whenever there was a significant sex difference among the sixty foods, meat was always more preferred by the males and with only one exception females preferred the sweet food more. Thus, these data parallel the research on lower animals; females have a greater sweet tooth and males prefer protein more. These data are also consistent with the research on the effects of hormones in animals; the differences appear only after puberty and are attenuated after menopause.

Because of the earlier research on humans and the effect of hormones upon salt preference thresholds, we analyzed the ratings of salty and bitter taste. Old females preferred salt significantly less than did all other subjects ($p < .001$). And, consistent with the earlier research, fifth-grade males liked salt more than college males and older subjects ($p < .001$). Fifth-grade and college females rated salt almost equally (2.16 and 2.18). Only the college group showed a significant sex difference in the ratings of bitterness, with males rating it higher. This sex difference was also found for rats in the data cited earlier.

Summary

Thus, it seems that the preference for sweets declines with puberty for males. This is opposite to the effect in rats, where the difference appears at puberty because the female preference increases. But the sex difference is the same, and is consistent with what little data there are on monkeys, where the young and the females also have a greater sweet tooth. The sex difference in protein, with males preferring meats more, also appears at puberty, and the male preference for red meats declines with age. So the data for food preferences in humans agree with some animal data: sex differences are greatest when both the inductive and the activational hormones differ the most. Activational estrogen increases finickiness and decreases food intake, while activational and inductive testosterone and activational progesterone lead to weight gains, though for different reasons.

Conclusions cannot yet be made, however. The effect of sex-role socialization upon these preferences in humans is yet to be evaluated, and it is undoubtedly important. Most people would identify meat eating and using bitters in cocktails as masculine; candy eating and the smell of flowers seems feminine. After all, it is men who give women candy for Valentine's Day, not vice versa. In food preference, as in most sex-role stereotypic traits, cause and effect have yet to be disentangled. Still, there may be a kernel of truth in the stereotype of food preferences, which sex roles have then exaggerated.

SUMMARY

The male human, like many male lower relatives, has a shorter life span than the female. Genes account for part of this difference, in that many disadvantageous traits are X-linked recessives. Both inductive and activational androgens are also involved, both directly and indirectly. Castration increases the life span of the male, particularly if done before puberty, presumably because of direct effects upon metabolism. However, inductive and activational effects of hormones also affect life span indirectly, by affecting behavior such as aggression and eating habits. Sex-role socialization, which encourages passivity in females and driving ambition and recklessness in males, also leads to sex differences in the incidence of deaths from accidents and heart attacks.

Diet and metabolism are also affected by inductive and activational hormones. Total body weight, the proportion of body weight that is fat, and food preferences are all affected by inductive and activational hormones. Some preliminary data also suggest that there may be a few consistent sex differences in food preferences in humans. The sexes, then, have different life expectancies, suffer from different diseases, and food does not even taste the same to them.

Glossary

Acetylcholine a compound released at some nerve endings that is active in the transmission of nerve impulses from one nerve to another.

Activational effect the effect of sex hormones circulating in the bloodstream after the critical period of development, either increasing or inhibiting the normal action of the brain and other organs. Activational effects are usually temporary and reversible.

Active avoidance a form of learning in which the subject must make a response to prevent or avoid a noxious stimuli.

Adrenal gland a gland that secretes hormones. The outer part of the gland, called the cortex, is embryologically derived from the lining of the coelom. It secretes various hormones, called corticosteroids, including androgens. The adrenal medulla, the inner part of the gland, secretes epinephrine and norepinephrine in times of stress or emergency.

Adrenocorticotropic hormone (ACTH) a hormone secreted by the anterior pituitary, that controls the amount of hormones secreted by the adrenal cortex.

Adrenogenital syndrome a condition produced by a genetically transmitted enzymatic defect in the functioning of the adrenal cortices of males or females. Abnormal function of the adrenal cortex starts in the fetus and unless treated continues chronically after birth. Females with this syndrome have ambiguous genitalia and if they survive, undergo masculinization. Males, if they survive, develop sexually during the first years of life.

Agency Bakan's male principle, referring to self-protection, self-assertion, self-expansion, separation, isolation, mastery, and repression.

Aggressive dependency dependence upon another person for aggressive reasons as, for example, becoming dependent so as to manipulate the other person.

Alpha frequency the brain frequency of electrical activity associated with a relaxed, awake state.

Alpha level the probability that the difference observed between two groups could be due to chance alone.

Amniocentesis the surgical insertion of a hollow needle through the abdominal wall and uterus of a pregnant female to obtain amniotic fluid, which is studied to determine the sex of the fetus or the presence of any chromosomal abnormality.

Anal stage the second stage of development in Freud's psychoanalytic theory, covering from one to three years of age. Pleasurable stimulation comes from retention and expulsion of feces.

Androgens male sex hormones, produced chiefly by the testis, but also by the adrenal cortex and, in small amounts, by the ovary. The major androgen is testosterone.

Androgyns individuals who have acquired masculine and feminine traits.

Androgyny attributing to oneself masculine and feminine traits in equal amounts, or attributing to oneself large numbers of traits of both sexes.

Anterior pituitary (adenohypophysis) that portion of the pituitary body embryologically derived from the hypophysis. It secretes FSH, LH, prolactin, ACTH, the growth hormone, and thyrotropin.

Antidiuretic hormone (ADH) a hormone secreted from the posterior pituitary. In mammals it stimulates water reabsorption, diminishing the volume of urine.

Aromatized converted chemically into one or more aromatic or strong smelling compounds. Testosterone can be aromatized into estrogen.

Autoimmune diseases diseases in which the body attacks itself.

Automatizers men with good speed of tapping and low spatial ability and who tend to have masculine body types.

Autosomes any ordinary chromosome, as contrasted to a sex chromosome.

Barr sex chromatin body (Barr body) the sex chromatin located at the edge of the nucleus of cells taken from individuals with more than one X chromosome. The Barr body is an inactivated X chromosome.

Biological bias the idea that genes and hormones affect the preparedness of the organism to respond in certain ways to certain kinds of stimuli or to associate certain responses with certain consequences. Hormones do not elicit behavior, they simply affect the probability of a response.

Cerebral asymmetry refers to the fact that different sides of the brain are reserved for or specialized for different functions.

Chromosomal gender sex as determined by the genes; females have two X chromosomes and males have one X and one Y.

Chromosomes bodies formed of chromatin in the nucleus of a cell during mitosis. They bear the genes, or determiners of heredity.

Circadian cycles cycles based on approximately twenty-four-hour periods.

Clitoris a small organ in the female analogous to the penis in males.

Cognitive-developmental theory a theory of personality stressing the stages of emotional and social development a child goes through in forming personality. The theory's emphasis is on cognitive maturation.

Cognitive structure rules for processing information or for connecting experienced events. Part of Kohlberg's theory.

Communion Bakan's female principle, a sense of being at one with other organisms, lack of separation, contact, cooperation, and removal of repression.

Consistency stage Kohlberg's first developmental stage, lasting from birth to three years, in which the child responds to new interests in a way consistent with past interests and behaviors.

Conversion hypothesis the theory that testosterone masculinizes the brain by being changed into estrogen by the fetal brain cells of males.

Corpus luteum a temporary endocrine gland formed by the action of LH upon the ruptured egg follicle. This gland secretes estrogen and progesterone throughout the last part of the menstrual cycle and, if fertilization has occurred, during the first part of pregnancy.

Cortex the outer or covering layer of a structure.

Corticosteroids hormones of the adrenal cortex that help to control blood levels of electrolytes, sugar, and antibodies, and also have anti-inflammatory and antiallergic actions. Also called corticoids.

Critical period a stage in development in which the organism is optimally ready to acquire certain learned responses.

Cross-over technique an experimental procedure in which the same person receives both the experimental drug and the control (placebo) at different times.

Delayed response learning learning to inhibit a response throughout a delay period. During the delay, the animal may be required to remember the response or stimulus last made or seen.

Deoxyribonucleic acid (DNA) the material of inheritance found in the chromosomes.

Distal attachment attachment expressed by looking at or talking to the parent, as opposed to touching.

Differentially reinforcing reinforcing a person in different ways for different behaviors according to gender.

Dominant a genetically determined characteristic of one parent that manifests itself in offspring to the exclusion of the gene carrying the contrasted recessive characteristic received from the other parent.

Double-blind procedure the experimental procedure in which neither the doctor nor the patient knows which patients receive the experimental drug and which the placebo.

Ejaculatory duct the duct through which semen is ejaculated in males.

Electra complex in Freudian theory, the emotional (sexual) attachment of a girl to her father.

Electroencephalogram (EEG) recordings of the electrical activity of the brain.

Erogenous zones areas of the body, very sensitive to irritation, but where certain stimulation also produces pleasure.

Estradiol an estrogenic hormone usually made synthetically and often used, combined with an ester, in treating menopausal symptoms.

Estrogens female sex hormones, produced chiefly by the ovary, but also by the adrenal cortex and, in some amounts, by the testis. The major estrogen is estradiol.

Estrous cycle the cycle of hormone levels and correlated behaviors in subprimate females, including regularly recurrent states of sexual excitability during which, in most mammals, the female will accept the male and is capable of conceiving. This cycle is not accompanied by regular periods of uterine bleeding, as is the menstrual cycle.

Evoked response a change in brain electrical activity evoked or elicited by the presentation of a stimulus.

Expressive roles roles emphasizing social intercourse, cooperation, and nurturance.

Fallopian tubes a pair of tubes conducting the egg from the ovary to the uterus.

Feminine behaviors behaviors having qualities defined by society as appropriate to a woman.

Fertilization the union of an egg and a sperm to form a zygote and initiate the development of an embryo.

Field dependency the inability to ignore irrelevant stimuli in making judgments, partic-ularly in spatial tasks. Tests of this include the rod-and-frame task and the embedded figures task. Field-dependent people have low spatial ability.

Follicles minute cellular sacs or coverings; usually refers to the sac around the egg in the ovary.

Follicle stimulating hormone (FSH) a gonadotropic hormone secreted by the anterior pituitary that stimulates the growth follicles and their oocytes, or eggs, in the ovary, and the formation of spermatozoa in testes.

46, XX the normal chromosome pattern in human females.

46, XY the normal chromosome pattern in human males.

Galvanic skin response (GSR) a change in the resistance of the skin to the passage of an electric current that often occurs in emotional states.

Gender constancy the ability to recognize that the sex of an individual is permanent.

Gender of external sex organs sex as determined by external appearance; having a penis in males and a vagina and clitoris in females.

Gender identity the sameness and persistence of one's individuality as male or female (or ambivalent) in greater or lesser degree, especially as it is experienced in self-awareness and behavior.

Gender of internal accessory organs sex as determined by the presence of a uterus and Fallopian tubes in females, and the presence of prostate glands, an ejaculatory duct, vas deferens, and seminal vesicles in males.

Gender of rearing sex as determined by the way a child is reared by her or his parents.

Gender role everything a person does and says to indicate to others and to himself or herself the degree to which he or she is male, female, or ambivalent.

Gene the unit of inheritance transmitted from one generation to another in the gametes. It controls the development of a characteristic in the new individual. It is the determiner of heredity.

Genetic mosaic an organism composed of cells of more than one karyotype.

Genital stage the last stage of development in Freud's psychoanalytic theory, during which adult sexuality is reached.

Genotype the internal genetic or hereditary constitution of an organism, without regard to the organisms's external appearance.

Germ cell a reproductive cell in a multicellular organism.

Gonadal gender sex as determined by the type of internal sex glands, testes or ovaries.

Gonadotropic hormones hormones secreted by the anterior lobe of the pituitary gland that control the activity of the gonads.

Hermaphrodite an individual whose sex is not clearly male or female because both male and female gonads are present.

Hormonal gender sex as determined by the presence of a male or female sex hormone pattern in the blood stream.

Hypothalamus a portion of the brain of special importance in regulating vital functions, including sex and eating. It also controls the pituitary by means of inhibiting and releasing factors.

Identification the process by which the child assimilates the values of the parents and sees himself or herself in some sense as the same as the parents.

Induce to put into action, as to induce a gene; opposite of repress.

Induction (genetic) occurs when the operator gene, the gene that controls the function of a set of related genes, is activated by some protein or metabolite, allowing the related genes to function, and the proteins for which they are the code to be manufactured.

Inductive effect the effect of sex hormones before birth, determining the development and connections of the brain, thus affecting the organism's later behavior. The effects are usually permanent and irreversible.

Inhibiting factors secreted by the hypothalamus to decrease the secretion of the appropriate anterior pituitary hormone into the blood stream.

Instrumental roles an emphasis on tasks, an orientation towards more distant goals and relationships between the family and the outside world.

Interaction a statistical term indicating that the influence of a particular variable depends upon the value of one or more others.

Karyotype the characteristics of the set of chromosomes (chromosomal sizes, shapes, and number) of a typical somatic cell of a given organism.

Klinefelter's syndrome (47, XXY and 48, XXXY) a chromosomal anomaly in males that causes a small penis, small testes, and sterility.

Latent stage the fourth stage of development in Freud's psychoanalytic theory, from age seven to puberty, when sexual urges are dormant.

Lateralization the tendency of the right and left cerebral hemispheres to control different functions.

Limbic system the old cortex, or paleocortex, as contrasted with the neocortex of the brain. Its functions pertain to those aspects of the human mind and behavior that are shared by lower species, including emotional behavior.

Locus of control feeling that one's life is determined primarily either by one's own behavior and characteristics (internal locus of control) or by luck, fate, and the influence of powerful other people (external locus of control).

Lunar cycle a cycle based on periods of approximately twenty-eight days.

Luteinizing hormone (LH) a gonadotropic hormone secreted by the anterior pituitary. In females it activates the estrogen-producing tissue of the ovaries, produces ovulation, and initiates corpus luteum development. In males, it activates the androgen-producing tissue of the testes. This hormone is also sometimes called the interstitial-cell stimulating hormone (ICSH).

Machiavellianism using exploitive and manipulative behaviors in interpersonal relations.

Mach scale a scale to measure Machiavellianism.

Masculine behaviors behaviors having qualities defined by society as appropriate to a man.

Maze learning learning the correct path through a puzzle box (maze) from the start box to the goal box.

Medulla the central part of an organ; the opposite of the cortex.

Menstrual cycle a cycle in which there is a regular period of discharge of blood, secretions, and tissue debris from the uterus of nonpregnant primate females at approximately monthly intervals.

Model the child's tendency to copy the behavior of significant persons in his or her environment.

Monoamine oxidase (MAO) an enzyme that affects the nervous system by breaking down monoamine neurotransmitters; the more MAO there is, the less active some portions of the brain will be.

Monomorphy having a single form or structural pattern for both sexes.

Monosomic having only one of a pair of chromosomes.

Müllerian inhibiting substance (MIS) a substance secreted by the fetal testis that causes the Müllerian structure adjacent to that testis to atrophy and degenerate.

Müllerian structures the structures in the fetus that degenerate in the male but develop into the uterus and Fallopian tubes in the female.

Multifactorial, sex-modified threshold model of inheritance the hypothesis that genetic, hormonal, and environmental conditions together determine the likelihood of the expression of a trait. The threshold for the appearance of the trait also depends upon gender. For example, males may have a lower threshold than females for spatial ability and for sociopathy.

Natural selection elimination of less fit individuals in the struggle to live.

Negative feedback effect a means of regulating the level of various hormones in the body. When the level of a sex hormone increases it causes a decrease in the level of a gonadotropic hormone, which in turn leads to a decrease in the sex hormone.

Nonspecific activational effects the effect of hormones on the brain by affecting cellular activity over wide areas.

Neonatal relating to or affecting the newborn, especially the human infant during the first month after birth.

Noradrenaline (norepinephrine) a crystalline compound that narrows the cavity of blood vessels and mediates transmission of sympathetic nerve impulses. This monoamine is also active in the synapses of the brain, especially in those areas affecting emotions and those areas which when stimulated electrically through implanted electrodes provide pleasure.

Object constancy the ability to recognize that objects remain the same despite differences in orientation.

Oedipus complex in Freudian theory, the emotional (sexual) attachment of a boy to his mother.

Oedipal period the period when the child develops a strong emotional (sexual) attachment to the parent of the opposite sex.

Oedipal-phallic phase according to Parsons, that phase of development in which the conscience is acquired and the child's emphasis shifts from his or her role in the mother-child system to that in the nuclear family.

Oral-dependent phase Parsons's first phase of development, in which the mother plays all the power roles with regard to her infant.

Oral stage first stage of development in Freud's psychoanalytic theory, lasting from birth to one year, in which the valued source of pleasurable stimulation comes from the mouth.

Ovaries the pair of female reproductive organs that produce eggs.

Ovulation the discharge of an egg from an ovary.

Ovum an egg, the sex cell of a female.

Oxytocin hormone secreted by the posterior pituitary that in mammals produces strong contractions of uterine muscle and ejection of milk.

Paramenstrual period the period from four or five days before to four or five days after the onset of the menses.

Parturition the action or process of giving birth to offspring.

Passerine a suborder of birds with the characteristic of perching.

Passive avoidance a form of avoidance learning in which the subject is given a noxious stimulus in a given place or after a given response. In order to avoid receiving the stimulus again, the subject must avoid that place or avoid making that response.

Penis the male organ of copulation that contains the ejaculatory duct.

Performance IQ intelligence as measured by tests on spatial tasks, reasoning ability, and the ability to apply knowledge.

Perinatal occurring during the period of pregnancy and just after birth.

Persistence the maintenance of a response even after the appropriate stimulus is no longer given. Persistence seems to be affected by androgen.

Phallic stage the third stage of development in Freud's psychoanalytic theory, lasting from three to seven years, in which pleasurable stimulation arises from masturbatory behavior.

Phenotype the external appearance of an individual, without regard to its genetic constitution.

Pheromones chemical substances that act as odiferous messengers between individuals. In mammals, pheromones serve as repellants, boundary markers, child-parent attractants, and sex attractants.

Photic driving exposure to flickering lights, which causes brain electrical activity to synchronize with the flicker frequency.

Pituitary an endocrine gland situated deep in the brain, important because it regulates many functions of the other endocrine glands of the body. Sometimes called the hypophysis.

Positive feedback effect a means of regulating the level of various hormones in the body where increases in the sex hormone lead to increases in the gonadotropic hormone, which lead to further increases in the sex hormones.

Posterior pituitary (neurohypophysis) that portion of the pituitary body embryologically derived from the brain. It secretes ADH and oxytocin.

Postpartum period the period following childbirth in women.

Precocial capable of a high degree of independent activity from birth.

Premenstrual syndrome the physical or emotional symptoms experienced by some women during the last three to five days of the menstrual cycle.

Prenatal occurring, existing, or being in a stage before birth.

Preoptic nucleus a group of cell bodies in the hypothalamus thought to be involved in body temperature and water regulation and sexual behavior.

Primary transsexual according to Person and Ovesey, those males who were not feminine as children but were withdrawn and gentle and who later requested sex-change surgery.

Progesterone one of two sex hormones chiefly characteristic of the female.

Progestins one of two classes of female sex hormones. The major progestin is progesterone.

Prolactin (luteotropic hormone, or LTH) a hormone secreted by the anterior pituitary that induces lactation in mammals.

Prostate gland a glandular body situated at the base of the male urethra. It secretes a fluid which is a major constituent of the ejaculatory fluid.

Proximal attachment touching and remaining close to the parent; contrast to distal attachment.

Pseudohermaphrodite an individual whose sex cannot be clearly defined; pseudohermaphrodites do not necessarily have gonads of both sexes, as do hermaphrodites.

Psychoanalytic theory Freud's theory of personality that stresses the importance of unconscious conflicts usually originating from developmental problems.

Puberty the period at which an organism is first capable of reproducing sexually, marked by maturing of the genital organs and development of secondary sex characteristics, and in the female by the first occurrence of menstruation.

Rapacious meat eating, living on prey.

Recessive a genetically determined characteristic of one parent that can be expressed in offspring if it is matched by the other parent or if it appears alone, but is not seen when associated with a dominant characteristic from the other parent.

Releasing factors secreted by the hypothalamus to increase the secretion of the appropriate anterior pituitary hormone into the blood stream.

Repress to inhibit the action of an object or gene.

Repression (genetic) occurs when the operator gene, the gene that controls the function of a set of related genes, is not activated by some protein or metabolite, such that the genes are not allowed to function, and the proteins for which they are the code are not manufactured.

Reticular formation a part of the brain that, when stimulated, produces cortical activation and behavioral arousal.

Sample size the number of subjects studied in an experiment.

Secondary sex characteristics those characteristics that distinguish one sex from the other but do not function directly in reproduction.

Secondary transsexual according to Person and Ovesey, those male homosexuals and transvestites who requested sex-change surgery.

Self-disclosure willingness to reveal intimate aspects of the self (emotions, motives, fears) to close friends.

Seminal vesicles pouches on either side of the male reproductive tract that temporarily store semen.

Sex chromosomes special chromosomes, different in males and females, that determine sex: the X and Y chromosomes.

Sex limited trait a trait coded for by a gene on an autosome, but expressed only or mostly in one sex or the other.

Sex linked trait a trait whose gene is located on one of the sex chromosomes.

Sex ratio the number of males for every hundred females.

Sexual dimorphism the presence of observable differences between the behavior and appearance of males and females of a given species.

Sexual selection the attraction to a member of the opposite sex, usually implying that one sex is more particular about the sexual partner than the other sex and will select partners with the desired characteristic more frequently.

Sex-typed behavior according to social-learning theory, behavior that receives different rewards as a function of the gender of the child exhibiting the behavior.

Significance level in statistics, the probability of rejecting the null hypothesis of a statistical test when it is true, that is, there is no difference between groups.

Social-learning theory a theory of personality stressing the effect on behavior of learning through differential reinforcement and modeling.

Space-form intelligence the ability to accurately visualize and locate objects in three-dimensional space.

Specific activational effects the effects of hormones on specialized receptor sites, which then induce changes in cellular activity in specific brain areas.

Spermatogenesis the formation of sperm.

Stages of emotional and social development developmental stages through which a child passes as she or he matures.

Target organ the organ on which the hormone has its greatest influence.

Testes the pair of male reproductive organs that produce sperm.

Testicular feminization describes a person with the chromosomes and internal gonads of a male but the external appearance of a female.

Testosterone the most biologically potent of the naturally occurring androgens. It is produced chiefly by the testes.

Transmitter agents chemical substances allowing one nerve to influence another at synaptic areas.

Transsexual a person living in the role of the opposite sex, before or after having attained hormonal, surgical, and legal sex reassignment.

Trimester a period of three months, particularly one of the three such periods in pregnant female humans.

Trisomic having three instead of two chromosomes in a set.

Turner's syndrome (45, X) a chromosomal anomaly in phenotypic females with the most typical symptoms being absence of ovaries and short stature. The genetic defect is a missing sex chromosome.

Two-way aboidance a form of avoidance learning in which, to avoid an unpleasant stimulus, the subject must shuttle back and forth across a low barrier each time a warning signal is made.

Uterus the organ of the female that contains and nourishes the fetus.

Vagina a canal in a female that leads from the uterus to the external orifice of the genital canal.

Variability a statistical term referring to differences among scores.

Vas deferens a duct containing sperm in males.

Verbal IQ intelligence as measured by tests of verbal usage, fluency, and comprehension.

Wolffian structures the embryonic structures adjacent to the testes that develop into the internal reproductive anatomy of the male.

X chromosome the sex chromosome that is characteristically paired with itself in females and with the Y sex chromosome in males.

X-linked recessive trait a recessive trait located on the X chromosome. This trait will always be expressed in the male, who has only one X chromosome, but it is only expressed in a female when both X chromosomes contain genes coded for it.

Y chromosome the sex chromosome characteristic of males.

References and Author Index _____

The page on which author and work are cited is shown in boldface.

Abraham, G. E. Ovarian and adrenal contributions to peripheral androgens during the menstrual cycle. *Journal of Clinical Endocrinology and Metabolism*, 1974, *39*, 340–46. **49**

Abramowicz, H. K., and Richardson, S. A. Epidemiology of severe mental retardation in children: Community studies. *American Journal of Mental Deficiency*, 1975, *80*, 18–39. **251**

Abramowitz, S. I., Abramowitz, C. V., Jackson, C., and Gomes, B. The politics of clinical judgment: What nonliberal examiners infer about women who do not stifle themselves. *Journal of Consulting and Clinical Psychology*, 1973, *41*, 385–91. **347**

Ågmo, A. Cyproterone acetate diminishes sexual activity in male rabbits. *Journal of Reproduction and Fertility*, 1975, *44*, 69–75. **124**

Alford, J. J., and Lewis, L. T. The influence of season on forcible rape rates. Personal communication, 1975. **165**

Allgeier, E. R. Beyond sowing and growing: The relationship of sex-typing to socialization, family plans, and future orientation. *Journal of Applied Social Psychology*, 1975a, *5*, 217–26. **222, 223**

Allgeier, E. R. Sexual and contraceptive socialization and attitudes among sex-typed and androgynous persons. Paper presented at the meeting of the World Population Society, Washington, November, 1975b. **222, 223**

Allport, G. W., Vernon, P. E., and Lindzey, G. *Study of values*. New York: Houghton Mifflin, 1951. **315**

Alper, T. G. Achievement motivation in college women: A now-you-see-it-now-you-don't phenomenon. *American Psychologist*, 1974, *29*, 194–203. **271, 275**

Alsum, P., and Goy, R. W. Actions of esters of testosterone, dihydrotestosterone or estradiol on sexual behavior in castrate male guinea pigs. *Hormones and Behavior*, 1974, *5*, 207–17. **124**

Altman, L. K. Study disputes data on girls' puberty. *New York Times*, March 26, 1976, p. 19. **123**

Altmann, M., Knowles, E., and Bull, H. D. A psychosomatic study of the sex cycle in women. *Psychosomatic Medicine*, 1941, *3*, 199–225. **145–146, 149, 150**

Altmann, S. A. Sociobiology of rhesus monkey, IV: Testing Mason's hypothesis of sex differences in affective behavior. *Behaviour*, 1968, *32*, 49–69. **73**

Anderson, C. O., Zarrow, M. X., and Denenberg, V. H. Maternal behavior in the rabbit: Effects of androgen treatment during gestation upon the nest building of the mother and her offspring *Hormones and Behavior*, 1970, *1*, 337–45. **96**

Anderson, M., and the Feminist Psychology Group. Sex role stereotypes and clinical psychologists. An Australian study. *Australian Psychologist*, 1975, *10*, 325–31. **347**

Andrew, J. M. Delinquency, sex, and family variables. *Social Biology*, 1976, *23*, 168–74. **291**

Andrew, R. J. Effects of testosterone on the behaviour of the domestic chick, I: Effects present in males but not in females. *Animal Behaviour*, 1975a, *23*, 139–55. **132**

Andrew, R. J. Effects of testosterone on the behaviour of the domestic chick, II: Effects present in both sexes. *Animal Behaviour*, 1975b, *23*, 156–68. **132**

Andrew, R. J. Effects of testosterone on the calling of the domestic chick in a strange environment. *Animal Behaviour*, 1975c, *23*, 169–78. **132**

Andy, O. J., and Peeler, D. F. Jr., and Foshee, D. P. Avoidance and discrimination learning following hippocampal ablation in the cat. *Journal of Comparative and Physiological Psychology*, 1967, *64*, 516–19. **81**

Angrist, S. S. The study of sex roles. *Journal of Social Issues*, 1969, *25*, 215–32. **210**

Anonymous. Effects of sexual activity on beard growth in man. *Nature*, 1970, *226*, 869–70. **136**

Archer, J. A further analysis of responses to a novel environment of testosterone-treated chicks. *Behavioral Biology*, 1973, *9*, 389–96. **132**

Archer, J. Sex differences in the emotional behavior of three strains of laboratory rat. *Animal Learning and Behavior*, 1974a, *2*, 43–48. **75**

Archer, J. Testosterone and behaviour during extinction in chicks. *Animal Behaviour*, 1974b, *22*, 650–55. **132**

Archer, J. Rodent sex differences in emotional and related behavior. *Hormones and Behavior*, 1975, *6*, 451–79. **75, 76, 82, 98**

Archer, J. Sex differences in the emotional behaviour of laboratory mice. *British Journal of Psychology*, 1977, *68*, 125–31. **75**

Ardrey, R. *African genesis*. New York: Atheneum, 1961. **328**

Arenson, S. J., and Bialor, G. B. Effects of sex of teacher and schedule of child's correct responses on teaching behavior. *Psychological Record*, 1976, *26*, 515–22. **304**

Argyle, M., Lalljee, J., and Cook, M. The effects of visibility on interaction in a dyad. *Human Relations*, 1968, *21*, 3–17. **311**

Aries, E. Male-female interpersonal styles in all male, all female and mixed groups. In A. G. Sargent (Ed.), *Beyond sex roles*, pp. 292–99. St. Paul: West 1977. **316, 317**

Arlin, M., and Brody, R. Effects of spatial presentation and blocking on organization and verbal recall at three grade levels. *Developmental Psychology*, 1976, *12*, 113–18. **253**

Arling, G. L., and Harlow, H. F. Effects of social deprivation on maternal behavior of rhesus monkeys. *Journal of Comparative and Physiological Psychology*, 1967, *64*, 371–77. **236**

Árvay, A., and Takács, I. The effect of reproductive activity on biological aging in the light of animal-experiment results and demographical data. *Gerontologica Clinica*, 1966, *8*, 36–43. **378**

Asdell, S. A., Doornenbal, H., Joshi, S. R., and Sperling, G. A. The effects of sex steroid hormones upon longevity in rats. *Journal of Reproduction and Fertility*, 1967, *14*, 113–20. **68, 377, 378, 382, 383**

Astrup, C. Maternal schizophrenia and the sex of offspring. *Biological Psychiatry*, 1974, *9*, 211–14. **373**

Atchley, R. C. Selected social and psychological differences between men and women in later life. *Journal of Gerontology*, 1976, *31*, 204–11. **336, 344**

Atkinson, J. W., Heyns, R. W., and Veroff, J. The effect of experimental arousal of the affiliation motive upon thematic apperception. *Journal of Abnormal and Social Psychology*, 1954, 49, 405–10. **304**

Atkinson, J. W., and McClelland, D. C. The projective expression of needs, II: The effect of different intensities of the hunger drive on thematic apperception. *Journal of Experimental Psychology*, 1948, *38*, 643–658. **264**

Bäckström, T., and Carstensen, H. Estrogen and progesterone in plasma in relation to premenstrual tension. *Journal of Steroid Biochemistry*, 1974, *5*, 257–60. **158**

Badiet, P. Women and legal drugs: A review. In A. MacLennan (Ed.), *Women: Their use of alcohol and other legal drugs*, pp. 57–81. Toronto: Addiction Research Foundation Press, 1976. **343**

Baenninger, R. Effects of day 1 castration on aggressive behaviors of rats. *Bulletin of the Psychonomic Society*, 1974, *3*, 189–90. **71, 93, 128**

Bailyn, L. Career and family orientations of husbands and wives in relation to marital happiness. *Human Relations*, 1970, *23*, 97–114. **279**

Bakan, D. *The duality of human existence: Isolation and communion in Western men*. Chicago: Rand McNally, 1966. **200, 220**

Baker, S. W., and Ehrhardt, A. A. Prenatal androgen, intelligence, and cognitive sex differences. In R. C. Friedman, R. M. Richart, and R. L. Vande Wiele (Eds.), *Sex differences in behavior*, pp. 53–76. New York: Wiley, 1974, **103, 105, 106**

Balish, E., Shih, C. N., Croft, W. A., Pamukcu, A. M., Lower, G., Bryan, G. T., and Yale,

C. E. Effect of age, sex, and intestinal flora on the induction of colon tumors in rats. *Journal of the National Cancer Institute,* 1977, *58,* 1103–6. **378**

Ballinger, C. B. Psychiatric morbidity and the menopause: Clinical features. *British Medical Journal,* 1976, *1,* 1183–85. **167**

Balswick, J. O., and Peek, C. W. The inexpressive male: A tragedy of American society. *Family Coordinator,* October, 1971, pp. 363–68. **218**

Bancroft, J., Tennent, G., Loucas, K., and Cass, J. The control of deviant sexual behaviour by drugs, I: Behavioural changes following oestrogens and anti-androgens. *British Journal of Psychiatry,* 1974, *125,* 310–15. **136**

Bandura, A. Influence of models' reinforcement contingencies on the acquisition of imitative responses. *Personality and Social Psychology,* 1965, *1,* 589–95. **186, 290**

Bandura, A., and McDonald, F. J. Influence of social reinforcement and the behavior of models in shaping children's moral judgments. *Journal of Abnormal and Social Psychology,* 1963, *67,* 274–81. **185**

Bandura, A., Ross, D., and Ross, S. A. Transmission of aggression through imitation of aggressive models. *Journal of Abnormal and Social Psychology,* 1961, *63,* 575–82. **185, 290**

Bandura, A., Ross, D., and Ross, S. A. Imitation of film-mediated aggressive models. *Journal of Abnormal and Social Psychology,* 1963a, *66,* 3–11. **186, 290**

Bandura, A., Ross, D., and Ross, S. A. Vicarious reinforcement and imitative learning. *Journal of Abnormal and Social Psychology,* 1963b, *67,* 601–7. **186, 290**

Bandura, A., and Walters, R. H. *Social learning and personality development.* New York: Holt, Rinehart and Winston, 1963. **183, 290**

Banerjee, U. Influence of pseudopregnancy and sex hormones on conditional behaviour in rats. *Neuroendocrinology,* 1971, *7,* 278–90. **133**

Barash, D. P. Some evolutionary aspects of parental behavior in animals and man. *American Journal of Psychology,* 1976, *89,* 195–217. **79, 361**

Barclay, A., and Cusumano, D. R. Father

absence, cross-sex identity, and field-dependent behavior in male adolescents. *Child Development,* 1967, *38,* 243–50. **246**

Bardwick, J. M. *Psychology of women.* New York: Harper and Row, 1971. **160, 183, 275, 300, 301, 323**

Bardwick, J. M. A predictive study of psychological and psychosomatic responses to oral contraceptives. In J. T. Fawcett (Ed.), *Psychological perspectives on population,* pp. 274–305. New York: Basic Books, 1972. **274–305.**

Bardwick, J. M. Some notes about power relationships between women. In A. G. Sargent (Ed.), *Beyond sex roles,* pp. 325–35. St. Paul: West, 1977. **143, 145, 229**

Barlow, P. The influence of inactive chromosomes on human development: anomalous sex chromosome complements and the phenotype. *Humangenetik,* 1973, *17,* 105–136. **39**

Barnes, R. H., Cunnold, S. R., Zimmerman, R. R., Simmons, H., MacLeod, R. B., and Krook, L. Influence of nutritional deprivation in early life on learning behavior of rats as measured by performance in water maze. *Journal of Nutrition,* 1966, *89,* 399–410. **81**

Barnett, R. C. Sex differences and age trends in occupational preference and occupational prestige. *Journal of Counseling Psychology,* 1975, *22,* 35–38. **273, 315**

Barr, G. A., Gibbons, J. L., and Moyer, K. E. Male-female differences and the influence of neonatal and adult testosterone on intraspecies aggression in rats. *Journal of Comparative and Physiological Psychology,* 1976, *90,* 1169–83. **61, 71, 78, 94**

Barr, M. L., and Bertram, L. F. A morphological distinction between neurones of the male and female and the behavior of the nucleolar satellite during accelerated nucleoprotein synthesis. *Nature,* 1949, *163,* 676–77. **26**

Barrett, R. J., and Ray, O. S. Behavior in the open field, Lashley III maze, shuttle-box, and Sidman avoidance as a function of strain, sex and age. *Developmental Psychology,* 1970, *3,* 73–77. **75, 80**

Barron, F. Originality in relation to personality

Barron, F. (*Continued*)
and intellect. *Journal of Personality*, 1957, 25, 730–42. **256**

Barry, H., III, Bacon, M. K., and Child, I. L. A cross-cultural survey of some sex differences in socialization. *Journal of Abnormal and Social Psychology*, 1957, 55, 327–32. **206, 207**

Bart, P. B. Depression in middle-aged women. In S. Cox (Ed.), *Female psychology: The emerging self*, pp. 349–67. Chicago: Science Research Associates, 1976. **167, 340**

Bar-Tal, D., and Saxe, L. Physical attractiveness and its relationship to sex-role stereotyping. *Sex Roles*, 1976, 2, 123–33. **271, 314**

Baruch, G. K. Sex-role stereotyping, the motive to avoid success, and parental identification: a comparison of preadolescent and adolescent girls. *Sex Roles*, 1975, 1, 303–9. **183, 194, 211, 269**

Baxter, J. C. Interpersonal spacing in natural settings. *Sociometry*, 1970, 33, 444–56. **310**

Bayley, N., and Oden, M. The maintenance of intellectual ability in gifted adults. *Journal of Gerontology*, 1955, 10, 91–107. **237**

Bayley, N., and Schaefer, E. S. Correlations of maternal and child behaviors with the development of mental abilities: Data from the Berkeley Growth Study. *Monographs of the Society for Research in Child Development*, 1964, 29, serial number 97. **239**

Beach, F. A. A review of physiological and psychological studies of sexual behavior in mammals. *Physiological Review*, 1947, 27, 240–307. **69**

Beach, F. A. Factors involved in the control of mounting behavior by female mammals. In M. Diamond (Ed.), *Reproduction and sexual behavior*, pp. 83–131. Bloomington: University of Indiana Press, 1968a. **69**

Beach, F. A. Retrospect and prospect. In F. A. Beach (Ed.), *Sex and behavior*, pp. 535–69. New York: Wiley, 1968b. **70**

Beach, F. A. Hormonal modification of sexually dimorphic behavior. *Psychoneuroendocrinology*, 1975, 1, 3–23. **93, 111**

Beach, F. A. Sexual attractivity, proceptivity and receptivity in female mammals. *Hormones and Behavior*, 1976, 7, 105–38. **64, 69, 123, 124, 125**

Beach, F. A., Kuehn, R. E., Sprague, R. H., and Anisko, J. J. Coital behavior in dogs, XI: Effects of androgenic stimulation during development on masculine mating responses in females. *Hormones and Behavior*, 1972, 3, 143–68. **70, 90**

Beatty, W. W., and Beatty, P. A. Effects of neonatal testosterone on the acquisition of an active avoidance response in genotypically female rats. *Psychonomic Science*, 1970a, 19, 315–16. **80, 100, 133**

Beatty, W. W., and Beatty, P. A. Hormonal determinants of sex differences in avoidance behavior and reactivity to electric shock in the rat. *Journal of Comparative and Physiological Psychology*, 1970b, 73, 446–55. **82, 100, 133**

Beatty, W. W., Gregoire, K. C., and Parmiter, L. L. Sex differences in retention of passive avoidance behavior in rats. *Bulletin of the Psychonomic Society*, 1973, 2, 99–100. **80**

Beatty, W. W., and O'Briant, D. A. Sex differences in extinction of food-rewarded approach responses. *Bulletin of the Psychonomic Society*, 1973, 2, 97–98. **80**

Beeman, E. A. The relation of the interval between castration and first encounter to the aggressive behavior of mice. *Anatomical Record*, 1947, 99, 570–71. **130**

Bell, B., Christie, M. J., and Venables, P. H. Menstrual cycle variation in body fluid potassium. *Journal of Interdisciplinary Cycle Research*, 1975, 6, 113–20. **147**

Bell, D. D., and Zucker, I. Sex differences in body weight and eating: Organization and activation by gonadal hormones in the rat. *Physiology and Behavior*, 1971, 7, 27–34. **385**

Belmaker, R. H., Murphy, D. L., Wyatt, R. J., and Lorizux, D. L. Human platelet monanine oxidase changes during the menstrual cycle. *Archives of General Psychiatry*, 1974, 30, 553–56. **147**

Belote, B. Masochistic syndrome, hysterical personality, and the illusion of a healthy woman. In S. Cox (Ed.), *Female psychology: The emerging self*, pp. 335–48.

Chicago: Science Research Associates, 1976. **342**

Bem, S. L. The measurement of psychological androgyny. *Journal of Consulting and Clinical Psychology,* 1974, *42,* 155–62. **221**

Bem, S. L. Sex-role adaptability: One consequence of psychological androgyny. *Journal of Personality and Social Psychology,* 1975, *31,* 634–43. **221, 307**

Bem, S. L. Beyond androgyny: Some presumptuous prescriptions for a liberated sexual identity. In J. Sherman and F. Denmark (Eds.), *Psychology of women: Future directions of research.* New York: Psychological Dimensions, in press. **221**

Bem, S. L. On the utility of alternative procedures for assessing psychological androgyny. *Journal of Consulting and Clinical Psychology,* 1977, *45,* 196–205. **221**

Bem, S. L., and Bem, D. L. Training the woman to know her place: The power of a nonconscious ideology. In M. H. Garskof (Ed.), *Roles women play: Readings toward women's liberation,* pp. 84–96. Belmont, Calif.: Brooks/Cole, 1971. **218**

Bem, S. L., and Lenney, E. Sex typing and the avoidance of cross-sex behavior. *Journal of Personality and Social Psychology,* 1976, *33,* 48–54. **222**

Bem, S. L., Martyna, W., and Watson, C. Sex typing and androgyny: Further explorations of the expressive domain. *Journal of Personality and Social Psychology,* 1976, *34,* 1016–23. **221, 222, 307**

Bender, A. E. Food preferences of males and females. *Proceedings of the Nutrition Society,* 1976, *35,* 181–89. **303, 388**

Bender, V. L., Davis, Y., Glover, O., and Stapp, J. Patterns of self-disclosure in homosexual and heterosexual college students. *Sex Roles,* 1976, *2,* 149–60.

Benedek, T. Sexual functions in women and their disturbance. In S. Arieti (Ed.), *American handbook of psychiatry,* Vol. 1, pp. 729–748. New York: Basic Books, 1959. **149**

Benedek, T. The psychobiology of pregnancy. In E. J. Anthony and T. Benedek (Eds.), *Parenthood: Its psychology and psychopathology,* pp. 137–51. Boston: Little, Brown, 1970. **159**

Benedek, T., and Rubenstein, B. B. The correlations between ovarian activity and psychodynamic processes, I: The ovulative phase. *Psychosomatic Medicine,* 1939a, *1,* 245–70. **149**

Benedek, T., and Rubenstein, B. B. The correlations between ovarian activity and psychodynamic processes, II: The menstrual phase. *Psychosomatic Medicine,* 1939b, *1,* 461–85. **149**

Bengelloun, W. A., Nelson, D. J., Zent, H. M., and Beatty, W. W. Behavior of male and female rats with septal lesions: Influence of prior gonadectomy. *Physiology and Behavior,* 1976, *16,* 317–30. **133**

Berens, A. E. Socialization of need for achievement in boys and girls. *Proceedings of the 80th Annual American Psychological Association Convention,* 1972, 273–74. **266, 271**

Berge, T., and Toremalm, N. B. Bronchial cancer—a clinical and pathological study, I: Histopathology and metastasis. *Scandinavian Journal of Respiratory Diseases,* 1975a, *56,* 109–19. **374**

Berge, T., and Toremalm, N. G. Bronchial cancer—a clinical and pathological study, II: Frequency according to age and sex during a 12-year period. *Scandinavian Journal of Respiratory Diseases,* 1975b, *56,* 120–26. **374**

Bermant, G. Behavior therapy approaches to modification of sexual preferences: Biological perspective and critique. In J. M. Bardwick (Ed.), *Readings on the psychology of women,* pp. 254–58. New York: Harper and Row, 1972. **331, 374**

Bermant, G., and Davidson, J. M. *Biological bases of sexual behavior.* New York: Harper and Row, 1974. **68, 124, 125, 136**

Bernard, B. K. Testosterone manipulations: effects on ranacide aggression and brain monoamines in the adult female rat. *Pharmacology, Biochemistry, and Behavior,* 1976, *4,* 59–65. **129**

Bernard, B. K., and Paolino, R. M. Temporal effects of castration on emotionality and shocks—induced aggression in adult male rats. *Physiology and Behavior,* 1975, *14,* 201–6. **128, 129, 132**

Bernard, J. *Academic women.* University

Bernard, J. (*Continued*)
Park: University of Pennsylvania Press, 1964. **226**

Bernard, J. Sex differences: An overview. New York *MSS Modular Publication,* 1973, Module 26, 1–18. **380**

Berndtson, W. E., Pickett, B. W., and Nett, T. M. Reproductive physiology of the stallion, IV: Seasonal changes in the testosterone concentration of peripheral plasma. *Journal of Reproduction and Fertility,* 1974, *39,* 115–18. **164**

Berry, J. L., and Martin, B. GSR reactivity as a function of anxiety, instructions and sex. *Journal of Abnormal and Social Psychology,* 1957, *54,* 9–12. **321**

Berry, J. W. Temne and Eskimo perceptual skills. *International Journal of Psychology,* 1966, *1,* 207–29. **244, 303**

Berry, J. W. Sex differences in behaviour and cultural complexity. *Indian Journal of Psychology,* 1976, 51, 89–97. **204, 207, 246**

Berry, J. W. Nomadic style and cognitive style. In M. H. McGurk (Ed.), *Ecological factors in human development, pp. 229–*45. Amsterdam: North-Holland, 1977. **246**

Bertram, B. C. R. Social factors influencing reproduction in wild lions. *Journal of Zoology,* 1975, *177,* 463–82. **64, 68, 122**

Bettelheim, B. *Symbolic wounds.* New York: Collier, 1962. **183**

Beuf, A. Doctor, lawyer, household drudge. *Journal of Communication,* 1974, *24,* 142–45. **217**

Beumont, P. J. V., Richards, D. H., and Gelder, M. G. A study of minor psychiatric and physical symptoms during the menstrual cycle. *British Journal of Psychiatry,* 1975, *126,* 431–34. **149**

Beutter, E., Yeh, M., and Fairbanks, V. F. The normal human female as a mosaic of X-chromosome activity: Studies using the gene for G-6-PD deficiency as a marker. *Proceedings of the National Academy of Science,* 1962, *48,* 9–16. **28**

Bevan, W., Daves, W. F., and Levy, G. W. The relation between castration, androgen therapy and pretest fighting experience to competitive aggression in C57 BL/10 mice. *Animal Behaviour,* 1960, *8,* 6–12. **130**

Bielert, C., Czaja, J. A., Eisele, S., Sheffler, G.,

Robinson, J. A., and Goy, R. W. Mating in the rhesus monkey (*Macaca mulatta*) after conception and its relationship to oestradiol and progesterone levels throughout pregnancy. *Journal of Reproduction and Fertility,* 1976, *46,* 179–87. **125**

Bieri, J. Parental identification, acceptance of authority, and within-sex differences in cognitive behavior. *Journal of Abnormal and Social Psychology,* 1960, *60,* 76–79. **246, 247, 256**

Bieri, J., Bradburn, W. M., and Galinsky, M. D. Sex differences in perceptual behavior. *Journal of Personality,* 1958, *26,* 1–12. **252, 240, 244**

Bigoness, W. J. Effect of applicant's sex, race, and performance on employers' performance ratings: Some additional findings. *Journal of Applied Psychology,* 1976, *61,* 80–84. **227**

Biller, H. B. Paternal and sex-role factors in cognitive and academic functioning. In J. K. Cole and R. Dienstbier (Eds.), *Nebraska symposium on motivation, 1973,* pp. 83–123. Lincoln: University of Nebraska Press, 1974. **211, 239, 242, 246, 255, 281**

Bing, E. Effect of childrearing practices on development of differential cognitive abilities. *Child Development,* 1963, *34,* 631–48. **239, 240, 253, 301, 317**

Birch, H. G., and Clark, G. Hormonal modification of social behavior, II: The effects of sex-hormone administration on the social dominance status of the female-castrate chimpanzee. *Psychosomatic Medicine,* 1946, *8,* 320–31. **74, 128, 129**

Birch, H. G., and Clark, G. Hormonal modification of social behavior. IV. The mechanism of estrogen-induced dominance in chimpanzees. *Journal of Comparative and Physiological Psychology,* 1950, *43,* 181–93. **129**

Birke, L. I. A., and Archer, J. Open-field behaviour of oestrous and dioestrous rats: Evidence against an 'emotionality' interpretation. *Animal Behaviour,* 1975, *23,* 509–12. **132**

Birnbaum, J. A. Life patterns and self-esteem in gifted family-oriented and career-committed women. In M. T. S. Mednick, S. S. Tangri, and L. W. Hoffman (Eds.), *Women and achievement: Social and motivational analyses*, pp. 396–419. New York: Halsted, 1975. **277, 278**

Black, H. Hormones used to treat depression. *Boston Globe*, September 29, 1975, p. 13. **140**

Blakemore, J. E. O., LaRue, A. A., and Olejnik, A. B. Sex-appropriate toy preference and its relationship to classification skills in young children. Private communication, 1976. **190**

Blizard, D. A. Lippman, H. R., and Chen, J. J. Sex differences in open-field behavior in the rat: The inductive and activational role of gonadal hormones. *Physiology and Behavior*, 1975, *14*, 601–8. **75, 98, 132**

Block, J. H., von der Lippe, A., and Block, J. H. Sex-role and socialization patterns: Some personality concomitants and environmental antecedents. *Journal of Consulting and Clinical Psychology*, 1973, *41*, 321–41. **220**

Block, J. H. Conceptions of sex role: Some cross-cultural and longitudinal perspectives. *American Psychologist*, 1973, *28*, 512–26. **203, 207**

Blood, R. O., Jr., and Wolfe, D. M. *Husbands and wives: The dynamics of married living*. New York: Free Press, 1960. **297**

Blum, A. H., and Broverman, D. M. Children's cognitive style and response modification. *Journal of Genetic Psychology*, 1967, *110*, 95–103. **141, 255**

Blum, G. S. A study of the psychoanalytic theory of psychosexual development. *Genetic Psychology Monographs*, 1949, *39*, 3–99. **180**

Blumer, D., and Migeon, C. Hormone and hormonal agents in the treatment of aggression. *Journal of Nervous and Mental Disease*, 1975, *160*, 127–37. **136, 387**

Blurton-Jones, M. G., and Konner, M. J. Sex differences in behavior of London and Bushman children. In R. P. Michael and J. H. Crook (Eds.), *Comparative ecology and behaviour of primates*, pp. 689–750. London: Academic Press, 1973. **240**

Bock, R. D. Word and image: Sources of the verbal and spatial factors in mental test scores. *Psychometrika*, 1973, *38*, 437–57.

Bock, R. D., and Kolakowski, D. Further evidence of sex-linked major gene influence on human spatial visualizing

ability. *American Journal of Human Genetics*, 1973, *25*, 1–14. **42, 108, 244**

Booth, A. Sex and social participation. *American Sociological Review*, 1972, *37*, 183–93. **303**

Born, G., Grützner, P., and Hemminger, H. Evidenz für eine Mosaik struktur der Netzhaut bei Konduktorinnen für Dichromasie. *Human Genetics*, 1976, *32*, 189–96. **41**

Borofsky, G., Slotlack, G., and Messe, L. Sex differences in bystander reactions to physical assault. *Journal of Experimental Social Psychology*, 1971, *7*, 313–18. **307**

Bossé, R., and Rose, C. L. Smoking cessation and sex role convergence. *Journal of Health and Social Behavior*, 1976, *17*, 53–61. **388**

Boúe, J., Boúe, A., and Lazar, P. Retrospective and prospective epidemiological studies of 1500 karyotyped spontaneous human abortions. *Teratology*, 1975, *12*, 11–26. **143**

Bouissou, M. F. Influence of body weight and presence of horns on social rank in domestic cattle. *Animal Behaviour*, 1972, *20*, 474–77. **71**

Boyatzis, R. E. Affiliation motivation. In D. C. McClelland and R. S. Steele (Eds.), *Human motivation: A book of readings*, pp. 252–76. Morristown, N.J.: General Learning Press, 1973. **304**

Brabant, S., and Garbin, A. P. Sex of student as defined by sex-typical experiences and persistence in higher education. *Journal of College Student Personnel*, 1976, *17*, 28–33. **274**

Bradley, A. J., McDonald, I. R., and Lee, A. K. Effects of exogenous cortisol on mortality of a dasyurid marsupial. *Journal of Endocrinology*, 1975, *66*, 281–82. **68**

Braginsky, D. D. Machiavellianism and manipulative interpersonal behavior in children. *Journal of Experimental Social Psychology*, 1970, *6*, 77–99. **298**

Brahen, S. L. Housewife drug abuse. *Journal of Drug Education*, 1973, *3*, 13–24. **349**

Brain, P. F., and Evans, C. M. Attempts to influence fighting and threat behaviors in adult isolated female CFW mice in standard opponent aggression tests using injected and subcutaneously implanted androgens.

Brain, P. F. (*Continued*)
Physiology and Behavior, 1975, *14,*
551–56.   **128**

Bridges, R. S., Zarrow, M. X., and Denenberg,
V. H. The role of neonatal androgen in
the expression of hormonally induced
maternal responsiveness in the adult rat.
Hormones and Behavior, 1973, *4,* 315–
22.   **96**

Brief, A. P., and Wallace, M. J., Jr. The impact
of employee sex and performance on the
allocation of organizational rewards. *Journal of Psychology,* 1976, *92,* 25–34.
227

Brindley, C., Clarke, P., Hutt, C., Robinson, I.,
and Wethli, E. Sex differences in the activities and social interactions of nursery
school children. In R. P. Michael and J. H.
Crook (Eds.), *Comparative ecology and
behaviour of primates,* pp. 799–828. New
York: Academic Press, 1972.   **293, 306**

Broadhurst, P. L. Determinants of emotionality
in the rat, I: Situational factors. *British Journal of Psychology,* 1957, *48,* 1–12.   **75**

Broitman, S. T., and Donoso, A. O. Maternal
and sex-related influences in locomotor
activity in rats following weaning. *Physiology and Behavior,* 1974, *12,* 309–12.   **75,
385**

Bronson, F. H., and Desjardins, C. Aggression
in adult mice: Modification by neonatal
injections of gonadal hormones. *Science,*
1968, *161,* 705–6.   **128**

Bronson, F. H., and Desjardins, C. Neonatal
androgen administration and adult aggressiveness in female mice. *General and
Comparative Endocrinology,* 1970, *15,*
320–25.   **93**

Bronson, F. H., and Desjardins, C. Steroid
hormones and aggressive behavior in
mammals. In B. E. Eleftheriou and J. P. Scott
(Eds.), *The physiology of aggression and
defeat,* pp. 43–63. New York: Plenum Press,
1971.   **122**

Brook, J. S., Whiteman, M., Peisach, E., and
Deutsch, M. Aspiration levels of and for
children: Age, sex, race, and socioeconomic correlates. *Journal of Genetic
Psychology,* 1974, *124,* 3–16.   **281**

Brookhart, J., and Hock, E. The effects of
experimental context and experimental
background on infants' behavior toward

their mothers and a stranger. *Child
Development,* 1976, *47,* 333–40.   **300**

Brooks, J., and Lewis, M. Attachment behavior
in thirteen-month-old opposite-sex twins.
Child Development, 1974, *45,* 243–
47.   **300**

Broverman, D. M. Generality and behavioral
correlates of cognitive styles. *Journal of
Consulting and Clinical Psychology,* 1964,
28, 487–500.   **141, 238**

Broverman, D. M., Broverman, I. K., Vogel, W.,
Palmer, R. D., and Klaiber, E. L. The au-
tomatization cognitive style and physical
development. *Child Development,* 1964,
35, 1343–1359.   **141, 245, 255**

Broverman, D. M., Klaiber, E. L., Kobayashi,
Y., and Vogel, W. Roles of activation and
inhibition in sex differences in cognitive
abilities. *Psychological Review,* 1968, *75,*
23–50.   **120, 133, 134, 140, 237, 255**

Broverman, I. K., Broverman, D. M., Clarkson,
F. E., Rosenkrantz, P. S., and Vogel, S. R.
Sex-role stereotypes and clinical judgments of mental health. *Journal of Consulting and Clinical Psychology,* 1970, *34,*
1–7.   **346**

Broverman, I. K., Vogel, S. R., Broverman,
D. M., Clarkson, F. E., and Rosenkrantz,
P. S. Sex-role stereotypes: A current
appraisal. *Journal of Social Issues,* 1972,
28, 59–78.   **183, 212, 213, 216, 217, 223**

Brown, L. M. Sexism in Western art. In J.
Freeman (Ed.), *Women: A feminist per-
spective,* pp. 309–22. Palo Alto, Calif.:
Mayfield, 1975.   **215**

Brown-Grant, K. On "critical periods" during
the post-natal development of the rat. In
M. G. Forest and J. Bertrand (Eds.), *Sexual
endocrinology of the perinatal period,* pp.
357–75. Lyon, France: Inserm, 1974.   **113**

Brown-Grant, K. A re-examination of the lordosis response in female rats given high
doses of testosterone propinate or estradiol
benzoate in the neonatal period. *Hormones
and Behavior,* 1975, *6,* 351–78.   **90**

Brown-Grant, K., and Sherwood, M. R. The
"early androgen" syndrome in the guinea
pig. *Journal of Endocrinology,* 1971, *49,*
227–91.   **90**

Buchsbaum, M. S., Henkin, R. I., and Christiansen, R. L. Age and sex differences in
averaged evoked responses in a normal

population, with observations on patients with gonadal dysgenesis. *Electroenceph-alography and Clinical Neurophys-iology,* 1974, *37,* 137–44.   **113**

Buchsbaum, M., Landau, S., Murphy, D., and Goodwin, F. Average evoked response in bipolar and unipolar affective disorders: Relationship to sex, age of onset, and monoamine oxidase. *Biological Psychiatry,* 1973, *7,* 199–212.   **352**

Buchsbaum, M., and Pfefferbaum, A. Individual differences in stimulus intensity response. *Psychophysiology,* 1971, *8,* 600–611.   **113**

Buck, R. W. *Human motivation and emotion.* New York: Wiley, 1976.   **158, 264, 291, 303, 362**

Buck, R. W., Savin, V. J., Miller, R. E., and Caul, W. F. Communication of affect through facial expressions in humans. *Journal of Personality and Social Psychology,* 1972, *23,* 362–71.   **317**

Buffery, A. W. H., and Gray, J. A. Sex differences in the development of spatial and linguistic skills. In C. Ounsted and D. C. Taylor (Eds.), *Gender differences: Their ontogeny and significance,* pp. 123–57. London: Churchill Livingston, 1972.   **81, 99, 237, 255, 257, 250**

Bugental, D. E., Love, L. R., and Gianetto, R. M. Perfidious feminine faces. *Journal of Personality and Social Psychology,* 1971, *17,* 314–18.   **311**

Burg, A. Visual acuity as measured by dynamic and static tests: A comparative evaluation. *Journal of Applied Psychology,* 1966, *50,* 460–66.   **323**

Burke, A. W., and Broadhurst, P. L. Behavioural correlates of the oestrus cycle in the rat. *Nature,* 1966, *209,* 223–24.   **132, 133**

Burke, R. J., and Weir, T. Some personality differences between members of one-career and two-career families. *Journal of Marriage and the Family,* 1976, *38,* 453–59. (b)   **277, 279**

Burke, R. J., and Weir, T. *Journal of Marriage and the Family,* 1976, *38,* 279–287(a).   **277, 278, 279, 345**

Burnight, R. G., and Marden, P. G. Social correlates of weight in an aging population. In N. Kiell, (Ed.), *The psychology of obesity,* pp. 92–105. Springfield, Ill.: Thomas, 1973.   **376, 377**

Butler, K. Predatory behavior in laboratory mice: Strain and sex comparisons. *Journal of Comparative and Physiological Psychology,* 1973, *85,* 243–49.   **71**

Byrne, D., Fisher, J. D., Lamberth, J., and Mitchell, H. E. Evaluations of erotica: Facts on feelings. *Journal of Personality and Social Psychology,* 1974, *29,* 111–16.   **330**

Byrne, D., Golightly, C., and Capaldi, E. J. Construction and validation of the food attitude scale. *Journal of Consulting Psychology,* 1963, *27,* 215–22.   **388**

Byrne, D., and Lamberth, J. The effect of erotic stimuli on sex arousal, evaluative responses, and subsequent behavior. In *Technical Report of the Commission on Obscenity and Pornography.* Vol. 8, pp. 41–67. Washington, D.C.: U.S. Government Printing Office, 1971.   **330**

Caballero, C. M., Giles, P., and Shaver, P. Sex-role traditionalism and fear of success. *Sex Roles,* 1975, *1,* 319–26.   **267**

Cadoret, R. J., Cunningham, L., Loftus, R., and Edwards, J. Studies of adoptees from psychiatrically disturbed biologic parents; II: Temperament, hyperactive, antisocial, and developmental variables. *Journal of Pediatrics,* 1975, *87,* 301–6.   **353**

Cadoret, R. J., Cunningham, L., Loftus, R., and Edwards, J. Studies of adoptees from psychiatrically disturbed biological parents, III: Medical symptoms and illnesses in childhood and adolescence. *American Journal of Psychiatry,* 1976, *133,* 1316–18.   **353**

Calabresi, E., De Giuli, G., Becciolini, A., Giannotti, P., Lombardi, G., and Serio, M. Plasma estrogens and androgens in male breast cancer. *Journal of Steroid Biochemistry,* 1976, *7,* 605–9.   **50**

Campbell, A., with Converse, P. and Rogers, W. The American way of mating: Marriage sí, children only maybe. *Psychology Today,* 1975, *8,* 37–43.   **338, 343**

Campbell, B. (ed.). *Sexual selection and the descent of man, 1871–1971.* Chicago: Aldine, 1972.   **361**

Campbell, P. B. Adolescent intellectual de-

Campbell, P. B. (*Continued*)
cline. *Adolescence*, 1976, *11*, 631–35. **239**

Cantor, J. R. What is funny to whom? The role of gender. *Journal of Communication*, 1976, *26*, 164–72. **296**

Cantor, N. L., and Gelfand, D. M. Effects of responsiveness and sex of children on adults' behavior. *Child Development*, 1977, *48*, 232–38. **301**

Caplan, P. J. Sex differences in antisocial behavior: Does research methodology produce or abolish them? *Human Development*, 1975, *18*, 444–60. **290, 358**

Carey, G. L. Sex differences in problem-solving performance as a function of attitude differences. *Journal of Abnormal and Social Psychology*, 1958, *56*, 256–60. **254**

Carlini, E. A., and Masur, J. Development of aggressive behavior in rats by chronic administration of *Cannabis sativa* (marijuana). *Life Sciences*, 1969, *8*, 607–20. **20**

Carlson, R. Sex differences in ego functioning: Exploratory studies of agency and communion. *Journal of Consulting and Clinical Psychology*, 1971, *17*, 267–77. **220**

Carlson, R. Understanding women: Implications for personality theory and research. *Journal of Social Issues*, 1972, *28*, 17–32. **220**

Carpenter, C. R. Sexual behavior of free-ranging rhesus monkeys. *International Journal of Comparative Psychology*, 1942, *33*, 143–62. **73**

Carter, C. O. Sex-linkage and sex-limitation. In C. Ounsted and D. C. Taylor (Eds.), *Gender differences: Their ontogeny and significance*, pp. 1–12. London: Churchill Livingston, 1972. **41, 42**

Carter, C. S., Clemens, L. G., and Hoekema, D. J. Neonatal androgen and adult sexual behavior in the golden hamster. *Physiology and Behavior*, 1972, *9*, 89–95. **90**

Carter, C. S., and Landauer, M.R. Neonatal hormone experience and adult lordosis and fighting in the golden hamster. *Physiology and Behavior*, 1975, *14*, 1–6. **90, 93**

Cassiman, J. J., Fryns, J. P., De Roover, J., and van den Berghe, H. Sex chromatin and cytogenetic survey of 10417 adult males and 357 children institutionalized in Bel-

gian institutions for mentally retarded patients. *Humangenetik*, 1975, *28*, 43–48. **33, 35**

Cathelineau, G. Effects des oestro-progestatifs sur la tolérance glucidique et l'insulino-secrétion. *Pathologie Biologie*, 1976, *24*, 625–29. **143**

Chafetz, J. S. *Masculine/feminine or human? An overview of the sociology of sex roles.* Itasca, Ill.: Peacock, 1974. **215**

Chambers, C. D., Inciardi, J. A., and Siegal, H. H. *Chemical Coping: A report on legal drug use in the United States.* New York: Spectrum Publications, 1975. **349**

Chambers, K. C. Hormonal influences on sexual dimorphism in rate of extinction of a conditioned taste aversion in rats. *Journal of Comparative and Physiological Psychology*, 1976, *90*, 851–56. **9, 383**

Chambers, K. C., and Sengstake, C. B. Sexually dimorphic extinction of a conditioned taste aversion in rats. *Animal Learning and Behavior*, 1976, *4*, 181–85. **9, 388**

Chamove, A., Harlow, H. F., and Mitchell, G. Sex differences in the infant directed behavior of preadolescent rhesus monkeys. *Child Development*, 1967, *38*, 329–35. **77, 131**

Chasen, B. Diagnostic sex-role bias and its relation to authoritarianism, sex-role attitudes, and sex of the school psychologist. *Sex Roles*, 1975, *1*, 355–68. **347**

Cherry, F., and Deaux, K. Fear of success vs. fear of gender—inconsistent behavior: A sex similarity. Paper presented at the meeting of the Midwestern Psychological Association, Chicago, May, 1975. **268**

Cherry, L., and Lewis, M. Mothers and two-year-olds: A study of sex differentiated aspects of verbal interaction. *Developmental Psychology*, 1976, *12*, 278–82. **208**

Chesler, P. *Women and madness.* New York: Doubleday, 1972. **218, 342, 350, 351**

Chiang, A., and Atkinson, R. C. Individual differences and interrelationships among a select set of cognitive skills. *Memory and Cognition*, 1976, *4*, 661–72. **252**

Childs, B. Genetic origin of some sex differences among human beings. *Pediatrics*, 1965, *35*, 798–812. **373**

Chodorow, N. Family structure and feminine personality. In M. Z. Rosaldo and L. Lamphere (Eds.), *Women, culture and society,* pp. 43–66. Stanford, Calif.: Stanford University Press, 1974. **200, 205, 207**

Cidlowski, J. A., and Muldoon, T. G. Sex-related differences in the regulation of cytoplasmic estrogen receptor levels in responsive tissues of the rat. *Endocrinology,* 1976, *98,* 833–41. **111**

Clancy, K., and Gove, W. Sex differences in mental illness: An analysis of response bias in self-reports. *American Journal of Sociology,* 1975, *80,* 205–16. **303, 334, 336**

Clark, G., and Birch, H. G. Hormonal modifications of social behavior, I: The effect of sex-hormone administration on the social status of a male-castrate chimpanzee. *Psychosomatic Medicine,* 1945, *7,* 321–29. **129**

Clarke, I. J. The sexual behaviour of prenatally androgenized ewes observed in the field. *Journal of Reproductive Fertility,* 1977, *49,* 311–15. **70, 90, 93**

Clemens. L. G., Shryne, J., and Gorski, R. A. Androgen and development of progesterone responsiveness in male and female rats. *Physiology and Behavior,* 1970, *5,* 673–78. **111**

Cloninger, C. R., Reich, T., and Guze, S. B. The multifactoral model of disease transmission, II: Sex differences in the familiar transmission of sociopathy (antisocial personality). *British Journal of Psychiatry,* 1975, *127,* 11–22.(a) **42, 353**

Cloninger, C. R., Reich, T., and Guze, S. B. The multifactorial model of disease transmission, III: Familial relationship between sociopathy and hysteria (Briquet's syndrome). *British Journal of Psychiatry,* 1975, *127,* 23–32. (b) **42, 353**

Coates, S. Sex differences in field independence among preschool children. In R. C. Friedman, R. M. Richart, and R. L. Vande Wiele (Eds.), *Sex differences in behavior,* pp. 259–74. New York: Wiley, 1974. **211, 244, 247, 255, 256**

Cochran, C. A., and Perachio, A. A. Dihydrotestosterone propinate effects on dominance and sexual behaviors in gonadectomized male and female rhesus monkeys. *Hormones and Behavior,* 1977, *8,* 175–87. **128, 135**

Cohen, D. Sex differences in spatial performance in the elderly: A review of the literature and suggestions for research. *Educational Gerontology: An International Quarterly,* 1977, *2,* 59–69. **237, 244**

Cohn, R. A., Barratt, E., and Pirch, J. H. Differences in behavioral responses of male and female rats to marijuana. *Proceedings of the Society for Experimental Biology and Medicine,* 1972, *140,* 1136–39. **320**

Coie, J. D., Pennington, B. F., and Buckley, H. H. Effects of situational stress and sex roles on the attribution of psychological disorder. *Journal of Consulting and Clinical Psychology,* 1974, *42,* 559–68. **347**

Coleman, J. S. *Adolescent society.* New York: Free Press, 1961. **273, 314**

Coles, M. G. H., Porges, S. W., and Duncan-Johnson, C. C. Sex differences in performance and associated cardiac activity during a reaction time task. *Physiological Psychology,* 1975, *3,* 141–43. **326**

Coltheart, M., Hull, E., and Slater, D. Sex differences in imagery and reading. *Nature,* 1975, *253,* 438–40. **245**

Commins, W. D. The effect of castration at various ages upon the learning ability of male albino rats. *Journal of Comparative Psychology,* 1932, *14,* 29–54. **133**

Constantinople, A. Masculinity-femininity: An exception to a famous dictum? *Psychological Bulletin,* 1973, *80,* 389–407. **211, 220, 342**

Cooperstock, R. Sex differences in the use of mood-modifying drugs: An explanatory model. *Journal of Health and Social Behaviour,* 1971, *12,* 238–44. **349, 377**

Cooperstock, R. Women and psychotropic drugs. In A. MacLennan (Ed.), *Women: Their use of alcohol and other legal drugs,* pp. 83–111. Toronto, Canada: Addiction Research Foundation of Ontario, 1976. **349, 377**

Coppen, A., and Kessel, N. Menstruation and personality. *British Journal of Psychiatry,* 1963, *109,* 711–21. **154, 155, 157**

Corah, N. L. Differentiation in children and their parents. *Journal of Personality,* 1965, *33,* 300–308. **42, 252**

Corey, S. M. Sex differences in maze learning

Corey, S. M. (*Continued*)
by white rats. *Journal of Comparative Psychology,* 1930, *10,* 333–38. **81**

Corso, J. F. Age and sex differences in pure-tone thresholds. *Journal of the Acoustical Society of America,* 1959, *31,* 498–507. **323**

Costrich, N., Feinstein, J., Kidder, L., Marecek, J., and Pascale, L. When stereotypes hurt: Three studies of penalties for sex-role reversals. *Journal of Experimental Social Psychology,* 1975, *11,* 520–30. **219, 347**

Couch, C. J. Family role specialization and self-attitudes in children. *Sociological Quarterly,* 1962, *3,* 115–21. **194**

Court-Brown, W. M., Harnden, D. G., Jacobs, P. A., Maclean, N., and Mantle, D. J. *Abnormalies of sex chromosome complement in man.* London: Her Majesty's Stationery Office, 1964. **29, 30, 33**

Court-Brown, W. M., Price, W. H., and Jacobs, P. A. Further information on the identity of 47, XYY males. *British Medical Journal,* 1968, *2,* 325–28. **38**

Crandall, V. J. Achievement. In H. W. Stevenson (Ed.), *Child Psychology,* pp. 416–459. Chicago: University of Chicago Press, 1963. **264**

Crandall, V. J. Sex differences in expectancy of intellectual and academic reinforcement. In C. D. Smith (Ed.), *Achievement related motives in children,* pp. 11–45. New York: Russell Sage Foundation, 1969. **281, 283**

Crandall, V. J., and Rabson, A. Children's repetitive choices in an intellectual achievement situation following success and failure. *Journal of Genetic Psychology,* 1960, *97,* 161–68. **265, 281, 301**

Crandall, V. J., and Sinkeldam, C. Children's dependent and achievement behaviors in social situations and their perceptual field dependence. *Journal of Personality,* 1964, *32,* 1–22. **244**

Crawford, M. P. The relation between social dominance and the menstrual cycles in female chimpanzees. *Journal of Comparative Psychology,* 1940, *30,* 483–513. **73**

Creutzfeldt, O. D., Arnold, P. M., Becker, D., Langenstein, S., Tirsch, W., Wilhelm, H., and Wuttke, W. EEG changes during spontaneous and controlled menstrual cycles and their correlation with psychological performance. *Electroencephalography and Clinical Neurophysiology,* 1976, *40,* 113–31. **143, 148, 151**

Critchlow, V., and Bar-Sella, M. E. In L. Martini and W. F. Ganong (Eds.), *Neuroendocrinology.* Vol. II, pp. 101–62. New York: Academic Press, 1967. **55**

Crook, J. H. Gelada baboon herd structure and movement: A comparative report. *Symposium Zoological Society of London,* 1966, *18,* 237–58 **77**

Crook, J. H. Sexual selection, dimorphism, and social organization in the primates. In B. Campbell (Ed.), *Sexual selection and the descent of man,* pp. 231–81. Chicago: Aldine, 1972. **65, 67, 77**

Cross, J. F., Cross, J., and Daly, J. Sex, race, age and beauty as factors in recognition of faces. *Perception and Psychophysics,* 1971, *10,* 393–96. **325**

Cross, K. P. *Beyond the open door: New students to higher education.* San Francisco: Jossey-Bass, 1971. **238, 240**

Cullberg, I. Mood changes and menstrual symptoms with different gestagen/estrogen combinations: A double-blind comparison with a placebo. *Acta Psychiatrica Scandinavica,* 1972 (Suppl. 236), 1–86. **143, 144, 158, 387**

Cummins, R. A., Budtz-Olsen, O. E., Walsh, R. N., and Worsley, A. Testosterone, early experience and behavioral arousal in a novel environment. *Hormones and Behavior,* 1974, *5,* 283–88. **133, 142**

Cunningham, L., Cadoret, R. J., Loftus, R., and Edwards, J. E. Studies of adoptees from psychiatrically disturbed biological parents: Psychiatric conditions in childhood and adolescene. *British Journal of Psychiatry,* 1975, *126,* 534–49. **353**

Curran, J. P. Differential effects of stated preferences and questionnaire rate performance on interpersonal attraction in the dating situation. *Journal of Psychology,* 1972, *82,* 313–27. **337**

Curtis, G. C., Fogel, M. L., McEvoy, D., and Zarate, C. Effects of weight, sex and diurnal variation on the excretion of 17-hydroxycorticosteroids. *Journal of Clinical Endocrinology and Metabolism,* 1968, *28,* 711–13. **163**

Curtis, R. C., Zanna, M.P., and Campbell, W. W., Jr. Sex, fear of success, and the perceptions and performance of law school students. *American Education Research Journal,* 1975, *12,* 287–97. **267, 268**

Czaja, J. A. Food rejection by female rhesus monkeys during the menstrual cycle and early pregnancy. *Physiology and Behavior,* 1975, *14,* 579–87. **384**

Czaja, J. A., and Goy, R. W. Ovarian hormones and food intake in female guinea pigs and rhesus monkeys. *Hormones and Behavior,* 1975, *6,* 329–49. **383, 384**

Dalton, K. Effect of menstruation on schoolgirls' weekly work. *British Medical Journal,* 1960, *1,* 326–28. **156**

Dalton, K. *The premenstrual syndrome.* Springfield, Ill.: Thomas, 1964. **158**

Dalton, K. Anti-natal progesterone and intelligence. *British Journal of Psychiatry,* 1968, *114,* 1377–82. (a) **105**

Dalton, K. Menstruation and examinations. *Lancet,* 1968, *2,* 1386–88. (b) **122, 156**

Dalton, K. Children's hospital admissions and mother's menstruation. *British Medical Journal,* 1970, *2,* 27–28 **157**

Dalton K. The influence of mother's menstruation on her child. In R. K. Unger and F. L. Denmark (Eds.), *Woman: Dependent or independent variable?* pp. 530–35. New York: Psychological Dimensions, 1975. **157**

Dalton, K. Prenatal progesterone and educational attainments. *British Journal of Psychiatry,* 1976, *129,* 438–42. **105, 242**

Damon, A., Nuttal, R. L., Salber, E. J., Seltzer, C. C., and MacMahon, B. Tobacco smoke as a possible genetic mutagen: Parental smoking and sex of children. *American Journal of Epidemiology,* 1966, *83,* 530–36. **373**

Dan, A. J. Behavioral variability and the menstrual cycle. Paper presented at the American Psychological Association Convention, Washington, D.C., September, 1976. **150, 361**

D'Andrade, R. G. Sex differences and cultural institutions. In E. E. Maccoby (Ed.), *The development of sex differences,* pp. 174–204. Stanford, Calif.: Stanford University Press, 1966. **198, 201, 202, 203**

Darwin, C. *The descent of man, and selection in relation to sex.* (2nd ed.) London: John Murray, 1874. **63**

David, D. S., and Brannon, R. (Eds.) *The Forty-nine percent majority: The male sex role.* Reading, Mass.: Addison-Wesley, 1976. **218**

Davidson, J. M. Effects of estrogen on the sexual behavior of male rats. *Endocrinology,* 1969, *84,* 1365–72. **124, 125**

Davidson, J. M., and Levine, S. Progesterone and heterotypical sexual behavior in male rats. *Journal of Endocrinology,* 1969, *44,* 128–30. **125**

Davidson, R. G., Nitowsky, H. M., and Childs, B. Demonstration of two populations of cells in the human female heterozygous for glucose-6-phosphate dehydrogenase variants. *Proceedings of the National Academy of Sciences,* 1963, *50,* 481–85. **28**

Davidson, R. J., and Schwartz, G. E. Patterns of cerebral lateralization during cardiac biofeedback versus the self-regulation of emotion: Sex differences. *Psychophysiology,* 1976, *13,* 62–68. **258**

Davidson, R. J., Schwartz, G. E., Pugash, E., and Bromfield, E. Sex differences in patterns of EEG asymmetry. *Biological Psychology,* 1976, *4,* 119–138. **258**

Davis, R., and Olsen, V. The career outlook of professionally educated women. *Psychiatry,* 1965, *28,* 334–45. **276**

Dawson, J. L. M. Effects of sex hormones on cognitive styles in rats and men. *Behavior Genetics,* 1972, *2,* 21–42. **80, 81, 133, 140, 242**

Dawson, J. L. M., Cheung, Y. M., and Lau, R. T. S. Effects of neonatal sex hormones on sex-based cognitive abilities in the white rat. *Psychologia,* 1973, *16,* 17–24. **75, 80, 86, 98, 100**

Deaux, K. *The behavior of women and men.* Belmont, Calif.: Brooks-Cole, 1976. **219, 283, 290, 291, 292, 294, 295, 307, 308, 311**

Deaux, K., and Emswiller, T. Explanation of successful performance in sex-linked tasks: What is skill for the male is luck for the female. *Journal of Personality and Social Psychology*, 1974, *29*, 80–85. **225**

Deaux, K., and Farris, E. Complexity, extremity, and affect in male and female judgments. *Journal of Personality*, 1975, *43*, 379–89. **227**

Deaux, K., and Farris, E. Attributing causes for one's own performance: The effects of sex, norms, and outcome. *Journal of Research in Personality*, 1977, *11*, 59–72. **284**

Deaux, K., and Taynor, J. Evaluation of male and female ability: Bias works two ways. *Psychological Reports*, 1973, *32*, 261–62. **227**

Deaux, K., White, L., and Farris, E. Skill versus luck, Field and laboratory studies of male and female preferences. *Journal of Personality and Social Psychology*, 1975, *32*, 629–36. **284**

DeFries, J. C., Vandenberg, S. G., and McClearn, G. E. Genetics of specific cognitive abilities. *Annual Review of Genetics*, 1976, *10*, 179–207. **42, 238**

Dennis, M. VMH lesions and reactivity to electric footshock in the rat: The effect of early testosterone level. *Physiology and Behavior*, 1976, *17*, 645–49. **112**

Denti, A., and Epstein, A. Sex differences in the acquisition of two kinds of avoidance behavior in rats. *Physiology and Behavior*, 1972, *8*, 611–15. **80**

Depner, C. E., and O'Leary, V. E. Understanding female careerism: Fear of success and new directions. *Sex roles*. 1976, *2*, 259–68. **269**

Desor, J. A., Greene, L. S., and Maller, O. Preferences for sweet and salty in 9- to 15-year-old and adult humans. *Science*, 1975, *190*, 686–87. **388**

Desor, J. A., Maller, O., and Turner, R. E. Taste in acceptance of sugars by human infants. *Journal of Comparative and Physiological Psychology*, 1973, *84*, 496–501. **388**

Deutsch, C. J., and Gilbert, L. A. Sex role stereotypes: Effect on perceptions of self and others and on personal adjustment. *Journal of Counseling Psychology*, 1976, *23*, 373–79. **341**

DeVore, I. Mother-infant relations in free-ranging baboons. In H. L. Rheingold (Ed.), *Maternal behavior in mammals*, pp. 20–52. New York: Wiley, 1963. **73, 77, 131**

Diamond, M. Progestogen inhibition of normal sexual behavior in the male guinea pig. *Nature*, (London), 1966, *209*, 1322–24. **91**

Diamond, M., Llacuna, A., and Wong, C. L. Sex behavior after neonatal progesterone, testosterone, estrogen, or antiandrogens. *Hormones and Behavior*, 1973, *4*, 73–88. **91**

Distler, L. S., May, P. R. A., and Tuma, A. H. Anxiety and ego strength as predictors of response to treatment in schizophrenic patients. *Journal of Consulting Psychology*, 1964, *28*, 170–77. **348**

Doering, C. H., Kraemer, H. C., Brodie, K. H., and Hamburg, D. A. A cycle of plasma testosterone in the human male. *Journal of Clinical Endocrinology and Metabolism*, 1975, *40*, 492–500. **139**

Doering, C. H., Brodie, H. K. H., Kraemer, H. C., Becker, H. B., and Hamburg, D. A. Plasma testosterone levels and psychologic measures in men over a 2-month period. In R. C. Friedman, R. M. Richart, and R. L. Vande Wiele (Eds.), *Sex differences in behavior*, pp. 413–31. New York: Wiley, 1974. **136**

Doering, C. H., Brodie, H. K. H., Kraemer, H. C., Moos, R. H., Becker, H. B., and Hamburg, D. A. Negative affect and plasma testosterone: A longitudinal human study. *Psychosomatic Medicine*, 1975, *37*, 484–91. **139, 140, 163**

Doherty, E. G. Length of hospitalization on a short-term therapeutic community: A multivariate study by sex across time. *Archives of General Psychology*, 1976, *33*, 87–92. **348**

Doherty, E. G., and Culver, C. Sex-role identification, ability, and achievement among high school girls. *Sociology of Education*, 1976, *49*, 1–3. **239, 256, 274**

Domash, L., and Balter, L. Sex and psychological differentiation in preschoolers. *Journal of Genetic Psychology*, 1976, *128*, 77–84. **185, 189**

Dorfman, P. W. Timing and anticipation: A developmental perspective. *Journal of Motor Behavior*, 1977, *9*, 67–79. **244**

Dornbusch, S. M. Afterword. In E. E. Maccoby (Ed.), *The development of sex differences*, pp. 204–22. Stanford, Calif.: Stanford University Press, 1966. **200**

Dörner, G., Stahl, F., Rohde, W., Halle, H., Rössner, P., Gruber, D., and Herter, U. Radioimmunologische Bestimmung des Testosterongehalts in Fruchtwasser männlicher und weiblicher Feten. *Endokrinologies*, 1973, *61*, 317–20. **47**

Dörner, G., and Staudt, J. Structural changes in the preoptic anterior hypothalamic area of the male rat, following neonatal castration and androgen substitution. *Neuroendocrinology*, 1968, *3*, 136–40. **112**

Doty, R. L. A cry for the liberation of the female rodent: Courtship and copulation in *Rodentia*. *Psychological Bulletin*, 1974, *81*, 159–72. **64, 123**

Doty, R. L., and Silverthorne, C. Influence of menstrual cycle on volunteering behaviour. *Nature*, 1975, *254*, 139–40. **149, 152**

Doughty, C., Booth, J. E., McDonald, P. G., and Parrott, R. F. Effects of oestradiol-17B, oestradiol benzoate and the synthetic oestrogen RU 2858 on sexual differentiation in the neonatal female rat. *Journal of Endocrinology*, 1975, *67*, 419–24. (a) **113**

Doughty, C., Booth, J. E., McDonald, P. G., and Parrott, R. F. Inhibition, by the antioestrogen MER-25, of defeminization induced by the synthetic oestrogen RU 2858. *Journal of Endocrinology*, 1975, *67*, 459–60. (b) **113**

Doughty, C., and McDonald, P. G. Hormonal control of sexual differentiation of the hypothalamus in the neonatal female rat. *Differentiation*, 1974, *2*, 275–85. **113**

Douvan, E. Independence and identity in adolescence. *Children*, 1957, *4*, 186–90. **273, 315**

Douvan, E., and Adelson, J. *The adolescent experience*. New York: Wiley, 1966. **273, 276, 277, 278**

Drewett, R. F. The meal patterns of the oestrous cycle and their motivational significance. *Quarterly Journal of Experimental Psychology*, 1974, *26*, 489–94. **384**

Drinkwater, B. L., Horvath, S. M., and Wells, C. L. Aerobic power in females. *Journal of Gerontology*, January, 1975, pp. 36–38. **320**

Drori, D., and Folman, Y. Environmental effects on longevity in the male rat: Exercise, mating, castration and restricted feeding. *Experimental Gerontology*, 1976, *11*, 25–32. **377, 378, 382**

Dubignon, J., Campbell, D., Curtis, M., and Partington, M. W. The relation between laboratory measures of sucking, food intake, and perinatal factors during the newborn period. *Child Development*, 1969, *40*, 1107–20. **388**

Dubois, P. H. The sex difference on the color-naming test. *American Journal of Psychology*, 1939, *52*, 380–82. **326**

Dubuc, P. U. Body weight regulations in female rats following neonatal testosterone. *Acta Endocrinologica*, 1976, *81*, 215–24. (a) **385**

Dubuc, P. U. Prepubertal estrogen treatment and sematic growth in rats. *Endocrinology*, 1976, *98*, 623–29. (b) **385**

Duke, M. P., and Nowicki, S. Locus of control and achievement—The confirmation of a theoretical expectation. *Journal of Psychology*, 1974, *87*, 263–67. **282**

Dunbar, R. I. M., and Dunbar, E. P. Dominance and reproductive success among female gelada baboons. *Nature*, 1977, *226*, 351–52. **73**

Dunnell, K., and Cartwright, A. *Medicine takers, prescribers and hoarders*. London: Routledge and Kegan Paul, 1972. **377**

Durber, S. M., Lawson, J., and Daly, J. R. The effect of oral contraceptives on plasma cortisol and cortisol binding capacity throughout the menstrual cycle in normal women. *British Journal of Obstetrics and Gynaecology*, 1976, *83*, 814–18. **143**

Dusek, J. B., Mergler, N. L., and Kermis, M. D. Attention, encoding, and information processing in low- and high-test anxious children. *Child Development*, 1976, *47*, 201–7. **253**

Dweck, C. S., and Bush, E. S. Sex differences in learned helplessness, I: Differential

Dweck, C. S. (*Continued*)
debilitation with peer and adult evaluators. *Developmental Psychology,* 1976, *12,* 147–56. **283**

Dweck, C. S., and Repucci, N. D. Learned helplessness and reinforcement responsibility in children. *Journal of Personality and Social Psychology,* 1973, *25,* 109–16. **283**

Dwyer, C. A. Test content and sex differences in reading. *Reading Teacher,* May 1976, pp. 753–57. **238**

Dyk, R. B., and Witkin, H. A. Family experiences related to the development of differentiation in children. *Child Development,* 1965, *36,* 21–55. **246**

Dyrenfurth, I., Jewelewicz, R., Warren, M., Ferin, M., and Vande Wiele, R. L. Temporal relations of hormonal variables in the menstrual cycle. In M. Ferin, F. Halberg, R. M. Richart, and R. L. Vande Wiele (Eds.), *Biorhythms and human reproduction,* pp. 171–201. New York: Wiley, 1974. **146**

East, M. E. The effects of the sex of the defendent, the sex of the subject-juror, and the family status of the defendent on judicial decisions. Paper presented at the meeting of the Midwestern Psychological Association, Chicago, May, 1973. **315**

Eaton, G. Effect of a single prepubertal injection of testosterone propinate on adult bisexual behavior of male hamsters castrated at birth. *Endocrinology,* 1970, *87,* 934–40. **90**

Eaton, G. G., Goy, R. W., and Phoenix, C. H. Effects of testosterone treatment in adulthood on sexual behavior of female pseudohermaphrodite rhesus monkey. *Nature, New Biology,* 1973, *242,* 119–120. **93**

Eaton, G. G., and Resko, J. A. Plasma testosterone and male dominance in a Japanese macaque (*Macaca fuscata*) troop compared with repeated measures of testosterone in laboratory males. *Hormones and Behavior,* 1974, *5,* 251–59. **135**

Edelman, I. S. Mechanism of action of steroid hormones. *Journal of Steroid Biochemistry,* 1975, *6,* 147–59. **42, 120**

Edelman, I. S., and Liebman, J. Anatomy of body water and electrolytes. *American Journal of Medicine,* 1959, *27,* 256–77. **320**

Edelsky, C. Subjective reactions to sex-linked language. *Journal of Social Psychology,* 1976, *99,* 97–104. **308**

Educational Testing Service. *GRE: Guide to the Use of the Graduate Record Examinations, 1973–74.* Princeton, N.J., ETS, 1972. **241**

Edwards, D. A. Mice: Fighting by neonatally androgenized females. *Science,* 1968, *161,* 1027–28. **93**

Edwards, D. A. Early androgen stimulation and aggressive behavior in male and female mice. *Physiology and Behavior,* 1969, *5,* 465–67.

Eeg-Olofsson, O. The development of the EEG in normal adolescents from the age of 16 through 21 years. *Neuropädiatrie,* 1971, *3,* 11–45. **113**

Ehrenkranz, J., Bliss, E., and Sheard, M. H. Plasma testosterone: Correlation with aggressive behavior and social dominance in man. *Psychosomatic Medicine,* 1974, *36,* 469–75. **138, 139, 140**

Ehrhardt, A. A. Maternalism in fetal hormonal and related syndromes. In J. Zubin and J. Money (Eds.), *Contemporary sexual behavior: Critical issues in the 1970's,* pp. 99–115. Baltimore: Johns Hopkins University Press, 1973. **103**

Ehrhardt, A. A. Prenatal hormonal exposure and psychosexual differentiation. In E. J. Sachar (Ed.), *Topics in psychoendocrinology,* pp. 67–82. New York: Grune and Stratton, 1975. **103, 105**

Ehrhardt, A. A., and Baker, S. W. Hormonal aberrations and their implications for the understanding of normal sex differentiation. Paper presented at the meeting of the Society for Research in Child Development, Philadelphia, March, 1973. **103,105**

Ehrhardt, A. A., and Baker, S. W. Fetal androgens, human central nervous system differentiation, and behavior sex differences. In R. C. Friedman, R. M. Richart, and R. L. Vande Wiele (Eds.), *Sex differences in behavior,* pp. 33–51. New York: Wiley, 1974. **103,105**

Ehrhardt, A. A., Epstein, R., and Money, J. Fetal androgens and female gender identity in the early-treated adrenogenital syndrome. *Johns Hopkins Medical Journal,* 1968, *122,* 160–67.

Ehrhardt, A. A., Evers, K., and Money, J. Influence of androgen and some aspects of sexually dimorphic behavior in women with the late treated adrenogenital syndrome. *Johns Hopkins Medical Journal*, 1968, *123*, 115–22. **103, 105, 137**

Ehrhardt, A. A., Grisanti, G. C. and Meyer-Bahlburg, H. F. L. Prenatal exposure to medroxyprogesterone acetate (MPA) in girls. *Psychoneuroendocrinology*, 1977, *2*, 391–98. **105,107**

Ehrhardt, A. A., and Money J. Progestin-induced hermaphroditism: I.Q. and psychosexual identity in a study of ten girls. *Journal of Sex Research*, 1967, *3*, 83–100. **104, 105**

Ehrman, L. Genetics and sexual selection. In B. Campbell (Ed.), *Sexual selection and the descent of man*, pp. 105–35. Chicago: Aldine, 1972. **64**

Ekehammar, B. Sex differences in self-reported anxiety for different situations and modes of response. *Scandinavian Journal of Psychology*, 1974, *15*, 154–60. **335, 336**

Ekehammar, B., Magnusson, D., and Ricklander, L. An interactionist approach to the study of anxiety: An analysis of an S-R inventory applied to an adolescent sample. *Scandinavian Journal of Psychology*, 1974, *15*, 4–14. **336**

Eliasson, M., and Meyerson, B. J. Sexual preference in female rats during estrous cycle, pregnancy and lactation. *Physiology and Behavior*, 1975, *14*, 705–10. **125**

Elliott, C. D. Noise tolerance and extraversion in children. *British Journal of Psychology*, 1971, *62*, 375–80. **323**

Ellis, H. D. Recognizing faces. *British Journal of Psychology*, 1975, *4*, 409–26. **325**

Ellis, H. D., Shepherd, J., and Bruce, A. The effects of age and sex upon adolescents' recognition of faces. *Journal of Genetic Psychology*, 1973, *123*, 173–74. **325**

Ellis, N. W., and Last, S. L. Analysis of the normal EEG. *Lancet*, 1953, *264*, 112–14. **113**

Elmore, P. B., and La Pointe, K. A. Effects of teacher sex and student sex on the evaluation of college instructors. *Journal of Educational Psychology*, 1974, *66*, 386–89. **227**

Elmore, P. B., and La Pointe, K. A. Effects of teacher sex, student sex, and teacher warmth in the evaluation of college instructors. *Journal of Educational Psychology*, 1975, *67*, 368–74. **227**

Elsberg, C. A., Brewer, E. D., and Levy, I. The sense of smell, IV: Concerning conditions which may temporarily alter normal olfactory acuity. *Bulletin of Neurological Institute of New York*, 1936, *4*, 31–34. **153**

Elwood, R. W. Paternal and maternal behaviour in the mongolian gerbil. *Animal Behaviour*, 1975, 23, 766–772. **79**

Eme, R., and Lawrence, L. Fear of success and academic underachievement. *Sex Roles*, 1976, *2*, 269–71. **267**

Engel, P., and Hildebrandt, G. Rhythmic variations in reaction time, heart rate, and blood pressure at different duration of the menstrual cycle. In M. Ferin, F. Halberg, R. M. Richart, and R. L. Vande Wiele (Eds.), *Biorhythms and human reproduction*, pp. 325–33. New York: Wiley, 1974. **146, 147**

Engel, R., Crowell, D., and Nishyima, S. Visual and auditory response latencies In neonates. In *Felicitation volume in honor of C. C. De Silva*. Ceylon: Kularatne, 1968. (Cited by Korner, 1973.) **113**

Erpino, M. J. Androgen-induced aggression in neonataly androgenized female mice: Inhibition by progesterone. *Hormones and Behavior*, 1975, *6*, 149–57. **93, 128**

Erskine, M. S., Stern, J. M., and Levine, S. Effects of prepubertal handling on shock-induced fighting and ACTH in male and female rats. *Physiology and Behavior*, 1975, *14*, 413–20. **321**

Eskilson, A., and Wiley, M. G. Sex composition and leadership in small groups. *Sociometry*, 1976, *39*, 183–94. **297**

Estes, R. D. Behavior and life history of wildebeest. *Nature*, 1966, *212*, 999–1000. **68**

Etaugh, C., and Turton, W. J. Sex differences in discrimination of forms by elementary school children. *Journal of Genetic Psychology*, 1977, *130*, 49–55. **244**

Evans, G. W., and Howard, R. B.. Personal space. *Psychological Bulletin*, 1973, *80*, 334–44. **310**

Eveleth, P. B. Differences between ethnic groups in sex dimorphism of adult height. *Annals of Human Biology*, 1975, *2*, 35–39. **198**

Everitt, B. J., and Herbert, J. Adrenal glands and sexual receptivity in rhesus female monkeys. *Nature,* 1969, *222,* 1065–66. **125, 126**

Exline, R. V. Effects of sex, norms, and affiliation motivation upon accuracy of perceptions of interpersonal preference. *Journal of Personality,* 1960, *28,* 397–412. **303**

Exline, R. V. Visual interaction—The glances of power and preference. In J. K. Cole (Ed.), Nebraska symposium on motivation, 1971, pp. 163–206. Lincoln: University of Nebraska Press, 1972. **311**

Eysenck, S. B. G., and Eysenck, H. J. The personality of female prisoners. *British Journal of Psychiatry,* 1973, *122,* 693–98. **335**

Fagan, J. F. III. Infants' recognition memory for faces. *Journal of Experimental Child Psychology,* 1972, *14,* 453–76. **325**

Fagan, J. F. III. Infants' delayed recognition memory and forgetting. *Journal of Experimental Child Psychology,* 1973, *16,* 424–50. **326**

Fagot, B. I., and Littman, I. Relation of preschool sex-typing and intellectual performance in elementary school. *Psychological Reports,* 1976, *39,* 699–704. **248**

Fagot, B. I., and Patterson, G. R. An *in vivo* analysis of reinforcing contingencies for sex-role behaviors in the preschool child. *Developmental Psychology,* 1969, *1,* 563–68. **185, 210**

Fairweather, H., and Hutt, S. J. Sex differences in a perceptual-motor skill in children. In C. Ounsted and D. C. Taylor (Eds.), *Gender differences: Their ontogeny and significance,* pp. 159–75. London: Churchill Livingstone, 1972. **327**

Falbo, T. The effects of sex and "masculinity" on person- and space-related perception. *Sex Roles,* 1975, *1,* 283–95. **304**

Falvo, R. E., Buhl, A., and Nalbandov, A. V. Testosterone concentrations in the peripheral plasma of androgenized female rats and in the estrous cycle of normal rats. *Endocrinology,* 1974, *5,* 26–29.

Feather, N. T., and Simon, J. G. Reactions to male and female success and failure in sex-linked occupations: Impressions of personality, causal attributions, and perceived likelihood of different consequences. *Journal of Personality and Social Psychology,* 1975, *31,* 20–31. **225, 227, 283**

Feder, H. H., Naftolin, F., and Ryan, K. J. Male and female sexual responses in male rats given estradiol benzoate and 52-androstan 17β-ol-3-one propinate. *Endocrinology,* 1974, *94,* 136–41. **124**

Feder, H. H., Phoenix, C. H., and Young, W. C. Suppression of feminine behavior by administration of testosterone propionate to neonatal rats. *Journal of Endocrinology,* 1966, *34,* 131–32. **90**

Feinblatt, J. A., and Gold, A. R. Sex roles and the psychiatric referral process. *Sex Roles,* 1976, *2,* 109–22. **348, 351**

Feldman-Summers, S., and Kiester, S. B. Those who are number two try harder: The effect of sex on attributions of casualty. *Journal of Personality and Social Psychology,* 1974, *30,* 846–55. **225**

Feldstein, J. H. Sex differences in social memory among preschool children. *Sex Roles,* 1976, *2,* 75–79.

Ferguson, L. R., and Maccoby, E. E. Interpersonal correlates of differential abilities. *Child Development,* 1966, *37,* 549–71. **248**

Ferin, M., Halberg, F., Richart, R. M., and Vande Wiele, R. L. (Eds.) *Biorhythms and human reproduction.* New York: Wiley, 1974. **145**

Fessler, R. G., and Beatty, W. W. Variations in postweaning environment and sensitivity to electric shock in male and female rats. *Behavioral Biology,* 1976, *16,* 535–38. **82**

Filene, P. G. *Him her self.* New York: Harcourt, Brace, Jovanovich, 1974. **359, 362**

Finney, H. C., and Erpino, M. J. Synergistic effect of estradiol benzoate and dihydrotestosterone on aggression in mice. *Hormones and Behavior,* 1976, *7,* 391–400. **128**

Fisher, J. D., and Byrne, D. Too close for comfort: Sex differences in response to invasions of personal space. *Journal of Personality and Social Psychology,* 1975, *32,* 15–21. **309**

Flavell, G. Webbing of the neck, with Turner's

syndrome in the male. *British Journal of Surgery*, 1943, *37*, 150–53. **32**

Floody, O. R., and Pfaff, D. W. Aggressive behavior in female hamsters: The hormonal basis for fluctuations in female aggressiveness correlated with estrous state. *Journal of Comparative and Physiological Psychology*, 1977, *91*, 443–64. **127, 128, 129**

Flora, C. B. The passive female: Her comparative image by class and culture in women's magazine fiction. *Journal of Marriage and the Family*, 1971, p. 33, 435–44. **214**

Ford, C. S., and Beach, F. *Patterns of sexual behavior.* New York: Harper and Row, 1951. **203**

Ford, D. Private Communication to K. B. Hoyenga.

Fortune, R. F. Arapesh warfare. *American Anthropologist*, 1939, *41*, 22–41. **199**

Fox, C. A., Ismail, A. A. A., Love, D. N., Kirkham, K. E., and Loraine, J. A. Studies in the relationship between plasma testosterone levels and human sexual activity. *Journal of Endocrinology*, 1972, *52*, 51–58. **136**

Frank, R. T. The hormonal causes of premenstrual tension. *Archives of Neurology and Psychiatry*, 1931, *26*, 1053–57. **154**

Frankenhaeuser, M., Dunne, E., and Lundberg, U. Sex differences in sympathetic-adrenal medullary reactions induced by different stressors. *Psychopharmacology*, 1976, *47*, 1–5. **321**

Franzwa, H. H. Female roles in women's magazine fiction, 1940–1970. In R. K. Unger and F. L. Denmark (Eds.), *Woman: Dependent or independent variable?*, pp. 42–53. New York: Psychological Dimensions, 1975. **214**

Fraser, G. R. Parental origin of the sex chromosomes in the XO and XXY karyotypes in man. *Annals of Human Genetics*, 1963, *26*, 297. **30**

Fraser, J. The female alcoholic. *Addictions*, 1973, *20*, 64–80. **226**

Fraser, W. The alcoholic woman: Attitudes and perspectives. In A. MacLennan (Ed.), *Women: Their use of alcohol and other legal drugs*, pp. 45–56. Toronto: Addiction Research Foundation Press, 1976. **343**

Freedman, J. L. Increasing creativity by free-association training. *Journal of Experimental Psychology*, 1965, *69*, 89–91. **254**

Fregly, M. J. Effect of an oral contraceptive on NaCl appetite and preference threshold in rats. *Pharmacology, Biochemistry and Behavior*, 1973, *1*, 61–65. **383**

Freire-Maia, A., Freire-Maia, D. V., and Morton, N. E. Sex effect on intelligence and mental retardation. *Behavior Genetics*, 1974, *4*, 269–72. **42**

French, E. G. Development of a measure of complex motivation. In J. W. Atkinson (Ed.), *Motives in fantasy, action, and society*, pp. 242–48. Princeton, N.J.: Van Nostrand, 1958. **264**

French, E. G., and Lesser, G. S. Some characteristics of the achievement motive in women. *Journal of Abnormal and Social Psychology*, 1964, *68*, 119–28. **274**

Freud, S. Some psychological consequences of the anatomical distinction between the sexes. *International Journal of Psychoanalysis*, 1927, *8*, 133–42. **178, 180, 328**

Freud, S. Female sexuality. In J. Strachey (Ed.), *Sigmund Freud: Collected papers.* (Vol. 5, pp. 252–72.) New York: Basic Books, 1959. (a) **178, 187, 328**

Freud, S. 'Civilized' sexual morality and modern nervousness. In E. Jones (Ed.), *The collected papers of Sigmund Freud*, pp. 76–99. New York: Basic Books, 1959b. **178, 328**

Freud, S. *New introductory lectures on psychoanalysis.* New York: Norton, 1965. (Originally published 1933.) **178, 327**

Freuh, T., and McGhee, P. E. Traditional sex role development and amount of time spent watching television. *Child Development*, 1975, *11*, 109. **217**

Fricke, H., and Fricke, S. Monogamy and sex change by aggressive dominance in coral reef fish. *Nature*, 1977, *226*, 830–32. **121**

Friedman, R. C., Richart, R. M., and Vande Wiele, R. L. (Eds.) *Sex differences in behavior.* New York: Wiley, 1974. **143**

Friedman, R. C., and Tendler, R. Discussion: Gender identity. In R. C. Friedman, R. M. Richart, and R. L. Vande Wiele (Eds.), *Sex differences in behavior*, pp. 327–31. New York: Wiley, 1974. **146, 147, 177**

Friedrich, L. K. Achievement motivation in college women revisited: Implications for

Friedrich, L. K. (*Continued*)
women, men, and the gathering of coconuts. *Sex Roles*, 1976, *2*, 47–61. **275**

Frieze, I. H. Women's expectations for and causal attributions of success and failure. In M. T. S. Mednick, S. S. Tangri, and L. W. Hoffman (Eds.), *Women and achievement: Social and motivational analyses,* pp. 158–71. New York: Halsted, 1975. **281, 283**

Frodi, A. Sex differences in perception of a provocation, a survey. *Perceptual and Motor Skills*, 1977, *44*, 113–14. **291**

Furman, R. H. Coronary heart disease and the menopause. In R. J. Ryan and D. C. Gibson (Eds.), *Menopause and aging,* pp. 39–55. Bethesda, Md.: National Institute for Mental Health, 1971. **379, 383**

Gabric̆, D., and Soljac̆ic, M. Effect of gonadectomy on taste preference for glucose solutions in rats. *Physiology and Behavior*, 1975, *15*, 145–48. **381**

Gadpaille, W. J. Research into the physiology of maleness and femaleness: Its contributions to the etiology and psychodynamics of homosexuality. *Archives of General Psychiatry*, 1972, *26*, 193–206. **374**

Gair, R. B. The high cost of losing. *Research Reporter*, 1975, *9*, 8–9. **122**

Galenson, E., and Roiphe, H. The emergence of genital awareness during the second year of life. In R. C. Friedman, R. M. Richart, and R. L. Vande Wiele (Eds.), *Sex differences in behavior,* pp. 223–31. New York: Wiley, 1974. **182**

Gandelman, R., and vom Saal, F. S. Pup-killing in mice: The effects of gonadectomy and testosterone administration. *Physiology and Behavior*, 1975, *15*, 647–51. **128**

Garai, J. E., and Scheinfeld, A. Sex differences in mental and behavioral traits. *Genetic Psychology Monographs*, 1968, *77*, 169–299. **237, 249, 261, 322, 323, 325, 326, 327**

Garrett, G. R., and Bahr, H. M. The family backgrounds of skid row women. *Signs: Journal of Women in Culture and Society*, 1976, *2*, 369–81. **335**

Garron, D. C. Sex-linked, recessive inheritance of spatial and numerical abilities, and

Turner's syndrome. *Psychological Review*, 1970, *77*, 147–52. **42**

Garske, J. P. Sex differences in cross-situational consistencies of personality traits. Paper presented at the Midwestern Psychological Association Convention, Chicago, May, 1977. **223**

Geffner, D. S., and Hochberg, I. Ear laterality performance of children from low and middle socioeconomic levels on a verbal dichotic listening task. *Cortex*, 1971, *7*, 193–203. **258**

Gentry, R. T., and Wade, G. N. Sex differences in sensitivity of food intake, body weight, and running-wheel activity to ovarian steroids in rats. *Journal of Comparative and Physiological Psychology*, 1976, *90*, 747–54. **383**

Gerall, A. A., Dunlap, J. L., and Wagner, R. A. Effects of dihydrotestosterone and gonadotropins on the development of female behavior. *Physiology and Behavior*, 1976, *17*, 121–26. **113**

Gerall, A. A., McMurray, M. M., and Farrell, A. Suppression of the development of female hamster behavior by implants of testosterone and non-aromatizable androgens administered neonatally. *Journal of Endocrinology*, 1975, *67*, 439–45. **113**

Gerall, A. A., and Thiel, A. R. Effects of perinatal gonadal secretions on parameters of receptivity and weight gain in hamsters. *Journal of Comparative and Physiological Psychology*, 1975, *89*, 580–89. **383, 385**

Gersoni-Stavn, D. (Ed.) *Sexism and youth.* New York: Bowker, 1974. **216**

Ghent, L. Developmental changes in tactual thresholds on dominant and nondominant sides. *Journal of Comparative and Physiological Psychology*, 1961, *54*, 670–73. **258**

Gibson, H. B., and Corcoran, M. E. Personality and differential susceptibility to hypnosis: Further replication and sex differences. *British Journal of Psychology*, 1975, *66*, 513–20. **337**

Gingrich, D. D. Sex, grade level, and religious-educational environment as factors in peer conformity. *Journal of Genetic Psychology*, 1973, *123*, 321–28. **294**

Ginn, R. O. Male and female estimates of

personal problems of men and women, *Journal of Counseling Psychology*, 1975, *22*, 518–22.(a) **351**

Ginn, R. O. Psychological androgyny and self-actualization. *Psychological Reports*, 1975, *37*, 886.(b) **224**

Glenn, N. D. Psychological well-being in the post-parental stage: Some evidence from national surveys. *Journal of Marriage and the Family*, 1975, *37*, 105–10. **339**

Glick, I. D. Mood and behavioral changes associated with the use of the oral contraceptive agents. *Psychopharmacologia*, 1967, *10*, 363–74. **140**

Goldberg, P. A. Are women prejudiced against women? *Transaction*, 1968, *5*, 28–30. **225**

Goldberg, P. A. Prejudice toward women: Some personality correlates. Paper presented at the meeting of the American Psychological Association, Hawaii, September, 1972. **216, 225**

Goldberg, S., and Lewis, M. Play behavior in the year-old infant: Early sex differences. In J. M. Bardwick (Ed.), *Readings on the psychology of women*, pp. 30–34. New York: Harper and Row, 1972. **208, 301**

Goldblatt, P. B., Moore, M. E., and Stunkard, A. J. Social factors in obesity. In N. Kiell (Eds.), *The psychology of obesity*, pp. 57–66. Springfield, Ill.: Thomas, 1973. **376, 377**

Goldman, P. S., Crawford, H. T., Stokes, L. P., Galkin, T. W., and Rosvold, I I. E. Sex-dependent behavioral effects of cerebral cortical lesions in developing rhesus monkey. *Science*, 1974, *186*, 540–42. **81**

Goldstein, A. G., and Chance, J. E. Effects of practice on sex-related differences in performance on embedded figures. *Psychonomic Science*, 1963, *3*, 361–62. **254**

Goldstein, A. G., and Chance, J. E. Visual recognition memory for complex configurations. *Perception and Psychophysics*, 1970, *9*, 237–41. **323**

Goldzieher, J. W., Moses, L. E., Averkin, E., Scheel, C., and Taber, B. Z. A placebo-controlled double-blind crossover investigation of the side effects attributed to oral contraceptives. *Fertility and Sterility*, 1971, *22*, 609–23. **144**

Golub, S. The magnitude of premenstrual

anxiety and depression. *Psychosomatic Medicine*, 1976, *38*, 4–12. **157, 159**

Gomes, B., and Abramowitz, S. I. Sex-related patient and therapist effects on clinical judgment. *Sex Roles*, 1976, *2*, 1–13. **347, 348**

Good, P. R., Geary, N., and Engen, T. The effect of estrogen on odor detection. *Chemical Senses and Flavor*, 1976, *2*, 45–50. **151, 153, 324**

Goodall, J. Chimpanzees of the Gombe Stream Reserve. In I. DeVore (Ed.), *Primate behavior*. New York: Holt, Rinehart and Winston, 1965. **72**

Goodenough, E. W. Interest in persons as an aspect of sex differences in the early years. *Genetic Psychology Monographs*, 1957, *55*, 287–323. **207**

Gordon, T. P., Rose, R. M., and Bernstein, I. S. Seasonal rhythm in plasma testosterone levels in the rhesus monkey (*Macaca mulatta*): A three year study. *Hormones and Behavior*, 1976, *7*, 229–43. **165, 361**

Gorski, R. A. The possible neural sites of hormonal facilitation of sexual behavior in the female rat. *Psychoneuroendocrinology*, 1976, *1*, 371–87. **121**

Gorzalka, B. B., Rezak, D. L., and Whalen, R. E. Adrenal mediation of estrogen-induced ejaculatory behavior in the male rat. *Physiology and Behavior*, 1975, *14*, 373–76. **118, 124**

Gough, K. The origin of the family. *Journal of Marriage and the Family*, November, 1971, pp. 760–71. **199**

Gouldner, A. W., and Peterson, R. A. *Notes on technology and the moral order*. Indianapolis: Bobbs-Merrill, 1963. **199**

Gove, W. R. The relationship between sex roles, marital status, and mental illness. *Social Forces*, 1972, *51*, 34–44. **345, 350**

Gove, W. R. Sex, marital status, and mortality. *American Journal of Sociology*, 1973, *79*, 45–67. **68, 344, 350, 351, 379**

Gove, W. R., and Tudor, J. F. Adult sex roles and mental illness. *American Journal of Sociology*, 1973, *78*, 812–35. **350**

Goy, R. W. Organizing effects of androgen on the behavior of rhesus monkeys. In R. P. Michael (Ed.), *Endocrinology and human behavior*, pp. 12–31. London: Oxford University Press, 1968. **70, 90**

Goy, R. W. Early hormonal influences on the development of sexual and sex-related behavior. In F. O. Schmitt (Ed.), *The neurosciences: Second study program*, pp. 199–207. New York: Rockefeller University Press, 1970. **70, 90, 93, 94**

Goy, R. W. The role of fetal hormones and early social experience on psychosexual orientation. Abstract of a paper presented at the Seminar on Long-Term Effects of Perinatal Hormone Administration, Tokyo, September, 1972. **87**

Goy, R. W., and Goldfoot, D. A. Experiential and hormonal factors influencing development of sexual behavior in the male rhesus monkey. In F. O. Schmitt and F. G. Worden (Eds.), *The neurosciences: Third study program*, pp. 571–81. Cambridge, Mass.: MIT Press, 1974. **90, 98, 236**

Goy, R. W., and Goldfoot, D. A. Neuroendocrinology: Animal models and problems of human sexuality. *Archives of Sexual Behavior*, 1975, *4*, 405–20. **69, 91**

Grady, K. L., Phoenix, C. H., and Young, W. C. Role of the developing rat testes in differentiation of the neural tissues mediating sexual behavior. *Journal of Comparative and Physiological Psychology*, 1965, *59*, 176–82. **90**

Gram, T. E., and Gillette, J. R. The role of sex hormones in the metabolism of drugs and other foreign compounds by hepatic microsomal enzymes. In H. A. Salhanick, D. M. Kipnis, and R. L. Vande Wiele (Eds.), *Metabolic effects of gonadal hormones and contraceptive steroids*, pp. 86–94. New York: Plenum Press, 1969. **321**

Grant, E. C. G., and Pryse-Davies, J. Effect of oral contraceptives on depressive mood changes and on endometrial monoamine oxidase and phosphates. *British Medical Journal*, 1968, *3*, 777–80. **144**

Gray, J. A. *The psychology of fear and stress*. New York: McGraw-Hill, 1971.(a) **75, 236, 335**

Gray, J. A. Sex differences in emotional behaviour in mammals including man: Endocrine basis. *Acta Psychologica*, 1971, *35*, 29–46.(b) **71, 73, 75, 98, 123, 132, 255, 321**

Gray, J. A., and Buffery, A. W. H. Sex differences in emotional and cognitive behaviour in mammals including man: Adaptive and neural bases. *Acta Psychologica*, 1971,*35*, 89–111. **76, 255, 256**

Gray, J. A., and Drewett, R. F. The genetics and development of sex differences. In R. B. Cattell and R. Dreger (Eds.), *Handbook of modern personality theory*. New York: Appleton-Century-Crofts, in press. **39, 92**

Gray, J. A., Drewett, R. F., and Lalljee, B. Effects of neonatal castration and testosterone injection on adult open-field behaviour in rats with atypical sex differences in defecation. *Animal Behaviour*, 1975, *23*, 773–78. **98**

Gray, J. A. and Lalljee, B. Sex differences in emotional behaviour in the rat: Correlation between open-field defecation and active avoidance. *Animal Behaviour*, 1974, *22*, 856–61. **75, 80**

Gray, J. A., Leon, J., and Keynes, A. Infant androgen treatment and adult open-field behavior: Direct effects and effects of injections to siblings. *Physiology and Behavior*, 1969, *4*, 177–81. **385**

Gray, P. Effect of the estrous cycle on conditioned avoidance in mice. *Hormones and Behavior*, 1977, *8*, 325–41. **132, 133, 134**

Green, R. *Sexual identity conflict in children and adults*. Baltimore: Penguin, 1974. **176, 177, 193, 248**

Greenberg, M., Rosenberg, I., and Lind, J. First mothers rooming-in with their newborns: Its impact on the mother. *American Journal of Orthopsychiatry*, 1973, *43*, 783–88. **306**

Greenblatt, R. B., Oettinger, M., and Bohler, C. S. S. Estrogen-androgen levels in aging men and women: Therapeutic considerations. *Journal of the American Geriatric Society*, 1976, *24*, 173–78. **165, 166**

Greene, L. S., Desor, J. A., and Maller, O. Heredity and experience: Their relative importance in the development of taste preference in man. *Journal of Comparative and Physiological Psychology*, 1975, *89*, 279–84. **388**

Greenough, W. T., Carter, C. S., Steerman, C., and DeVoogd, T. J. Sex differences in dendritic patterns in hamster preoptic area. *Brain Research*, 1977, *126*, 63–72. **112**

Greidanus, T. B. W. V. Pregnene-type steroids and impairment of passive avoidance behavior in rats. *Hormones and Behavior,* 1977, *9,* 49–56. **133**

Griffiths, A. W., Richards, B. W., Zaremba, J., Abramowicz, T., and Stewart, A. Psychological and sociological investigation of XYY prisoners. *Nature,* 1970, *227,* 290–92. **38**

Griffitt, W. Response to erotica and the projection of response to erotica in the opposite sex. *Journal of Experimental Research in Personality,* 1973, *6,* 330–38. **330**

Griffitt, W. Sexual experience and sexual responsiveness: Sex differences. *Archives of Sexual Behavior,* 1975, *4,* 529–40. **330, 331**

Gross, A. In the section called "From the APA notebook." *Behavior Today,* 1972, *3,* 2. **315**

Grounds, D., Davies, B., and Mowbray, R. The contraceptive pill, side effects and personality: Report of a controlled double blind trial. *British Journal of Psychiatry,* 1970, *116,* 169–72. **144**

Guardo, C. J. Personal space in children. *Child Development,* 1969, *40,* 143–51. **309**

Guardo, C. J., and Meisels, M. Factor structure of children's personal space schemata. *Child Development,* 1971, *42,* 1307–12. **309**

Gummow, L. J. Postnatal androgenization influences social behavior of adult rats tested in standard male and female sexual paradigms. *Behavioral Biology,* 1975, *13,* 385–99. **100**

Gump, J. P. Sex-role attitudes and psychological well-being. *Journal of Social Issues,* 1972, *28,* 79–92. **338**

Gurwitz, S. B., and Dodge, K. A. Adult's evaluations of a child as a function of sex of adult and sex of child. *Journal of Personality and Social Psychology,* 1975, *32,* 822–28. **227**

Gustafsson, J. Å., Gustafsson, S. A., Ingelman-Sundberg, M., and Stenberg, Å. Neonatal differentiation of hepatic steroid metabolism in the rat. *International Symposium on Sexual Endocrinology,* 1974, *32,* 233–44. **87**

Guttman, D. Women and the concepts of ego strength. *Merrill-Palmer Quarterly of Behavior and Development,* 1965, *2,* 229–40. **200**

Guttman, R. Genetic analysis of analytical spatial ability: Raven's Progressive Matrices. *Behavior Genetics,* 1974, *4,* 273–84. **42**

Guttman, R., Lieblich, I., and Gross R., Behavioral correlates of estrous cycle stages in laboratory mice. *Behavioral Biology,* 1975, *13,* 127–132. **132**

Gyermek, L. Pregnanolone: A highly potent, naturally occurring hypnotic anesthetic agent. *Medical Proceedings of the Society for Experimental Biology,* 1967 *125,* 1058–62. **121, 133**

Haas, R. Sexual selection in *Nothobranchius guentheri* (Pisces: Cyprinodontidae). *Evolution,* 1976, *30,* 614–22. **69**

Haavio-Mannila, E. Convergences between East and West: Tradition and modernity in sex roles in Sweden, Finland, and the Soviet Union. *Acta Sociologica,* 1971, *14,* 114–25. **202**

Haccoun, D. M., Allen, J. G., and Fader, S. The effects of sex and emotion on selection of helping responses by peers. *Journal of Counseling Psychology,* 1976, *23,* 17–21. **307**

Hacker, H. M. Women as a minority group. *Social Forces,* 1951, *30,* 60–69. **227**

Hacker, H. M. Women as a minority group twenty years later. In R. K. Unger and F. I. Denmark (Eds.), *Women: Dependent or independent variable?,* pp. 103–12. New York: Psychological Dimensions, 1975. **228**

Hakstian, A. R., and Cattell, R. B. An examination of adolescent sex differences in some ability and personality traits. *Canadian Journal of Behavioral Science,* 1975, *7,* 295–312. **211, 237, 244, 253, 295, 326**

Halas, C. M. Sex-role stereotypes: Perceived childhood socialization experiences and the attitudes and behavior of adult women. *Journal of Psychology,* 1974, *88,* 261–75. **278**

Hall, C. A modest confirmation of Freud's theory of a distinction between the superego of men and women. *Journal of Abnormal and Social Psychology,* 1964, *69,* 440–42. **181**

Hall, K. R. L. Behavior and ecology of the wild patas monkey (*Erythrocebus patas*) in Vgonda. *Journal of Zoology,* 1966, *148,* 15–87.   **77**

Hall, K. R. L., and DeVore, I. Baboon social behavior. In I. DeVore (Ed.) *Primate behavior.* New York: Holt, Rinehart, and Winston, 1965.   **73**

Hall, K. R. L., and Mayer, B. Social interactions in a group of captive patas monkeys (*Erythrocebus patas*). *Folia Primatologica,* 1967, *5,* 213–36.   **72**

Hall, M. C., and Van de Castle, R. L. *The content analysis of dreams.* New York: Appleton-Century-Crofts, 1966.   **181**

Hamburg, D. A. Psychobiological studies of aggressive behavior. *Nature,* 1971, *230,* 19–23.   **73**

Hamburg, D. A., Moos, R. H., and Yalom, I. D. Studies of distress in the menstrual cycle and the postpartum period. In R. P. Michael (Ed.), *Endocrinology and human behavior,* pp. 94–116. London: Oxford University Press, 1968.   **149, 150, 158, 160**

Hamerton, J. L., Canning, N., Ray, M., and Smith, S. A cytogenetic survey of 14,069 newborn infants. *Clinical Genetics,* 1975, *8,* 223–43.   **29, 30, 33, 36, 38**

Hamilton, J. B. The role of testicular secretions as indicated by the effects of castration in man and by studies of pathological conditions and short lifespan associated with maleness. *Recent Progress in Hormone Research,* 1948, *3,* 257–322.   **68, 373, 374, 376, 378, 382, 388**

Hamilton, J. B., Hamilton, R. S., and Mestler, G. E. Duration of life and causes of death in domestic cats: Influences of sex, gonadectomy, and inbreeding. *Journal of Gerontology,* 1969, *24,* 427–37.   **68, 377**

Hamilton, J. B., and Mestler, G. E. Mortality and survival: Comparison of eunuchs with intact men and women in a mentally retarded population. *Journal of Gerontology,* 1969, *24,* 395–411.   **68, 377**

Harding, C. F., and Feder, H. H. Relation between individual differences in sexual behavior and plasma testosterone levels in the guinea pig. *Endocrinology,* 1976, *98,* 1198–1205.   **122**

Hardyck, C., Goldman, R., and Petrinovich, L. Handedness and sex, race, and age. *Human Biology,* 1975, *47,* 369–75.   **258**

Harford, T. C., Willis, C. H., and Deabler, H. L. Personality correlates of masculinity-femininity. *Psychological Reports,* 1967, *21,* 881–84.   **341**

Hariton, E. B., and Singer, J. L. Women's fantasies during sexual intercourse: Normative and theoretical implications. *Journal of Consulting and Clinical Psychology,* 1974, *42,* 313–22.   **331**

Harkness, R..A. Variations in testosterone excretion by man. In M. Ferin, F. Halberg, R. M. Richart, and R. L. Vande Wiele (Eds.), *Biorhythms and human reproduction,* pp. 469–78. New York: Wiley, 1974.   **163**

Harley, J. P., Kalish, D. I., and Silverman, A. J. Eye movements and sex differences in field articulation. *Perceptual and Motor Skills,* 1974, *38,* 615–22.   **252**

Harlow, H. F. Sexual behavior in the rhesus monkey. In F. A. Beach (Ed.), *Sex and behavior,* pp. 234–265. New York: Wiley, 1965.   **72, 73, 77**

Harlow, H. F., and Lauersdorf, H. E. Sex differences in passion and play. *Perspectives in Biology and Medicine,* 1974, *17,* 348–60.   **73**

Harris, G. W. Sex hormones, brain development and brain function. *Endocrinology,* 1964, *75,* 627–48.   **90, 385**

Harris, G. W., and Jacobsohn, D. Functional grafts of the anterior pituitary gland. *Proceedings of the Royal Society of London,* 1952, *139,* Series B, 263–76.   **55**

Harris, G. W., and Levine, S. Sexual differentiation of the brain and its experimental control. *Journal of Physiology,* 1965, *18,* 379–400.   **91**

Harris, L., and Associates. *The Virginia Slims women's opinion poll.* 1970.   **331, 363**

Harris, L. J. Sex differences in spatial ability: Possible environmental, genetic and neurological factors. In M. Kinsbourne (Ed.), *Hemispheric, asymmetrics of function.* Cambridge, Eng.: Cambridge University Press, in press.   **259**

Harris, M. B. Mediators between frustration and aggression in a field experiment. *Journal of Experimental Social Psychology,* 1974, *10,* 561–71.   **90, 292, 293**

Harris, M. B. The effects of sex, sex-stereotyped descriptions and institution on evaluations of teachers. *Sex Roles*, 1976, *2*, 15–21. **227**

Harris, S. Influence of subject and experimenter sex in psychological research. *Journal of Consulting and Clinical Psychology*, 1971, *37*, 291–94. **19**

Hart, B. J. L. Gonadal androgen and sociosexual behavior of male mammals: A comparative analysis. *Psychological Bulletin*, 1974, *81*, 383–400. **124, 127, 128**

Hart, B. L. Neonatal dihydrotestosterone and estrogen stimulation: Effects on sexual behavior of male rats. *Hormones and Behavior*, 1977, *8*, 193–200. **385**

Hartlage, L. C. Sex-linked inheritance of spatial ability. *Perceptual and Motor Skills*, 1970, *31*, 610. **42**

Hartley, R. E. Children's concepts of male and female roles. *Merrill-Palmer Quarterly*, 1959, *6*, 83–91. (a) **182, 217**

Hartley, R. E. Sex role pressures and the socialization of the male child. *Psychological Reports*, 1959, *5*, 457–68. (b) **193**

Hatotani, N. Endocrinological studies on periodic psychosis. In K. Lissák (Ed.), *Hormones and brain function*. New York: Plenum Press, 1973. **155**

Hattendorf, K. W. A study of the questions of young children concerning sex: A phase of an experimental approach to parent education. *Journal of Social Psychology*, 1932, *3*, 37–65. **183**

Hawkins, R. A., and Oakey, R. E. Estimation of oestrone sulphate, oestradiol-17β and oestrone in peripheral plasma: Concentrations during the menstrual cycle and in men. *Journal of Endocrinology*, 1974, *60*, 3–17. **50**

Hayashi, S. Failure of intrahypothalamic implants of an estrogen antagonist, ethamoxytriphetol (MER-25), to block neonatal androgen-sterilization. *Proceedings of the Society for Experimental Biology and Medicine*, 1976, *152*, 389–92. **113**

Hayman, A. S. Legal challenges to discrimination against men. In D. S. David and R. Brannon (Eds.), *The forty-nine percent majority: The male sex role*, pp. 297–320.

Reading, Mass.: Addison-Wesley, 1976. **226**

Heilbrun, A. B., Jr. Sex differences in identification learning. *Journal of Genetic Psychology*, 1965, *106*, 185–93. **182**

Heilbrun, A. B., Jr. Sex-role identity in adolescent females: A theoretical paradox. *Adolescence*, 1968, *3*, 79–88. (a) **341**

Heilbrun, A. B., Jr. Sex role, instrumental-expressive behavior, and psychopathology in females. *Journal of Abnormal Psychology*, 1968, *73*, 131–36. (b) **182, 223, 341**

Heilbrun, A. B., Jr. Parent identification and filial sex-role behavior: The importance of biological context. In J. K. Cole and R. Dienstbier (Eds.), *Nebraska symposium on motivation, 1973*, pp. 125–94. Lincoln: University of Nebraska Press, 1974. **182, 190, 194, 210, 341**

Heilbrun, A. B., Jr. Identification with the father and sex-role development of the daughter. *Family Coordinator*, October, 1976, pp. 411–16. (a) **210, 341**

Heilbrun, A. B., Jr. Measurement of masculine and feminine sex role identities as independent dimensions. *Journal of Consulting and Clinical Psychology*, 1976, *44*, 183–90. (b) **341**

Heilman, R. D., Brugmans, M., Greenslade, Imperato-McGinley, J., Peterson, R. E., and androgen-mediated aggressive behavior in mice to flutamide, an anti-androgen. *Psychopharmacology*, 1976, *47*, 75–80. **128**

Helmreich, R., and Stapp, J. Short forms of the Texas Social Behavior Inventory (TSBI), an objective measure of self-esteem. *Bulletin of the Psychonomic Society*, 1974, *4*, 473–75. **336**

Helson, R. Women mathematicians and the creative personality. *Journal of Consulting and Clinical Psychology*, 1971, *36*, 210–20. **256**

Helzer, J. E., and Winokur, G. A. Family interview study of male manic-depressives. *Archives of General Psychiatry*, 1974, *31*, 73–77. **352**

Henderson, L. F., and Lyons, D. J. Sexual differences in human crowd motion. *Nature*, 1972, *240*, 353–55. **310**

Hendricks, S. E., and Weltin, M. Effect of estrogen given during various periods of prepuberal life on the sexual behavior of rats. *Physiological Psychology*, 1976, *4*, 105–10. **91**

Henkin, R. I. Sensory changes during the menstrual cycle. In M. Ferin, F. Halberg, R. M. Richart, and R. L. Vande Wiele (Eds.), *Biorhythms and human reproduction*, pp. 277–85. New York: Wiley, 1974. **150, 151, 153**

Henley, N. M. Status and sex: Some touching observations. *Bulletin of the Psychonomic Society*, 1973, *2*, 91–93. **311**

Henshel, A. M. Swinging: A study of decision making in marriage. In J. Huber (Ed.), *Changing women in a changing society*, pp. 123–29. Chicago: University of Chicago Press, 1973. **297**

Herbert, J. Hormones and reproductive behavior in rhesus and talapin monkeys. *Journal of Reproduction and Fertility*, 1970, *11* (Suppl.), 119–40. **125, 126**

Herbert, J., and Trimble, M. R. Effect of oestradial and testosterone on the sexual receptivity and attractiveness of the female rhesus monkey. *Nature*, 1967, *216*, 165–66. **125, 126**

Herman, B. H., and Hyde, J. S. Effects of chronic testosterone administration on fighting behavior in adult female wild mice genetically selected for differences in agression. Paper presented at the meeting of the Midwestern Psychological Association, Chicago, May, 1976. **128, 130**

Hetherington, E. M. A developmental study of the effects of sex of the dominant parent on sex-role preference identification and imitation in children. *Journal of Personality and Social Psychology*. 1965, *2*, 188–94. **185, 189, 190, 210**

Hewes, G. W. The anthropology of posture. *Scientific American*, 1957, *196*, 123–32. **310**

Hicks, R. E., and Kinsbourne, M. Human handedness: A partial cross-fostering study. *Science*, 1976, *192*, 908–10. **258**

Hilger, W. N., Jr., and Rowe, F. A. Olfactory bulb ablation: Effects on handling reactivity, open-field behavior, and agonistic behavior in male and female hamsters *Physiological Psychology*, 1975, *3*, 162–68. **112**

Hill, C. T., Rubin, Z., and Peplau, L. A. Breakups before marriage: The end of 103 affairs. *Journal of Social Issues*, 1976, *32*, 147–68. **347**

Hill, M. K., and Lando, H. A. Physical attractiveness and sex-role stereotypes in impression formation. *Perceptual and Motor Skills*, 1976, *43*, 1251–55. **314**

Hinsull, S. M., and Bellamy, D. Development and involution of thymus grafts in rats with reference to age and sex. *Differentiation*, 1974, *2*, 299–305. **376**

Hochreich, D. J. Sex-role stereotypes for internal-external control and interpersonal trust. *Journal of Consulting and Clinical Psychology*, 1975, *43*, 273. **282**

Hochschild, A. R. A review of sex role research. *American Journal of Sociology*, 1973, *78*, 1011–29. **18, 316**

Hoffman, L. R., and Maier, N. R. F. Social factors influencing problem solving in women. *Journal of Personality and Social Psychology*, 1966, *4*, 382–90. **253, 254**

Hoffman, L. W. Early childhood experiences and women's achievement motives. *Journal of Social Issues*, 1972, *28*, 129–55. **265, 271**

Hoffman, L. W. Fear of success in males and females: 1965 and 1971. *Journal of Consulting and Clinical Psychology*, 1974, *42*, 353–58. **266, 267, 268**

Hoffman, L. W. Fear of success in 1965 and 1974: A follow-up study. *Journal of Consulting and Clinical Psychology*, 1977, *45*, 310–21. **269, 277, 307**

Hoffman, M. L. Sex differences in moral internalization and values. *Journal of Personality and Social Psychology*, 1975, *32*, 720–29.

Hoffman, M. L. Identification and conscience development. *Child Development*, 1971, *42*, 1071–82. **181, 314, 315**

Hokanson, J. E., Willers, K. R., and Koropsak, E. Modification of autonomic response during aggressive interchange. *Journal of Personality*, 1968, *36*, 386–404. **292**

Hollander, D. A., Slaymaker, F. L., and Foley, J. M. Attribution of maleness or femaleness by children to gender-free figures. Paper presented at the meeting of the Midwestern

Psychological Association, Chicago, May, 1975. **178**

Holmes, D. S., and Jorgensen, B. W. Do personality and social psychologists study more men than women? *Representative Research in Social Psychology*, 1971, *2*, 71–76. **18**

Hook, E. B. Behavioral implication of the human XYY genotype. *Science*, 1973, *179*, 139–50. **35, 37**

Horner, M. The motive to avoid success and changing aspirations of college women. In J. M. Bardwick (Ed.), *Readings on the psychology of women*, pp. 62–67. New York: Harper and Row, 1972. (a) **265, 267, 268, 266**

Horner, M. Toward an understanding of achievement-related conflicts in women. *Journal of Social Issues*, 1972, *28*, 157–75. (b) **265, 267**

Horner, M. Why bright women fear success. In C. Tavris (Ed.), *The female experience* pp. 55–57. Del Mar, Calif.: Communications Research Machines, 1973. **265, 266, 267**

Hoyenga, K. B., and Hoyenga, K. T. Inductive androgens and weight, activity, dominance, and taste preferences. Paper presented at the meeting of the Midwestern Psychological Association, Chicago, May 1977. **93, 385**

Hoyenga, K. T., and Hoyenga, K. I. B. Experiential factors in the deprivation-induced enhancement of saccharin intake. *Animal Learning and Behavior*, 1973, *I*, 244–46. **384, 386**

Hrdy, S. B., and Hrdy, D. B. Hierarchical relations among female Hanuman langurs (Primates: Colobinae, *Presbytis entellus*). *Science*, 1976, *193*, 913–15. **73**

Hubbert, H. B. The effect of age on habit formation in the albino rat. *Behavior Monographs*, 1915, *2*, 1–55. **80**

Hudson, P. T. W. The genetics of handedness—A reply to Levy and Nagylaki, *Neuropsychologia*, 1975, *13*, 331–39. **258**

Hughes, R. N. Behaviour of male and female rats with free choice of two environments differing in novelty. *Animal Behaviour*, 1968, *16*, 92–96. **76**

Hutchinson, R. R., Ulrich, R. E., and Azrin, N. H. Effects of age and related factors on the pain-aggression reaction. *Journal of*

Comparative and Physiological Psychology, 1965, *59*, 365–69. **127**

Hutt, C. *Males and females*. Baltimore: Penguin, 1972.(a) **236, 250, 306, 319, 321, 322, 323, 326**

Hutt, C. Neuroendocrinological, behavioural, and intellectual aspects of sexual differentiation in human development. In C. Ounsted and D. C. Taylor (Eds.), *Gender differences: Their ontogeny and significance*, pp. 73–121. London: Churchill Livingston, 1972. (b) **143, 250, 252, 253, 292, 306**

Ikard, W. L., Bennett, W. C., Lundin, R. W., and Trost, R. C. Acquisition and extinction of the conditioned avoidance response: A comparison between male rats and estrous and non-estrous female rats. *Psychological Record*, 1972, *22*, 249–54. **80, 133**

Imanishi, K. Social organization of subhuman primates in their natural habitat. *Current Anthropology*, 1960, *1*, 393–402. **73**

Imperato McGinley, J., Guerrero, L., Gautier, T., and Peterson R. E. Steroid 5α reductase deficiency in man: An inherited form of male pseudohermaphroditism. *Science*, 1974, *186*, 1213–15. **175**

Imperato/McGinley, J., Peterson, R. E., and Gautier, T. Gender identity and hermaphroditism. *Science*. 1976, *191*, 872. **175**

Ingerslev, M., Jeppesen, T., and Ramsing, E. M. Secondary amenorrhea and oral contraceptives. *Acta Obstetrica Gynecologica Scandinavica*, 1976, *55*, 233–38. **142**

Iscoe, L., and Carden, J. A. Field dependence, manifest anxiety, and sociometric status in children. *Journal of Consulting Psychology*, 1961, *25*, 184. **336**

Itani, J. On the acquisition and propagation of a new food habit in the natural group of Japanese monkeys at Takasaki Yama. *Journal of Primatology*, 1958, *I*, 84–98. **381**

Ivey, M. E., and Bardwick, J. M. Patterns of affective fluctuation in the menstrual cycle. *Psychosomatic Medicine*, 1968, *30*, 336–44. **149**

Izard, C. E., and Caplan, S. Sex differences in emotional responses to erotic literature. *Journal of Consulting and Clinical Psychology*, 1974, *42*, 468. **330**

Jackaway, R., and Teevan, R. Fear of failure and fear of success: Two dimensions of the same motive. *Sex Roles*, 1976, *2*, 283–93. **284**

Jackson, D. M. *Personality research form manual*. New York: Research Psychologists Press, 1967. **296, 305**

Jacobs, G. H. Visual sensitivity, significant within—species variation in a nonhuman primate. *Science*. 1977, *197*, 499–500. **82**

Jacobs, P. A. Epidemiology of chromosome abnormalities in man. *American Journal of Epidemiology*, 1977, *105*, 180–91. **38**

Jacobs, P. A., Brunton, M., Melville, M. M., Brittain, R. P., and McClemont, W. F. Aggressive behavior, mental subnormality and the XYY male. *Nature*, 1965, *208*, 1351–52. **37**

Jacobs, P. A., Price, W. H., Court-Brown, W. M., Brittain, R. P., and Whatmore, P. B. Chromosome studies on men in a maximum security hospital. *Annals of Human Genetics*, 1968, *31*, 339–58. **38**

Jacobs, P. A., Price, W. H., Richmond, S., and Ratcliffe, R. A. W. Chromosome surveys in penal institutions and approved schools. *Journal of Medical Genetics*, 1971, *8*, 49–58. **37**

James, W. P. T., and Trayhurn, P. An integrated view of the metabolic and genetic basis for obesity. *Lancet*, 1976, *2*, 770–72. **382**

Janowsky, D. S., Berens, S. C., and Davis, J. M. Correlations between mood, weight, and electrolytes during the menstrual cycle: A renin-angiotensin-aldosterone hypothesis of premenstrual tension. *Psychosomatic Medicine*, 1973, *35*, 143–54. **158**

Jarvik, L. F. Human intelligence: Sex differences. *Acto Geneticae Medicae et Gemellologiae*, 1975, *24*, 189–211. **237, 261**

Jay, P. Mother-infant relations in langurs. In H. L. Reingold (Ed.), *Maternal behavior in mammals*, pp. 282–304. New York: Wiley, 1963. **77**

Jean, Cl., André, M., Jean, Ch., Berger, M., Turckheim, M. De., and Veyssière, G. Estimation of testosterone and androstenedione in the plasma and tests of cryptorchid offspring of mice treated with oestradiol during pregnancy. *Journal of Reproductive Fertility*, 1975, *44*, 235–47. **110**

Jenni, D. A., and Jenni, M. A. Carrying behavior in humans: Analysis of sex differences, *Science*, 1976, *194*, 859–60. **311**

Jenni, M. A. Sex differences in carrying behavior. *Perceptual and Motor Skills*, 1976, *43*, 323–30. **310**

Jennings, W. A. Estrous anorexia: Single-tube intake and barpress rate in the albino rat. *Physiological Psychology*, 1973, *I*, 369–72. **384**

Jensen, A. R., and Rohwer, W. D., Jr. The Stroop color-word test: A review. *Acta Psychologia*, 1966, *25*, 36–93. **326**

Jensen, G. D. Human sexual behavior in primate perspective. In J. Zubin and J. Money (Eds.), *Contemporary sexual behavior: Critical issues in the 1970's*, pp. 17–31. Baltimore: Johns Hopkins University Press, 1973. **236**

Jensen, G. D., Bobbitt, R. A., and Gordon, B. N. Sex differences in the development of independence of infant monkeys. *Behaviour*, 1967, *30*, 1–14. **78**

Jensen, K. Differential reactions to taste and temperature stimuli and newborn infants. *Genetic Psychology Monographs*, 1932, *12*, 361–477. **324**

Johansson, G. Sex differences in catecholamine output in children. *Acta Physiologica Scandinavica*, 1972, *85*, 569–72. **321**

Jones, B. M., and Jones, M. K. Alcohol effects in women during the menstrual cycle. *Annals of the New York Academy of Sciences*, 1976, *273*, 576–87. **148, 320**

Jones, B. M., Jones, M. K., and Paredes, A. Oral contraceptives and ethanol metabolism. *Alcohol Technical Reports*, 1976, *5*, 28–32. **143, 320**

Jones, M. C., and Mussen, P. H. Self-conceptions, motivations and interpersonal attitudes of early- and late-maturing girls. *Child Development*, 1958, *29*, 491–501. **292, 304, 342**

Jones, S. E. A comparative proxemics analysis of dyadic interaction in selected subcultures of New York City. *Journal of Social Psychology,* 1971, *84,* 34–44. **309**

Joslyn, W. D. Androgen-induced social dominance in infant female rhesus monkeys. *Journal of Child Psychology and Psychiatry,* 1973, *14,* 137–45. **383**

Jost, A. The role of fetal hormones in prenatal development. *The Harvey Lectures,* 1961, *55,* 201–26. **47**

Kaess, W. A., and Witryol, S. L. Memory for names and faces: A characteristic of social intelligence? *Journal of Applied Psychology,* 1955, *39,* 457–67. **325**

Kagan, J., and Freeman, M. Relation of childhood intelligence, maternal behaviors and social class to behavior during adolescence. *Child Development,* 1963, *34,* 899–911. **255, 256, 273**

Kagan, J., and Kogan, N. Individual variation in cognition processes. In P. H. Mussen (Ed.), *Carmichael's manual of child psychology,* pp. 1273–1365. New York: Wiley, 1970. **243, 244, 246, 251, 336**

Kagan, J. and Moss, H. A. *Birth to maturity: A study in psychological development.* New York: Wiley, 1962. **15–17, 239, 271, 272, 292, 299, 300, 302**

Kagan, J., Sontag, L. W., Baker, C. T. and Nelson, V. L. Personality and I.Q. change. *Journal of Abnormal and Social Psychology,* 1958, *56,* 261–66. **239, 317**

Kakolewski, J. W., Cox, V. C., and Valenstein, E. S. Sex differences in body-weight changes following gonadectomy of rats. *Psychological Reports,* 1968, *22,* 547–54. **383**

Kane, F. J., Lipton, M. A., and Ewing, J. A. Hormonal influences in female sexual response. *Archives of General Psychiatry,* 1969, *20,* 202–9. **160**

Kangas, J., and Bradway, K. Intelligence at middle age: A thirty-eight-year follow-up. *Developmental Psychology,* 1971, *5,* 333–37. **237**

Kanner, A. D. Femininity and masculinity: Their relationships to creativity in male architects and their independence from each other. *Journal of Consulting and Clinical Psychology,* 1976, *44,* 802–5. **256**

Kaplan, H. B. Self-derogation and childhood family structure. *Journal of Nervous and Mental Disease,* 1970, *151,* 13–23. **336**

Kaplan, H. B. Self-derogation and social position: Interaction effects of sex, race, education and age. *Social Psychiatry,* 1973, *8,* 92–99. **336**

Kaplan, H. B., and Pokorny, A. D. Sex-related correlates of adult self-derogation: Reports of childhood experiences. *Developmental Psychology,* 1972, *6,* 536. **336**

Karsch, F. S., Dierschke, D. J. and Knobil, E. Sexual differentiation of pituitary function: Apparent difference between primate and rodents. *Science,* 1973, *179,* 484–86. **57**

Kashiwagi, T., McClure, J. N., and Wetzel, R. D. Premenstrual affective syndrome and psychiatric disorder. *Diseases of the Nervous System,* 1976, *37,* 116–19. **155, 157**

Katcher, A. The discrimination of sex differences by young children. *Journal of Genetic Psychology,* 1955, *87,* 131–43. **182**

Kawakami, M., and Sawyer, C. H. Neuroendocrine correlates of changes in brain activity thresholds by sex steroids and pituitary hormones. *Endocrinology,* 1959, *65,* 652–68. **120, 121**

Kawakami, M., and Sawyer, C. H. Effects of sex hormones and antifertility steroids on brain thresholds in the rabbit. *Endocrinology,* 1967, *80,* 857–71.

Kawashima, S., and Shinoda, A. Spontaneous activity and learning ability of neonatally estrogenized rats. Abstract of a paper presented at the Seminar on Long-term Effects of Perinatal Hormone Administration, Tokyo, September, 1972. **100**

Kearley, R. C., van Hartesveldt, C., and Woodruff, M. L. Behavioral and hormonal effects of hippocampal lesions on male and female rats. *Physiological Psychology,* 1974, *2,* 187–96. **80, 112**

Kelly, J. A., and Worell, L. Parent behaviors related to masculine, feminine, and androgenous sex role orientations. *Journal of Counseling and Clinical Psychology,* 1976, *44,* 843–51. **223**

Kenshalo, D. R. Changes in the cool threshold associated with phases of the menstrual cycle. *Journal of Applied Physiology,* 1966, *21,* 1031–39. **150, 153**

Kenshalo, D. R., Nafe, J. P., and Brooks, B. Variations in thermal sensitivity. *Science,* 1961, *134,* 104–5. **323**

Keogh, B. K. Pattern copying under three conditions of an expanded spatial field. *Developmental Psychology,* 1971, *4,* 25–31. **246**

Keskiner, A., Zalcman, M. J., and Ruppert, E. H. Advantages of being female in psychiatric rehabilitation. *Archives of General Psychiatry,* 1973, *28,* 689–92. **345, 348**

Kessler, S., and Moos, R. H. The XYY karyotype and criminality: A review. *Journal of Psychiatric Research,* 1970, *7,* 153–70. **37**

Key, M. R. *Male/female language.* Metuchen, N.J.: Scarecrow Press, 1975(a). **308, 311**

Key, M. R. The role of male and female in childrens books—Dispelling all doubt. In R. K. Unger and F. L. Denmark (Eds.), *Woman: Dependent or independent variable?,* pp. 56–70. New York: Psychological Dimensions, 1975(b). **214**

Keys, W., and Ormerod, M. B. Some sex-related differences in the correlates of subject preference in the middle years of secondary education. *Educational Studies,* 1977, *3,* 111–16. **242**

Kilham, W., and Mann, L. Level of destructive obedience as a function of transmitter and executant roles in the Milgram obedience paradigm. *Journal of Personality and Social Psychology,* 1974, *29,* 696–702. **295**

Kimura, D. Speech lateralization in young children as determined by an auditory test. *Journal of Comparative and Physiological Psychology,* 1963, *56,* 899–902. **258**

King, M. C. The politics of sexual stereotypes. *Black Scholar,* March–April, 1973, pp. 12–23. **218**

Kinsey, A., Pomeroy, W. B., Martin, C. E., and Gebhard, H. *Sexual behavior in the human female.* New York: Pocket Books, 1965. **330**

Kitay, J. I. Pituitary-adrenal function in the rat after gonadectomy and gonadal hormone replacement. *Endocrinology,* 1963, *73,* 253–60. **118**

Klaiber, E. L., Broverman, D. M., Vogel, W., Abraham, G. E., Stenn, P. G. Effects of testosterone on mental performance and EEG. In *influence of hormones on the ner-* *vous system; The proceedings of the International Society of Psychoneuro-endocrinology,* pp. 341–53. Basel, Switz.: Karger, 1971. **142, 255**

Klaiber, E. L., Broverman, D. M., Vogel, W., and Kobayashi, Y. Rhythms in plasma MAO activity, EEG, and behavior during the menstrual cycle. In M. Ferin, F. Halberg, R. M. Richart, and R. L. Vande Wiele (Eds.), *Biorhythms and human reproduction,* pp. 353–67. New York: Wiley, 1974. **142, 147, 148, 151, 161**

Klaiber, E. L., Broverman, D. M., Vogel, W., and Mackenberg, E. J. Rhythmns in cognitive functioning and EEG indices in males. In M. Ferin, F. Halberg, R. M. Richart, and R. L. Vande Wiele (Eds.), *Biorhythms and human reproduction,* pp. 481–93. New York: Wiley, 1974. **140, 148**

Kleinke, C. L., Bustos, A. A., Meeker, F. B., and Staneski, R. A. Effects of self-attributed and other-attributed gaze on interpersonal evaluations between males and females. *Journal of Experimental Social Psychology,* 1973, *9,* 154–63. **311**

Kline, N. S., and Shah, B. K. A pattern of antidepressive effect of tryptophan and imipramine in males and females. *Diseases of the Nervous System,* 1974, *35,* 481–83. **320**

Knobil, E. Maturation of the neuroendocrine control of gonadotropin secretion in the rhesus monkey. *International Synposium on Sexual Endocrinology of the Perinatal Period,* 1974, *32,* 205–18. **57**

Knox, C., and Kimura, D. Cerebral processing of nonverbal sounds in boys and girls. *Neuropsychologia,* 1970, *8,* 227–37. **253**

Kobayashi, T., Kobayashi, T., Kato, J., and Minaguchi, H. Cholinergic and adrenergic mechanisms in the female rat hypothalamus with special reference to feedback of ovarian steroid hormones. In G. Pincus, T. Nakao, and J. F. Tait (Eds.), *Steroid dynamics,* pp. 303–37. New York: Academic Press, 1966. **120**

Kohlberg, L. A cognitive-developmental analysis of children's sex-role concepts and attitudes. In E. E. Maccoby, (Ed.), *The development of sex differences,* pp. 82–173. Stanford, Calif.: Stanford University Press, 1966. **186, 188, 189, 210**

Kohlberg, L. Stage and sequence: The

cognitive-developmental approach to socialization. In D. A. Goslin (Ed.), *Handbook of socialization theory and research*, pp. 347–480. Chicago: Rand McNally, 1969. **186, 187, 188, 302**

Kohlberg, L., and Ullman, D. Z. Stages in the development of psychosexual concepts and attitudes. In R. C. Friedman, R. M. Richart, and R. L. Vande Wiele (Eds.), *Sex differences in behavior*, pp. 209–22. New York: Wiley, 1974. **186, 189, 211**

Kohlberg, L., and Zigler, E. The impact of cognitive maturity on the development of sex-role attitudes in the years 4–8. *Genetic Psychology*, 1967, *75*, 84–165. **189**

Kohn, M. L. Social class and parental values. *American Journal of Sociology*, 1959, *64*, 337–51. **211**

Komarovksy, M. Cultural contradictions and sex roles. *American Journal of Sociology*, 1946, *52*, 182–89. **218**

Komarovsky, M. Cultural contradictions and sex roles: The masculine case. *American Journal of Sociology*, 1973, *78*, 873–84. **218**

Kopacz, F. M., II, and Smith, B. D. Sex differences in skin conductance measures as a function of shock threat. *Psychophysiology*, 1971, *8*, 293–303. **321**

Kopell, B. S. The role of progestins and progesterone in brain function and behavior. In H. A. Salhanic, D. M. Kipnis, and R. L. Vande Wiele (Eds.), *Metabolic effects of gonadal hormones and contraceptive steroids*, pp. 649–67. New York: Plenum Press, 1969. **121, 140, 148, 151**

Kopell, B. S., Lunde, D. T., Clayton, R. B., and Moos, R. M. Variations in some measures of arousal during the menstrual cycle. *Journal of Nervous and Mental Disease*, 1969, *148*, 180–87.

Korner, A. F. Sex differences in newborns with special reference to differences in the organization of oral behavior. *Journal of Child Psychology and Psychiatry*, 1973, *14*, 19–29. **322, 388**

Korner, A. F. Methodological considerations in studying sex differences in the behavioral functioning of newborns. In R. C. Friedman, R. M. Richart, and R. L. Vande Wiele (Eds.), *Sex differences in behavior*, pp. 197–208. New York: Wiley, 1974. **320, 322**

Köster, E. P., and Koelega, H. S. Sex differences in odour perception. *Journal of the Society of Cosmetic Chemists*, 1976, *27*, 319–27. **324**

Kow, L. M., and Pfaff, D. W. Induction of lordosis in female rats: Two modes of estrogen action and the effects of adrenalectomy. *Hormones and Behavior*, 1975, *6*, 259–76. **125**

Krail, K. A., and Leventhal, G. The sex variable in the intrusion of personal space. *Sociometry*, 1976, *39*, 170–73. **309**

Krasnoff, A. and Weston, L. M. Pubertal status and sex differences: Activity and maze behavior in rats. *Developmental Psychology*, 1976, *9*, 261–69. **75, 80, 132, 133**

Kreuz, L. E., and Rose, R. M. Assessment of aggressive behavior and plasma testosterone in a young criminal population. *Psychosomatic Medicine*, 1972, *34*, 321–32. **138**

Kristal, J., Sanders, D., Spence, J. T., and Helmreich, R. Inferences about the femininity of competent women and their implications for likability. *Sex Roles*, 1975, *1*, 33–40. **219**

Krzanowski, M. Short- and long-term rhythms in testicular function in the bull. In M. Ferin, F. Halberg, R. M. Richart, and R. L. Vande Wiele (Eds.), *Biorhythms and human reproduction*, pp. 447–56. New York: Wiley, 1974. **164**

Kubo, K., Gorski, R. A., and Kawakami, M. Effects of estrogen on neuronal excitability in the hippocampal-septal-hypothalamic system. *Neuroendocrinology*, 1975, *18*, 176–91. **121**

Kühl, J. F. W., Lee, J. K., Halberg, F., Haus, E., Günther, R., and Knapp, E. Circadian and lower frequency rhythms in male grip strength and body weight. In M. Ferin, F. Halberg, R. M. Richart, and R. L. Vande Wiele (Eds.), *Biorhythms and human reproduction*, pp. 529–48. New York: Wiley, 1974. **163**

Kummer, H. Two variations in the social organization of baboons. In P. C. Jay (Ed.), *Primates: Studies in adaptation and variability*, pp. 293–312. New York: Holt, Rinehart and Winston, 1968. **77, 78**

Kurtenes, W., and Greif, E. B. The develop-

Kurtenes, W. (*Continued*)
ment of moral thought: Review and evaluation of Kohlberg's approach. *Psychological Bulletin*, 1974, *81*, 453–70. **189**

Kushnick, T., and Colondrillo, M. 49, XXXXY patient with hemifacial microsomia. *Clinical Genetics*, 1975, *7*, 442–48. **35**

Kusumi, T. T. Triple mosaicism of X chromosomes in bipolar affective disorder. *American Journal of Psychiatry*, 1976, *133*, 719. **29**

Kutner, S. J., and Brown, W. L. History of depression as a risk factor for depression with oral contraceptives and discontinuance. *Journal of Nervous and Mental Disease*, 1972, *155*, 163–69. **142**

Laidlaw, J. Catamenial epilepsy. *Lancet*, 1956, *2*, 1234–37. **148**

Lake, D. A., and Bryden, M. P. Handedness and sex differences in hemispheric asymmetry. *Brain and Language*, 1976, *3*, 266–82. **259**

Lamb, M. E. Fathers: Forgotten contributors to child development. *Human Development*, 1975, *18*, 245–66. (a) **195**

Lamb, M. E. Physiological mechanisms in the control of maternal behavior in rats: A review. *Psychological Bulletin*, 1975, *82*, 109–19. (b) **130**

Lamb, M. E. Proximity seeking attachment behaviors: A critical review of the literature. *Genetic Psychology Monographs*, 1976, *93*, 63–89. **300**

Lamb, M. E. Father-infant and mother-infant interaction in the first year of life. *Child Development*, 1977, *48*, 167–81. **307**

Lancaster, J. B. In praise of the achieving female monkey. In C. Tavris (Ed.), *The female experience*, pp. 5–9. Del Mar, Calif.: Communication Research Machines, 1973. **73**

Lancaster, J. B. Sex roles in primate societies. In M. S. Teitelbaum (Ed.), *Sex differences: Social and biological perspectives*, pp. 22–61. New York: Anchor Press, 1976. **73, 77, 361, 381**

Landy, E. E. Sex differences in some aspects of smoking behavior. *Psychological Reports*, 1967, *20*, 575–80. **181**

Lanouette, W. J. Everyday math baffles many.

National Observer, August 2, 1975, p. 5. **241**

Lansdell, H. The effect of neurosurgery on a test of proverbs. *American Psychologist*, 1961, *16*, 448. **258**

Lansdell, H. A sex difference in effect of temporal-lobe neurosurgery on design preference. *Nature*, 1962, *194*, 852–54. **258**

Lansdell, H. The use of factor scores from the Weschler-Bellevue scale of intelligence in assessing patients with temporal lobe removals. *Cortex*, 1968, *4*, 257–68. **258**

Lansky, L. M. The family structure also affects the model: Sex-role attitudes in parents of preschool children. *Merrill-Palmer Quarterly*, 1967, *13*, 139–50. **193**

Lao, R. C., Upchurch, W. H., Corwin, B. J., and Frossnickle, W. F. Biased attitudes toward females as indicated by ratings of intelligence and likeability. *Psychological Reports*, 1975, *37*, 1315–20. **219**

Larwood, L., O'Neal, E., and Brennan, P. Increasing the physical aggressiveness of women. *Journal of Social Psychology*, 1977, *101*, 97–101. **291**

Laschet, U. Antiandrogen in the treatment of sex offenders: Mode of action and therapeutic outcome. In J. Zubin and J. Money (Eds.), *Contemporary sexual behavior: Critical issues in the 1970's*, pp. 311–19. Baltimore: Johns Hopkins University Press, 1973. **137**

Laschet, U., and Laschet, L. Antiandrogens in the treatment of sexual deviations of men. *Journal of Steroid Biochemistry*, 1975, *6*, 821–26. **136**

Latane, B., and Bidwell, L. D. Sex and affiliation in college cafeterias. *Personality and Social Psychology Bulletin*, 1977, *3*, 571–74. **303**

Lattime, E. C., and Strausser, H. R. Arteriosclerosis: Is stress-induced immune suppression a risk factor? *Science*, 1977, *198*, 302–3. **378**

Laws, J. L. A feminist review of marital adjustment literature: The Rape of the Locke. *Journal of Marriage and the Family*, 1971, *33*, 483–515. **337, 338**

Laws, J. L. The psychology of tokenism: An anlaysis. *Sex Roles*, 1975, *1*, 51–67. **228**

LeBoeuf, B. J., and Peterson, R. S. Social

status and mating activity in elephent seals. *Science,* 1969, *163,* 91–93. **64**

Lee, C. T., Griffo, W., Braunstein, A., Mars, H., and Stein, J. Progesterone antagonism of aggression-promoting olfactory signals: A time-dependent phenomenon. *Physiology and Behavior,* 1976, *17,* 319–23. **128**

Lee, C. T., and Naranjo, J. N. The effects of castration and androgen on the social dominance of BALB/cJ male mice. *Physiological Psychology,* 1974, *2,* 93–98. **128, 130**

Leeton, J. The relationship of oral contraception to depressive symptoms. *Australian and New Zealand Journal of Obstetrics and Gynaecology,* 1973, *13,* 115–20. **144**

Leff, D. N. Boy or girl: Now choice not chance. *Medical World News,* 1975, *16,* 45–56. **226**

Leifer, A. D., Leiderman, P. H., Barnett, C. R., and Williams, J. A. Effects of mother-infant separation on maternal attachment behavior. *Child Development,* 1972, *43,* 1203–18. **306**

Leifer, M. Psychological changes accompanying pregnancy and motherhood. *Genetic Psychology Monographs,* 1977, *95,* 55–96. **160**

Le Magnen, J. Physiologie des sensations—Un cas de sensibilité olfactive se présentant comme un caratère sexuel secondaire féminin. *Comptes Rendus de l'Academie des Sciences,* 1948, *226,* 694–95. **151, 324**

Le Magnen, J. Physiologie des sensations—Variations spécifiques des seuils olfactifs chez l'Homme sous actions androgène et oestrogène. *Compte's Rendus de l'Academie des Sciences,* 1949, *228,* 947–48. **151, 324**

Le Magnen, J. Physiologie des sensations—Nouvelles données sur le Phènomène de l'exaltolide. *Comptes Rendus de l'Academie des Sciences,* 1950, *230,* 1103–5. **151, 153, 324**

Le Magnen, J. Les Phénomènes olfacto-sexuels chex l'homme. *Archives des Sciences Physiologiques,* 1952, *6,* 125–60. (a) **324**

Le Magnen, J. Les phénomènes olfacto-sexuels chez le rat blanc. *Archives des Science Physiologiques,* 1952, *6,* 295–331. (b) **324**

Lenney, E. Women's self-confidence in achievement settings. *Psychological Bulletin,* 1977, *84,* 1–13. **282**

Leon, M., Numan, M., and Moltz, J. Maternal behavior in the rat: Facilitation through gonadectomy, *Science,* 1973, *179,* 1018–19. **130, 131**

Lerner, R. M., Orlos, J. B., and Knapp, J. R. Physical attractiveness, physical effectiveness, and self-concept in late adolescents. *Adolescence,* 1976, *43,* 313–26. **314, 337**

Leshner, A. I., and Collier, G. The effects of gonadectomy on the sex differences in dietary self-selection patterns and carcass compositions of rats. *Physiology and Behavior,* 1973, *11,* 671–76. **381, 383**

Leshner, A. I., Siegel, H. I., and Collier, G. Dietary self-selection by pregnant and lactating rats. *Physiology and Behavior,* 1972, *8,* 151–54. **383, 384**

Lesser, G. S. Achievement motivation in women. In D. C. McClelland and R. S. Steele (Eds.), *Human motivation: A book of readings,* pp. 202–21. Morristown, N.J.: General Learning Press, 1973. **271, 273, 274, 276, 277**

Lesser, G. S., Krawitz, R. N., and Packard, R. Experimental arousal of achievement motivation in adolescent girls. *Journal of Abnormal and Social Psychology,* 1962, *66,* 59–66. **273, 274, 275**

Lever, J. Sex differences in the games children play. *Social Problems,* 1976, *23,* 478–87. **295**

Levine, S. V. Differential response to early experience as a function of sex differences. In R. C. Friedman, R. M. Richart, and R. L. Vande Wiele (Eds.), *Sex differences in behavior,* pp. 87–98. New York: Wiley, 1974. **132, 236**

Levine, S. V., Kamin, L. E., and Levine, E. L. Sexism and psychiatry. *American Journal of Orthopsychiatry,* 1974, *44,* 327–36. **336, 350**

Levine, S., and Mullins, R. F., Jr. Estrogen administered neonatally affects adult sexual behavior in male and female rats. *Science,* 1964, *144,* 185–87. **91**

Levinson, R. M. From Olive Oyl to Sweet Polly Purebread: Sex role stereotypes and televi-

Levinson, R. M. (*Continued*)
sion cartoons. *Journal of Popular Culture,* 1975, *8,* 561–72. **215**

Levinson, R. M. Sex discrimination and employment practices: An experiment with unconventional job inquiries. *Social Problems,* 1976, *23,* 533–43. **226**

Lev-Ran, A. Sexuality and educational levels of women with the late-treated adrenogenital syndrome. *Archives of Sexual Behavior,* 1974, *3,* 27–32. **104, 105**

Levy, D. M. Control-situation studies of children's responses to the difference in genitalia. *American Journal of Orthopsychiatry,* 1940, *10,* 755–62. **181**

Levy, J., and Reid, M. Variations in writing posture and cerebral organization. *Science,* 1976, *194,* 337–39. **259**

Lewin, A. Y., and Duchan, L. Women in academia: A study of the hiring decision in departments of physical science. *Science,* 1971, *173,* 892–95. **226**

Lewis, M. Parents and children: Sex-role development. *School Review,* 1972, *80,* 229–40. **207, 208**

Lewis, M., and Weinraub, M. Sex of parent X sex of child: Socioemotional development. In R. C. Friedman, R. M. Richart, and R. L. Vande Wiele (Eds.) *Sex differences in behavior,* pp. 165–89. New York: Wiley, 1974. **210, 300, 301, 326**

Lewis, V. G. , Money, J., and Epstein, R. Concordance of verbal and nonverbal ability in the adrenogenital syndrome. *The Johns Hopkins Medical Journal,* 1968, *122,* 192–95. **103, 105**

Lewittes, D. J., Moselle, J. A., and Simmons, W. L. Sex role bias in clinical judgments based on Rorschach interpretations. *Proceedings of the 81st Annual Convention of the American Psychological Association,* 1973, 495–96. **347**

Liberson, C. W., and Liberson, W. T. Sex differences in autonomic responses to electric shock. *Psychophysiology,* 1975, *12,* 182–86. **321, 323**

Lincoln, G. A., Guiness, F., and Short, R. V. The way in which testosterone controls the social and sexual behavior of the red deer stag (*Cervus elaphus*). *Hormones and Behavior,* 1972, *3,* 375–396. **128, 164**

Lipman-Blumen, J. How ideology shapes women's lives. *Scientific American,* January, 1972, pp. 34–42. **316**

Lipsett, M. B. Steroid secretion by the testes in man. In V. H. T. James, M. Serio, and L. Martini (Eds.), *The endocrine function of the human testes.* Vol. II, pp. 1–9. New York: Academic Press, 1974. **50**

Lisk, R. D. Neonatal hormone manipulation in the mouse: Effects on the hormonally mediated maternal nest. Abstract of a paper presented at the Seminar on Long-term Effects of Perinatal Hormone Administration, Tokyo, September, 1972. **96**

Litteria, M. Increased incorporation of [³H]-lysine in specific hypothalamic nuclei following castration in the male rat. *Experimental Neurology,* 1973, *40,* 309–15. (a) **112**

Litteria, M. Inhibitory action of neonatal androgenization on the incorporation of [³H]-lysine in specific hypothalamic nuclei of the adult female rat. *Experimental Neurology,* 1973, *41,* 395–401. (b) **112**

Litteria, M., and Thorner, M. W. Alterations in the incorporation of [³H]-lysine into proteins of the medial pre-optic area and specific hypothalamic nuclei after ovariectomy in the adult female rat. *Journal of Endocrinology,* 1974, *60,* 377–78. (a) **112**

Litteria, M., and Thorner, M. W. Inhibition in the incorporation of [³H]-lysine in the Purkinji cells of the adult female rat after neonatal androgenization. *Brain Research,* 1974, *69,* 170–73. (b) **112**

Litteria, M., and Thorner, M. W. Inhibition in the incorporation of [³H]-lysine into the proteins of specific hypothalamic nuclei of the adult female rat after neonatal estrogenization. *Experimental Neurology,* 1975, *49,* 592–95. **112**

Litteria, M., and Thorner, N. W. Inhibitory action of neonatal estrogenization on the incorporation of [³H]-lysine into cortical neuroproteins. *Brain Research,* 1976, *103,* 584–87. **112**

Little, B. C., Matta, R. J., and Zahn, T. P. Physiological and psychological effects of progesterone in man. *Journal of Nervous and Mental Disease,* 1974, *159,* 256–62. **141, 142, 381**

Little, B. C., and Zahn, T. P. Changes in mood

and autonomic functioning during the menstrual cycle. *Psychophysiology,* 1974, *11,* 579–90.   **146, 148, 149**

Livson, F. The pinch of stepping out of stereotype. (Discussed by M. Casaday in *Psychology Today,* 9, 1976, pp. 102–3.)   **218**

Lockheed, M. E. Female motive to avoid success: A psychological barrier or a response to deviancy? *Sex Roles,* 1975, *1,* 41–50.   **268**

Lockheed, M. E., and Hall, K. P. Conceptualizing sex as a status characteristic: Applications to leadership training strategies. *Journal of Social Issues,* 1976, *32,* 111–24.   **296**

Logothetis, J., Harner, R., Morel, F., and Torres, F. The role of estrogens and catemenial exacerbations of epilepsy. *Neurology,* 1959, *9,* 352–60.   **148**

Lombardi, J. R., and Vandenbergh, J. G. Pheromonally induced sexual maturation in females: Regulation by the social environment of the male. *Science,* 1977, *196,* 545–46.   **122**

Longuski, P., Cudillo, C. A., and Stern, J. J. Effects of estradiol on feeding and locomotion in REM deprived rats. *Physiology and Behavior,* 1976, *16,* 97–99.   **303**

Loranger, A. W. X-linkage and manic-depressive illness. *British Journal of Psychiatry,* 1975, *127,* 484–88.   **41, 352**

Lorenz, K., and Leyhausen, P. *Motivation of human and animal behavior: An ethological view.* New York: Van Nostrand, 1973.   **76**

Lubin, B., Gardener, S. H., and Roth, A. Mood and somatic symptoms during pregnancy. *Psychosomatic Medicine,* 1975, *37,* 136–46.   **159**

Luce, G. G. *Biological rhythms in human and animal physiology.* New York: Dover, 1971.   **158, 165**

Luisada, P. V., Peele, R., and Pittard, E. A. The hysterical personality in men. Paper presented at the meeting of the American Psychiatric Association, Honolulu, May, 1973.   **348**

Luckey, E. G., and Nass, G. B. A comparison of sexual attitudes and behavior in an international sample. *Journal of Marriage and the Family,* 1969, *31,* 364–79.   **203, 204**

Lumia, A. R., Rieder, C. A., and Reynierse, J. H. The differential effects of reinforcement and testosterone on aggressive responding in pigeons: Species typical and adversive aspects of pigeon aggression. *Bulletin of the Psychonomic Society,* 1973, *1,* 165–66.   **130**

Lynn, D. B. The process of learning parental and sex-role identification. *Journal of Marriage and the Family,* 1966, *28,* 466–70.   **192, 193, 194**

Lyon, M. F. Gene action in the X-chromosome of the mouse (*Mus musculus L.*). *Nature,* 1961, *190,* 372–73.   **26, 28**

Lyon, M. F. X-chromosome inactivation and developmental patterns in mammals. *Biological Review,* 1972, *47,* 1–35.   **28, 30**

McArthur, L. Z., and Eisen, S. V. Achievements of male and female storybook characters as determinants of achievement behavior by boys and girls. *Journal of Personality and Social Psychology,* 1976, *33,* 467–73.   **272**

McArthur, L. Z., and Resko, B. G. The portrayal of men and women in American television commercials. *Journal of Social Psychology,* 1975, *97,* 209–20.   **215**

MacBrayer, C. T. Differences in perception of the opposite sex by males and females. *Journal of Social Psychology,* 1960, *52,* 309–14.   **181**

McCall, R. B. Childhood IQ's as predictors of adult educational and occupational status. *Science,* 1977, *197,* 482–83.   **274**

McCance, R. A., Luff, M. C., and Widdowson, E. E. Physical and emotional periodicity in women. *Journal of Hygiene,* 1937, *77,* 571–611.   **150**

McClearn, G. E., and DeFries, J. C. *Introduction to behavioral genetics.* San Francisco: Freeman, 1973.   **64**

McClelland, D. C. *The achieving society.* Princeton, N.J.: Van Nostrand, 1961.   **264, 265**

McClelland, D. C. *Power: The inner experience.* New York: Halsted, 1975.   **298, 303**

McClelland, D. C., Atkinson, J. W., and Clark, R. A. The projective expression of needs, III: The effect of ego-involvement, success,

McClelland, D. C. (*Continued*)
and failure on perception. *Journal of Psychology*, 1949, *27*, 311–30.   **263, 264**

McClelland, D. C., Atkinson, J. W., Clark, R. A., and Lowell, F. L. *The achievement motive.* New York: Appleton-Century-Crofts, 1953.   **265**

McClelland, D. C., and Watt, N. F. Sex-role alienation in schizophrenia. *Journal of Abnormal Psychology*, 1968, *73*, 226–39.   **342**

McClelland, D. C., and Winter, D. G. *Motivating economic achievement.* New York: Free Press, 1969.   **264**

McClintock, C. G., Messick, D. M., Kuhlman, D. M., and Campos, F. T. Motivational bases of choice in three-choice decomposed games. *Journal of Experimental Psychology*, 1973, *9*, 572–90.   **295**

McClintock, M. K. Menstrual synchony and suppression. *Nature*, 1971, *229*, 244–45.   **123**

Maccoby, E. E. Sex differences in intellectual functioning. In E. E. Maccoby (Ed.), *The development of sex differences*, pp. 25–55. Stanford, Calif.: Stanford University Press, 1966.   **13, 239, 255, 274**

Maccoby, E. E., and Jacklin, C. N. Stress, activity, and proximity seeking: Sex differences in the year-old child. *Child Development*, 1973, *44*, 34–42.   **300**

Maccoby, E. E., and Jacklin, C. N. *The psychology of sex differences.* Stanford, Calif.: Stanford University Press, 1974.   **185, 192, 194, 196, 205, 209, 236, 237, 239, 240, 241, 244, 246, 249, 250, 251, 252, 253, 255, 266, 271, 273, 282, 290, 291, 292, 293, 294, 295, 296, 297, 299, 302, 303, 307, 323, 324, 325, 326, 335, 336, 357**

McCollom, R. E., Siegal, P. B., and Van Krey, H. P. Responses to androgen in lines of chickens selected for mating behavior. *Hormones and Behavior*, 1971, *2*, 31–42.   **124**

Mc Cullough, J., Quadagno, D. M., and Goldman, B. D. Neonatal gonadal hormones: Effect on maternal and sexual behavior in the male rat. *Physiology and Behavior*, 1974, *12*, 183–88.   **96**

MacDonald, A. P., Jr. Anxiety, affiliation, and social isolation. *Developmental Psychology*, 1970, *3*, 242–54.   **303**

McDonald, T. W., Annegers, J. F., O'Fallon, W. M., Dockerty, M. B., Malkasian, G. D., Jr., and Kurland, L. T. Endogenous estrogen and endometrial carcinoma: Case-control and incidence study. *American Journal of Obstetrics and Gynecology*, 1977, *127*, 572–80.   **143**

McDowell, A. A., and Brown, W. L. Sex and radiation as factors in peripheral cue discrimination learning. *Journal of Genetic Psychology*, 1963, *102*, 261–265.   **81**

McDowell, A. A., Brown, W. L., and McTee, A. C. Sex as a factor in spatial delayed-response performance by rhesus monkeys. *Journal of Comparative and Physiological Psychology*, 1960, *53*, 429–32.   **81**

McEwen, B. S., Denef, C. J., Gerlach, J. L., and Plapingu, L. Chemical studies of the brain as a steroid hormone target tissue. In F. O. Schmitt and F. G. Worden (Eds.), *The neurosciences: Third study program,* pp. 599–620. Cambridge, Mass.: MIT Press, 1974.   **111**

McEwen, M. K. Counseling women: A review of the research. *Journal of College Student Personnel*, 1975, *16*, 382–88.   **216, 336**

McGee, M. G. Laterality, hand preference, and human spatial ability. *Perceptual and Motor Skills*, 1976, *42*, 781–82.   **244, 258**

McGinnies, E., Nordholm, L. A., Ward, C. D., and Bhanthumnavin, D. L. Sex and cultural differences in perceived locus of control among students in five countries. *Journal of Consulting and Clinical Psychology*, 1974, *42*, 451–55.   **282**

McGlone, J., and Davidson, W. The relation between cerebral speech laterality and spatial ability with special reference to sex and hand preference. *Neuropsychologia*, 1973, *11*, 105–13.   **259**

McGlynn, R. P., Megas, J. C., and Benson, D. H. Sex and race as factors affecting the attribution of insanity in a murder trial. *Journal of Psychology*, 1976, *93*, 93–99.   **226**

McGuinness, D. Equating individual differences for auditory input. *Psychophysiology*, 1974, *11*, 113–20.   **323**

McGuinness, D. Away from a unisex psychology: Individual differences in visual sensory and perceptual processes. *Perception*, 1976, *5*, 279–94.   **323, 324**

McGuinness, D., and Lewis, I. Sex differences in visual persistence: Experiments on the Ganzfeld and afterimages. *Perception,* 1976, *5,* 295–301. **324**

McIntyre, A. Sex differences in children's aggression. *Proceedings of the 80th Annual Convention of the American Psychological Association,* 1972, 7, 93–94. **290, 292**

McKeachie, W. J. Motivation, teaching methods and college teaching. *Nebraska symposium on motivation, 1961,* pp. 111–42. Lincoln: University of Nebraska Press, 1962. **264, 275, 298**

McKenna, W., and Kessler, S. J. Experimental design as a source of sex bias in social psychology. *Sex Roles,* 1977, *3,* 117–28. **18**

Mackey, W. C. The adult male-child bond: An example of convergent evolution. *Journal of Anthropological Research,* 1976, *32,* 58–73. **79, 201**

McKinney, T. D., and Desjardins, C. Postnatal development of the testis, fighting behavior, and fertility in house mice. *Biology of Reproduction,* 1973, *9,* 279–94. **127**

MacKinnon, D. W. The nature and nurture of creative talent. *American Psychologist,* 1962, *17,* 484–95. **251, 256**

MacKinnon, I. L., MacKinnon, P. C. B., and Thompson, A. D. Lethal hazards of the luteal phase of the menstrual cycle. *British Medical Journal,* 1959, *1,* 1015–17. **155, 157**

McLaughlin, M. The doctor shows. *Journal of Communication,* 1975, *25,* 182–84. **215**

Maclean, N., Court-Brown, W. M., Jacobs, P. A., Mantle, D., and Strong, J. A. A survey of sex chromatin abnormalities in mental hospitals. *Journal of Medical Genetics,* 1968, *5,* 165–72. **29**

McNemar, Q., and Stone, C. P. The sex difference in rats on three learning tasks. *Journal of Comparative and Physiological Psychology,* 1932, *14,* 171–80. **80**

Macrides, F., Bartke, A., and Dalterio, S. Strange females increase testosterone levels in male mice. *Science,* 1975, *189,* 1104–5. **122**

Madigan, F. C. Are sex mortality differentials biologically caused? *Milbank Memorial Fund Quarterly,* 1957, *35,* 203–23. **373**

Maeroff, G. I. Males excel in tests. *New York Times,* October 13, 1975, p. 32. **237**

Magalhães, H. M., and Carlini, E. L. deA. Effects of perinatal testosterone treatment on body weight, open field behavior and Lashley III maze performance of rats. *Acta Psychologica, Latin-America,* 1974, *24,* 317–27. **98, 385**

Majeres, R. L. Sex differences in clerical speed: Perceptual encoding vs. verbal encoding. *Memory and Cognition,* 1977, *5,* 468–76. **326**

Makosky, V. P. Sex-role compatibility of task and of competitor, and fear of success as variables affecting women's performance. *Sex Roles,* 1976, *2,* 237–48. **270, 277**

Manning, A. *An introduction to animal behavior.* London: Addison-Wesley, 1967. **65**

Manning, A., and Thompson, M. L. Postcastration retention of sexual behavior in the male BDF₁, mouse: The role of experience. *Animal Behaviour,* 1976, *24,* 523–33. **117**

Manosevitz, M., and Joel, U. Behavioral effects of environmental enrichment in randomly bred mice. *Journal of Comparative and Physiological Psychology,* 1973, *85,* 373–82. **75**

Marcel, T., and Rajan, P. Lateral specialization for recognition of words and faces in good and poor readers. *Neuropsychologia,* 1975, *13,* 489–97. **258**

Marcus, R. F. The effects of children's emotional and instrumental dependent behavior on parental response. *Journal of Psychology,* 1976, *92,* 57–63. **301**

Marinari, K. T., Leshner, A. I., and Doyle, M. P. Menstrual cycle status and adrenocortical reactivity to psychological stress. *Psychoneuroendocrinology,* 1976, *1,* 213–18. **143, 147**

Marks, H. E. Body weight as a determinant of saccharin consumption in the orchidectomized male hamster (*Mesocricetus auratus*). *Bulletin of the Psychonomic Society,* 1974, *3,* 11–13. **383**

Marques, D. M., and Valenstein, E. S. Another hamster paradox: More males carry pups and fewer kill and cannibalize young than do females. *Journal of Comparative and Physiological Psychology,* 1976, *90,* 653–57. **129**

Marrone, B. L., Gentry, R. T., and Wade, G. N.

Marrone, B. L. (*Continued*)
Gonadal hormones and body temperature in rats: Effects of estrous cycles, castration and steroid replacement. *Physiology and Behavior,* 1976, *17,* 419–25. **381**

Marshall, J. C., Reed, P. I., and Gordon, H. Luteinizing hormone secretion in patients presenting with post-oral contraceptive amenorrhoea: Evidence for a hypothalamic feedback abnormality. *Clinical Endocrinology,* 1976, *5,* 131–43. **142**

Marx, J. L. Estrogen drugs: Do they increase the risk of cancer? *Science,* 1976, *191,* 838–40, 882. **143**

Masica, D. N., Money, J., Ehrhardt, A. A., and Lewis, V. G. I.Q., fetal sex hormones and cognitive patterns: Studies in the testicular feminizing syndrome of androgen insensitivity. *Johns Hopkins Medical Journal,* 1969, *124,* 34–43. **108**

Maslow, A. H. Dominance-feeling, behavior, and status. *Psychological Review,* 1937, *44,* 404–29. **317**

Maslow, A. H. Dominance, personality, and social behavior in women. *Journal of Social Psychology,* 1939, *10,* 3–39. **317**

Maslow, A. H. Self-esteem (dominance-feeling) and sexuality in women. *Journal of Social Psychology,* 1942, *16,* 259–94. **331**

Mason, J. W. Psychologic stress and endocrine function. In E. J. Sachar (Ed.), *Topics in psychoendocrinology,* pp. 1–18. New York: Grune and Stratton, 1975. **122**

Mason, J. W., Brady, J. V., and Tolliver, G. A. Plasma and urinary 17-Hydroxycorticosteroid responses to 72-hour avoidance in the monkey. *Psychosomatic Medicine,* 1968, *30,* 608–30. **122**

Mason, W. A., Green, P. C., and Posepanka, C. J. Sex differences in affective-social responses of rhesus monkeys. *Behaviour,* 1960, *16,* 74–83. **73**

Masters, J. C., and Wilkinson, A. Consensual and discriminative stereotype of sex-type judgments by parents and children. *Child Development,* 1976, *47,* 208–17. **187**

Masters, W. H., and Johnson, V. E., *Human sexual response.* Boston: Little, Brown, 1966. **152, 329, 330, 331**

Masur, J., and Benedito, M. A. C. Inversion by apomorphine of the tendency of female rats to be defeated by males when competing for food in a straight runway. *Behavioral Biology,* 1974, *10,* 527–31. (a) **71**

Masur, J., and Benedito, M. A. C. Winning among rats in a food competition situation as a sex-related behavior. *Behavioral Biology,* 1974, *10,* 533–40. (b) **71**

Mathes, E. W., and Kahn, A. Physical attractiveness, happiness, neuroticism, and self-esteem. *Journal of Psychology,* 1975, *90,* 27–30. **314, 337, 338**

Mathews, K. E., and Cooper, S. Deceit as a function of sex of subject and target person. *Sex Roles,* 1976, *2,* 29–38. **315**

Matousek, M., and Peterson, I. Frequency analysis of the EEG in normal children and adolescents. In P. Kellaway and I. Peterson (Eds.), *Automation of clinical electroencephalography,* pp. 75–102. New York: Raven Press, 1973. **113**

Matsumoto, A., and Arai, Y. Effect of estrogen on early postnatal development of synaptic formation in the hypothalamic arcuate nucleus of female rats. *Neuroscience Letters,* 1976, *2,* 79–82. **111**

Matsumoto, S., Sato, I., Ito, T., and Matsuoka, A. Electroencephalographic changes during long term treatment with oral contraceptives. *International Journal of Fertility,* 1966, *11,* 195–204. **143**

Maüsle, E., and Fickinger, G. Ultramorphometric studies of the adrenal cortex of adult rats after neonatal administration of sex steroids. *Acta Endocrinologica,* 1976, *81,* 537–47. **87**

Mayr, E. Sexual selection and natural selection. In B. Campbell (Ed.), *Sexual selection and the descent of man,* pp. 87–104. Chicago: Aldine, 1972. **64**

Mazanec, N., and McCall, G. J. Sex, cognitive categories, and observational accuracy. *Psychological Reports,* 1975, *37,* 987–90. **253**

Mead, M. *Male and Female.* New York: William Morrow, 1949. **199**

Mead, M. *Sex and temperament in three primitive societies.* New York: Dell, 1949 (first published in 1935). **198**

Mednick, M. T. S. Social change and sex-role inertia: The case of the Kubbutz. In M. T. S. Mednick, S. S. Tangri and L. W. Hoffman

(Eds.), *Women and achievement: Social and motivational analysis*, pp. 85–105. New York: Halsted, 1975. **202**

Megargee, E. I. Influence of sex roles on the manifestation of leadership. *Journal of Applied Psychology*, 1969, *53*, 377–82. **297**

Mehrabian, A. Male and female scales of the tendency to achieve. *Educational and Psychological Measurement*, 1968, *28*, 493–502. **265, 282, 309**

Mehrabian, A. Verbal and nonverbal interactions of strangers in a waiting station. *Journal of Experimental Research in Personality*, 1971, *5*, 127–38. **311**

Meijer, A. Psychological factors in maternal grandparents of asthmatic children. *Child Psychiatry and Human Development*, 1975, *6*, 15–25. **374**

Meisels, M., and Guardo, C. J. Development of personal space schemata. *Child Development*, 1969, *40*, 1167–78. **309**

Meissner, W. W. Comparison of anxiety patterns in adolescent boys: 1939–1959. *Journal of Genetic Psychology*, 1961, *99*, 323–29. **336**

Melges, F. T. Postpartum psychiatric syndromes. *Psychosomatic Medicine*, 1968, *30*, 95–108. **181**

Mendlewicz, J., Fleiss, J. L., and Fieve, R. R. Evidence for X-linkage in the transmission of manic-depressive illness. *Journal of the American Medical Association*, 1972, *222*, 1624–27. **352**

Meyer, J., and Sobieszek, B. Effect of a child's sex on adult interpretations of its behavior. *Developmental Psychology*, 1972, *6*, 42–48. **208**

Meyer-Bahlburg, H. F. L., Boon, D. A., Sharma, M., and Edwards, J. A. H. Aggressiveness and testosterone measures in man. *Psychosomatic Medicine*, 1974, *36*, 269–74. **138, 182**

Meyer-Bahlburg, H. F. L., Grisanti, G. C. , and Ehrhardt, A. A. Prenatal effects of sex hormones on human male behavior: Medroxyprogesterone acetate (MPA). *Psychoneuroendocrinology*, 1977, *2*, 383–90. **105**

Meyer-Bahlburg, H. F. L., McCauley, E., Schenck, C., Aceto, T., Jr., and Pinch, L. Cryptorchidism, development of gender

identity, and sex behavior. In R. C. Friedman, R. M. Richart, and R. L. Vande Wiele (Eds.), *Sex differences in behavior*, pp. 281–299. New York: Wiley, 1974.

Myerson, B. J., Lindstrom, L. H., Nordstrom, E., and Ågmo, A. Sexual motivation in the female rat after testosterone treatment. *Physiology and Behavior*, 1973, *11*, 421–28. **125**

Michael, R. P. Gonadal hormones and the control of primate behavior. In R. P. Michael (Ed.), *Endocrinology and human behavior*, pp. 69–93. London: Oxford University Press, 1968. **123, 129**

Michael, R. P. Behavioral effects of gonadal hormones and contraceptive steroids in primates, In H. A. Salhanick, D. M. Kipnis and R. L. Vande Wiele (Eds.), *Metabolic effects of gonadal hormones and contraceptive steroids*, pp. 706–21. New York: Plenum Press, 1969. **77, 78, 125, 126, 236**

Michael, R. P. Hormonal factors and aggressive behavior in the rhesus monkey. In The influence of hormones on the nervous system: The proceedings of the International Society of Psychoneuroendocrinology, pp. 412–23. Basel, Switz.: Karger, 1971. **128, 129**

Michael, R. P. Hormonal steroids and sexual communication in primates. *Journal of Steroid Biochemistry*, 1975, *6*, 161–70. **125, 126**

Michael, R. P., and Bonsall, R. W. Periovulatory synchronisation of behaviour in male and female rhesus monkeys. *Nature*, 1977, *265*, 463–65. **361**

Michael, R. P., Setchell, K. D. R., and Plant, T. M. Diurnal changes in plasma testosterone and studies in plasma corticosteroids in non-anesthetized male rhesus monkeys (*Macaca mulatta*). *Journal of Endocrinology*, 1974, *63*, 325–35. **125, 163**

Michael, R. P., and Wilson, M. I. Mating seasonality in castrated male rhesus monkeys. *Journal of Reproduction and Fertility*, 1975, *43*, 325–28. **165**

Michael, R. P., Wilson, M. I., and Plant, T. M. Sexual behaviour of male primates and the role of testosterone. In R. P. Michael and J. H. Crook (Eds.), *Comparative ecol-*

Michael, R. P. (*Continued*)
ogy and behaviour of primates, pp. 235–313. New York: Academic Press, 1973. **117**

Michael, R. P., and Zumpe, D. Evironmental and endocrine factors influencing annual changes in sexual potency in primates. *Psychoneuroendocrinology*, 1976, *1*, 303–13. **165, 361**

Michael, R. P., and Zumpe, D. Effects of androgen administration on sexual invitations by female rhesus monkeys (*Macaca mulatta*). *Animal Behaviour*, 1977, *25*, 936–44. **126**

Michelini, R. L., Passalacqua, R., and Cusimano, J. Effects of seating arrangement on group participation. *Journal of Social Psychology*, 1976, *99*, 179–86. **308**

Miettinen, O. S., Neff, R. K., and Jick, H. Cigarette-smoking and nonfatal myocardial infarction: Rate ratio in relation to age, sex and predisposing conditions. *American Journal of Epidemiology*, 1976, *103*, 30–36. **379**

Milgram, S. Behavioral study of obedience. *Journal of Abnormal and Social Psychology*, 1963, *67*, 371–8. **294**

Miller, A. G. Role of physical attractiveness in impression formation. *Psychonomic Science*, 1970, *19*, 241–43. **314**

Miller, M. M., and Reeves, B. Dramatic TV content and children's sex-role stereotypes. *Journal of Broadcasting*, 1976, *20*, 35–50. **217**

Milton, G. A. Sex differences in problem solving as a function of role appropriateness of the problem content. *Psychological Reports*, 1959, *5*, 705–8. **254**

Minnigerode, F. A. Attitudes towards women, sex-role stereotyping and locus of control. *Psychological Reports*, 1976, *38*, 1301–2. **282**

Minuchin, P. Sex role concepts and sex typing in childhood as a function of school and home environments. *Child Development*, 1965, *36*, 1033–48. **183, 189, 194, 211**

Mischel, W. A social-learning view of sex differences in behavior. In E. E. Maccoby (Ed.), *The development of sex differences*, pp. 56–81. Stanford, Calif.: Stanford University Press, 1966. **183, 184**

Mishell, D. R., Thorneycroft, I. H., Nagata, Y., Murata, T., and Nakamura, R. M. Serum gonadotropin and steroid patterns in early human gestation. *American Journal of Obstetrics and Gynecology*, 1973, *117*, 631–39. **387**

Mislow, J. F., and Friedhoff, A. J. A comparison of chlorpromazine-induced extrapyramidal syndrome in male and female rats. In K. Lisśak (Ed.), *Hormones and brain function*, pp. 315–326. New York: Plenum Press, 1973. **320**

Mitchell, G., and Murphy, J. B. A survey of female patients in Carstairs State Hospital. *British Journal of Psychiatry*, 1975, *127*, 445–47. **351**

Mitchell, G. D. Attachment differences in male and female infant monkeys. *Child Development*, 1968, *39*, 611–20. **72, 78**

Mitchell, G. D. Paternalistic behavior in primates. *Psychological Bulletin*, 1969, *71*, 399–417. **77**

Mitchell, G. and Brandt, E. M. Behavioral differences related to experience of mother and sex of infant in the rhesus monkey. *Developmental Psychology*, 1970, *3*, 149. **74, 78**

Mitchell, G. D., Reppenthal, G. C., Raymond, E. J., and Harlow, H. F. Long-term effects of multiparous and primiparous monkey mother rearing. *Child Development*, 1966, *37*, 781–91. **236**

Molfese, D. L., Nuñez, V., Seibert, S. M., and Ramanaiah, N. V. Cerebral asymmetry: Changes in factors affecting its development. Paper presented at the New York Academy of Sciences conference on the Origins and Evaluation of Language and Speech, New York, September, 1975. **113**

Moltz, H., and Wiener, E. Effects of ovariectomy on maternal behavior of primiparous and multiparous rats. *Journal of Comparative and Physiological Psychology*, 1966, *62*, 382–387. **131**

Money, J. Two cytogenetic syndromes: Psychologic comparisons. 1. Intelligence and specific-factor quotients. *Journal of Psychiatric Research*, 1964, *2*, 223–31. **32, 35**

Money, J. Psychologic approach to psychosexual misidentity with elective mutism:

Sex reassignment in two cases of hyperadrenocortical hermaphroditism. *Clinical Pediatrics*, 1968, *7*, 331–39. **103, 173, 174**

Money, J. Prenatal hormones and intelligence: a possible relationship *Impact of Science on Society*, 1971, *21*, 285–90. **99**

Money, J. Prenatal hormones and postnatal socialization in gender identity differentiation. In J. K. Cole and R. Dienstbier (Ed.), *Nebraska symposium on motivation, 1973*, pp. 221–95. Lincoln: University of Nebraska Press, 1974. (a) **173, 174**

Money, J. Two names, two wardrobes, two personalities. *Journal of Homosexuality*, 1974, *1*, 65–70. (b) **103, 173**

Money, J. Gender identity and hermaphroditism. *Science*, 1976, *191*, 872. **175**

Money, J., Athanasiou, R., and Tobach, E. Eve first, or Adam? A review of M. J. Sherfey, *The nature and evolution of female sexuality. Contemporary Psychology*, 1973, *18*, 593–95. **329**

Money, J., and Clopper, R. R., Jr. Psychosocial and psychosexual aspects of errors of pubertal onset and development. *Human Biology*, 1974, *46*, 173–81. **374**

Money, J., and Ehrhardt, A. A. *Man and woman, boy and girl*. Baltimore: Johns Hopkins University Press, 1972. **4, 30, 32, 33, 34, 102, 104, 108, 126, 136, 173, 174, 200, 327, 331**

Money, J., Ehrhardt, A. A., and Masica, D. N. Fetal feminization induced by androgen insensitivity in the testicular feminizing syndrome: Effect on marriage and maternalism. *Johns Hopkins Medical Journal*, 1968, *123*, 105–14. **108**

Money, J., and Granoff, D. IQ and the somatic stigmata of Turner's syndrome. *American Journal of Mental Deficiency*, 1965, *70*, 69–77. **30**

Money, J., Hampson, J. L., and Hampson, J. G. An examination of some basic sexual concepts: The evidence of human hermaphroditism. *Bulletin of the Johns Hopkins Hospital*, 1955, *97*, 301–319. **173**

Money, J., and Lewis, V. IQ, genetics and accelerated growth: adrenogenital syndrome. *Bulletin of the Johns Hopkins Hospital*, 1966, *118*, 365–73. **103, 105, 106**

Money, J., and Schwartz, M. Fetal androgens

in the early treated adrenogenital syndrome of 46, XX hermaphroditism: Influence on assertive and aggressive types of behavior. *Aggressive Behavior*, 1976, *2*, 19–30. **90, 104, 105, 114**

Montagu, A. *The natural superiority of women*. New York: Collier, 1970. **353, 376**

Montagu, J. D., and Coles, E. M. Mechanism and measurement of the galvanic skin response. *Psychological Bulletin*, 1966, *65*, 261–79. **321**

Monti, P. M., Brown, W. A., and Corriveau, D. P. Testosterone and components of aggressive and sexual behavior in man. *American Journal of Psychiatry*, 1977, *134*, 692–94. **136, 139, 140**

Moore, M. Aggression themes in a binocular rivalry situation. *Journal of Personality and Social Psychology*, 1966, *3*, 685–88. **299**

Morgan, B. S. Intimacy of disclosure topics and sex differences in self-disclosure. *Sex Roles*, 1976, *2*, 161–66. **303**

Morgan, E. *The descent of woman*. New York: Bantam Books, 1972. **328, 331**

Morris, D. *Naked apes: A zoologist's study of the human animal*. New York: McGraw-Hill, 1969. **328**

Morton, J. H., Additon, H., Addison, R. G., Hunt, L., and Sullivan, J. A. A clinical study of premenstrual tension. *American Journal of Obstetrics and Gynecology*, 1953, *65*, 1182–91. **147, 149, 151, 154, 155, 387**

Moss, H. A. Sex, age, and state as determinants of mother-infant interaction. *Merrill-Palmer Quarterly*, 1967, *13*, 19–36. **208**

Moss, H. A. Early sex differences and mother-infant interaction. In R. C. Friedman, R. M. Richart, and R. L. Vande Wiele (Eds.), *Sex differences in behavior*. New York: Wiley, 1974, 149–63. **209**

Moss, R. L. Changes in bar-press duration accompanying the estrous cycle. *Journal of Comparative and Physiological Psychology*, 1968, *66*, 460–66. **133**

Mostow, E., and Newberry, P. Work role and depression in women: A comparison of workers and housewives in treatment. *American Journal of Orthopsychiatry*, 1975, *45*, 538–48. **346**

Moyer, K. E. Sex differences in aggression. In

Moyer, K. E. (*Continued*)
R. C. Friedman, R. M. Richart, R. L. Vande Wiele (Eds.), *Sex differences in behavior,* pp. 335–72. New York: Wiley, 1974. **127, 128, 138, 139, 140**

Mulford, H. A., and Salisbury, W. W. II. Self-conceptions in a general population. *Sociological Quarterly,* 1964, *3,* 115–21.

Mundy, J. Women in rage: A psychological look at the helpless heroine. In R. K. Unger and F. L. Denmark (Eds.), *Women: Dependent or independent variable?* pp. 196–214. New York: Psychological Dimension, 1975. **218**

Munsinger, H. Most California college women already know that the surface of still water is always horizontal. *American Journal of Psychology,* 1974, *87,* 717–18. **249**

Murdock, G. P. Comparative data on the division of labor by sex. *Social Forces,* 1935, *15,* 551–53. **201**

Mussen, P. H. Some antecedents and consequents of masculine sex-typing in adolescent boys. *Psychological Monograph,* 1961, *75,* (No. 506). **342**

Mussen, P. H. Long-term consequents of masculinity of interests in adolescence. *Journal of Consulting Psychology,* 1962, *26,* 435–40. **342**

Mussen, P. H. Early sex role development. In D. A. Goslin (Ed.), *Handbook of socialization theory and research,* pp. 707–29. Chicago: Rand McNally, 1969. **185, 189, 210, 211**

Myrsten, A. L, Hollstedt, C., and Holmberg, L. Alcohol-induced changes in mood and activation in males and females as related to catecholamine excretion and blood-alcohol level. *Scandinavian Journal of Psychology,* 1975, *16,* 303–10. **320**

Nadler, R. D. A biphasic influence of progesterone on sexual receptivity of spayed female rats. *Physiology and Behavior,* 1970, *5,* 95–97. **125**

Nadler, R. D. Sexual cyclicity in captive lowland gorillas. *Science,* 1975, *189,* 813–14. **64, 125, 126**

Naftolin, F., Ryan, K. J., and Petro, Z. Aromatization of androstenedione by the diencephalon. *Journal of Clinical Endocrinology,* 1971, *33,* 368–70. **113**

Nakamura, C. Y., and Anderson, N. H. Avoidance behavior differences within and between strains of rats. *Journal of Comparative and Physiological Psychology,* 1962, *55,* 740–47. **80**

Nance, J. *The gentle Tasaday.* New York: Harcourt Brace Jovanovich, 1975. **202**

Nance, D. M., and Gorski, R. A. Neurohumoral determinants of sex differences in the hypothalamic regulation of feeding behavior and body weight in the rat. *Pharmacology, Biochemistry and Behavior,* 1975, *3,* 155–62. **384**

Nance, D. M., Shryne, J. E., Gordon, J. H., and Gorski, R. A. Examination of some factors that control the effects of septal lesions on lordosis behavior. *Pharmacology, Biochemistry and Behavior,* 1977, *6,* 227–34. **112**

Nanko, S. Dermatoglyphic study of forty males with 47, XXY karyotype. *Japanese Journal of Human Genetics,* 1975, *20,* 109–21. **35**

Narins, P. M., and Capranica, R. R. Sexual differences in the auditory system of the tree frog. (*Eleu Thero dactylus cogui*). *Science,* 1976, *193,* 278–80. **63, 82**

Nash, J. *Development psychology: A psychobiological approach.* Englewood Cliffs, N.J.: Prentice-Hall, 1970. **112**

Nash, S. C. The relationship among sex-role stereotyping, sex-role preference, and the sex difference in spatial visualization. *Sex Roles,* 1975, *1,* 15–32. **228, 248, 256**

Nathanson, C. A. Illness and the feminine role: A theoretical review. *Social Science and Medicine,* 1975, *9,* 57–62. **379**

Netter, F. H. *The Ciba collection of medical illustration: Endocrine system and selected metabolic diseases.* Vol. 4. New York: Ciba Pharmaceutical Company, 1965. **27, 30, 31, 35, 45, 46, 47, 48, 49, 50, 51**

Neugarten, B. L. *Middle age and aging.* Chicago: University of Chicago Press, 1968. **211**

Neumann, F., Steinbeck, H., and Hahn, F. D. Hormones and brain differentiation. In L. Martini, M. Mott, and F. Fraschini (Eds.), *The hypothalamus,* pp. 569–603. New York: Academic Press, 1970. **96**

New Scientist. More divorce and less salary

for women science Ph.D.s. 1976, *69,* 130. **278**

Newsweek. The women's touch. January 6, 1975, p. 35. **290**

Newton, N. Interrelationships between sexual responsiveness, birth, and breast feeding. In J. Zubin and J. Money (Eds.), *Contemporary sexual behavior: Critical issues in the 1970's,* pp. 77–98. Baltimore: Johns Hopkins University Press, 1973. **53**

Nicholls, J. G. Causal attributions and other achievement-related cognitions: Effects of task outcome, attainment value and sex. *Journal of Personality and Social Psychology,* 1975, *31,* 378–89. **281, 283**

Nielsen, J. *Klinefelter's syndrome and the XYZ syndrome: A genetical, endocrinological and psychiatric-psychological study of 33 hypogonadal male patients and 2 patients with karyotype 47, XYY.* Copenhagen: Munksgaard, 1969.

Nielsen, J., and Christensen, A. L. Thirty-five males with double Y chromosome. *Journal of Psychological Medicine,* 1974, *4,* 38–37. **36, 37, 38**

Nielsen, J., and Tsuboi, T. Electroencephalographic examinations in the XYY syndrome and in Klinefelter's syndrome. *British Journal of Psychiatry,* 1974, *125,* 236–37. **33, 36**

Nilsson, L., and Sölvell, L. Clinical studies on oral contraceptives—A randomized, double-blind, cross-over study of 4 different preparations. *Acta Obstetrica Gynecologia Scandinavica,* 1967, *46,* (Suppl. 8). **144**

Nisbett, R. E., Braver, A., Jusela, G., and Kezur, D. Age and sex differences in behaviors mediated by the ventromedial hypothalamus. *Journal of Comparative and Physiological Psychology,* 1975, *88,* 735–46. **381**

Nisbett, R. E., and Gurwitz, S. B. Weight, sex, and the eating behavior of human newborns. *Journal of Comparative and Physiological Psychology,* 1970, *73,* 245–53. **324, 388**

Nisbett, R. E., and Temoshok, L. Is there an "eternal" cognitive style? *Journal of Personality and Social Psychology,* 1976, *33,* 36–47. **282**

Noble, R. G., and Alsum, P. B. Hormone dependent sex dimorphisms in the golden hamster (*Mesocricetus auratus*). *Physiology and Behavior,* 1975, *14,* 567–74. **124, 125**

Nöel, B., Duport, J. P., Revil, D., Dussuyer, I., and Quack, B. The XYY syndrome: Reality or myth? *Clinical Genetics,* 1974, *5,* 387–94. **36, 37**

Noirot, E., Goyens, J., and Buhot, M. -C. Aggressive behavior of pregnant mice toward males. *Hormones and Behavior,* 1975, *6,* 9–17. **127**

Norman, R. D. Sex differences in preferences for sex of children: A replication after 20 years. *Journal of Psychology,* 1974, *88,* 229–39. **226**

Notman, M. T., and Nadelson, C. C. Medicine: A career conflict for women. *American Journal of Psychiatry,* 1973, *130,* 1123–27. **238, 240**

O'Bryant, S. L., and Brophy, J. E. Sex differences in altruistic behavior. *Developmental Psychology,* 1976, *12,* 554. **306**

O'Connor, J. F., Shelley, E. M., and Stern, L. O. Behavioral rhythms related to the menstrual cycle. In M. Ferin, F. Halberg, R. M. Richart, and R. L. Vande Wiele (Eds.), *Biorhythms and human reproduction,* pp. 309–24. New York: Wiley, 1974. **155, 156**

Oetzel, R. M. Annotated bibliography. In E. E. Maccoby (Ed.), *The development of sex differences,* pp. 223–31. Stanford, Calif.: Stanford University Press, 1966. **220, 315**

Ohno, S. *Sex chromosome and sex linking genes.* New York: Springer-Verlag, 1967. **26, 28**

Oldfield, R. C. The assessment and analysis of handedness: The Edinburgh inventory. *Neuropsychologia,* 1971, *9,* 97–113. **258**

O'Leary, V. E. Some attitudinal barriers to occupational aspirations in women. *Psychological Bulletin,* 1974, *81,* 809–26. **265, 276, 336**

Omark, D. R., and Edelman, M. S. A comparison of status hierarchies in young children: An ethological approach. *Social Science Information,* 1975, *14,* 87–107. **296**

O'Neill, S., Fein, D., Velit, K. M., and Frank, C. Sex differences in preadolescent self-

O'Neill, S. (*Continued*)
disclosure. *Sex Roles*, 1976, *2*, 85–88. **303**

Ortner, S. B. Is female to male as nature is to culture? In M. Z. Rosaldo and L. Lamphere (Eds.), *Woman, culture and society*, pp. 67–87. Stanford, Calif.: Stanford University Press, 1974. **199, 200, 205**

Oster, G. Auditory beats in the brain. *Scientific American*, 1973, *229*, 94–102. **150**

Ounsted, C., and Taylor, D.C. (Eds.) *Gender differences: Their ontogeny and significance.* London: Churchill Livingston, 1972. (a) **32, 380**

Ounsted, C., and Taylor, D. C. The Y chromosome message: A point of view. In C. Ounsted and D. C. Taylor (Eds.), *Gender differences: Their ontogeny and significance,* pp. 241–62. London: Churchill Livingston, 1972. (b) **36**

Ounsted, M. Gender and intrauterine growth with a note on the use of the sex proband as a research tool. In C. Ounsted and D. C. Taylor (Eds.), *Gender differences: Their ontogeny and significance,* pp. 177–201. London: Churchill Livingston, 1972. **373**

Outzen, H. C., and Pilgrim, H. I. Differential mortality of male and female germfree C_3H mice introduced into a conventional colony. *Proceedings of the Society for Experimental Biology and Medicine*, 1967, *124*, 52–56. **377**

Owen, D. R. The 47, XYY male: A review. *Psychological Bulletin*, 1972, *78*, 209–33. **36, 37**

Page, T., Harris, R. H., and Epstein, S. S. Drinking water and cancer mortality in Louisiana. *Science*, 1976, *193*, 55–57 **374**

Paige, K. E. Effects of oral contraceptives on affective fluctuations associated with the menstrual cycle. *Psychosomatic Medicine*, 1971, *33*, 515–37. **143, 149, 158**

Paige, K. E. Women learn to sing the menstrual blues. In C. Tavris (Ed.), *The female experience,* pp. 17–21. Del Mar, Calif.: Communications Research Machines, 1973. **158**

Palti, H., and Adler, B. Anthropometric measurements of the newborn, sex differences, and correlations between measurements. *Human Biology*, 1975, *47*, 523–30. **319**

Pande, C. G. Sex differences in field-dependence: Confirmation with Indian sample. *Perceptual and Motor Skills*, 1970, *31*, 70. **244**

Pandey, J., and Griffitt, W. Attraction and helping. *Bulletin of the Psychonomic Society*, 1974, *3*, 123–24. **307**

Panek, P. E., Deitchman, R., Burkholder, J. H., Speroff, T., and Haude, R. H. Evaluation of feminine professional competence as a function of level of accomplishment. jblPsychological Reports, 1976, *38*, 875–80. **227**

Pangborn, R. M. Influence of hunger on sweetness preferences and taste thresholds. *American Journal of Clinical Nutrition*, 1959, *7*, 280–87. **324**

Papalia, D. E., and Tennent, S. S. Vocational aspirations in preschoolers: A manifestation of early sex role stereotyping. *Sex Roles*, 1975, *1*, 197–99. **190**

Pardue, L. H. Familial unipolar depressive illness: A pedigree study. *American Journal of Psychiatry*, 1975, *132*, 970–72. **352**

Parke, R., and O'Leary, S. Mother-father-infant interaction in the newborn period: Some findings, some observations, and some unresolved issues. In K. Riegel and J. Meacham (Eds.), *The developing individual in a changing world: Social and environmental issues.* (Vol. 2, pp. 653–663.) The Hague, Holland: Mouton, 1976. **307**

Parlee, M. B. Comments on "Roles of activation and inhibition in sex differences in cognitive abilities." *Psychological Review*, 1972, *79*, 180–84. **260**

Parlee, M. B. The premenstrual syndrome. *Psychological Bulletin*, 1973, *80*, 454–65. **156**

Parlee, M. B. Stereotypic beliefs about menstruation: A methodological note on the Moos menstrual distress questionnaire and some new data. *Psychosomatic Medicine*, 1974, *36*, 229–40.

Parlee, M. B., and Rajagopal, J. Sex differences on the embedded-figures test: A cross-cultural comparison of college students in India and in the United States. *Perceptual and Motor Skills*, 1974, *39*, 1311–14. **158, 244**

Parsons, T., and Bales, R. F. *Family, socialization and interaction process.* New York: Free Press, 1955. **191, 192, 200**

Pátkai, P., Johannson, G., and Post, B. Mood, alertness and sympathetic-adrenal medullary activity during the menstrual cycle. *Psychosomatic Medicine,* 1974, *36,* 503–12. **19, 150**

Patty, R. A. Motive to avoid success and instructional set. *Sex Roles,* 1976, *2,* 81–83. **270**

Paulson, M. J. Psychological concomitants of premenstrual tension. *American Journal of Obstetrics and Gynecology,* 1961, *81,* 733–38. **157**

Payne, A. P. Neonatal androgen administration and aggression in the female golden hamster during interactions with males. *Journal of Endocrinology,* 1974, *63,* 497–506. (b) **67, 71, 93**

Payne, A. P. A comparison of the effects of neonatally administered testosterone, testosterone propinate and dihydrotestosterone on aggressive and sexual behavior in the female golden hamster. *Journal of Endocrinology,* 1976, *69,* 23–31. **90, 91, 93, 113**

Payne, A. P. Changes in aggressive and sexual responsiveness of male golden hamster after neonatal androgen administration. *Journal of Endocrinology,* 1977, *73,* 331–37. **90, 91, 93**

Payne, A. P., and Swanson, H. H. The effects of neonatal androgen administration on the aggression and related behaviour of male golden hamsters during interaction with females. *Journal of Endocrinology,* 1973, *58,* 627–36. **67, 93, 128**

Payne, A. P. The aggressive response of the male golden hamster towards males and females of differing hormonal status. *Animal Behaviour,* 1974, *22,* 829–35. (a) **67, 71**

Pederson, D. M., Shinedling, M. M., and Johnson, D. L. Effects of sex of examiner and subject on children's quantitative test performance. *Journal of Personality and Social Psychology,* 1968, *10,* 251–54. **254**

Pennington, V. M. Meprobamate (Miltown) in premenstrual tension. *Journal of the American Medical Association,* 1957, *164,* 638. **154**

Penrose, L. S. Medical significance of finger-prints and related phenomena. *British Medical Journal,* 1968, *2,* 321–25. **39**

Peplau, L. A. Fear of success in dating couples. *Sex Roles,* 1976, *2,* 249–58. **269, 295**

Peretz, E., Goy, R. W., Phoenix, C. H., and Resko, J. A. Influence of gonadal hormones on the development and activation of the nervous system of the rhesus monkey. In *Influence of hormones on the nervous system: The Proceedings of the International Society of Psycoendocrinology,* pp. 242–54. Basel, Switz.: Karger, 1971, pp. 401–411. **125**

Perez-Lopez, F. R., L'Hermite, M., and Robyn, C. Gonadotropin hormone releasing tests in women receiving hormonal contraception. *Clinical Endocrinology,* 1975, *4,* 477–85. **142**

Perloff, R. M. Some antecedents of children's sex-role stereotypes. *Psychological Reports,* 1977, *40,* 463–66. **217**

Persky, H. Reproductive hormones, moods, and the menstrual cycle. In R. C. Friedman, R. M. Richart, and R. L. Vande Wiele (Eds.), *Sex differences in behavior,* pp. 455–66 New York. Wiley, 1974. **138, 139, 142, 152, 157**

Persky, H., O'Brien, C. P., Fine, E., Howard, W. J., Khan, M. A., and Beck, R. W. The effect of alcohol and smoking on testosterone function and aggression in chronic alcoholics. *American Journal of Psychiatry,* 1977, *134,* 621–25. **139**

Persky, H., Smith, K. D., and Basu, G. K. Relation of psychologic measures of aggression and hostility to testosterone production in man. *Psychosomatic Medicine,* 1971, *33,* 265–77. **138, 140, 165**

Person, E. S., and Ovesey, L. The psychodynamics of male transsexualism. In R. C. Friedman, R. M. Richart, and R. L. Vande Wiele (Eds.), *Sex differences in behavior,* pp. 315–25. New York, Wiley, 1974. **176, 177**

Peterson, A. C. Physical androgyny and cognitive functioning in adolescence. *Developmental Psychology,* 1976, *12,* 524–33. **141, 238, 244, 245, 246**

Petit, C. Medical mystery solution proposed.

Petit, C. (*Continued*)
   San Francisco Chronicle, June 26, 1976,
   p. 12. **143**
Petre-Quadens, O., and DeLee, C. Sleep-
   cycle alterations during pregnancy, postpartum, and the menstrual cycle. In M.
   Ferin, F. Halberg, R. M. Richart, and R. L.
   Vande Wiele (Eds.), *Biorhythms and human
   reproduction,* pp. 335–52. New York: Wiley,
   1974. **150**
Pettigrew, T. *A profile of the Negro American.*
   Princeton: Van Nostrand, 1964.
Pfaff, D. W. Morphological changes in the
   brains of adult male rats after neonatal
   castration. *Journal of Endocrinology,* 1966,
   36, 415–16. **112**
Pfaff, D. W. Nature of sex hormone effects
   on rat sex behavior: Specificity of effects
   and individual patterns of response.
   *Journal of comparative and Physiological
   Psychology,* 1970, *73,* 349–58. **124, 125**
Pfaff, D. W., Diakow, C., Zigmond, R. E., and
   Kow, L. M. Neural and hormonal determinants of female mating behavior in rats.
   In F. O. Schmitt, and F. G. Worden, (Eds.),
   The neurosciences: Third study program,
   pp. 621–46. Cambridge, Mass.: MIT Press,
   1974. **90, 91, 111**
Pfaff, D. W., and Zigmond, R. E. Neonatal
   androgen effects in sexual and nonsexual
   behavior of adult rats tested under various
   hormone regimes. *Neuroendocrinology,*
   1971, *7,* 129–145. **98**
Pfeiffer, C. A. Sexual differences of the
   hypophyses and their determination by the
   gonads. *American Journal of Anatomy,*
   1936, *58,* 195–226. **90**
Pheterson, G. I., Kiesler, S. B., and Goldberg,
   P. A. Evaluation of the performance of
   women as a function of their sex, achievement, and personal history. *Journal of Personality and Social Psychology,* 1971, *19,*
   114–18. **225**
Philippe, P., and Yelle, L. Effect of family size
   on mother's longevity. *Annals of Human
   Biology,* 1976, *3,* 431–39. **378**
Phillips, A. G., and Deol, G. S. Neonatal
   gonadal hormone manipulation and emotionality following septal lesions in weaning
   rats. *Brain Research,* 1973, *60,* 55–64.
   112
Phillips, A. G., and Deol, G. S. Neonatal

androgen levels and avoidance learning in
   prepubescent and adult male rats. *Hormones and Behavior,* 1977, *8,* 22–29. **98,
   99, 100**
Phillips, D., and Segal, B. Sexual status and
   psychiatric symptoms. *American Sociological Review,* 1969, *34,* 58–72. **346**
Phoenix, C. H. Prenatal testosterone in the
   nonhuman primate and its consequences
   for behavior. In R. C. Friedman, R. M.
   Richart, and R. L. Vande Wiele (Eds.), *Sex
   differences in behavior,* pp. 19–32. New
   York: Wiley, 1974. **98**
Phoenix, C. H., and McCauley, E. Discussion:
   Stress and early life experience in non-
   humans. In R. C. Friedman, R. M. Richart,
   and R. L. Vande Wiele (Eds.), *Sex differences in behavior.* pp. 143–45. New York:
   Wiley, 1974. **81, 131**
Pietarinen, G. J., Leichter, J., and Pratt, R. F.
   Dietary folate intake and concentration
   of folate in serum and erythrocytes in
   women using oral contraceptives. *American Journal of Clinical Nutrition,* 1977, *30,*
   375–80. **143**
Pietras, R. J., and Moulton, D. G. Hormonal
   influences on odor detection in rats:
   Changes associated with the estrous cycle,
   pseudopregnancy, ovariectomy, and administration of testosterone proprinate.
   Physiology and Behavior, 1974, *12,* 475–
   91. **82, 151, 324**
Plank, E. M., and Plank R. Emotional components in arithmetic learning as seen
   through autobiographies. In R. S. Eissler
   (Ed.), *The psychoanalytic study of the child.*
   Vol. 9, pp. 274–93. New York: International
   University Press, 1954. **256**
Plant, T. M., Zumpe, D., Sauls, M., and Michael, R. P. An annual rhythm in the plasma
   testosterone of adult male rhesus monkeys
   maintained in the laboratory. *Journal of
   Endocrinology,* 1974, *62,* 403–4. **167**
Pleck, J. H. Masculinity-femininity: Current
   and alternative paradigms. *Sex Roles,*
   1975, *1,* 161–78. **211**
Polani, P. E. Abnormal sex chromosomes
   and mental disorder. *Nature,* 1969, *223,*
   680–86. **39**
Polani, P. E. Chromosome phenotypes—Sex
   chromosomes. In F. C. Fraser, V. A. Mc-
   Kuisick (Eds.), *Congenital malformations,*

pp. 233–50. Princeton, M.J.: *Excerpta Medica,* 1970. **39**

Polani, P. E. Errors of sex determination and sex chronosome anomalies. In C. Ounsted and D. C. Taylor (Eds.), *Gender differences: Their ontogeny and significance,* pp. 13–39. London: Churchill Livingstone. 1972. **30, 36**

Polani, P. E. Some experiments of nature with sex. *British Journal of Psychiatry,* 1974, *125,* 559–67. **30**

Pollack, E. I., and Sachs, B. D. Masculine sexual behavior and morphology: paradoxical effects of prenatal androgen treatment in male and female rats. *Behavioral Biology,* 1975, *13,* 401–411. **91**

Pollack, E. S., Rednick, R. W., and Taube, C. A. The application of census socioeconomic and familial data to the study of morbidity from mental disorders. *American Journal of Public Health,* 1968, *58,* 83–9. **340**

Porteus, D. S. *Porteus maze test: Fifty years application.* Palo Alto, Calif.: Pacific Books, 1965. **244, 252**

Potkay, C. R., and Merrens, M. R. Sources of male chauvanism in the rat. *Journal of Personality Assessment,* 1975, *39,* 471–79. **347**

Powell, A., Thompson, N., Hall, D. J., and Wilson, L. Parent-child concordance with respect to sex and diagnosis in schizophrenia and manic-depressive psychosis. *British Journal of Psychiatry,* 1973, *123,* 653–58. **352**

Powell, B. J. Prediction of drug action: Elimination of error through emotionality. *Proceedings of the 75th Annual Conference of the American Psychological Association,* 1967, 69–70. **80**

Prescott, R. G. W. Estrous cycle in the rat: Effects of self-stimulation behavior. *Science,* 1966, *152,* 796–97. **133**

Preston, F. S., Bateman, S. C., Short, R. V., and Wilkinson, R. T. The effects of flying and of time changes on menstrual cycle length and on performance in airline stewardesses. In M. Ferin, F. Halberg, R. M. Richart, and R. L. Vande Wiele (Eds.), *Biorhythms and human reproduction,* pp. 501–12. New York: Wiley, 1974. **122**

Price, W. H., Brunton, M., Buckton, K., and Jacobs, P. A. Chromosome survey of new patients admitted to the four maximum security hospitals in the United Kingdom. *Clinical Genetics,* 1976, *9,* 389–98. **35, 37**

Price, W. H., and Whatmore, P. B. Behavior disorders and pattern of crime among XYY males identified at a maximum security hospital. *British Medical Journal,* 1967, *1,* 533–36. **38**

Procacci, P., Buzzelli, G., Passeri, I., Sassi, R., Voegelin, M. R., and Zoppi, M. Studies on the cutaneous pricking pain threshold in man: Circadian and circatrigintan changes. *Research and Clinical Studies in Headache,* 1972, *3,* 260–76. **150, 163, 323, 325**

Proctor, E. B., Wagner, N. N., and Butler, J. C. The differentiation of male and female orgasm: An experimental study. *American Psychological Proceedings,* 1973, *8,* (No. 1), 411–12. **330**

Pugh, T. F., Jerath, B. K., Schmidt, W. M., and Reed, R. B. Rates of mental disease related to childbearing. *New England Journal of Medicine,* 1963, *268,* 1224–28. **160**

Purvis, K., and Haynes, N. B. Short-term effects of copulation, human chorionic gonadotropin injection and non tactile association with a female on testosterone levels in the male rat. *Journal of Endocrinology,* 1974, *60,* 429–39. **122**

Quadagno, D. M., Albelda, S. M., McGill, T. E., and Kaplan, L. J. Intracranial cycloheximide: Effect on male mouse sexual behavior and plasma testosterone. *Pharmacology, Biochemistry and Behavior,* 1976, *4,* 185–89. **122**

Quadagno, D. M., Briscoe, R., and Quadagno, J. S. Effect of perinatal gonadal hormones on selected nonsexual behavior patterns: A critical assessment of the nonhuman and human literature, *Psychological Bulletin,* 1977, *84,* 62–80. **93, 115, 128, 129, 132**

Quadagno, D. M., McCullough, J., Ho, G. K. H., and Spevak, A. M. Neonatal gonadal hormones: Effect on maternal and sexual behavior in the female rat. *Physiology and Behavior,* 1973, *11,* 251–54. **79**

Quadagno, D. M., and Rockwell, J. The effect of gonadal hormones in infancy on mater-

Quadagno, D. M. (*Continued*) nal behavior in the adult rat. *Hormones and Behavior,* 1972, *3,* 55–62.   **79, 96, 130**

Quadagno, D. M., Shryne, J., Anderson C., and Gorski, R. A. Influence of gonadal hormones on social sexual, emergence, and open field behaviour in the rat (*Rattus norvegicus*). *Animal Behaviour,* 1972, *20,* 732–40.   **78, 96, 100**

Rabb, G. B., Woolpy, J. H., and Ginsburg, B. E. Social relationships in a group of captive wolves. *American Zoologist,* 1967, *7,* 305–11.   **71**

Raboch, J., and Stárka, L. Coital activity of men and the levels of plasmatic testosterone. *Journal of Sex Research,* 1972, *8,* 219–24.   **136**

Radloff, L. Sex differences in depression: The effects of occupation and marital status. *Sex Roles,* 1975, *1,* 249–65.   **338, 339, 344**

Ragavi, L. Sex chromosomes, handprints and sexual behavior. Paper read at the meeting of the American Association for the Advancement of Science, Boston, 1969. (Cited by A. Mazur and L. S. Robertson, *Biology and social behavior,* New York: Macmillan, 1972.)   **39**

Raisman, G., and Field P. M. Sexual dimorphism in the preoptic area of the rat. *Science,* 1971, *173,* 731–33.   **111**

Raisman, G., and Field, P. M. Sexual dimorphism in the neuropil of the preoptic area of the rat and its dependence on neonatal androgen. *Brain Research,* 1973, *54,* 1–29.   **111**

Ramaley, J. A. Effects of prior androgen exposure upon adrenal function in maturing rats. *Steroids,* 1974, *24,* 281–93.   **87**

Ransom, T. W., and Ransom, B. S. Adult male-infant relations among baboons (*Papio anubis*). *Folia Primatology,* 1971, *16,* 179–95.   **72**

Raskin, A. Age-sex differences in response to antidepressant drugs. *The Journal of Nervous and Mental Disease,* 1974, *159,* 120–130.   **320**

Rebelsky, F., and Hanks, C. Fathers' verbal interaction with infants in the first three months of life. *Child Development,* 1971, *42,* 63–68.   **208**

Reddy, V. V. R., Naftolin, F., and Ryan, K. J. Conversion of androstenedione to estrone by neural tissues from fetal and neonatal rats. *Endocrinology,* 1974, *94,* 117–121.   **113**

Rees, L. Psychosomatic aspects of the premenstrual tension syndrome. *Journal of Mental Science,* 1953, *99,* 62–73.   **157**

Regestein, Q. R., Williams, G. H. and Rose, L. I. Influence of perinatal progesterone on sexual activity in the male guinea pig. *Journal of Psychiatric Research,* 1975, *12,* 149–51.   **91**

Reich, T., Clayton, P. J., and Winokur, G. Family history studies, V: The genetics of mania. *American Journal of Psychiatry,* 1969, *125,* 1358–69.   **352**

Reich, T., Winokur, G., and Mullaney, J. The transmission of alcoholism. In R. R. Fieve, D. Rosenthal, and H. Brill (Eds.), *Genetic research in psychiatry,* pp. 259–71. Baltimore: Johns Hopkins University Press, 1975.   **42, 352**

Reik, T. *The creation of woman.* New York: McGraw-Hill, 1960.   **183**

Reinartz, K. F. The paper doll: Images of American woman in popular songs. In J. Freeman (Ed.), *Women: A feminist perspective,* pp. 293–308. Palo Alto, Calif.: Mayfield, 1975.   **215**

Reinberg, A., Lagoguey, M., Chauffournier, J. M., and Cesselin, F. Circannual and circadian rhythms in plasma testosterone in five healthy young Parisian males. *Acta Endocrinologica,* 1975, *80,* 732–43.   **164, 165, 167**

Reinisch, J. M. Prenatal exposure of human foetuses to synthetic progestin and oestrogen affects personality. *Nature,* 1977, *266,* 561–62.   **104, 106, 110, 245**

Rekers, G. A., Amaro-Plotkin, H. D., and Low, B. P. Sex-typed mannerisms in normal boys and girls as a function of sex and age. *Child Development,* 1977, *48,* 275–78.   **310**

Rekers, G. A., and Yates, C. E. Sex-typed play in feminoid boys versus normal boys and girls. *Journal of Abnormal Child Psychology,* 1976, *4,* 1–8.   **187**

Repucci, N. D. Parental education, sex differences, and performance on cognitive tasks among two-year-old children. *De-*

velopmental Psychology, 1971, *4*, 248–53. **208, 252**

Resko, J. A. Androgen secretion by the fetal and neonatal rhesus monkey. *Endocrinology*, 1970, *87*, 680–87. **47**

Resko, J. A., Feder, H. H., and Goy R. W. Androgen concentration in plasma and testes of developing rats. *Journal of Endocrinology*, 1968, *40*, 485–91. **47**

Restak, R. The danger of knowing too much. *Psychology Today*, 1975, *9*, 21 ff. **4**

Retherford, R. D. Tobacco smoking and sex ratios in the United States. *Social Biology*, 1974, *21*, 28–38. **379**

Richards, M. P. M. Effects of oestrogen and progesterone on nest building in the golden hamster. *Aminal Behaviour*, 1969, *17*, 356–61. **96**

Richards, M. P. M., Bernal, J. F., and Brackbill, Y. Early behavioral differences: Gender or circumcision? *Developmental Psychobiology*, 1976, *9*, 89–95. **322**

Richter, C. P. Periodic phenomena in man and animals: Their relation to neuroendocrine mechanisms (a monthly or nearly monthly cycle). In R. P. Michael (Ed.), *Endocrinology and human behavior*, pp. 284–309. New York: Oxford University Press, 1968. **163, 164**

Roberts, J. Binocular visual acuity of adults. *Public Health Service Publication N.O. 1000*, (Series 11, No. 3), 1964. **323**

Roberts, S., Kenney, N. J., and Mook, D. G. Over-eating induced by progesterone in the ovariectomized, adrenalectomized rat. *Hormones and Behavior*, 1972, *3*, 267–76. **384**

Robinson, A. Sex chromatin in newborns. *American Journal of Human Genetics*, 1975, *27*, 118. **28**

Robinson, E. Effect of crowding and litter size on several behaviors of white rats. *Psychological Reports*, 1975, *37*, 599–606. **75**

Robinson, J. A., Scheffler, G., Eisele, S. G., and Goy, R. W. Effects of age and season in sexual behavior and plasma testosterone and dihydrotestosterone concentration of laboratory-housed male rhesus monkeys (*Macaca mulatta*). *Biology of Reproduction*, 1975, *13*, 203–10. **165**

Rodin, E. A., Grisell, J. L., Gudobba, R. D., and Zachary, G. Relationship of EEG background rhythms to photic evoked responses. *Electroencephalography and Clinical Neurophysiology*, 1965, *19*, 301–53. **113**

Rodin, J. Menstruation, reattribution and competence. *Journal of Personality and Social Psychology*, 1976, *33*, 345–53. **157, 159**

Rogers, L. J. Persistence and search influenced by natural levels of androgens in young and adult chickens. *Physiology and Behavior*, 1974, *12*, 197–204. **132**

Romney, A. K. Variations in household structure as determinants of sex-typed behavior. In F. A. Beach (Ed.), *Sex and behavior*, pp. 208–20. New York: Wiley, 1965. **207**

Rosaldo, M. Z. Woman, culture, and society: A theoretical overview. In M. Z. Rosaldo and L. Lamphere (Eds.), *Woman, culture, and society*, pp. 17–42. Stanford, Calif.: Stanford University Press, 1974. **199**

Rose, R. M., Bernstein, I. S., Gordon, T. P., et al. Androgens and aggression: A review and recent findings in primates. In R. L. Holloway (Ed.), *Primate aggression, territoriality and xenophobia*, pp. 275–304. New York: Academic Press, 1974. **127**

Rose, R. M., Bernstein, I. S., and Gordon, T. P. Consequences of social conflict on plasma testosterone levels in rhesus monkeys. *Psychosomatic Medicine*, 1975, *37*, 50–61. **122**

Rose, R. M., Gordon, T. P., and Bernstein, I. S. Plasma testosterone levels in the male rhesus: Influences of sexual and social stimuli. *Science*, 1972, *178*, 643–45. **122**

Rosen, B., and Jerdee, T. H. The influence of sex-role stereotypes on evaluations of male and female supervisory behavior. *Journal of Applied Psychology*, 1973, *57*, 44–48. **298**

Rosen, B., Jerdee, T. H., and Prestwich, T. L. Dual-career marital adjustment: Potential effects of discriminatory managerial attitudes. *Journal of Marriage and the Family*, 1975, *37*, 565–72. **225, 226**

Rosenberg, B. G., and Sutton-Smith, B. *Sex and identity*. New York: Holt, Rinehart and Winston, 1972. **185, 191**

Rosenberg, B. G., and Sutton-Smith, B. Family structure and sex-role variations. In J. C. Cole and R. Dienstbier (Eds.). *Nebraska symposium on motivation, 1973*, pp. 195–220. Lincoln: University of Nebraska Press, 1974. **211**

Rosenberg, F. R., and Simmons, R. G. Sex differences in the self-concept in adolescence. *Sex Roles*, 1975, *I*, 147–59. **272, 303, 336**

Rosenberg, K. M., and Sherman, G. F. Testosterone induced pup-killing behavior in the ovariectomized female rat. *Physiology and Behavior*, 1974, *13*, 697–99. **93, 128**

Rosenberg, K. M., and Sherman, G. F. Influence of testosterone on pup killing in the rat is modified by prior experience. *Physiology and Behavior*, 1975, *13*, 669–72. (a) **71, 93**

Rosenberg, K. M., and Sherman, G. F. The role of testosterone in the organization, maintenance and activation of pup-killing behavior in the male rat. *Hormones and Behavior*, 1975, *6*, 173–79. (b) **71, 93**

Rosenberg, M. The biologic basis for sex role stereotypes. *Contemporary Psychoanalysis*, 1973, *9*, 374–91. **19**

Rosenberg, P. A., and Herrenkohl, L. R. Maternal behavior in male rats: Critical times for the suppressive action of androgens. *Physiology and Behavior*, 1976, *16*, 293–97. **96**

Rosenblatt, J. S., and Aronson, L. R. The decline of sexual behavior in male cats after castration with special reference to the role of prior sexual experience. *Behavior*, 1958, *12*, 285–338. **117**

Rosenblum, L. A. Sex differences, environmental complexity and mother-infant relations. *Archives of Sexual Behavior*, 1974, *3*, 117–28. **78**

Rosenthal, L., and Klapper Z. Mother Jones' feminist quiz. *Mother Jones*, 1977, *2*, 31–4, and 38. **182**

Rosenthal, R. On the social psychology of the psychological experiment: The experimenter's hypothesis as an unintended determinant of experimental results. *American Scientists*, 1963, *51*, 268–83. **19**

Rosenthal, R. *Experimenter effects in behavioral research*. New York: Appleton-Century-Crofts, 1966. **19**

Rosenthal, R., Archer, D., DiMatteo, M. R., Koivumaki, J. H., and Rogers, P. L. Body talk and tone of voice: The language without words. *Psychology Today*, September, 1974, pp. 64–68. **303**

Rosenthal, R., and Fode, K. L. The effect of experimenter bias on the performance of the albino rat. Unpublished manuscript, Harvard University, 1960. **19**

Rosenthal, R., and Jacobson, L. *Pygmalion in the classroom: Teacher expectations and pupil's intellectual development*. New York: Holt, Rinehart and Winston, 1968. **19**

Rosenthal, R., and Lawson, R. A longitudinal study of the effects of experimenter bias on the operant learning of laboratory rats. Unpublished manuscript, Harvard University, 1961. **19**

Rosner, M. Women in the kibbutz: Changing status and concepts. *Asian and African Studies*, 1967, *3*, 35–68. **205**

Ross, M. H., and Bras, G. Food preference and length of life. *Science*, 1975, *190*, 165–67. **382**

Ross, S., and Walters, J. Perceptions of a sample of university men concerning women. *Journal of Genetic Psychology*, 1973, *122*, 329–36. **228**

Rossi, A. S. Barriers to the career choice of engineering, medicine, or science among American women. In J. A. Mattfeld and C. G. Van Aken (Eds.), *Women and the scientific profession*, pp. 51–127. Cambridge, Mass.: MIT Press, 1965. **274, 276, 278, 279, 338**

Rossi, A. S. Maternalism, sexuality and the new feminism. In J. Zubin and J. Money (Eds.), *Contemporary sexual behavior: Critical issues in the 1970's*, pp. 145–73. Baltimore: Johns Hopkins University Press, 1973. **330**

Rothbart, M. K., and Rothbart, M. Birth order, sex of child, and maternal help-giving. *Sex Roles*, 1976, *2*, 39–46. **301**

Rotter, J. Generalized expectancies for internal versus external control of reinforcement. *Psychological Monographs*, 1966, *80*, 1–28. **282**

Rowell, T. E. Baboon menstrual cycles affected by social environment. *Journal of Reproduction and Fertility*, 1970, *21*, 133–41. **129**

Roy, E. J., Maass, C. A., and Wade, G. N. Central action and a species comparison of the estrogenic effects of an antiestrogen on eating and body weight. *Physiology and Behavior*, 1977, *18*, 137–40. **383**

Roy, E. J., and Wade, G. N. Role of estrogens in androgen-induced spontaneous activity in male rats. *Journal of Comparative and Physiological Psychology*, 1975, *89*, 573–79. **132, 383**

Roy, E. J., and Wade, G. N. Estrogenic effects of an antiestrogen, MER-25, on eating and body weight in rats. *Journal of Comparative and Physiological Psychology*, 1976, *90*, 156–66.

Rubin, J. Z., Provenzano, F. J., and Luria, Z. The eye of the beholder: Parents' views on sex of newborns. *American Journal of Orthopsychiatry*, 1974, *44*, 512–19. **207**

Ruble, D. N. Premenstrual symptoms: A reinterpretation. *Science*, 1977, *197*, 291–92. **158**

Ruble, D. N., and Higgins, E. T. Effects of group sex composition on self-presentation and sex-typing. *Journal of Social Issues*, 1976, *32*, 125–32. **210**

Russell, P. A. Sex differences in rats' response to novelty measured by activity and preference. *Quarterly Journal of Experimental Psychology*, 1975, *27*, 585–89. **76**

Ryan, A. J. Gynecological considerations. *Journal of Health, Physical Education, and Recreation*, January, 1975, pp. 40–44. **156**

Sachs, B. D., Pollack, E., Schoelch-Krieger, M., and Barfield, R. J. Sexual behavior: Normal male patterning in androgenized females. *Science*, 1973, *181*, 770–72. **90**

Sackett, G. P. Sex differences in rhesus monkeys following varied rearing experiences. In R. C. Friedman, R. M. Richart, and R. L. Vande Wiele (Eds.), *Sex differences in behavior*, pp. 99–122. New York: Wiley, 1974. **236**

Safilios-Rothschild, C. A cross-cultural examination of women's marital, educational, and occupational options. *Acta Sociologica*, 1971, *14*, 96–113. **203**

Salmon, U. J., and Geist, S. H. Effect of androgens upon libido in women. *Journal of Clinical Endocrinology and Metabolism*, 1943, *3*, 235–38. **137**

Sanchez-Franco, F., Garcia, M. D., Cacicedo, L., Martin-Zurro, A., and Del Rey, F. E. Influence of sex phase of the menstrual cycle in thyrotropin (TSH) response to thyrotropin-releasing hormone (TRH). *Journal of Clinical Endocrinology and Metabolism*, 1973, *37*, 736–40. **147**

Sanday, P. R. Female status in the public domain. In M. Z. Rosaldo and L. Lamphere (Eds.), *Women, culture and society*, pp. 189–206. Stanford, Calif.: Stanford University Press, 1974. **199**

Sands, D. E. Further studies on endocrine treatment in adolescence and early adult life. *Journal of Mental Science*, 1954, *100*, 211–19. **136, 138, 140, 387**

Sands, D. E., and Chamberlain, G. H. A. Treatment of inadequate personality in juveniles by dihydroisoandosterone: Prelimary report. *British Medical Journal*, 1952, *3*, 66–68. **138**

Sassenrath, E. N., Rowell, T. E., and Hendrick, A. G. Perimenstrual aggression in groups of female rhesus monkeys. *Journal of Reproduction Fertility*, 1973, *34*, 509–11. **129**

Schachter, S., and Singer, S. E. Cognitive, social and physiological determinants of emotional state. *Psychological Review*, 1962, *69*, 379–99. **117**

Schiavi, R. C., Davis, D. M., White, D., Edwards, A., Igel, G., and Fisher, C. Plasma testosterone during nocturnal sleep in normal men. *Steroids*, 1974, *24*, 191–202. **163**

Schmidt, G. Male-female differences in sexual arousal and behavior during and after exposure to sexually explicit stimuli. *Archives of Sexual Behavior*, 1975, *4*, 353–65. **330**

Schmidt, G., and Sigusch, V. Sex differences in responses to psychosexual stimulation by films and slides. *Journal of Sex Research*, 1970, *6*, 268–83. **330**

Schmidt, G., and Sigusch, V. Women's sexual arousal. In J. Zubin and J. Money (Eds.), *Contemporary sexual behavior: Critical issues in the 1970's*, pp. 117–43. Baltimore: Johns Hopkins University Press, 1973. **330**

Schmidt, G., Sigusch, V., and Schäfer, S. Responses to reading erotic stories: Male-female differences. *Archives of Sexual Behavior,* 1973, *2,* 181–99. **330**

Schneider, R. A., Costiloe, J. P., Howard, R. P., and Wolf, S. Olfactory perception thresholds in hypogonadal women: Changes accompanying administration of androgen and estrogen. *Journal of Clinical Endocrinology and Metabolism,* 1958, *18,* 379–90. **324**

Schneider, R. A., and Wolf, S. Olfactory perception thresholds for citral utilizing a new olfactorium. *Journal of Applied Physiology,* 1955, *8,* 337–42. **151, 153, 324**

Schoelch-Krieger, M., and Barfield, R. J. Independence of temporal patterning of male mating behavior from the influence of androgen during the neonatal period. *Physiology and Behavior,* 1975, *14,* 251–254. **90**

Schuckit, M. A., Daly, V., Herrman, G., and Hineman, S. Premenstrual symptoms and depression in a university population. *Diseases of the Nervous System,* 1975, *36,* 516–17. **157**

Schultz, D. P. The human subject in psychological research. *Psychological Bulletin,* 1969, *72,* 214–28. **18**

Schulze, I. Sex differences in the acquisition of appetitively motivated learning in rats. *Physiology and Behavior,* 1976, *17,* 19–22. **80**

Sclafani, A., and Gorman, A. N. Effects of age, sex and prior body weight on the development of dietary obesity in adult rats. *Physiology and Behavior,* 1977, *18,* 1021–26. **382, 387**

Scott, J. P., and Fuller, J. L. *Dog behavior: The genetic basis.* Chicago: University of Chicago Press, 1965. **71, 72, 75**

Scouten, C. W., Grotelueschen, L. K., and Beatty, W. W. Androgens and the organization of sex differences in active avoidance behavior in the rat. *Journal of Comparative and Physiological Psychology,* 1975, *88,* 264–70. **100, 133**

Scruton, D. M., and Herbert, J. The reaction of groups of captive Talapoin monkeys to the introduction of male and female strangers of the same species. *Animal Behaviour,* 1972, *20,* 463–73. **72**

Sears, R. R. Doll play aggression in normal young children: Influences of sex, age, sibling status, father's absence. *Psychological Monographs,* 1951, *65* (No. 6). **290**

Sears, R. R. Dependency motivation. In M. R. Jones (Ed.), *Nebraska symposium on motivation, 1962,* pp. 25–64. Lincoln: University of Nebraska Press, 1963. **300, 301**

Sears, R. R. Development of gender role. In F. A. Beach (Ed.), *Sex and behavior,* pp. 133–63. New York: Wiley, 1965. **290**

Sears, R. R., Rau, L., and Alpert, R. *Identification and child rearing.* Stanford, Calif.: Stanford University Press, 1965. **210**

Seavey, C. A., Katz, P. A., and Zalk, S. R. Baby X: The effect of gender labels on adult responses to infants. *Sex Roles,* 1975, *1,* 103–9. **208**

Selander, R. K. Sexual selection and dimorphism in birds. In B. Campbell (Ed.), *Sexual selection and the descent of man,* pp. 180–230. Chicago: Aldine, 1972. **63**

Seligman, M. E. P. On the generality of the laws of learning. *Psychological Review,* 1970, *77,* 406–18. **8**

Seligman, M. E. P. *Helplessness: On depression, development and death.* San Francisco: Freeman, 1975. **118, 158**

Selmanoff, M. K., Goldman, B. D., Maxson, S. C., and Ginsburg, B. E. Correlated effects of the Y-chromosome of mice in developmental changes in testosterone levels and intermale aggression. *Life Sciences,* 1977, *20,* 359–66. **140**

Selye, H. *The stress of life.* New York: McGraw-Hill, 1956. **118, 158**

Selye, H. *Hormones and resistance.* Berlin: Springer-Verlag, 1971(a). **320, 378**

Selye, H. Protection by estradiol against cocaine, coniine, ethylmorphine, LSD, and strychnine. *Hormones and Behavior.* 1971, *2,* 337–41. (b) **320, 378**

Seyfried, B. A., and Hendrick, C. When do opposites attract? When they are opposite in sex and sex-role attitudes. *Journal of Personality and Social Psychology,* 1973, *25,* 15–20. **219, 347**

Shaffer, D. R., and Wegley, C. Success orientation and sex-role congruence as determinants of the attractiveness of competent women. *Journal of Personality,* 1974, *42,* 586–600. **219**

Shaffer, J. W. A specific cognitive deficit observed in gonadal aplasia (Turner's syndrome). *Journal of Clinical Psychology,* 1962, *18,* 403–6. **32**

Shagass, C., Overton, D. A., and Straumanis, J. J., Jr. Sex differences in somatosensory evoked responses related to psychiatric illness. *Biological Psychiatry,* 1972, *5,* 295–309. **113**

Shagass, C., and Schwartz, M. Age, personality, and somatosensory cerebral evoked responses. *Science,* 1965, *148,* 1359–61. **113**

Shainess, N. A re-evaluation of some aspects of feminity through a study of menstruation: A preliminary report. *Comparative Psychiatry,* 1961, *2,* 20–26. **149**

Shapiro, B. H., and Goldman, A. S. Feminine saccharin preference in the genetically androgen insensitive male rat pseudohermaphrodite. *Hormones and Behavior,* 1973, *4,* 371–75. **385**

Shaver, P., Pierson, L., and Lang, S. Converging evidence for the functional significance of imagery in problem solving. *Condition,* 1974, *3,* 359–75. **252**

Shaw, J. M. *The things I want: Poems for two children.* Tallahassee: Friends of Florida State, 1967. **3**

Sheldrake, P., Cormack, M., and McGuire, J. Psychosomatic illness, birth order and intellectual preference, I: Men. *Journal of Psychosomatic Research,* 1976, *20,* 37–44.(a) **374**

Sheldrake, P., Cormack, M., and McGuire, J. Psychosomatic illness, birth order and intellectual preference, II: Women. *Journal of Psychosomatic Research,* 1976, *20,* 45–49.(b) **314**

Shepherd, M., Cooper, B., Brown, A. C., and Kalton, G. W. *Psychiatric illness in general practice.* London: Oxford University Press, 1966. **336**

Sherfey, M. J. *The nature and evolution of female sexuality.* New York: Random House, 1966. **329**

Sherfey, M. J. On the nature of female sexuality. In J. B. Miller (Ed.), *Psychoanalysis and women,* pp. 136–53. New York, Penguin, 1973. **329, 331**

Sheridan, C. L., and King, R. G., Jr. Obedience to authority with an authentic victim. *Proceedings of the 80th Annual Convention of the American Psychological Association,* 1972, 165–66. **294**

Sherman, J. A. Problem of sex differences in space perception and aspects of intellectual functioning. *Psychological Review,* 1967, *74,* 290–99. **243, 244**

Sherman, J. A. *On the psychology of women: A survey of empirical studies.* Springfield, Ill.: Thomas, 1971. **142, 160, 167, 182, 183, 210, 300, 315, 327, 331**

Sherman, J. A., and Fennema, E. The study of mathematics by high school girls and boys: related variable. *American Educational Journal,* 1977, *14,* 159–68. **242**

Shiavi, R. C., Davis, D. M., White, D., Edwards, A., Igel, G., and Fisher, C. Plasma testosterone during nocturnal sleep in normal men. *Steroids,* 1974, *24,* 191–202.

Shipley, T. E., Veroff, J. A projective measure of need for affiliation. *Journal of Experimental Psychology,* 1952, *43,* 349–56. **304**

Siegler, D. M., and Siegler, R. S. Stereotypes of males' and females' speech. *Psychological Reports,* 1976, *39,* 167–70. **308**

Sigalow, S., and Reuter, J. Sex-role stereotyping and preference for activities in elementary children. Paper presented at the meeting of the Midwestern Psychological Association, Chicago, May, 1975. **183**

Silbergeld, S., Brast, N., and Noble, E. P. The menstrual cycle: A double-blind study of symptoms, mood and behavior, and biochemical variables using Enovid and placebo. *Psychosomatic Medicine,* 1971, *33,* 411–28. **144, 149**

Silverstone, J. T. Psychosocial aspects of obesity. In N. Kiell (Ed.), *The psychology of obesity: Dynamics and treatment,* pp. 67–74. Springfield, Ill.: Thomas, 1973. **336, 377**

Silverthorne, C., Micklewright, J., O'Donnell, M., and Gibson, R. Attribution of personal characteristics as a function of the degree of touch on initial contact and sex. *Sex Roles,* 1976, *2,* 185–93. **311**

Simmel, C. C., Cheney, J. H., and Landy, E. E. Visual vs. locomotor response effects of satiation to novel stimuli: A sex difference in rats. *Psychological Reports,* 1965, *16,* 893–96. **76**

Simmons, R. G., and Rosenberg, F. Sex, sex roles, and self-image. *Journal of Youth and Adolescence,* 1975, *4,* 229–58. **183, 193, 236, 272, 303, 336**

Simpson, J. L., Morillo-Cucci, G., Horwith, M., Stiefel, F. H., Feldman, F., and German, J. Abnormalities of human sex chromosomes, VI: Monozygotic twins with the complement 48, XXXY. *Humangenetik,* 1974, *21,* 301–8. **33, 35**

Singer, J. E., Westphal, M., and Niswander, K. R. Sex differences in the incidence of neonatal abnormalities and abnormal performance in early childhood. *Child Development,* 1968, *39,* 103–22. **374**

Singer, S. L., and Stefflre, B. Sex differences in job values and desires. *Personnel and Guidance Journal,* 1954, *32,* 483–84. **315**

Sjödén, P. O., and Södderberg, U. Sex-dependent effects of prenatal 2-, 4-, 5-tri-chlorophenoxy-acetic acid on rats open-field behavior. *Physiology and Behavior,* 1972, *9,* 357–60. **75**

Slaby, R. G., and Frey, K. S. Development of gender constancy and selective attention to same-sex models. *Child Development,* 1975, *46,* 849–56. **185, 190**

Slánská, J., Plevová, J., Benesová, O., Tikal, K., and Hvizdosová, J. Alteration of psychosomatic reactivity after a single therapeutic dose of pentobarbital in relation to the sex of probands. *Activosa Nervosa Sup.* (Prague), 1974, *16,* 218–20. **320**

Slater, J., and Blizard, D. A. A reevaluation of the relation between estrogen and emotionality in female rats. *Journal of Comparative and Physiological Psychology,* 1976, *90,* 755–64. **132, 383**

Slob, A. K., and van der Werff ten Bosch, J. J. Sex differences in body growth in the rat. *Physiology and Behavior,* 1975, *14,* 353–61. **385**

Smals, A. G. H., Kloppenborg, P. W. C., and Benraad, T. J. Body proportions and androgenicity in relation to plasma testosterone levels in Klinefelter's syndrome.

Acta Endocrinologica, 1974, *77,* 387–400. **33**

Smith, C. P. Fear of success: Qualms and queries. In F. L. Denmark (Ed.), *Women: A PDI research reference work.* Vol. 1, pp. 141–56. New York: Psychological Dimensions, 1976. **277**

Smith, S. L. Mood and the menstrual cycle. In E. J. Sachar (Ed.), *Topics in psychoendocrinology,* pp. 19–58. New York: Grune and Stratton, 1975. **155, 156, 158**

Smith, S. L., and Sauder, C. Food cravings, depression, and premenstrual problems. *Psychosomatic Medicine,* 1969, *31,* 281–87. **151, 157, 387**

Smith, W. I., Powell, E. K., and Ross, S. Food aversions: Some additional personality correlates. *Journal of Consulting Psychology,* 1955, *19,* 145–49.(a) **388**

Smith, W. I., Powell, E. K., and Ross, S. Manifest anxiety and food aversions. *Journal of Abnormal and Social Psychology,* 1955, *50,* 101–4.(b) **388**

Smolensky, M. H., Reinberg, A., Lee, R. E., and McGovern, J. P. Secondary rhythms related to hormonal changes in the menstrual cycle: Special reference to allergology. In M. Ferin, F. Halberg, R. M. Richart, and R. L. Vande Wiele (Eds.), *Biorhythms and human reproduction,* pp. 287–306. New York: Wiley, 1974. **143, 145, 148**

Södersten, P. Effects of an estrogen antagonist, MER-25, on mounting behavior and lordosis behavior in the female rat. *Hormones and Behavior,* 1974, *5,* 111–21. **384**

Södersten, P. Estrogen-activated sexual behavior in male rats. *Hormones and Behavior,* 1973, *4,* 247–56.(a) **124, 125**

Södersten, P. Increased mounting behavior in the female rat following a single neonatal injection of testosterone propinate. *Hormones and Behavior,* 1973, *4,* 1–17.(b) **385**

Solberg, D., Butler, J. C., and Wagner, N. N. Sexual behavior during pregnancy. *New England Journal of Medicine,* 1973, *288,* 1098–1103. **160**

Solomon, D., and Kendall, A. J. Final report: Individual characteristics and children's performance in varied educational settings. *Spencer Foundation Report,* 1976. **271**

Solomon, H., and Yager, J. Authoritarianism and graffiti. *Journal of Social Psychology,* 1975, *97,* 149–50. **293**

Soltan, H. C., and Bracken, S. E. The relation of sex to taste reactions. *Journal of Heredity,* 1958, *49,* 280–84. **324**

Somerville, B. W. The influence of progesterone and estradiol upon migraine. *Headache,* 1972, *12,* 93–102. **148, 158**

Sommer, B. Menstrual cycle changes and intellectual performance. *Psychosomatic Medicine,* 1972, *34,* 263–69. **142, 155**

Sommer, B. The effect of menstruation on cognitive and perceptual-motor behavior: A review. *Psychosomatic Medicine,* 1973, *33,* 515–34. **153, 156**

Sommer, R. Studies in personal space. *Sociometry,* 1974, *37,* 423–31. **310**

Sopchak, A. L., and Sutherland, A. M. Psychological impact of cancer and its treatment, VII: Exogenous sex hormones and their relation to life-long adaptations in women with metastatic cancer of the breast. *Cancer,* 1960, *5,* 857–72. **137**

Soto, D. H., and Cole, C. Prejudice against women: A new perspective. *Sex Roles,* 1975, *1,* 385–93. **227**

Soulairac, M.-L., and Soulairac, A. Comportement sexuel et tractus génital du rat mâle adulte après oestrogénisation postnatale précoce. *Annales d'Endocrinologie (Paris),* 1974, *35,* 577–78. **91**

Southam, A. L., and Gonzaga, F. P. Systemic changes during the menstrual cycle. *American Journal of Obstetrics and Gynecology,* 1965, *91,* 142–65. **145, 146, 147, 148**

Southren, A. L., and Gordon, G. G. Rhythms and testosterone metabolism. *Journal of Steroid Biochemistry,* 1975, *6,* 809–13. **163**

Spence, J. T. The thematic apperception test and attitudes toward achievement in women: A new look at the motive to avoid success and a new method of measurement. *Journal of Consulting and Clinical Psychology,* 1974, *42,* 427–37. **267, 268**

Spence, J. T., and Helmreich, R. Who likes competent women? Competence, sex-role congruence of interests, and subjects' attitudes toward women as determinants of interpersonal attraction. *Journal of Applied Social Psychology,* 1972, *2,* 197–213. **218**

Spence, J. T., Helmreich, R., and Stapp, J. A short version of the attitudes toward women scale (AWS). *Bulletin of Psychonomic Society,* 1973, *2,* 219–20. **228**

Spence, J. T., Helmreich, R., and Stapp, J. Ratings of self and peers on sex role attributes and their relation to self-esteem and conceptions of masculinity and femininity. *Journal of Personality and Social Psychology,* 1975, *32,* 29–39. **221, 223, 341**

Spiro, M. E. *Children of the Kibbutz.* Cambridge, Mass.: Harvard University Press, 1958. **205**

Spreitzer, E., Snyder, E. E., and Larson, D. Age, marital status, and labor force participation as related to life satisfaction. *Sex Roles,* 1975, *1,* 235–47. **338, 343**

Stafford, R. E. Sex differences in spatial visualization as evidence of sex-linked inheritance. *Perceptual and Motor Skills,* 1961, *13,* 428. **41, 42, 245**

Stafford, R. E. An investigation of similarities in parent-child test scores for evidence of hereditary components. *Princeton Educational Testing Service,* 1963. **41, 42**

Stafford, R. E. Hereditary and environmental components of quantitative reasoning. *Review of Educational Research,* 1972, *42,* 183–201. **42, 240, 241, 242**

Staines, G., Tavris, C., and Jayaratne, T. E. The queen bee syndrome. In C. Tavris (Ed.), *The female experience,* pp. 63–66. Del Mar, Calif.: Communications Research Machines, 1973. **228**

Staudt, J., and Dörner, G. Structural changes in the medial and central amygdala of the male rat, following neonatal castration and androgen treatment. *Endokrinologie,* 1976, *67,* 296–300. **112**

Stauffer, J., and Frost, R. Male and female interest in sexually-oriented magazines. *Journal of Communication,* 1976, *26,* 25–30. **330**

Stearns, E. L., MacDonnell, J. A. Kaufman, B. J., Padua, R., Lucman, T. S. Winter, J. S. D., and Faiman, C. Declining testicular function with age. *American Journal of Medicine,* 1974, *57,* 761–66.

Stearns, E. L., Winter, J. S. D., and Faiman, C. Effects of coitus on gonadotropin, prolactin

Stearns, E. L. (Continued)
and sex steroid levels in man. Journal of Clinical Endocrinology and Metabolism, 1973, 37, 687–91.(a)   **57, 122, 136**

Stearns, E. L., Winter, J. S. D., and Faiman, C. Positive feedback effect of progestin upon serum gonadotropins in estrogen-primed castrate men. Journal of Clinical Endocrinology and Metabolism, 1973, 37, 635–38.(b)

Steele, D. G., and Walker, C. E. Female responsiveness to erotic films and the "ideal" erotic film from a feminine perspective. Journal of Nervous and Mental Disease, 1976, 162, 266–73.   **331**

Stein, A. H., and Bailey, M. M. The socialization of achievement orientation in females. Psychological Bulletin, 1973, 80, 345–66.   **242, 256, 265, 271, 274, 281, 283**

Stein, G., Milton, F., Bebbington, P., Wood, K., and Coppen, A. Relationship between mood disturbances and free and total plasma tryptophan in postpartum women. British Medical Journal, 1976, 2, 457–59.   **161**

Stein, L. S., del Gaudio, A. C., and Ansley, M. Y. A comparison of female and male neurotic depressives. Journal of Clinical Psychology, 1976, 32, 19–21.   **348, 349**

Stephens, W. N. The family in cross-cultural perspective. New York: Holt, Rinehart and Winston, 1963.   **199, 203**

Stern, E., Forsythe, A. B., Youkeles, L., and Coffelt, C. F. Steroid contraceptive use and cervical dysplasia: Increased risk of progression. Science, 1977, 196, 1460–62.   **143**

Stern, J. J., Cudillo, C. A., and Longuski, P. A. Estradiol benzoate, norepinephrine, and weight regulatory behavior in female rats. Physiological Psychology, 1976, 4, 45–49.   **383**

Sternglanz, S. H., and Serbin, L. H. Sex role stereotyping in children's television programs. Developmental Psychology, 1974, 10, 710–15.   **215**

Stewart, A. J., and Rubin, Z. The power motive in the dating couple. Journal of Personality and Social Psychology, 1976, 34, 305–9.   **298**

Stewart, A. J., and Winter, D. G. Arousal of the power motive in women. Journal of Consulting and Clinical Psychology, 1976, 44, 495–96.   **297**

Stewart, C. N., and Brookshire, K. H. Shuttle box avoidance learning and epinephrine. Psychonomic Science, 1967, 9, 419–20.   **80**

Stewart, J., Skvarenina, A., and Pottier, J. Effects of neonatal androgens on open-field behavior and maze learning in the prepubescent and adult rat. Physiology and Behavior, 1975, 14, 291–95.   **75, 80, 98, 100**

Stocking, S. H., and Zillmann, D. Effects of humorous disparagement of self, friend, and enemy. Psychological Reports, 1976, 39, 455–61.   **296**

Stoll, C. S. Female and male: Socialization, social roles, and social structure. Dubuque, Iowa: Brown, 1974.   **210, 373**

Stoller, R. J. Sex and gender. New York: Science House, 1968.   **176, 177, 182**

Strauss, E. B., Sands, D. E., Robinson, A. M., Tindall, W. J., and Stevenson, W. A. H. Use of dihydroisoandrosterone in psychiatric treatment: A preliminary survey. British Medical Journal, 1952, 3, 64–66.   **138**

Struve, F. A., Saraf, K. R., Arko, R. S., Klein, D. F., and Becka, D. R. Electroencephalographic correlates of oral contraceptive use in psychiatric patients. Archives of General Psychiatry, 1976, 33, 741–45.   **143**

Sugiyama, Y. An artificial social change in a Hanuman langur troop. Primates, 1966, 7, 41–72.   **78**

Sugiyama, Y. Social organization of Hanuman langurs. In S. A. Altmann (Ed.), Social communication among primates, pp. 221–236. Chicago: University of Chicago Press, 1967.   **78**

Sugiyama, Y. Social behavior of chimpanzees in the Budongo Forest, Uganda. Primates, 1969, 10, 197–225.   **73**

Sutherland, H., and Stewart, I. A critical analysis of the premenstrual syndrome. Lancet, 1965, 1, 1180–83.   **154, 155**

Svare, B., Davis, P. G., and Gandelman, R. Fighting behavior in female mice following chronic androgen treatment during adulthood. Physiology and Behavior, 1974, 12, 399–403.   **128**

Swanson, H. H. Sex differences in behaviour

of hamsters in open field and emergence tests: Effects of pre- and post-pubertal gonadectomy. *Animal Behaviour*, 1966, *14*, 522–29. **75, 98, 132**

Swanson, H. H. Alteration of sex-typical behavior of hamsters in open field and emergence tests by neo-natal administration of androgen or oestrogen. *Animal Behaviour*, 1967, *15*, 209–16. **75, 98**

Swanson, H. H. Interaction of experience with adrenal and sex hormones on the behaviour of hamsters in the open field test. *Animal Behaviour*, 1969, *17*, 148–54. **75, 98**

Syme, L. A., and Syme, G. J. The role of sex and novelty in determining the social response to lithium chloride. *Psychopharmacologia*, 1974, *40*, 91–100. **78**

Tangri, S. S. Determinants of occupational role innovation among college women. *Journal of Social Issues*, 1972, *28*, 177–99. **269, 277**

Tangri, S. S. Implied demand character of the wife's future and role innovation: Patterns of achievement orientation among college women. In M. T. S. Mednick, S. S. Tangri, and L. W. Hoffman (Eds.), *Women and achievement: Social and motivational analysis*, pp. 239–54. New York: Halsted, 1975. **269, 277**

Tanner, J. M. Physical growth. In P. M. Mussen (Ed.), *Carmichael's manual of child psychology*. Vol. 1, pp. 77–155. New York: Wiley, 1970. **319, 320**

Tarttelin, M. F., Shryne, J. E., and Gorski, R. A. Effects of testosterone propinate treatment of neonatally ovariectomized rats on growth and subsequent responsiveness to oestrogen. *Acta Endocrinologica*, 1976, *82*, 652–60. **385**

Taub, J. M., and Berger, R. S. Diurnal variations in mood as asserted by self-report and verbal content analysis. *Journal of Psychiatric Research*, 1974, *10*, 83–88. **161**

Taylor, D. C., and Ounsted, C. The nature of gender differences explored through ontogenetic analyses of sex ratios in disease. In C. Ounsted and D. C. Taylor (Eds.), *Gender differences: Their ontogeny and significance*, pp. 215–40. London: Churchill Livingston, 1972. **374, 376, 380**

Taylor, G. T. Influence of female's sexual cycle on aggressiveness in male rats. *Journal of Comparative and Physiological Psychology*, 1976, *90*, 740–46. **361**

Taynor, J., and Deaux, K. When women are more deserving than men: Equity, attribution, and perceived sex differences. *Journal of Personality and Social Psychology*, 1973, *28*, 360–67. **227, 284**

Tea, N. T., Castanier, M., Roger, M., and Scholler, R. Simultaneous radio-immunoassay of plasma progesterone and 17-hydroxyprogesterone normal values in children, in men and in women throughout the menstrual cycle and in early pregnancy. *Journal of Steroid Biochemistry*, 1975, *6*, 1509–16. **50**

Telegdy, G., and Stark, A. Effect of sexual steroids and androgen sterilization on avoidance and exploratory behaviour in the rat. *Acta Physiologica Academiae Scientiarum Hungaricae, Tomus*, 1973, *43*, 55–63. **133**

Tennes, K., Puck, M., Bryant, K., Frankenburg, W., and Robinson, A. A developmental study of girls with trisomy X. *American Journal of Human Genetics*, 1975, *27*, 71–80. **29**

Terkel, J., and Rosenblatt, J. S. Hormonal factors underlying maternal behavior at parturition: cross transfusion between freely moving rats. *Journal of Comparative and Physiological Psychology*, 1972, *80*, 365–71. **130**

Terman, L. M., and Miles, C. C. *Sex and personality*. New York: McGraw-Hill, 1936. **211, 342**

Terman, L. M., and Oden, M. H. *The gifted child grows up*. Stanford, Calif.: Stanford University Press, 1947. **237**

Terres, G., Morrison, S. L., and Habicht, G. S. A quantitative difference in the immune response between male and female mice. *Proceedings of the Society for Experimental Biology and Medicine*, 1968, *127*, 664–67. **376**

Theilgaard, A. Cognitive style and gender role. *Danish Medical Bulletin*, 1972, *19*, 276–82. **30, 32, 33, 35**

Thoman, E., Leiderman, P., and Olson, J.

Thoman, E. (*Continued*)
Neonate-mother interaction during breast feeding. *Developmental Psychology*, 1972, *6*, 110–18. **208**

Thomas, H., Jamison, W., and Hummel, D. D. Observation is insufficient for discovering that the surface of still water is invariantly horizontal. *Science*, 1973, *181*, 173–74. **249**

Thompson, A. W. S. Prescribing of hypnotics and tranquillizers in New Zealand. *Pharmaceutical Journal of New Zealand*, 1973, *35*, 15–18. **349**

Thompson, G. B. Sex differences in reading attainments. *Educational Research*, 1975, *18*, 16–23. **237**

Thompson, W. R. Exploratory behavior as a function of hunger in "bright" and "dull" rats. *Journal of Comparative and Physiological Psychology*, 1953, *46*, 323–26. **76**

Thor, D. H., Ghiselli, W. B., and Ward, T. B. Infantile handling and sex differences in shock-elicited aggressive responding of hooded rats. *Developmental Psychobiology*, 1974, *7*, 273–79. **71**

Thornhill, R. Sexual selection and paternal investment in insects. *American Naturalist*, 1976, *110*, 153–63. **68**

Tidball, M. E. Perspective on academic women and affirmative action. *Educational Record*, 1973, *54*, 130–35. **269**

Tidball, M. E., and Kistiakowsky, V. Baccalaureate origins of American scientists and scholars. *Science*, 1976, *193*, 646–52. **269**

Tiger, L. *Men in groups*. New York: Random House, 1969. **328**

Timiras, P. S. Estrogens as 'organizers' of CNS function. In *Influence of hormones on the nervous system: The proceedings of the International Society of Psychoendocrinology*, pp. 242–54. Basel, Switz.: Karger, 1971. **111**

Timonen, S., and Procópe, B. J. The premenstrual syndrome; Frequency and association of symptoms. *Annales Chirurgiae et Gynaecologiae Fenniae*, 1973, *62*, 108–16. **154, 155**

Tobin, S. M. Emotional depression during pregnancy. *Obstetrics and Gynecology*, 1957, *10*, 677–81. **160**

Tollman, J., and King, J. A. The effects of testosterone propinate on aggression in male and female C57/BL/10 mice. *British Journal of Animal Behaviour*, 1956, *4*, 147–49. **128**

Tolman, E. C., Ritchie, B. F., and Kalish, D. Studies in spatial learning; II: Place versus response learning. *Journal of Experimental Psychology*, 1946, *36*, 221–29. **81**

Tolar, A., Kelly, B. R., and Stebbins, C. A. Assertiveness, sex-role stereotyping, and self-concept. *Journal of Psychology*, 1976, *93*, 157–64. **295, 336**

Tomilin, M. I., and Stone, C. P. Sex difference in learning abilities of albino rats. *Journal of Comparative Psychology*, 1933, *16*, 207–19. **80, 81**

Tomlinson-Keasey, C. Role variables: Their influence on female motivational constructs. *Journal of Counseling Psychology*, 1974, *21*, 232–37. **270, 277**

Tonks, C. M., Rack, P. H., and Rose, M. J. Attempted suicide and the menstrual cycle. *Journal of Psychosomatic Research*, 1968, *11*, 319–23. **155, 159**

Toran-Allerand, C. D. Sex steroids and the development of the newborn mouse hypothalamus and preoptic area *in vitro:* Implications for sexual differentiation. *Brain Research*, 1976, *106*, 407–12. **111**

Torda, C., and Wolff, H. G. Effects of steroid substances on synthesis of acetylcholine. *Proceedings of the Society of Experimental Biology and Medicine*, 1944, *57*, 327. **120**

Torrance, E. P. Changing reactions of preadolescent girls to tasks requiring creative scientific thinking. *Journal of Genetic Psychology*, 1963, *102*, 217–23. **254**

Treadway, C. R., Kane, F. J., Jr., Jarrahi-Zadeh, A., and Lipton, M. A. A psychoedocrine study of pregnancy and puerperium. *American Journal of Psychiatry*, 1969, *125*, 1380–86. **160, 161**

Tresemer, D. Fear of success: Popular but unproven. In C. Tavris (Ed.), *The female experience*, pp. 58–62. Del Mar, Calif.: Communications Research Machines, 1973. **269, 270**

Tresemer, D. The cumulative record of research on "fear of success." *Sex Roles*, 1976, *2*, 217–36. **282**

Tresemer, D., and Pleck, J. Sex-role boundaries and resistance to sex-role change. *Women's Studies,* 1973, *1,* 18. **279**

Triandis, H. C., and Osgood, C. E. A comparative factorial analysis of semantic structures in monolingual Greek and American college students. *Journal of Abnormal and Social Psychology,* 1958, *57,* 187–96. **199**

Trigg, L. J., and Perlman, D. Social influences on women's pursuit of a nontraditional career. *Psychology of Women Quarterly,* 1976, *1,* 138–50. **277, 278**

Trimble, M. R., and Herbert, J. The effect of testosterone or oestradiol upon the sexual and associated behaviour of the adult female rhesus monkey. *Journal of Endocrinology,* 1968, *42,* 171–85. **128**

Trivers, R. L. Parental investment and sexual selection. In B. Campbell (Ed.), *Sexual selection and the descent of man,* pp. 136–72. Chicago: Adline, 1972. **63**

Trupin, E. W. Correlates of ego-level and agency-communion in stage REM dreams of 11–13 year old children. *Journal of Child Psychology and Psychiatry,* 1976, *17,* 169–80. **220**

Tryon, R. C. Studies in individual differences in maze ability, II: The determination of individual differences by age, weight, sex and pigmentation. *Journal of Comparative and Physiological Psychology,* 1931, *12,* 1–22. **80**

Tsuang, M. T. Sex chromatin anomaly in Chinese females: Psychiatric characteristics of XXX. *British Journal of Psychiatry,* 1974, *124,* 299–305. **29**

Tsuang, M. T. Sex chromatin anomaly among Chinese psychiatric inpatients compared to schoolchildren. *Acta Psychiatrica Scandinavica,* 1975, *51,* 88–91. **29**

Tsuang, S. H., and Heckman, M. G. Klinefelter syndrome, immunological disorders, and malignant neoplasm. *Archives of Pathology,* 1974, *98,* 351–54. **33**

Tuch, R. H. The relationship between a mother's menstrual status and her response to illness in her child. *Psychosomatic Medicine,* 1975, *37,* 388–94. **157**

Turner, J. W., Jr. Influence of neonatal androgen on display of territorial mating behavior in the gerbil. *Physiology and Behavior,* 1975, *15,* 265–70. **93, 128**

Tyler, L. *The psychology of human differences.* (3rd ed.) New York: Appleton-Century-Crofts, 1965. **326**

Uddenberg, N. Reproduction adaptation in mother and daughter: A study of personality development and adaptation to motherhood. *Acta Psychiatrica Scandinavica,* 1974 (Suppl. 254), 1–115. **159, 160, 161**

Uddenberg, N., and Nilsson, L. The longitudinal course of para-natal emotional disturbance. *Acta Psychiatrica Scandinavica,* 1975, *52,* 160–69. **160, 161**

Udry, J. R., and Morris, N. M. Distribution of coitus in the menstrual cycle. *Nature,* 1968, *200,* 593–96. **149, 150**

Udry, J. R., Morris, N. M., and Waller, L. Effect of contraceptive pills on human sexual activity in the luteal phase of the human menstrual cycle. *Archives in Sexual Behavior,* 1973, *2,* 205–15. **152**

Unger, R. K., and Denmark, F. L. (eds.) *Women: Dependent or independent variable?* New York: Psychological Dimensions, 1975.

Urbina, S., and Grey, A. Cultural and sex differences in the sex distribution of dream characters. *Journal of Cross-Cultural Psychology,* 1975, *6,* 358–63. **181**

U.S. Department of Health, Education, and Welfare. National ambulatory medical care survey: May 1973–April 1974. *Monthly Vital Statistics Report,* 1975, *24,* (Suppl. 2). **377**

U.S. Department of Justice. *Survey of inmates of local jails.* Washington, D.C.: U.S. Government Printing Office, 1972. **351**

Vale, J. R., Ray, D., and Vale, C. A. The interaction of genotype and exogenous neonatal androgen and estrogen: Sex behavior in female mice. *Developmental Psychobiology,* 1973, *6,* 319–27. **91**

Valenstein, E. S., Kakolewski, J. W., and Cox, V. C. Sex differences in taste preference for glucose and saccharin solutions. *Science,* 1967, *156,* 942–43. **381**

Valle, F. P., and Bols, R. J. Age factors in sex differences in open-field activity of rats.

Valle, F. P. (*Continued*)
Animal Learning and Behavior, 1976, *4*, 457–60. **132**

Vandenberg, S. G., McKusick, V. A., and McKusick, A. B. Twin data in support of the Lyon hypothesis. *Nature*, 1962, *194*, 505–6. **13**

Van den Berghe, P. *Age and sex in human societies: A biosocial perspective.* Belmont, Calif.: Wadsworth, 1973. **67, 198, 199, 202**

van De Poll, N. E., and van Dis, H. Hormone induced lordosis and its relation to masculine sexual activity in male rats. *Hormones and Behavior*, 1977, *8*, 1–7. **125**

van Keep, P. A., and Kellerhals, J. M. The aging woman: About the influence of some social and cultural factors on the changes in attitude and behaviour that occur during and after the menopause. *Acta Obstetricia et Gynecologica Scandinavica Supplement*, 1975, *51*, 17–27. **167**

van Lawick-Goodall, J. The behavior of free-living chimpanzees in the Gombe Stream Reserve. *Animal Behavior Monographs*, 1968, *1*, 1–311. **73, 381**

Vaught, G. M. The relationship of role identification and ego strength to sex differences in the rod-and-frame test. *Journal of Personality*, 1965, *33*, 271–83. **244, 248, 256**

Vermeulen, A. The hormonal activity of the postmenopausal ovary. *Journal of Clinical Endocrinology and Metabolism*, 1976, *42*, 247–53. **163**

Vermeulen, A., Verdonck, L., and Comhaire, F. Rhythms of the male hypothalamo-pituitary-testicular axis. In M. Ferin, F. Halberg, R. M. Richart, and R. L. Vande Wiele (Eds.), *Biorhythms and human reproduction*, pp. 427–45. New York: Wiley, 1974. **163, 165**

Veroff, J., McClelland, L., and Ruhland, D. Varieties of achievement motivation. In M. T. S. Mednick, S. S. Tangri, and L. W. Hoffman (Eds.), *Women and achievement: Social and motivational analysis*, pp. 172–205. New York: Halsted, 1975. **264, 266**

Vessey, M. P. Gender differences in the epidemiology of non-neurological disease. In C. Ounsted and D. C. Taylor (Eds.),

Gender differences: Their ontogeny and significance, pp. 203–13. London: Churchill Livingston, 1972. **374, 378**

Vierling, J. S., and Rock, J. Variations in olfactory sensitivity to Exaltolide during the menstrual cycle. *Journal of Applied Physiology*, 1967, *22*, 311–15. **151, 153**

Vilberg, T. R., Revland, P. B., Beatty, W. W., and Frohman, L. A. Effects of cyproterone acetate on growth and feeding in rats. *Pharmacology, Biochemistry and Behavior*, 1974, *2*, 309–16. **384**

Vollmer, F. Sex differences in expectancy of examination results. *Scandinavian Journal of Psychology*, 1975, *16*, 152–55. **281**

Vollmer, F., and Almås, R. Sex differences in achievement motivation. *Scandinavian Journal of Psychology*, 1974, *15*, 310–13. **266, 283**

vom Saal, F. S., Svare, B., and Gandelman, R. Time of neonatal androgen exposure influences length of testosterone treatment required to induce aggression in adult male and female mice. *Behavioral Biology*, 1976, *17*, 391–97. **92, 93, 130**

Vroegh, K. Masculinity and femininity in the elementary and junior high school years. *Developmental Psychology*, 1971, *4*, 254–61.

Waber, D. P. Sex differences in cognition: A function of maturation rate? *Science*, 1976, *192*, 572–73. **245, 259**

Wachs, T. D. Visual exploratory behavior as a function of early handling, sex, and level of auditory prestimulation. *Developmental Psychobiology*, 1974, *7*, 385–92. **76**

Wada, J. A., Clark, R., and Hamm, A. Cerebral hemispheric asymmetry in humans. *Archives of Neurology*, 1975, *32*, 239–46. **259**

Wade, G. N. Gonadal hormones and behavioral regulation of body weight. *Physiology and Behavior*, 1972, *8*, 523–34. **381, 383**

Wade, G. N. Some effects of ovarian hormones on food intake and body weight in female rats. *Journal of Comparative and Physiological Psychology*, 1975, *88*, 183–92. **384**

Wade, G. N. Sex hormones, regulatory

behaviors, and body weight. In J. S. Rosenblatt, R. A. Hinde, E. Shaw, and C. Beer (Eds.), *Advances in the study of behavior*. Vol. 6, pp. 201–79. New York: Academic Press, 1976. **131, 381, 383, 384, 385**

Wade, G. N., and Zucker, I. Hormonal and developmental influences on rat saccharine preferences. *Journal of Comparative and Physiological Psychology*, 1969, *69*, 291–300.(a) **384, 385**

Wade, G. N., and Zucker, I. Taste preferences of female rats: Modification by neonatal hormones, food deprivation, and prior experience. *Physiology and Behavior*, 1969, *4*, 935–43. (b) **382, 384, 385**

Wadsworth, M. E. J., Butterfield, W. J. H., and Blaney, R. *Health and sickness: The choice of treatment*. London: Tavistock, 1971. **377**

Wakoh, T., and Hatotani, N. Endocrinological treatment of psychoses. In K. Lissák (Ed.), *Hormones and brain function*, pp. 491–498. New York: Plenum Press, 1973. **155**

Walberg, H. J. Physics, femininity, and creativity. *Developmental Psychology*, 1969, 1, 47–54. **303, 315**

Waldron, I. Why do women live longer than men? *Journal of Human Stress*, 1976, *2*, 2–13. **379, 380**

Waldron, I., and Johnston, S. Why do women live longer than men? *Journal of Human Stress*, 1976, *2*, 19–29. **380**

Walker, E. L., and Heyns, R. W. *The anatomy for conformity*. Englewood Cliffs, N.J.: Prentice-Hall, 1962. **275, 295**

Ward, I. L. Differential effect of pre- and postnatal androgen on the sexual behavior of intact and spayed female rats. *Hormones and Behavior*, 1969, *1*, 25–36. **90, 385**

Washburn, S. L., Jay, P. C., and Lancaster, J. B. Field studies of Old World monkeys and apes. *Science*, 1965, *150*, 1541–47. **72, 373, 374**

Waters, C. W., Waters, L. K., and Pincus, S. Factor analysis of masculine and feminine sex-typed items from the Bem Sex-Role Inventory. *Psychological Reports*, 1977, *40*, 567–70. **224**

Watson, J. S. Operant conditioning of visual fixation in infants under visual and auditory reinforcement. *Developmental Psychology*, 1969, *1*, 408–16. **323**

Wax, R. H. The experiment as a social occasion. *Society*, 1975, *13*, 86–87. **19**

Waxenberg, S. E. Psychotherapeutic and dynamic implications of recent research on female sexual functioning. In G. D. Goldman and D. S. Milman (Eds.), *Modern woman: Her psychology and sexuality*, pp. 3–24. Springfield, Ill.: Thomas, 1969. **137**

Waxenberg, S. E., Drellich, M. G., and Sutherland, A. M. The roles of hormones in human behavior, I: Changes in female sexuality after adrenalectomy. *Journal of Clinical Endocrinology and Metabolism*, 1959, *19*, 193–202. **137**

Weaver, D. D., Gartler, S. M., Boué, A., and Boué, J. G. Evidence for two active X chromosomes in a human XXY triploid. *Humangenetik*, 1975, *28*, 39–42. **33**

Weber, P. G., and Weber, S. P. The effect of female color, size, dominance and early experience upon mate selection in male convict cichlids, *Cichlasoma nigrofasciatum Günther* (pisces, cichlidae). *Behaviour*, 1975, *56*, 116–35. **64**

Weeke, J., and Hansen, A. P. Serum TSH and serum T_3 levels during normal menstrual cycles and during cycles on oral contraceptives. *Acta Endocrinologica*, 1975, *79*, 431–38. **143**

Weinstein, S. Intensive and extensive aspects of tactile sensitivity as a function of body part, sex, and laterality. In D. R. Kenshalo, (Ed.), *The skin senses*, pp. 195–218. Springfield, Ill.: Thomas, 1968. **323**

Weintraub, W., and Aronson, H. Patients in psychoanalysis: Some findings related to sex and religion. *American Journal of Orthopsychiatry*, 1974, *44*, 102–8. **345, 348, 350**

Weissman, M. M. The epidemiology of suicide attempts, 1960 to 1971. *Archives of General Psychiatry*, 1974, *30*, 737–46. **351**

Weisstein, N. Psychology constructs of the female or, the fantasy life of the male psychologist. In M. H. Garskof (Ed.), *Roles women play: Readings toward women's liberation*, pp. 68–83. Belmont, Calif.: Brooks-Cole, 1971. **19**

Weitz, S. Sex differences in nonverbal com-

Weitz, S. (*Continued*)
munication. *Sex Roles,* 1976, *2,* 175–84.
296, 304, 311

Weitzman, L. J. Sex role socialization. In J. Freeman (Ed.), *Women: A feminist perspective,* pp. 105–44. Palo Alto, Calif.: Mayfield, 1975. **218**

Weitzman, L. J., Eifler, D., Hokada, E., and Ross, C. Sex-role socialization in picture books for preschool children. *American Journal of Sociology, 1972, 77,* 1125–50. **214**

Westoff, C. F., and Rindfuss, R. R. Sex preselection in the United States: Some implications. *Science, 1974, 184,* 633–36. **226**

Weston, P. J., and Mednick, M. T. S. Race, social class, and the motive to avoid success in women. *Journal of Cross-Cultural Psychology,* 1970, *1,* 283–91. **268**

Wetzel, R. D., Reich, T., McClure, J. N., Jr., and Wald, J. A. Premenstrual affective syndrome and affective disorder. *British Journal of Psychiatry, 1975, 127,* 219–21. **157**

Whalen, R. E., and Edwards, D. A. Hormonal determinants of the development of masculine and feminine behavior in male and female rats. *Anatomical Record, 1967, 157,* 173–80. **90**

Whalen, R. E., Edwards, D. A., Luttge, W. G., and Robertson, R. T. Early androgen treatment and male sexual behavior in female rats. *Physiology and Behavior,* 1969, *4,* 33–39. **90, 111**

Whalen, R. E., and Nadler, R. D. Suppression of the development of female mating behavior by estrogen administered in infancy. *Science,* 1963, *141,* 273–74. **91**

Whalen, R. E., and Rezak, D. L. Inhibition of lordosis in female rats by subcutaneous implants of testosterone, androstenedione or dihydrotestosterone in infancy. *Hormones and Behavior,* 1974, *5,* 125–28. **113**

Whetton, C., and Swindells, T. A factor analysis of the Bem sex-role inventory. *Journal of Clinical Psychology, 1977, 33,* 150–53. **224**

Whiting, B. B. (Ed.), *Six cultures: Studies of child rearing.* New York: Wiley, 1963. **205**

Whiting, B. B., and Edwards, C. P. A cross-cultural analysis of sex differences in the

behavior of children aged three through eleven. *Journal of Social Psychology,* 1973, *91,* 171–88. **205, 281, 289, 301, 306**

Whiting, J. W. M. Menarcheal age and infant stress in humans. In F. A. Beach (Ed.), *Sex and behavior,* pp. 221–33. New York: Wiley, 1965. **122**

Whitsett, J. M., and Vandenbergh, J. G. Influence of testosterone propinate administered neonatally on puberty and bisexual behavior in female hamsters. *Journal of Comparative and Physiological Psychology,* 1975, *88,* 248–55. **90**

Widdowson, E. M. The responses of the sexes to nutritional stress. *Proceedings of the Nutrition Society,* 1976, *35,* 175–80. **377, 382**

Wilcock, J., and Fulker, D., Avoidance learning in rats: Genetic evidence for two distinct behavioral processes in the shuttlebox. *Journal of Comparative and Physiological Psychology,* 1973, *82,* 247–53. **80, 237**

Wilkie, F. L., and Eisdorfer, C. Sex, verbal ability, and pacing differences in serial learning. *Journal of Gerontology, 1977, 32,* 63–67.

Will, J. A., Self, P. A., and Datan, N. Maternal behavior and perceived sex of infant. *American Journal of Orthospsychiatry,* 1976, *49,* 135–39. **207, 208**

Willemsen, E., Flaherty, D., Heaton, C., and Ritchey, G. Attachment behavior of one-year-olds as a function of mother vs. father, sex of child, session, and toys. *Genetic Psychology Monographs,* 1974, *90,* 305–24. **300**

Williams, G. C. *Sex and evolution.* Princeton, N.J.: Princeton University Press, 1975. 62, 63, 64, 68.

Williams, J. H. Sexual role identification and personality functioning in girls: A theory revisited. *Journal of Personality, 1973, 41,* 1–8. **210**

Willis, F. N., Jr. Initial speaking distance as a function of the speakers' relationship. *Psychonomic Science,* 1966, 5, 221–22. **310**

Willis, F. N., Jr., and Williams, S. J. Simultaneous talking in conversation and sex of speakers. *Perceptual and Motor Skills,* 1976, *43,* 1067–70. **308**

Wills, T. A., Weiss, R. L., and Patterson, G. R. A

behavioral analysis of the determinants of marital satisfaction. *Journal of Consulting and Clinical Psychology*, 1974, *42*, 802–11. **337**

Wilmore, J. H. Body composition and strength development. *Journal of Health, Physical Education and Recreation*, January, 1975, 38–40., pp. **320**

Wilson, A. P., and Vessey, S. H. Behavior of free-ranging castrated rhesus monkeys. *Folia Primatologica*, 1968, *9*, 1–14. **131**

Wilson, J. G., and Wilson, H. C. Reproduction capacity in adult male rats treated prepuberally with androgenic hormone. *Endocrinology*, 1943, *33*, 353–60. **91**

Winchel, R., Fenner, D., and Shaver, P. Impact on coeducation on "fear of success" imagery expressed by male and female high school students. *Journal of Education Psychology*, 1974, *66*, 726–30. **268, 269**

Winer, J. A., Dorus, W., and Moretti, R. J. Sex and college year differences in students' presenting psychiatric complaints. *Archives of General Psychiatry*, 1974, *30*, 478–83. **351**

Winokur, G. The types of affective disorders. *Journal of Nervous and Mental Disease*, 1973, *150*, 82–90. **330, 348, 350, 351, 352**

Winokur, G., and Cadoret, R. The irrelevance of the menopause to depressive disease. In E. J. Sachar (Ed.), *Topics in psychoendocrinology*, pp. 59–66. New York: Grune and Stratton, 1975. **167**

Winokur, G., and Tanna, V. L. Possible role of X-linked dominant factor in manic depressive disease. *Diseases of the Nervous System*, 1969, *30*, 89–94. **352**

Winston, F. Oral contraceptives, pyridoxine, and depression. *American Journal of Psychiatry*, 1973, *130*, 1217–21. **144**

Winter, D. G., Stewart, A. J., and McClelland, D. C. Husband's motives and wife's career level. *Journal of Personality and Social Psychology*, 1977, *35*, 159–66. **280**

Wise, D. A., and Pryor, T. L. Effects of ergocornine and prolactin on aggression in the postpartum golden hamster. *Hormones and Behavior*, 1977, *8*, 30–39.

Witelson, S. F. Sex and the single hemisphere: Specialization of the right hemisphere for spatial processing. *Science*, 1976, *193*, 425–27. **259**

Witelson S. F., and Paille, W. Left hemispheric specialization for language in the newborn: Neuroanatomical evidence of asymmetry. *Brain*, 1973, *96*, 641–46. **259**

Witkin, H. A., and Goodenough, D. R. Field dependence and interpersonal behavior. *Psychological Bulletin*, 1977, *84*, 661–89. **247**

Witkin, H. A., Mednick, S. A., Schulsinger, R., Bakkestrøm, E., Christiansen, K. O., Goodenough, D. R., Hirschhorn, K., Lundsteen, C., Owen, D. R., Philip, J., Rubin, D. B., and Stocking, M. Criminality in XYY and XXY men. *Science*, 1976, *193*, 547–55. **35, 38**

Witryol, S. L., and Kaess, W. A. Sex differences in social memory tasks. *Journal of Abnormal and Social Psychology*, 1957, *54*, 343–46. **325**

Wolf, T. M. Effects of live adult modeled sex-inappropriate play behavior in a naturalistic setting. *Journal of Genetic Psychology*, 1976, *128*, 27–32. **190**

Wolf, V. C. Age and sex performance differences as measured by a new nonverbal visual perceptual test. *Psychonomic Science*, 1971, *25*, 85–7. **244, 254**

Wolff, P. H., and Hurwitz, I. Sex differences in finger tapping: A developmental study. *Neuropsychologia*, 1976, *14*, 35–41. **326**

Wolkind, S. N. The components of "affectionless psychopathy" in institutionalized children. *Journal of Child Psychology and Psychiatry*, 1974, *15*, 215–20. (a) **351**

Wolkind, S. N. Sex differences in the aetiology of antisocial disorders in children in long term residential care. *British Journal of Psychiatry*, 1974, *125*, 125–30. (b) **351**

Wong, P. T. P. A behavioral field approach to instrumental learning in the rat, I: Partial reinforcement effects and sex differences. *Animal Learning and Behavior*, 1977, *5*, 5–13. **80**

Wood, R. Sex differences in mathematics attainment at GCE ordinary level. *Educational Studies*, 1976, *2*, 141–60. **241**

Woodrow, R. M., Friedman, G. D., Siegelaub, A. B., and Collen, M. F. Pain tolerance: Differences according to age, sex and race. *Psychosomatic Medicine*, 1972, *34*, 548–56. **323**

Work, M. S., Grossen, N., and Rogers, H. Role

Work, M. S. (*Continued*)
of habit and androgen level in food-seeking dominance among rats. *Journal of Comparative and Physiological Psychology*, 1969, *69*, 601–7. **130**

Work, M. S., and Rogers, H. Effect of estrogen level on food-seeking dominance among male rats. *Journal of Comparative and Physiological Psychology*, 1972, *79*, 414–18. **128**

Wright, P., and Crow, R. A. Menstrual cycle: Effect on sweetness preferences in women. *Hormones and Behavior*, 1973, *4*, 387–91. **151, 387**

Wynn, V. T. Measurements of small variations in "absolute" pitch. *Journal of Physiology*, 1972, *220*, 627–37. **150, 163**

Yalom, I. D., Green, R., and Fisk, N. Prenatal exposure to female hormones. *Archives of General Psychiatry*, 1973, *28*, 554–61. **108**

Yang, R. K., Federman, E. J., and Douthitt, T. C. The characterization of neonatal behavior: A dimensional analysis. *Developmental Psychology*, 1976, *12*, 204–10. **319, 322**

Yarbrough, K. M., and Howard-Peebles, P. N. X-linked nonspecific metal retardation. Report of a large kindred *Clinical Genetics*, 1976, *9*, 125–30. **41**

Yen, S. S. C., Tsai, C. C., Vandenberg, G., and Siler, T. Causal relationships between the hormonal variables in the menstrual cycle. In M. Ferin, F. Halberg, R. M. Richart, and R. L. Vande Wiele (Eds.), *Biorhythms and human reproduction*, pp. 219–38. New York: Wiley, 1974. **54, 55**

Yen, W. M. Sex-linked major-gene influences on selected types of spatial performance. *Behavior Genetics*, 1975, *5*, 281–8. **42**

Yorburg, B., and Arafat, I. Current sex role conceptions and conflict. *Sex Roles*, 1975, *1*, 135–46. **274**

Young, F. A., and Brown, M. Effects of test anxiety and testing conditions on intelligence tests scores of elementary school boys and girls. *Psychological Reports*, 1973, *32*, 543–49. **272**

Zanna, M. P., and Pack, S. J. On the self-fulfilling nature of apparent sex differences in behavior. *Journal of Experimental Social Psychology*, 1975, *11*, 583–91. **218**

Zeldow, P. B. Clinical judgment: A search for sex differences. *Psychological Reports*, 1975, *37*, 1135–42.

Zeldow, P. B. Effects of nonpathological sex role stereotypes on student evaluations of psychiatric patients. *Journal of Consulting and Clinical Psychology*, 1976, *44*, 304. **347**

Zieger, G., Lux, B., and Kubatsch, B., Sex dimorphism in the adrenal of hamsters. *Acta Endocrinologica*, 1974, *75*, 550–60. **321**

Zillmann, D., and Stocking, S. H. Putdown humor. *Journal of Communication*, 1976, *26*, 154–63. **246**

Zimmerman, B. J., and Koussa, R. Sex factors in children's observational learning of value judgments of toys. *Sex Roles*, 1975, *1*, 121–33. **191**

Zondek, L. H., and Zondek, T. The influence of complications of pregnancy and of some congenital malformations on the reproductive organs of the male foetus and neonate. In M. G. Forest and J. Bertrand (Eds.), *Sexual endocrinology of the perinatal period*. pp. 79–96. Lyon, France: Inserm, 1974. **110**

Zucker, I. Hormonal determinants of sex differences in saccharin preference, food intake and body weight. *Physiology and Behavior*, 1969, *4*, 595–602. **383**

Zuckerman, M., and Wheeler, L. To dispel fantasies about the fantasy-based measure of fear of success. *Psychological Bulletin*, 1975, *32*, 932–46. **269, 270**

Zuckerman, S. *The social life of monkeys and apes*. London: Kegan Paul, 1932. **73**

Zumoff, B., Fukushima, D. K., Weitzman, E. D., Kream, J., and Hellman, L. The sex difference in plasma cortisol concentration in man. *Journal of Clinical Endocrinology and Metabolism*, 1974, *39*, 805–8. **53**

Zurif, E. B., and Bryden, M. P. Familial handedness and left-right differences in auditory and visual perception. *Neuropsychologia*, 1969, *7*, 179–87. **258**

Index _____